GAY BOY'S LIFE

Published by Michael Anastasio
New York, NY
Printed in the United States of America
Cover Photos by Michael Anastasio
Design by Bert Green

Library of Congress Cataloging-in-Publication Data
Anastasio, Michael
Gay Boy's Life

ISBN 979-853-970-404-9

GAY BOY'S LIFE

by Michael Anastasio

For
All the boys who didn't survive . . .
. . . to write their own memoirs.

Randy
Chase
Ron
Don
Art
Warren
Steve
Dennis
Scott
Preston
Jimmy
Jimmy
Paul
Joey
Charlie
Jerry
Jeff
Bob
Terry
Tom
David
Michael
&
An Entire Generation of Gay Men
Lost But Not Forgotten

HEAVEN

Patrick Phillips

It will be the past
and we'll live there together.

Not as it was to live
but as it is remembered.

It will be the past.
We'll all go back together.

Everyone we ever loved,
and lost, and must remember.

It will be the past.
And it will last forever.

Patrick Phillips
The author of "HEAVEN"
From his book, "BOY"
Published in 2004 by
University of Georgia Press
Has graciously given his
Permission for its use here.

CONTENTS

If

the journey

leads

to

self-realization,

there are no wrong choices

or wrong roads

for the destination

is

always

the same.

.

PREFACE

AS A GAY MALE in his late-sixties, I have lived forty years longer than I had at once anticipated. As the first news story appeared in 1981about a disease that was killing gay men, I, along with so many others, knew I was doomed. I was wrong about myself. So many others were not. I began this book writing about one who was not. A very special one; my best friend, Randy. As a single unit of two conjoined souls, while navigating the mostly uncharted waters of being young and gay and out in the 70s, we found ourselves riding the crest of a wonderful wave we never imagined ending.

As gay baby boomers, Randy and I, along with an entire generation of kindred spirits, were on the front lines at the dawn of the sexual revolution. **When I came out at 18 in 1969, the entire world was 18. Or so it seemed.** There were legions of us, an endless supply arriving daily, hitting the streets and bars and parks and… well, just about everywhere. Young and gay and horny, we pushed the boundaries and rewrote the rules as we explored the new socio-sexual terrain of being gay post-Stonewall. We had arrived. And we were having sex. A lot of sex. Almost overnight the shameful, closeted "Love that dare not speak its name" was out and proud and shouting. They couldn't shut us up. Even with the prejudices and discrimination of the day, it was great to be gay in the '70s. Newly unencumbered from the restrictive past, we did it all.

What we didn't know, while we were doing it all, was that a sinister, yet-to-be-named -upper-case-acronym of a tidal wave was lurking offshore ready to sweep us from our happy but surprisingly inconstant gay world. The wave crashed down on us with such force; such ferocity; out of nowhere; without warning. We were no match for it. The sand shifted below, and we, along with our happy gay life, were swept away. Had the capricious universe shifted the tidal wave slightly this way, or that, Randy or any one of my other exceptional lost friends might just as well be writing about me. Such is the nature of tidal waves and I suppose, the universe.

I have wanted for years to write all about it; about the joy and sorrow, the sex and death. My stories. Having heard me tell my stories and share my observations and philosophies, my niece Starr would ask me to get it all down on paper. "Uncle Mike, you need to write your stories," she'd say almost pleading, "share your beautiful words with others. People need to hear them and be inspired by them." Year after year she'd give me journal after journal by way of encouragement. I'd give it a go but with random notes written down longhand in a journal here or on a scrap of paper there, I couldn't get them out of my head and on to paper. About five or six years ago my husband Eric gave me an iPad. Using it synched with my iPhone (on which I had started a "List of Stories" I wanted to write about), I was suddenly in business. I could write anywhere, anytime.

Around that time, Eric and I watched the new version of The Normal Heart. One scene in particular, paralleling an actual in-flight experience, about which I had imagined writing (it was already on my iPhone list), resurrected dormant memories and their attendant repressed emotions, reminding me exactly why I had never gotten around to writing about it. It was, in a word, unbearable and writing it would mean reliving it. I wasn't sure I was ready. **Time however does heal all wounds; even though scars remain, they do so to remind us that we have loved.** Focused then, not on the wounds but on the scars and the love, and the loving memories they evoke, with a special pair of dates (Randy's 60th birthday and the 25th anniversary of his passing) fast approaching, I knew it was time, at long last, to write about Randy. And me.

On a typically grey and damp January morning in Amsterdam, in the warmth of our friend Sander's apartment (which he had graciously allowed our use), with Eric reading in the chair across from me, I sat down to write. Upon meeting Sander, not so long before, I was filled with thoughts of Randy. Perhaps it was his height. Or his body type. His sweetness or his sensitivity. Maybe it was the smoking. I couldn't put my finger on exactly why, but when I was with Sander I simply felt Randy. We had had conversations about Sander's older brother lost to AIDS and the devastating effect it had on Sander, his gay younger brother. Considering the similarities to Randy, those conversations evoked in me thoughts of what it may have been like for Randy if I had been taken instead. All of the above came together to provide an environment that almost forced me to begin writing. Armed with a hot cup of coffee and a stroopwafel, and surrounded by ghosts (both mine and Sander's), I pulled up my "List of Stories," synched to iPages, and created a new document called, "Randy & me."

Friends who read *All About Randy & Me* encouraged me to expand it into a book with all the pre- and post-Randy stories I've told over the years. Having come out in the Stonewall Summer of '69, my gay life has paralleled the gay movement itself; and having lived in major cities all over the country, I do have the stories. Younger friends continually ask me to write them, "It's important," they tell me, "they're our history." I did see an opportunity: my story—their history—could perhaps show younger generations of gay boys that we are more similar than dissimilar. While times change, not everything does. A young friend once thanked me for my "courage" in paving the way for him and his generation. I thanked him, but with a little shrug I stated, "You know Pete, I never thought of it as courage, I was just horny." I was being cute but it was sort of true. I did what I needed to do to have sex. If that broke laws and barriers and paved the way for other gay boys who'd come later, so much the better. I was among the many who watched friend after friend suffer and die as we loved them and cared for them until they left us one by one in numbers beyond belief. That was not easy. I will take credit for that. Having been there and being among the few to survive it, I am among the few to write about it. About them. So I have. Written all about it. And them. Honestly. Personally. The funny. The tragic. The sexy. The spiritual. And most important to me, all of it...GAY.

If I seem to go overboard in the descriptions of my lost friends, I hope you'll indulge me. I am not exaggerating. They were I assure you, every bit as beautiful, funny, sexy, talented and accomplished as I lovingly remember and portray them; an extraordinary lot poised to change the world. I'm afraid the world just wasn't ready. I do dream of an alternate world where they didn't die and I am certain it is a better one than the one we find ourselves in now. As an optimist who holds reincarnation as a truth—a simple fact of life—I am convinced of their inevitable return and of the new Renaissance they will bring with them to lighten our current darkening age. I hope I live to see the beginnings of it. If I don't, I expect to return in time to enjoy its fruits. If by chance it hasn't started by the time I join all my angels waiting on the other side, I humbly offer to lead the charge.

There are those who refuse to be defined by their sexuality; I am not among them. I came into this world two things: naked and gay. I have always loved being both. Every memory, even my earliest, is colored by my being a gay male. It is my essence. The core of my being. My driving force. Without question, I was born this way. It is another simple fact of my life. I embrace the universe that embraced me with the blessing of being gay and, even with all its ups and downs, I am ever-grateful for this, my gay boy's life.

A comedian friend, named Vincent, starts his act with this joke: "I knew I was gay when I was in the womb...I looked around and thought, 'I could do something with this space!'"

That's me. I'm pretty certain that even in the womb, somehow I knew.

LOUISVILLE

I

was given

BOYS' LIFE

magazine

which

proudly proclaimed on its cover

"For All Boys,"

but

I

found little

of

my own boy's life

within its pages.

December 31, 1950

The Eggnog Kid

OK, though I wasn't 'technically' there, I figure it must've gone something like this:

MIKE AND BERNICE ANASTASIO, who do not drink, are home from the neighbors' New Year's Eve party after consuming too much eggnog and in Bernice's case, her annual Manhattan. Their two young children, Frank and Carmen, are with their grandparents so Mike and Bern have the house to themselves and are feeling festive...and frisky. Or, at least Mike is. Bernice is mostly giddy. So, with opportunity in the air, Mike has removed them from the party well before the arrival of the new year. Mike's plan is working. He is about to get lucky. This is not a common occurrence at 4262 Poplar Level Road and on this special night, ever-head-over-heels-in-love Mike cannot think of a happier way to ring in 1951.

At the stroke of midnight, under a rattling "sick call" crucifix on the wall above their bed and to the burst of the neighborhood kids' rainbow-colored fireworks lighting their bedroom window, Mike and Bernice, party hats askew, conceive a child at the exact midpoint of the Twentieth Century.

Come September, "The Eggnog Kid" (as my father christened me, to my mother's eternal embarrassment) entered this world, naked and gay. And probably smiling at a handsome orderly.

I was later officially christened Michael Lee Anastasio.

1967

Clarity

THAT'S ME! A lightning bolt of recognition flashed through my brain, illuminating the darkness as I read, for the first time, the word 'homosexual.' "That's it! That's me!" **I realized this irrefutable fact with a resounding certainty and a connection to that deepest part of me where the truth is safely kept.** "There's a word for it," I thought, "It has a name. A name for me." The name was 'homosexual.' I had been flipping through our most recent copy of *LOOK* Magazine, this particular one, *An entire issue about....The American Man*. The article I'd stopped at and was currently devouring was entitled, *The Sad "Gay" Life of the Homosexual*. I might have passed right by it but for the photo of a handsome man wearing an earring and a black leather hat. It was the earring. As the title might suggest, it wasn't exactly the most positive accounting of gay life in the early sixties but I didn't care. At fifteen years old I'd finally found a word that explained who I was. What I was. And, what I was, I found out on that winter afternoon, in the privacy of my upstairs bedroom, was a homosexual. I went to the dictionary for verification. There it was, 'homosexual: of, relating to, or characterized by a tendency to direct sexual desire toward another of the same sex.' Where had this word been all my life; this crucial bit of information previously denied me? It was not a new word; our dictionary was really old yet there it was, "homosexual." Mr. Webster had heard about it. Why hadn't I? **In that one precious Webster-validated moment, my world, wobbling along off its axis for all my short life, suddenly, firmly and permanently shifted into place.** Clarity was a wonderful thing after spending a young lifetime in an uninformed, uneducated fog about my very being. Suddenly I not only knew what I was, but I also learned there were others like me. I was not alone. And there was that other word, "Gay." I was also gay. I liked that word better. It reminded me of Fred Astaire and Ginger Rogers and all the old black and white 1930s musicals I loved watching with my mother. **Oh yeah, I was gay.**

Understanding early on there was a basic difference between myself and apparently everyone else, I constantly looked for some indication I wasn't alone. It wasn't there. Nothing in my little 1950s-1960s Louisville, Kentucky sphere indicated there was anyone else who felt the way I did. Any other boys who found boys interesting in that special, indefinable way. Everything in my world from TV shows to advertising, along with friends and family told me I was just like everyone else even though I knew this to be untrue. I was alone and confused. That is until *LOOK* Magazine with its life-saving article about homosexuals, arrived that January afternoon. The article described the sad existence these sexually depraved creatures lived, mostly under the cloak of darkness. Somehow the negativity of the article didn't interest me. What did interest me were the subtle sexual references and especially the information that these "admitted homosexuals" would gather at gay bars in San Francisco and New York. I made a plan. Since I'd decided in my naïveté there was one gay bar in New York and the other one was in San Francisco, first chance I got, I'd pack my bags and hop on a flight out of Louisville and move to one of those cities. **Like Dorothy in *The Wizard of Oz*, I yearned for a place to fit in.** New York most probably would be the place where I could be an "admitted homosexual" along with all the other ones I'd read about. Once I made it to my own Emerald City, I'd find the gay bar (singular) and meet those who were the same as me, different in the same way I was. I'd become the newest member of their underground sub-culture. There was nothing I wanted more.

My "difference" had expressed itself, as early as five or six years old, as I was greatly interested in my older brother's friends. Frank, six years my senior and quite athletic, had a cadre of similarly athletic, and to my young precocious and ever appreciative eyes, dreamy friends. I remember quite clearly, one hot humid southern evening on a brightly lighted neighborhood baseball diamond, being fascinated by the way a snug, sweaty, increasingly transparent t-shirt clung to the chest of one those older boys, the wet cloth clearly defining his smooth flat pecs along with two prominent little nipples. **I remember how those nipples made me feel; it was a sensation warm and wonderful that went to a "special" place where it gave me a "special" feeling deep within the core of me.** It was a feeling I enjoyed immensely and I just couldn't take my eyes away from that lean athletic older boy with his wet t-shirt and wonderful nipples. While I knew how good that cotton-clad chest made me feel — I wanted desperately to see it without the shirt — I also knew without question, this was information I had to keep to myself. A built-in self-preservation system told me not to share my "special" feelings with anyone. Let the withholding begin.

I would need to keep other similar thoughts regarding my "difference" to myself. Arriving home after my first day of first grade I was asked if I'd made a girl friend. Which little girl did I like best? Now, I knew I had had my eye on a particularly adorable blond haired, blue eyed classmate named Ronnie, but even at the age of six I knew I couldn't say his name. There was a Phil too, also adorable, now that I think about it. Instead of either of those names, I'd blurted out a suitable answer, "Susan," the little girl in the class who I thought was the prettiest. **I knew I was supposed to like little girls and my self-protective inner voice, coming**

from a much wiser place than my six year old mind could possibly comprehend, told me to keep my actual preferences to myself. Though a by-nature honest little boy, I would answer dishonestly. Forced to do so by that protective inner voice and the sub-currents of the world around me, I had no choice. Let the lying begin.

I had to keep quiet about Tommy too. **Tommy Scott, my first love, who, with his towhead blond, blue-eyed, classically athletic beauty had dominated my adolescent desire.** He was a dead ringer for the beautiful male angels in our family bible. We talked about going to the seminary to become Dominican priests and I imagined a lifetime with the two of us in our black and white habits, paired-up for eternity. More than admire Tommy, or even desire him, I wanted to be him. A trim golden boy and natural athlete, he was everything I was not. The summer would burnish his gold — tanning his smooth skin and whitening his already impossibly white blond hair buzzed so short it created a luminous halo, making him even more desirable and ever-unattainable. He was a year younger but I looked up to him, hoping desperately he was hiding the same romantic feelings for me but certain he was not. We'd ride bikes, climb trees, pitch tents, wrestle and do all sorts of boy things together, perpetuating my one sided love affair. He was being a boy. I was having a relationship. On hot summer nights, Tommy and I would camp out together in our backyards. **There we'd lie, in the tight musty confines of an evening-damp, army-green tent who's heavy sagging sides seemed determined to push us together.** In the midnight darkness with a cacophony of crickets, katydids, cicadas and tree frogs playing a heated, lushly romantic nighttime symphony for two, as we lay there pressed together side by side, I had wanted desperately to reach under the covers and touch him; or caress him; or hold him; or kiss him; or... I did none of those things. I could not. The risk of exposing myself to potential ridicule and loss of my best friend was far too great. This wonderful-horrible secret, along with so many others, would have to be kept, guarded with my life. There was a piece of me that I couldn't share even with my best friend.

That would someday change. There would come a day, years later, when I would learn there were others like me. And years after that, just as soon as I could, I would board a plane out of Louisville and go to that place, somewhere, perhaps over the rainbow. Or at the least, at the end of it. I could see it. I'd just have to be patient and wait, certain there would come a day in that special place, when I would find other friends. I was certain too, that someday I would find a new best friend from whom I'd keep no secrets. **We could share everything because this best friend would be, in that very "special" way, just like me.**

RANDY

1989

Going Back

RANDY was sitting in the window seat, curled in on himself, his now rapidly balding head resting against the vibrating fuselage wall. I studied my best friend intently as he sat there hunched over, swallowed up by his big oversized beige cardigan. Eyes half-lidded. Staring blankly. Not asleep. Not awake, but something in between. I had seen him in that same state in that same baggy, ratty, threadbare sweater everyday for I don't know how long. You hear a lot about comfort food. This was comfort clothing. I think that particular sweater was the one thing able to give his shivering skeletal frame some actual relief, and he had worn it almost exclusively those final, bone chilling days in San Francisco. My sharp, bright, fastidious friend, previously meticulous about his appearance, had, at only thirty-four years old, faded into an old man who had shed all his vanity in favor of comfort. Where was my perfectly groomed friend who had cared so much about the cut and color of his hair, the perfect trim of his beard, the precise amount of starch in his signature white button down Oxford cloth shirts, the sharp crease in his Brooks Brothers trousers, the high polish on his shoes? **This new version of Randy had different priorities, more basic ones: comfort and survival.** I sat in the middle seat watching this barely recognizable man, intently trying to find my dear friend. Trying to find in what now seemed to be a withered old man, that sweet, fresh faced young boy I'd met fifteen short years before. A disease nobody completely understood had accelerated the aging process well beyond those thirty-four short years and had taken my best friend away leaving something of a functioning shell of a person in his place. An old man, four years my junior, I no longer knew. I looked at Randy and tried to determine his thoughts. Funny, this was someone whose every thought I at one time knew. Could simply intuit. As he could, mine. I could no longer read his thoughts, or his feelings. **Now all I could find was resignation.** Not surprising given the physical challenges he'd already faced and others expected to come. I looked beyond my friend catching the first glimpse of Chicago out the window. Was he searching for it too? Did he realize (or care) that the rapidly approaching grid of streets and assemblage of buildings that lay down there before us, was indeed, our Chicago, the city that had played such a prominent role in our shared story? The city that had become our home and had shaped so much of who we were. The city where we'd now change planes on our way back to Louisville, our hometown.

Where was my best friend with whom I could communicate without a word, the friend of those glorious Chicago days? And where was that sweet, impossibly naive boy I'd met years before on a summer night in Louisville? **Back when a limitless future lay ahead of us; back when Chicago was more than a place to change planes; back when dying was just a word; back when all things seemed possible.**

1973

Funny The Things You Remember…

DIANA ROSS's "Touch Me In The Morning" was playing on the jukebox. It was a Saturday night, early summer, 1973, at Badlands Territory, our local gay bar. The disco upstairs hadn't opened yet so the first floor bar was pretty crowded. Gay bars in cities the size of Louisville always had two floors. On the entry floor you'd find the main bar decorated in one of several themes: Parisian Whorehouse — especially popular down south, English Hunt/Library — found throughout New England and university towns, Western Rodeo — predictably out west and mid-west, Industrial Mineshaft — big cities, Bare Minimum To Get The Doors Open — almost anywhere but especially in smaller towns and strip malls. The Badlands main floor theme was a sort of hybrid: Rough Hewn Western Cowboy meets Industrial Mineshaft.

The secondary floor either upstairs or down, is where you'd find the dance floor. It was always this way, a holdover from the bad old days (a mere four or five years before) when same sex dancing was illegal. And enforced. Raiding police would be required then to run either upstairs or down, giving the same-sex couples time to separate men from men and women from women and switch to legal heterosexual couples. If there was a show bar it would also be located on the second level.

I was on the crowded first floor, leaning against a rough hewn lumber pilaster and exposed brick wall, drink in hand — no doubt either Kahlúa and cream or more probably, "Dubonnet over ice" — in homage to Barbra's Katie Morosky in *The Way We Were*, my favorite film of that year. With Ms Ross (my other favorite singer, this being just slightly pre-Bette Midler) singing about love and loss, I was checking out the boys, happy to be full-time, one hundred percent gay again after a recent, unexpected and ill-fated two year heterosexual-ish detour.

I was waiting for the upstairs disco to open and was feeling cute and sexy in my favorite bright red v-neck tennis-style sweater with the two white stripes around the left bicep. I looked down to check out my brand new cream-colored gabardine trousers making sure the cuffed wide legged bells were breaking "just so" over my platform saddle shoes. Hey, it was the seventies. **When I looked up again there was a determined young face, big eager clear blue eyes, perfect pore-less skin and full lips just inches from mine.** A pretty-boy. Smiling. I was startled. "Where's Ron tonight?" was his opening line, "Is he coming out later?" No introduction. No "Hi, what's your name?" Or "Hi my name is…" Just "Where's Ron?" I didn't know how to answer because I didn't know who or what the boy was talking about. Seeing the puzzled look on my face, he went on, slightly annoyed, "Ron Bianchi! You were with him last night. I saw you." There was impatience in his voice and those big blue eyes demanded an answer. "Is he coming out tonight?" Oh, of course. The handsome Mr. Bianchi. Louisville's oh-so tall and oh-so popular answer to Rock Hudson. The night before I'd been hanging with Ron at the Badlands and apparently this boy had had an eye on us. Well, at least, on one of us. Ron, an EBT (everybody's type) with his movie star good looks and sparkling charisma was the older brother of a high school classmate of mine. We were friends. We weren't, however, friends enough for me to know his momentary whereabouts or precise plans for that night. I let the boy know as much. Left to my own devices, that would have been the end of it but, for whatever reason, the kid became stuck to me — a piece of human flypaper. **I could not get rid of him. And I tried.** At every turn, there he was in all his youthful eagerness. I was being used for my friendship with Ron, the object of the boy's desire and I knew it. We spent the evening together, attached, except for the moments he'd sidle up to Ron, who, to the boy's delight, did finally show up.

I went out in those days (if I wasn't meeting friends) pretty much for one reason: to find sex. Once again, it was the seventies. For whatever reason, I felt no sexual spark for this boy and clearly his interests lay elsewhere. I really wanted to move on. I was dressed to kill. I wasn't out to make a friend, I was out to make a conquest. I couldn't shake the kid, so I made a friend. As it turned out, my persistent new friend was housesitting for an older acquaintance, and as the evening wore down, he asked me back to the apartment. Never one to let go of an evening, and with other prospects slim, I agreed. I also agreed, at his insistence and against my better judgement, to show the kid, on the way, where Ron lived. Was he some kind of stalker? We started out with the kid following me, then after the requisite Ron apartment drive-by, me following the kid. Driving behind him I worried that his invitation might have a sexual component to it. While I was no Ron Bianchi, I was another, though only 21, older man and Italian to boot, so it was quite likely the boy might have intentions on me, his second choice. Well, this "second choice" did not find him sexually attractive and that was that. I was concerned I was about to dash the hopes of an eager young boy. I needn't have worried. As it turned out, he shared the same concern; he was just as disinterested.

I don't know precisely when or why or just what it was that bonded us that night but we became fast friends; "attached at the hip" friends as we would come to be referred to time and again. It certainly didn't hurt that I was friends with Ron, the object of his current pursuit. It was more than that. **Something to this day I've never been able to quite put my finger on, created in one night, a bond that would last forever.** He was certainly the little brother I never had and I the big brother he'd never had. There was more to it than that though. Something strong and permanent. We spent the early morning hours sharing our hopes and dreams for the future, things we liked, places we'd like to go, things we'd like to do, guys we'd like to do, things we'd like to do with them, pretty much anything that came to mind. We talked about our "first times." We'd both done "it" in Louisville's Cherokee Park. I expressed my love of Chicago and hope of someday living there and he shared, with a roll of his eyes and a heavy sigh, his desire to live "Anywhere but Louisville." We had that in common.

He was a natural talker, free with his feelings and I a natural listener so we made quite a good match from the start. I am not entirely sure that he, ever in his short life, had had anyone's ear to the extent and for the amount of time that he had mine that night. I learned while listening until way past dawn, that his name was William Randal Riede, and with another roll of the eyes, "Though everybody calls me Randy." We found out we'd gone to the same high school. "Years apart," he would, throughout the course of our friendship, be quick to point out, verbally stretching the word "y-e-e-e-a-a-a-a-r-s" for emphasis, making it seem like way more than the four years that actually separated us. I had graduated from St. Xavier High School the spring of '69 before he started there the following fall. He was a recent graduate from St. X and at 18 was illegally in the Badlands, having had some sort of "relationship" with the guy at the door who would look the other way as Randy presented his I.D. I, being a mature 21, felt significantly older. I was immediately fascinated by this eager, bright, affable young boy who, I learned, had been a state swimming and diving champion. He was a champion tennis player as well, unless I'm confusing the "champion" part with his mother, something more easily done than you'd think. Anyway, he did play tennis. He had also enthusiastically helped raise his younger brothers and sisters. Ask him anything about swimming, diving, tennis or childcare and he was a master of in-depth information. Anything else seemed to puzzle him. A casual reference to say, Katharine Hepburn or

Bette Davis would elicit a "Katharine who?" or "Betty who?" Seriously? There was a human on this planet (and especially a gay male human) who had never even heard these names before? I'm not sure he'd ever even been to a movie. Certainly none of the classics. "Get this kid to a showing of *All About Eve*. Stat!" He knew almost nothing of pop culture, Broadway shows, classic movies, gay icons or anything else that comprised the conversations of most of the gay men I knew. Any such references just winged their flighty way over his head. Barbra and Judy were just names to him. Seriously? Barbra Streisand? The Greatest Star? Never even heard the name? He also couldn't sing one show tune. He had quite possibly never heard one. **He had grown up so focused on a world of school, sports and family, he seemed to have missed everything else.** He was an excellent student, a trophied and sweatered athlete, a devoted son and a devoted brother; beyond that his world seemed to have stopped. To my would-be mentor's eyes he was fertile ground. There were seeds to plant. Barbra seeds. Judy seeds. Movie seeds. Broadway seeds. Art seeds. Design seeds. Brunch seeds. Gay seeds! Ever the gardener, I saw fresh earth and I was ready to till, plant, tend and harvest. And so I would. There were worlds of things, things I held precious, things beyond his current scope of imagination, to introduce to this wide-eyed eager young boy. I had been waiting for this moment all my life. **I'd be Auntie Mame to his young Patrick. Two more names he wouldn't recognize.**

1963...

The Greatest Star

ON ONE OF OUR FAMILY VISITS to New York during the early 60s, I was with my cousin Anthony in his bedroom listening to tape recordings a friend of his had brought over. The origins of the recordings I do not know, but they were of a young singer, female, whose voice and manner of singing was like nothing I'd ever heard. Even though the recordings were not particularly good — they were kind of scratchy and I think, there might have been voices in the background — still, the singer's voice was so clear and the songs so fresh and dramatic, that that moment in an upstairs bedroom in Springfield New Jersey, would freeze in my memory and make me a fan forever. I don't recall how Anthony's friend had come by these recordings — he wasn't old enough to have gotten into a bar to record them himself — but he told us all about her. Her name was Barbra "Not Barb-a-ra," he was quick to add, and she was absolutely everything to him. There was in fact a conflict in his own home at that moment. His family was readying themselves for vacation and it was decided that he could not bring his big cumbersome tape recorder along. He told us, as he had told his parents in no uncertain terms, "If Barbra doesn't go, I don't go!" **I loved his determination and in retrospect I think this is probably the first time I had ever met another gay boy.** Even though I knew nothing of the gay world or other gay people — indeed at that point I didn't even know the word 'gay' existed in that context — I connected not only to this other boy but also, and I think this is important, because of him, to this singer he so fiercely loved.

From that moment I was also fiercely in love with Barbra Streisand. I watched along with my mother as my new favorite singer performed on *The Garry Moore Show* and asked to stay up late to see her on *The Tonight Show*. I kept my eyes out for any press mentions or photos from New York events, Broadway openings, film premieres, etc. Once at a backyard family gathering I overheard some grown-up mention being in New York and seeing "That Bar-ba-ra Streis-land" going into a theater. Horrified by the mispronunciation, I was nevertheless consumed with envy.

One evening out shopping with the rest of our family in Bacon's Department Store I had in my pocket a few dollars to burn. My brother and I wandered off to the record department. Flipping through the stacks of LP albums I came across The Barbra Streisand Album. My heartbeat increased as I snatched the prize out of its bin and clutched it to my chest. Why hadn't I known this was available? Looking back it's hard to imagine a time when the singular "Album" could be used for a Barbra Streisand record but at that point there was only one. At about the same time my older brother Frank was approaching, waving an album he'd found. He excitedly called out, "Meet The Beatles," like that was supposed to mean something to me. He seemed just as excited about his find as I was with mine. One problem. He of empty pocket knew I had money to spend and had decided he'd get me to buy his album for him. He was disappointed to see I had made a choice of my own but I think he was convinced his was an easy sell. I was typically a pretty agreeable pleaser, especially when it came to pleasing my big brother. On this occasion however, there was no way he was going to get that three or so dollars out of the often easily manipulated me. He tried shaming me. He snatched Barbra away and gave her a quick once-over. "You mean, you're gonna buy an album of dumb old songs sung by some big nosed girl when you could go home with The Beatles?" heavy emphasis on the word "Beatles," again like those fours strangers on his album were anything to me. Big mistake. Insulting Barbra was certainly no way to win me over. I wasn't budging. There was no chance I'd leave Bacons that night without Barbra. The Beatles could stay just where they were. Barbara made her way back to Ardmore Drive where she would be mine forever. I couldn't wait to get home and listen to my very own Barbra Streisand album.

I wasn't disappointed. I put Barbra on the turntable of my small portable record player and sat enraptured by the voice, the phrasing and intonation and sheer perfection of what I was hearing. **I could have put her on the big console stereo in the living room and gotten way better sound, but I wanted instead the intimacy of just Barbra and me, alone in my room, a private performance in my private upstairs inner sanctum.** I read the album notes which said "…each song is like a one-act musical." I couldn't have agreed more, even though I didn't really know exactly what a one act musical was like. I listened over and over and over memorizing not just every word but every breath and every nuance this talented singer brought to each song. She sang "Happy Days Are Here Again" like they were gone forever. Who would think of doing such a thing, singing an up-beat, happy, let's-get-out-of-the-depression-presidential-campaign song so down-beat and with such irony that you felt her heartbreak and loss. I could feel, in fact, in each song, each emotion she felt and wanted me to feel. That was her genius and that is, I suppose, what captured me from the start. Even though Barbra herself was quite young she was "older" to me and when she sang, I knew she had already experienced the emotions she expressed through her singing. Through her, I experienced them too. **I knew someday I would feel exactly about love (and other things still a mystery to me) as she did. When Barbra sang the words "How does the wine taste…" somehow I knew she wasn't singing about wine.** I wanted to taste it too. Whatever it was. She held that kind of power over me and connected somehow to my little gay boy sensibilities — an undeniable gay sense of the dramatic — and in so doing connected me (unknowingly at the time) with a gay world of men with similar sensibilities who felt the way I already did about love and life and Barbra. Remembering my cousin Anthony's friend, the one who'd introduced me to her — though I didn't understand exactly what it was — I knew we shared something special; with each other and with Barbra. **She didn't fit in and neither did we.** I didn't grasp this first hint that I might not be alone in the world. To this day I can't explain it but she made me feel like everything would be alright and that somewhere there was a place for a boy like me and wherever that was, there would be more boys like me. And she'd be there too. Someday, in fact, many years later, Barbra would record the song, "Somewhere," from the Broadway show West Side Story confirming my little boy belief that yes, there is a place for us.

The next albums came in rapid-fire succession. The years went on and Barbra made appearances on *The Ed Sullivan Show*, received an Emmy Award for her first TV special, and The Academy Award for her first film role in *Funny Girl*. Others would eventually learn what I'd known from the start about "that strange girl singer with the big nose." I'd now have to share her with the world. Eventually I would do so enthusiastically, preaching the gospel of Barbra to anyone who'd listen.

I stayed a big fan throughout out all the years, straying only once (during the 70s) when I'd become disenchanted with her more contemporary, less classic choices. They just didn't fit her. She was clearly trying to be something, someone, she wasn't. Someone I didn't recognize. The lyrics "Come rub it on my belly like guava jelly," made me wonder just who she was now singing for and sent me running for the exits. My Bette Midler defection lasted until Barbra came to her senses some years later with a classical album.

We've been together ever since.

1973...

NoSex

THE BABY BOOM was booming sexually. We were young. We were horny. We were on the front lines of a revolution. I became a happy foot soldier in that sexual revolution. I'd go out for an evening at either a cruise bar or a dance bar or failing that, any one of a number of cruise locations. I'd meet someone, drag him home (or go to his place.) I'd have sex, maybe chat a bit, have sex again and at some point, perhaps put on his t-shirt (t-shirt switching was a thing then) and depart, pretty much knowing if he'd fall into boyfriend, fuck buddy, friend, or never-to-be-seen-again status. Most of my "new acquaintances" fell quite happily into the fuck buddy category and eventually, when the flames of passion dimmed (which for me, with rare exception, was pretty much inevitable — and soon) crossed over to friend status. Those I chose to see again but not sexually, typically went directly to friend. The never-to-be-seen-again I might see out and the only thing familiar about him would be his (formerly my) t-shirt.

It was a time — I don't like admitting this but it's true — when nothing was as important as my next orgasm. Yep, there it is. Not pretty but it's honest. Whenever I stepped out of the door it was with the hope and possibility of sex. Make that probability. And with that probability around every corner, it was difficult to focus my interest toward any situation or person that didn't offer it. Sex was surely an obsession and I passed up many prospective friendships and opportunities because they lacked the potential for sex. **Had Randy not been so persistently stuck to me the night we met, I'd probably have missed the greatest friendship of my life.** It does make me wonder what else I might have overlooked but I don't spend much time with regret. That first night, Randy's insistence overcame my indifference and we were able to skip over the sex part and move right to friendship. While we were generally each other's types, there was never any sexual chemistry between us. Throughout our entire friendship, we'd have to explain this lack of attraction over and over to friends who never quite bought our sexual disinterest in each other. We seemed like such a couple. But we weren't. We never had sex. Not on that first night. Not years later sharing cold winter nights, high and relaxed, horny and home alone with just each other. Not ever. Being "just friends," the usual hurdles of sexual compatibility, jealousy, or romance never needed to be cleared. Sex is a powerful force, especially for two such sexual creatures as we. **Sex could short-circuit the best of friendships; it never intruded into ours.** Even "our types" were polar opposites, so we never competed for the same guys. We were a match made in sex heaven, able to cruise together without ever stepping on the other's toes.

1973...

Dizzy Is As Dizzy Does

RANDY WAS SMART (a lot smarter than I, though I never let on that I knew.) He made an excellent student, an eager agreeable sponge ready to soak up anything I had to impart. Over and over I'd authoritatively share some sort of something that I knew (or thought I knew) and he'd always say in astonishment, "How do you know these things?" My mentor's heart would burst with happiness! In spite of his high IQ, Randy had a naïveté that was absolutely charming. He was, to use my favorite word for it, "Dizzy." A tall, sweet, loony Laverne to my shorter, bossier Shirley. Many of our friends would, in later years, point out, the resemblance which was in many ways, uncanny. **Randy was not insulted by my use of the word dizzy at all, and in fact stated, with a little pride, that it was a family trait.** He was right. I'd find this out for myself upon eventually meeting his family. With the exception of his father who seemed as normal as any father, they were to a one, the dizziest group of people I had ever met. Visits to their home always reminded me of one of those sitcoms, probably starring Bob Newhart, with one character who was the rock-solid center of the action — in this case, Randy's dad, a rational, fixed planet, and orbiting around him, a dizzy off-kilter solar system of looniness — Randy's mom, brothers and sisters and of course, Randy. Even his grandmother. And none of them, apart from Randy seemed aware. I loved my visits with these wonderfully smart, kind, loving and yes, dizzy people. I fell in love with them all just as instantly as I had fallen for their equally smart, kind, loving and dizzy older brother. As the youngest in my family (thereby little brother and little sister deprived) I'd hit the familial jackpot. I happily felt like a big brother in their house. While I'd classify Randy's love of his siblings as maternal, mine was definitely fraternal. They were sweet and endlessly entertaining. I felt loved in their presence. And thoroughly entertained.

It was clear just how much Randy had been influenced by his mother. She was the greatest driving force in his life and would always remain so. Jean had an athletic-beauty that I think Randy ascribed to his whole life. He was essentially her male clone. She was a tennis player. A tennis pro, I believe, and she looked like one. One of the handsomer ones. Randy adored her. I thought she was about the coolest mom I'd ever met. She, along with her entire family, was kind to me and always accepting of me. She was the first person I can think of who actually treated me like an adult. And a gay adult at that, which was especially good for me since we didn't speak of "it" in my own home. Growing up the baby in that home, by now in my early twenties, I still felt ever the little boy in most circles, especially in familial situations. With Jean, I was a grownup. We understood each other. **I always saw her as having handed Randy off to me in a move so deft, he never even noticed. An easy lob, right into my court.** She had raised him to be the unique individual he'd become by the time I found him. The heavy lifting was done. All I had to do was add a little polish. Gay polish. I'm pretty sure she was quite grateful for me when I happened into her son's life. Not that she stepped out of Randy's life in any way. She was there for him in every way and every day. Until the end. She was the smart and charmingly dizzy voice inside Randy's head. It was a good voice and Randy wisely consulted and followed it.

But back to the dizziness. I remember once during a conversation with Randy, his referring to something as being "Out of congress." Seeing the puzzled look on my face he stopped mid-sentence with, "What?" In response I said, "I'm not sure I heard you correctly. Did you say, 'out of congress?' I don't know that expression." I made a face. "What does it mean?" It was now my turn to get a puzzled look from him. "What does it mean?" he parroted me and added, "You say it all the time," and, adding for emphasis, "all the time." I was still puzzled as he continued impatiently, "It means something that doesn't belong, something that is out of context. 'Out of congress.' Something that doesn't make sense is 'out of congress.' Really, you do say it all the time." I continue to stare blankly not remembering ever having said the words, "Out of congress." I thought about the phrase and it did make sense, sort of, but I really couldn't remember having ever heard it much less having said it. Randy decided to clarify. "Well, actually, I guess I haven't heard you say 'out of congress.' But you're always using its opposite, saying something is 'In congress,' he continued while waving his hands, "You're always saying, this is 'in congress' or that is 'in congress.'" He stood there obviously pleased with himself at this clarification. "In congress, in congress," I said to myself over and over and it made no more sense than "out of congress." When had I ever said, "In congress" to describe anything? I continued to ponder the words, "In congress, in congress, in congress." **Suddenly I heard it. "Incongruous?" I shouted out, startling Randy a bit.** "Incongruous is the word I'm using," I laughed and sounded it out, "in-con-gru-ous, one word, not 'in congress,' in-con-gru-ous," once again sounding it out for him, "something that doesn't belong with everything else."

In congress. I had to laugh. Though I was saying, "inconguous," dizzy Randy was hearing, "In congress" and had decided that it meant the exact opposite of what incongruous actually means. He then craftily came up with it's opposite which ended up meaning the same thing. Dizzy yes, and yet, somehow, still...smart. Just like his mom.

I would see in Randy, throughout our years together, both his parents: his mother's sweet dizziness and athleticism always balanced with his businessman dad's smart practicality. He was clearly a combination of both parents, a perfect blend of their very individual sensitivities. I loved the dichotomy of Randy's inner-Jean and inner-Keller and wonder, especially as I age, if my own parents — my inner-Bernice and inner-Mike are as apparent in me.

1962

My Mother's Hands

MY MOTHER had beautiful hands. "A pianist's hands" is how she'd have described them on someone else. And though she had played the piano as a young woman, as a adult, her fingers were more likely to be working the keys of a typewriter. While subsequent to my brother's, my sister's and my arrival, she was no longer a secretary, she was still in the frequent habit of using a typewriter. I would sit in rapt little boy amazement watching the lovely fingers of this lovely woman I loved so much as they deftly struck each key without her ever once looking at them. Ever. And she never missed. Ever. How was it possible? I didn't know. I tried to figure it out as I examined her fingers which somehow seemed to know where each key was located and strike it with such swift authority there was no room for error. How did they know which key was which? These wise fingers of hers? Seeing that the keys weren't even in alphabetical order I decided that my mother's fingers weren't just beautiful, they were magic.

They were thin and elegant as well, the ring finger of her left hand adorned with a modest but sparkling diamond engagement and wedding ring combination circa 1945 and on her right, a lovely passed-down family diamond ring she'd received for her high school graduation. She had long ideally shaped fingernails highly-arched, each with a perfect "moon" and always, always meticulously manicured.

The manicure was a Saturday night ritual. Seated at our dinette table in front of the TV, a big heavy turquoise and cream not-so-portable portable, mom would surround herself with all her manicure paraphernalia. And me, her ever-observant little gay son. She would be watching any one of the Saturday night black and white TV offerings and in turn would be fervently watched by me, as she would go to work on her nails. First there was the cotton ball removal of last week's chipping-away polish. This was the only part I didn't enjoy as the strong chemical odor of the nail polish remover made me hold my nose, scrunching up my face and leaning way back. When that smelly business was over, I would pull myself up close to watch the filing and shaping, a sound — more of a feeling — that sent shivers through my body. She performed this spine tingling task with the sureness and dexterity of a concert violinist. This was followed by the rather mundane soaking and cuticle push back. After that, came the color application — my favorite part — a task at which mom was a real pro. Swift and sure, working from the pinkie to the thumb, she colored each nail in three steady, perfectly applied strokes. Always three. One stroke up each side of the nail and the last one right up the middle. Suddenly there were ten perfectly painted nails gleaming wet with the light from the milk-glass early American fixture hanging above us. The color was usually some seasonal red or pink variation or occasionally clear, allowing those perfect moons to show. With the polish applied, all that was left was the drying. She would hold her hands up in the air, fingers fluttering, while *The Snows of Kilimanjaro* (or some other "Saturday Night at the Movies" movie) played out or the June Taylor Dancers made black and white kaleidoscopic patterns on the floor of the Jackie Gleason stage. **It was all a Saturday night ritual in preparation for a Sunday morning ritual — mass.**

Mass. Those were the days when families went to church on Sunday morning in their "Sunday best." My mother always said, "We may not be the richest family in the parish, but that doesn't mean we can't be the best dressed," and best dressed we were. Jackets and ties and well-pressed shirts, crisply-creased slacks and high-polished shoes for my dad, my brother Frank and me and perfectly coordinated dresses, hats, shoes and bags for mom and my sister Carmen. For her own wardrobe choices, my mom would often consult me — her gay-in-training son. Hearing "Mikey, come in here," I knew an opinion was needed. Mom had weight issues — unhappily passed on to me — and was overly critical of her appearance, though I thought she was beautiful and elegant in everything she wore. I entered my parents' bedroom to find her in front of a mirror, trying on a new dress for the first time as I sat down on their bed. Turning this way and that, eyes focused on the mirror, she asked, "What do you think? Belt or no belt?" She modeled it one way, then the other. I could see disapproval in her reflection. "Belt," I answered resolutely. "Oh, I don't know," she sighed, deeply discontented looking at her belted form, "I look like a pillow tied in the middle." Having already given my solicited opinion I could only add, "Well, what's worse, to look like a pillow tied in the middle or to look like a pillow?" She shot me "a look," that bounced right off the mirror hitting its mark, but she wore it belted. With bag and shoes to match.

And gloves. My mother came from a generation of women who always wore gloves. Mom had an array of soft kid gloves suited to each season and occasion in shades of grey, black, navy, tan, bone and white and in varying lengths. Her gloves fit tightly, so tightly in fact that even putting them on and taking them off was something of a ritual. She couldn't just slip them on. They were too tight for that. I'd watch her as she'd pull the glove onto her hand and then work each finger of each glove starting with the tip of the little finger, smoothing the supple kid and working it down the length of the finger toward the palm. She'd do the same with each finger working from pinkie to thumb and then finally, smoothing the rest of the glove over the palm and back of her hand and over her wrist and up her forearm. **Seeing she'd been observed at this, Mom would dependably say with a wink, "There's nothing worse than baggy gloves," in a prim, high-pitched voice that made me feel she was quoting someone else.** At the end of this task, usually performed right before heading out the door, her lovely hands, fresh manicure, diamonds and all, would be elegantly hidden from my appreciative eyes, clad in soft supple kid and ready to go.

On the way to church, ever-observant I would blurt out, "Are those new earrings? They're really pretty." I'd get another "look," this one shot quickly over her shoulder, and my question would go unanswered. It was rhetorical anyway as I *knew* they were new. Dad, who made the money in our house but didn't handle it, wasn't always clued-in on new purchases. On arrival at St. Stephen's, as we were approaching the doors to the church, Mom would already be reversing the glove ritual. But only on her right hand. She would crisply pull at each finger of the right glove so that, by the time she'd reached the church doorway, her glove would be totally removed. She could dip her now bare, perfectly manicured hand into the holy water font located just inside the entry. Then, reverently and ever so elegantly she'd make the sign of the cross with the moistened fingers of her exposed right hand. We would all do the same, less elegantly, following her lead, and proceed as a family to file in to our always front row pew, my dad pulling up the rear. Mom would make her way to her place in the pew and while kneeling, she'd deposit her purse and right glove on the seat behind her. The rest of us would follow and kneel in unison.

That's the way it was. **When you found your seat in a Catholic Church you couldn't just sit down but were required to kneel first and silently say some prayers. Like there wasn't enough praying to come. I usually faked it.** I knew I was *supposed* to be praying but no one could tell if you were *actually* praying or not and I was always way too busy looking around at all the visual treats the place had to offer. While I didn't much care for mass and prayers, I did love our church with all its embellishments — every pretty thing to capture the imagination of a visually-inclined young religious gay boy. With an audio background of lilting organ walk-in music, there were big lavish flower arrangements, fine embroidered linens, crystal goblets and cruets, gold bells, gold chalices and gold candelabras with tall gold-capped white candles being lit by really cute older altar boys in their long black cassocks and starched white surplices — Catholic drag I found so appealing. Someday I'd be old enough to wear a long black dress in church and get away with it. There were colorful statues including The Blessed Virgin Mary and a handsome, blond-haired, blue-eyed St. Stephen who was my favorite. **There was also a well-muscled, nearly-naked, decidedly hunky, unfortunately crucified Jesus that attracted much of my attention as well.** His body was so lean and muscular and his alabaster skin was so smooth and shiny that you could almost overlook (with a twinge of Catholic guilt) the agony in his pained expression, all the blood and the fact he was nailed to two pieces of wood.

Most memorable of all, in the ecclesiastical beauty of that Sunday morning experience were my mother's hands.

My mother's hands. I would divert my gaze her way to find those two elegant hands devoutly folded in prayer, pressed together. One gloved. One bare. Long beautiful fingers of her exposed, perfectly manicured right hand with that single sparkling diamond, silhouetted against her other, gloved hand. **She presented an indelible image of hand pressed against hand, a perfect pair, one gloved, one bare.** Those praying hands would burnish themselves onto my mind's eye, leaving me with a clear image of pure elegance that would stay forever. One gloved, one bare. Surely I thought, God must have also appreciated the beauty and grace of those hands, the care and effort that had gone into their perfect presentation. **Most certainly the prayers her hands were so fervently offering (I was quite certain she wasn't faking it) would be heard, and their gracious requests, granted.**

That's how I will always remember those hands. My mother's hands. The hands that fed me, bathed me, changed my diapers, administered my cough medicine, parted and combed my hair, happily signed my birthday cards and not so happily, my report cards. The hands that would someday pen a letter of acceptance of my lifestyle, one she could never really understand but would try so hard to support. Lovely, elegant, hands that grew the finest roses in the tri-state area and would carefully create those abundant flower arrangements on the altar. Graceful, praying hands that made their way through a thousand rosaries and that will, I am quite certain, welcome me when I cross over from this life to the next. **The same hands that made our dinners, laundered and pressed our clothes, cleaned our house and provided so much motherly care, now, in church, one gloved, one bare, beautifully and elegantly pressed together, in prayer. For us.**

1963

My Father's Shoes

I WAS HIDING, afraid someone would see me. As I emptied a small garbage can into a larger garbage can, I did so out of sight. The clanking sound echoed in the terrazzo floored nighttime emptiness of St. Stephen Martyr Catholic School, briefly drowning out the distant sound of children playing outside. I was helping my father clean classrooms on a Friday night and I was making absolutely certain I couldn't be seen by any of those children in the playground just outside the locked school doors. If they recognized me they'd wonder why I was inside the school on a Friday night when they were all outside playing. They would wonder what I was up to in there and I didn't want them see me and to find out what I was doing. Find out that I was helping my father clean classrooms. Find out that my dad was a janitor. And I was a janitor's son. Well, in truth my father wasn't a janitor. He was a produce manager at the A&P but he had a second, part-time job cleaning classrooms at my school which to my mind, pretty much made him a janitor and me a janitor's son. I couldn't let them know this. I adored my father and would do anything to spend time with him and in truth I was happy being there with him and being the "good helper" a term he'd consistently use to describe me. I was happy to help, took pride in my work and basked in the praise he'd give me for a job well done. **I just didn't want anyone else to know about it. I was a snob.**

Louisville is a mostly Catholic city divided by parishes. Ours was St. Stephen's, a parish divided by class. **You either lived in the wealthier meticulously landscaped Audubon Park or you didn't.** We didn't. I was consummately aware of this unfortunate fact of my life. Audubon Park was a place for other people to live and for us it was a place to drive through on our way to the fairgrounds or to the stores and fast food places on Preston Highway. Or in the springtime it was a place to bicycle around and see all the abundant dogwoods and redbuds in bloom; azaleas too. I was prone to imagining myself living in one of those solid, two and three story brick and stone homes — mansions to my eyes — surrounded by lushly landscaped yards overflowing with all those magnificent flowering trees. They had sidewalks in Audubon Park. Actual sidewalks. And real estate set aside just for trees and flowers and birds. Audubon Park, as its name might suggest was a "bird sanctuary." Oh how I loved those two words. They held a festival each year when the dogwoods bloomed; just think, a festival, when the dogwoods bloomed. My imagined lifestyle in that lovely sanctuary did not fit in any way with my current janitorial duties assisting my hard working dad. Of this I was quite certain.

So that was my father, a blue collar perfectionist, the kind of man who would get up before dawn, work a hard, eight hour plus day, come home, take a short nap, have dinner with his family, then go off to his second job and work just as hard at that one. All for his loved ones. He was a giver who would do anything to provide for his wife and children and he would do it all with dedication and without complaint. **That is who he was: a good, loving, hard working, tireless provider of a dad.**

And that was me, the kind of boy embarrassed that his father had to clean classrooms to support us; secretly wishing he was another kind of father, one who would come home in a big expensive car and wearing a suit. One who would loosen his tie, make himself a drink and put his feet up on a well-upholstered ottoman in a professionally decorated den. Just like in the movies and TV shows and, I supposed, in all those houses I coveted in Audubon Park. **And that is who I was: Veda in *Mildred Pierce*.**

Dad was a study in contrasts. He was a giant of a man standing just over 5 feet tall in his tiny size 6 shoes. He wanted everything for his family and wanted nothing for himself. He doted on and was fiercely protective of the family he created and oddly detached from the family he'd grown up with. Kind and tender hearted he could become close to murderous when anyone in his family was harmed in any way. He was a man uncomfortable with the words "I love you," yet proved his deep love every day with his every act. **He would carefully work his way through a bag of potato chips picking out the broken pieces, leaving the whole, unbroken ones for his wife and children.**

Dad lived to serve. His country. His employer. His friends. And especially, his family. And anyone anywhere who needed his help. He was an inexhaustible runner. He picked car-less neighbors up, took them to church and brought them back home. On those same Sunday mornings he would make the rounds of four different German bakeries in the area because each of us preferred a particular kuchen from one, the cream puffs from another, the brownies from yet another and so on. He shopped daily for my grandmother (his mother-in-law) who would direct him to three different grocery stores and just as many pharmacies because of her clipped coupons and brand preferences. He fell in love at first sight with my mother and held a love that never wavered until the day he died. For 54 years he could not pass her anywhere in the house without a peck on the cheek, a hug and something sweet whispered in her ear always about her being "the most beautiful woman in the world."

And he embraced his gay son. **When in 1969 he found out I was gay, he assured me he had always loved me and always would.** He never judged me. Ever. He once told me that, though a parent "Can't love one child more than another," he knew my being gay had given me a "tougher row to hoe" and he couldn't be prouder of me and the way I was living my life. This from a quiet man of so few intimate words.

That was my father, Michael Salvatore Anastasio, a provider who by the way he lived and loved was loved, admired and even adored by virtually everyone. A man small in stature who nevertheless cast an amazingly long shadow and whose goodness looms over me to this day. It is a goodness that humbles and shames me when I think of how I, as a young boy, under appreciated him, wanting him to be something other than what he was, when, he always accepted me for exactly who and what I was.

I am occasionally told that I am like my dad. When that happens I graciously accept the compliment but I know deep down it isn't true. I wasn't blessed with his unending gift of selflessness. In an ego driven world it is perhaps the rarest of qualities. Dad was just that — selfless. And so very rare.

He was a man who by his words and example made it impossible to fill his enormous size 6 shoes.

1969

Out & Out-ed

WHEN I WAS LITTLE and convinced I was the only boy who felt the way I did about other boys, I held the belief that if I ever acted on this feeling, if I ever told on myself, if I ever let on in any way about this basic difference between myself and all the other boys, I'd surely be sent to a psychiatrist and declared sexually perverse and insane. Off I'd be shuttled to one of those horrible stark looney bins I'd seen in the type of movies that ran in the middle of the afternoon or after the late night news. It was a childish view of my predicament but reasonable enough given the lack of early 1960s information from which I was making such assessments. From my first grade crush, I knew I had to keep my secret a secret. Keep the information close and guard it, for my very existence depended on my never revealing my true self. I was different from every Ronnie or Phil or Tommy that I secretly longed for and that was a secret I would just have to carry to my grave. **It was that or living a life cast out, unloved and forgotten, a tidied-away embarrassment, forever clad in a dingy white hospital gown, endlessly roaming the gray halls of a institution with high fences, bad lighting, barred windows, malevolent attendants and drooling, howling inmates. I watched too much television.**

When I eventually learned there were other boys like me and I was not in immediate danger of being locked up, I realized that I would be able to let certain people in on my secret but only others like me and mostly for sexual purposes. Anyone else, especially my beloved mother and father, must be kept in the dark. Even after I realized I'd probably not be locked away, I was still pretty certain I could not tell my family for the high risk of losing their love; or tell my friends for risk of ridicule and rejection. I especially kept at arms length any friends I found physically attractive as I just couldn't take the chance of exposing myself. Even though there might be others like me, I wouldn't find them among my friends but would be resigned to living in a part-time underground sexual world of clandestine meetings with strangers in semi-public places. Or so it seemed.

All that changed toward the end of the summer of 1969. The summer I turned 18. The summer that gave us the Walk On The Moon and Woodstock was also the summer of The Stonewall Revolution and though news of that fateful weekend did not make it to my eyes or ears at the time, my personal experience of coming out fell along the same timeline. There was another revolution just starting, a sexual one and I would find myself at the right age, at the right place, at the right time, with the right mindset. Right on the front lines. The first week away at school, I met another Michael, also from Louisville, who recognized my gayness immediately and, after hitchhiking home together (my parents would have passed-out and died), introduced me to the gay social circuit in our hometown. Or at least the flaming gay twinkie circuit. I don't think we used the word twinkie then but it certainly is descriptive. We were generally referred to as "chicken" by each other and by the older gentlemen (at the time even twenty-somethings were older gentlemen.) They were more than happy to include us, though still not drinking age, in the small private parties held in their Louisville homes. This was what I consider to be my Coming Out. I had already been out sexually for about two years but in 1969 I became part of a larger social world — the gay world. The social and sexual facets of being gay had now merged and just like that, I was part of a clandestine subculture that I happily embraced as it embraced me. Just out of high school and finally finding "my people" I not only felt desired, I felt emancipated. Annette was my given 'girl name.' They were always alliterative and I had no choice in the matter. I was having a ball being openly gay with all my new openly gay friends in this subversive parallel universe right in my own hometown. It was a new world with new mannerisms, new activities, a lot of pronoun shifting and an entirely new vocabulary. Well, the vocabulary was essentially the same. Cruising, camping, trick, wreck, rim, number, girl, sister, queen, read, drag, chicken, fluff, top, bottom, heaven, were all words familiar to me but in this new and exciting world-where-I-belonged, the meanings had changed. **Suddenly the mere mention of the words box, basket or package could give me an involuntary erection.**

Once I had naively thought that there were only two gay bars in the entire world. Now I found out that there were two or three right in Louisville. My hometown. Who knew? We were too young to get in these bars but it was certainly nice to know they were there — waiting for the stroke of midnight, September 4, 1972. There were other places where under-drinking-age gay boys went to hang out together (and make themselves available to older gay boys and men.) One was a downtown hotel lounge with a flaming-flamboyant gay pianist where we could order our cokes — at what to me was an outrageously inflated price of $1.50–listen to the piano music and be out and gay together; a kind of twinkie cafe society. Another hangout was the cafe area in the front of Masterson's Restaurant in Old Louisville. We'd hang out there for hours on Saturday nights "camping it up" and lip syncing to "Sugar, Sugar" or "I'm Gonna Make You Love Me" or whatever other suitable diva song came on. When a heterosexual couple would enter the cafe (especially if the guy was really hot) we'd call out, "Ditch the bitch and make the switch," to him, loud enough to amuse ourselves but not so loud he'd actually hear. **I was living a double life: in the daytime, still the dutiful pre-coming out son and at night a freshly-out 18 year old gay boy determined to spread his wings.** Masterson's was the only place where the two circles of the Venn diagram of that double life overlapped. Not only was Masterson's the young gay boy Saturday night hangout but it was also, coincidentally, the restaurant my family went to every Sunday right after mass. I lived in constant fear that one of the waitresses who were endlessly entertained by the campy Saturday night "girls" would pull a double-shift, work on Sunday, see me, and blow my cover. I would leave Masterson's with my "sisters" at about midnight or later, an out gay boy, and return twelve or so hours later with my family, a closeted son. It was necessary to walk right through the cafe to get to the main restaurant and I would do so, head down, eyes firmly cast on the patterned carpet, hoping no one would recognize me.

I couldn't reconcile the two facets of my life and was constantly worried about how and when they might collide. I had always been a good loving son and now I found myself lying over and over to my parents about my whereabouts and friendships. An honest kid forced into dishonesty. I wasn't happy about this but I just couldn't tell them. I was afraid of rejection I suppose, and loss of their love, but I was even more afraid if they found out, they'd try to keep me from this exciting new life. **Finding myself a denizen of an underworld called "gay," I savored every minute of its social and sexual subversion and jealously guarded my membership in it.** So I kept my beloved parents in the dark. How could I possibly come out to them? It was 1969. The word 'gay' itself had only just come out of the closet.

They surely noted the changes. My wardrobe switched from high school preppy to trendy and a little flamboyant. My hair changed dramatically; remember "The Shag?" They could have been writing off the changes to my being in college but they surely noted that my old high school friends who still came around occasionally, also now in college, were not changing in the same way. And I know they observed that I was less inclined to see my old friends and I was spending all my time with new friends they never somehow got around to meeting. I would talk about these friends with few details, but was careful never to bring them home. I couldn't. They were a flamboyant group and would certainly have "given me away." To a one, my "chicken" group were self-described "flamers" and though I wondered how I fit in, and tried, I felt I didn't quite belong. They were my only link to this exciting new world and I clung to them desperately all the while feeling out of place. I tried "Girl this" and "Miss Thing that" but none of it sat comfortably with me. I didn't feel like a girl. And it certainly wouldn't sit well with my parents. I couldn't bring home these boys who'd seem to them, more girl. I wondered if I'd ever meet any "More-presentable-to-my-parents" gay boys who, like me, didn't use makeup or feel an endless need to "camp it up." To me, being gay was about sex and that behavior wasn't sexy. I was still feeling out of place. **While I may have found my people, I had yet to locate my tribe.**

One weekend away from school, my dad picked me up from wherever in Louisville I had managed to get myself. On the drive home he said he had something to talk to me about. My dad, not one to "discuss" things had never before said these words to me. Ever. My ears perked up as I got a terrible sinking feeling in my gut. His next words, rather long in coming, confirmed what my innards had already told me. "Someone," he said, "who called himself a 'concerned party,' called me at work and wanted me to know that you have been seen around town with 'known homosexuals' and that I should do something about it 'before they turn you into one.'" He stopped there and a dead silence fell between us. **My heart was suddenly and quite literally in my throat. I could feel it there, beating wildly where the fluttering wings of a million or so butterflies below had pushed it.** My brain shifted into overdrive with questions. Who was this person? How did he know about me and my friends? Who told him? Where had he seen us? How did he know who my dad was? Dad's name? Where he works? What should I say? Was denial an option?

My dad clearly knew when it was time to be quiet. We sat there side by side, silent in the dark watching the approaching road. There was suddenly a new landscape out there in that darkness ahead, uncharted territory I hadn't planned on exploring yet. Until I was ready. Was I ready? Was the time now? It kinda had to be. The deafening silence had to be broken. In the nighttime darkness I watched my father's face or what I could see of him reflected in the windshield, looking for some indication he had more to say. It became clear he was not going to speak further. I would have to be the one to break the silence. I sat there feeling suddenly naked and gay in front of my own father, stripped of all the protective clothing I'd layered on myself, all the lies, determined to ever-avoid such a moment. Without any more thought I simply blurted out, "Its true, I guess I have been seen around town with known homosexuals because I am also a known homosexual." Still looking straight ahead, "Nobody can turn me into one, Dad, I already am one." More frozen silence. I had surprised myself with those two bold declarative statements and, taking a cue from my dad, I said no more. It was now his turn as I awaited for god-knows-what kind of response. After an eternity he finally broached the silence between us with, "You are my son. I have always loved you and always will. We have to talk to your mother." That was it. It was done. Half done at least, there was still my mom but the moment I had so dreaded had come and gone. The air was cleared and it suddenly occurred to me that I wouldn't have to lie anymore. Wrong. I wouldn't have to cover up my whereabouts and hide my friends away from the two people who meant the most to me in the world. Also wrong. Unaware of my own naïveté, I optimistically pondered all of this on the silent drive home.

It was never clear to me whether or not my dad had shared the information with my mother before sharing it with me. I couldn't imagine he had kept it from her before our discussion but by the time the three of us sat down together to talk, she knew. There was much talk as to the "how" and "why" of my being gay. They both felt that somehow they'd caused it. They had failed me. It was their fault. I assured them they were not the cause but if they had been, I'd be grateful. I was being honest but they didn't buy it. My mother in particular decided that she had said one too many times, "Mikey was always too pretty to be a boy." She was sure her gender-altering description of my babyhood had something to do with it. The end result of the conversation was the decision that I should see a therapist. Oh my god a psychiatrist! **My long dormant looney bin fear rose up and reared its ugly straight-jacketed head.** The brief thought of institutionalization flashed through my brain but it became clear their intent was not in locking me away, but simply needing another opinion — a professional one. I agreed to see a therapist.

As I sat in Dr. Connelly's wood paneled waiting room staring at a framed picture of a particularly glowing doe eyed Holy Family — Jesus, Mary and Joseph — I knew I was in trouble and wondered if it was too late to run. I suspiciously eyed the waiting others, a rather ordinary looking bunch as mismatched as the furniture we were seated on, and tried to determine what was wrong with each of them. And what would he find wrong with me? **Once seated across from my inquisitor, I just sat there silently fixated on a crucifix that was not centered between the windows behind him.** He asked me lots of questions about my gay life and my gay loves and how I felt about all of it; even my gay sex. He perked up with an optimistic show of interest when I happened to mention the dissatisfaction I felt with my first in-bed gay sex. When I explained it had to do with an overly pimpled backside (and not the actual boy-on-boy sex) that turned me off, he seemed disappointed. As it turned out he was really quite nice and not a bit threatening; and for a Catholic, not particularly judgmental. Maybe I could put to rest all my howling inmates fears. Much to my surprise, my parents reported that he had proclaimed me "pretty well adjusted" and they really shouldn't worry too much about me.

From then on, my parents adopted a posture of acceptance and containment. And silence. At their insistence, I agreed reluctantly that this information would not be shared with anyone. Not even my brother and sister. Life would go on as it had before and we'd all just ignore my homosexuality — pretend it away. No questions asked. No answers given. I sort of understood this. It was easier that way. For all of us, I guess. Talking about homosexuality was tantamount to talking about sexuality, something about which my exceedingly Catholic parents and their generation were never comfortable. I really thought my brother and sister, both older but still from my own generation, could handle it, but I'd made my promise. From that point on, my parents accepted any "friends" I brought into the house with no questions asked. Ever. They did not want to think of these boys as anything but friends. Once I had moved away from Louisville and brought these boys home for the weekend, they were completely disassociated with anything we might be doing up in my bedroom right above their sleeping heads. I suppose this did make life easier (and less embarrassing) but it drove a wedge between us. **As I embarked upon this new life, one about which the two people I loved the most, clearly wanted to know nothing and therefore play no part, I did so, alone.** The other two people I loved most, my brother and sister, were to be excluded from the truth, and my life, as well. Not only would this alienate me from them but gave me the uneasy sense that my parents somehow were trying to protect them from me and from this unpleasant truth about me.

Life did go on, but I was changed forever. I was OUT! While my parents tried their best to ignore my sexual orientation, I embraced it and proceeded with the determination of a suddenly unrestrained charging bull. **Every new social situation now held the potential for sex.** Open to every exciting thing this new world presented, I joyfully anticipated my social and sexual future.

1969

Lying My Way Into A New Year

THE NEW YEAR was on its way and my Louisville chicken friends and I had a plan. We wanted desperately to spend New Year's Eve in a gay bar. But we were all under age. We had heard there was a bar we could get into in Cincinnati, the larger Ohio City just an hour and a half drive from our little Louisville. The bar was actually a boat named the *Chaperon* and, I guess, since it was in the middle of the Ohio River and not attached to either Kentucky or Ohio, neither state's age restrictive drinking rules applied. Eighteen year olds could board the *Chaperon*. We didn't know why exactly, and didn't care. **What we did know was that we "just had" to see in the gay 70s in a gay bar.** If that gay bar happened to be floating on the Ohio River, cool!

This presented a problem. Still living with my parents since being outed to them only months before, they had become quite adept at pulling in the reins on my social activities. They wanted to know my whereabouts at all times — I became a truly proficient liar — and they tightened my curfews. While they never said so, it was clear that they were dedicated to the task of curtailing as much as was possible any of my new gay activities: social or heaven forbid, sexual. **Now out to them, a cold war was on and rather than the lying and subterfuge being over, it began to hit new heights.**

Telling them my real plans for New Year's Eve was out of the question. I could just imagine it: "Hey Mom and Dad, just so you to know, I'll be driving to Cincinnati with a flaming bunch of teenage queens you haven't met and staying up til all hours partying and god-knows-what-else on a floating gay bar in the middle of the Ohio River on New Years Eve." Their heads would have exploded. I'd have to come up with a whopper of a story to cover this plan.

Thankfully I had become quite good at this kind of deception and improbably got some assistance from the Church. On the church calendar, New Year's Day is a "Holy Day of Obligation," requiring good Catholics to get up and go to mass; a total buzz-kill effort to keep the fold from having too much of a good time on New Year's Eve, no doubt. I figured out a way to use this to my best interests. I told my parents that I'd been invited to a New Year's Eve party that a bunch of my old high school friends (subtext: straight, familiar and dependably respectable) were having. Since it was a New Year's Eve party, it would undoubtedly run quite late so the whole lot of us (subtext: good Catholic kids that we were) planned to attend the 5:00am mass at Holy Spirit Church (adding in the poshest and classiest of all the Louisville parishes was a typical sort of flourish I'd become so proficient at.) After mass then, we'd probably go to breakfast. I figured that'd give me until about 7:30am to get to Cincinnati with my gay buddies, ring in the New Year on the boat, get up to whatever other activity we (or I) might be lucky enough to find post-cruise and get back to Louisville. **It was a perfectly crafted lie meticulously laced together with an unthreatening combination of heterosexual and ecclesiastical familiarity, delivered with great sincerity.** They bought it.

The whole gay group of us piled into my friend Michael's car and off we went to our big gay New Year's Eve adventure in Cincinnati. Dressed in our festive best — it was the year of the chocolate brown shirt so I was in mine along with my brand new brown and copper striped flairs — we cranked the car radio up and lip-synched our way to Cincinnati "doing drag" to Bobbie Gentry's "Fancy" and The Supremes' "Someday We'll Be

Together" and the like. I just couldn't wait to board that floating gay bar and we could not make that hour and a half trip to Cincinnati fast enough. We were all filled with the excitement of not only experiencing our first gay bar but also of who we might meet — and in what romantic and sexual situations we might find ourselves. It was, after all, New Year's Eve. One of my friends insisted we each find someone before midnight as it would be "too too tragic" if we had only "our sisters" to kiss as the new year rang in. My mind reeled and my ever dependable teenage penis hardened in my flairs at the possibility.

We arrived at the *Chaperon* which turned out to be a well past its prime smoke-stacked stern-wheeled river boat. We parked the car on the steeply inclined cobblestoned bank of the Ohio River and approached the boat in the fervent hope that eighteen year olds really were allowed on. We boarded with no problem. **I was in my first gay bar, albeit a floating one but still, I was in my first gay bar!** The boat filled up pretty quickly and we shoved off at about 9pm. the *Chaperon* was a little shabby, decked with hanging Christmas lights all around and didn't look entirely seaworthy or even river-worthy but I didn't care. I was in a gay bar. At last. Words simply fail to describe the feeling of elation; the overwhelming sense of possibility. It was so much fun dancing surrounded by nothing but other gay boys, and a few girls. It was a pretty eclectic and kind of seedy bunch but once again, who cared? I was in a gay bar. I watched male couples slow-dance together and I almost giggled. It looked strange to me. At some point I found myself dancing next to a really cute boy. In not too long a time we were dancing with each other rather than side by side. Danny, if I remember his name correctly, had enormous brown eyes with way too many eyelashes, a crooked smile that turned up boyishly at the corners and a lean athletic build. We danced and danced and when a slow song came on, we pressed ourselves together. He smelled of The Baron cologne. While boy-on-boy slow dancing may have looked odd at first, it felt wonderful. By this time I'd slow danced with many a girl but it never felt like this. Earlier on the trip up, one of my friends suggested that if we slow-danced with another boy, "the thing to do is to press your leg into his crotch to show him you're interested." As we were dancing I could feel Danny's thigh pressing into my own crotch. He must be interested! His interest was rewarded with a spontaneous stiffening in those brand new flairs. I returned the favor and felt him hardening against my thigh. His warm breath was in my ear. I didn't want that slow dance to end. Ever. Later in the evening still lost in Danny's arms he suddenly said, "Look," and pointed to a window. It was snowing. Really snowing! Snow was all we could see out every window. We were dancing together in a twinkle-lighted reverse snow globe — a snowy floating fairyland. It was nearly midnight when Danny took my hand and, rushing us through the dancing crowd, pulled me outside with him. As the clock struck midnight, our New Year rang in, to the muffled sound of the celebrating inside. **With the snow swirling around us in the shivering cold, in the middle of the Ohio River, on the bow of an ancient old riverboat plowing its way through the snowy night, I was warmed and kissed by another boy in a wildly romantic, sexy New Year's Eve moment that has yet to be matched these many years hence.**

It was 1970, a brand new decade full of possibility and the experience of my first gay bar, Danny, and that kiss had made all the planning, all the lying and deceit well worth the effort. It was all, in the gay vernacular of the time, "Heaven." Danny was heaven. The *Chaperon* was heaven. The snow was heaven. 1970 was already heaven and I was in heaven. Gay heaven. Until we came ashore. **The snow that was softly romantic while we were aboard the *Chaperon* suddenly became a harshly inconvenient blizzard.** Our car, parked on that cobblestone incline was going nowhere. There was too much snow, too much ice and an incline way too steep to get out. Even if we could have moved the car we'd have never made the snowy drive back to Louisville. We were stuck in Cincinnati. A kindly older gentleman who had wisely not parked on the incline and was "interested" in one of our group, drove us to a nearby motel and got two rooms. We gladly sacrificed our friend to the older man for a ride and a warm, dry, semi-private place to spend the night with a new pair of add-on boys we'd collected. On the way, I fretted about what I was going to tell my parents. I was stuck in Cincinnati and would not be coming home. I needed a reason. I thought out some new convoluted lie to heap on my earlier convoluted lies, but it was all too complicated. As far as they were concerned, I was still in Louisville. Had I been certain the blizzard had extended to Louisville, I could have used the snow to stay put wherever I was supposed to be, there. But there was no way of knowing. I had to come clean...at least about the Cincinnati part.

From that overcrowded motel room, I bit the bullet and called, knowing my parents would be sound asleep. Also knowing that phone calls in our house meant bad news; phone calls in the middle of the night meant tragic news. My mom groggily answered the phone and after assuring her that I was fine, the extemporane-ous lying began. I started into my explanation as to why I wasn't coming home. I lied that only a couple of people had shown up for the party in Louisville. Since there really wasn't a party, one friend had known about another party in Cincinnati that we could go to. I heard my mother whisper to my dad, "He's in Cincinnati." And from my dad in the background, "WHAT THE HELL IS HE DOING IN CINCINNATI?" He was clearly unhappy. I continued on with the story of the snow and how we thought it too dangerous to try to get back to Louisville that night. There was, by the way, no snow in Louisville. Not a flake. I don't think they bought a word of my story, not even the snow.

It had all gone so wrong so fast. The snow. The ice. My lying. My angry parents. My first horizontal gay sex — finally — but with a boy disappointingly covered from his shoulders to his butt in a horror show of dick-limping teenage pimples. I didn't even know back acne was a thing. Could you catch it? To make matters worse, upon leaving the motel room, a few of my "friends" decided at the last minute to trash it. I'd never seen or imagined such a thing. I watched from the hallway, horrified, as they vandalized the place, tossing the mattresses off the beds, turning over furniture and ripping down the draperies. I thought of the kind, unsuspecting gentleman asleep in his room, who'd paid for our's and would undoubtedly be expected to pay for the damage. I swore I'd get new friends. **The 70s which had started with such sweet promise had soured and curdled.**

When I finally made it home, it was to a silent house. They were on to me. I was sure they knew the entire thing was a big homosexual lie from convoluted beginning to tragic end — something I'd manufactured in order to pursue my new deviant sexual lifestyle. 1970 would begin with a wary sense of silence in the Anas-tasio household. Surely my parents were pondering this new person living under their roof. Meanwhile, in his upstairs bedroom, "This new person," listening to Barbra Streisand singing "He Touched Me," despite all the parent drama, was aglow remembering the dancing, the bulging pants and that perfect midnight moment on the bow of an old riverboat with the kiss that had made it all worthwhile. **He *had* touched me, in a way I'd never been touched and, just like Barbra sang, "nothing, nothing, nothing" would ever be the same.** But what of my dear parents? The poor things. They were just not equipped for any of this. How were they supposed to know how to deal with a gay son? Their eighteen year old darling who was now apparently driven (and in the "wrong" direction) only by his penis? I'm sure they didn't like knowing I even had one. There was certainly no parental instructional manual for this. Not in a brand new 1970. No sir. They were winging it and so was I. Heading into a gay new year and a gay new decade, how was I supposed to deal with them? I had changed but they hadn't. Honesty was not an option. The more honestly I tried to pursue my new lifestyle, the more adept they became at curtailing it. Neither was conformity to a forever tossed off heterosexual "norm" an option. It was too late for that. **Having tasted my life as it was meant to be — there were more Dannys out there — I was ready for a feast. I wouldn't be starved out.**

My poor parents. They tried so hard to ignore my homosexuality but it was in the habit of rearing its "ugly" head and biting them in their own self interests. In February 1971 having moved on to the University of Kentucky in Lexington, I returned home for a weekend visit. My mom and dad had a new favorite sitcom about a "lovable" bigot trying to cope with all the societal changes around him. They assured me I'd love it. The character's family was constantly challenging him on his prejudices. They loved how the show used humor to strip away the thin veneer of the main character's bigotry. The fact that his narrow views rather closely aligned with those of my sister's husband, also made the character, Archie Bunker, relevant in our house. On Saturday evening we sat down together to watch *All In The Family*. In one of those moments when the universe was clearly showing itself in my favor, wouldn't you know the episode was about homosexuality and intolerant Archie's homophobia. The elephant in the room which my parents had gone to such great lengths to pretend away was right there on their TV screen announcing itself. "The love that dare not speak its name" was shouting at them through their new favorite sitcom — which they'd sat me down to watch — and exposing my mom and dad's homophobia right along with Archie's. It was an uncomfortable thirty minutes and there was no discussion afterwards. Their favorite new sitcom had betrayed them.

I'm certain they were hoping my being gay was "Just a phase" something that would work it's way out with my eventual return to the "normal" son they'd known and loved all along. Or the son they *thought* they'd known and loved all along. I'm quite certain, especially with my mother praying rosary after rosary, they held onto the hope and prayer that god would return their beloved little Mikey to the heterosexual fold.

Quite unwittingly, I ended up playing right into those silent prayers.

1970

Continuing Education

IN THE SPRING OF 1970, one of my twinkie friends was invited to a Derby party. There existed in those days a gay party circuit and Louisville, with its Kentucky Derby, was part of the circuit. While I knew nothing of it at the time, Louisville would become, for one weekend each year, the hot destination for gays from around the world. I attended that Derby party as my friend's plus one. Held in a big home on Lexington Road in the posh neighborhood of St. Matthews, it was right around the corner from where my childhood choir director (and early crush) Mr. Ellis had lived. I was totally unprepared for what greeted us as I stepped through the garden gate with my friend and I found myself at my first big gay party: men, stunning men, muscular athletic men, sexy masculine men, by the hundreds, men from all around the world packed the place. Colorfully well-dressed with drinks in hand, they lined the wooden walls of the large backyard garden, traversed its large brick patio and over-filled the rooms of the house as well. **We were local 'chicken' dazzled by this brand-new-to-us glamorous homosexual rooster pen.** Overwhelmed at first and thoroughly intimidated — I was only 18 in this sea of older, sophisticated and experienced men — much to my own shy surprise, we were both quite popular. My age was not the liability I'd thought, but an asset instead. Who knew? I certainly had no idea the sexual power I could have wielded in those days and it's just as well, I suppose.

The scope of my tiny gay world increased exponentially, with that one party where I suddenly found I was attractive and attracted. I discovered, quite literally, a whole world of handsome, kind, attentive, sexy gay men. It was a gay universe much larger than anything I had ever imagined. I met a man from Australia and instantaneously fell in love with him and his accent. In addition to all the "foreigners," there were also a lot of local gays: architect, restaurant owner, doctor and even a pilot of the *Belle of Louisville* where I ended up that night. Sex on a landmark riverboat. **I'd located my tribe.**

And my tribe had located me. I found myself, post Derby, welcomed into an entirely new circle of friends, mostly older with apartments and homes of their own where I was welcome to hang out pretty much whenever I wished. **In the process of being friended by these men, I was given a blueprint for my future.** They were, to a one, smart, witty, handsome and accomplished with gorgeous homes and wonderful lives. They set flawless tables and threw fabulous parties. I'd never before seen driveways and patios lined with tiki torches or a self-service wall of diner-style drink machines filled with a frothing rainbow of alcoholic beverages. They traveled to sunny exotic places surrounded by boys, and had lots and lots of sex. **They were gay role models; I wanted to grow up to be just like them and could imagine a day when I would have a place of my own and like them, fill it with lots of gay boys.** These were the men who took me to my first ballet. My first orchestra concert. I was a hungry sponge as they taught me about design, taste, theater, smart thrift store shopping, entertaining and so many other things that galvanize gay men together in an often hostile world, things I still hold dear. They were wonderfully generous and kind. And sadly, during the 80s and into the 90s, one by one, most of them would die.

College had started in 1969 with Murray State University. After an unfortunate 60s-style campus protest gone awry, I was asked not to return. Something about "inciting a riot." After only one semester. Don't ask. This wasn't bad news however, having felt, since the moment I'd arrived at MSU in the wilds of western Kentucky, I had made a big mistake. I took the next semester off and enjoyed my new gay friends and new gay life in Louisville; well, as much as I could get away with since I still lived with my parents and they were still trying their best to limit my activities. Needing further education, and more autonomy, I decided to go back to school. I set off in the fall of 1970 for the University of Kentucky in Lexington where I found a new group of gay friends. They helped me fake the date on my driver's license to get me into the local gay bar downtown. The Living Room had a well lighted front entrance right on Main St, but no one ever used it, preferring to enter under the cloak of darkness at the rear entrance, off the unlighted parking lot. Approaching that dark lot on my first trip there, my friend Glenn instructed me to park a bit further away where I could back the car up against a building so my license plate wouldn't show; in those days in Kentucky we only had plates on the rear of the car. **He told me the police would ride by and take down the numbers of any license plates they could see in order to put the car owners' names on a list of "suspected homosexuals."** That was Kentucky circa 1970. The possibility scared me to death, particularly since the car was registered to my father and his name was Michael too. It didn't stop me from going however. I would just be careful.

The main bar of The Living Room, decorated in a scarlet on scarlet flocked Parisian Brothel look was primarily for cruising. The upstairs was for dancing and drag shows. That is where I saw my first drag show and where I made my first drag queen friends, Wilfred and Leo. Wilfred and Leo were the Mutt and Jeff of African

American drag queens; Wilfred being a good six foot six skinny inches tall. Add to that stilettos and a wig and he was easily seven feet. Leo was a petite five foot two or so. I learned how to be fearless from these two. They taught me by example how to be different and the courage it takes to openly be who you are and live how you must. And were those girls talented! They did their own hair and makeup and made their rather extravagant outfits. Wilfred, who's drag name was Crystal Blue, even did his own from-behind-the-stage announcing. In a husky masculine voice several registers below his usual, he'd announce, "And now…put your hands together and welcome to the stage…if you will…the tall and tantalizing, persuasive Crystal Blue," and off she'd trot onto the stage, suddenly Crystal. Wilfred taught me about "shrimp and biscuit." The bane of existence for any drag queen in those early days, especially big girls like Wilfred, was finding high heels large enough. Since high heels were made for women, they were always way too small. A big drag queen's too-large-for-the-shoes feet would inevitably require a sandal style, open at the front and rear. Just as inevitably, the toes would hang over the front in what my clever drag queen friend described as "shrimp." The heel (typically ashy) would hang over the back of the shoe creating what truly looked like a big biscuit. Hence "shrimp and biscuit." Silly visual imagery — typically gay campy humor — that has remained forever embedded in my consciousness.

It was at the Living Room where every night when the bar was ready to close, upstairs they'd play "United We Stand Divided We Fall." It was a popular new song and happened to be the motto on our own Kentucky state flag. We would all rise and stand with our arms around each other swaying and singing together in a lovely show of solidarity. In that little upstairs dance room, in that little gay bar in little Lexington, KY, there'd be drag queens and businessmen, bartenders and hustlers, students and professors, college boys and senior citizens, all sorts and types. **We'd join together, as one, singing a song of mutual support before heading back out into the uncertain, often hostile world outside where we would, no longer bound to each other, singularly and vulnerably go about our small town southern lives.**

Pulling out of the bar's parking lot, you'd glance up at your rear view mirror to see a pair of headlights following. It could be an interested guy who'd followed you out of the bar; more likely, it was a police car. You'd drive terrified of being pulled over while knowing you would. After several blocks, the inevitable red lights would start to flash and you and your increasing heart rate and sweating palms would pull over. There was so much to be afraid of. He might notice the altered date on your driver's license. Even when he didn't, he'd still ask all the same questions: "Where did you just come from?" You knew he knew the answer to that one, he'd followed you out of the parking lot. "What goes on in there?" Why, you wondered to yourself, was he so interested? "What were you doing in there?" Stress the word "doing." "How much did you have to drink?" You'd then be instructed, wildly beating heart, sweating palms and all, to step out of the car and walk a straight line, touch your nose and do god knows what else. After finding no infractions he'd allow you to get back in your car and drive away, same sweaty palms gripping the steering wheel and heart still beating wildly. He would continue to follow for several blocks before finally turning off. Just to intimidate.

1970...

An Unexpected Left Turn

HAD I EVER HEARD THE TERM "SOUL MATE," and understood its meaning I might have also understood my instant attraction to Dawn. I saw her from well-across the room in the cavernous Reynolds Building, a former tobacco warehouse converted to art studio. It was the first day of my first art class during my first year at the University of Kentucky. We, all of us art students, were sitting, some in folding chairs and some on the floor in a loose circle surrounding our young instructor, a blond, long haired, cute, bell-bottomed, hippie-looking artist who seemed not much older than any of us, his students. I watched her from the opposite side of that circle. I knew her. I couldn't say how, but I did already, know her. I could not take my eyes away. She had a short, for lack of a better word, 'pixie' haircut, Titian red, that gave her a boyish look, a singularly pretty boyish look with enormous pale green eyes and extraordinarily long thick eyelashes — a prettier young Shirley MacLaine type. Or was it Leslie Carón? Was it that resemblance that made her familiar? I think not. Whatever the case, it was a face I recognized instantly; though I had never seen it before, I knew it by heart. It was emblazoned onto my memory as though I had seen it a thousand times, grown up with it even. A face that, at first glance, was already familiar. Around her neck was a multi-color Indian bead choker. She was wearing a pale green oversized sweatshirt, tight Capri-style peddle-pushers in a bright print and trim white sneakers — a well executed 1950s Parisian chic. It was the only chic in that shabby circle of freshman art students. She was a standout, glowing as if lit from within, setting herself apart from all the rest of the other rather disheveled and forgettable students, myself included, who were gathered around listening to instructions on our first assignment. She was, in Kentucky parlance, a "thoroughbred." I was captivated from the get-go. I was, quite simply…hers.

There was some sort of mishap with a folding chair in which she got a "grundgie," to use our teacher's word, on her leg just above the ankle. She was embarrassed, I think as much by the word "grundgie" as by the mishap itself, but it gave me the opportunity to come to her first aid with a Kleenex. Her name was Dawn. "Of course it is," I thought. "Dawn." It fit. I'd have committed it to memory but I didn't need to. Like her face, it was already there. Remembered. Pre-burnished onto my mind's eye in a sparkling script... Dawn…waiting for the day we would actually meet.

We walked from class and I think we fell pretty madly in love with each other in a matter of blocks. I told her I was gay but it didn't seem to matter. To either of us. "Love conquers all," is what she'd say again and again. She believed it. She also loved Italian men. Now as gay goes I am as gay as you can get. A 'perfect Kinsey 6,' with absolutely no sexual attraction for the opposite sex. But, somehow we managed to navigate the heterosexual waters around us. We also, when I got pressed in to it, had pretty good sex. I know some of it was ego on my part as no one, male or female, had ever found me as attractive as Dawn had. That can work wonders on a needy ego. She'd also once used the "b" word, "beautiful," to describe me. Well actually, it was my bare feet. My feet? I'd never even noticed them. Such a compliment can go a long way for a boy who had a lifelong obsession with beauty but never found beauty anywhere in himself. She had called my feet "beautiful" and I would never look at them in the same way. It was much more, though than that. We had a significant, very special connection that at the time I didn't understand and couldn't explain. What did I know, at nineteen about 'Soul Mates?'

Dawn was also from Louisville and the first time we went back for a visit, her father picked us up in Lexington. With "Your Song" by a brand new recording artist named Elton John playing on the radio, we made our way home. "Your Song" immediately became "our song" and we'd sing it together constantly. Of course I was grilled about this new young woman in my life who I had endlessly talked about: how pretty she was, how fun she was, all the things we'd done together. I was, sadly and inadvertently giving my parents false hope for a potential return to heterosexuality. Who could blame them? Dawn was the red-headed answer to their many prayers.

When it was time to return to school, my father drove me to Dawn's house so her dad could then drive us back to Lexington. Not sure of the location, we gave ourselves plenty of 'get lost' time. We didn't get lost so we arrived earlier than expected. I saw two red headed boys playing frisbee in a front yard and knowing Dawn had two bothers I had my dad pull into the driveway. This had to be the place as the boys were dead ringers for Dawn, short tousled red hair and all. As I opened the car door, one of the boys saw me. He looked shocked and frightened and letting out a squeal he covered his face and ran for the front door. That's when I realized the boy was not Dawn's brother but was actually Dawn. I had never seen her without makeup and she, running to the house, was determined I wouldn't. She needn't have worried as I found her somewhat boyish look attractive. Without makeup she was even more boyish. It was the eyelashes. Being a redhead her light blond eyelashes without mascara, though long and thick, practically disappeared. That was the first and last time I ever saw Dawn without mascara.

I met Dawn's mother that evening and she was a hoot. She was British and was always seated in the same corner of the sofa, drink in hand in varying stages of tipsy every time I ever saw her. I don't think she even stood up to greet me, or my father. The sofa was permanently hollowed out where she sat. I'm not certain she ever approved of me but I was drawn to her probably because she was European (my second European ever) and therefore exotic by my small world standards. And sarcastically funny in that wry, snarky and amusingly new to me, British way.

Back at school Dawn and I became inseparable. Best friends. With benefits. And when we weren't together, we'd be on the phone for hours, falling asleep with each other, neither wanting to be the one to hang up. She gave me a nickname: Maca. **She said I gave her the "issy-foos" and, snuggling up to me and breathing the made-up word into my ear in such a soft sensual way, she made me understand it immediately.** She was softly seductive and sexily sensual. She tried so hard. She always thought of herself in competition with all the men I had been with before her and the ones that she assumed (correctly) with whom I was still having sex. It was 1970, three years post-the summer of love and there was an air of sexual permissiveness, fluidity and exploration that our relationship fit quite nicely into. We were a product of our baby boomer, counter-cultural, sexual revolution, 'anything goes' era.

1971

Straight Boy

HE WAS TALL, BLOND AND HANDSOME and, with a sexy athletic walk, was headed right toward me on the sidewalk in front of my Lexington, Kentucky rooming house. His pale blue eyes seemed to connect with mine before he surprisingly turned onto the sidewalk leading up to the house. My house. Was it his house too? This tall blond god? I lagged back a bit waiting to see and sure enough he put a key in the front door and disappeared inside. I followed, pausing briefly to glance through the opened French doors and smile a "hello" to my ancient landlady — apparently "our" ancient landlady — as she sat in the living room of her boarding house. She was there day and night having (it seemed) nothing better to do than monitoring the comings and goings of her residents. I heard the blond god's footfalls preceeding me up the stairs and a door — his door — open and close. The athletic broad-shouldered blond boy lived in the room right next to mine. It was an instant crush and I was suddenly Judy Garland in *Meet Me In St. Louis,* loving "The Boy Next Door" more and more each day.

Subsequent to that first sighting, I would hear his comings and goings past my room and it wasn't too long before I'd engineered, in the hallway outside our shared bathroom, a "chance" meeting with the boy next door. Jack and I hit it off immediately. We began to hang out together — a lot — mostly in his room since it was significantly larger. We'd talk until all hours of the night. He had a girlfriend back home and I had just met Dawn, so we were just straight boys hanging out together; except for the fact that I wasn't straight. And I was falling in love.

I knew I had to tell him that I was gay but had trouble finding the words. We'd quickly become such good friends. **It's always like this. When you first meet someone new, it's too early to share such a confidence and then, once you're friends, it's too late. It's as if you've been concealing a major truth when in actuality, you're only trying to assess the right time, worried of course, about rejection.** Or worse. Once I finally did find the right time and words to tell him that his new best friend was gay, he was pretty shocked and reacted by holing himself in his room for a few days of "burning things," is how he put it. He must've had a fireplace though I don't remember one. It didn't take him long to come around and we continued our friendship. We named our South Limestone Street boarding house "Tacky Terrace" and he nursed me through a mild case of mono — a bonding experience and collegiate rite of passage. **Jack was a voice major with a big booming operatic voice and also a rough and tumble rugby player — an unlikely artistic and muscular dichotomy I found irresistible.** Plus, his singer's diaphragm control gave him abs of steel. I would attend his choral concerts as well as his rugby matches. Those rugby players — "It takes leather balls to play rugby" — in their tight little short shorts and rugby shirts were some of the biggest, beefiest, sexiest boys on campus. My little green and white Nash Rambler became the team mascot (along with myself) and hauled some of the boys and most of the equipment around. **I was in sweaty dirty athletic love. With a little opera on the side.**

When summer break arrived, I returned to Louisville as did Dawn while Jack stayed on in Lexington for summer classes. He began a search for an apartment we could share. I had three requirements: a quiet street, an eat-in kitchen and a lot of closet space. With some reservation, I left the search in Jack's hands. He called one day excited with the news that he'd found the perfect apartment that met all my criteria. He had to rent it immediately because apartments, especially ones "as good as this one, go fast." Some weeks later I was able to get away and visit Lexington and see our new apartment. Jack had done his homework. It was on a lovely quiet tree lined street. It was clear he wanted me to like the new place as much as he as he began to show it off. "Look at this closet," he said as he opened the door to an exceedingly generous entryway closet. I was impressed. As he led me into a sizable living room we quickly turned right into the kitchen. "Look at that," he said as he proudly pointed to the sweetest little built-in breakfast nook. I was charmed. Back in the living room Jack swung open another door to another large closet. "Wow," was all I could say. He'd really done a great job. He crossed the living room and opened one more door. I stuck my head in and exclaimed, "Now this is a closet!" "No," he answered, "this is a bedroom!" A bedroom? It had no windows. "It has no windows!" I bellowed in opposition. "Does too," was his answer as he pointed to a tiny transom at ceiling height that opened into the building's interior hallway. Ignoring this technicality I continued, rather harshly if I'm honest, "If we try to wedge even a double bed in here it'll touch all four walls!" It was true. The "room" was, without exaggeration, that small. "Not a problem," Jack stated proudly, "my dad's gonna build us bunk beds for twin size mattresses, not those puny little bunk ones," adding, "it'll be great!" I was unconvinced. Seeing the disappointment on my face he reminded me, "I got you everything you asked for." True enough. Clearly in my list of requirements I had forgotten to mention a bedroom.

Jack's dad did build us bunk beds — rather sturdy ones from 2 x 4s. I took the top. We christened the building "Adequate Arms" and started our next year of college life together in our nearly perfect little apartment with our closet bedroom and before either of us knew it, we were having closet sex. Yep, somehow I had gotten my horny way. I can't remember exactly how it happened the first time but one collegiate night when straight boy Jack, separated from his hometown girlfriend and having been turned down by one or more of his campus girlfriends, horny as only a college-age boy can be, acquiesced and allowed me to have my way with him. It would happen regularly thereafter; his lying back and allowing me to "do him," oftentimes (and I am not proud of this) while he was on the phone with one or another of his many girlfriends. That made it super-hot for me and perhaps "less gay" for him. I didn't care. I was getting what I wanted. **My first straight boy dick.** Even the fact he'd (in straight boy fashion) named it "Irwin" couldn't turn me off. I was in love with Irwin too.

Jack said he loved me and that's why he could do with me the things we did. I understood since I was having the same experience with Dawn. I loved her and our sex was a product of that love. He was also, think, worried about me and the trouble I might get into cruising on campus. Or going out to the gay bar. As long as he kept "my horns clipped" I'd stay home and out of impending doom. He cared that much for me. And he was getting a lot of really good blow jobs. Jack's sex with me didn't make him gay any more than mine with Dawn made me straight. We were a product not only of our love for each other but of the sexual revolution happening all around us. Things had become sexually fluid. Even in Lexington, Kentucky.

At one point Jack bought a motorcycle. We named it "Momo" and off we'd go on adventure after adventure — me with my arms wrapped around his waist (girlfriend-style) as we'd explore the back-hills of Kentucky. Now I was Patty Duke in *Me Natalie.* We'd go camping together (sleeping naked) and in the musty confines of an old army tent I'd do all the things to him that I'd fantasized doing to my childhood friend Tommy in our Ardmore Drive backyard tent sleepovers. **It was Grade A fantasy fulfillment having campground sex by the fire with a willing, horny straight boy in the woods.** And a bit scary as these were the deep backwoods of Appalachian Eastern Kentucky and we weren't always smart in our campground choices. In 1971, on one such camping trip, "strangers" that we were, after being stared at by the locals throughout dinner at the Main Street greasy spoon, we made the mistake of seeing exactly the wrong movie in the theater next door; *Straw Dogs* with Dustin Hoffman. It's an uber-violent film about a young couple harassed and worse by a vicious group of local red-neck stereotypes. We spent a terrified overnight back at the campsite clinging to our fears (and probably each other) worried about whatever violent toothless forces lay just beyond our woefully inadequate tent flaps.

Over time my relationship with Dawn grew and I, taking another break from education, would return with her to Louisville. I never imagined my relationship with Jack could be anything more than a loving friendship (with sex), so we parted as good friends. He moved on too and after a few years, as was inevitable in those days of growth, change and relocation, we lost track of each other.

1972

Back Into The Gay Lane

BACK IN LOUISVILLE and away from Jack, I spent more and more of my time with Dawn and her friends and less time in my gay world. All our straight friends were coupling up and getting engaged and it just seemed to be the thing to do despite 'the gay thing.' The Christmas I presented her with a diamond engagement ring, of course, she presented me with a gold signet ring. We were always on the same page that way. The inside inscription, '*Love Dawn*' though diminished through the years is still legible in the ring which to this day, I still wear.

We both loved old movies and the classic movie houses that showed them. We had a particular fondness for Fred Astaire and Ginger Rogers. Dawn was Ginger to my Fred. We'd go out dancing dressed to the nines, she in the full-skirted "petunia dress" she'd made herself and modeled after Ginger's from *The Gay Divorceé*. We loved Katharine Hepburn and couldn't see *The Philadelphia Story* enough. **Dawn was my own personal Tracy Lord. "My she was yare," quick-witted, funny, elegantly above it all, incendiary and most of all a firm believer, against all odds, in True Love.** We adored Audrey Hepburn and shared an absolute fixation with *Breakfast At Tiffany's*. More than once we would find ourselves crying together under a single umbrella in the rain just like Holly and Paul, trying to hold on to a relationship that was clearly doomed from the start.

We both loved Barbra Streisand and had *What's Up, Doc?* memorized. She wore her long hair up, just like Barbra's Judy Maxwell. We especially loved *On A Clear Day* and saw this musical about reincarnation, appropriately, over and over and over again. **Whenever it looked like we might not make it together, Dawn would quote Daisy Gamble with, "If you miss me in this life, you can catch me in the next." She was quite certain we were destined for each other and if it couldn't be in this life, then, there would just have to be another time for us. She would recite that quote over and over throughout our relationship in sad and quiet resignation.**

We continued as a straight couple, hanging out with other straight couples and doing straight couple things but more and more I really began to miss the gay life that I had inhabited so comfortably and appropriately before our meeting. While I was able to have sex with her I missed the thrill of sex. I missed the hunt. I missed the carnal attraction that I had with men. Most of all I missed the passion. **I needed someone to give me "the issy-foos." I was, after all, gay and being gay was my favorite thing about myself.** I'd somehow lost track of that. As much as I loved Dawn, the passion just wasn't there and it couldn't be manufactured. I also missed the social aspect of the gay world. I missed the bars and parties and the fun. I loved being gay and I loved being surrounded by other gay men. At dances that weren't half as much fun as a night at a gay bar, I'd dance with Dawn but over her back I'd check out the asses of other guys dancing with their girlfriends. It just didn't seem fair to her. To either of us. More and more I'd find my way back to my gay bars or after dropping her off at her place, to Cherokee Park looking for some quick sex. I missed my former life and was having a dual existence with a foot in both worlds, doing complete justice to neither. Dawn's green-eyed jealousy didn't help either and my being gay gave her twice the opportunity to be jealous. All other men and even women were suspect. We were at some Catholic function and I suppose throughout the meal I gave a bit too much attention to a handsome young priest seated at our table. "If I grow a red beard," she snidely said to me later that evening, "would you look at me that way?" Like her mother, she could have a sarcastic side.

I realized that I couldn't keep up this double-life, so I made the heartbreaking decision to break up with Dawn. I had to let her go so she could pursue her own happiness. And I, mine. It was clear, to me at least, that we could never find our complete happiness with each other. Love, apparently does not conquer all. I think the breakup was devastating to Dawn and I am afraid she carried that hurt far longer than perhaps she should have. She did marry, though, quite happily and with her handsome Italian husband, raised two predictably beautiful children, a girl and a boy. She adored my also devastated parents as much as they adored her and she stayed in touch with them after I left Louisville. Whenever I'd return to Louisville, we would meet for lunch. Over the years our lives took different, quite divergent paths. By the time she died of cancer in 2012 we had become "Christmas card friends." My sister having read the obituary in Louisville's newspaper, notified me of Dawn's death the night before her funeral. Too late to make it.

Not long ago, I was going through boxes of stored away things trying to lighten my load. I came across a stack of old Barbra Streisand albums, vinyl records I could never bring myself to throw away. For some reason I pulled out the *On A Clear Day* album. As I slid the record from the sleeve, along with it came a big optimistic yellow envelope. On it was written, "Maca" in Dawn's unmistakable handwriting. There was a card inside and in the same hand as the envelope were the words "If you miss me in this life you can catch me in the next. Love, Dawn." She must have slipped the card in that particular album expecting it to be found within days at its next playing but the card had remained there, waiting to be discovered some forty years later as a reminder that *our* time was yet to come. **Catch you in the next, soul mate.**

1973

Friendship, Dreams & Weed Grow In A Storybook Cottage

AS THE BABY OF MY FAMILY, I suppose my parents expected me to live with them in my Louisville home forever. I had other ideas. At the ripe old age of twenty-one, post–Dawn and once again resolutely homosexual, having to explain my whereabouts (especially late-night whereabouts) to my parents had gotten pretty old. In our traditional Roman Catholic household that never spoke of sex, I couldn't say to them, "I probably won't be home tonight as I'll be fucking god knows what guy I haven't even met yet, god knows where, until god knows when…and then…if I get lucky…there might be somebody else…someplace else." No, that wouldn't work. I was anxious to get out on my own and not have to account for my every hour. I was ready to be adult, autonomous and free; sexually free. **After my unsuccessful turn into the straight lane, I was ready to be full-speed ahead in the wonderfully curvy gay one.** It's where I belonged all along and I wanted every social, sexual and romantic experience I could have at every rest-stop along that homo-highway. Once again I was Dorothy and if I was going to live my life the way I wanted, I had to get out of Kansas and away from my own Aunt Em and Uncle Henry. No matter how much they loved me, under their roof I couldn't be me.

I didn't know how I was going to get out of the house where I was born, I just knew I would. Would it take a tornado too?

It was right around this time that I'd met Randy and we'd become fast friends spending as much time as we could together, for two gay boys living under their parents' respective roofs. We had flirted with the possibility of finding an apartment together but his being only 18 years old, jobless and on his way to college, it didn't seem likely that his parents would be too pleased with the idea.

Eventually a friend named Doug told me of an opportunity to share a house owned by a University of Louisville professor going away on an extended European sabbatical. The house in question, a stone cottage actually turned out to be a real stunner, a storybook carriage house tucked away in one of Louisville's lovely rolling wooded residential neighborhoods in an area known as The Highlands. **It was truly an enchanted cottage of the fairy tale variety and one of Louisville's oldest residences.** We'd heard it was the only surviving structure on the old George Rodgers Clark estate. It had thick stone walls, sparkling leaded and stained glass windows, a soaring cathedral style ceiling with heavy rough hewn beams and a huge stone fireplace. It appeared to have been plucked from some fairy tale medieval village and inexplicably deposited in Dundee Estates. **The house was tastefully furnished — antiques, bauhaus furniture pieces, books and art — in a way that only a highly educated tasteful gay man of a certain age would.**

Randy or no Randy, I leapt at the chance. I packed up and left my sad parents in tears — especially my poor grieving mother — the night I departed the home where I'd grown up. It was nothing short of tragic for her but I was suddenly free and began having the time of my life. I was finally able to come and go at will. Staying up all night I could binge on an entire bag of Oreos or staying out all night I could binge on an entire night of sex. I could bring guys home. Lots of guys. Day or night. Anyone and anytime I liked. I especially loved meeting a boy at the bar downtown or the woods of Cherokee Park and have my new friend follow me home in his car along the winding wooded roads, up and down hills, over a stone bridge which crossed a babbling brook and eventually pulling up to that wonderful little stone cottage. He'd be fully seduced before we'd even crossed the threshold. I was suddenly living my own fairy tale in a fairy tale cottage. Somehow things just work out for me.

Not too long into the carriage house stay, my flight attendant roommate Doug decided to make a career change which would move him to a culinary institute in Southern Indiana. Did I know of anyone who could take his place? Did I! **I presented the opportunity to Randy and he moved right in.** By this time he'd picked up a part-time job at a suburban department store and because his parents had met and become comfortable with me, they presented no problems. Though they were much younger and cooler (especially with his homosexuality) than my parents, he was still happy to get away and gain a new level of independence. Thus started our coupledom. We were now living in our storybook cottage about to create some stories of our own.

We were instantly the best of roommates. We began to have the time of our still short lives. Together. We shared some odd unspoken language that would keep us constantly amused and continue for the rest of our lives together. We could communicate without a word. A mere shared glance could crack us up. We found each other endlessly funny. Returning to the carriage house after some outing, within seconds I'd be out of my clothes and into a pair of gym shorts. Knowing my love of being as close to naked as possible and my penchant for quick sex anywhere, he'd observe in astonishment, "I have never known anyone who can get out of clothes as fast as you." I'd proudly reply, "It's a gift," with a self-satisfied shrug. We'd break up. I'd say I did something "Lickety-split," and he'd make the awfullest face. "I don't like that expression," he'd say, "it makes me think of lesbian sex." I'd respond with my own horrified face. "Well doesn't it you?" he'd ask. "Well now it will," I'd exclaim in horror and we'd roll on the floor. We were such fans of irony you would have thought we had invented it. Our unifying language, a quirky perspective and a similar sense of the absurd, galvanized us. Whatever made one giggle, giggled the other. A mutual observation of some silly absurdity and a simple shared glance without a word exchanged, would send us into uncontrollable fits of shared convulsive howls. **It was a once-in-a-lifetime kind of side-splitting laughter that takes your breath away, hurts you from the inside-out and creates the strongest of friendships.**

It could also have had something to do with the weed (some of it ever-struggling to grow on a windowsill.) There was weed involved. Our mutual love of pot smoking — I've yet to roll a joint as well as he — was something else we shared. It was as natural to us as breathing and eating. To this day, though the incidence is far less frequent, I can't roll a joint or fill a bowl without thoughts of Randy. He was the most capable, motivated, driven, highly functioning pot smoker I would ever know.

We felt so grand, so grown-up in our elegant temporary digs. While our windowsill pot plant may have struggled, our friendship grew in that fairytale cottage, blossomed and flourished during that time together. We became the best of "partners in crime," a duo doing virtually everything together. Well, that is when Randy wasn't studying. Ever the student that I was never, he did a lot of studying. We had a great family of friends and our home became a meeting place for all of them. There were lavish Christmas events, birthdays, and impromptu gatherings. And a lot of sex.

During those early days together, with Randy studying and working, I'd spend many a weekend in Chicago, my favorite city and a mere six hour drive north of Louisville. I'd return from these trips with stories of my weekend adventures and created in Randy, a love for a glamorous city which he'd yet to visit. I'd regale him with stories of fabulous gay discos, hot gay leather bars, urban gay beaches, sexy gay bathhouses, fabulous stores and restaurants and a sophisticated high rise life with gorgeous apartments full of gay boys. I'd also tell him about all the sex to be found not only in Chicago but with the many truckers along the way and back. Randy, no stranger to rest stop sex, was sold.

We'd spend many evenings fantasizing about our future life together in Chicago, visualizing ourselves there doing all the things Chicagoans do; especially gay Chicagoans. I'd be working on the top floor of a department store, preferably Marshall Fields, and he'd be an administrative assistant to a high-powered CEO. We'd live together in a super-chic high rise Chicago apartment somewhere along the Gold Coast. Together, we'd enjoy the perfect Chicago life, living way above a glittering city that at the time we could only dream about. Randy's current student status and my job planning A&P grocery stores didn't quite support the dream but we could both see it all just the same. **Any night could find us toe to toe, in front of our enormous roaring fireplace, sometimes high, sometimes not, sometimes silly and sometimes serious but always sharing with each other our hopes and dreams for a future that at the time seemed not only certain, but limitless.**

1973

Coco & The Bachelor

ONE EVENING Randy and I were at the home of our friends Donna and Enzo, a soon to be married heterosexual couple. They were our best pot smoking buddies. Italian Enzo in fact, taught me how to roll a joint in one of those funny little rolling machines. Enzo wasn't home that night when under a smoke-fueled haze, two decisions were made, one that turned out well and the other not so much. Not all decisions made under the influence do. Anyway, while passing a joint and listening to Procol Harum's "Whiter Shade of Pale," Randy blurts out "This is your processional!" I wasn't sure what he was talking about. "Donna, I could play this as you go down the aisle. Listen to the organ. Slow it down a bit. It's a perfect wedding processional." Apparently at some earlier conversation to which I wasn't privy it had been determined that Randy would play at Donna and Enzo's upcoming wedding. Oh yeah, Randy could play the organ. And the piano. Taught himself. Donna listened and agreed. He was right. He played it at their wedding several weeks later. **In Randy's hands it was the hauntingly perfect choice for a 1970s wedding in a little stone chapel in the woods with a bride in a peasant dress and flowers in her hair.**

We should have stopped there. Unfortunately we also decided, no Donna decided, that since Randy and I had the best residence of anyone she knew — the carriage house — we should host Enzo's bachelor party. Bachelor party? I was skeptical. Weren't those things alcohol-fueled boozy nights of heterosexual debauchery? Super 8 porn films? Naked ladies jumping out of cakes? That's what happens at bachelor parties. Mayhem and destruction! I'd seen the movies. I knew what drunken straight men were like and I wanted no part of it. Donna assured me that wasn't the case. "Enzo and his friends are different. It'll be a civilized evening of a few friends, a few drinks and no more than a few hours." Grasping my hand in reassurance she pleaded, "Just make him feel a little special and send him on his way." I clearly remember a sad plaintive face and the batting of eyelashes. "Please, would you do this for Enzo...for me?" Were those lips actually pouting? "No one else has volunteered," she said in a soft forlorn voice. This time taking my other hand in hers, her eyes directly fixed on my own, and in a suddenly no-nonsense businesslike manner, "It's really up to the two of you." She fell quiet and I thought that was it and we could just move on but she shifted her glance over to Randy who, smoking with his face buried in an old copy of Vogue, was doing his best to avoid the conversation. She began to make her case there. Gently squeezing my hand now and back to the soft pleading voice, she continued, "Randy, you know how touched he'd be if you volunteered. Honored, really. It'd mean so much to him." Shifting her focus back to me, "Michael, you know it would. And you could suggest it yourselves. He wouldn't even know I'd asked." More pouting of the lips. I'm gay. I'm immune to this kind of feminine coercion and yet I could feel myself being reeled in. Randy too. And then, in a somewhat sterner voice full of gravitas, "You know how he loves the two of you. If you don't do it poor Enzo won't have a bachelor party." That did it. She'd landed us. We did adore big sweet handsome Enzo so, against our better judgement, and my firm protestations, worn down by and falling victim to Donna's feminine bullying, we agreed. The second we had I knew it was a mistake. **Two gay boys giving a bachelor party for a straight guy and his straight friends, none of whom we knew? In an elegant home that was not ours? What could go wrong?**

The night arrived. We set up a small wine bar in the kitchen, put out a few bowls of peanuts and pretzels, chips and dip and some pigs in blankets. We were ready for our handful of Enzo well-wishers and armed with an ironclad plan that had the lot of them in and back out the door by 11pm. Midnight at the latest. We could then go off to the Badlands as we normally would. Things didn't quite go according to our carefully crafted plan. Out of nowhere, legions of straight guys descended upon us. Along with them, cases of beer, vodka, gin, bourbon, scotch. Our driveway and front yard had become a parking lot. There were even more cars parked up and down the tree-lined streets of our usually quiet little neighborhood.

The evening got away from us pretty fast. We lost all ability to control our own home. Randy and I sat there horrified as the partiers, consuming more alcohol than I knew was possible, were clearly settling in for an entire night of revelry. We'd become totally side-lined, side-glancing each other unable to get any of these guys to move on or move anywhere. Rather than hosts, we were simply servants, there to pick up after them and try, against all odds, to keep up in our futile attempt against wet bottle and glass rings forming on someone else's fine mahogany furniture. It was well past midnight, after hours of "pussy" talk, when, after slipping out unbeknownst to us, a couple of the drunken partygoers returned from downtown Louisville with a prostitute.

Coco burst through the front door and immediately took over. She called herself "An exotic dancer." In front of her wide-eyed, captivated audience (with two noticeable exceptions,) for what seemed an eternity, she danced "exotically" to the hoots and hollers of her horny drunk and enraptured audience. Our dining room, which was a step higher than the living room, provided a perfect stage for her 'performance.' And perform she did, making her bumping and grinding way back and forth, humping our dining table and wriggling every rounded glistening body part she owned. **How had this happened? We should have been at our comparatively peaceful gay bar downtown by then, not watching this nearly-naked woman defiling the homo-sanctity of our dining room with her bare and overly ample bouncing breasts to the whistles and cheers of her horny boozed-up audience.** I sat there fuming, remembering Donna's words, "Enzo and his friends are different. It'll be a civilized evening of a few friends, a few drinks and no more than a few hours." Yeah...right! More fuming. By now, Coco after writhing on lap after grateful lap, democratically sharing herself with each partygoer, finally wriggled her way over to Enzo. She of course gave the groom-to-be special attention. Very special. Shockingly special. And he was giving it right back to her. Who was this man? What had happened to dear sweet mild mannered Enzo? After having watched her for an eternity of bumping and grinding and the removal of what little clothing she'd arrived in, the groom-to-be was clearly horned-up and ready. Enzo, grinding right back into her and encouraged by everyone in the room (with the same two notable exceptions) swept Coco's naked glistening body (was that glitter or sweat?) into his arms. Buoyed by the chants and cheers from his friends, he carried her up the stairs and right into Randy's bedroom slamming the door behind them. **Randy's horrified look — I can still see it — said it all! "My sheets!"** I, on the other hand was thinking, if she ever got wind of this, how the whole nasty thing was not going to go down well with Donna, the bride. Somehow I knew that we, as the party hosts, would be held responsible for the groom's debauchery. Wouldn't you know, the bride came down with a yeast infection or vaginitis or some sort of hideous communicable, sexually transmitted malady during the honeymoon. Enzo had to fess-up and well, I was right. It was all our fault. How could we have allowed things to get so out of hand? We'd promised her, after all, a civilized evening. Hadn't we?

Randy bought new sheets.

1974...

Steve McQueen

NO, NOT *THAT* STEVE MCQUEEN. This Steve McQueen wasn't even really a Steve. Because his last name was McQueen, the nickname Steve had been given him and it stuck. Steve wasn't everybody's cup of tea. To say the least. He was weird. To say the least. He was an odd combination of: Boring — extraordinarily boring as he was an actuary, the most boring profession; Tasteless — or to be more precise, without taste. He had no taste bad or good. He wore only beige, tan, beige, brown or beige; Strange — he was into meditation, yoga, chanting, strange "natural" nutrition and some totally "out there" spiritual beliefs and practices — this was still the early '70s, a decade and a half ahead of the emerging New Age; Sexually Perverse — he was into hardcore S&M, really hardcore, dungeons and meat hooks and masters and slaves and god knows what all else I never wanted to know about and he always wanted to share. **He was a bossy bottom of biblical proportions, two years my junior.** Socially Perverse, he was direct, abrasive, insulting, and honest to a fault, having no verbal filter, saying the most awful things to people; and Crazy — combine all the above.

Steve instantly repelled most people. Randy in particular. Chalk and cheese, as the Brits say. He was a recent transplant from Tennessee and we met at a party of a mutual friend. I say mutual friend, but I can't think of who it could have been because I may have been Steve's only friend. He seemed to have alienated everyone else. Randy in particular. For some reason though, he and I really hit it off. Possessed of all the above mentioned qualities, he was like no one I'd ever met before. I was fascinated by him and all the craziness that I'd never experienced in another human being. There was a bit of an ego stroke as well because (and this is what I believe he saw in me) he was convinced, if to this day I understand it correctly, that I was some deity named "Lord Michael." He was certain that I had a mission here on earth that someday I'd realize. And fulfill. Suspect as it seemed to me at the time, still, it did make me feel special. It wouldn't last though, as he would, in true

Steve McQueen fashion, append the remark with the dismissive "If you can ever manage to pull your shit together." **I thought he was nuts but somehow I still liked him in spite of and because of (in equal contradictory parts) the craziness.** He was the fearless outrageous looney little brother I'd never had. He was fresh and new and different and opened doors to worlds I hadn't imagined. He pushed me to do things that might otherwise have scared me but for his extreme confidence. I learned from him and I loved spending time with him. But only him. I could not add one other friend as he would inevitably say something awful, that would instantly alienate them and cause them to turn and run in the other direction. And vow never to return. And question how I could possibly be friends with this strange and abrasive person. For any event, if Steve was coming, they weren't. He was instantly repellant to, it seemed, everyone but me.

As it had been with Randy at our first meeting, this younger man fascinated me from the start. Also similar to Randy, there was no sexual spark between us. **He was quick to tell me that he could never have sex with me because of my curly hair. Curly hair was on his mile-long list of absolute sexual deal breakers.** That was fine by me as I had no sexual interest in him either. Since Randy was so busy at the time with work and school, Steve moved right into the void. And Randy hated him for it. Of course it didn't help that Steve had made the mistake of saying, to his face, among surely other insulting things, that Randy (who was always a bit concerned about his feminine side showing) should "Butch it up a little." That did not sit well.

Steve and I started hanging out a lot. We'd spend most of our time together at his place as Randy was never happy to come home from a long day of school and his part-time job at Stewart's Department Store, to find Steve at ours. Steve's apartment was a nearly empty (save for a sofa, a tv, and a bed) wall to wall beige carpeted box in one of those equally beige and indistinguishable suburban brick complexes. With his beige car parked right outside he was a perfect fit.

As luck would have it for Randy, Steve was filled with wanderlust and Louisville couldn't interest him for long. His first move was to Atlanta and I'd spend many a weekend flying down to visit him there, going to the bars, and baths, hiking up to Stone Mountain and just getting high and hanging out. After his brief stint in Atlanta, Steve was on to Los Angeles to move in with a new boyfriend. Los Angeles was a place I'd never been so I excitedly said yes to the opportunity to make the road trip with him. I flew to Atlanta and we headed off in that beige beater, taking a detour through Chattanooga, his hometown, then on to LA via the southern route. Texas was endless, with fast food and fast sex (at truck stops and rest stops) breaking the desert monotony. With Gloria Gaynor's "Never Can Say Goodbye" blasting from the 8 track tape deck, against all odds, in that rattle trap of a car, we made it all the way to LA. With the "Protection of Lord Michael" whose intercession Steve would constantly invoke with some sort of "Lord Michael to the left, Lord Michael to the right, Lord Michael above, Lord Michael below…" chant, we crossed the country without major incident. I'd be sitting in the car rolling my eyes, and at the same time, endlessly amused.

Steve's new boyfriend waiting in LA was hot. He was another Michael. At the time, Steve could "only have relationships with Michaels" and at one point briefly, changed his name to Michael — don't ask. **Hot LA Michael was a golden blonde-haired, blonde-mustachioed, blue-eyed, muscular, sweet Adonis and well worth relocating 3,000 miles for.** Hot Michael lived in a small apartment complex overlooking a high school. One day during one of my subsequent visits, Steve and I noticed a fairgrounds carnival had been built on the school property and went down the hill to investigate. This being Hollywood, we could see they were shooting a film and we sat on the hillside and watched take after take. I had no idea what we had been watching until many months later sitting in a theater, at the end of the film *Grease* there was the same school carnival. I recognized it instantly. We had been able to watch the whole thing from our perch on the hillside above the school and behind the apartment complex, not knowing what we were witnessing.

At the end of that first LA visit, the three of us flew up to San Francisco and I fell in love with the city to which I would eventually move. **It was Halloween in San Francisco — something of a redundancy in a place where every day was Halloween.** Polk Street and the Castro were great big giant sexy street parties. Nearly everyone was in costume, many of which despite the evening chill, were quite minimal, sexily exposing lots of skin and muscle. I had never seen that level of creativity or public near-nudity. At one point as I was standing un-costumed in my plaid shirt, jeans, construction boots and bomber jacket minding my own business, two drag queens approached. Slipping their arms in mine with the line, "Finally a real man," they dragged me off with them. We toured the festival together, the three of us arm in arm. A Channel 4 newscaster came up at one point and interviewed me while flanked by my two new drag buddies. I told him how I was visiting from the Midwest, this was my first San Francisco Halloween and in fact only a few hours from then, I'd be boarding the redeye for Chicago to change planes for home. Later, after saying my goodbyes to Steve and Hot Michael, as I waited to board my flight at the San Francisco Airport, Channel 4 News came on in the waiting area. There I was up on the TV screen arm in arm with my drag queens talking about flying home through Chicago. I slouched somewhat self consciously, surrounded by my fellow Chicago bound travelers in the same clothes I was wearing on TV. I caught a judgmental look or two. I didn't care. I was on TV!

There came a time when Steve became obsessed with *The Front Runner*. It was a novel about a gay high school track and field star named Billy Sive who ends up having a relationship with his track coach. Required reading for any gay man at the time. Steve was not only obsessed with the book, he became obsessed with the idea of playing the role of Billy. He was absolutely convinced that he was born to play the role. In true Steve style, he had decided it was his mission here on earth. He began working out endlessly in order to condition himself for the role. He bought the same style shoes that Billy wore in the novel and he ran constantly in them. He sent letter after letter to Paul Newman who had supposedly optioned the book and would play the coach. **I tried to be as supportive as possible in this highly unlikely quest; I did not share in his certainty that playing Billy was simply a fait accompli.** I actually thought he was bonkers but I did my best to encourage him and would listen endlessly about all the ways he was conditioning himself and preparing for the role. Each letter contained photos of Steve's physical progress. Well, whether or not Paul Newman was ever actually interested in the film I do not know. I do know Steve never heard from Mr. Newman, never played Billy and the film was never made.

Steve wrote letters throughout our entire friendship. Many letters. He travelled a lot around the country and would write from wherever he happened to be. Long strange rambling letters each with the request, no, the demand that I save every one of them. The letter writing continued after he moved to Atlanta and then LA and then back to Chattanooga. I did, as I was told, save his letters and I have them still, tied up neatly with a gold cord. I took them out recently and re-read them. I was astonished. So much of what I have learned over the years about the universe, about spirituality was in those letters. Ideas I thought I had come up with on my own were there. Some of them verbatim. **I had adopted some of his "craziness" over the years.** It occurred to me that all the time he was telling me his crazy whacked out notions of the universe, he had been planting seeds. Way ahead of his time spiritually — the meditation, the yoga, the "strange" spiritual practices — he had seen in me fertile ground and he had gone about the work of planting his seeds. Sadly he lost patience waiting for a time when, nourished by my own spiritual awareness, those seeds would grow. **I was a**

slow learner so deciding that I might never "get my shit together" Steve finally gave up on me. I disappointed him one too many times and in one final letter he cut his losses and moved on. I, while not truly appreciating any of this at the time, was a little relieved to allow him out of my life. I had had enough of explaining him to my other friends; explaining our strange friendship and my strange attraction to this strange being. He demanded a kind of loyalty that was difficult, really impossible for me to give at that time, in the face of all my friends he had alienated and all my misgivings about his various "oddities." He was never concerned about what other people thought of him but I was still years away from that level of self-esteem. I had also had enough of not being the person he wanted me to be and feeling constantly, curly hair and all, inadequate. In that one final goodbye letter, he disappointedly dismissed me and our friendship forever. That was the last of Steve McQueen. Over the years I wondered if Steve survived AIDS. Decades later through the determined help of a friend in Australia, (that's another story) I learned he had not.

1974

TruckerSex

MY LOVE AFFAIR WITH CHICAGO started when I was a young teenager visiting my childhood friend Tommy. His family had moved there after his father's job transfer from Louisville. They lived in Lombard actually, which was a small suburban village west of the city. While I can't remember too much about Lombard, I can recall most everything about Chicago. Tommy and I were allowed to make the short train trip in to the city thus starting my life-long love affair with it. **I felt an instant connection with Chicago that I had never experienced any place else.** And I'd been to New York. There was something, I don't know, organic, or perhaps spiritual about that connection. Chicago was big and glamorous and yet felt instantly comfortable. I knew my way around it's logical pattern of streets. I had found my soil and a sense of being where I was supposed to be. That was something I had never felt before and the feeling never wavered during the subsequent years when I would make frequent visits and eventually live there. Chicago was definitely my kind of town.

Young gay boys from Louisville would typically migrate to either Chicago or Atlanta each city being more exciting and having a larger gay population than Louisville. I, with my more northern sensibility always chose Chicago. So in the days before I made my eventual move there, and with its manageable six hours driving time, I would spend many weekends in Chicago. The drive was always worth it. I would get off work in Louisville at 4:30 on a Friday afternoon and hop in my little blue Gremlin with its Levi's interior. With the sunroof rolled back and the windows down (weather permitting) off I'd go. By 10:30 I'd be parking somewhere near the Bistro, my favorite gay dance club. I reasoned those were six hours I'd typically do nothing much in Louisville, so I might just as well do nothing much in a straight 70 mph line and end up in Chicago.

And a straight line it was — a boring flat straight line. There was nothing much of interest during those six hours of mostly flat Indiana. Things would get a little interesting around Gary. If, that is, you consider the gates of Hell interesting. **Gary Indiana was the ugly price you had to pay to reach the glory that was Chicago.** As you approached in the dark of night it really did seem like the gates of hell with its dreary skyline of refineries and their grimy smokestacks belching stinky sulfuric clouds you could see, smell and almost taste. And there were flames. Actual flames, everywhere you looked, exposed and lighting the murky night sky full of those heavy, greenish, smokey clouds piled one on the other. The yellow and orange of those open fires eerily illuminated everything below. It wasn't pretty but it did at least provide respite from the unending sameness of the rest of Indiana.

About the only other breaks during those five flat hours between Louisville and Gary were the rest stops. And truck stops. And truckers. Truckers are a horny bunch and in those early days of the sexual revolution, with free sex everywhere, sexual orientation didn't really seem to matter. **You never knew when you were going to get lucky and have either a little outdoor sex or maybe even be invited into a trucker's lair in his cab right behind the drivers seat. There are little bedrooms in there.** Occasionally when driving you'd pass a trucker and glance over (and up through the sunroof, as trucks sit quite a bit higher) and make eye contact. After passing each other several times, he might simply pull off at the next rest stop and you would follow or sometimes he might even gesture to you as you pass, that you should pull off and then he'd follow. It was exciting and it was sexy: perhaps a bit dangerous but also fun, hot and so worth the risk. And it went a long way in breaking up the long, tediously flat Indiana drive.

The trips *to* Chicago were better because Chicago and all it's limitless possibilities lay ahead. Returning trips meant the weekend was over with the work week and far-less interesting Louisville as the destination. On one of these horny endless trips home, I was on auto-pilot (probably playing with myself if I'm being honest) and not paying much attention. There were a lot of trucks (and of course truckers) so there was opportunity in the air but I hadn't connected with anyone…yet. With the monotony of the drive getting to me and my mind elsewhere (focused no doubt between my legs,) I looked up to see the truck right in front of me had stopped. Stopped! Dead! I slammed on my brake and in the same instant I instinctively glanced up into my rear view mirror to see another truck barreling down on me. Fast! I immediately jerked the steering wheel sharply to the right, abruptly getting out of the way into the breakdown lane, just as the truck behind barreled right through the spot that I had just vacated, stopping inches short of ramming the rear of the unmoving truck ahead. **Had I not responded so quickly, I and my little Gremlin would have been squashed between the trucks. Gay roadkill.**

For some reason when I turned sixteen and became eligible to drive, my parents decided that I should have professional driving instruction. I think this was a first in our family. I luckily ended up with a supremely qualified instructor who taught me many techniques I employ to this day. Chief among them was a reflex motion that he programmed into me and had me practice over and over. Were it not for that very thorough driving instructor who made his 16 year old student practice and practice the reflex motion of hitting the brake and immediately looking up in the rear view mirror to check behind, I'd have met my maker on I-65 S that day. It was a reflex that served me well that fateful day and does to this day, a day I wouldn't have seen had it not been for his thorough training.

It took me more than a few minutes to recover from my near-death experience. I sat distressed, pondering my own mortality for quite awhile before I somewhat tentatively pulled out of the breakdown lane and back into traffic. Still shaken, it took me awhile to get back up to speed but I eventually did and got on with getting home. I wasn't so shaken that I didn't glance now and again at the truckers I would pass as I picked up speed. I mean, I wasn't dead yet so I might as well get off if I could. As I was passing one of the drivers, he glanced down at me and with an enormous sexy and enthusiastic smile he started waving me over, signaling me to pull off onto the breakdown lane. He was really good looking, rugged and sexy and waving me over with his requisite tanned, golden haired and muscular forearm. He apparently didn't want to wait until the next truck stop. He wanted me and he wanted me immediately. Woof! I was about to get lucky. Right in the breakdown lane. I had a good feeling about this and could already see Randy's look of envy when, once home, I'd inevitably share the story with him as I always did. I slowed my car and as directed, pulled off the road. He did the same following me into the breakdown lane. I was excited. We both coasted to a stop. I checked my breath, fluffed my crotch and stepped out of my car and saw my handsome hunky trucker with a major package between his legs, already out of his cab and coming toward me. With his right hand outstretched, he greeted me with, "I just wanted to shake your hand!" A handshake? I was confused. "That was some pretty damn nice driving you did back there!" As he grabbed my hand and shook it, I soon realized he must have been the trucker behind me who earlier hadn't killed me "back there" when I swerved out of his way. **He continued, "You saved your life, mine and I don't know who all else's but alls I know is, yessir, I just had to shake your hand! That was some mighty fine, damn nice driving!"**

Well, it wasn't exactly what I was expecting. A firm trucker handshake instead a firm trucker...oh well, never mind. Still, it was nice to get a compliment on my driving skills from one who does it for a living. And I could return home to Randy, happy to be alive and able to tell him another exciting but quite different type of trucker story.

1974

The Problem With Potential

AROUND THE TIME the professor who owned "our" storybook carriage house was due back from his sabbatical, Randy and I heard of a potential available apartment. I say potential because it actually did not exactly quite exist. Yet. Rod and Ron, a gay couple and recent transplants from Texas, were renovating an enormous house in Old Louisville, one of the largest preservation districts in the country and my favorite section of the city. **Old Louisville was a once grand Victorian neighborhood with huge houses, mansions really, wide, stately tree lined streets and the most bohemian mix of people you could find in Louisville.** If you were young and hip that's where you wanted to be. With its many old homes and cheap rents it was a fixer-upper of a neighborhood right at the precipice of being up and coming. Full of potential. Gay heaven. For me at least. We looked at the space (also full of potential) and loved it. Well, I loved it. Randy was skeptical. First off, while I loved the romance of the old and the potential in the raw, Randy preferred the slickness of the new and the certainty in the finished. There was nothing slick or finished about this space. The cavernous old mansion was divided into three units: a commercial basement unit already renovated and leased, and above, two un-renovated residential units. One unit, un-renovated where Rod and Ron were living, was on the first floor. The upper two (arguably best) floors would be the rental unit. Also un-renovated. It was big, lofty and light-filled, with high vaulted ceilings and a fireplace in the living room. There were huge French windows, enormous bedrooms, a big kitchen, big bathrooms and plenty of closets. It was quite grand. Or it would be. Eventually. When it was finished. It was "Very New York," a phrase people in Louisville used quite frequently to designate anything thought to be "big city." I'd read of the loft spaces in New York's Soho district that artists were flocking to and imagined this loft to be similar. The space was under demolition. You really had to use your imagination to see past the piles of debris, caving-in ceilings, and the filthy paint spattered, hundred year old wooden floors, and imagine the Architectural Digest masterpiece with the state-of-the-art kitchen that Rod and Ron described to us. I could see it clearly. Randy not so much. **Because of our timing, we would have to move in during the renovation work.** Rod and Ron assured us they'd accelerate the construction schedule and concentrate solely on our space before they worked on their own. I was sold. Randy remained skeptical. He'd have preferred something new and sensible. Something in a modern building, with a modern kitchen, wall to wall carpeting, air conditioning and everything else of his dreams. "And no dirt. Please, after the carriage house, all I want is something that stays clean and is easy to maintain," pleaded my friend who knew he couldn't depend on me for much help in the housecleaning arena. I hadn't noticed that the carriage house had any cleaning issues. Not fully understanding Randy's contribution, things just seemed to clean themselves. He would not have agreed. My job, as I saw it, was to keep things in their place. Maintain order, I believed at the time, and things will just stay clean. Once again, Randy would not have seen it that way at all.

I had been on house tours in Old Louisville and my inner-interior designer saw the potential in a space transformable into one of these designer dream homes. It would be our designer dream home. A magazine-ready apartment like the ones I'd coveted during those tours was all I could see as I looked around that demolished wreck of a space. I somehow managed to convince Randy of this dream. Or did I just wear him down? Whatever the case, against his better judgement and bound by my own enthusiasm and sense of adventure, we moved into our rough and raw but "full of potential" new home.

Potential can only take you so far. Living in a construction zone was not a pleasant experience. To say the least. More of a horror show. Especially to poor Randy. No kitchen, unfinished bathrooms (mine was missing its door,) bedrooms with no doors, closets with no rods or shelves, windows that didn't work and everything, everything covered in a thin layer of ubiquitous ashy construction dust. White dirt. Everywhere. Wipe it away and it'd seem to regenerate itself right before your eyes. And in your nose. To make matters worse, shortly after work had commenced, Rod and Ron had some major disagreement and split up. Ron returned to Texas leaving Rod to complete the job on his own. It became clear that Ron who had departed was probably the more construction-savvy of the two. Or more likely, Rod's heart just wasn't in it anymore. He was now working alone so work that was already slow, became slower and more slap-dash. If a corner could be cut it was cut. Every detail, simplified. The walls got painted and the white shag carpeting installed, and I think I got some closet doors but little else was accomplished. There was still no kitchen, state of the art or otherwise. The bathrooms went untouched. I'd stare at the bare bulb dangling from the center of the living room ceiling and find it harder and harder to believe that a chandelier would ever hang there. **Rod had clearly lost interest and Randy and I were clearly losing patience.**

1974

To Make Matters Worse

ONE SATURDAY MORNING, after a typical Friday night of dancing and debauchery, in my as–yet unfinished second floor bedroom, in our as–yet unfinished designer apartment, only a few hours after having finally gotten to bed, I was rudely awakened by the tinny sound of bullhorn–amplified yelling outside my window. **Who's up at this ungodly hour and why are they making this ungodly noise outside my window?** I dragged my naked ass, morning wood and all out of bed and over to the window. I looked down and saw, through my groggy stupor, the sidewalk in front of our building crowded with people carrying signs, yelling and chanting and waving their fists in the air. At me and my morning nakedness. Or so it seemed. I hurriedly ran to my "en–suite" bathroom (with no door.) Dick in hand, still sleepy and confused, I peed and watched (my bathroom did have a window) as those total strangers were picketing our house. We were being picketed! Baffled, I continued watching as they marched back and forth along the sidewalk, signs waving and yelling at anyone who'd listen. What were they yelling and why in the world were they picketing me? Or us? What had we done? Homosexuals in the neighborhood? No couldn't be. Old Louisville was overrun with gay boys. No, they wouldn't be picketing us. We increase property values.

I shook off the last drops and ran to Randy's bedroom in the rear of the house where he was sleeping, blissfully unaware of the unpleasantness in the front. I woke him from his sound sleep and dragged his sleepy undie–clad ass back with me to see this new horrifying development. While we couldn't quite understand what the scratchy bull–horned chanting was yelling up at us, after having located my glasses, upon closer scrutiny of the signs, I began to make out their messages. "Abortion Is Murder!" "Baby Killers!" All sorts of lovely anti–abortion slogans and photos of fetuses were being paraded back and forth right in front of our house. And screamed at us. Fists shaking in the air. Apparently they thought for some reason, we were baby killers. Us? Given neither of us had clearly ever had an abortion or ever would, why us? Would they picket individuals about their personal views on abortion? How would they even know our personal views on abortion? How about Rod downstairs? Did Rod have something to do with this? Was he...? What would...? Or what...? Puzzled, we looked at each other and together came to the same conclusion. Oh no. Simultaneously our thoughts went further downstairs. The renters in the basement apartment. The commercial space on the lower level. The little unobtrusive door on the side of the building with the little equally unobtrusive sign. A sign that read, "Alternatives." We thought of the women we'd sent around to the side of the house after their having mistakenly rung our bell at the front; the unhappy tentative faces that we'd previously not given much thought to. The company we knew nothing about except for that small, ever so discreet sign on the door. "Alternatives!" we said in unison, "Shit," added Randy, keeping an eye on the situation, "it's an abortion clinic!" It was my turn, "We live above a goddamn abortion clinic!" **Yep, Rod and Ron had rented to us, less than a year post–Roe v. Wade, a full–of–potential apartment right over an abortion clinic.**

"Don't these people have anything better to do on a Saturday morning?" I asked, watching the hubbub below, "it's practically still the middle of the night..." Before I could finish, Randy who had retrieved his glasses shouted "That's Madge Macdonald!" I stared at him, incredulous. "You know them?" "*One* of them," he replied, "The Uber–Catholic with the bullhorn. That's my father's boss's wife, Madge!" With that he ran back to his bedroom to grab a bathrobe and slippers. I heard him rush down the stairs and the front door slam behind him. **I watched my nineteen year old friend below, belching smoke from his just-lighted long-overdue morning cigarette; a determined locomotive on a direct line to its destination, "Madge the Uber-Catholic with the bullhorn."** His bathrobe was flying in the wind and bedroom slippers flapping. He was yelling at her, his arms and hands waving wildly in the air. I could hear the shouting but not what was being said. This went on for a bit. Whatever he had to say proved effective because the picketers, Madge included, moved away from the front of the house and around the corner to the side where the clinic door was actually located. On his return, I asked what he'd said to them. "I told them that it's illegal to picket a private residence especially with bullhorns on a quiet Saturday morning, and that if they didn't move around the corner immediately and stop with the fucking bullhorns I was going to call the cops on their Catholic asses!" Randy was not a fan of Catholicism. I was impressed. I asked him how he knew that picketing a residence and bullhorns were illegal. Exhaling cigarette smoke, he said with a shrug, "Just guessing," as he turned, hopped over the ever-present rolls of carpeting and around the growing stack of empty paint cans, and headed back to the quiet sanctuary of his bedroom.

The picketing went on for the duration of our time there but only along the side of the house. Never in front and never again with bullhorns. We eventually came to recognize some of the regulars and would give a quick wave hello and goodbye to them as we'd come and go. They seemed nice enough, though thoroughly misguided.

That was the anti-abortion straw that broke our Old Louisville camel's back. Between the barely begun, never ending renovation work, "The abortion mill" as my older teaser of a brother took delight in calling it, and the relentless picketing, we decided it was time to move on. This time I left it up to Randy to choose something new and sensible which he did. Modern building, modern kitchen, wall to wall carpeting, air conditioning, and best of all, easy to keep clean; everything this time, of Randy's dreams. We moved right in and settled into our new and I suppose improved, potential-free digs.

1971 – 1975

Chicago Chicago Chicago

THERE'S A BETTE DAVIS FILM called, *Beyond The Forest*, in which her character Rosa Moline dreams of getting out of the small town where, in a horrible long black fright-wig, she famously declares, "What a dump" in regards to her current surroundings. Convinced of finer things than the dumpy Loyalton, Wisconsin had to offer her, she dreams day and night about fleeing to nearby Chicago. Rosa would hear, "Chicago, Chicago, Chicago," like a locomotive in her head urging her on.

"Chicago, Chicago, Chicago."

I could identify with poor Rosa. I dreamed day and night of Chicago, a glittering place just six hours beyond my reach. Like Rosa of Wisconsin or even Dorothy of Kansas, I had my sites set elsewhere. Rosa wanted out of Loyalton. Dorothy wanted out of Kansas. And I wanted out of Louisville. A good portion of my childhood saw me looking toward New York (or even San Francisco) but at some point, the geographically closer

Chicago had moved to number one. **Chicago became for me, like Dorothy's someplace over the rainbow, an almost mythical place where all my dreams would surely, someday be realized.** It held that kind of allure with its magnificent architecture, glamorous lakefront, sexy beaches, fine department stores, sophisticated restaurants and hot gay clubs. Above all else, for me at least, it was all those big-city, high-rise-dwelling gay boys, many of whom I had already gone home with and had tasted, if for only a matter of hours or sometimes days, what it was like to be one of them and live their ultra-urban sky-scraping lives. That taste of life in the big glamorous sexy city gave me an unquenchable hunger for more. I just wanted to live in Chicago. I didn't think to ask for more.

On my many weekend visits, after a long Saturday or Sunday at Oak Street Beach, I'd find myself on a street corner in the shadow of The John Hancock Tower, a dark massive exoskeleton-ed behemoth that had supplanted The Empire State Building as my favorite skyscraper. **I'd look to my right to see people in their bathing suits and then to my left to see others in tuxedos and evening gowns. Sand and diamonds. It was that kind of place.** There was a special sort of energy there — glamorous and sexy in equal parts — and I knew I wanted to somehow, someday plug into it for more than a weekend. I'd walk the serene tree-lined streets of the Gold Coast and imagine myself actually living there. I'd have a fabulous apartment most likely way up high in this high rise city. I'd have the perfect job and lots and lots of hot boys at my disposal whenever and wherever I wanted them. I could see it. I could feel it. I just had to be patient. I knew I had to live there and someday be a part of this magnificent city. There would come a time, I was certain, that I would not have to get in a car on Sunday afternoon and drive six hours south to live in a lesser place devoid of sunny beaches and glittering evening activities and men; smart, sexy sophisticated men by the tens of thousands. I would live among them and I was equally certain that my best friend Randy would be there to share all of it with me. I could see it. I could hear it, "Chicago, Chicago, Chicago."

How I'd manage to obtain my big city dream — one I'd held fast to since childhood — I did not know, but manage it I would. I was a city boy through and through, identifying with my Italian father's roots in New York City. My mother's German roots went back to a tiny little farming community not far across the river in Southern Indiana. I felt no connection to it and had no interest in anything even remotely rural. Mariah Hill was remote and it was rural and most certainly it was not for me. As far as I was concerned, the Indiana of my German roots was nothing more than what I had to "get through," on my drive to Chicago, my ultimate big city destination just beyond its northern border.

Mid-1960s

Mariah Hill - Probably Not A Good Idea

MARIAH HILL, INDIANA, a township quite literally not on the map (that is not until the I-64 Interstate was completed nearby) was a no stoplight, wide place in a country road with a population of "nearly 500 souls." All of them Catholic. This is where my German grandmother was born. **Mariah Hill had one church (Catholic), one cemetery (Catholic), one school (Catholic), and one IGA market (non-denominational I suppose but still, with its Mary Help Of Christians church**

calendar hung on the wall behind the cash register, like everything else, pretty Catholic). There were two long, parallel, dusty dirt roads along one of which all my socially-distanced relatives lived. It was a minuscule place overlooked not only by map makers but by just about anyone else who visited its far more illustrious neighboring Indiana towns of Dale, Ferdinand, Jasper, Saint Meinrad and the not to be missed, Santa Claus.

My grandmother was the only one of her immediate family to have escaped Mariah Hill, leaving her sister Nora behind and finding her way, after marriage, to the much larger and more cosmopolitan Louisville, Kentucky about two hours driving time away. Louisville is where my mother was born and after marrying my relocated New Yorker dad, where she gave birth to my brother Frank, my sister Carmen and lastly, me.

There were yearly family pilgrimages from Louisville to Mariah Hill, usually just my grandparents, parents, brother, sister and myself. There were other trips which included all the Louisville aunts, uncles and cousins. These were usually planned around special events such as "First Masses," as the Mariah Hill branch of our Catholic family tree had yielded more than its share of priests (and nuns as well.) This was a real sticking point for my ever-competitive ever-disappointed grandmother whose own family — we — never produced a single cleric. Oh, a few got close — my brother Frank included — but no Catholic cigar. For these special occasion trips to the other side of the Ohio River, there would be a familial car and station wagon caravan along the circuitous Indiana State Road 62. It was an impossibly hilly, serpentine route that wound its way around the lumpy Southern Indiana region known as the Floyd Knobs. **It was a looping roller coaster of a road that could cause any child the severest case of car sickness; and did.** There were several inevitable emergency sickness stops along the way for each of the queasy cousins (between the Catholicism and the Baby Boom, there were legions of us) to violently eject their breakfasts one by one and sometimes in unison as we made our collective green faced way to Mariah Hill. It was an agonizing experience for those of us of delicate stomachs, remediated only by the sight of the St. Meinrad Seminary twin steeples which signaled that Mariah Hill was just around the corner and that the endless nauseating trip would soon be over.

A rite of passage among the Louisville cousins was a summer visit to Aunt Nora's Mariah Hill farm. "Farm" always seemed a slight over-description of the smallish patch of land she shared with my Uncle Jesse. It consisted of a house, a somewhat dilapidated looking garage/barn, an outhouse, chicken pen, grape arbor and a curiously overdone outdoor geode-encrusted stone shrine to The BVM (Blessed Virgin Mary) complete with goldfish pond — a close match to my grandmother's in Louisville. There was not much more. My cousins and now that I think about it, in particular my brother Frank, had raved about their summer weeks spent in Mariah Hill. When it came my turn to go, I'd guess around twelve years old, I was more than a bit skeptical. Displaced New Yorker that I was (and gay to boot,) I was inclined toward indoor pastimes like sleeping late, watching movie musicals on television, eating, shopping, going to the movies, going to restaurants or designing ladies' clothes. **There were also the endless auto-erotic hours I'd spend with my secret collection of photos I'd surreptitiously purloined from the men's underwear and swimwear pages of soon to be discarded Speigel catalogs.**

The accounting I'd heard of the Aunt Nora country sabbaticals included none of the above activities — clearly there'd be no *South Pacific* on TV — and consisted mostly of outdoor enterprises such as farming and athletics. Having absolutely no interest in either, I lacked motivation regarding my own proposed Mariah Hill visit. By that time I had set my sights on more cosmopolitan places like Chicago, New York, San Francisco, Boston and Ft. Lauderdale. Places I'd mostly just seen in movies that you had to get on a plane to get to.

Mariah Hill made none of my short lists of places I wanted to spend any of my precious summer vacation time. The one thing that did interest me though was my Aunt Nora's cooking. She was always in the kitchen and I had enjoyed every bite I'd ever taken from Aunt Nora's fresh and well-cooked bountiful spreads. Being a spreading "healthy" eater, I'd happily gobbled up everything she'd ever laid out. She was especially known for her absolutely sublime fried chicken — there was none better. Anywhere. Imagining a week of that moist and crispy-delicious chicken, thick milk gravy and fresh homemade biscuits, was nearly enough to tip the scales in favor of my going. Also helping was my overly healthy (and slightly prurient) imagination which had conjured up afternoons of all-boy skinny dipping with naked country cousins and their country friends; or even the possibility of frisky fun of the "I'll show you mine if you'll show me yours" variety in heated haylofts. I imagined there'd maybe even be, hay rides under the stars, just like in a Judy Garland and Mickey Rooney movie. **Motivated then by the promise of good food, naked outdoor fun, and MGM romance, still with some reservation, I was in.**

Full of hope and misgivings about the rural weeks that lay ahead but ruled mostly by my emerging libido and stomach, little city boy Mikey was loaded onto a bus that would make that circuitous, nausea-inducing trip over and around the hills of Southern Indiana. It would subsequently deposit my reluctant self a few hours later in front of the Mariah Hill IGA/Post Office. The IGA was a small weathered building greatly in need of a paint job. It had the requisite elevated and covered porch running the length of its facade. On it was a rocking chair or two where I waited in the heated still air to be collected by my Uncle Jesse, while swatting away innumerable flies. The fly population of Mariah Hill I was already learning, outnumbered by millions, the people population. The only place I could remember having even come close to the fly density of this still and breeze-less place, was the animal barn at the Kentucky State Fair which, as I sat there and thought about it, had also smelled curiously like Mariah Hill. The beauty of that animal and fly infested barn on the fairgrounds though, was my ability to exit quickly; which I had, holding my nose and gagging all the way. This wasn't the case with Mariah Hill. There'd be no exit, quick or otherwise. I was committed. **My only thought in this super-quiet, insect-infested place where all I could hear was the buzz from those incessant flies and the distant sound of a tractor was, "I wanna go home."**

After being collected by my Uncle Jesse, I arrived at their home on the farm down the road, a bit disoriented and homesick. My ever-aproned Aunt Nora was hard at work preparing dinner so that brightened my mood a bit. I didn't see any chicken frying but whatever was cooking smelled great and took my mind off thoughts of fleeing back to Louisville. She wiped her hands on a dish towel ever at her waist and greeted me with a big kiss and hug and took me straight upstairs to a little bedroom that I loved up in the eaves over the kitchen. Aunt Nora was the sweet version of my rather sour grandmother. Kind and loving, she was all things her sister was not. I hadn't much thought of this particular upside — some greatly needed grandmotherly love — when I had been contemplating the pluses and minuses of a potential Mariah Hill stay.

The heart of Aunt Nora and Uncle Jesse's home (and just off the front porch) was a room that was mostly kitchen but also dining room, living room and TV room (a small seldom used black and white on a rolling stand, over in the corner.) In this regard country home design was way ahead of its city counterpart having come up with the open-plan concept of great rooms long before its current popularity. Anyway, this is the room where everything happened. All meals were cooked and eaten there and most of the socializing took place. There was a small parlor as I recall but I never saw it used. **The front screen door opened right into this room and family members and neighbors came and went without so much as a knock**

on the door; no doorbell to announce a visitor, just the slam of the door behind them. I doubt the door had a lock.

Full from dinner on my first night and sitting on a glider on the flower-bordered wraparound porch with Aunt Nora, I was feeling a bit less homesick and a little more comfortable in my new rural surroundings. The growing sounds of a warm summer night in the country along with the additional warmth of my dear great aunt made me think this whole Mariah Hill thing might no be so bad. Until morning.

Morning came at about five o'clock. That's 5:00am! Who even knew five o'clock came twice in the same day? Apparently farm people don't like to sleep. Not in the morning at least. They had gone to bed at a surprisingly early 9pm and I, who was used to staying up late in the summer, watching movies I probably shouldn't and snacking in front of the TV, was expected to go to sleep as well. I lay in my bed in that cozy warm little upstairs room with a rare evening breeze billowing the sheer curtains toward me and the bed springs squeaking with my every move. Staring at the inclined mini-floral wallpapered ceiling, playing with myself — my favorite pastime — I wished I had brought my secret photo collection with me. I could have put those sexy near-naked men to good bed-spring-rattling use. I had eventually, at what hour I do not know, drifted off to sleep and found myself awakened to "Mikey, ya gonna sleep all day?" hollered up the stairs at that ungodly hour. I dragged my sleepy little city kid ass out of bed and down the steps to a big country breakfast that I decided was probably worth the early rise. After breakfast it was announced that it was "Chicken day." Well, as a big Shirley Temple fan, I had watched with my sister Carmen, Rebecca Of The Sunnybrook Farm enough times to figure out what that meant. **I imagined myself lovable little Shirley, outside in a straw hat, with my hair in tightly wound braids, and wearing something gingham. I had a particular affection for blue and white. With a sunny attitude, a song in my heart and ready to tap dance at a moment's notice, I'd be out in the chicken yard with Aunt Nora spreading chicken feed to dozens of hungry waiting birds.** I'd do this from a ribbon wrapped woven wicker basket. Later being sent to the henhouse I'd use my multipurpose basket to happily collect farm-fresh eggs of varying photogenic shades of tans and beiges and present them to my grateful great aunt. Then there might be enough time for a bit more chicken feeding and then, a big lunch followed by a nap on the front porch glider. Not quite.

"Chicken day" as it turned out wasn't so much about us feeding the chickens as it was about the chickens feeding us. My little city boy sensibility was in no way prepared for what was about to happen. To me or the chickens. One of my older-from-across-the-street-country-cousins, who had joined us for breakfast took me out to the chicken yard, a fenced-in area just outside the kitchen door and across the gravel driveway. Going through the gate my not distant enough cousin instructed, "Catch one of those chickens and bring it over here." Catch a chicken? Me? With what? My bare hands? Touch a chicken? And then what? **I hadn't seen Shirley Temple do this.** I actually tried to chase one down and was hopelessly inept at the task, the squawking chicken being faster and craftier than my chubby little self. I was beginning to believe my country cousin was playing a trick on me. His condescending chuckle confirmed it. I side-eyed him to let him know I was on to him. He then took a long pole with a hook on the end and easily snatched a wildly protesting chicken by the neck, pulling it toward him. He gave me the hook to hold and feeling like an accessory to a crime, I watched as he, holding the squawking chicken by its head and feet, laid it upside-down on a piece of wood slanted at a forty-five degree angle and attached to the fence post and to the ground. He placed its horrified upside-down head between two parallel nails sticking out of the wood and stretched its protesting body out tight. With the two nails now doing part of the work, and his right hand free, he picked up an ax lying on the ground. I watched in horror as he gave one quick sure whack squarely on the poor chicken's outstretched unprotected neck, forever severing its head from its wriggling body. He then flung the poor thing, blood spurting from the fatal neck wound, right past me where it landed with a thud on the ground. I immediately came to understand the expression "Like a chicken with its head cut off." I hadn't given any real thought to what that actually meant until that unfortunate morning. **I watched transfixed as that poor headless chicken carcass ran blindly around the chicken yard, wings crazily flapping like some deranged headless lunatic, falling and running and tumbling and flapping and spurting and spurting.** Horrified by what I had just witnessed, along with the squawking protests of the remaining (I'm pretty certain equally horrified) chickens, I heard another whack and another poor unfortunate was flung past me to repeat the entire headless scenario. And another and another. I was soon surrounded by bloody chicken carnage. The yard was full of headless spurting birds most of which had tired of their crazy flapping run and were lying on the ground with their little webbed chicken feet pumping the air as if riding little chicken bicycles to a shared eternity in chicken heaven. The eyes of the tidy little pile of decapitated chicken heads, though resigned to their fate, still looked up at me in accusation. I wanted to go home.

The bloodbath thankfully was over but, sadly, chicken day was not. There was plucking to be done. My aunt had prepared a big vat of scalding hot water for the chicken carcasses to be dipped in. Then, along with my aunt and two female cousins — I guess this was "women's work" though there I was anyway — we went about the sweaty stinky task of liberating those poor dead carcasses from their filthy feathers. When at last my participation in the horrifying events of chicken day was complete, in the afternoon-heated attic room, I was allowed to take to my bed, physically exhausted and emotionally drained. When it was time for lunch I was called down to the kitchen. I immediately saw that Aunt Nora had been busily preparing...of course... wait for it...fried chicken. Aunt Nora's fried chicken. What else? The one thing in Mariah Hill I was most looking forward to was now, not surprisingly, a lot less appealing. I sat there staring at my individual fried-up, crispy-crusted chicken part that had only hours earlier been an essential piece of a living little being routinely enjoying its morning not knowing it would be it's last. I could hear its surviving friends and family members still happily clucking away just outside the window blissfully unaware of their own eventual fate. And that of their recently departed loved one on a plate in front of me. I couldn't do it. Somehow, Aunt Nora's fabulous fried chicken, even with that legendary milk gravy, had lost its appeal. Pass the biscuits please. I wanted to go home.

It became clear to me not long after the chicken enterprise that these weeks in Mariah Hill were less about country fun and more about indentured servitude. There were apparently no child labor laws in effect in the early sixties in Southern Indiana. I was put to work doing all kinds of farm chores. Every menial task they could conjure up. This was hard labor. Sweating in that ever-still air, under the hot Indiana sun and being terrorized by all those horrible horse flies, I learned among other things how to dig post holes, stretch fencing and feed pigs. And of course, behead and pluck chickens. There were acres of weeds to be cleared and I learned the difference between a sickle and a scythe and how to use both. These were not skills I'd need for my future occupation of either commercial artist or fashion designer. Neither was my newly acquired ability to handle a post-hole digger, though it did come in handy later when my best friend Tommy and I wanted to bury our Time Capsule in my backyard. All of the chores I accomplished alongside my older male cousins from across and up the street. They were the ones with whom I'd imagined the naked swimming hole frolicking and overheated hayloft fun. Never happened. There was work to do and we were the ones to do it. Never naked. I can't even remember a shirt being removed. We'd be sweatily slaving away clearing weeds taller than my own short self and one of the cousins would take note of a passing airplane way up in the sky with "Look a plane!" All work would stop to take in this rare event of the modern outside world crossing high over Mariah Hill. As a city kid who happened to live on the flight path of our local airport I'd roll my eyes and be reminded of those old Tarzan films where the natives would spot a plane overhead, point to it and yell, "Iron bird." I mean, I loved planes but come on. **The iron bird would pass, its vapor trail silently slicing the clear Mariah Hill sky in two and the show would be over.** It was time to bat away the flies, get back to work and sweat some more. I'd go to bed each night so exhausted that I suppose it was just as well that I'd left my "special" photo collection at home. I wouldn't have had the energy reserve to get my typically horny little self off. I wanted to go home.

One younger cousin, Billy, became quite attached to me. He was my sweet little helper. No matter where I went, he was right at my side. Though considerably younger, he knew his way around farm life and therefore became invaluable to me. For my short time in Mariah Hill, Billy became the little brother I never had and the rural mentor I surely needed. We used to sit on a glider on his parents' front porch and have wonderful conversations mostly about his curiosity about "Big City Life." Once during one of our conversations, Billy gushed, "I can't wait 'til I'm as big as you." My big brother heart swelled but the glow was quickly extinguished by his mother, my caustic cousin Bernita who happened to be passing by at exactly the wrong moment. Hearing Billy's vocal wish to be "…as big…" as me, her corpulent city cousin, Bernita venomously responded, "Oh lord, let's hope not!" as the screen door slammed behind her. Bernita was not my friend. I wanted to go home.

As the sticky summer days crept on at a glacial hazy hot and humid pace, it became apparent there'd be endless work and no evening hay rides or sunny skinny dipping or hot hayloft shenanigans in the land of the iron bird. I did want to go home and finally asked to go back to Louisville earlier than planned. The unfortunate event of my accidentally hitting little Billy square in the forehead with a hammer — I should have known he'd be standing there right beside me, he was always standing right beside me — blood pouring down his sweet surprised face — sealed the deal. It was decided, before I could do any more damage, that I'd be put on the next morning's bus back to Louisville. I was going home.

It was clear that Mariah Hill had been a mistake. There were surely other sunny, skinny dipping places for me. I was certain of that. I was also certain they weren't to be found in Southern Indiana. I would go there someday, wherever "there" might be. I had pictures in my special photo collection from a Life magazine fashion spread of men (and women too though I cut them out) in the tiniest swimsuits I'd ever seen, posing in places with exotic names like Mykonos and Ibiza. I had no idea where these far off places were (where people went around practically naked and there'd probably be no chickens,) but I knew I'd find them. Someday. I'd simply have to grow up, keep my eyes and ears open and wait patiently for more information. And get through my last night in Mariah Hill.

Lucky for me the timing of my departure was perfect as that last evening turned out to be what must have been the biggest event of the entire Mariah Hill social calendar. Earlier that day the first and only street lamp in the entire town had been installed on a telephone pole near Aunt Nora and Uncle Jesse's farmhouse. At dusk, the community emerged, toting folding lawn chairs and assembled at the foot of the telephone pole with its newly-installed light fixture. **As the summer night grew darker, the semi-circular rows of seated opening night attendees waited in breathless anticipation for the lamp's inaugural lighting.** As the evening dissolved from dusk to dark, suddenly the mercury vapor started to spark and came alive.

In seconds it was a fully illuminated streetlight. The crowd, eyes cast upward, broke into spontaneous applause! Some seconds later, as the clapping subsided, one by one the chairs were folded up and the people of Mariah Hill, along with their brand-new mercury vapor shadows, began to depart. It was time to go.

It was time to go.

mid-1960s

Porn-ish

PORNOGRAPHY (of a sort) made an early appearance in my life. In addition to our family bible and it's naked male angels, saints, sinners and Adams, there was also the arrival of the new Spiegel or Penney's catalogs which would find me rushing off to the bathroom or up to my bedroom. I'd go directly to the index and search for the men's underwear and swimwear pages. Finding them I'd spend an eternity devouring the handsome nearly-naked men with their bulging packages. I'd often "borrow" my sister's Seventeen magazines — the summer issues were the best — and get lost in them as they'd always have the "dreamiest boys." When it was time for the catalogs and magazines to be thrown out, I'd surreptitiously confiscate them, take them to my room and cut out and save my favorite photos. Being a horny and artistically inclined little kid, I'd take the best of these photos, oftentimes the ones from the summer Sea and Ski or Coppertone ads, and trace them onto onion skin paper purloined from my mother's stationery drawer. I'd conveniently leave off the swimsuits and draw in genitalia and body hair which, since I had none at the time, I found endlessly fascinating. I was developing into quite the erotic writer as well and created fantasy stories about exotic islands off the coast of France inhabited by only naked males or about weekends in a New York City populated only by boys in their underwear. I visualized and wrote in great detail about tanned muscular men running around naked on beaches, among the palm trees and flowers and tighty-whitey clad boys swarming the nighttime streets of New York City. **With my perpetual little kid horniness and vivid sexual imagination, I ended up creating my own little homemade porn collection (though the word 'porn' was unknown to me at the time.)** I would secret all of this away in a secret box, tied up in a secret way, hidden in a secret location in the wall behind a piece of moveable fiberboard in the rear of my clothes closet. I'd visit that box with great frequency. Over time the contents of the box would expand to near bursting.

Then there was gay porn-in-plain-sight brought to me by the (he must've been gay) film director Joshua Logan. While I had no idea who Joshua Logan was, I was clearly a young aficionado of his work. His films, including *South Pacific, Ensign Pulver* and *Tall Story*, reliably had the best big-screen beefcake that had ever met my eyes. My mother was a huge fan of movie musicals and while I certainly followed suit, *South Pacific* took me to new heights of musical connoisseurship. From the first frame, the screen is packed with some of the hottest male physique models of the time. Most every production number — "There Is Nothing Like A Dame" is my favorite — was layered with shirtless, muscled, bulging, skimpily clad hunks. There are oftentimes nearly-naked men just hanging around the edges and backgrounds of the numbers. I couldn't see *South Pacific* enough. My mother was so proud. The same was true of *Ensign Pulver*, a comedy also chock-full of scantily clad hunks. In fact, I thought I recognized a few from *South Pacific*. My older brother Frank took me to see that one and I was eternally grateful to him. While he was watching a military comedy, I was enjoying a gay porn-fest. I'd ask him over and over if we could go see it again. *Tall Story* had only one memorable scene but it was a good one. Jane Fonda chases Anthony Perkins into the men's locker room and is faced with a stunning, flirtatious boy who rounds the corner of the lockers wearing only a sexy smile, with a towel in hand, obscuring only his genitals. It's a scene that instantly burnished itself onto my ten year old gay brain. I made my mother promise to tell me whenever *Tall Story* was on TV explaining to her, "I just love Anne Jackson, she's my favorite actress." She played the coach's wife and I was probably her only thirteen year old "fan." And speaking of genitals, in *It's a Mad Mad Mad Mad World*, not directed by Joshua Logan, I could swear I saw Dick Shawn's balls! Twice! In Cinerama! Oh how I longed to go back for a second viewing — it had flashed by so quickly — to see if I really saw what I was certain I saw.

Actual pornography didn't make it to my eyes until I was about fourteen. I was allowed to go to downtown Louisville on my own by then and did so with some frequency, loving the independence my trips afforded me. Downtown was exciting, glamorous and sexy and I went whenever I could. Downtown had possibilities, of what order I wasn't quite certain but I was certain there were things going on there that did not go on in our neighborhood. I'd impatiently wait at the end of our street for the downtown bound Camp Taylor bus, excited about being on my own. As the bus would make its serpentine way through the streets of Louisville, it would briefly ramp up onto the North-South Expressway giving me a clear view of the taller buildings of downtown. My pulse would quicken as we'd close in on the destination: the corner of 4th and Walnut, the center of downtown where I'd proceed to do some shopping, have lunch and perhaps catch a movie at one of Louisville's many movie theaters along 4th Street, just as I had with my mom when I was younger. I'd sit alone at the serpentine counter of the Stewart's Department Store Luncheonette, lower level, order my Benedictine Sandwich and potato salad, scan the room of mostly working girls, ladies who lunch and some blue haired gems and feel decidedly grown up and autonomous. I'd always sit at a table when I was with my mother but I'd eyed that counter many times — where there'd often be a handsome single gentleman or two — and imagine myself there on my own someday.

At the end of my afternoon, I'd walk the few blocks of a still thriving downtown to the Blue Motor Coach bus station located at its seedier end. This was a slightly frightening area where, in my youth, my mother would take my hand or, if she was already holding it, squeeze it tighter. There were certain undefinable businesses that, though I couldn't put my finger on just why, greatly interested me. I'd see flashy signs for places with names like "The Savoy Theater" and wonder, with its pink naked lady neon, if "Savoy" was a dirty word. Now, old enough to be on my own, I passed a heavily made-up gypsy woman sitting in an open doorway in a head scarf, big hoop earrings and scores of bracelets with an oversized deck of cards in her hand saying, "Leetle boy, come here, you luuk hongry." I quickly skipped past her, making a mental note to not walk down that side of the street again and ran to the bus station to wait for another Camp Taylor bus that would safely return me to Ardmore Drive. On one occasion, on the other side of the street, I passed a magazine store called Liberty News. It was only a few doors away from the bus station. Needing to kill some time, I went in. It was cool, dingy and darkish in there and I was met at the door by a musty magazine store fragrance that to this day I recognize immediately upon entering stores that sell magazines and paperbacks. The place was empty but for one man seated under a cloud of smoke behind a raised sales counter and a few men clustered in a corner adjacent to that counter. Upon closer inspection I saw the men were looking at magazines with naked women on the covers. Some unseen gravitational force pulled me into that same corner. Looking between two of the men, I could see that all of the magazines in that section had naked women on them. Well, almost all. My eyes quickly shot to some nudist magazines which had in addition to naked women, naked men. **Naked men!** I froze and stared at those magazine covers, my heart in my throat, frightened I was being too obvious but at the same time not able to open my eyes wide enough or take them away. After I don't know how long, scared of being found out, I forced myself to move away and left the store.

Walking to the bus station I knew I had to see one of those magazines — have one — but how? I was just a kid. Nobody is going to sell a magazine like that to me. If I tried to buy one they'd surely throw me out. **Those naked men haunted me after that and I vowed to go back to Liberty News the next time I went downtown.** Prior to this, the closest I'd come to male nudity were the muscle men magazines at our neighborhood drug store. After peddling my way there, I'd cruise the magazine racks and surreptitiously peruse the pictures of the shiny, sleek muscle men but was way too intimidated by the pinched-faced old lady at the cash register to ever buy one. I found the pics of these seductive shiny men endlessly entertaining. While there was at best some captivating delineation showing in their skimpy posing suits and some asscheeks exposed and perhaps even a glimpse of a pubic hair, there was no nudity. One could only imagine what prizes lay beneath the clingy fabric. Still, it was well worth the bicycle trip to Rueben's Pharmacy to be able to ogle these gorgeous photos just as they were.

Those downtown nudist magazines were different. They showed everything! On the cover! At the next possible opportunity, I made another trip in to town. While I may have done some shopping or other business as usual, my main focus was Liberty News and those nudist magazines. Eventually making my way to Liberty Street, I walked back and forth before getting up the nerve to go in. When I eventually did, without any clear plan, I casually made my adolescent way around that adult place trying as best I could to blend in unnoticed. I'd pick up a magazine here, flip through it, put it down, move on and pick up another there. I repeated the same charade as casually as possible, over and over making my way everywhere around that store, everywhere that is, except the corner up by the sales counter where my actual interest lay and where once again men had gathered to look at their magazines. I didn't give so much as a glance in that direction focused instead on whatever Better Homes and Gardens or Popular Mechanics I happened to be holding. After an eternity of this subterfuge, I eventually, ever so nonchalantly, sidled up to the group of men and, heart beating wildly, picked up the first nudist magazine I saw and just as casually began to peruse it. **Oh my god naked men! On every page! Naked men! Walking around — naked. Swimming — naked. Lying in the sun — naked. Playing volleyball — naked. Croquet — naked.** There was even a naked beauty contest. Shiny naked men holding big shiny trophies. There were women too but they barely registered with of all the penises and hairy buttocks spread before me just going about their outdoor day to day lives, exposed and photographed. My heart was threatening to beat right out of my chest, my palms were moistening and I felt a familiar (and at that particular moment, unwanted) swelling in my pants. I was about to blow my cover. I briefly considered sticking the magazine under my shirt and making a run for it but felt certain all eyes were on me and I'd never get away with it. **I'd never stolen anything but as far as I could see, theft was the only way for me to obtain this coveted piece of age-restricted contraband.** I'd loved to have marched right up to the man at the sales counter and boldly forked over the $2.99 and run, but I hadn't the courage. I reluctantly put the magazine back where I'd found it and once again, frustrated, left the store empty-handed. But not defeated. I vowed, "Next time!"

Of course, my next trip downtown brought me right back to Liberty News determined this time to walk out with that magazine. As I purposely strode down Liberty Street, I was a worried mess. What would they do to a kid who tried to buy such a magazine? What if I do get it, and they don't put it in a paper bag? What, even if they do bag it, if someone asks me what's in the bag? What if it slips out of the bag on the bus? How will I get it into the house? The mounting worries however could not keep me out of the store and away from those magazines. I just had to have one and all its naked men. I did the back and forth on Liberty Street once again until I got up the courage to do what I knew I had to. I went in and repeated the same slow, lengthy round the store deception until it brought me to that once again overpopulated corner of the shop. Shoving my sweaty left hand into my pants pocket where a carefully rolled-up dedicated three dollars waited, I worked up my nerve and walked straight to the nudist mags. I picked one up and without even looking at it, marched right up to the sales counter eyes cast down, laid it on the counter along with my three dollars and hoped the man silently smoking wouldn't ask me how old I was, or throw me out or perhaps even call the police. My eyes, which couldn't meet his, focused instead on the cylinder of ash growing at the end of the cigarette dangling from his lips. I now had a new worry. What if it breaks away and falls on my new treasure? I imagined myself having to go back to the magazine rack for another unspoiled one. **Fixed in place and willing the ashes to stay put, I didn't know what to expect from this quiet smoking man. Perhaps he would call the cops and they'd put me in stockades just a few blocks away in the City Hall Plaza as a warning to all the other precocious horny underage boys with prurient same-sex interests.** Who knew?

Without a word, ash still growing at the end of his cigarette, the man unceremoniously flattened and counted the cash, put it away and snapped a penny change onto the counter. He then quietly slipped the magazine into a flat brown paper bag its exact size, folded the end of the bag over and sealed it with a small piece of scotch tape. I stood there eyes now focused on that little piece of tape; frozen. What's next? I hadn't planned past this point. Was that it? Had I done it? Shocked at the ease of the transaction, I reached up, still not making eye contact, slipped the brown package off the counter, tucked it up under my arm, snatched up the penny and made a hasty breathless exit, my feet keeping time with my ever increasing heartbeat.

That was it! I had my magazine! I was home free! No I wasn't. I still had to get it home. On the longest bus trip of my life, with that unopened brown-paper-bagged treasure on my lap, I wanted desperately to rip it open right then and there and devour those naked male bodies. Scanning the other passengers faces, I tried to look innocent but felt they all knew I had a lap-full of forbidden naked men. **I ran my finger over that little reassuring inch of scotch tape, grateful for how it had managed to alleviate my fear about the magazine's being accidentally exposed somehow before getting it home.** As I rushed from the bus stop to our house, I stuck the magazine up under my shirt. Smuggling it in, I moved as quickly as I could past my mom in dinner prep mode, hoping that the crinkling sound I could hear from the paper bag wouldn't give me away. I gave her a clipped "hello" and went right upstairs to my bedroom. I couldn't wait another minute to see all those men publicly exposed at play in their sexy nakedness and quietly lifted the piece of tape, slipping the magazine out of its paper bag. I devoured it. The cover alone was worth all the planning and the well-oiled execution. The pages inside were full of also well-oiled, masculine, total nudity and oh so much better than the Spiegel catalog. These men and boys, many of them muscled and handsome, some smooth, some hairy, were frolicking naked in the great outdoors having the time of their lives. Oh how I wanted to join them. Pulling off my clothes I could at the very least be naked with them. They would be my new constant companions and I'd have my horny adolescent way with them time and again. **I was already a masturbation prodigy working the medium like a gifted artist and with my new nudist magazine, I achieved even greater heights.** I so wanted to frolic naked with these naked men and boys.

Stroking away I visualized myself right square among them, just as naked, playing in the sunny great outdoors, exposed, happy and horny as I'd jerk my stiff young penis and explode over and over.

During the next year or so, subsequent trips to my new favorite magazine store went a lot easier. On one such occasion, now a regular, in looking for yet another nudist magazine I spied a new addition to the merchandise mix. It was a magazine called *Avanti* and it had a sexy handsome naked man on the cover. With an erection! Right on the cover! Hard! I almost passed out on the cold dirty tile floor of Liberty News. I'd never seen a man's erection. I had seen my own of course, many times, but never a man's. Without a moment's hesitation, I grabbed it, paid for it and got home as quickly as I could. *Avanti* was full of handsome sexy naked men (this time only men) all of them better looking than the ones in the nudist magazines. They all had gorgeous muscular shining bodies like the men in the muscle magazines but these men were naked, totally naked showing off their full round bare buttocks, hard, erect penises and quite unexpectedly an occasional bonus of a well-lighted pink posterior pucker. That was the end of the nudist magazines. By now I had learned the words "homosexual" and "gay" and these new gay magazines were an important bridge taking me from observer to participant in a new-to-me gay world. I could now totally imagine myself naked and gay among all these equally naked and gay men. My copy of *Avanti* became the new crown jewel of my growing porn collection and the men on those pages my constant sexual companions. There were also ads for all sorts of male oriented merchandise — sexy clothing, sexy accessories, sexy posters and other semi-pornographic material. Oh, for a checking account and a post office box of my own. In addition to these new male-only magazines — there came others — Liberty News started carrying gay fiction, novels that described in great detail, cover to cover torrid man on man sex. I would no longer have to write my own stories. **I couldn't get enough of these books, reading and re-reading my favorite passages on the dog-eared pages some of which unfortunately and quite frequently (the magazines as well) got stuck together (oddly enough) right at the best parts.** The sexy artwork on the covers of these works of erotic male fiction was reason enough to buy them.

My precocious sexual interest wasn't limited to drawings and photos. I was just as obsessed with living, breathing male beauty and as much skin as I could manage to see. Preoccupied with male nudity and near-nudity, summer would find me on my bike following the sound of lawn mowers that would inevitably lead me to shirtless older boys, earning their summer cash while sweating through their high school gym trunks, occasionally barefooted, though I found this particularly foolhardy with sharp metal blades. There was also the occasional boy washing his car, often clad only in a skimpy swimsuit and especially, on super hot days, soaking wet. If I was lucky I'd come across two or more boys washing a car or cars together, frisky with each other and a garden hose. I'd go back and forth or circle the block catching as many glimpses as possible, wanting them and wanting to be them in their sexy older boyishness.

High School freshman gym class provided some covert ogling, especially when sharing the locker room with the more developed upperclassmen. **I landed a volunteer position as a football team "manager" whose only real responsibility was keeping the stinky locker room tidy. I'd loiter around the shower room eyes wide open, waiting for wet used towels to be tossed at me by naked football players otherwise unaware of my presence. Or stares.**

There were also quick glimpses of usually hidden treasures at the occasional public swimming pool locker/change/shower room, the best of which was at Lincoln Lake in Southern Indiana not too far from Mariah Hill. The German side of our family would hold its annual reunion at Lincoln State Park. This was my favorite event of the summer. The park itself was nothing special and while it was fun being with members of our extended family and all those Catholic cousins most of whom I really liked, my real interest lay in the beach-adjacent, gender-specific bath house. The men's bathhouse had a large shower and changing area surrounded by a wall but with no roof. Open to the sun and the sky and the breezes it felt more outdoors than in and made me feel as if I were in the great outdoors, naked, with a lot of other naked boys and men. There was a constant flow of them, stripping out of their clothes and into their bathing suits, showering, parading around naked, snapping towels and showing off. Something about this place, with its roofless outdoor quality and all the sunshine and breezes, made for friskier behavior than I'd ever witnessed anywhere else. I couldn't get my young eyes open wide enough to take in all the bending and bouncing and posing and posturing. **It was as if I had stepped right onto the pages of my cherished nudist magazines and there I was, sharing in their frolicking male nakedness.** I took a lot of showers at Lake Lincoln, getting into and out of my swimsuit, spending more time in that bath house than anywhere else at our family reunion. It was not only the highlight of our family reunion, but of my entire summer. My Aunt Pat's German potato salad, coming in a distant second, was the one thing that could pull me away.

Lake Lincoln's bath house inspired a lot of fantasies about other places where I imagined I might find boys who, like me, were attracted to other boys; there we would gather to be naked in the great outdoors and play together. My teenage masturbatory fantasies were rife with these sunny and sexy imaginary places. In my youthful naïveté, I hadn't imagined that such boys and such places might actually exist. That happy discovery was still years away.

1975

Where The Boys Are

AT 23 YEARS OLD I finally made it to Florida. I had dreamed of the day when I would experience the palm-treed land of *Where The Boys Are.* The 1960 film had been, since my early landlocked youth, my primary point of reference for the sunshine state. **It had taught me that Florida was *the* place for sun and fun, filled with palm trees and beaches, parties and swim-suited boys, and, most important-to-me, rampant youthful sexuality.** It was all strictly heterosexual of course, but I'd necessarily gender-switch myself with Yvette Mimieux and my youthful same-sex Florida fantasy would be complete. In truth, I was probably more Dolores Hart; or Paula Prentice. Anyway, as the plane approached the runway at the Palm Beach airport, on that inaugural visit, I spotted my first palm tree and excitedly pointed it out to my friends Margaret and Pat who, being Florida veterans, met my enthusiasm with a shared "This is going to be a long ten days." I was finally in Florida — the ever-in-school Randy having stayed behind in Louisville — and in Palm Beach no less. Well, we called it Palm Beach. We actually stayed farther north in a condo in Juno Beach. More Palm Beach-ish. It was a place long on palm trees and beaches but short on parties, tanned boys and sex. Still, I had a ball with my two girlfriends, going in to Palm Beach each day shopping and each evening to the restaurants. We loved pretending we were of the Rolls Royce driving, Gucci wearing (if only a belt) Palm Beach upper crust, denizens of the fabulous Breakers where we'd go for drinks and dancing in the Arabian-tented Alcazar Lounge overlooking a sparkling ocean. We'd dine at The Flame where they served the best crispy Duck l'Orange with wild rice on earth. Or Nino's where the waiter would light the wrappers from the amaretto cookies and flaming, they would lift off magically, ascending into the air, hover there overhead for a moment before turning to ash, extinguishing themselves and softly floating back down to earth — or tabletop. Other nights it'd be drinks and dining at Ta-Boo rubbing elbows with the celebrities. We were told there were celebrities. We did all of this dressed to the nines improbably transported to this monied place in our rented red Plymouth Duster. We thought we were fabulous, despite the Duster. Pat was forever referring to Palm Beach as "The Land of Rolls Royces" so I'd have hoped for more; but a Duster was what we could afford. **We'd sing along with Minnie Ripperton's "Lovin' You" or Labelle's "Lady Marmalade" as we'd cross the bridge onto that immaculate, perfectly manicured dream of an island where royal palm trees stood in royal rows and each single blade of grass was tended to.**

Two words: "Worth Avenue!" We covered every square inch of that fabled shopping street and would spend far more at the tony Palm Beach stores and shops than we could afford. We called it Palm Beach Fever. You were convinced you were rich and acted accordingly. Once infected there was no turning back. Money was suddenly no object. Worth Avenue was our daytime playground. Slaves to fashion and our credit cards, we'd run up our charge accounts and pay for it all later.

Toward the end of our stay the weather took a nasty turn and the predictions made it clear our remaining time in Palm Beach(ish) would be a washout. Margaret and Pat decided to cut their losses and return to Louisville a day early. I couldn't give up on Florida that easily so with a definite plan in mind, I decided to stay. While Palm Beach was a dream place it wasn't exactly my dream. It was fun enough with all the dining and shopping and it had palm trees galore but it was more "Where The Boys Aren't." There was another place in Florida that I was pretty sure could fulfill my youthful Florida expectations. Or even my childish Mariah Hill fantasies. Or, dare I hoped, exceed them.

I dropped the girls off at the Palm Beach Airport on Sunday morning and in a torrential rainstorm pointed the little red Duster south in the general direction of Key West. I didn't even have a map. I just figured I'd head south. There was only one road. And Key West was the southernmost point in Florida, so, heading south, how could I not get there?

As far away from the rest of the straight world as you can get, Key West had become a live and let live, hedonistic free-to-be-gay destination of gay guest houses, gay bath houses, gay clubs and gay boys. I'd seen advertisements and articles in gay publications. And I'd heard the stories. **I'd been imagining such a place for most of my life and was quite certain this was an island where the boys were and that it was tailor-made for me.**

I had no idea how long the drive would be, but armed with the fervent belief there was something special waiting for me there, I became a pilgrim possessed. I was on a personal quest to get to that little island and spend my final vacation day (singular) looking for my own holy grail. Whatever it might be, I just *knew* it was there. Hours into the trip on the harrowing narrowing road linking the tiny islands — occasionally only one lane at many of the bridges where cars were held at either end, I was cursing myself and my foolishness. While driving at a crawl in a fierce rainstorm with the Duster's woefully inadequate windshield wipers, I was doubting my sanity. "Crazy," I kept mumbling to myself as sheets of rain, heavier than I had ever experienced, pummeled the car and along with those awful wipers, made visibility nearly impossible. "This is crazy!" Wave after wave of water attacked the car from above and both sides of the road nearly swamping it. Moving at a crawl, I felt in immediate danger of being swept away! Everything was water. I couldn't see ahead and I couldn't see behind. How absolutely insane was it of me to make such a trip, at a snail's pace for a one night stay in a place I had never been, a place I knew little about and had no accommodations awaiting me? And it would most likely be raining. Things typically had a way of working out for me but I wasn't thinking of that. I wasn't thinking at all. I just pressed on. **Had I known how many more hours of this stormy insanity lay ahead, I'd have turned back. I am so glad I didn't.**

After several hours of that nightmarish road trip I finally made my way onto the last bridge that would take me to the island of my dreams. From the higher vantage point of the bridge's crest, I saw, just ahead, an improbable patch of blue opening up in the threatening stormy gray sky around it. It was right over Key West. After the horrors of that drive, a miraculous welcoming beam of radiant sun light was shining through that one small blue hole in the dark sky, lighting the island below setting it apart from its darkened surroundings. Key West was already showing its glistening magic to me as it welcomed me forth. Suddenly I was Dorothy and that beam of sunlight was pointing the way to a gleaming Emerald City. I could hear a chorus singing inside my head, "You're out of the woods you're out of the dark you're out of the night. Step into the sun step into the light. Keep straight ahead for the most glorious place on the face of the earth and the sky…" I sang out loud along with those optimistic voices as I descended the arc of the bridge and made my way to that "most glorious place."

The rain had stopped entirely as I left the bridge and enthusiastically looked around but my enthusiasm began to wane. My first impression of the island was a little less than glorious. Had I made a mistake? **It all seemed sort-of-warehouse-boat-storage-industrial-tacky; it had a temporary corrugated aluminum quality giving the first impression that, at a moment's notice, you could fold it all up and take it somewhere else.** Eventually a small sign pointing to Old Town gave me hope. I followed the subsequent signs along the water, past an airport and a small beach. After a right turn and then a left I found myself in a more populated area. On Truman Avenue now, as I passed it's intersection with Margaret Street, I chuckled at a sign that read, "Margaret Truman Launderette." I was charmed and in fact, everything I saw from that point on was charming and quaint. It was all, suddenly, right in tune with what I had expected or at least had hoped to find. A couple of blocks farther I made a right turn onto Duvall Street, a charming little main street of palm trees and shops. Suddenly I knew I was right in the heart of where I wanted to be.

I parked at the first available space. It was now a cloudless sunny day as I headed toward Duval Street. Approaching the cutest bike shop I'd ever seen, I decided that a bike might be the best way to determine my whereabouts. I needed after all to find some accommodation for the night. It had to be gay and I wasn't entirely sure I'd recognize a gay guesthouse if I saw one. The tanned bike rental guy was cute, barefoot and shirtless as he waved me away to explore the heart of Old Town Key West. I did this by looping a square block at a time and then widening it to include another square block outside the first one. And then another. I continued in this vein, passing cottage after cottage, all picket fenced and palm treed, and flowered; everywhere flowers. Bougainvillea spilled over fences and walls. The cracked sidewalks buckled-up and the picket fences along with their tropical vegetation followed right along. The love affair was on. I continued, dazzled and charmed at every turn by everything I saw until I noticed a sign with a sea horse logo on it. It said "The Monster." Under the seahorse was a tacked-on sign which read, "Tea Dance - Today 4pm." Tea Dance! Tea Dance was already a tradition in the gay world, having had its initial start in Fire Island, not too many years before. They were late afternoon parties (at tea time) typically in resort-ish places. I'd never been to one but

I'd heard of them. The words, "Tea Dance" meant The Monster must be a gay club and tea dance only about an hour away. I chained up my bike, went in and got a stool at the bar. **I ordered a Piña Colada from a sexy bartender who insisted on giving me a "free float." I didn't know what that was but I was certain I wanted it.** Turned out it was just a little extra rum on top. My generous bartender was not only barechested but barefooted and had on the tiniest little clingy swimsuit. Yup, it was a gay bar alright. I was home; in my first gay bar in Key West.

Soon the near empty space started to fill up and I wasn't there even an hour before, much to my surprise, I heard my name being shouted at me. Key West magic. I turned to see a friend named Tim who I met and had gone home with on one of my weekends in Chicago. We had stayed friends and occasional fuck buddies. He had his cute and blond new boyfriend (we apparently had the same taste in men) in tow. I stood eyes attached to the adorable boyfriend but listening to Tim, a get-things-done kinda guy who had a string of questions for me. "When did you arrive?", "How long are you staying?", "Where are you staying?" In response to my lack of housing he said, "I'm pretty sure there's a room available at the Cypress House. A guy checked out this morning and I don't think anyone new has checked in." "Cypress House!" My heart did a little flip-flop at the very name. I immediately imagined a sultry sexy place steeped in sun-bleached, sub-tropical atmosphere with sun-bleached, sub-tropical gay boys, naked and near-naked, all over it. I could see the gay glamour and sexy decadence and I was there already. Right in the middle of it. "Cypress House is only a few blocks away," it was Tim bringing me back from my reverie, "Lets go now and make sure the room's still there," and he added, "Don't worry. We'll get back to t-dance in plenty of time. You won't miss a thing." He leaned over to kiss his boyfriend with, "Chip, keep our barstools warm, honey. We'll be back before you miss us." As we hurried off to Cypress House in the tropical perfection of a late Key West afternoon, I thought, "Chip. Of course it would be 'Chip.'"

Cypress House was a stately silver-gray, weathered, cypress mansion which had been (I was told) disassembled in the Bahamas and reassembled in Key West. It was so one with its environment you'd never have guessed it was from anywhere else. Embraced by magnificent old Palm trees and tropical vegetation and weathered to a silvery perfection, it had that mossy, organic quality of having just sprouted out of the Key West soil and grown up right there. We checked with the proprietor, a handsome, darkly tanned, also weathered to perfection, barefoot, bare chested, sexy gay man, in a tiny pair of loose gym shorts and nothing else. Key West standard gay business wear, I came to learn.

The room was still available. I paid for it, sight unseen, told Jim I'd meet him back at The Monster after I'd ditched my bike, relocated my car to the Cypress House and put my luggage in the room. The room. My first room in Key West was, is quite possibly still, my all time favorite. It was a long narrow bright white room located right by the long narrow lap pool, paralleling it actually. It was sparsely but perfectly furnished in what I would eventually christen, "Key West Smart Gay Simplicity." It had a white on white wood paneled and beamed vaulted ceiling with a white slowly revolving ceiling fan. The wall facing the pool had jalousie windows that ran the entire length of the room. They were cranked open to let in the sounds and fragrances of a Key West poolside evening. To say the room had a view of the pool would be an understatement. There was a small perfectly appointed bathroom with no shower. In one more bit of magic for me and my slightly exhibitionistic tendencies, there was an outdoor shower right outside my door. **I'd have no choice but to take my showers outdoors, under the sun, in full view of anyone who cared to watch.**

I unpacked a few things, took a shower — of course — watched only by a slow moving roach the size of a Sherman tank; I later learned it was a Palmetto Bug. And it could fly. Wishing I'd paid more attention to what others were wearing at The Monster, I ended up in a my favorite white Lacoste, navy blue piped-in-white gym shorts and Adidas sneaks. Within minutes I was right back to Tea Dance at The Monster where we danced for hours, indoors and out. We went straight to dinner at a kind of treehouse restaurant where the host politely and ever so nonchalantly removed a sleeping cat from my chair (a first for me) and deposited it undisturbed on another chair at a neighboring table. I was absolutely charmed. I learned that night about Key West cats and how they were said to all be descendants of Ernest Hemingway's cats and therefore revered. After dinner in what became through the years a near-ritual, we went back to the house, hung out by the pool and got to know other guests, changed outfits, got a little high, changed outfits again and eventually returned to The Monster for more dancing. I had never been to a place where you would transition so seamlessly from indoors to out that you'd suddenly and quite unexpectedly find yourself dancing under the stars. The Monster was as magical as the island itself and I danced until near dawn.

Getting a little lost taking the long way back to the Cypress House, I learned very quickly about the possibilities for sex around nearly every corner on your way home. There were boys all over the place similarly finding their way back to their guesthouses a little high or not, a little drunk or not but all of them, like me, in the early morning darkness of the tropical heat, horny. It could take a very long time to get home. The humid nighttime air was heavy with the smell of frangipani trees and the scent of sex. I was on a quest now, a mission to clip my horns and have my first nighttime outdoor tropical sex. Strolling down Fleming Street, I saw a boy sitting on a pastel front porch of the most charming little cottage I'd yet to see. He was sitting there in the heat of that night, legs spread wide, softly lighted by an accommodating nearby streetlight. On closer inspection I could see he was slowly stroking his hard penis which was standing out of the leg opening of his shorts. He took his hand away, leaned back spread his legs wider and gave me a sweet crooked smile. I'd never had a friendlier invitation, and though somewhat hesitantly, I made my way up the short walkway, and took it. We had sex right there on the porch using a conveniently placed twin mattress over in the corner. I didn't know if the boy actually lived there, was staying there or if he had just stopped, affording himself the convenience of the cottage, the porch, the mattress and me. It didn't matter. **I'd had my first outdoor naked Key West sex on a warm humid night, with a sexy, available boy who was as horny for me as I for him.** Knowing my long drive down that stormy inhospitable road had been well worth the effort, I could have satisfyingly left the island right then and there. I am so glad I didn't.

With only a few hours sleep I was up and out early the next morning. These would be my only daylight hours in Key West and I wasn't going to sleep them away. Not indoors at least. I was lying by the pool, sun-warmed, happy and content, sleepily slipping in and out of consciousness when I heard a voice next to me say, "Do they always do that?" I didn't understand the question but as I opened my eyes and glanced in the general direction of the voice, on the previously empty lounge chair next to me was a long, lean, naked boy, oiled and glistening, with a tanned body and an adorably sweet smiling boyish face topped off by tousled sand colored hair. How long had I been asleep? I glanced down and was excited to see that this naked boy was excited to see me. "So, do they?" He was pointing to my feet and the habit I've had since childhood, of constantly moving them in a kind of out of synch windshield wiper fashion at odds with each other and my otherwise still body. I was only slightly embarrassed but was happy to have provided him with an opening line. "Oh, them," I replied, "They have a mind of their own. Two... actually." I gave a self-deprecating smile that I hoped he'd find charming. We hit it off instantly, Hepburn and Tracy style with the type of back and forth banter that comes from a shared wit and an instant ease with each other. His name was Rod. Rod! He was from San Francisco. San Francisco! I was torn between looking into Rod from San Francisco's sparkling blue eyes or feasting my own brown ones on Rod's rod, hard and proudly standing between his legs. I had to pinch myself as I thought, " I am lying by a pool in Key West with a hot naked boy with a boner pointed right at me." I had spent my life dreaming of such a moment. Feeling his touch, I glanced down to see his fingers walking up my leg toward the growing bulge in my tan-line preserving swimsuit. I'd have been naked too, but given these were my final Florida sun hours, I was determined to return to Louisville with razor-sharp tan-lines dark as I could get them. "How long are you staying in Key West?" he asked as his fingers invaded the leg opening of my suit. "About four hours," I declared to his look of astonishment and a firm squeeze as he wrapped his fingers around my hardened penis. "I have a flight outta Palm Beach tonight. Gotta be at work tomorrow morn..." my voice trailed off with a deep intake or air as the pleasure of more squeezes made further speaking impossible. "Nooooo," he said stretching out the word and then adding, "Call your boss." He delivered his directive directly into my eyes as he continued his insistent squeezes down there. As I tried to offer the many reasons why I had to get back, once again, with three firmer squeezes, timed to his command, "Call...your...boss." I tried once more to counter his firm order, but his firm grasp on my now rock-hard-on made it difficult to form the words. What could I say? I was lying by a pool in Key West getting a slow deliberate hand-job from a sexy naked very insistent gay boy named Rod who had just leaned in and pressed his lips to mine, invading my mouth, his tongue keeping time with his determined squeezes. I called my boss.

Miracle of miracles! He said yes. I must have caught my boss in a particularly good mood or I effectively employed my "charm offensive" as it has been called or perhaps the planets had aligned in a favorable way. **Whatever the case, and against all odds, I was staying in Key West for another three days.**

Those three days went by like a movie montage where a young couple in love, soft dissolve from one happy romantic activity to another. There was:

- Breezy **getting-to-know-you-sex** on crisp white sheets during a perfectly timed afternoon thunderstorm in that wonderful little pool-adjacent room;

- Dinner at Claire **under a canopy of sparkling twinkle-light-laced-trees** to the romantic sound of Shirley Horn softly singing in the background;

- Sunburnt chlorinated **sex by the pool** watched only (as far as we knew) by the tall elegantly curving palm trees swaying above us;

- An out of the way weathered little thrift shop where we nakedly shared a fitting room, in and out of item after item, where I purchased **the perfect vintage 1950s rayon tropical printed swim trunks** — classic with palm trees, sailboats and all;

- A speed boat ride to the Dry Tortugas bouncing over the waves while **laying naked side by side on the bow**, kissing, while stroking each others' erect penises;

- Subsequent **sandy sunburnt sex on one of the beaches** of the Dry Tortugas;

- The best sandwich you could have in your life shared on the front porch of a tiny little off the beaten track storefront called **La Bodega**;

- A most unusual (and believe it or not, romantic) cemetery where we made out by a tombstone that read, **"See I Told You I Was Sick"**;

- A little dockside restaurant/shack where I enjoyed **my first Conch Chowder** and **first slice of Key Lime Pie** and wondered how I'd ever lived my entire life without either and without this special man who introduced me to both;

- Dancing at The Monster pressing our aching hardness against each other, kissing and **blissfully unaware of the people around us and even the stars above**;

- Romantic walks, openly hand-in-hand all around the island discovering the charming tree and bougainvillea lined streets, big impressive Victorian homes, tiny beach shacks and funky little shops (often side by side) and occasionally tripping on the **charmingly buckled sidewalks of Key West**;

- The best broiled fish sandwich I would experience in my life, **grilled to perfection and served by a sexy suntanned cook wearing only an apron exposing his smooth untanned butt cheeks**, while we sat under a thatched palm roof, both in our microscopic euro-style swimsuits at a microscopic euro-style beach named "The Sands" where we spent the day warmed by the sun, watching a glistening, absolutely golden nearly-naked boy loll around the sand in and out of the water polishing himself to suntanned perfection;

- **Falling in love and lust with each other and with that wonderful magical little island, a place so far away from everywhere else that you could simply be and do whatever you wanted, with whomever you wanted, however you wanted, wherever you wanted, whenever you wanted.**

It was all too wonderful. As I had headed off to that mythical little island, I'd done so with the hope of a fun twenty-four hours; I didn't think to ask for more. All too soon though, it was time to hop in the little red Duster and get myself back to the Palm Beach Airport for my late night flight. We said our goodbyes and promised, even with the nearly 3,000 miles between us, to keep in touch. **With the knowledge we wouldn't and a lump in my throat, I drove away from Rod, The Cypress House and that wonderfully magical sunny place full of palm trees and boys.** As I reached the crest of the first bridge, the one where, a few days earlier, I had caught my initial glimpse of the sunny little island ahead, I glanced in the rear view mirror. There it was, reflected for just a moment, sparkling away like the jewel it was, before it just as quickly disappeared as the little red Duster descended the other side of the hill. In sharp contrast to the stormy drive down, the drive back would be sparklingly clear. I was able to appreciate that glittering, super thin line of road and bridges and islands that connected Key West to the mainland. **It was a stretched-out diamond necklace with the last and the most precious of the sparkling jewels, receding now behind me.** I determined in that moment to return to that gem of a place as often as possible for, I was quite certain, there'd be more magic waiting there for me. I'd return over and over to explore the many ways my "own special island" would have of manifesting its magic. I was certain Key West would once again and for as many times as I wished to return, open its arms to me the way it had on my very first visit. I was a grateful seed that had found its tropical soil. My own personal heaven.

1975

Key West & Cats & Mr. Williams

STILL AGLOW with all my fresh memories, during the drive back I was reminded of something I'd seen just that afternoon out by the pool before I took my last semi-public shower. I was lying there with Rod at my side, on that blistering hot afternoon determined to get every final ray of sun available to me and my tan-lines before returning to the cold north. I spotted one of Mr. Hemingway's cats lazily making its way along the top of the greenery-crested wall that separated the Cypress House pool area from whatever lay beyond. She was barely moving at a heat-induced, lethargic pace under the burning Key West sun. That is until she reached the roof a small outbuilding at the corner. As she stepped onto the corrugated metal she skittered across the sun heated surface so quickly that she seemed to have for that moment become another cat entirely from the sluggish one I'd seen only seconds before. It suddenly hit me. "Look," I whispered to Rod, my fingers tapping him awake, "A cat on a hot tin roof!" And so she was. I'll just bet that Tennessee Williams, who spent a lot of time in Key West, had witnessed the same thing, saw the metaphor in it, named the cat "Maggie," and wrote all about her.

INDIANAPOLIS

I'd

drift off

to sleep

surrounded

by the

nighttime sparkle

of my

dream city,

imagining

my own eventual existence

in this

steel and glass

high-rise-heaven.

1975

Closing In On Chicago

WITH OUR EXIT from all the challenges of Old Louisville, Randy and I were quite comfortable in his happy dream home in New(er) Louisville where our lives became a lot easier. The absence of construction dust and abortion protesters and the presence of working bathrooms and an actual kitchen with real appliances made all the difference. We happily went about our lives together until an unexpected opportunity presented itself — A&P offered me a job transfer to Indianapolis. The offer represented a chance for a better job, higher salary, some upward-mobility, and a location two hours closer to Chicago. If I couldn't live in Chicago I could at least get there faster. While Randy had yet to visit the city of my dreams, through all my stories, it had become the city of his dreams as well. We shared our mutual intent of moving there together. So I relocated my twenty-four year old self two hours closer to our dream, leaving Randy and our shared Louisville life behind. It was exciting and at the same time, sad. Everything was new and exhilarating but I immediately missed the comfort and warmth of the life we enjoyed together.

Despite the separation from Randy, Indianapolis proved to be a good move. In addition to those two hours saved on the trip to my beloved Chicago, it had also given me a much greater sense of independence than I had ever known before. This was a city where I knew no one so I would socially have to make my way myself. I'd never before enjoyed this level of autonomy. It was both scary and exciting to be twenty-four and on my own.

It didn't take long for me to find a near north neighborhood I liked right along Meridian Street which bisected the city into East and West Sides. It had grand old homes and some of the nicest old high rise and low rise apartment buildings classically filled with the expected mix of gay men and old ladies. I set my sights on The Admiral, a stately old yellow brick eleven story Art Deco "Very New York" faded beauty looking nothing like anything around it. The building tapered gracefully at the top stepping back with symmetrical terraces all around. I imagined the apartments up there. Were they penthouses? They must be penthouses. I imagined the people who must live in them; **I imagined me in my own — Lauren Bacall stepping out onto my own private living room-adjacent terrace.** I made an in-person visit to the rental office where a rather sour shriveled woman seemed to take great joy in informing me that there was a "very long waiting list" for The Admiral. I filled out an application anyway and was dismissed from her office with low hopes. The next morning I received a phone call at the work number I'd listed. It was Miss Sour telling me there was a one bedroom apartment available. Would I like to see it? Yes! A week or so later I moved into my lovely new apartment on the seventh floor, a few floors shy of the penthouses, and no terrace, but still with a glorious view and parquet floors. I happily settled in to my new home above my new city.

I needn't have worried about making it socially. During one of my first weeks at The Admiral as the brass grill in the open European-style elevator started to close I heard the click of heels on the marble lobby floor. I put my hand in the way to reverse its direction and pushed the door open to see a handsome, well-dressed, and somewhat short gentleman perhaps about ten years my senior. With gay men, age is impossible to tell for certain. "Thanks, he said eyeing me up and down, as I held the door open for him, "I'm Bob," and pointing up, "I live in the penthouse." My ears perked up. "The Penthouse." Singular. Could both the floors and all those terraces belong to one residence? It must be huge. Sizing me up as gay, and fresh meat to boot, he insisted that he throw a welcome to Indianapolis party to introduce me to all his friends. I was thrilled and totally unaware of Bob's position in the Indianapolis gay world and the significance of his parties. He was the Perle Mesta or Brooke Astor of the Indy gay social circle, presiding over it from his lofty penthouse atop the appropriately named Admiral. Clearly I had moved into the right building. Things just seem to work out for me.

My initial visit to Admiral Bob's penthouse gave me a huge case of apartment envy. While I loved my little one bedroom apartment, it would tidily fit in one of the many corners of Bob's rambling two story mansion in the sky. There were living rooms and sitting rooms and bedrooms, all decorated in the latest big city gay chic. "Very New York." There were also fireplaces and terraces galore. The largest of the terraces spanned most of the entire top of the building and became my new summertime hangout. Bob generously gave me a key to the place with come and go as I liked privilege. And I liked coming and going with great regularity. I'd put the cast album of the brand new Broadway show *A Chorus Line* on the sound system, smoke a joint, slick myself in Bain de Soleil and bake my way to a golden brown. The height of The Admiral, comparative to its neighbors, gave the top deck total privacy and I could lay out naked if I wanted and have sunshine sex with myself or with any surprise visitor who, like me, had come and go access to Bob's penthouse. Lover of flowers that I was, I also watered and plucked my way through all the many container plants on the terrace. Gardening in the sky was both new and wonderful. **The fact that I could do it in a speedo or even naked if I liked, just increased the appeal and guaranteed Bob not only a gorgeous rooftop garden but a sometimes naked gardener.**

When the night of my welcome to Indy party arrived I met what seemed to be just about every gay male in Central Indiana. I dragged one of them, a golden bearded, blue eyed artist back down to the seventh floor to spend the night. We spent the next day together and on Monday morning I had to go off to work but he, being an artist, didn't. I told him to just stay in bed and let himself out whenever he got up. What I didn't know, being new to the place was that when I locked the door from the outside, I locked him inside. How would I know? After much banging and yelling and the subsequent phone calls from my new old lady neighbors to the building super, my date was sprung. I immediately gained the dubious reputation in gay Indianapolis as someone who, if you went home with, just might try to lock you in.

During this time, Randy and I would speak on the phone often and share stories of things we'd done, guys we'd met and experiences each had had — ones that in prior days we'd have had, together. Life moved on. I switched jobs and found myself working in a department store — L. S. Ayres — on the top floor. It wasn't Chicago but I was getting closer to my dream. My four years working in Indianapolis fit nicely into Randy's getting his undergraduate business degree. I made frequent trips to Louisville and Randy would occasionally visit Indianapolis on the rare weekend when school and work would allow. More frequently he would drive to Indy and the two of us would continue on to Chicago. With our good Chicago parking karma, we'd usually find a well-located, well-lighted spot to park the car with our stuff in it. We'd start together at the Bistro, my favorite dance bar where I'd likely end up meeting somebody and dancing the night away to "Ring My Bell," "Rock The Boat," "Rock Your Baby" or some other current favorite dance hit. By this time Randy would have headed off to the Gold Coast, a leather bar around the corner where he'd be doing god-knows-what, probably in the basement. In the bars, I was typically the dancer, he was the cruiser.

We'd usually make these trips to Chicago for the weekend without a place to stay and typically neither of us would have a problem finding someone to go home with. We'd always have a meeting place and time for the next day set up in advance: Oak St Beach in the summer or in the just opened Water Tower Place on rainy or winter days. If all else failed one or the other could leave a note under the windshield wiper of the car and we'd eventually meet up.

If neither hooked up with someone, we'd end up at Man's Country, a bath house up on North Clark St. "The Tubs" as they were lovingly called, were the default back-up plan. They were great sexy fun and always a welcome alternative. If one of us found someone to go home with while the other hadn't, he'd negotiate a place for the other in a spare room or on a sofa. This worked better if Randy found a new friend since he was into older (hence more monied and established) gentlemen who were more likely to have space for my third wheel. None of my younger new friends ever had much. As Randy's third, I spent a few nights on some of the sleekest Bauhaus sofas in some of the most fabulous Miesian sky-scraping glass boxes in Streeterville and the Gold Coast. **I'd drift off to sleep surrounded by the nighttime sparkle of my dream city, imagining my own eventual existence in this steel and glass high-rise-heaven.** I'd wake up some time later to a spectacular sun drenched cityscape, reinforcing my distant dream of living in such a gleaming glamorous place. Though two hours closer, the big city life I'd dreamed of as a little boy and a young man was still beyond my grasp.

1976

Malcolm & The Golden Child

INDIANAPOLIS is where I met Malcolm. We were at a party given by a mutual friend and we hit it off immediately. Similar to Dawn, at first meeting, there was a familiarity about Malcolm that I couldn't quite put my finger on until it hit me. Mr. Ellis. I had had a 7th grader crush on the handsome new choir director at St. Stephen's about a dozen years before. He was a glamorous older man, from Austria, and I had been smitten at first sight. Handsome Malcolm possessed the same sort of well-dressed sophistication, sharp wit and sparkle that Mr. Ellis had had in abundance. And kindness. He treated me with a sort of dignity (for lack of a better word) just as Mr. Ellis had and I was instantly drawn to him.

Our whirlwind romance was off and running. At some point Malcolm told me that during our initial conversation as I rattled off what I did for a living and where I did it, he realized that I worked at the same department store, in the same office, in the same job, and as it turned out, sitting in the same chair as his former lover, Bud. The same chair! And the same age. What were the chances? This unlikely piece of serendipity appealed to our shared sense of the dramatic. And wonder. Bud still worked at Ayres and I'd met him several times. The fact that he was the store "glamour-boy" (I had had my own eye on him,) caused instant feelings of inadequacy on my part. I felt like a downgrade. **A former English teacher and life-long film buff, Malcolm was movie star handsome, a hopeless romantic and a firm believer in the happy ending.** We saw a lot of each other and had a wonderful time together. While I had yet to take note of it myself, the continued serendipity Malcolm would frequently observe in my life, fascinated him. Watching, sometimes in amazement, how events seemed to unfold consistently in my favor, he would eventually christen me "The Golden Child."

Malcolm was a big personality, good company and a great story teller. I was never quite certain how much was true and how much was embellishment in many of his tall-ish tales. **"It makes for good story-telling," he'd say with a shrug whenever I'd question the veracity of any particularly outrageous detail in one of his stories.** Whether complete truth or partial fiction, I'd still listen intently, not wanting to miss a word as he'd artfully construct each story bringing it to its typically amazing or amusing conclusion. We laughed so much.

Film buff Malcolm had two side by side apartments, one in which he lived and one set up theater-style in which he showed favorite old classic films. Being well ahead of the video tape era, these films were on 16mm film stock and projected onto the silver screen, in Malcolm's words, "as god intended." I loved classic movies and I loved movie nights and I loved Malcolm; in my fashion. We were, however, on different wavelengths. While I was in love in my fashion, he was in love in *his* fashion. Being way too immature for his idea of a relationship, I tried not to notice his apparent affection and I am certain I sent many a mixed message. In so doing, I am also certain I misled him. Malcolm was kind and generous but more than a decade older than I, a gap that at the time seemed, to me at least, insurmountable. And he was serially monogamous. A relationship in Indianapolis was out of the question for non-monogamous Chicago-bound me. There was an as yet un-specified glamorous new career, bars and boys and god knows what else waiting just a few hours away. I was just getting started and couldn't entertain for one second the possibility of staying in Indianapolis in a com-mitted monogamous relationship. My destiny lay three hours to the north and most certainly would be shared with my best friend, Randy. I just never got around to communicating all this to Malcolm. Indianapolis was a necessary stepping stone toward my unshakable Chicago goal and I am quite certain I stepped on Malcolm and his tender devoted heart in the process. He deserved better. After nearly four years in Indianapolis I head-ed off to Chicago, without looking back, leaving a disappointed and depressed Malcolm behind. **As it had been with Dawn, my immaturity and level of self-esteem (or lack thereof at the time) wouldn't allow me to consider that I might have had such a profound effect on another human being.** Had I understood this, I hope I'd have behaved better and been more grown-up and sensitive to his feelings. I'd find out later in life how bleak those days were for depressed Malcolm who was not a man inclined to-ward depression. He found a sense of purpose helping to raise an adopted nephew and was able eventually to move on. He is now in a long-term committed-relationship and being a fiercely loyal friend, he has kept our friendship going through to the present.

1963

The Soft Focus Mystery Of Mr Ellis

MR. ELLIS arrived as a breath of fresh air at St. Stephen Martyr Catholic Church and School. We had not seen the likes of him before in our Louisville, Kentucky parish and for me and my twelve year old's emerging gay sensibility, it was love at first sight. He was from Austria — a "foreign" country. He was tall, impeccably groomed and perfectly dressed, movie star handsome with dark wavy hair and a smart, worldly, sophistication about him that immediately set him apart from all our other garden variety parishioners. **Mr. Ellis had the quality of always appearing to be in soft-focus, like Doris Day in all her close-ups. He spoke perfect English in a deep velvety rich Austrian accent and he was to be our new organist and choir director.**

It was the beginning of the 1963-64 school year and Mr. Ellis's first priority was to create a boys' choir he'd model after the famous Vienna Boys Choir of his hometown. I couldn't wait to tryout for the choir and sing for this handsome exotic visitor. With my as yet unchanged soprano voice and ability to read music (I had studied the accordion — don't ask) I not only made it into the choir but was selected by Mr. Ellis himself as its President — one of the happiest moments of my up until then short and rather uneventful life. While his reasoning for choosing a 7th grader as President was for continuity's sake as it would provide for a two year presidency, I actually held onto the notion it was because I was his favorite and he wanted me with him for two whole years. Another Michael, an 8th grader, was appointed Vice President.

Having followed in the shadow of my older, overachieving brother and sister through St Stephen's, I, as a comparatively non-academic type, was finally able to establish myself beyond the disappointing underachiev-ing-little-brother persona I had "enjoyed" with the nuns in our school. **It was my personal renaissance at St. Stephen's and I relished every mass, wedding, even funeral at which we would sing.** It got me out of class too. Under Mr. Ellis's extraordinarily capable direction and accompanied by his organ artistry, our well rehearsed, angelic voices would rise from the choir loft at the rear of our church, lifting the heavily beamed ceiling heavenward. No mass was too demanding for us. No piece, however complex, seemed above our little heads.

Saturday morning rehearsal time was my favorite weekly event. We'd work on new pieces with Mr. Ellis, a good and patient teacher, honing them to perfection. They were glorious works and I loved every moment spent practicing to get them just right. It thrilled me to be able to make glamorous Mr. Ellis happy. After rehearsal for those of us who would linger, Mr. Ellis would pull out all the stops, literally, and play our church organ as no one had ever played that instrument before! Or, I imagine, since. His feet shod in the supplest black leather would fly over the pedals as his fingers worked the black and white multilayered keyboards. In what was to my young eyes and ears a superhuman effort, he created the most exceptional music my young ears had ever heard — a veritable blast of heavenly sound. **How I loved the way his playing filled every corner of our church, his rich full resonant notes touching the old soul in my young body.**

After the organ recital, we'd adjourn to the school cafeteria where Mr. Ellis would prepare tea for us and we would have, as I came to learn later in life, high tea. Having grown up a southerner with iced tea year round I had prior to this, thought of hot tea as something you were given only when sick. I learned from Mr. Ellis that drinking hot tea, especially in the afternoon, was *the* thing to do in Europe and I felt so sophisticated doing it. To this day both the fragrance of tea brewing and its subsequent taste fill me with thoughts and memories of my boys' choir days, those Saturday mornings, the singing, the masses, and of course, Mr. Ellis, and my ever growing affection for and devotion to him.

My father, chauffeur to us all, would pick me up after rehearsals and together we would drive Mr. Ellis home. We would also do this after mass on Sundays. Mr. Ellis neither had a car nor could he drive one. This was another of his exotic features. Grown-ups drove. That's what they did. But this grown-up didn't. I imagined in his native Austria he'd always been chauffeured around in long black limousines like the ones at our neighborhood funeral parlor. Or perhaps where he came from they still used horse drawn carriages with top hatted drivers. I could certainly imagine his dapperness being driven around in one of those. **These highly detailed**

fantasies, supported by my love of old movies and ignorance of modern European culture, intrigued me and my youthful emerging gayness no end.

Mr. Ellis lived in St. Matthews; an East End of Louisville neighborhood much tonier than our own. Between his home and ours was Louisville's spectacularly landscaped Cherokee Park — the crown jewel in Frederick Law Olmsted's "Emerald Necklace" a series of lushly green parks and tree-lined parkways that wound its way through my hometown. My dad was an expert in finding his way through Cherokee Park. It's circuitous roads, which baffled lesser navigators than my father, wind themselves around and through some of the most expensive and perfectly landscaped real estate in Louisville. With its rolling hills and verdant valleys, babbling brooks and stone bridges, open fields and dense forests, it was my favorite place in my entire hometown. Mr. Ellis seemed to know a lot about trees and was able to name virtually all of them as we made our seasonal way through the heavily wooded green, then red and golden, then barren park. We both shared a particular affection for birch trees with their multiple-clump, paper-white trunks. We had something in common. We had the same favorite trees. Before learning their real name I had always called them "scenic trees." He seemed to appreciate this and, for my sake I think, always referred to them with a slight wink in his eye as "scenic trees." This preferential commonality and his deference to my own terminology increased my ever growing affection for this smart accomplished and worldly man and made me feel that much closer to him. I was surely in love.

Arriving on the other side of Cherokee Park at Mr Ellis's home on Braeview Road — a virtual mansion to my youthful eyes — always took my breath away. It was a three story federal masterpiece that sat atop a small hill with a long driveway taking you up to its semi-circular Corinthian columned portico. He was "staying with friends" and my young gay mind reeled at the thought of who these mysterious, wealthy and undoubtedly glamorous "friends" might be. I could only imagine what must have gone on behind that stately facade with its impressive front door. The elegant dinners. The smart parties. The piano playing. The champagne drinking. Tuxedoes and evening gowns. Satin and sequins. Emeralds and pearls. **Repartee out-sparkling even the diamonds.** Partying and singing and dancing until dawn — just like in my favorite old black and white 1930s movies I loved watching with my mom. I so wanted to know more about this wonderful man and his wonderful friends in that wonderful house.

I was never to find out about those friends or much else about Mr. Ellis for that matter. One cold November morning, VP Michael and I were called out of our classes to Mr. Ellis's office. He greeted us in a serious almost grave manner which was completely out of character for him. This was most certainly not going to be good news; I stood there, braced. He said in a completely straightforward manner, "I have some rather bad news," I knew it. I listened intently as he continued, "Father Weiker has asked this morning for my resignation and I think it is best that I comply." Those were his only words. Cold and direct. So unlike him. That was it. No further explanation given. I was sent back to class with tears in my eyes. I can't remember ever actually saying goodbye. I don't think I fully comprehended that that moment might be the last time I would ever see or hear from Mr. Ellis. **My kind and gracious, handsome soft-focus friend and mentor was gone. Just like that; vanished the way a wonderful dream disappears with the harsh morning light.**

As an insult to this injury, my all-too-brief golden age at St. Stephen's followed Mr. Ellis right out the door. Shortly after his abrupt departure, a new organist and choir director was brought in. Mrs. King who was much more comfortable at the piano than at an organ was, I suppose, nice enough. But who could have ever filled the supple leather shoes of the wonderfully elegant, larger than life Mr. Ellis? Gone were the organ solos and high tea and the incomparable European flair he brought to everything he did. Gone was the glamour, the mystery, the fun. **Mr. Ellis had left a vacancy much too big to be filled by a sweet natured little church lady in sensible shoes and a tidy hairdo.** Under her tutelage the boys choir continued but without a President or Vice President. Mrs. King saw no need for officers so my tenure as President came to a quick end and my newfound status was over as abruptly as it had begun.

Christmas was on its way by this time and Mrs. King who prior to this had not shown anyone individual attention chose me for the solo at Midnight Mass in what was my favorite Christmas Carol: "Angels We Have Heard On High." Perhaps she felt sorry for my loss of the presidency or maybe my voice was right. I don't know but what I do know is, I was feeling kind of special again. In addition to the fact that I would have the solo, the choir was going to be not up in the choir loft at the rear of the church but right down front, in the sanctuary. We'd be in front of the St Joseph Altar (stage left, house right) so the entire congregation would be able to see exactly who was singing. In other words — the big time. Had Mr. Ellis still been there to coach and conduct us everything would have been perfect.

Loving a good surprise, I decided that I would keep this all a secret and make my big Christmas Eve solo a big Christmas Eve surprise. It would be my special Christmas present for the entire family. I now had an additional reason for that childhood I-can't-wait-for-Christmas impatience. I practiced and practiced to get my "Glo-o-o-o-o-o-o-o-o-o-o-o-o-o-o-o-ri-a in Ecelsis Deo" to its sweetest highest pitch-perfect soprano flawlessness. I was poised and ready and counting the days until my midnight mass debut. As I waited impatiently for my surprise solo performance, only a few days before Christmas, the phone call came.

The Cathedral of The Assumption in Downtown Louisville was, as usual, having a Christmas Midnight Mass. The mass, as usual, would be celebrated by the Archbishop. What was unusual was the request that my brother Frank, six years my senior and a seminarian, be a server to the Archbishop at this mass. This was not only an extraordinary opportunity for a young priest-to-be but what a feather in our family's Catholic cap! Talk about "The Big Time." There was just one small problem: "What to do about Mikey." While of course my parents knew nothing of my surprise solo, they did know I had a commitment to sing with our boys' choir at St. Stephen's Midnight Mass. To resolve this unfortunate scheduling conflict, it was decided that while the rest of the family would trot off to the cathedral to see my brother downtown with the Archbishop, I would need to honor my singing commitment; my grandparents would take me with them to our church that Christmas Eve. It's a good thing that the cathedral seating was by invitation and limited to just immediate family or I'm pretty sure my grandparents would have gone as well leaving me to be dropped off like an extra poinsettia plant at our church door that night.

I was to suffer a double Christmas Eve indignity then. Not only would my family not be there to hear me sing my big surprise solo, but I, who absolutely adored Catholic pomp, would be the only one of us who would not get to attend Christmas Midnight Mass at the cathedral downtown.

So at the much smaller and less important St. Stephen's Midnight Mass, I believe my grandfather had dozed off by the time my big solo came around and I don't remember my grandmother so much as look up from her prayer book or even glance my way as I competently sang my well-practiced solo. Certainly nothing was said about it on the drive home and the conversation back at our house that early Christmas morning was mostly about how wonderful the service at the Cathedral had been. How impressive it was. How grand the music and flowers and the vestments, the pomp and circumstance. And how well my brother had performed serving the Archbishop. It seemed I was the only one without a story to tell. I just couldn't tell them about my solo and never did.

Like the tree in a forest falling with no one around, if a little boy sings and his loved ones aren't present to hear it, did it actually happen? Though my memory is clear, still, at times, I've wondered. Without my family to listen proudly and lavish their praise and affection on me later, had I sung at all? Without applause, is there ever really a performance?

I stood in the sanctuary that Christmas Eve, joylessly singing, eyes searching the congregation for someone, anyone who might appreciate my solo. I had looked and looked past my dozing grandfather and praying grandmother and over the heads of the other parishioners, searching for my European Mr. Ellis's soft focus presence; for the approval I'd surely find in his handsome eyes. **I'd hoped that somehow, someway he would have known I'd be singing and had made his car-less way to St. Stephen's for that special midnight mass.** My searching eyes did not find him in the congregation that Christmas Eve. There was only a church full of preoccupied parishioners and Mrs. King conducting a choir of enthusiastic little boys with a sad and disappointed chubby little soloist giving it his best.

1975

Indy Sidney

DURING MY FIRST WEEKS at The Admiral, I was still parking outside. There was an underground parking garage on the property but my new space had yet to be vacated by a soon to be departing tenant. One evening as I approached the property in my blue Levi's Gremlin (don't ask,) I was following, in sharp contrast, a silver vintage Porsche convertible driven by a chic looking and fashionably wind-blown young woman wearing big Jackie O sunglasses. It was late-summer in Indianapolis — still top-down weather. I stopped behind her as she waited for the garage door to open.

As the door lifted, she pushed her sunglasses up headband style and disappeared into the dark garage. I drove my car around and pulled into one of the outside spaces. As I shut off the car and began pulling my things together, I saw the chic young lady come up the steps leading out of the garage. Entering the sunlight she dropped her sunglasses back down and walked the short distance to the entry of our building. **She was quite pretty, smartly attired and I instantly assessed her to be a high powered department store or cosmetics executive.** A super-smart standout in Indianapolis. I took note of the Bloomingdales shopping bag she was carrying. Bloomingdales was, at the time, the coolest of cool department stores. There was not, however, a Bloomingdales in Indianapolis. She slipped into The Admiral and had vanished before I made my way to the lobby. I silently congratulated myself for having gotten into a building that housed such an attractive and chic set. It wasn't just old ladies after all.

The next time I saw my chic neighbor some weeks or months later, I was once again right behind her car as she waited for the garage door to open. This time as she drove her Porsche in, I followed and pulled into my new parking space. Exiting our cars, we said "hello" and walked together to the building, she introducing herself as Sidney and I to her as Mike. She had a dazzling smile that could have easily sold lipstick. Or toothpaste. We briefly chatted in the lobby, mostly about her length of residence in the building, its inhabitants and apartments. "I'm in 203. Would you like to see it?" And with that I followed her up to the second floor.

As Sidney opened her door, she called out in a loud voice, "Anastasio are you hungry?" My first thought was: "She's calling me by my last name?" Then... "How would she even know my last name?" Then... "I could eat a little something." It became readily apparent when a large grey cat jumped into her arms that she had been speaking not to me but to her cat, Anastasia. It was her cat's current state of hunger that was in question. Not my own. There was another cat, a male, named Ivan. Both Russian Blues with Russian names.

We were friends from the get-go and hung out together a lot. She loved antiques (everything in her apartment in fact, still had its original price tag affixed) as well as fashion, fine things and so much of what I held dear. We would occasionally watch TV together. I had a TV. She did not. I learned that far from being a high powered executive, cosmetics or otherwise, she was actually a first grade school teacher. I'd have never guessed. No one would. Sidney was also, much to my surprise and delight, not nearly as sophisticated as I'd initially thought but along with her polished air of big city smartness, there was a wide-eyed, gullible, midwestern girl quality that was absolutely charming. At 25 years old she seemed on one hand so world-wise and on the other, so naive. **And then there was the laugh. A big loud one-of-a-kind uncontrollable combustible head turning blast that spontaneously erupted from somewhere deep within her. It could be heard blocks away. She couldn't suppress it if she'd tried.** That laugh was Sidney's alone and probably my favorite thing about her. I loved making her laugh and did it with great regularity.

My sexuality didn't enter the conversation. I'm not sure during those early days of friendship whether or not Sidney was holding out any romantic aspirations — perhaps. Having made my ill-fated heterosexual detour a few years earlier, I was now more firmly footed than ever in my own homosexuality, not ready to navigate those waters again.

Speaking of my homosexuality, I began seeing a long, lean and shockingly blue-eyed Indiana boy named Steve. Steve and I spent a lot of time together. We met in winter. Of that I am certain because the first time we slept together and each time thereafter, it snowed. We decided at some point that sex, or at least our sex, caused snow storms. It was a long winter of enormous blizzards as the snow stacked up around The Admiral. Come spring, Steve found his own apartment in the building and moved in.

Sidney, Steve and I became inseparable. We'd often squeeze the three of us into Sidney's two seater convertible (it was a lot more fun than my Gremlin or whatever Steve was driving) and, three for the road, off we'd go. Cabins in the woods, whitewater rafting, lake outings, antiquing, state fairs or just an evening trip to the neighborhood diner, saw us happily heading off on one adventure after another.

No mention was made of the fact that two of our three were having a romantic/sexual relationship right under the nose of the unaware, naive third. I remember Steve and I discussing this and wondering if Sidney had a clue — whether her smart sophisticated woman had picked up on it or more likely had her inexperienced Indiana girl missed the entire thing? It was the latter. While I am unclear about how we managed it, we did at some point surprise her with the information. It was a mere blip and the three of us remained friends and partners in crime.

At some point, the smart sophisticated Sidney became disenchanted with her first grade teaching job. Actually it was precisely at the point where she found herself at her supplemental waitressing job counting out knives and forks as if doing so for her first graders; discontent was inevitable. A similar level of discontent entered into her waitressing job at Sam's Attic, a block from The Admiral, a restaurant where people actually ate in bed. Hey...the seventies. It was a place where (this happened — I saw it) while taking an order, a waitress (not Sidney) caught, out of the corner of her eye, a cockroach crawling up the wall just behind her, and, without missing a beat, she nailed it with her order pad and immediately resumed writing. **Sidney's chic smartness was no more at home with restaurant roaches than with first graders.** She wanted (and was clearly intended for) more. As with most academic types, when faced with indecision about her life's direction, she decided to go back to school and enrolled in the Masters of Education program at Purdue University in West Lafayette Indiana.

Sidney quit both jobs a week or two before departing for Purdue. During this time she was making the most of saying how much she enjoyed being "unemployed" and happily worked the information into any conversation. Just before her departure, I invited her downtown for a goodbye lunch at our favorite restaurant, The King Cole. My treat. Ayres Department Store, my current employer, was just a block away.

As we were waiting in line to be seated, an Ayres Buyer friend of mine joined us in line with his lunch party. His name was Jim and I introduced him to "my friend Sidney." "Nice to meet you 'friend Sidney,'" said Jim as he extended his hand, "and what do you do?" As was her new custom, Sidney proudly announced, "I'm unemployed." She had no idea who Jim was but I knew that not only was he our store's cosmetics buyer but there happened to be an Ayres store in West Lafayette. I saw an opportunity. Knowing that Sidney was going to need a job there, I added to her answer, "Jim, maybe you could help," I explained nodding toward my friend, "Sidney is moving to West Lafayette and will be needing a job." Sidney explained her situation to Jim and he suggested she come to see him in his office the next day.

You never know when a simple action on your part, as seemingly insignificant as a lunch invitation, might be a life-changing event for someone else.

Sidney moved from The Admiral leaving the two remaining musketeers, Steve and me, to sit in tears on the floor of her dark empty apartment sharing the mutual loss of our third. She started her new life studying at Purdue University and working at her new job behind a cosmetics counter at L. S. Ayres. She was so good at selling the products (she had already been a loyal user for years) that she took a flat business and drove it through the roof. The Ayres and cosmetics execs took notice.

After completing her Master's degree and still not knowing exactly what she wanted to do with her life, Sidney moved back to Indianapolis and took a job selling the same cosmetics line at the Glendale Ayres store — the company's largest counter in the state. By this time I had moved on to Chicago. Under the watchful eye of the company executives, Sidney was just as successful there as she had been in West Lafayette.

More on Sidney's continued rise later...

1976

Bi-coastal Va-gay-tion

HAVING MEMORIZED the entire score to *A Chorus Line,* the hottest show on Broadway, I couldn't wait see it in New York. I had played the album incessantly up at Admiral Bob's penthouse, especially when sunning on the roof terrace, committing it to memory before I saw the actual production. Having tried and failed at getting Randy away from his studies, I made plans to meet other friends in New York for the big July 4th, 1976 Bicentennial celebration and after multiple long-distance phone calls with long hold times, had been able to score tickets to *A Chorus Line.* At last! My excitement faded however when I subsequently read that the original cast was pulling up stakes and moving west to the new production opening in Los Angeles on July 1. I wouldn't be seeing the original company; the company on the cast recording I was so in love with. No wonder I'd been able to get tickets. I was pissed.

This got me thinking, "How about a two week vacation doing both New York and Los Angeles?" A bi-coastal vacation. This excited me. I could attend the bicentennial in New York and see *A Chorus Line* there as originally planned, and then, just a week later, fly out to Los Angeles and see the original cast there. Oh yes, this was a great idea! My friend Steve McQueen was still living in Los Angeles and I'd been wanting to visit. It worked out perfectly. I was able to take the time off from work, procure tickets for the Los Angeles production and re-book my flights. I could stay with Steve and his hunky boyfriend Michael and we could do a long weekend in Palm Springs before my return to Indianapolis. Another great idea. I had never been to Palm Springs which was quickly developing into a gay playground. My bi-coastal gay holiday was set.

A Chorus Line, in New York with the replacement cast, was wonderful. Being so familiar with the original cast recording, I was amazed that it was exactly the same as that recording. I actually wondered if perhaps there'd been some sort of mix-up and the original cast was still in New York. Checking the Playbill told me otherwise. Still, the entire cast looked as they had in the photo on the album cover and every voice the same as those I'd listened to ad infinitum. It occurred to me that there must be an enormous pool of talent in New York to be able to cast a show with performers essentially identical in talent, voice, looks and even height.

New York was the place to be the weekend of July 4, 1976. It was the best of times during the worst of times in a bankrupt city. A fleet of tall ships sailed into the New York Harbor along with a spectacular array of fireworks and, if memory serves, even The Queen of England got involved. And of course the city filled up with boys, boys and more boys from around the country and the world. Christopher Street in Greenwich Village was overrun. There was endless cruising up and down the street. Sex was immediately available wherever you wanted it. There was also endless activity where Christopher Street met the river and the piers. **During the day, hundreds of gay boys could be found crammed-in, many naked, on the old abandoned piers, sunning themselves and some even having sex.** Right there in the open on a sunny New York afternoon. During the night, those same crumbling piers were alive with cruising gay boys who faced the threat of danger in the form of muggers, policemen and holes that you could fall right through. One false step and, splash, you were in the Hudson River. It happened. Still, we went there. We were just careful. There were also dozens of empty trucks parked along West Street under the West Side Highway where scores of horny gay boys would get off together all night long. It was all dark and seedy and so sexy.

One of my most vivid memories of that weekend was a visit to Man's Country gay bathhouse, advertised on an enormous billboard (two of them actually, stacked) at the gayest corner in New York — Christopher Street and 7th Avenue. It was the bathhouse cousin to my Chicago favorite of the same name. It was my first visit to this one and I was astonished to find a big red tractor trailer — the real thing — cab and all, inside the bathhouse where you could indulge your truckersex fantasies in and around it. I had sex in the cab with a blond mustachioed Adonis who was a near-twin to my friend Steve's hunky LA boyfriend Michael who I'd be seeing the next week. The blond "Steve-twin" was naked but for a black leather jacket that he kept pushing in my face demanding in a super-deep voice, "Smell the leather, smell the leather." In the tight confines of the truck cab I could smell the leather but found his insistence about it more funny than sexy. He certainly got off on it. I could tell because without warning he shot buckets of semen all over my face. **You don't forget your first sticky, soaking surprise "facial." I quite nearly drowned.**

Days later, out in Los Angeles *A Chorus Line* with the original cast was sheer perfection and exactly the same as New York's. Though I was thrilled to finally see the original cast, I had to admit I could barely tell the difference. Since seeing *A Chorus Line* in those days was the thing to do; seeing it twice in one week at two different Shubert Theaters, in two different cities, on two different coasts made me the envy of all my friends. I got a lot of mileage telling the story and both Playbills took up residence on my living room coffee table where they stayed for quite sometime.

The week in LA was loads of fun. Steve and Mike and I hung out at all the bars and "bookstores" up and down Santa Monica Boulevard. We danced the nights away at Studio 1, a super-fun mega-disco where I met Wayland Flowers and his puppet Madame and danced with my favorite Colt model at the time, Clay Winslow. I learned my way around that big sprawling smoggy city. On the weekend we went to Palm Springs as planned. **I fell instantly in love with this sleepy sexy place dramatically surrounded by palm trees and mountains where, around every corner, you could have a fresh date shake or gay boy sex.** Both if you were lucky. The place was crawling with gay boys absolutely everywhere. Our gay guesthouse — more of a gay playground — was packed with them and we were a frisky bunch. I especially loved all the mid-century (though I don't think we used the term at the time since we were still sort of mid-century) homes dotting the desert landscape.

One evening in the local gay bar I met a slightly older, hot and handsome man. He was one of those persons that you *knew* at a glance was highly educated and quite wealthy. Unfortunately he seemed intent on impressing me with both. His hotness began to chill the more he talked about himself with multiple, increasingly more obnoxious references to his apparent wealth. After my having related my newfound love of Palm Springs architecture, he suggested we go out to his car, share a joint and take a ride through the neighborhoods and he could point out his most and least favorites. He assured me there were some superb architectural masterpieces I'd love and super-tacky gems I'd love to hate. **Though previous to this invitation I'd been finishing my drink and planning my escape, I jumped at the chance.** Out in the parking lot I could see we were making a bee-line to a waiting sable brown Rolls-Royce Silver Shadow. I became instantly excited about the potential of having my first ride ever in a Rolls-Royce but was also skeptical, wondering if this tour of Palm Springs had been engineered as just another device to impress me. "Oh my god you drive a Rolls-Royce!" is what I would have said under any other circumstances, but I held my tongue, not giving this guy the validation he surely wanted. He opened the passenger door and as I slipped in, he just couldn't help himself, tipping his hand by asking, "Have you ever been in a Rolls-Royce before?" Without missing a beat I answered, "Well, never in the *front* seat." I don't know where that came from but as he closed the door I think he did so, deflated just a bit. The funny thing was, without all the veiled references to his wealth, I would have been totally impressed by this handsome, impeccably dressed, erudite gay man with a spectacular set of wheels.

The nighttime architectural tour driving around Palm Springs in a Rolls-Royce, baked, was, I have to say, a lot of fun. We "oooh'ed and aaah'd" and laughed in equal measure as we coursed our way around that desert city in that fabulous car. My rich friend ended up being a lot more fun stoned and I eventually did make it to the back seat of that Rolls-Royce. We got naked and had sex there after he pulled off at the end of a deserted desert road; I could smell the leather — this time, fine upholstery. **Sex in the back of a Rolls-Royce, high, and high up a mountainside with a spectacular midnight view of a sparkling Palm Springs below was a series of fabulous firsts for me.**

On my last day hanging out by the pool with my lean, naked, tan, long-haired blond surfer boy from the night before, I noticed something happening with my left eye. When I'd blink, my vision was blurry for a second or two. The eye itched as well and I'd constantly lift my sunglasses to rub it. It felt a little tender and swollen too. Eventually I went back to my room to check it out in the mirror. My eye, definitely swollen, was also quite red and weepy. I kept an eye on it (so to speak) as it continued to get worse. As the evening drew on, the white part of my eye had been replaced with scarlet red. The swelling was worse and the clear fluid escaping the eye had become less translucent. Yuk. **I had kept my sunglasses on camouflaging the situation as best I could as we made our way back to Los Angeles International where Steve and Mike dropped me off for the "red eye" (you can't make this shit up) that would take me back to Indianapolis through Chicago.**

By the time I got home, my condition had deteriorated to something out of a horror film. What little of my eye that could still be seen through the swelling was a pure crimson red. My eyelashes were dripping with — there's no other word for it — sorry — pus. Rather than go straight to work from the airport as planned, I went straight to a doctor who's name I'd gotten on a "help me" phone call to my coworker, Ken. I instantly fell in love with Ken's doctor. He was a short tubby ancient little man in a white coat with a stethoscope around his neck and glasses that were so thick his eyes were completely obscured. One or the other would make a brief blurry appearance behind the thick glass as his head would move, but never together and never making direct contact. Those super-thick lenses mostly reflecting the light, gave him the appearance of a humorous cartoon character line drawing. He was so kind and if he was as repulsed by my appearance as I was, it didn't show. He was a true old pro as he asked me question after question. "You know," he said matter-of-factly, "this is probably way out there but..." he paused for the right words, "since...uh...you're just back from vacation...could you have...uh...been mixing it up with...uh...the ladies while you were away?" The ladies? Not likely. What was he getting at? "Again...uh...I'm not saying this is what it is...and I'm probably way off track here...but you can't be too careful when it comes to your eyes." (In retrospect, "come" being an unfortunate choice of words.) He continued, "I...uh...think we need to test you...for...a...sexually transmitted disease." What? Gonorrhea? In an *eye*? Gonorrhea in *my* eye? This can happen? I had never heard of such a thing and was instantly disgusted by the possibility. How in the world could this have happened? Where...? Who...? In the blink of an eye (sorry,) I remembered the "smell the leather" guy, back in New York, the week before, the TubSex I'd had with the blond Adonis in the truck cab who shot all over my face. **I'd wiped about a quart of my seminally-blessed friend's sticky thick goop from my eyes, but not quickly enough or thoroughly enough, apparently.** That had to be it. Well, yes, of course, that was it. My first facial was also my first case of gonorrhea. In. My. Eye. I include this thoroughly gross story as a cautionary tale and public service announcement: Listen up people! You can get gonorrhea in your eye! You're welcome.

Back at work, my (thankfully gay) coworker Ken (who'd recommended the doctor) stood there looking at my patched eye, appropriately appalled by my story. Over the years, having heard so many of these Monday morning accountings of my weekend and vacation adventures, he stood there shaking his head as always and said, "I think you could find truffles." I laughed and thanked Ken for the doctor referral that he was now probably embarrassed to have made. Before the doc gave me a shot of penicillin, he had asked if I was allergic to it. "Ya gotta be careful with this stuff," he said as he readied me for the big shot in my ass, "I didn't know I was allergic the first time they gave it to me. Well, my feet swelled-up so bad, it was like walkin' on an acre of tits!" I laughed out loud as I felt the needle prick my asscheek and I instantly pictured this little line drawing of a white-coated cartoon doctor with thick round spectacles, arms stretched-out for balance, tottering, trying to make his wobbly way over a lumpy "acre of tits."

1970 – 1985

TubSex

BATHHOUSES WERE HOT. In absolutely every sense of the word, from the sexual climate to the actual climate, bathhouses were hot. Any trip to a new city was incomplete without a visit to the local "tubs" as we called them. In smaller cities, you'd be the fresh new face and there'd be a crop of boys hungrily waiting for it and all your other fresh new body parts. After a short time there was nothing fresh or new about me in Indianapolis so I preferred the ones in Chicago. **Some bathhouses, like Man's Country in Chicago were large urban multi-floor complexes while in smaller cities, other much smaller single floor versions could be found in a suburban strip mall sandwiched in between the One Hour Martinizing and a Cut 'n Curl.** You'd typically have to wait in line, sometimes very long lines in cities with large gay populations. At peak hours, post-bar-closing time in San Francisco for instance, the early morning zig-zag queue could go down the block and around the corner. There was an awful lot of cruising and pre-tubs connecting during the wait to get in. When you finally made it to the little lobby and up to a small window, a typically cheerful, probably mustachioed hottie likely in a super-tight white tank top with the company logo would give you the choice of a room or a locker. I was a locker boy, more of a hunter. Rooms were for the hunted. After you'd made your choice, the attendant would take your money, check your valuables, give you a towel and a locker key and with a buzz of the door you were in.

In. A wall of dense male sexuality hit you and your increasing heart rate immediately on the other side of the doorway. Eight hours of an all male sexual Disneyland with a hard-hitting disco beat awaited as you'd excitedly pass, on your way to the lockers, hot boys cruising in their skimpy towels. Long lean smooth bodies, thick muscular hairy ones, every legal age and type you could imagine, and many you might not, sweatily traversing the space, most of them barely covered by and bulging through those little white towels just like the one in your hand. Some boys, towels casually tossed over the shoulder, were completely naked. All searching for the same thing. **You could actually, quite literally, smell sex in the air. And chlorine.** Once out of your clothes and into your towel you were off, to get off. As many times as your body and the night would permit. As you'd head out into the semi-darkness there'd be a familiar semi-hard, heavy-hung stirring down below. You were never more aware of your penis than here and now. The sexual anticipation of what lay ahead was excruciatingly exciting. As you nonchalantly stepped over and around copulating bodies here and there, knowing the endless possibilities that lay ahead; there were decisions to be made as you squeezed yourself down there. Where to go first?

You might start off in the wet area where you could shower in a communal sexily lit shower room, show off, beat off or play with lots of wet naked boys and have some good clean fun. **This was also where you'd learn that everybody looks good through glass block.** You could hit the steam room where you'd follow the labyrinthian pathways in a dense cloud of steam feeling your way through as anonymous hands made their way under your towel, if you still happened to have it on, or you could make your way under someone else's towel squeezing, jerking or poking around until, with your other hand, you'd find another and then another and another and still another. You just didn't have enough hands. If you were feeling somewhat less proactive you could just stand there in the fog leaning against a hot slippery tile wall and wait for others to find you. Lots and lots of others. Through the hot thick steam, mouths would find mouths or penises or any other body parts made available by the accommodating others. Groups large and small would form in the dimly lit steam at the dead end of a cul-de-sac for hot penetrating pliable group sex.

You could also shed your towel and settle into the hot bubbling water of the whirlpool, what Randy and I to referred to as "The Giant Petrie Dish," where hands (yours or someone else's) under the water, found their way to places dark and deep or hard and slick and all wonderfully, bubblingly hot. Or with your arms out along the rim of the tub you could simply stretch out and wait for any number of exploring hands to go to work on your hard equipment. If you weren't interested in a guy interested in you, a wink and a smile and the standard "just resting" would usually move him on to someone else. If that didn't work, a polite removal of his hand would send a more direct message. Sometimes if the other guy was just too aggressive and not responding to any of the above, you'd just simply up and move somewhere else. There was always somewhere else.

Next might be the dry heat of the sauna where under its slightly brighter lighting, the games were more visual. A boy might be sitting there in the dry hot heat, legs spread, fully tumescent, cock-ringed, proudly displaying himself for your appreciation. Or use. This was a place for the big boys. Or you could be the big boy, stretched out horizontally naked on the dry hot wood planking, with your hands clasped behind your head, eyes closed, towel opened, cock standing tall proud and hard, waiting to be appreciated. Or used. There would always be someone to appreciate you. Or use you, over and over again for as many times and as long as you'd like.

There were video rooms where porn films (and later when the technology had developed, videos) were shown 24/7. The rooms were typically set up amphitheater style with scores of horny guys, dimly lit by the flickering light from the screen. They'd be settled in among throw pillows on the carpeted stepped platforms, legs spread, cocks hard, eyes fixed on the screen, all masturbating in unison. **You could watch the movie or watch the jackers. Either way there was a show going on.**

There were also orgy rooms, big dark sweaty spaces, fully occupied and waiting for you to feel your way through. The orgy rooms were oftentimes fitted with big vinyl covered beds, slings and other fetish equipment and encouraged, as the name might imply, lots of group activities of every stripe. The name "orgy room" always seemed a bit redundant since every room by definition with its group activities would become an orgy room. The entire bathhouse was an orgy room.

Then there were the glory holes. These were small booths, large enough for one (well, maybe two if "friendly") with holes conveniently drilled in the partitions dividing them. You could enter the booth, close the door behind you and push your equipment through the hole and have it manipulated by some hungry nameless faceless stranger on the other side or you could be the hungry nameless faceless stranger manipulating whatever had been graciously pushed through the partition to you. It was always shocking and I have to admit — sexy — stepping into a booth and seeing a gleaming rock hard dick and balls by itself, just a sexual organ sticking out of a wall attached to nothing, no face, no body, no personality, no name, no questions asked or answered, just a piece of flesh and blood, hard horny and waiting, ready for use of any kind, by anyone. **If you were into anonymous sex, you couldn't find any sex more anonymous; I always cheated though and would get a good look at the boy next door before he entered the booth next door.** You could also squeeze into one booth with a buddy, each sticking his equipment through the holes and be attended to by some energetic stranger with, on his side, twice as much on his grateful hands as he expected. While on your side, you'd be making out with your buddy and attending to whatever of his body parts were still on your side of the partition.

Then there were the private rooms. You could walk corridor after corridor of them, all with built-in beds, side tables, dim-able lighting and lockable doors. This was a literal "bedroom community" a neighborhood if you will, with street after street of these small cubicle homes or at least that's how I always saw it. **Randy and I used to joke that they should give the corridors street names like Bottom Boulevard and Top Terrace or perhaps Popper Place and Lube Lane or Hard Cock Court and Big Dick Drive or Anal Avenue and Penis Parkway. I could go on and on. You didn't after all, want the place to get too serious.** The private rooms belonged to the guys who had chosen a room rather than a locker when they checked in. Some doors would be closed (nobody home or somebody busy.) Some doors would stand wide open with the lighting cranked way up in full invitation, some doors only open a few, more tentative, inches with the lighting way down. You'd slowly walk the corridors peering into room after room. The body position of the occupant left little doubt as to what type of sexual activity he was looking for. When you found the right face, the right body or body part or body position, the right outfit (jock strap, speedo, leather harness, blindfold, hand cuffs, white socks, sneakers, baseball cap) even the right lighting, or any combination of the above that appealed to you, you'd stop, make eye contact and perhaps reach down and squeeze yourself through your towel registering your interest or even pull your towel aside and flash your own goods. It was then up to the room occupant to welcome you in or away. The nod of a head, the flash of a smile or the flash of a penis would be ways of extending the sexual invitation for you to cross the threshold. One boy might gently nudge the door open with his foot in a universal gesture of welcome while another might just as gently tap it closed; others might slam it shut. **While there was bathhouse etiquette to be followed, not everyone was kind.** If you got the OK, you'd go in, shut the door behind you, drop your towel and get on with whatever you wanted to get on with. If it turned out to be not quite what you were looking for, there were many others to choose from. You'd get up, politely excuse yourself and with a wink and a "thanks" and perhaps a little peck on the lips, a pat on a butt or a tug on a dick, you'd exit and move on to the next interesting room. And the next. And the next. It wasn't unusual to go in, mount a round proffered ass, ride it to ecstasy, maybe unload maybe not, pull out and leave without exchanging a word or in some cases, even seeing the face at the other end. And on you'd go to find the next inviting boybutt upturned spread and waiting. It went on this way all night long. Lots of walking. Little talking. A lot of in and a lot of out. You'd cruise the corridors too. Boys passing and eyeing and groping each other with the smell of lube and poppers hanging heavy in the air and the sounds of sex: orgasmic cries, barked orders, lots of "oh yeahs," "fuck me's," ass slaps and messy wet sounds — pouring over the walls of the rooms.

In warmer climates such as Florida, there would typically be an outdoor pool area where you could, after having shared a joint, lie back relaxing on a lounge chair, and enjoy just being naked outdoors and playing with yourself. With the stars and the swaying palm trees overhead you could have your dick sucked by one guy while, with a dick in each hand, jerk two other kissing guys off, and be deep-kissed by yet another. There was space to group-up and spread-out, out there.

Sometimes in between orgasms you'd take a break and visit the food and refreshment area if there was one. It was usually not much more than some vending machines and a few tables and chairs, with bad lighting, a potted or hanging plant or two, perhaps an aquarium or believe it or not, a noisy caged parrot with a propensity for barking S&M orders. You could actually socialize and meet guys there. Or, if you needed to rest, you could go there to get away for a bit as this was typically, save for the fish and that talkative bird, the least populated spot in the entire bathhouse.

There might also be a gym, just a few machines or large and fully equipped, where you could work out naked or jocked with other naked jocks and perhaps indulge yourself in a high school student/coach gym class fantasy or two, and in the process pump your muscles up for the next go around.

Occasionally there'd be a disco, where you could happily dance away the hours with any number of hot naked or almost naked boys. You could meet someone on the dance floor, sexy slow dance with him, kissing and groping, rubbing against each other, cocks rising and towels dropping. You most probably would eventually move to the carpeted perimeter where you'd find big upholstered sofas and lots of soft cushions tossed around the floor, provided just for the purpose of more tossing around. You could, après sex, fall asleep in your sexy stranger's arms, drifting off blissfully unaware of your surroundings. **Eventually (minutes later? hours later?) with a kiss from your sexy stranger, you awaken to the sound of Grace Jones singing "La Vie en Rose" and eventually realize your erect penis is being manipulated by some other sexy stranger's mouth or hand. La Vie en Rose indeed.**

CHICAGO

Having achieved

all

my professional

dreams,

and

my own

personal golden age,

along with

my best friend,

I

settled in

for a lifetime.

1978

We Made It

AFTER RANDY completed his degree, he accepted a job. In Chicago, of course. He was hired to be the executive secretary to the president of the American Association of Senior Physicians. His dream job. He moved there expecting that with my affection for that city (and probably underestimating my affection for him) I'd soon follow. Randy had already survived one of the harshest winters in Chicago history (there were phone calls with cries of "Your face can actually freeze," and "It's snowing again, I can't believe it's snowing again") by that time, I had read an article about the new chairman at Marshall Field's and the changes he hoped to make there. I made a phone call looking for a job. Within weeks I had landed one in their store design department. Weeks after that I moved in with Randy. **My little boy dream of working on the top floor of a major department store in a big city was coming true.** I'd be designing Marshall Field's stores. And I'd be living in Chicago. After all the years of hoping and dreaming, my Dorothy had finally made it to her Emerald City. Suddenly all my dreams were coming true, and all of it facilitated by Randy's move north. I hadn't imagined it could be so easy. Things just seem to work out for me.

Randy had a one bedroom apartment so I temporarily moved just my clothes and bed. His bedroom was big enough to accommodate both our double beds dormitory style. It was the perfect arrangement. Well, Randy would be quick to note, except on chili night. We lived that way until his lease was up and we found our dream apartment on Lincoln Park West. It was a rambling two bedroom two bath with an entry hall, high ceilings, a fireplace, built-in linen storage, cedar closet and spectacular lake, park and city views. It was in a sumptuous near north building perfectly situated between my two favorite bus routes in my favorite neighborhood. The living room was large enough for Randy's newly acquired high gloss black Yamaha grand piano. **The building even had a glamorous name: The 2000 Building. It was a high-rise from a glorious past with a name that seemed to embrace the future.** I could imagine the two of us ringing in a new millennium there. We could both see "2000 Lincoln Park West" looking especially fabulous, engraved in black on Tiffany blue-bordered ivory stationery.

The first night in our huge new apartment, after months of living on top of each other in a much smaller one bedroom, we were like a set of conjoined twins suddenly separated. In fact, as we prepared to go out that night, Randy conjoined me in my bathroom, even though he now had a bathroom of his own. I think it had as much to do with separation anxiety as it did the stated reason that I had the only shower curtain at that point. In the kind of error that can occur when you're in new unfamiliar surroundings, we locked ourselves in that bathroom. Laverne and Shirley style. Trapped. We didn't go out that night. We couldn't. Instead we spent our first night together in our brand new dream apartment locked in the windowless back bathroom fearing for our lives. Beating on the walls and screaming for help, we realized that our effort was futile. In such a sound old building, there was no hope of our being heard. We sat there together laughing, crying, talking, and shouting for help. What an ironic twist to our dream-come-true apartment story, to eventually just die there huddled together on that cold black and white tile floor. On night one. No one would miss us. No one knew us. No one would say, "Where are those two handsome young men in 1101?" It was our first night. No one had even seen the two handsome young men in 1101. We lay there in despair as we imagined that after months of nonpayment of rent, we'd be found by building management, clinging to each others' lifeless, deteriorating bodies. We did have water so we knew we could survive for awhile. "I suppose for protein we could suck each other off," I offered as we eyed each other mutually shuddering at the thought. "Will you eat me to survive if I die first?" asked Randy. I was horrified and made a vomit face but we laughed as we speculated which of us would be more likely to eat the other if he survived longer. "When you do eat me," I asked, "where will you start?" His responding downward glance followed by his "you have to ask?" look gave answer to my rhetorical question. This is how we entertained our frightened selves trapped in that bathroom on our first night in our dream apartment.

Well, no one died and no one had to eat anyone. After I don't know how many hours of jiggling and coercing, pushing and pulling, the lock or the doorknob or something finally gave way in the early morning hours and set us free. We would live to tell the story and would live to see what The 2000 Building had in store for us now that it had decided to release us.

We easily settled in to our wonderful new life in our grand new apartment in our spectacular old building in our glorious new neighborhood. **It was heaven with a Gold Coast view.** Each of us with his dream job living together in our dream apartment in our dream city. The lake with its endless view and many moods, the zoo with its exotic pink flamingoes in their habitat we could see from our living room windows, and its lions whose roars would lull us to sleep at night, the park and marinas and gay men by the thousands. It was all right outside our sumptuously chandeliered (there were even crystal chandeliers in the elevators,) Aubusson carpeted, Chippendale furnished, mahogany and marble lobby with its bronze revolving door and canopy over the sidewalk. We were embarking together on our shared dream. Things really do have a way of working out. **We were excited, hopeful, content, happy and just naïve enough to think…believe… it would all go on forever.**

1978

Chicago Morning

IT IS MORNING IN CHICAGO just after my move from Indianapolis. Randy is seated at the dining table trying to enjoy, unmolested, the *Chicago Tribune*, *The Today Show*, a cigarette, our view of North Hampden Court and his breakfast. I enter from the general direction of the bathroom, with a purpose, making a bee-line to him while brandishing a magazine at him. I can tell he's already trying to ignore me and my gay skin mag with its multi-page, pictorial coverage of the annual lifeguard competition in Sydney, Australia.

"We're moving!" I say to him leaving no room for dissent. Randy turning a page, drawing on his cigarette and not looking away from his newspaper, exhales and responds, "I know…Lincoln Park West…first of the month." I respond immediately and emphatically, "No…Sydney, Australia…as soon as possible."

Now, cigarette down and spoon in hand, eating his cereal, Randy, again without benefit of glancing up, continues to peruse his paper and responds with a dismissive, "Mmmmmmm hmmmmmm."

Not at all satisfied with this response, I slap the magazine down in front of my disinterested roommate and on top of his *Tribune*. It is opened to one of the many pages filled with photographs of dozens of tanned, muscular, hunky Australian lifeguards with their already skimpy speedos rolled to practically nothing and pulled up into the cracks of their ample asses showing off the entirety of their smooth round muscular untanned butt cheeks. "Look at that!" I shout, "That's how they wear their speedos in Australia! **They go around like that. In public! Bare-assed! Look at those tan lines! Look at those butts! Look, over here, wait…"** as I **flip to another page, "…pubes!"**

I push the magazine closer to Randy, tapping one particular photo, "We're moving."

Randy casually flips through the pages of bulges and butts, and, still registering no interest whatsoever in them, states in his suddenly adopted parent-to-child voice, "I'm not entirely sure that the way in which a bunch of Australians wear their swimsuits is really an adequate reason to relocate our lives ten thousand miles to the other side of the planet." He casts a quick side-glance up at me — for effect — and right back down to his paper as he shoves the magazine aside, with all its full-color, nearly-naked beefcake glory, and — for effect — summarily pushes it again like some smelly dishrag.

I pick up the magazine and head out to the kitchen to get my coffee, "Well, I can't think of a better reason. I'm checking airfares today."

As I exit the kitchen, coffee and magazine in hand, Randy takes a long deep drag on his cigarette, exhales, and with a slight shake of his head, rolls his eyes heavenward, takes a sip from his coffee mug, turns up the volume of *The Today Show*, and goes back to his newspaper.

1973…

Platonic Lovers

PERFECT PAIRING that we were, Randy and I came to refer to ourselves as "platonic lovers." Throughout our friendship, our friends would constantly accuse us of covering up (for what possible motive I do not know) some wild love affair we were having. They would urge us again and again to come out and admit that we were lovers. We couldn't because we weren't. Never had been. They wouldn't buy it. **The platonic lover arrangement was one that kept us both happily single for quite some time.** We had during our cohabitation in Louisville and Chicago all the best trappings of a couple: friendship, companionship, respect, mutual support, endless amusement, true affection and best of all, love. We managed then to escape the possible downsides of romantic relationships: jealousy, infidelity, sexual incompatibility, withholding of affection, "cheating," etc. Of course we both had romantic fantasies of finding that perfect someone, but we never seemed to find a situation better than what we had with each other. Mona's Law from Armistead Maupin's *Tales Of The City* states "You can have a hot job, a hot apartment & a hot lover but you can't have all three at same time." Well we nearly had all three. Perhaps even better. At twenty-four and twenty-eight, Randy and I had the hot jobs of our dreams, the hot apartment of our dreams and and as many hot lovers as we could each handle, and still have a special someone to love and come home to every night.

Arriving home after work was in fact one of my favorite things about our life together. Randy would get home before me and his way of decompressing was to play the piano. At the end of my evening commute, I'd walk up to one of the grandest buildings along Lincoln Park West, go through the bronze revolving door, hear the clicking of my heels across the marble floors, occasionally hushed at my crossing one of the richly-colored oriental carpets. I would hear the resonant sound from the gongs of an antique grandfather clock as I boarded the walnut and beveled-mirrored elevator. **At the 11th floor, the doors would open and I'd be greeted with the lushly romantic sound of Debussy's "Clair de Lune" wafting down the hallway and welcoming me home.** I was decompressed by the time I'd reached our door.

Randy was quite the pianist. Self-taught. Admittedly more of a technician than an artist, he relied on me, of virtually no musical training, to help him with the expression of the notes he was reading. I loved his playing and I loved being able to help him improve if I could. Though the music was mostly new to him, the pieces were like old friends to me. He worked for months on "Laura," my favorite movie theme. I, who knew it so well, was able to help him with the nuance of the music. He eventually played it exactly as I remembered it from the film; note for note and nuance for nuance. It was lovely having my own personal pianist willing to learn and play any piece of my choosing. *The Cole Porter Songbook* was next.

Sexually speaking, Randy and I were attracted to opposite types. We could go out together for a night of cruising and never vie for the same man. There was never any competition. I was attracted to younger men and Randy to older. Both our attractions were established, early in our lives. Mine by the crush I'd had on my athletic, younger George Peppard-ish, sports playing childhood angel of a friend, Tommy and Randy's by the crush he'd had on his virile, athletic, older Robert Mitchum-ish, tennis playing dad. As a Catholic boy he'd also developed a strong priest fixation and had had his share of clerics and even the brothers who taught at our high school included.

One evening out in Chicago we'd gone our separate ways on the hunt, I to my favorite dance club and Randy to his favorite "daddy bar." We'd both scored — BIG-time — and unbeknownst to each other had hauled back our respective Tommy and Dad fantasies. Each was the perfect embodiment of our types. They both stayed the night — always a good sign and we invited them to stay for breakfast. Sharing our mutual good fortune about this, Randy and I happily worked away in the kitchen, preparing brunch that Sunday afternoon for our new love interests now seated together in the dining room. With several peeks around the corner, it became readily apparent that in bringing these two fantasy prizes together to our breakfast table we had made a major tactical error. Our fantasies, it seemed, were each others' fantasies. Made sense. My boyish younger man-who's-into-older-daddy types and Randy's-older-daddy-type-who's-into-boyish younger-men. It was an unintentional match made in heaven. While Randy and I were busily preparing a perfect hollandaise in the kitchen, out in the dining room our perfect guests were busily falling in perfect love. **We watched unable to do anything as they nearly consummated their new love right there over of the Eggs Benedict and Potatoes Lyonnaise.** We and our Julia Child-Silver Palate brunch creation were no match for the romantic forces at our table and, at that point, were well beside the point. They ate and ran. For months, perhaps years, we would see the happy result of our unintentional matchmaking all over gay Chicago and received no credit whatsoever for having brought them together.

1979

The Golden Age

MY LIFELONG LOVE AFFAIR with department stores started when I was young. I cherished the regular trips to downtown Louisville with my mother and for me, the highlight of our downtown days together was shopping at Stewart's, Louisville's premiere department store. It was a grand dame department store at a time when every city had one. **Stewart's was the glamorous beating heart of downtown Louisville, as far as I was concerned.**

There were annual trips downtown with the entire family to see the Stewart's Christmas windows, Christmas decorations and a visit with Santa Claus — OK, not all of it was wonderful as that loud fat bearded man scared me to death. There were other stores in a still flourishing downtown Louisville as well, all decorated for the season and wonderful in their own right and with their own windows but no other store quite matched up to the glamour of Stewart's. In the springtime you'd step in through the always revolving doors to be met with a long wide island planted with real spring flowers taking up most of the main aisle and running all the way back to the escalators. In the center of the island reaching up to the high ceiling was a huge tree with its pink spring apple-blossom-burdened-branches reaching out in all directions. From one of the branches was hung a swing, it's rope supports entwined with flowers and on the swing a delicate young woman with flowers in her hair and wearing something pastel and diaphanous, swinging to-and-fro over the flowers and reflected in a small pond of real water below. Surrounded by chirping birds, she was modeling hosiery sold at the well attended counters just to her left. The scent from all those live flowers mixed with the perfumed fragrances emanating from the cosmetics department and the chocolate scents from the candy counters. There were other things I loved: the chandeliers, the elevators, the escalators, the pneumatic tubes that magically sent your money (or pink Stewart's charge plate) somewhere and just as magically delivered a receipt and change right back. I especially loved the mysterious electronic sounding bells that seemed to be ringing out coded messages to those-in-the-know and delighted in the fact that Stewart's was the only place I knew of that had a notions counter. I didn't have a notion as to what notions were but I was glad Stewart's had them. And there were the restaurants: the elegant Art Deco right-out-of-the-movies Orchid Room on the sixth floor at the top of the escalators and my favorite, the streamlined Luncheonette tucked away in a corner of the lower level with its ever changing four season tree mural and serpentine counter.

Everything was pretty. Everything was glamorous. And most of it was for sale even if you couldn't afford it. **I wanted nothing more as a boy than to work in such a place and I set my sights on the top floor of Stewart's where I'd someday have a studio office (like I'd seen in the movies.)** I'd be like Katharine Hepburn in *The Desk Set*. Or Lauren Bacall in *Designing Woman*. I could see myself sitting at a big drawing board illustrating ladies' fashions for Stewart's newspaper ads. I was quite specific in my fantasies and was certain, without a doubt, when I was old enough they'd become reality. Somehow. I didn't think to ask for more.

My actual work trajectory took a slightly different track but ended me right where I'd asked to be on the top floor of a department store. Twice actually. But never Stewart's. At L. S. Ayres, the grande dame of Indianapolis department stores, even better than my original dream, rather than drawing clothes, I was actually designing the stores. At a big drawing board. Three years working for Ayres and learning retail store design prepared me for the day when I made the fateful phone call that moved me to Chicago and the grandest grande dame of them all, Marshall Field & Company. My timing was perfect. The phone call had been instigated by an article I read in a retail trade magazine about the new CEO of Marshall Field's. He was young and had been hired to dust off the rather dowdy image Field's had acquired over the former few decades. I saw an opportunity for some good work and upward mobility. **Within a few weeks I was working in Chicago. At Marshall Field's. On the top floor. At a big drawing board. Just like in the movies. Just like in my dreams.**

The Store Design office was an airy sky-lighted studio space filled with plants, ever-changing art, antiques and contemporary furnishings and decoration. The department was made up of an array of gay men — fun and quirky — and a constantly coffee making secretary named Virginia who was mostly mother. The general climate was more cocktail party (without the alcohol) than office and I wonder sometimes how we got any work done. But we did.

The 13th floor where the studio was located incorporated an entire Chicago block with: our store design offices, visual merchandising offices, display/prop storage, seasonal decorations (it was always Christmas on the 13th floor,) mannequins, in-house construction, art restoration, bakeries, ice cream kitchens and the candy kitchen that produced Marshall Field's famous Frango Mints. We'd occasionally sneak into the candy kitchen and "liberate" a full tray of the deliciously salty (salt was their secret ingredient) chocolate Frango Mints before they'd been cubed, coated and boxed. The 13th floor was a fantasy world exceeding anything I had ever imagined as a little Louisville boy with big city ambitions. It even exceeded the movies. My big city dreams hadn't been big enough.

Right off I was given a new Junior's Department to design and it was quite unlike anything Field's had seen before. It caught the attention of Mr. Kelly the new CEO and within a short time he had sought me out and taken me under his wing. It was a match made in my own professional heaven as the two of us developed a great working relationship. It wasn't all smooth sailing. My boss, a handsome silver haired Scandinavian a few years from retirement was a bit threatened and threw a few roadblocks in my way. I can't blame him. **I was a bit of an upstart with a sense of predestination and I couldn't be reigned in.** I had the ear of the CEO anytime I wanted and used it. I was among the few who could knock on his office door without an appointment and discuss whatever it was I was working on or happened to be on my mind.

The honeymoon was on. **During that time my favorite words were, "Walk with me."** That's what Mr. Kelly (Phil, though I always had trouble using his first name) would say when he'd run into me in the store, "Michael, walk with me." We'd walk the floors of Marshall Field's together — CEO and subordinate, as he'd pick my brain about everything we saw. "Do you like this?", "What do you think of that?", "What can you do with this?", "Can we make that any better?", "Would you wear that?", "Got any ideas?" He was absolutely dedicated to lifting the rather dowdy image of Marshall Field's and welcomed new energy and new ideas. We were well-tuned to each other and that made us the best of working partners. My equivalent in the Visual Merchandising (display) Department was another 'infante terrible' named Terry. We couldn't stand each other at first. But I think when we realized neither was a threat to the other, we actually became friends and worked together beautifully. Terry and I were the only two non-officers regularly in attendance in the walnut paneled board room store planning meetings.

Having achieved all my professional dreams, and my own personal golden age, along with my best friend, I settled in for a lifetime. My future was set in my favorite department store in my favorite city. I could easily see a Vice Presidency and a gold watch for my thirty-five golden age years of devoted service.

1979

Finding Heaven At The Oasis

THE FIRST TIME I saw Key West's Oasis Guesthouse I was a guest of a guest.

One Chicago winter, probably 1979 or 1980, work had been crazy busy and it seemed there'd be no time for a warm weather getaway. Suddenly I could see an opening where I might just be able to get myself down to Key West for a week or so. Anyone who has endured a brutal Chicago winter will understand why I seized the opportunity. Guesthouse choices were critically important in Key West and planning ahead was imperative. There were so many at the time (15? 20? or more) each with its own distinct personality. They were all popular and they filled up fast. In those days I usually stayed at Cypress House, Curry House or Lighthouse Court but they were booked, so I had to take what I could get and a place called Sea Isle was what I got. I knew nothing about Sea Isle but they had a room available so Sea Isle it was. The fact that there was space available when all of the other guesthouses were full was not encouraging.

As I settled in at Sea Isle which was actually nicer than I'd imagined, and readied myself for my first night out, thoughts about dinner made me realize I was on vacation alone. I'd never gone on vacation alone. Dinner on vacation alone? I was horrified. What had I done? I projected further. Drinks alone? After that, clubs alone? Vacationing alone? I clearly hadn't thought this through a few days before as I hurriedly made my last minute plans. Key West vacations were typically group activities planned and choreographed well in advance. I'd have to wing it. Alone.

I had no alternative other than hit the streets by myself. I set out from Sea Isle waving goodbye to the kindly looking older gentlemen who had been by the pool when I checked in and were still installed there (as they would be my entire stay — day and night) enjoying their cocktails. I headed off to Duvall Street the social center of the island. Well, I needn't have worried about the alone thing. Within the first three or four blocks on Duvall Street I ran into friends from Chicago. We went to dinner. We spent the rest of the night at the strip club where the really sexy stripper boys, boners-to-the-wind, would always go all the way. We parted having made plans to meet the next day at Queer Pier aka Dick Dock which was a long narrow pier where boys stretched out, soaking up the sun, all naked and gay. The pier must have had a real name but no one used it. Or knew it for that matter. It was "Queer Pier" or "Dick Dock" and I could never decide which nickname was cuter. Key West with its coral reefs had no real beaches for sunning and the one small man-made exception called The Sands filled up pretty quickly. Key West was primarily a pool community so if you wanted to lie out in the sun anywhere beyond the pool at your guesthouse and you hadn't gotten up early enough for some space on The Sands, Queer Pier/Dick Dock was where you'd head.

The next morning at breakfast before heading off to Queer Pier, I met the older Sea Isle gentlemen. They were a sweet, friendly couple, I'd say in their mid to late forties or fifties — I was in my late twenties. They were a quick witted jovial pair from the upper Midwest — Wisconsin or Minnesota, I think, one a school teacher and one a school principal. They had been together for quite awhile and seemed to be a perfect match, laughing at the same things and prone to finishing each other's sentences.

The school teachers were much like so many of the other gay gentlemen who had taken me under their collective wings since my coming out ten years before, an immature and naïve seventeen year old. I'd had so many of these terrific friendships with older, wiser, experienced men who taught me all about the gay world I was stepping into. We were inter-generational buddies. Though not attracted to these men sexually, I'd always valued their friendship, mentorship and generosity in sharing themselves and their experience with me. There also seemed to be something about me that attracted them. **It was my relative immaturity I think, and what they perceived as my wide eyed naïveté that made them want to protect me, the little gay lamb, from the big gay slaughter.** I was always in good hands. It was that way with these two gentlemen right off the bat. After I'd related my disbelief at being on vacation alone, giving me a once over, one offered, "Darlin' not for long." The other also sizing me up, "Oh, girl, you're gonna do just fine." Their reassurance was comforting and as it turned out, they were correct.

At Dick Dock where my friends from the night before did not show up, I scored big. Literally. Lying next to me was a 6'-5" gay god. We started talking. His name was Stefan. He worked for Lufthansa Airlines and had been a swimmer for The Netherlands in the 1972 Olympics. He was tall. He was handsome. He was smart. He was originally from South Africa. He had a dazzling smile and the tiniest little speedo. I would stay glued to him for days; I'd see to that. As the sun made its way to the other side of the island, we departed Dick Dock and I brought my prize back to Sea Isle parading him past my ever-present teacher duo. They sat straight up in their lounges, drinks in hand and their eyes wide as saucers. I introduced Stefan to them and just before disappearing into my room, I gave them an amazed "Oh my god can ya believe it?" look over my shoulder. After a sweaty hour or two we came out for a dip in the pool. My Olympic swimmer was doing laps and I was smitten. As were my cocktail sipping friends. It went on that way for days. I don't think I spent a night in my own room. The schoolteachers loved teasing me, "Darlin' those Sea Isle people love you," one said snickering, "You don't know it but they're rentin' your room out every night," snickers turning to laughter, and from the other, "They're turnin' twice the revenue on you!" They thought this was hilarious; even funnier when I had to change rooms. When I'd made my last minute plans I'd been told I'd need to change rooms midway through my stay. I was way too busy to remember such a detail. When it came time for the move, in my absence, that lovely couple helped the Sea Isle staff transfer my things. When I returned that evening and walked in on someone else in my old room, they couldn't contain their glee; one of them pointing and laughing, "Oh my god she doesn't even know which room she's in!" And from the other, "Good thing she's pretty."

It was Stefan who introduced me to the Oasis. Toward the end of the week he suggested we go there one afternoon to use the pool. I had heard about it and knew its reputation as the nicest, most luxurious of all the Key West guesthouses. Stefan was staying at the much smaller and pool-less Gideon Lowe House just around the corner. There was an arrangement which allowed Gideon Lowe Guests to use the Oasis pool. **So, as a guest of a guest, I would get my first glimpse of the fabled Oasis.**

From Fleming Street, all that could be seen of the Oasis was a low pale yellow wall topped by a small white picket fence and above it, a tall, well manicured ficus hedge and above that, a row of tall stately palm trees. An inconspicuous white gate was set into the wall under a ficus arch and a small equally inconspicuous sign reading "Oasis" just to the right of it. Stefan opened the gate with a pass key and standing proudly before us was an impressive pale yellow two story traditional Bahamian mansion. It had white railed verandas on both levels with slowly circulating ceiling fans. We followed a stone path flanked by thick tropical vegetation along the right side of the house to the hushed sound of some light jazz/samba soundtrack emanating from somewhere in the near distance ahead. After having seen the traditional front of the house I was unprepared for what lay behind as the narrow shaded path opened up to the sunny total fantasy that was the rear of the house. A shimmering rectangular pool punctuated at one corner with a stone horse's head was the centerpiece of this hidden oasis. **On the pool, stretched out face down on an aquamarine float was a golden naked boy, lazily making his way around the pool surface, his bare gleaming white ass cheeks in sharp contrast to his golden tan and the blue sparkling pool surrounding him.** Forming a backdrop for this display of perfection was a high wall of tropical vegetation along with a row of tall gently swaying-to-the-music palm trees backed by an almost unseen weathered cypress wood fence peeking through the foliage. Just in front of that was a row of sleek lounges in the same sun-silvered cypress on which lay sleek sun-tanned glistening male houseguests some naked, some in tiny swimsuits. Some were reading. Some were sleeping. Some were watching the floating boy. Until our arrival. As Stefan and I stepped into that sunny space, in a perfectly choreographed move, heads turned, sunglasses slid down noses, rested there briefly as the eyes behind them scanned us, and then, again in perfect synchronicity, were slowly pushed right back to where they'd been before our arrival. Cute barefoot boys, dressed in tight white short shorts, tight white tank tops cropped to show their smooth tanned bellies, (all embellished with the Oasis logo) crisscrossed the space delivering towels and drinks and such here and there. **These young accommodating Florida boys, all of them sun bleached, tan, usually blond and sexy, were found in similar jobs all over the island; they were as much a part of the Key West landscape as the palm trees and wooden houses.** The boys smiled their welcome as the Oasis wrapped its arms around us. I glanced to the left to see a small white canvas-walled outdoor gym and working out under a cascading waterfall of fuchsia bougainvillea blossoms, was a suntan-oiled, jock-strapped muscle-boy, lying back, legs spread wide, everything bulging as he pressed a barbell overhead. Spotting him was his naked muscle-buddy straddling the bench, his pendulous privates hanging right above his friend's face. Above, on the next level was a long rectangular seating area surrounded by a low white stucco wall with that same bougainvillea spilling over the full length of it. Above the seating area, covering it entirely, was a white canvas canopy — an Arabian style tent swooping up from its four corners to a single tall thin flagpole towering over the peak. **At the top of the pole flew a long thin triangular pennant rippling in the soft breeze of a crystal blue Key West sky.**

Turning to the left my eyes widened as I took in the spectacular rear of the house. It was three stepped-back stories of crenelated white stucco Moroccan fantasy with that same fuchsia bougainvillea spilling over the entire length of each level. A spiral staircase with a towering blossoming cactus next to it welcomed us up to the second level which was dotted here and there with more naked gay boys enjoying their afternoon. A white stucco staircase, curving elegantly to the left and then back just as elegantly to the right, made its steep way from the second level to the third where presumably there'd be more naked men. Topping it all, mounted on the peak of the third level, was, quite unexpectedly, a unicorn head made of gleaming white metal. I was breathless as we located two lounges on the second level. I was home.

If you'd overlay my love of good design with my love of places where men would gather to be naked and gay, you'd get the Oasis, as sophisticated as it was sexy. Had I sat down to a drawing board myself, I couldn't have designed it better. **Two circles of the Venn diagrams of my life — unerring good taste and gay male nudity — overlapped that life-changing day; I had found my own tasteful, exotic and**

erotic heaven. Stefan and I spent only one perfect afternoon there sunning and floating and enjoying our time together but I knew without question that I would return.

All too soon we were at the end of Stefan's month long Key West stay — we'd met during his last week. It was the end of our time together. While he spent his final day making the rounds saying goodbye to all his old friends, I spent the day at Dick Dock making new ones. Especially notable was an adorable tow head blond, blue-eyed boy named Jeff. He was on spring break. From high school, no less. He was 18, no less. I demanded I.D. He was staying in a tent at a campground with schoolmates who didn't know he was gay. He'd gone off on his own and found Dick Dock and I found him. Never one to miss an opportunity with a sweet-smiling tow head surfer type, I took him back to Sea Isle. The schoolteachers' jaws dropped as we entered the pool area. Having seen me with Stefan for days, their gaze followed me and my new young friend to my room where we disappeared for a couple of hours of sunburnt sex. He was so blond, so fair, so smooth, and so in need of aloe applied absolutely everywhere.

I'd committed earlier to dinner with Stefan who'd be leaving on the first flight out the next morning. Not wanting to lose Jeff (perhaps forever) to his straight campground, I told him about my dinner plans and encouraged him to stay until my return. I knew it was only dinner with Stefan; we would not be spending the night together. Hearing Stefan's knock, I opened the door to see, well behind him, the astonished faces of the schoolteachers. Cocktails in hand, they were clearly looking past Stefan for the young blond boy, now fast asleep. Installed on their designated lounges the entire time, they were certain he hadn't left. With heads shaking, amazed and amused, they watched me walk off with Stefan knowing the blond boy was still in my room. The next day, reminding me over and over about my having been afraid to be on vacation alone, as they watched blond Jeff doing laps in the pool, they told me that I was their new hero.

1980

Father Johnny

LOVE DID FIND RANDY once during our Chicago days. Johnny was slightly older than I. He was tall, athletic and handsome. And sexy. He was the all-man version of the boy-next-door. The dad next door would be more like it. He pushed all of Randy's buttons with his sexy sparkle and mischievous smile. He was a professor at Loyola, smart, and he seemed to have been designed and supplied by a benevolent god just for Randy. **He was one of the most charming, attractive and smart men either of us had ever met and he had a secret.** There was something mysterious about Johnny, something that we both knew he was withholding. And I knew what it was. He was a priest. I was certain of it. He had to be a priest. As a Catholic boy who'd grown up with a seminarian older brother I'd been exposed to many priests and would-be priests. I could spot one a mile away. There was something about Johnny that reminded me of my brother's priest and seminarian friends; something that made me dead certain he was a priest and hiding it from Randy who was not quite as certain. It made sense. Loyola, where he taught, was a Catholic university. He was a teaching priest, something of which, I supposed, Loyola had legions. He was always suspiciously circumspect about details of his life. There were times when he was unavailable with no real explanation. They certainly never went to Sunday brunch. He only saw Randy out or at our place. Randy had never seen or been invited to his...a rectory no doubt. And you could easily imagine Johnny in a roman collar. Gorgeous and sexy. We both agreed on this point. Case closed. **Of course my suggestion of Johnny's priesthood only fanned the flames of desire for Randy and his priest fixation.**

When, after months of seeing each other, Randy shared my suspicions with Johnny; he laughed the suggestion away. While Randy remained uncertain, I was convinced. Mr. Perfect was Rev. Perfect. I started calling him, "Father Johnny" anytime Randy and I spoke of him. Randy chose to ignore all the signs subtle and not so subtle that Johnny was hiding his priesthood and instead fell absolutely madly in love with him. From all indications the feeling was mutual. "So what if he is a priest," Randy would say. They could not get enough of each other. I eventually began to overlook my suspicions as my own initial crush on him blossomed and took over.

Randy, having found his perfect love, resurrected his life-long picket-fenced His & His fantasy, of a dream house (something stone and substantial and probably in Evanston) that came with the perfect man, an abundant garden, an in-ground pool and a golden retriever. If that didn't work for Father Johnny, Randy wouldn't be opposed to something a little more professorial out by the Loyola campus. No matter the geography, Randy, ever the planner, was planning his future. As they say, "When man plans..."

One day as he was walking down Clark Street, Randy saw Johnny parallel parking before their date. For whatever reason, rather than rushing up to the car as he normally would, Randy stood back and watched. He saw Johnny get out of the car, close the driver's door and open the rear passenger door. He then saw Johnny remove a child's car seat, open the trunk, toss it in and close the trunk. A child's car seat. Johnny was not a priest. Father Johnny was a father alright, just a different kind of father...and husband. It should have been obvious but neither of us had ever given that possibility a thought. All the signs that pointed me to ordained should have instead pointed to married. Johnny was married.

When confronted by what Randy had seen, Johnny confessed that yes, he was married. He told Randy however that the marriage was over. He no longer loved his wife and that it was just a matter of time before he got out of the marriage. He would then be free. He just couldn't say when. He had to think of his child. Of course. In other words, the same story that every married man having an affair has told every lover. "It's over. We're just going through the motions. It's just a matter of time." They continued on for awhile but it became clear that Johnny was never going to leave his wife. He actually liked things as they were. Fine for him but not enough for Randy. When forced to decide, Johnny turned back to his loveless marriage with his unsuspecting wife, leaving a devastated Randy in his wake.

The film *Making Love* came out not long after the breakup. It was a movie about a married man who discovers his homosexuality and eventually leaves his wife. In retrospect, probably not the best choice of film for Randy in his current state of romantic bereavement. Neither of us had thought this through. At the end of the film when the theater lights came up, I looked over to Randy who was immobilized in convulsive weeping. It was one of the only two times I would ever see Randy cry and was the moment when I fully appreciated the level of loss he had endured with Johnny's departure. It was not easy to recover from the loss of his dream man and along with him his dream life. **Real life moved on and eventually, Randy with it, to face other unimaginable losses ahead.**

1981

Kim & The Super & Officer Kaloskagathos

UNLIKE RANDY, I had no real desire or need for a full-time boyfriend; apart from, that is my many perfect-man fantasies. They were just that though; fantasies. Though far from perfect myself, I was still notoriously incapable of sustaining sexual attraction for any length of time in anyone who didn't meet the perfection of these fantasy-men. **It likely was none too healthy, but the perfection I'd find in the pages of my skin magazines or in other forms of pornography, or with my eyes closed, the legions of these fantasy boys who lived in the real estate I'd happily turned over to them in my head, had I suppose, soured me on anything less.** I quite frequently preferred the sexy perfection of these fantasy figures and fantasy situations, a bottle of poppers, some Vaseline and my right hand to most of reality.

I did however manage to have several ongoing more-than-just-a-fuck-buddy-less-than-perfect-part-time relationships. These boys were not only sexual partners but were also friends. Often dear friends. I'd go out looking for trouble, find it and drag it home for sex. Or go home with it. Post-sex, I'd have a new friend. Kim was one of my favorites who I brought home for sex and became not just fuck buddies but great friends as well. What I suppose we now call "friends with benefits." **So that was Kim — a tall, blond, fun friend with frequent benefits.** He was a flight attendant and an often time bed buddy. We didn't actually date (or at least I didn't think so) but we saw each other a lot and had a fun, easy and sexy friendship. He always made me laugh.

Kim's schedule as a flight attendant was different from my 9 to 5 work schedule, so quite frequently when he would stay over, I'd get up and go off to work leaving him in bed. He would eventually get up and at his own leisure, let himself out. One such morning, well after I had departed, I received a phone call from an excited Kim. "Michael you are not gonna believe what just happened! I was still in bed and I heard your front door open. I actually thought it was you or Randy coming back until I heard a voice say something about 'checking the plumbing,'" he continued breathlessly, "I heard footsteps coming back to your bedroom. I was naked of course and there was no time to get dressed so I jumped out of bed and hid in your closet. I didn't want to scare the guy." On the other end of the line I imagined naked Kim, probably with his early morning wood, hiding in my closet. I was both amused and a little turned on, or the very least curious, because I really didn't know what was coming next — naked fly-boy and plumber — a porn scenario for sure. My excited fuck buddy continued, "So I'm standing naked in your closet looking through the slats and I see this guy in a gray uniform come into your bedroom but he does not go to the bathroom where the plumbing is, nope, instead he goes right over to the dresser and takes my wallet and watch! Like a crazy mad man I jump out of the closet, naked as a jay bird, and chase him down the hall! I must've scared him to death cause he was running and screaming like a little girl with his hands up over his head!" I'm listening stunned and open-mouthed. "He dropped my wallet and watch and ran out the door and it slammed shut behind him. Since I got my stuff back and I was a little underdressed I didn't follow him." There was a short pause while he let me digest his story. "And then I called you." I stood in my office stunned. A thieving plumber in The 2000 Building? Kim was right, I didn't believe it. But I believed him.

Once convinced he wasn't playing some sort of joke, before I headed home, I promptly called Margery our building Manager, and then Randy relaying Kim's story to both. Once Randy was convinced I wasn't playing some sort of a joke, he headed home as well. **When I arrived, Margery was waiting with Officer Kaloskagathos; sweet, devastatingly beautiful Officer Kaloskagathos was there to file the police report.** There was no sign of a plumber but I'd somehow forgotten about him for the moment. Officer Kaloskagathos was a handsome, wide-shouldered, classic Greek god squeezed into a super-tight second skin of a police uniform. As he removed his hat, revealing a full head of thick, shiny, wavy black curls, he extended his hand and with a sparkling Pepsodent smile, gave me a sexy "Hello." His equally sparkling eyes, the color of the Aegean, were framed with thick black eyelashes and focused directly on mine. I was dazzled and instantly in lust. As I followed Margery and Officer Kaloskagathos to the elevator, my eyes locked on his firm, muscular, round, abundant ass taunting me from his tight blue uniform pants. Unable to take my eyes away from this favored body part, I stayed focused there as my one-sided love-lust went into full-bloom. Somehow I failed to notice that Randy had arrived but once I did, as we entered the elevator, I managed to introduce him to Officer Kaloskagathos who responded to my massacre of his name with the same sexy sparkling smile as he shifted it to Randy and with a nod, said, "Hello." As the elevator doors closed behind us, I took note of Randy's taking note of my sexy new police-officer-love-interest.

Up in the apartment, a now clothed Kim was waiting for us. **My theatrically inclined friend and fuck buddy flew into his story, acting out the entire hilarious scenario from bed to closet to front door.** It was really entertaining. I especially enjoyed his impersonation of the frightened super (turns out it was the building superintendent) running down the hall all the way to the front door, arms flailing and "Screaming like a little girl." Made me wish I'd been there for the actual naked version.

Officer Kaloskagathos asked a lot of questions and took a lot of notes. He was certainly thorough. Did he seem especially interested in the details surrounding Kim's being naked in my bed? It seemed so. I wanted to think so. Did he imagine himself naked in my bed? I certainly had. In great detail. Every cop fantasy I'd ever entertained flashed across my single-minded brain. I could tell I was not alone in my thoughts. As he wrote his report, biceps bulging, we all looked on lasciviously. Margery included. I'd spied her in what I was certain was a quick fluff mode, surreptitiously checking her hair in our entryway mirror and reapplying her lipstick. I stood there devising a plan to somehow manage to get all the others, including Margery and her shimmering lips, out of the apartment.

"Officer Kaloskagathos and I can take this from here," I heard myself saying in a register somewhat deeper than my usual as I opened the door and politely shoved everyone else to the other side of it. Closing the door firmly, I flipped the lock and turned around, casting my hungry eyes on my sexily-smiling officer, who was already unbuttoning his stressed out shirt, exposing the Greek perfection of his smooth, tanned pecs and perfectly patterned chest hair. My eyes widened as did the opening of his shirt as button after button popped from its hole, revealing a black treasure trail welcoming my eyes and me down further, past his low-riding gun belt to his uniform-tight bulging crotch. He already knew where my bedroom was and just as I reached out for his gleaming belt buckle to unlock the treasure that lay below, with a sexy wink and a nod, he headed off down the hallway. I happily followed, stepping over pieces of discarded police uniform while stripping my own clothes away. I turned the corner and took in the sight of my naked policeman; it was the same perfection I'd seen for years in Ancient Greek statuary but Officer Kaloskagathos was real and on his back excited, hard and hanging, his hairy muscular legs spread wide in welcome. He'd left his policeman's hat on, and, sexily pushing it back, once again released those shining black curls to cascade over his forehead. He flashed that wicked greek smile again as he handcuffed himself to the bed. I jumped right in. **We had torrid afternoon sex to the sound of his police radio squawking from the nightstand where it had been deposited along with his gun.**

Sadly none of that happened.

Gentlemanly Officer Kaloskagathos remained ever-professional and the unwitting object of my vivid cop fantasies. Nothing more and never again to be seen. The building super, who was apparently just months away from retirement, lost his job and pension. Hero Kim received threats from the Super's awful lawyer son but Kim stood his ground and nothing ever came of it. Apparently for months, maybe even years before this event, there had been items mysteriously disappearing from apartments all over The 2000 Building. Thanks to Kim's bold and naked intervention, the mystery had been solved, the building got a new super, and I got to add sexy perfect Officer Kaloskagathos to my collection of other perfect fantasy boyfriends.

1976 – 1983

Sun & Sex & Shopping

KEY WEST gave birth to my "Three S'es of a Perfect Vacation." **Rife with sun, sex and shopping that perfect little island set my personal "Three S" standard for every vacation to come.** Sun, Sex and Shopping were in abundance in Key West; I'd find all three virtually everywhere on that extraordinary made-to-measure little island.

The intense Key West sun was, without exception, the most dependable I'd ever found for developing the perfect tan. Something that was critically important to me. Over the years I learned how to use that accommodating sun and had become something of a suntanning professional. If only you could make a living at such a thing. Wearing my little speedo and an ultra-thin coat of Bain de Soleil Gel, I'd slip onto an aquamarine float moored on the edge of the guesthouse pool and slip off into the water creating not even a ripple. Whether on my back or stomach, I'd stay in constant motion with the least amount of effort, allowing the rays to find every inch of my rotating exposed skin. I'd flip over now and then, adjusting the lines of my swimsuit, and when necessary, apply sunscreen to any "hot spots," creating by vacation's end, the perfect seamless tan with razor sharp tan lines. Away from the pool, the ever-reliable Key West sun would find you wherever you were. At The Sands or Queer Pier, on a sailboat or even just walking around the streets of Key West you had to always be aware of the intensity of the rays from that magnificent subtropical fire ball and use them wisely. Bake in it and you will fry. And burn. And peel. And go home a big mess. A little Key West sun goes a long way and I've found it's the best, most efficient-for-tanning-sun anywhere.

My favorite sun and sex playground was the pool area of any Key West gay guesthouse. I would happily spend the lion's share of my vacation time there. While others might go off to visit the Hemingway House or the Key West Lighthouse, I would contentedly spend my days in and out of the pool; in and out of my swimsuit. Over the years, I'd stayed at or visited (under varying circumstances) most of them. Each had its own personality; each custom made for me; a place to be appropriately naked and gay. **There I could experience without judgement or concern, my true natural sexual self. The Key West gay guesthouse was the one place that not only tolerated sexuality but also embraced and celebrated it; was even designed for it.** It was a place where recreational sex was, well...recreational; just as god had intended. There, for ten days, I could be exactly who I was meant to be in an environment that supported that kind of authenticity for anyone willing to embrace and be embraced by the wonderfully tolerant universe of the Key West all male gay guesthouse. Being in a place that supports such authenticity, set my soul free in an environment where, best of all, the sexual me and the spiritual me aligned (though it took me a while to understand that part of it) and were allowed to coexist, supporting each other and melding together as one.

Some of my favorites:

Curry House was small and intimate and run by a super-hot couple who set the tone for the sexy environment there. There was lots of "I'll show you mine if you'll show me yours" activity between the management and clientele. Staying there circa early '90s, as I was lying on my back floating on the pool I heard a voice excitedly say, "You're him." There was a silvered older gentleman looking at me. I'd have cast him as a coach in any sex video. He went on, "When I made my reservation I was looking at the brochure and saying how I wanted the guy on the cover to be here and there you are, floating away!" I knew the photo to which he was referring. The Curry House full color brochure had a photo of a long and lean man relaxing in a little speedo on a float on the pool. I too loved that photo and the man in it, but apart from the float, the color of my red speedo and perhaps the sunglasses, I saw little similarity. But if the older gentleman did, well I was ready to go for it. He was very visual — I could relate — and I became something of an obsession for him. He saw that I skipped rope for exercise and asked if I'd skip rope for him and while at it, let my penis escape my gym shorts. "Sure, Coach." I obliged rolling them at the waistband a little, and gave him the bouncing, fully erect show he'd asked for. "Anything for you, Coach!" I could see his approval as it shot right out at me. I was a live porn show for an enthusiastic audience of one. Another day he asked if I could float naked on the pool on my stomach this time and spread my legs. I happily gave him the view he wanted and he happily jerked himself off once again. **Firmly believing in karma, and our ability to create our own future, I had the thought that when I become his age there will be someone young and hunky waiting to do the same things for me.** I immediately visualized it.

Shortly after my gentleman friend departed Curry House another older gentleman, this time British, checked in with three — count 'em — three boys, giving me a really bad case of boy-toy envy. That evening, with thoughts of those adorable boys and a towel around my hips, I made my usual trip out under the stars to the hot tub. At any gay guesthouse anywhere this is a good idea. As I approached the bubbling tub of men, I was rewarded with the sight of the British gentleman and his bait...I mean...boyfriends. The three adorable boys were even more adorable, naked. Each possessed the kind of working-class British accent that I find to this day, inordinately sexy. I hopped right into the hot tub with the lot of them and started playing. The four of us were having the best time kissing and groping, poking and prodding, while the older gentleman sat at the edge of the bubbling water quietly watching us and stroking himself. All was super sexy until he opened his mouth. Out came sexual instructions in a British accent so posh, if I closed my eyes, I thought Elizabeth II, her royal self, had just joined us in the hot tub. With my love of a sexy working-class British accent, it never occurred to me how an upper crust British accent might be the polar opposite. With the unanticipated surprise of Her Royal Highness poshly instructing me to "Suck his cock" in a perfectly proper, dulcet and archly bossy (and yes) queenly British voice, I went royally limp. I am not one for taking directions in sex anyway and from that voice…well, all sexiness was out the window. With the mood broken and the arrival of more guys, I departed. Back in my wonderful little pitched-ceiling room up in the eaves of Curry House, with thoughts of those wet naked Brit boys, I took matters into my own hand.

The next morning as I ate breakfast by the pool, the British contingent came down and sat at a table to themselves. There was one boy that I particularly had my eye on both the night before and that morning. **He had tousled shaggy hair somewhere between sandy and strawberry blond, the palest green eyes, a sprinkling of freckles across his nose and bare shoulders and the kind of smooth pale translucent skin that sends shivers up my spine and desire down my groin.** He sat there at breakfast with the rest of his party, shirtless and in a peach-fuzzed-asscrack-revealing speedo and sneakers. Was he noticing my noticing him as I made my way to the coffee urn for a refill? I couldn't tell. I wanted to think he was checking me out but again, I couldn't tell. I left breakfast and went back to my room to ready myself for a day by the pool. I was almost set to leave when I heard a knock at the door. "Housekeeping," I thought.

I opened the door to see my adorable green-eyed British boy, now in a tank top (why had he bothered?) standing there. Before I could say anything, in the accent that drives me wild he said, "Ahm sorry fer comin' up here an disturbin' yer like this, but… ah jus couldn' help me self." I grabbed him by the tank top, pulled his hunky gingerness through the door and kicking it closed with my foot, I pushed him down on the bed and dropped down on him stripping him naked. We spent I don't know how long making that hot little top floor room hotter. I devoured him and his accent and every inch of his freckled ginger sweetness. Pink nipples. Pink penis. Pink everything. He never even got his sneakers off. He eventually left a spent and exhausted me, to catch up with his group. He apparently wasn't supposed to be going "rogue" like that but I guess he just couldn't help himself.

Lighthouse Court circa 1978 was perhaps too big to be called a guesthouse. A small formerly-family motel it had been transformed into more of a gay compound retaining absolutely no motel look or feel. It had lushly tropical private grounds and quite a few more rooms than the average gay guest house which meant quite a few more gay guests. It got its name from the Key West Lighthouse which was on the adjacent property. The Lighthouse itself was a big tourist attraction and I always thought they owed a great deal of their income to the Lighthouse Court and all its sunning naked denizens. You would lie by the pool stretched out in the sun and see tourists (mostly women) up on the observation deck which encircled the top of the Lighthouse's tower. Though the lookout was 360 degrees, the quadrant closest to Lighthouse Court was the most popular. Binoculars would scan the island and, as they made their way to the grounds of the Lighthouse Court they'd slowly and deliberately drop, becoming stationary for a moment or two or however long it took to check out every naked or nearly-naked gleaming body there. **Satisfied, the binoculars would eventually pan back up and continue on. This happened all day long. Observation deck indeed.** I usually would take a room at the rear of the compound conveniently located by the hot tub. It was a great place to make new friends, especially after midnight. There were always so many new friends to be made at Lighthouse Court. As a seasoned Key West veteran, I loved telling newcomers all the things to do and places to go on the island. I'd make restaurant recommendations, give directions to the baths, Dick Dock, The Sands and anything else they might be looking for. **It was at Lighthouse Court that someone named me "The Pied Piper of Key West" as I'd set out for late afternoon expeditions to perhaps the cemetery or evening dinner with up to a dozen or so new friends at a time.** It was also the place while floating on the pool

I first heard the recording artist, Sade. Her "Smooth Operator" and the rest of that album couldn't have been more perfectly in tune with the relaxed sexy vibe of a Key West guesthouse afternoon. It can be the depths of winter but when I hear Sade, I'm right back at Lighthouse Court happily floating away.

The Oasis circa 1980 was gay heaven on earth. I've already described it's stunning design. I'll just add that everything about that design supported everything that I ever really needed or wanted in a vacation spot. The rooms were crisp and white and tastefully Spartan. You'd open the closet door to find the hangers spaced three fingers apart. Always. It was that kind of place. The rooms were appointed "just so," in a comfortable spare and perfectly designed utilitarian way. Add to all of that a constantly changing array of the sexiest men and boys of all ages and you had a gay paradise. It was aptly named for it was indeed, a gay oasis in the desert of a heterosexual world. **I'd wake up each day under a slowly moving ceiling fan hearing the faint strains of light classical music, the clinking of glasses and the murmured deep-voice sound of male conversation in the distance wafting in through an open window.** Mr. Haydn or Brahms or some other long gone composer was announcing that breakfast was being served. I'd shake the sleep off, grab a towel and flip flops and head to the shower. I've never been a shower first thing in the morning person but in Key West things were different. There was an outdoor shower by the pool. It got a lot of use in the mornings. Like many of my housemates, I would stroll out clad only in my towel casually passing the breakfast area. I'd nod or smile or if I knew someone, wave. I'd head straight to the shower at the far corner of the pool. I'd drop my towel on the nearest lounge chair and make my naked way to the shower which was enclosed by a thin peek-a-boo wall of living bamboo. After a quick shower under the sun — still my favorite way — I'd step out naked and wet, drying off in full view of anyone at breakfast who'd care to look. The ever-changing stream of morning showerers was the best part of breakfast at the Oasis. Or any Key West guesthouse. You never wanted to miss breakfast where you could also catch up with other guests with whom you'd made friends and where you got to know any newcomers who might have checked in the night before. Fresh squeezed orange juice, homemade breakfast, sexy boys, classical music, bougainvillea, palm trees and light morning breezes made it the best breakfast experience I've ever had.

After breakfast I'd return to my room and prepare myself for a day at the pool. I would toke up on weed, slip on my swimsuit and grab a pool towel. Into my baseball cap or pith helmet — straw with a turquoise strap, an instant favorite purchased years before in Key West — I would toss my room key, sunglasses, Bain de Soleil, pipe and lighter, and a bottle of poppers (you never knew when opportunity would knock.) Feeling the embracing effects of the weed, and the dense warm air I would greet my fellow sun-worshippers and spread my towel first and then myself on a lounge chair. The cooperative Florida sun always worked quickly on my skin type as I'd turn over every fifteen minutes or so. After awhile I'd grab a float and from that point on, could be found on it and off it enjoying once again, my favorite pastime. **A little high from the weed, feeling sun-warmed and sexy and effortlessly moving my way around the pool I was in my own personal heaven, perfectly balancing the sexy with the divine.** I could see now and then, the appreciative reaction from one or more of my similarly clad or naked housemates; their reactions registered not so much from their faces but from between their legs where they'd be giving themselves an appreciative squeeze. I, in my tan-line-saving swimsuit, would do the same. **Tan-lines notwithstanding, I always felt sexier in a wet clingy swimsuit rather than naked, leaving just enough to the imagination.** There'd be plenty of naked time later, when the sun got lower in the sky. I would flip some cooling water onto myself and in the process make my clingy swimsuit clingier, leaving just a little less to the imaginations of any appreciative onlooker.

For lunch, I had the same routine every day. I'd grab some money and my house key and head out to Fleming Street still wearing only my speedo, and sunglasses. Key West was that kind of place. I'd barefoot my way to a small bodega just a couple of doors away where I'd buy a banana and a bottle of grape juice. That was lunch. It was all I ever had and all I ever wanted. I'd walk right back and enjoy my banana and juice by the pool.

The rest of the afternoon would find me floating, socializing and making new friends in, out of or around the pool. **There were surely other daytime pursuits on that little island but none that I'd rather pursue.** When the sun would finally leave the pool area (around 3:30 to 4:00pm) I'd gather my things and head up the iron spiral staircase to the woven hammock on the second outdoor level. I'd spread my towel out, strip out of my bathing suit and stretch out. Naked. I'd light my pipe and take a toke or two. My routine was well known in the house and just prior to my relocating myself, some of the other guests would quietly relocate themselves to spots with good views. Seriously. This always surprised and delighted my needy ego. **Lying on the hammock gently swaying back and forth, legs spread wide, hanging heavy, I'd enjoy the effect of the weed, the hot humid air, the tingling sensation of a day's worth of sun on my skin, the hungry eyes around me, and the feeling of being contentedly sexy; this was the one place in the world where I truly felt sexy.**

Comfortably settled into my hammock which hung from a beam at the edge of a shade providing porch above, I would effortlessly rock back and forth from sun to shade and back to sun. In and out. **Sun and shade.** I would squeeze some Bain de Soleil out and apply a thin glistening coat, the golden gel melting into the heat of my newly golden arms, shoulders, pecs, torso, and legs. I'd apply a more liberal amount to my slowly swelling cock-ringed penis. In seconds it'd be stiff, proudly standing at attention, slick and shiny, swaying there with me, back and forth. Sun and shade. Demanding my attention. Aching for it. Aware of the rapt eyes around me, I'd press the gleaming chrome cock ring into me, making my shining golden penis stand taller, more monumental than it actually was. They were there for a cock show and I was happy to provide it; delighted in fact. **My penis is the one thing, the only thing about me that I have found absolutely beautiful; it isn't the biggest but damn, it's one of the prettiest I've seen and I have seen a lot of 'em.** I delighted in showing it off here and now for all those appreciative eyes. Nowhere would it ever be harder than here. Turned on now even more, I would give it a good squeeze. And another. And another. The squeezes would become a slow stroking motion, exciting myself and in so doing, the others gathered and watching. I'd take my time enjoying every long slow stroke. My breathing would deepen and my breaths quicken as would the fist action on my slick thrusting rock hard penis. This could go on for quite awhile. In and out. Sun and shade. Squeeze after squeeze. Thrust after thrust.

When it became time, with my breathing deeper, my pulse quickening, and my penis tingling, release seemed imminent. I'd reach into my baseball cap where I'd deposited the bottle of poppers. Those who have used them will understand; those who haven't probably won't. I closed the left nostril and breathed in from the little brown bottle with the right. I repeated on the other side. Replacing the cap and depositing the bottle where I'd found it, I waited for the effects of my particular, easily obtained over-the-counter-sex-aid-of-choice to kick in. In a rush, the balance would shift and suddenly, briefly I would become transported to a world of raw sexual desire. "Poppered-up" and focused now on my penis and only my penis and the pleasure it was giving me, nothing was more important than my imminent orgasm. I was pure sexual energy. Carnal desire. Lust. I was suddenly in a universe where for that moment, nothing mattered but the sheer pleasure I was giving myself. My left fist joined in above my right as my strokes became longer and the squeezes harder.

My penis which swelled to even greater girth and length was now the rock-hard pleasure-core of entire existence, sending wave after wave of pleasure throughout my entire body; the pure essence of who I was at that particular moment of approaching ecstasy. In that instant, connecting with the divine, everything about me, everything about this place was in service of the exquisite moment when, in an act both carnal and spiritual, my buttocks would tighten, my hips would buck into the air and pleasure-thrusting, I would, in sheer sexual tingling ecstasy, suddenly release rope after thick rope of white creamy semen shooting out of the tip of my engorged throbbing cock, shooting in an arc well over my head. **Fucking the air over and over again, I'd buck — toes curled, leg and ass muscles tight, balls bouncing — with spasm after spasm of deep unbridled auto-erotic climax, sending my seed out into the universe, covering myself in my own hot liquid in splash after milky splash.**

As the last of the pearly fluid would seep from my throbbing dickhead, my body would convulse in a series of sexual aftershocks. My fingers wrapped around and fused to my dick-shaft would barely graze the reddened flaring more-sensitive-than-ever still-leaking knob, pulsing and glistening above my clenched fists. It responded in kind with squeeze after satisfying squeeze. Shivers of self-gratification emanating from the pleasure between my legs would run up and down the entire length of my being. As the shaking would begin to subside, my fingers would loosen on my thick and now rubbery penis leaving it to stand alone and then hang thick and heavy, between my relaxing legs. My muscles would become increasingly limp as my body would flatten and melt into the embrace of the hammock and the universe, exhausted and satisfied. **Aware once again of the light breezes caressing my body, I would softly and predictably drift off into a floating dreamland state of safe, sexual, spiritual fulfillment, rocking to and fro, sun and shade, in and out, naked and gay, happy and content. Completely satisfied.**

The Coconut Grove which was right next door had several high terraces overlooking the Oasis, providing ample opportunity for houseguests there to get involved in my daily routine. While I never stayed at the Coconut Grove, it was pointed out by some fellow houseguests at the Oasis, that if its owners were smart, they'd pay me to stay at the Oasis to ensure their guesthouse would stay booked. I laughingly gave brief consideration to the possibilities of jerking off for a living, and, though a great pastime or even hobby, I dismissed it as, though loads of fun, not a particularly dignified career goal. Anyway, the Coconut Grove with its less expensive rates, drew a decidedly younger crowd. It reliably housed some adorably cute collegiate types — a never ending ever-changing array of younger men usually interested in the slightly older gentlemen of the Oasis. For many boys, the "Daddies" around the Oasis pool were the best reason to stay at the Coconut Grove.

During one of my stays at the Oasis there were two particularly cute, sexy and very rambunctious boys next door. I couldn't help noticing these two always hanging out (sometimes quite literally) on the top deck. I couldn't ignore the boys next door if I'd wanted, they were so blatant in their voyeurism. One of my friends at the Oasis asked if I had noticed that I had a couple of "fans" over at the Coconut Grove. Noticed? They had binoculars! All day long I'd catch them out of the corner of my eye, loving the attention. At one point after doing a particularly sensual job of devouring my daily banana, I could hear from above, "Oh my god he's having sex with it." Mindlessly picking at the banana's little blue Chiquita label and eventually peeling it off, with no place to put it, I stuck it on my arm. One of them squealed as he snatched the binoculars from his friend, "Look, he put the banana sticker on his bicep!" They didn't miss much. I'd glance up occasionally and smile while just going about my day of floating, sunning and enjoying being watched and appreciated until it was hammock time. I went up the spiral staircase as usual and stretched out naked on the hammock for their bug-eyed enjoyment. And of course, my own. The boys were glued to the edge of the railing and my every move, passing the binoculars back and forth. They gasped out loud as I greased myself up and did my thing. I especially loved showing my dick off and shooting my wad for them. As I lay there in my hammock spent and about to drift off, one of the two launched a paper airplane my way. It landed right next to me. I looked up, and they were anxiously awaiting my retrieval of it. I had to give the boy snaps for accuracy as I didn't even have to get out of the hammock. I opened up the folds of the airplane and read on the yellow legal pad paper, "YOU ARE NOTORIOUS!" I had to laugh. I looked up and gave them a big smile, a self-deprecating shrug and a thumbs up. As I started to drift off, another paper airplane landed next to me. This boy was good! "WAS IT FUN?" the note asked, "WILL I SEE YOU OUT TONIGHT?"

Of course we met that night at the Copa and of course I paid a little visit to The Coconut Grove — two on one. The next afternoon after reaching my hammock, the entire scenario was repeated although there were no paper airplanes the second time around. The day after that, with some encouragement from me, the two of them stripped and stood buck ass naked at the edge of the top deck, hard dicks to the wind, jerking off with me as we all three shot together. **Both houses came to a complete standstill.**

I saved the paper airplanes.

Oh. Shopping. Can't get so carried away with the first two "S's" that I forget the third S: Shopping. I have always loved shopping and never more so than on vacation. There is something about shopping on vacation, especially in a tropical location or in a far off land with shops carrying merchandise you'd never find back home. **Key West was an island full of one-of-a-kind, only-in-Key West shops full of one-of-a-kind, only-in-Key West finds.** They were often tucked away here and there where you'd likely just happen upon them around some tropical corner. Most of course were on Duvall Street where you could spend hours in and out of them, finding the most wonderful stuff. There was Fast Buck Freddie's which, while it called itself a department store, was unlike any department store I'd ever seen. It was a whacked out sort of place that was part Henry Bendel, part Fred Segal and part acid trip. I would swear the merchandise changed daily as they had a way of keeping the store fresh no matter how frequently you visited. There was Last Flight Out which used as its logo, the romantic old DC 3 airplanes you used to fly into and out of Key West in the old days. **The name referred to those who were so reluctant to leave the paradise that was Key West that they wouldn't leave until "the last flight out."** I could understand that. Last Flight Out had all sorts of specialized resort merchandise. I still have a favorite cherished baseball cap with its DC 3 logo. Then there was Peaches for the very best swimwear ever, and later on, Hot Tops, a cool hip hat store opened by the former owners of the Oasis. One of my favorite shops carried only boat and marine merchandise — ship clocks, boat hardware, nautical maps, woven nets, glass floats, fishing line in every strength and every color of the rainbow, stuff like that that I couldn't get enough of. I'd spend hours there. I even loved the drug stores and apothecaries as they carried exotic Florida-only brands you'd never see up north. I'd stock up on Florida Water for its light scent that, once back up north, would instantly return me to my favorite little island. It supposedly had medicinal properties but I bought it for that scent and its tropical packaging.

Shopping in Key West was a "must" not only for the merchandise available, but for the only-in-Key West boys available as there were boys, boys, and more boys, everywhere. You weren't always shopping for merchandise. Any shopping trip could lead right back to sex. And probably sun. Boys, mostly shirtless and tanned, in tiny shorts and speedos, sneakers and flip-flops were up and down the streets and in the stores. **Shopping and cruising went hand in hand. You could hardly do one without the other. Why would you?** There was groping to be had behind the garment racks and sex to be had in the fitting rooms. Occasionally the more accommodating shopkeeper (for some reason the antique store owners were particularly horny) might even put the "Back in 15 Minutes" sign on the door, lock it and take you to the stock room for a little afternoon Florida fun. Shopping in Key West was surely a "must."

One more thing...

During one of my final stays in Key West, in the weekly local gay magazine, I read a piece of "one-handed" fiction. It was written from the point of view of a guy living across the street from a popular unnamed gay guesthouse. He wrote descriptively about a sexy barefoot man who would dependably emerge from the guesthouse at the same time every day wearing only a tiny revealing speedo. He would watch this man make the short trip to the little bodega down the street and back. The writer would wait each day for the man to appear, watch him make his way down the street and fantasize about sex with this fantasy man. I'm sure there were others who have made similar trips to similar bodegas but I couldn't help but wonder if the writer had seen my daily trips from the Oasis to pick up my lunch and felt motivated to write a story about it. Given the slightest chance I might have inspired a piece of gay erotic fiction, I certainly hope so.

1978 – 1981

Julia, Cathy, Lily, Tammy Faye & Ernest

IN OUR KITCHEN with its view of Lake Michigan, Randy and I threw ourselves into cooking. My mother had been a phenomenal cook and her ever-observant Mikey had attended her over-the-shoulder-cooking school. I learned some of her best recipes that way but the process of cooking always put me off. While creating her culinary masterpieces (mostly Italian or German) she would destroy the entire kitchen. Tidy little Virgo I, had then equated cooking with disaster and decided early on that no dish, no matter how yummy, was worth the mess of making it. **Randy taught me the fine art of "cleaning as you go," and it changed the way I felt about cooking.**

We loved learning new dishes and went through the Silver Palette Cookbook recipe by recipe. Cooking together became one of our favorite pastimes along with all the dinner parties and brunches. We loved entertaining. We also thrived on cooking shows and absorbed everything we could learn from Julia Child. We watched her religiously — typically stoned — I highly recommend it. We would roll a joint then roll on the floor in convulsive laughter all the while picking up tips on making the perfect roux or a curdle-free hollandaise sauce. **We'd oftentimes find ourselves in the kitchen together, baking while baked.** We, in fact, became masters at baking and our pound cake was legendary. Our crepes rivaled the Magic Pan's, though we always had to throw out the first one. We studied The Berghoff's creamed spinach and experimented until we got ours to be the perfect consistency and exact flavor; nutmeg, we decided, was the key ingredient. We thought our chili and quiche were the best in town. We weren't above a little trailer park cooking and got raves for our 'Dirt Pudding.' We invested in a second food processor. We made our own mayonnaise.

On any Saturday or Sunday afternoon, especially during the cold Chicago winters, when we weren't watching Ms. Child, you'd probably find us in front of the TV, predictably upholding a gay stereotype by watching ice skating, swimming, diving or gymnastics competitions. Especially if it happened to be an Olympic year. Randy wasn't the only dizzy one in our household and he loved catching me in my own occasional empty-headedness. We were watching an Olympic competition when Cathy Rigby's commercial for Stay-Free Maxi Pads came on. I simply tossed off a casual remark registering my surprise that anyone, especially a well known and beloved olympic gymnastics champion would go on TV and tell the world she had an enormous vagina. I probably used a word that was less clinical than "vagina." "Twat," I think was the word, "huge twat." **Randy, leaning away like I was suddenly contagious, gave me one of his "You're an idiot" looks.** "What?" was my response. He stated in his everybody-but-you-knows-this voice, "Maxi pads are not for women with large genitals," and then he added, "They're for heavy days!" Another blank look from me. "Days when a woman's menstrual flow is heavier." Well this was news to me. Heavier than what? What did I know about menstrual flow, heavy or otherwise? And how did he? I did get him to admit that the genital size thing (something in the gay male world we quite frequently make reference to) made some sense since she had been a gymnast for a long time, spending the better part of her life doing splits and straddling beams and horses and such. I imagined such activities could take quite a toll down there. After all my "Dizzy Randy" stories, he loved telling that one and got a lot of mileage out of it.

We also loved watching late night "religious" programming...again, stoned. We especially loved Tammy Faye Bakker and her husband Jim well before they reached national prominence. We'd sit in front of the television baked and in hysterics waiting for the moment when Tammy Faye's globbed-on eye makeup would begin to melt down her kewpie doll face in mascara-black tears of joy, as she shared the "good news" about her personal relationship with her personal savior. **Tammy Faye was high drama, low humor and she never disappointed with her straight man husband Jim at her side.** Our other absolute favorite was a toupee-wearing, polyester-upholstered, neckless faith healer named Ernest Angley. He would heal people right there on TV. Right in front of our eyes! Healing hands on foreheads in that shoe polish black wig. The lame walked. The deaf heard. The mute spoke. And we laughed. And laughed and laughed until our insides hurt. That Ernest Angley was real entertainment. We spent many a cold Chicago night toking up and being endlessly entertained by these televangelistic charlatans.

We also both shared an unwavering love and affection for Lily Tomlin and listened to her *This Is A Recording* album with Ernestine the telephone operator enough times together to have memorized it word for word. We'd find myriad ways to interject her quotes into everyday conversation and be endlessly amused by ourselves. And by Edith Ann our other favorite Lily Tomlin character whose voice and intonation we'd work on constantly. Randy even perfected her pbbbbttthhh raspberry sound which ever-alluded me.

There was a huge overlap of what Randy and I both found funny. **We were forever laughing at the exact-same things — silly absurdities that seemed to pass by most others but made us convulse with laughter.** We'd share the same oblique perspective and appreciation for the same funny nuances no matter how minute. Oftentimes without sharing a word, a simple glance at something would send the two of us into convulsive spasms of laughter.

1980

Church? Probably Not A Good Idea

YOU NEVER KNEW when our shared sense of the absurd would rear its silly head. Randy and I were invited to hear a friend sing in a choral concert in a big (Presbyterian, I think) church on Michigan Ave. It seemed like a good idea at the time; supporting a friend; but probably not a good idea. I don't think I'd ever been in such an archly conservative church environment, ever, and it didn't bring out the best in me. **Having started out a devout Catholic boy, very much into all the pomp and circumstance my given religion had to offer, once I escaped, I somehow ended up an irreverent church cut-up.** I had always loved the theatricality of religion — the music, and costumes, and pageantry and was quite seriously awestruck by it. I wouldn't miss a midnight mass for its drama or a May procession for its beauty. Older, having developed a healthy dose of cynicism, I no longer took any of it seriously.

The event Randy and I were attending was not a church service. It was just a concert, yet you could hear the proverbial pin drop in the super-hushed, stiffly conservative, packed with people, gothic ecclesiastic environment. Only a cough now and then echoing through the high-ceilinged nave or an occasional click of a heel on the highly polished stone floor, would break the absolute silence.

Now, years before, my Episcopalian one-time fiancé Dawn taught me a game to play in church. We'd do it at weddings mostly. You take the hymnal — Protestant preferably as Catholic ones are never as much fun — anyway, you take the hymnal, kindly provided just for this purpose, from the little shelf-thing where it lived, and open it to any random page. You would then read the title of the hymn and append it with "under the bedsheets." Hilarity would ensue. For instance "My Savior Will Rise Again...Under The Bedsheets." Or "Jesus Is Coming....Under The Bedsheets." Or "I Need Thee Ev'ry Hour...Under The Bedsheets." Well, I could go on and on but you get the picture. Juvenile, yes, but always amusing. **Fun guaranteed to enliven any otherwise boring church visit.**

So there I sat with Randy in exactly the kind of arch-churchy environment that never brought out the best in me. I was feeling a bit giggly (and about twelve years old) just being there. Randy was only too familiar with this reality about me and was doing his best to ignore me. I reached for the hymnal. Randy, also being all too familiar with the hymn game, slapped my hand like a mother of a three year old and made a point of going back to ignoring me. I reached for it again, got slapped again but managed to get hold of the hymnal anyway. I opened it and of course a really choice title was staring right up at us. He made the mistake of glancing over. I no longer remember the title but it was a good one — something about sheep I think — and, caught off-guard, he broke up right along with me. All bets were off at that point and I continued flipping for more gems. And found them. With both of us stifling, as best we could, our guffaws, Randy finally snatched the book away from me, placed it back in it's little shelf thingie and we settled back down...somewhat. **This left me wanting more.**

Sometimes the universe presents you with exactly what you need exactly when you need it. Or at least want it. There was a space in the pew in front of us and the stiffest of ushers stiffly ushered a minuscule old lady into it. She, adorably swallowed up in her mink collared coat, settled right in and right in front of me. Hovering just above the wooden pew, was her tidy little mink-to-match pillbox hat. My eye went immediately to a coral-colored satin band perfectly matching her coral coat and encircling the base of the hat. It wasn't the band however that caught my attention but the equally coral bow made from the same satin. Once again nothing too unusual about a bow except that this particular satin bow had been made by a teeny tiny little unexpected taxidermied mink paw pinching the fabric, creating the little bow. I let out a yelp! I couldn't help it. Nothing could prepare you for such a thing. It took me totally by surprise, this tiny little pressed-into-service, over-achieving mink remain. **After a sharp intake of breath and another stifled yelp, (heads turning here and there) I continued my suppressed snickering and elbowed Randy who was trying even harder to ignore whatever it was that was noisily going on just to his right.** Another elbow and a flick of my head and he followed my glance right to the bow. And the paw. Unprepared for this he let out a howl worse than mine. It echoed throughout the entire church. We were back out on Michigan Avenue before the concert ever began.

No matter how devout a little Catholic boy I'd been — and I was, in love with all the pomp and circumstance — church, in my older irreverent state, was no longer a good idea.

1962

Easter Spectacular

IT'S GOOD FRIDAY and ever-observant Catholic I, am in my bedroom, my upstairs inner sanctum where I could be alone with my many precious activities that require participation by no one but my eleven year old self. I am busily sewing a couple of small purple fabric shrouds — yes, shrouds — and doing so seated in front of an altar. The altar is a white gothic affair made of molded plastic and trimmed all over in gold. It is quite beautiful, I think, and somewhat resembles the altar in Louisville's equally gothic cathedral downtown. It is made in two slip-together parts and stands about two feet tall. The lower portion of the altar has an ivory colored relief of the Last Supper flanked by two gold spiral columns. Centered on the upper part is a small tabernacle with a working hinged door — also gold. Inside is a removable gold plastic chalice. Above all that are three tall connected open gothic arches in which stand from left to right, an angel (praying and ivory colored,) Christ (crucified and gilded,) and another angel (playing a harp and also ivory colored.) The three arches are topped with gold trimmed ziggurat embellishments and the center one topped with a small gold cross pointing the way toward heaven. There are also four tall gold plastic candlesticks each a with tall thin white plastic candle permanently lit with a red plastic flame. I had made antique lace handkerchiefs into linens for the altar. It was all quite grand and very Catholic. And pretty gay. I absolutely loved that altar which had been a present from my parents the Christmas before. I'd actually asked for an Infant of Prague statue from Tonini's, the same Catholic gift shop (one of my favorite shopping stops in Louisville) where the altar presumably was purchased. I got the altar instead. **My parents had intuited that since the Infant of Prague, a kind of dress up baby Jesus, came with several gold jeweled crowns and interchangeable lace and embroidered dresses, and capes, my interest in him was more closely related to his being more of a doll than a religious article. They were on to me.** While my dear parents hadn't quite come to the complete realization they had an eleven year old flaming gay boy under their roof, they'd already become quite adept at redirecting me away from 'girlish" interests. So I had received instead, that Christmas, the more suitably masculine altar. They hadn't anticipated the antique lace linens; nor my penchant for dress-up. Being Infant of Prague-less, I dressed myself up instead in all sorts of homemade Catholic drag and had thrown myself into my altar, holding masses and all sorts of other Catholic-ish ceremonial events. I had even made a 'jewel' encrusted bishop's mitre — look it up. I would do all of this entertaining myself (and the occasional friend or cousin I could coerce into attending) in the sanctuary of that upstairs bedroom gobbling up all the leftover 'communion hosts' I'd cut from slices of white bread using a jigger glass borrowed from our kitchen cabinet downstairs.

So on this particular Good Friday I was alone, up in my room, in high-prep for Holy Week. I was a devout little Catholic and loved the drama of Holy Week. **Our pastor, Father Weiker had a flair for the dramatic that matched my own.** On Holy Thursday, the day of The Last Supper, apart from all the washing and kissing of feet — one time my dad's...poor Father Weiker — things would be pretty much the same as always. But on Good Friday, the day that Christ was crucified, we'd walk into a church dramatically changed. In an effort to illustrate and observe the gravity of our lord's crucifixion, Father Weiker had the altar and entire sanctuary stripped of all ornamentation. Lavish flower arrangements...tossed out. Gold candelabras... polished and closeted. Delicate lace linens...laundered, pressed and folded away. Crystal water and wine goblets...washed, drying and out of sight. Potted palms...sunning somewhere outdoors. The place was barren, bereft of anything I considered pretty or important. Even my beloved life-size statues standing high on their ledges atop the wall that separated the sanctuary from back-of-the-house sacristy, had been sheathed in purple shrouds. These statues were like friends, so familiar in their beaming countenances and giving me something to look at to get me through all those typically boring masses. Now, the Blessed Virgin Mary, the quintessence of grace, wearing her requisite blue and white and a heavenward eternally suffering look, was hidden from my eyes. Jesus, crimson-robed, long-haired and handsome, pointing to his sacred heart which was inexplicably on fire was also covered-up. And I could no longer feast my young eyes lovingly on cute, blond St. Stephen, our unfortunately martyred, youngish, sandy-haired namesake, my favorite of the four. The old, bearded and beige St. Joseph I didn't miss so much but I did miss, held in his arms, the little beaming infant Jesus with his tiny outstretched arm, and finger in baby blessing but now just a pointed bulge in a big purple bag. **My four sacred friends were now lumpy purple ghostly globs. It was all quite strange and rather ghoulish and emphasized the uncovered crucified Jesus in agony on his special day.** Add to this spartan atmosphere, the silencing of the big organ in the choir loft along with the church bell outside and the other bells on the altar. And no choir. It was a serious time for total austerity. While I adored the dramatic effect, I missed all the prettiness. My little gay self was devoutly obsessed with pomp and circumstance, music and all the pretty hoopla of the Catholic Church. These distractions were the real reason to go to church, as far as I was concerned. Their absence, though dramatic, gave me an inescapable feeling of "What are we doing here and how long til we can leave?" This made Good Friday and Holy Saturday services endless and unbearable, until, that is, Easter Midnight Mass which was my favorite event of Holy Week and of the entire ecclesiastical calendar. And for good reason...the aforementioned Father Weiker's flair for the dramatic.

Holy Saturday night we'd find the church in the same austere state — the hushed sanctuary stripped and the statues shrouded. The mass would start in silence without bells, music, singing or any fanfare. Father Weiker and a meager two altar boys, still in the requisite black of mourning, would silently enter, sanctuary left, and get things started with a dreary, atonal, stripped-down opening. There was all sorts of glum clerical stuff to get through during the first fifteen minutes or so and all of it performed with cast-down faces as drearily, flatly and quietly as possible. I thought we'd never get through it all. The wait was excruciating. And, somehow... wonderful.

Finally, at midnight, it was time for some high–Catholic drama — a real resurrection was about to take place. Places! Showtime!

I sat in restless anticipation as Father Weiker, with the organ still silenced, would sing, a-cappella, "Gloria in ecelsis De-e-e-o." Immediately and in sharp contrast to the days before, the organ unheard since Thursday, fully unstopped, blasted out in a way that nearly peeled the skin off your face. The choir, along with it, burst into a full-throated Gloria equal to the organ blast. The bells, both the big one outside the church and the smaller ones on the altar inside, started ringing. While all this was going on, out of the wings from the sacristies — sanctuary right and left, rushed legions of altar boys dressed in white satin robes with gold fringe. They were hurriedly crisscrossing the sanctuary decorating it with potted palms and linens, flower arrangements and candelabras, gold chalices and crystal goblets. Within seconds, during all that lavish organ music blasting, the choir singing the Gloria and the bells ringing, the altar would be restored to its full glory, candles lighted. Within seconds! **But even better, happening at the same time as all the above, was my favorite part.** The purple shrouds, the ones that had been hiding my beloved statues would suddenly, magically fly off, up into the air, instantly revealing my four hidden figures. The "magic" was provided by my grandfather and three other of his sturdy male parishioner friends who were out of sight behind the wall and below the statues with long unseen poles hooked into small loops at the top rear of the shrouds. When the bells started the purple shroud flew! My grandfather always claimed St. Joseph, as that baby Jesus outstretched hand, forefinger extended, increased the degree of difficulty on that particular statue.

Father Weiker who at the start of all of this had sneaked off, sanctuary left, in his austere black vestments suddenly returned triumphant in shimmering lamé gold and white drag to continue the mass in a fully-restored sanctuary with full organ, full choir in full Gloria, bells still ringing inside and out and dozens of altar boys blocked and ready. All the church trappings I knew and loved were restored and the entire transformation had taken less than a minute. Now THAT'S Entertainment. A true Easter Spectacular. Sometimes I loved being Catholic. Oh thank you, Father Weiker!

My little gay-boy-in-waiting was dazzled by all the hoopla and nothing during the rest of the church year could match up to this one perfect moment of religious theater. The May Procession came close in its sheer outdoors scale and warm springtime floral prettiness, but a Mary statue being hauled around the parking lot lacked the drama of an Easter Midnight resurrection.

So back to that particular Good Friday morning up in the privacy of my bedroom, I was devising a way to approximate as closely as I could figure, this holy piece of theatricality with my own altar. I had removed all candelabras and linens. That was easy. I had found some purple fabric and was sewing little purple shrouds to cover the angel statues. Also easy. That'd get me through Good Friday and Holy Saturday but how to recreate the midnight transformation? I would be in church at midnight so it would have to occur in my absence. I couldn't find a way to deal with the candelabras and the linens so I guessed I'd just have to put them back on the altar before leaving for midnight mass. I pondered the purple shrouds covering my beloved angels. They were the most important part. I studied the altar and the shrouds. Those statues had to be revealed. At midnight. With bells if possible. I pondered the problem awhile and suddenly I had it! I got my sewing kit back out and ran to my bedside table and grabbed my trusty Baby Ben wind-up alarm clock. I threaded the needle with white thread (to blend in with the altar) and attached a long thread to the top of each of the shrouds. I ran the threads up over the top of the altar. I placed the alarm clock behind the altar and attached the threads to the wind-up thingie on the back of it. I then set the alarm for midnight. At midnight then, the alarm would sound and the thingie would turn wrapping the threads around its stem thereby lifting the shrouds off the statues. **There'd be bells ringing and shrouds flying; I was pretty proud of myself.** My Virgo-in-training decided that I needed to do a test run. Good thing. It all went off perfectly until…uh-oh… the alarm ran down before the shrouds could get all the way off the statues and didn't come close to clearing the top of the altar. The threads were wrapping too tightly. More pondering. Once again I had it and ran to the closet in the basement where all our kid art supplies were kept. I found a popsicle stick. **Popsicle sticks were an artistic staple in any late 1950s and early 1960s household with children. You could do or make anything with popsicle sticks and our household was littered with the results: lopsided picture frames, flammable ashtrays and pen and pencil holders that wouldn't stand up.** I cut the popsicle stick down to about an inch, carefully cut Vs into the ends and snugly taped it to the wind-up thingie on the alarm clock. I taped the strings to the popsicle stick and ran a second test. As the alarm went off and the thingie started to go round and round, the popsicle stick did just as I intended. The threads fell into place in the Vs and the extra girth of the stick took up several times as much string as before. The shrouds, easily revealing my angels, cleared the altar and fell behind it. I was ready. I did the final set up on Saturday afternoon. I double and triple checked to be certain everything was set and ready. My Baby Ben alarm clock was wound tightly and I went off to church with my family that night, secure in the knowledge that at midnight, while I'd be experiencing my favorite event of the Catholic calendar, the same event would be playing out, in my absence, on my own private altar, in my own private sanctuary. I returned from Easter midnight mass to proudly see my angels uncovered.

Hopefully next Christmas I'd get that Infant of Prague statue.

1980

Why Is It Funny?

STRANGELY, there were times when Randy wouldn't get the joke. It was an odd dichotomy. For all his appreciation of the sublimely esoteric in humor, an appreciation I'm so happy we shared, in your average garden variety funny-to-everyone-else situations, Randy never got the joke. It was that dizzy/smart thing again. I mean, this was a man who kept a "Funny File" a folder filled with funny silly items he'd culled from newspapers, friends' and co-workers' notes, magazines, work-related silliness, etc. In some instances, his sense of humor seemed so elevated. And yet, in other circumstances, a joke, or something that would amuse absolutely everyone else, would fly right over his head. **You could almost see it wing its way above him as his puzzled face would try to catch it. It never would.** Sitting around with a group of friends, (this being Chicago, an advertising city chock full of witty copy writers of whom we knew more than our share) someone would tell a story or make an observation, remark or just say something funny, breaking up all our friends. All, that is, except Randy. I could easily read the bewilderment on his face; see him processing the information as everyone else in the room was breaking up. He'd always respond with a puzzled "hunh?" Later, in private when he would ask me about it, I'd have to explain to him why it was funny. That never worked. You can't tell someone why something is funny and expect he'll suddenly find it funny. He just wouldn't get it. During the course of an evening with friends, Randy's puzzled "hunh" would occur with such frequency, that after God-knows-how-many-times, and right in front of all the others, I'd said a little too loudly, **"Randy...turn it up to 'Group'!"** I'd make a little hand gesture against my torso, turning up an imaginary dial connected to an imaginary hearing aid. This would break everyone up. Everyone, that is, except of course, Randy. He'd glare at me like the traitor I was. I'd cast my eyes shamefully downward and would always wonder if this time I'd gone too far.

We loved watching an old British sitcom (well, it's old now, I guess it was current then) called *Good Neighbors* on Public Television. It was about two very dissimilar best friend couples in suburban England living next door to each other. We wouldn't miss an episode. There was one particular episode though, that struck a little too close to home. I guess I always knew Randy's not being in on the joke bothered him but never knew just how much until the episode where Margo, one of the four lead characters (and the one I had always identified as Randy) didn't get the joke. She was always just outside the humor. Just the way Randy was. The other three characters would be breaking up constantly over this or that, and poor Margo would sit there baffled, trying to find the humor but just not getting it. Just like Randy. Were I as empathetic in those days as I am now, my heart would have gone out to poor Margo rather than finding her situation so funny. And to poor Randy as well who was clearly saddened by his identifying with Margo's plight. Margo, puzzled, would sit ingesting the same stories, watching the others laughing hysterically and ask, "Why is it funny?" She would plead, almost in tears, "Please tell me why it's funny!" Randy was Margo alright. I found the episode hysterically funny. Predictably, Randy did not.

1980

Randy's Brain

IN OUR RELATIONSHIP, Randy was the talker and I, the listener. He loved sharing every detail of his daily experiences and his many observations and he constantly sought out my counsel. Randy thought he needed my advice and perhaps I was helpful now and then, but most of all he just needed to talk. And to be listened to. I was that greatly-needed ear. Randy's mom was his other sympathetic ear, but I of course was more immediately available without long distance charges. Often it didn't take much more than my simply being present. A "mmmm...hmmmm" now and then from me was all that was necessary to keep these one-sided conversations going. Many a night, Sominex Riede as I would call him, would lay next to me in my bed, telling me about his day or his hopes and dreams or whatever else might have been on his mind. He would talk me right to sleep before heading off to his own bed in his own room. He'd feel better and I'd sleep like a rock.

I was fascinated by Randy's brain. He was something, I think, of a savant. He was a whiz at the daily crossword puzzle which he'd always complete (insisting you could only write in a word connected to another already filled-in one) all the while doing something else. He'd insist Jeopardy responses be put in a question form.

He was a young man who had taught himself how to play the piano and the organ, how to take shorthand and how to crochet. In a true case of role reversal, eventually teaching his grandmother. What boy had ever taught his grandmother to crochet? He also taught himself how to knit. Well, to be honest he had a little help with the knitting.

One especially cold winter, Randy wasn't challenged enough by his full time job, working to complete his MBA at Loyola University, and working toward becoming a Master in his Contract Bridge League. He needed something else to do with his brain and his hands. There was smoking (both cigarette and weed) but that wasn't enough. He decided on knitting. So in the nose- and ear-biting cold of a Chicago Saturday afternoon, the two of us trudged through the snow up Clark Street to a yarn store. He bought some skeins of yarn in a tasteful combination of cream and beige and asked for a couple of pointers on how to knit. To the skeptical and somewhat (if I read them correctly) condescending attitude of the yarn store ladies, he exited the store with a shopping bag full of supplies, determination and hope. I remember sitting in our living room watching him, legs crossed and studying at the dining table, occasionally highlighting lines in his MBA text books, taking drags from a cigarette or a joint all the while his hands would be working like some sort of knitting machine as a perfectly manufactured sweater magically emerged. Two to three weeks (or so) after Randy walked out of the yarn store, I accompanied him back with his finished sweater. I wanted to see the looks on the yarn store ladies' smug faces. He had even improvised a series of stripes across the chest to "make it his own" and proudly showed them off as he presented his work. I can still remember the lady behind the counter, the especially skeptical one, with her glasses at the end of her nose closely inspecting his workmanship, still skeptical. "I've been knitting all my life…" she stated more to the sweater than to Randy, as she pulled and tugged at the stitches. Her eyes narrowed as she glanced up at him in a steely look over the top edge of her eyeglasses and added, "…but I have never had a stitch that tight and even." She clearly remained skeptical as she added an emphatic, "…ever!"

Randy bought more yarn.

1980...

ParkSex

SEX IN PARKS was one of the great joys of summer in the city life. There has never been anything quite like meeting some sexy stranger on a hot summer night under the stars in a park or in the heat of an afternoon under a blazing sun in a lush wooded environment, pants down, naked and gay, sweaty and hard, "doing it" right then and there. Outdoor sex is anonymous, quick, convenient, efficient, a little dangerous and hot and always takes me back to Louisville's Cherokee Park and my very first sexual encounter — exciting and frightening in equal parts — when I was fifteen. **With nature all around, the sound of birds singing and chirping, leaves and sticks crunching underfoot, the fresh green smell of opportunity in the hushed, cool, forest air, I'm back in Cherokee Park and all I can think of is getting naked and getting off.**

In Chicago there were any number of places where gay men would congregate day and night to indulge in the illicit but oh-so-fun activity. The best place Randy and I knew for the exciting nocturnal activity was, quite conveniently, located right across the street in lushly-landscaped Lincoln Park. The Bushes, as the cruising area was called, was a nighttime sexual fun-fest filled with gay men by the scores quietly coursing through the labyrinth-like narrow leafy pathways cut through the vegetation over and around hills and valleys surrounding the Lincoln Park Lagoon. Straight people would never think of going into the woods at night. Why would they? Gay boys on the other hand had plenty of reason. **We'd head out on a steamy summer night wearing as little as possible, only gym shorts for me — I always liked being one article of clothing away from naked.** Once in the park, the opportunity for sex was down every path and around every corner, or bush. The anticipation of what lay ahead was palpable. There was the guarantee of some stranger (or strangers) in there waiting for some hot steamy outdoor pleasure. There was always a sense of danger, I guess. A turn-on for some but not for me. If there was a real sense of danger, my ever-reliable dick would soften, turn and run. If we were afraid, the fear — of cops? muggers? — was not enough to keep us out of that park at night. Cautious, I suppose is what we were. I guess the sexual drive and the excitement of the outdoor location were just way too strong. We felt more or less safe. We'd heard of an occasional arrest or mugging but they were few. In the face of semi-public summertime horniness it was worth the risk.

Once Randy and I were in the park we'd split up and go our separate ways. **With a background soundtrack of crickets and katydids and the distant car horns or an occasional siren on The Outer Drive, we'd follow the web of moonlit paths into the thicket of trees and men in our horny, hopeful pursuit of late night outdoor sex.** We were rarely disappointed as there were legions of similarly horny sexy gay boys to choose from — a whole baby-boom generation's worth of sex hungry hunters all walking the same wooded paths in the same relentless pursuit. Around any bend or in any open clearing there could be a sexy stranger or group of strangers in any level of undress from an open zipper to completely naked, waiting. I wasn't much of a fan of "zipper-sex" as I called it, preferring my playmates and me to be as close to naked as possible. After splitting up, Randy and I would hope to not see each other again but more than once, we would have to quickly avert our glances as we would come across the other participating in some sort of one on one or group activity. This was startling at first but we got used to it. We'd occasionally acknowledge each other with a "woof" of appreciation or envy for the other's current conquest and then quickly look away and move on through the bush to the next clump of trees and the next guy. There was always another clump of trees and always another guy.

There was also fun to be had during the day farther up Lincoln Park at an area known as the Belmont Rocks. Boys would lie out in the sun behind a low rock wall on various levels of rocks that stepped down to the lake like a linear amphitheater in this semi-secluded northern end of the park. There was a lot of showing off happening there with boys bulging in their speedos and oftentimes letting their penises hang out the leg openings, playing with themselves, stroking their hard cooks for each other and getting off together. With an accommodating self-designated lookout perched on the stone wall, occasionally some guys would actually get totally naked and have sex with each other right there in the broad daylight out in the open on those rocky steps. It was bold, brazen and incredibly sexy doing this in a semi-public location with other naked and gay, tanned and horny guys watching and jerking off. **With the summer sun beating down on all the sexy activity, the waves of Lake Michigan, crashing behind the entire scene, provided an unparalleled dramatic backdrop.**

This was all just part of our unbridled sexual play of the times. For me it had all started quite early and I took it somewhat for granted that it would always be this way. We never really imagined — or at least I hadn't imagined — there'd come a time when recreational sex would be not so loose and carefree, easy to find and… well…recreational. And fun — oh was it fun! I can still hear my Chicago friend Charlie leaning over to me once at some sort of sex event and saying with a shake of his head, in his strong southern accent that years of living in the north hadn't diminished, "Darlin', if straight people knew all of what we are up to, they'd re-fire up the ovens."

1967

FirstSex

IT HAPPENED in my beloved Cherokee Park; the same one I used to drive through with my dad at the wheel, taking choir director Mr. Ellis home post-singing. Eventually I was allowed to ride my bike all the way there if accompanied by a friend or cousin. As I got a little older it was less of a big deal and quite frequently I'd peddle my way out the lushly greened Eastern Parkway to enjoy my favorite park on my own. My parents might not have known about that. I loved the way my British ten speed took the hills and curves as I'd fly by the densely verdant scenery. A bike, for me, was synonymous with independence and freedom. I'd feel free and so alive shifting gears and coursing around my beloved park with the wind blowing through my hair and caressing my shirtless body — it was the one place I dared to be shirtless like the older more athletic boys. I'd pull up my already short high school gym shorts exposing even more leg to the sun and wind, feeling grown-up and sort of sexy while peddling my fifteen year old self around that public place. I had learned my way through the park, over its sturdy stone bridges and around its monuments and came to know all its many circuitous tree-lined roads by heart. **It was a boy's bicycling love affair with a park that shifted into high gear the summer of 1967.**

During those bike trips through the park I had noticed from time to time certain spots where cars were parked along the road for no apparent reason. This stood out to me as odd. And interesting. There weren't any tennis courts around, no playgrounds or any other destination to account for the cars. And yet, there they were. Where were the drivers of these vehicles? And what were doing? There was, upon closer inspection, a bicycle or two chained up to posts here and there. This intrigued me and was probably the first time I'd employed what I came to appreciate as an innate, nearly infallible gay tracking system enabling me to sniff out cruise spots, nude beaches, or other gay sex spots like some horny gay divining rod. It's a gift. Wanting to know more about whatever was going on with those cars and bikes, I rode my bike over to a grassy knoll across the road from one of the spots, hopped off and sat and watched for awhile. Now and again a car would pull up, the driver (always male) would get out and walk over to an opening in the bushes, and disappear into the woods. Once again, this intrigued me. A lot. It happened time and again. Occasionally a man would emerge from the opening in the wood, go directly to his car and quickly leave. I was fascinated. **I was a horny little fifteen year old and watching these men go into the woods aroused something in me. There was something going on in there.** I didn't know exactly what those guys were up to in there but the whole milieu interested me greatly. I returned to my spot on the knoll and to two other similar locations in the park, over and over and each time it was the same. More cars. More men. More trekking off into the woods. More quick departures. Once while perched on my usual spot I saw a particularly attractive shirtless man drive up in a convertible and get out. Did he glance over at me as he headed off into the woods? I wasn't sure but I decided it was time to investigate. I put my t-shirt on, chained my bike to a metal signpost and hesitantly entered the wooded path.

The temperature dropped several degrees as I proceeded on the cool shaded path. I followed it becoming aware of the crackling noise of dried branches and leaves crunching under my sneakered feet and upsetting the balance of this quiet place. I tried to lighten my step as I continued to follow the circuitous path. It narrowly cut its way under the dense forest of trees and through the brush twisting and turning up hill and down. The well-defined path split several times forcing me to choose a direction. I didn't see anything or hear anyone and felt very much alone save for the birds I could hear chirping and singing all around me. Thinking I'd taken a wrong turn, and fearing I was going too deep into the woods, I thought about retreating, but didn't. I continued on, passing a clearing or two. As I rounded a bend into another clearing, I stopped in my tracks as I saw two men, both with their pants down, playing with each other's penises. Out in the open! In broad daylight! I froze. They didn't seem disturbed by my walking in on them and in fact seemed happy to see me. I didn't know what to do but stare, until I nervously turned and headed off down another path deeper into the woods. Nervous and excited and kind of scared, I was torn between running for my bike and pressing on. I pressed on. With my previously ill-defined suspicions suddenly confirmed, there was no turning back. The narrow path I was following got even narrower and less defined as I felt my bare legs being scratched by underbrush and low branches. I worried about poison ivy. I had to push an occasional branch out of my way to continue. Ever more aware of the loud crunching under my sneakers, I tried even harder to lighten my step. The path finally opened up into yet another small clearing. There he was. Just across from me stood the handsome shirtless, convertible-driving man, now also pantless. He was totally naked! Well, his shorts were down around his ankles but apart from that and his sneakers he was naked and his penis was sticking straight out at me. Once again I froze. But this time I didn't run in the other direction. I just stood there, unable to move, heart beating wildly, staring at the beauty of this boldly naked man and his big erection. He gave me a wry smile, looked down at his hard-on, gave it a squeeze and looking back up at me, once again, flashed that smile. I didn't know what to do but I could feel a familiar rising in my own shorts. Still smiling and with a nod of his head, he invited me over. I hesitated and thought about running away. **I was torn in half by equal parts of excitement and fear; I couldn't run and I couldn't take my eyes off of the sight of the naked man now squeezing his erection right in front of me.** He nodded again and this time waved me over. Looking around to see if there was anyone else about, I hesitantly moved toward the handsome naked stranger in the woods. As I got up close to him he stepped out of his shorts and nakedly closed the space remaining between us until we were in touching distance. He reached out and gave my hardened crotch a squeeze as I took in a quick deep breath. I could have cum right then. My breathing got harder as he continued to squeeze me down there. He pressed up against me and I felt his arm wrap around the back of my neck and pull my face to his. He pressed his lips to mine and started kissing me, his tongue probing my mouth. I had never been kissed like that before and in fact didn't know that it was possible to be kissed like that. And what it could do to me. How it could make me feel. I felt scared and pulled away. I was scared, not of the kiss or the hand squeezing my now aching crotch, but scared of being caught with this naked stranger in this outdoor public place. But more than scared, I was excited. More excited than I had ever been in my young life. I did not want this to stop. I was no stranger to masturbation and had discovered several ways to make myself feel something like this at home alone in my room with my homemade porn stash but this was different and so much better. **I wanted this, whatever this was.** The naked stranger started pulling my t-shirt off over my head and I let him do it. I felt his hands at the waistband of my shorts and in one quick move my shorts and underpants were down at my ankles. In an instant I was naked too. Naked! Outdoors! In Cherokee Park! With an older naked man. I looked around frightened that someone might see us but the fear was quickly overcome by the pleasure I was feeling as he began squeezing my rock hard penis. "You're a big little boy aren't-cha?" he whispered in my ear. I had never before had anyone else's hand on my penis and I was sure it had never before been this big and hard. It was almost painful at first but mostly it was pleasure. As he continued to squeeze me down there, it became pure pleasure. And excitement. It excited me even more looking down to see my rock-hard pink flesh being squeezed by his manly fist; to see that special part of me in someone else's hand. I started clenching my buttocks, bucking my hips and pushing myself into his fist over and over again, experiencing for the first time what it actually felt like to fuck something rather than jerk off. It was new and different and wonderful! And felt so much better. He started kissing me again and this time I kissed back, pushing my own tongue into him, trying in a way to...to consume him. He squeezed my hardness down below with each thrust of his tongue above, making my breathing come quicker and quicker. I reached around tentatively touching and then squeezing his muscular butt cheek, my fingertips finding his furry furrow down there, going deeper, moving lower, finding...then touching his...that's when it happened. **My entire body went rigid and tingled to an extent it had never tingled before.** It was like those times alone in my room but much more intense. My butt cheeks clenched and my body started to convulse. My mouth still locked on his, gasped for air. My thrusting increased as my knees weakened and I felt myself begin to unload in his fist, uncontrollably shooting my stuff all over the ground, our shoes, his legs, my legs and my bunched-up shorts and underpants. It was me all over the place rather than the neat little well-controlled puddle I'd typically make in a Kleenex alone in my room while imagining something just like this. I couldn't stop. His kissing and his squeezing made me lose all control of myself as I continued fucking his fist. **Each knee-buckling ejaculation ignited every previously untouched pleasure cell throughout my young inexperienced body, all of them linked directly to my thrusting penis in the tight fist of this sexy older man.** I just kept coming and coming and coming and coming. With his tongue deep inside my mouth, I was still gulping for air and groaning in unbridled ecstasy with my fingers deep between his asscheeks, and his hand squeezing the last drops out of me.

As I finally started to slow down and come back to earth, the man stopped squeezing me, looked down at my dripping cock in his hand and with that same sly sparkling smile said, "Well, little boy, that didn't take long, did it?" Now suddenly aware of my surroundings, the older man with his hand still on my rock hard dick and feeling certain we'd been watched by god knows whom, with his words still hanging in the air above us, I was back to being scared. Really scared! This time there was no passion to override the fear. Just fear. I hurriedly pulled up my thoroughly dampened underpants and shorts, looked around the ground for my t-shirt, grabbed it and ran without so much as a nod back to the naked stranger. I followed the circuitous path back out as best I could while, in a futile effort to eliminate any evidence of our act, I brushed dirt from my t-shirt. I got out of the woods and on my bike and pedaled my fifteen year old ass out of that park in record time. I headed home feeling frightened, though of exactly what I wasn't sure. I had done it! I had finally done "IT!" I loved what had just happened and was excited about what I had just done with the handsome naked stranger in the woods. **I was frightened I suppose of who might have seen us and how they'd punish us**

for what we'd just done together in that public place. Afraid of unseen angry judgmental eyes. Afraid of being arrested and thrown into jail. The shocking embarrassment I'd bring upon my unsuspecting family. Despite the level of fear I was feeling, and even as I rapidly distanced myself from the scene of our "crime," I was already plotting my inevitable return to that scary but exciting place.

1981

The Elevator Party

LOCATED IN CHICAGO'S OLD TOWN, right between The Gold Coast, to the south, and "Boystown" to the north, our apartment in The 2000 Building was perfectly situated to be a gathering place for our friends who mostly lived in one of the three neighborhoods. We threw a big, lavish once-a-year summer party that took months of planning and smaller, spontaneous ones as well.

One summer weekend, toward the end of an Oak Street Beach day with friends, the discussion turned to what to do with the remainder of the night. **I decided it would be a great idea to have a barbecue on the roof of our building.** Randy, not a beach person, wasn't around to consult on this, but it wasn't unusual for either of us to make spontaneous plans without the other's knowledge or consent. I told everyone about our enormous roof terrace that was rarely used. It had spectacular views of the lake, the park and downtown and was convenient to all, so it was agreed on the spot that a rooftop barbecue was indeed a good idea. We assigned tasks for who would bring what and arranged to meet a couple of hours later at the apartment. As planned, we assembled at the apartment and went up to the roof. After a few add-ons there ended up being about two dozen of us.

I left a note downstairs for Randy telling him to come up and join us. As our barbecue was beginning to wind down, he returned home and joined us briefly, but since he had a brand new "friend" in tow, he went right back down to our empty apartment to get to know his new "friend" better. Neither Randy nor his friend made a reappearance at the gathering on the roof deck after that.

As so frequently happens in Chicago, the temperature unexpectedly dropped and we brought the barbecue to a quick end sometime around midnight. Our white glove building was always maintained to perfection so I made sure we cleaned the place thoroughly before departing. Not a crumb was left behind. We even took the barbecue grill, after thoroughly dousing the coals with water and placed it completely out of sight behind a low wall. **As we departed, I surveyed the space to be certain there wasn't a trace of anything to show we'd ever been there.** I wanted no complaints from the building.

As we began piling into the freight elevator I remember my younger-but-somehow-more-mature-friend, Jim, always the voice of reason, say something about how perhaps we shouldn't all get in the elevator at the same time. Something about, I don't know, too many people, too much weight. **You know, the kind of suggestion that kills the party mood just when you're hoping to only move it to a fresh and frisky venue.** It seemed to me to be a lot more fun if all of us just crammed in. And so we did, at my insistence, against Jim's better judgement, all of us, cram in. I pressed the button for the 11th floor. As the elevator descended, something felt odd. An avid bicycle rider, I used the freight elevator a lot, hauling my bike up and down. I knew it well. On this ride something didn't feel right. A "strange slow descent" as Jim puts it, "like dropping into pudding." I could not describe it better. As the 11th floor passed right by and the group of us plummeted, in that "pudding" sort of way, toward the sub-basement, clearly something was very wrong. **I'd always imagined elevator free-falls as fast and harrowing replete with wild eyes, arms crazily grasping at the walls and terrified screams. A plunging to your death kind of thing.** This ride however had been slow and spongy until we eventually settled at the bottom of the elevator shaft. So there we were, twenty some odd gay boys with coolers, half eaten watermelons, bags of food, blankets, folding chairs and tables and who knows what else crammed in and stranded somewhere in the sub-basement netherworld beneath the elegant 2000 Building. We rang the alarm for hours. Jim remembers we were stuck "for maybe 20 minutes" but I'd swear it was longer. With "the voice of reason" in my ear, perhaps it just seemed so. There was no response.

In the meantime, Randy had finished whatever it was he had been doing with his new friend and had sent him on his way. He then decided to join our party up on the roof. He went up. There was no one there. Not only was there no one there but no sign that anyone had ever been there. No people. No tables. No chairs. No barbecue. Not a trace of the party that he was certain he'd witnessed a short time before. Perplexed, he went back to the apartment. No one there. Back up to the roof. No one. He went down to the front desk and asked if a bunch of guys had left recently. Nope. The night desk guy had just recently come on duty, so he hadn't been there for the arrival of these "supposed" partygoers. Randy walked around the building. No one. Finally back up to the apartment and still no one there. It was all very confusing and right out of "The Twilight Zone." A rooftop party of more than two dozen gay boys had vanished. Or had it happened at all? Poor Randy was confounded.

I don't know who finally heard the alarm bell but the building superintendent was eventually summoned. At last we heard the door well above our heads release. Once opened we saw an angry, disgruntled face that had no doubt been dragged out of bed somewhere across town and was now surveying our gay huddled masses. "You know why this happened!" was all this unhappy man had to say. A ladder was dropped down and we were one by one pulled up and hauled out.

Once we had made our reappearance, relieved to find there really had been a rooftop party, Randy was no longer doubting his sanity. Later he wasn't amused when a hefty charge for elevator repair appeared on our next rent bill because "somebody" had decided to "throw a party" in our freight elevator. Luckily that same "somebody" managed to talk his way out of the repair charge. **"The Elevator Party" as it came to be known, became something of a Chicago legend.**

1973 – 1983

Somebody

RANDY AND I had devised, in the days of our cohabitation, a sort of third roommate named *Somebody*. *Somebody* took the blame for all the small household infractions, the kind of things, habits really, that might annoy and cause friction between two home-sharing souls. "*Somebody* left dirty dishes in the sink again last night, we don't want cockroaches," would be something Randy might say to forgetful me. "*Somebody* left a nasty smelling ashtray full of cigarette butts smoldering and stinking on the coffee table... again," would be something non-smoker I might say to smoker Randy.

Somebody had the habit of not cleaning the coffee maker, leaving wet umbrellas or shoes or boots in the entryway, or not taking them off and tracking winter salt stains onto our shiny and prized parquet floors. *Somebody* was fond of dropping cigarette butts into toilet bowls, leaving them there nastily un-flushed. *Somebody* would let the plants go unwatered. *Somebody* would over-water the plants. *Somebody* would hang gym-sweaty t-shirts, socks and jockstraps to dry where they clearly didn't belong; would leave post-sex or masturbation detritus in unexpected places; would never fluff the sofa cushions or fold the afghan. *Somebody*, it seemed, was responsible for every annoying little infraction around our house.

Thinking only with his penis, *Somebody* might drag home the type of person Randy really didn't like encountering unexpectedly on his way to the bathroom. *Somebody* even had the habit of leaving his dildo in the upper rack of the dishwasher, a "surprise " I never became accustomed to.

Yep, *Somebody* had a lot of nasty little habits and got blamed for everything and in so doing, always kept the peace in our household.

1980...

PhoneSex

THE ADVOCATE was a gay publication. Actually *The Advocate* is gay publication but now a mainstream glossy magazine. In the seventies it was more of a counter culture newspaper which had two sections that conveniently separated. The first section printed on white paper was the more political and social part of the publication. The white section, with all the 'acceptable" gay news, arts, culture and advertising, could be left out anywhere for anyone to see. **This section ended up in the living room on the coffee table with Vanity Fair and GQ.** The pink section, with all its ads for sexual products, erotic stories, erotic photos, ads for varied sexual products and lots and lots of erotically oriented classified ads wasn't for general consumption. **This section ended up in the bedroom under the bed with the porn, poppers and lube.**

The pink section's classified ads were mostly ads placed by boys looking for sex. The ads could be pretty amusing, describing all sorts of fetishes, fantasies and sexual situations desired. They were also full of all sorts of abbreviations. **I guess in placing the ads you had to pay by the letter so in order to keep costs down, thrifty gays had abbreviated practically everything.** It was fun trying to decipher them. Randy and I would endlessly entertain ourselves creating hilarious alternate versions using the letters provided, laughing at all our manufactured possibilities. We were so easily amused. Oh how I wish I had held onto just one of those pink sections. They were priceless. Once while perusing the pink section I asked Randy, "Have you noticed how many professors place these ads? They must be an inordinately sexual bunch. Is there something about the teaching profession," I wondered aloud, "that creates such horny men?" In response I got one of his blank-eyed puzzled "What are you talking about?" looks so I showed him ad after ad where guys identified themselves as "Prof." In his all-too-familiar-to-me, everybody-knows-this-but-you-voice he answered, "They're professionals, Michael, not professors, professionals." "Oh, professionals," I repeated processing the information, "pretty much everybody then," and with a shrug, "makes sense." What did I know? I guess it was the upper case 'P' that threw me off. Anyway, I think that was the conversation that actually instigated our little abbreviation game.

Once while scouring the 'pink pages' (as we called them) I came across an ad that stated "F u wnt t hv a gd tm n th phn, cl 000-000-000. Hmmmm, 'phn'? I thought this one through before taking it to Randy. Phn? Phone? Good time? On the phone? What would you...? Wait a minute...sex? On the phone? Sex on the phone. SEX ON THE PHONE! Why hadn't I thought of that? This was the coolest new thing I'd ever heard of. Sex on the phone. Keep in mind this is nearly a decade before phone sex lines were invented. I thought it through and the idea really appealed to me. I was pretty verbal during sex, loving some good dirty talk now and then; I could get nasty with the best of them. I had been told I could get a guy off just by talking. **Being since childhood something of a chronic masturbator, it was easy to see that sex on the phone could be the perfect hybrid of two of my greatest talents: dirty talk and jacking off.** I determined in a flash that this was for me and I couldn't wait until the next time I'd be home alone. So one horny night when Randy was out somewhere, alone in the privacy of my room behind a closed door, I excitedly, and somewhat nervously, with a cum towel, bottle of poppers, a tub of Vaseline and a bottle of baby oil at my side, gave the number a call. To the "hello" on the other end (in Minnesota I believe) in a voice several registers lower than my usual, I identified myself as "Joe." Joe? Where did that come from? Out of nowhere — and quite extemporaneously — I had a sexy new name. Joe. I liked it. I went on to say that I was answering the ad for a good time on the phone. A blaring TV got turned down on the other end and the suddenly sexy voice (also lowered) began asking questions about my looks, my likes, my size (I'm not talking about height even though as I recall he did eventually get around to that as well.) That's all it took. Suddenly we were off! And we got off. Boy was that fun. It was clear my new phone friend had done this more than a few times and he certainly knew how to keep a conversation going. Wow! Who'd have thought? Sex on the phone. I, or Joe, as it turned out, was a natural at this. Like the proverbial duck to water, I waded right in and paddled my sexy-ass way around this brand new sexy-ass pond. I had located a new talent. Joe was one horny fucker and had only one thing on his mind — getting off. After my new phone friend and I had gotten off and he had registered his disbelief that it was my first time — proud? yes! — he asked me if I would like some telephone numbers of other guys he was certain would like to hear from me. Would I? He gave me a list of telephone numbers with some pretty vivid descriptions of what each guy was into. I couldn't write them down fast enough and wasted no time using the numbers. Within weeks I was happily involved in a nationwide web of phone sex buddies. I was hooked. Literally. I was building up quite a long list of my own, with phone numbers, names (first names only, made up, I imagine, like my own,) ratings, sexual preferences, scenarios, fetishes, fantasies and kinks. I made sort of a grid. I was also building up quite a long distance bill but I didn't care, I was having the time of my life!

It became readily apparent that there were some very real advantages to phone sex. I certainly didn't have to look my best. Hell, I didn't have to shower, comb my hair or even check my breath. **Also…and this was the best part, I could be anybody I wanted to be or anybody they wanted me to be.** I had long-lived in a sexual fantasy world in my head; now I could share it. I became a sexual chameleon. On one call I'd be a horny six foot-two blonde-haired blue-eyed smooth college swimmer hung like a horse in a tiny wet spee-do. On the next call I'd be a big muscled hairy top daddy with big low hanging bull balls in a leather jock. I could be almost anybody's total fantasy man. I could indulge myself in any fantasy I wanted and most that they wanted. They wanted a smooth choirboy for an angelic fuck in the church choir loft? I was he. They wanted a beefy, muscular, tattooed, cigar smoking, smelly, un-shaved and un-showered truck driver with a penchant for dirty outdoor rest stop sex, hey that was me too. I was the priest-confessor, the daddy, the wrestling coach, the arresting officer or the army drill sergeant. Whatever they wanted, I was it. I was astounded at some of the things they could come up with. I was astounded at some of the things I could come up with. I had always enjoyed an active masturbatory life which had been contained mostly to skin mags and erotic fiction — porn videos still being years away. Phone sex introduced me to the anything-goes world of shared sexual fantasy and whether it was his fantasy or mine, I was a natural.

I also learned, and this was key, that the phone made it possible, at long last, for a man to fake an orgasm. This talent I developed (and it was indeed a talent) was especially handy when I was ready to wrap things up and move on from a call that wasn't going particularly well. Once I had lost interest in a caller, I'd pick up the momentum, grunting and groaning with a lot of heavy breathing, all the time getting louder and louder. "OH! OH!! OH!! YEAH! YEAH! UNHUNH…YEAH…YEAH…OH…SHIT…OH! OH YEAH! OH MAN! YEAH! FUCK! FUCK! FUCK! YEAH! OH! OHHHH! OHHHHH! OHHHHHHHHHHHHHHHHH!!!!!!!! Wow, man, that was hot. Thanks. Really great! Yeah. See ya. Bye." Then, after striking through that number, it was right on to the next one on my list. I got really really good at faking it years before Harry ever met Sally. I could have taught Meg Ryan a few things about heavy breathing with "loads of technique."

And there was the convenience. I never had to go farther than the arms length to my bedside nightstand. Instead of throwing myself out into a freezing Chicago winter night and standing around a smoky bar or disco for hours in the relentless pursuit of sex, I could stay home in the comfort and warmth of my own home, get high, dial any one of my phone friend favorites and get off with exactly the sex I desired at the moment. Again and again, as many times as I'd like. And…I could indulge in this new perfect pastime and still, not miss Tammy Faye Bakker on TV.

It was also, as it turned out, the perfectly timed pastime.

Yep, my new phone sex pastime was hot, fun, convenient, and it just may have saved my life. You see, there was a bug out there. A bug none of us knew about. A bug spread sexually. It was by this time making its way through the bloodstreams of many unsuspecting gay boys. It would prove to be a relentless killer, sparing no one and was being passed on, through sex, unbeknownst to any of us. Who knows, I might one night have decided to go out looking for sex and in so doing brought the bug home and given that nasty evil latent little critter a place to grow and flourish. And eventually kill me. Instead I had chosen to stay home and indulge myself in my new fun, sexy and as it happened, safe phone pastime, thereby saving my life. Who knows? It's as if the universe sent me phone sex at the perfect moment in the history of gay sex. Certainly it was the perfect moment in my personal history as I had been at the peak of my multiple-partner sexual activity when I started staying home to hang out with my phone buddies. I was having safe sex long before the term was coined. Things just seem to work out for me.

Concurrent with my phone sex phase something else started to happen. I started having a bout of impotence. Curiously, the impotence was only when I was having sex in person. Never on the phone. With my phone friends I was always rock hard but in person, with another human being...limp. This annoyed the hell out of me at the time. Prior to this I had had the 'Old Faithful' of penises, the greatest asset an unwavering top can have. Reliable 24/7. But not anymore. I couldn't figure it out and I didn't like it but the fact was, on the phone I was a steel piston, but in person with another human being, over-cooked spaghetti. I remember thinking "Thank heaven for phone sex." Thank heaven indeed. **In retrospect I was given a two step fail-safe, anti-bug protection device.** Time and again I'd consider my new and unfortunate sexual disability, compare it with the fun of fantasy sex on the phone and decide to not risk the embarrassment of going out and going limp. Instead I'd just stay in and play on the ever-dependable telephone. Even impotence became another way that things just seem to work out for me, and quite possibly, the way the universe chose to protect me.

1951...

The Karma Kid

I DON'T KNOW, "Things just seem to work out for me." Randy would roll his eyes at this, my response to his question as to why I wasn't worried about some upcoming, 'potentially catastrophic,' (to use words he might) event in my near future about which he felt I was insufficiently concerned. He'd heard it god knows how many times before and it was always the same. I 'should' be worried about something but I wasn't (not enough at least) and it infuriated him. **Well, infuriated is probably a bit strong but he just couldn't understand my lack of concern for some situation he'd deemed worthy of more attention than I was prepared to give it.** It drove him crazy. Time and again Randy would show far more concern than I for some potential catastrophe that loomed ahead. When bringing this to my attention, as I would begin to answer, he'd jump in with a hand-stop-sign and an, "I know. I know. Things just seem to work out for you." Then he'd stand in awe as an unbelievable chain of events would somehow, inexplicably and against all odds turn things in my favor as I stood passively by totally unconcerned with all the inherent potential tragedies that had been possible. Shaking his head in disbelief he'd mutter the words, sometimes aloud and sometimes to himself, "Things just seem to work out..." and he would christen me, "The Karma Kid."

Things *did* just seem to work out for me, "The Golden Child," as my Indianapolis friend Malcolm had named me years before. Happily, that's just the way it was. Had always been. My older brother used to call me "The What Me Worry? Kid," a reference to *Mad Magazine*'s Alfred E. Neuman and his famous slogan. I was never prone to worrying about the future and as it usually turned out, when the future became the present, things had usually worked themselves out. I had witnessed in my mother so much worry that seemed to ruin her present and did nothing to improve her future that I suppose I just chose the other path, (or perhaps it wasn't a choice, I'm not quite sure) always believing that things would work out for me. I didn't think to ask for more.

This lack of concern was my nature. I have felt at times that I was somehow supposed to be apologetic about this reality of mine. I am not. I have been ever-grateful and haven't taken these things for granted but I also never thought to question as to the how or the why. It's not as if things didn't go wrong in my life. They did. With some regularity. I just never saw the sense in worrying about it. And in the end, things would work out.

I had never been a person searching for answers to the great mysteries of life; not prior to the mid-to-late-80s at least, when the challenges became far greater and introspection more frequent. Had I been, I'd probably have tried to find a deeper meaning to it all. At the time I didn't. Someday I would. In years to come, I would develop a philosophy (based on years of my own observations and experience) that the universe is, when all is said and done, designed for our happiness. When we accept and are appreciative of what the universe has provided — good or bad — and when we make any move toward our own happiness — doing what is intrinsic to our true and individual natures — we accommodate the universe in its goal, aligning ourselves with it and giving it the ability to work in our favor. **Just as it was designed; for us and our happiness.** Early on I learned the ability to not question the process — long before I began to understand the process — to accept things as they were and not worry about it. Randy was right. I was The Karma Kid. Things did just seem to work out for me.

1980

Old Friends

I LOVED MY CHICAGO COMMUTE. Living on the edge of Lincoln Park, adjacent to the zoo and right on the bus line, to the roar of our beasty neighbors, I'd board the bus in the shadow of the 2000 Building. The bus route wound its way south through pastoral Lincoln Park and onto busy Lake Shore Drive with its shimmering lake to the east and to the west, the towering wall of the high-rise, high-style Gold Coast. As "The Drive" took its dramatic turn east, we'd proceed south onto Michigan Avenue — aptly named, "The Magnificent Mile." Anchored at the north by the elegant grand dame Drake Hotel, "The Mile" proceeded south past the sleek and sexy Playboy Tower — an Art Deco treasure — and the impossibly tall, dark and handsome John Hancock Center. Next came the white marble-clad Water Tower Place and across the avenue, the stone, castle-like fire-surviving Water Tower itself. Then it was past such venerable names as I Magnin and Saks Fifth Avenue and on toward a bridge flanked by The Tribune Tower on the left and The Wrigley Building to the right, creating a majestic gleaming gothic gateway to downtown. **On days when the bridge was up, when it finally descended, it was as if a drawbridge had been lowered, allowing access to a mythical kingdom.** Once over the river, there you were: in the Kingdom of Downtown Chicago, where I was lucky enough to work in its grandest palace — Marshall Field's. I've yet to witness a lovelier commuting experience anywhere. It was a dream journey gorgeous in any season.

Quite frequently Randy and I would take the trip on Saturday mornings around 11am or so. The bus would be filled with ladies of "a certain age," many, old friends no doubt. They were mostly blue haired, sensibly coiffed, sensibly outfitted, sensibly shod and sensibly scented with Estée Lauder's "Youth Dew." We called it "The Yenta Express." **With a day of shopping and lunching ahead, these downtown-bound passengers possessed a no-nonsense uniformity of personal presentation that would suggest one common brain.** And likely, one common destination: Marshall Field's where the workers in the Walnut Room were readying the place to absorb the lion's share of them.

One cloudy Saturday morning Randy and I boarded the bus and, to our delight, it was packed (we never expected to find a seat) with dozens of our interchangeable blue haired favorites. As the lot of us were making our way through the park there was a sudden deafening, crackling din in the bus — a startling, nearly ear-shattering sound echoing off the metal and glass of the vehicle's interior. Unobserved by the two of us, a sudden shower had begun to rain spot the bus windows and, as if on cue, every lady, to a one, in perfect synchronization, had snapped open her purse and withdrawn one of those folded up cellophane rain bonnets. In perfectly choreographed unison after a noisy quick opening-up flick of the bonnet, in that cellophane-caused cacophony, within seconds, every head was clad. The bus, suddenly quiet again, was filled with row after uniform row of see-through pastel plastic bubbleheads, providing a bus-full of cellophane hairdo preservation. It was as if at some predetermined "certain age" women were issued those fold-up rain bonnets and given exact instructions on their usage. Looking out over the cellophaned old lady landscape, and careful to *not* share even a glance at each other, we could hardly contain ourselves.

We loved those dear ladies in their worsted wool suits, pearls, sturdy shoes, smart little handbags and sturdy, uncompromising hairdos. **Our favorite pastime on those trips in, was pointing out our future old lady selves; we found this endlessly amusing.** I'd scan the bus until my eyes fell upon a tall thin fastidious looking starched and studious retired-librarian-type with sharp blue eyes, pinched face, perfect posture and impeccable tailoring. Surreptitiously pointing to her and with a devilish smirk, I'd say, "There she is. That's you," singing the words "iiiiiiis" and "yoooou." Not to be outdone, Randy, searching the old lady-scape would locate a shorter, darker, sturdier, probably curly haired, bossy looking one with her determined brown eyes locked in judgement on some unspecified thing. With a finger point, an eye roll, a nod in her direction and an arch of his eyebrow, he didn't have to say anything. But then with another nod to her advanced years and of course to the four year disparity in our ages, he'd slowly mouth, "And sooner than you think!" I'd shoot him back a narrow-eyed look and we'd break up into mutual spontaneous laughter.

Were we actually prone at the time to imagining the future, I guess we'd have seen ourselves old and gray like our cherished ladies, retired and still the best of friends. We'd ride into town to share another lunch at Marshall Field's and another day of shopping and boy watching in our favorite city. Perhaps later, we'd take in a movie at Water Tower Place and after that, high tea and scones at The Drake. Still later, surrounded by our shopping bags, we'd share cocktails and hors-d'oeuvres at The Pump Room before heading home, exhausted. Back on Lincoln Park West we'd put on a pot of tea, kick off our shoes and rub our aching arches high above our beloved Chicago with its moody Lake Michigan and wooded Lincoln Park Zoo and our dear old aging lions roaring their welcome home.

While we hadn't really given much thought to our actual futures, I think we simply expected to enjoy our senior years together as we had our junior ones. We had found happiness with each other and knew we'd be good together even into our senior years, if no other spouses had presented themselves. Or even if they had. Never for a moment did we give thought to the possibility that we might not reach those ages. **We had quite simply expected to grow old together and hadn't imagined a universe with other plans.**

1981

Nothing Good's Gonna Last Forever

WHILE WE ENJOYED those happy, silly, wonderful times, I don't think we were completely aware of the absolute magic in them. How wonderfully precious they were. We were too young for gratitude and we had no real concept of the future, just perhaps an expectation for more of what we already had. That was 'pretty good enough' for us. We hadn't given a thought to those days not going on forever and were absolutely unaware our lives were about to change in a dramatic, unexpected and tragic way. "Tragic" was a word we'd use to describe a bad haircut or an unfortunate choice of outfit. What did we know of tragedy? Inexperienced in the world of loss, we'd be forced to grow up and face a new and harsh reality we could not, even in our worst nightmares, have imagined.

It was New Years Eve 1980 at our friend Roger's party in his lavish loft on Halstead Street. 1981 was only minutes away and I was moaning on in Randy's ear about how I wished the '80s were over. I was ready for a new edition of the Gay 90s. **"There's something horrible out there Randy. I don't know what it is but I know it's terrible. It's on its way and I wish the 80s were over."** "Oh, Ronald Reagan you mean," was his response. Well yes, there was that. Ronald Reagan was soon to be inaugurated, and there was a not so subtle conservative shift happening in the social environment. While I could feel the cultural landscape changing around us, it was more than that, worse than that. Something — I couldn't put my finger on it — but real nonetheless. "Whatever it is, it is awful. Really awful," I tried to explain but couldn't come up with any concrete reason, just an unrelenting, inescapable feeling of dread. At twenty-nine years old, the first time in my life I was afraid, really afraid of the future. This new pessimism was a total about-face from the eternal optimist I'd been since early childhood. "So, what do you want to do, wish an entire decade of your life away? You'd be forty for Christ sakes!" Randy, who'd turn twenty-five in three weeks, spat out at me, "Or a decade of my life for that matter." And then after a long drag on his cigarette, "You're not gonna make me ten years older. Thirty-five? Just kill me." He was right of course, about wishing away the years, but his light attitude regarding my new darkness couldn't allay this newfound sense of doom that I simply couldn't shake.

On that precise New Year's Eve, thirty years since my unexpected conception, had I been given the opportunity to fast forward until whatever it was that loomed ahead of us had passed, I think I'd have done it. Or better yet, hit the pause button. Freeze my life before the clock struck midnight and 1981 had a chance to commence. Keep our magical Chicago existence, our great apartment, our great friends, our great sex lives, our great jobs, a democrat in The White House and our pretty near perfect life just as it was. Forever. Given the choice to keep things as they were — freeze our lives (even our rent) right in the middle of what I now consider to have been our golden age — I'd have jumped at the opportunity. Especially with this newfound pessimism. My fear for the future and the potential loss it would bring was that overwhelming and still, unexplainable. Perhaps it was simply that things as they were, were just too perfect. I was too happy. Too content. How long could it stay that way? **I was afraid of losing it all, really afraid, probably for the first time, that things were not going to work out for me. Or, and I couldn't explain this either, for any of us.**

It was later that year, in the summer, when I read a small article in The Chicago Tribune about gay men in New York and San Francisco contracting some mysterious illness and dying from it. **A disease that was**

attacking only gay men? How is that possible? All of them getting the same rare form of skin cancer or some rare form of pneumonia? And they were dying? All of them? I knew from that moment I was doomed. We all were. Whatever they had done, I had done. Wherever they had done it, I had been there too. Whatever infected them would surely infect me. And Randy. And all our friends. And lovers. And fuck-buddies. It probably already had. Venereal disease ran rampant through the gay community. We all knew this. We'd all had it. Randy and I like so many others, would, as a matter of habit, go to the VD clinic to be tested every four to six weeks without fail. In fact, the workers at the clinic knew us by our first names and loved us (and our antics — think Laverne and Shirley go to the VD clinic.) They assumed we were lovers because we were always tested together. And treated if necessary.

Now, if there was some new gay angel of death, it would certainly not pass over the two of us. When would it visit our door, this new horror? We waited and worried as more and more cases were reported. And more and more deaths. We were suddenly and unwittingly thrust into a serious and uncertain new reality guided by fear and ignorance of this new malady. Our lives and the lives of most everyone we knew would never be the same. Life had to go on but it would go on changed. Forever. Every day, every decision was colored by this horrible new reality, this new probability of our lives being foreshortened. **Our carefree attitudes, especially toward sex, and unrelenting optimism for a better tomorrow faded, only to be replaced with an escalating feeling of dread and a diminishing sense of hope.** The specter of suffering and death lurked around every corner ominously waiting to snatch us, all of us, from our previously happy, hopeful lives and bury us six feet under.

It seemed almost no one, beyond or own, cared. We were poised to fight this thing pretty much alone under the largely contemptuous and judgmental glare of the ever more conservative non-gay public. They, along with the press and especially our government would take a stance somewhere between unconcerned and derisive. While President Reagan ignored us, and we were already dying by the thousands, they were making jokes and laughing about us in White House press briefings.

The new and horrible disease which was to become the overriding specter of our lives was alternately referred to as "The Gay Cancer," GRID (Gay Related Immune Deficiency) or the 4H Disease (because it attacked Homosexuals, Hypodermic users, Hemophiliacs and Haitians.)

The joke within the gay community went:

"What's the hardest part about getting AIDS?"

"Trying to convince your parents you're Haitian."

Gallows humor but ya gotta laugh through your fears.

Later, that's what they would call it: AIDS, Acquired Immune Deficiency Syndrome. It was an all-powerful four letter uppercase acronym that would rule our lives forever more. It was poised to wipe most of us out, attacking our immune systems and our entire way of life. In some circles, AIDS was casually and derogatorily referred to as the "gay plague."

1982

Speaking Of Gay Plagues...Ronald

WHILE ON A Marshall Field's business trip to San Francisco I met Ronald. He was young, charming beyond his years, tall, smart, sexy and impeccably dressed. He was also jobless, aimless, a liar, a user and a thief, but I was thinking with my penis so I failed to notice any of these shortcomings. He seemed totally smitten with me and that ego-feed was enough. He was also great sex, accommodating my every whim. Ronald was very big on little gifts — a pen here, some cologne there — small surprises he'd always show up with. The honeymoon was on and against all good judgement, I brought him back to Chicago with me. What I thought would be a visit of about a week or so turned into something a bit more open-ended. He seemed intent on staying in Chicago and I couldn't manage to get him to move on. Did I mention the sex? Well it was a lot of fun and I just couldn't quite bring myself to throw him out even as it became clearer and clearer that he was using me. He wasn't contributing in any way to the household and he showed no interest in getting a job in Chicago or returning to San Francisco.

Randy didn't like Ronald from the start — he loathed him actually — and saw him for exactly who he was. Randy also didn't like having a third unwanted and unplanned-for roommate. I actually wasn't so thrilled with it either but, there he was. I couldn't blame Randy for his unhappiness with the situation. Or for my lack of a backbone. My having brought Ronald into our home and my inability to get him to leave drove the first real wedge into our relationship. **It was a mistake that I'd look at years later, mystified by my own actions; and inactions. Did I mention the sex?**

For some time, Randy had been toying with the idea of getting a place of his own. He'd never lived alone and I'm quite certain had wondered how it would be to *not* live with someone who was pretty much ruled by his penis. Ronald pushed Randy off that ledge. That and a lease which was coming up for renewal with a sizable rent increase was enough to make the decision for him. We both found new apartments. Randy moved into his and I, not more than eight blocks away, I into mine; thank heaven we bought that second food processor. Ronald came along with me but shortly thereafter I finally managed to get rid of him. Once I began to (inevitably) lose interest in him sexually, with my sex-clouded vision suddenly cleared, I was able to see how dishonest he was and how I'd been used. I packed his bags and moved him out. A month or so after Ronald's departure came the bills. He'd opened charge accounts in my name at Saks Fifth Avenue and Lord & Taylor and had spent liberally. Wonderful boy. I began to think of all those "little gifts" he'd show up with and wondered if he'd stolen them. Especially the hand carved wooden toothbrush. Lovely as it was, who gifts a toothbrush? Ronald's departure also saw the departure of my cherished home made porn collection that I'd created during my horny childhood years and hidden away in my bedroom closet. I was never certain he took that box full of my adolescent sexual yearnings but its having disappeared at the same time as Ronald, seems to make him the prime suspect.

Ronald was a major learning experience for me and the greatest test to my relationship with Randy. Generous, forgiving Randy and contrite, repentant Michael survived dishonest, freeloading Ronald and became even better friends in the process. I came to understand that a good relationship broken and then well-repaired, becomes stronger and better equipped to stand the test of time. "The Ronald Incident" as it came to be known, in the end, served Randy well as it gave him the impetus to move out on his own, and test the waters of his new maturity and autonomy. He found out he could live on his own far better than he'd imagined. **This new level of independence and self-reliance would serve him well for the challenges that lay ahead.**

1983

Making My Exit Right Along With The Golden Age

MY ARRIVAL at Marshall Field's aligned with the tail end of what was arguably the golden age of department stores. Lucky I was to have barely caught it. For nearly four years I excitedly walked through the doors at 111 State Street every morning, thrilled to be entering that great fabled palace of commerce. **It was my dream job; Marshall Field's was my dream store and I was enjoying my own personal and professional golden age.** The industry however was changing quickly from a merchant driven business to a Harvard MBA one, driven by numbers and statistics rather than instinct and experience. As the sands of commerce shifted, the entire nature of the animal changed. One by one, departments that didn't produce their sales per square foot were dropped in favor of more profitable fashion, cosmetics and accessories. Not coincidentally these were the departments that set one store apart from the other and gave each company its individuality. For those of us who were in love with department stores, it was a recipe for retail disaster. Along with this unhappiness came an inevitable series of corporate buyouts and takeovers. Stores started gobbling up other stores. And worse.

Not long after Randy and I had made our individual moves, with the evil specter of that new "gay disease" threatening to tear the fabric of our lives, something else sinister was approaching. As I was just settling into my new home (and Randy into his) there was a hostile takeover of Marshall Field's. With the threat of being liquidated by a "corporate bandit," in a matter of weeks the company was saved by a "white knight" and instantly changed hands. All this in the course of a week's time. **The stabile work environment that supported the dream job that I somewhat naively expected to last forever, and the life plan I had built upon it, abruptly ended.**

With the intervention of Mr. Kelly, the new ownership, deeming store design in Chicago redundant, offered me a job in their New York headquarters. It would be a lateral move with no increase in salary. While I'd always held onto the hope of living in New York someday, the timing just didn't seem to be right. And the cost of living so much higher. My ego also got in the way as I had come to be something of a star at Marshall Field's and in New York I'd just be one more in a large stable of designers. Mr. Kelly was a bit disappointed that I turned it down. "Michael, I really wish you'd taken the New York job but since you didn't, I do not want you leaving the protective umbrella of Marshall Field's until you are up and running with your new company," he generously offered. "Take all the time you need while you're still on our payroll to get established," and then he added, "please don't tell anyone else in the company about this conversation." Of course, at his request, I kept his generosity to myself, until now.

My first client was a store design firm in Columbus Ohio that hired me as a designer for a new department store in Tokyo. After working for them a few weeks they offered me a Vice Presidency and a move to San Francisco, my other favorite city. A little frightened about being out in the professional world on my own, I made the decision to leave my beloved Chicago. Once again I'd be heading off to a new job and a new life in a new city leaving my best friend Randy behind. And once again I'd be doing so with the hope he'd eventually join me.

Our friend Roger gave me a huge going away party in his loft. Randy presided over it and roasted me while he was wearing his signature white button down Oxford cloth shirt, this time with an enormous "L" he had embroidered on it, "Laverne" style. At the same time, there were more and more reports of gay men dying. Some in Chicago and other cities but the lion's share were either in New York or San Francisco.

Shirley was moving on, right into the belly of the beast.

My Louisville friend Margaret made the drive to the West Coast with me in my brand new company provided BMW 318i. I had never been a "car person" but I had to admit, I felt pretty special driving this graphite colored "ultimate driving machine." This would be my second cross country road trip and a much more luxurious one than when I did so with my friend Steve in his less than reliable old beater not so many years before.

In San Francisco at thirty-one years old, I'd once again be on my own in a new city. Knowing no one. Though I was excited to be moving to San Francisco, a city I'd come to love, I would be leaving my beloved Chicago and Randy with great reservation. **I had thought myself settled in Chicago for a lifetime and suddenly I was pulling up stakes and abandoning my favorite city, my best friend and most of my old dreams.** I had to accept there'd be new dreams farther west in San Francisco, "Everybody's Favorite City," and allow for the possibility and the hope that it could become my new favorite.

Once relocated, I was instantly homesick for Chicago, Marshall Field's and especially Randy. I couldn't do anything about the first two but I could work on Randy. I would try my best to convince him to leave Chicago as well. Describing San Francisco in lushly romantic and sexy detail, I hard-sold him on this new city by the bay much as I had done with Chicago before ever he'd seen it. It seemed to be working. He started to become excited by the idea of San Francisco, and the thrill of a new adventure. Since he wasn't particularly happy with his job, he agreed the timing did seem right to leave Chicago. It was time to try something new, he decided, and if I said San Francisco was all that great then, well, ok. I'd been right about Chicago. He was in. What could go wrong? We decided at whatever time he wrapped things up in Chicago, he'd put his things in storage and make his way west. Once again we'd do the roommate thing only this time he'd move in with me in my one bedroom and we'd eventually get a bigger place.

Well, that was the plan.

SAN FRANCISCO

It

was

rapidly becoming

a place

trying its best

to put on a brave face,

desperate

to retain

its old sparkle

while preparing

to die.

CHASE

1993

Into The Past...

I FELL IN LOVE WITH CHASE the night before he died.

It was the evening of October 22, 1993. As I sat on our bed in our Boston apartment with my back against the wall, in my "human chair" position, arms wrapped around Chase's skeletal frame leaning up against me, I could hear his mumbling something. He'd been mumbling a lot recently, sometimes making sense sometimes not. I leaned in as he repeated himself. Facing away from me in his soft, shaky voice he said, "You're so comfortable." I leaned in closer. "You're so comfortable I'd like to take you to the past with no judgement." I wrapped my arms a little tighter and leaned in, to get my ear closer to his mouth, as I wasn't quite sure of what I had heard. He repeated his words, making certain that I heard him correctly, "You're so comfortable. You're so comfortable I'd like to take you to the past with no judgement." I pondered the words, "No judgement," as an unexpected warmth washed over me and a tear escaped my eye. **I tightened my hold on Chase's frail body and finally, on the eve of our tenth anniversary, just in the nick of time, I fell in love.**

1983

What's New?

IT WAS THE EVENING of October 23, 1983. Being new to San Francisco, I was having a drink alone at my favorite neighborhood gay bar in Pacific Heights. The Alta Plaza, a "skirt and sweater bar" was not far from my new apartment at Broadway and Franklin Streets. My new home was also in Pacific Heights. Sort of. "Pacific Heights-ish" as I liked to call it. Pacific Heights is a quite small sought after San Francisco neighborhood whose borders are stretched by those (like myself) claiming to live there.

The bar that night was crowed as usual. **With Madonna's "Holiday" or some other gay-favorite-of-the-day playing on, the waitress with her tray held high above her head pushed her way through the thicket of men saying "Make a hole, make a hole boys, make a hole."** Just as she passed I was approached by a boy making good use of the "hole" she had just created while moving through the packed space. He introduced himself and asked if I'd like to join him and his friends. I was delighted not only because the boy happened to be really cute but also being new to the area, I had no friends. I was introduced around as we joined the seated group of four or five and was quite happy to be meeting new boys in my new home. There was nothing significant that I could have attached to that moment other than having made new acquaintances and the promise and hope to see each other again in the future.

The future played out about a week later at the Friday post-work cocktail hour at Sutter's Mill, a downtown "business suit" gay bar. I was standing alone in my Brooks Brothers' business drag, again not knowing anyone, when a smiling semi-familiar face approached. This was a first for me to actually recognize a face in a San Francisco bar. And a first to be recognized. He was tall, handsome, dark-haired, green-eyed and immaculately dressed. He had a slightly exotic look I couldn't quite put my finger on but was at odds with his otherwise preppy presentation. His face beamed with recognition but I couldn't quite place it. He introduced himself as "Chase" and reminded me that he was among the group I had met at the Alta Plaza that evening a week before. Oh, of course. I was delighted to have finally been in a bar in my new city and actually have known someone. We chatted and had a couple of cocktails together. He was funny and smart and the conversation was light and easy. I invited him to dinner and he enthusiastically accepted. Where did we go to dinner that night? "Funny the things you remember." Chase would have said Caffe Sport but I'm not sure. "And the things you don't." I do remember his responding quite positively to my brand new BMW as we drove off to wherever it actually was we dined that night. "318i? I didn't even know they were out yet," he'd said with what I took to be a touch of envy, while stroking the dashboard. He responded just as well to my Pacific Heights(ish) location as we pulled into the parking garage tucked under the building. As the automatic garage door closed behind us, we shared our first kiss, a long probing passionate one, right then and there in the dimly lit garage.

Upstairs in my apartment, a rambling white stuccoed space with high ceilings, some beamed, some vaulted, and a breathtaking view of the bay, and the Golden Gate Bridge, I dimmed the lights (dimmer installation being the first order of business for any gay man moving into a new place) and we shared another kiss. **I put on my new favorite album, Linda Ronstadt's *What's New?* a lushly (and as it happened appropriately) romantic collection of old standards with the likes of "Someone To Watch Over Me" and "What'll I Do?"** To the flashing pulse of the beacon from Alcatraz regularly lighting the living room, we proceeded to get to know each other much much better. During all the kissing and groping and clothing removal, Chase confessed that it was he who had sent the boy over at the Alta Plaza with the invitation to join his group. He had spotted me earlier that evening and had put someone else on the job. So this had all been masterminded. And delegated. Successfully. I was flattered. With Ms. Ronstadt sweetly singing on, we made our now naked way to the bedroom that the two of us would share from that night forward.

That's right. He never left. I wasn't in the market for a relationship but Chase it seemed, was. He'd fallen in love. I didn't know whether it was me or the Brooks Brothers suit, the BMW, the Pacific Heights address or perhaps a combination of all of those things but something made it instantaneous. For him. It wasn't that way for me and I suppose that says more about me than it does him. He was quite attractive, we were sexually compatible and I enjoyed being with him but I just wasn't at that point in my life, relationship oriented. I fully embraced my single-hood and my notorious inability to sustain sexual interest for any length of time, always preferring the promise of whatever might be just around the corner. In a brand new city with so much fresh new meat around so many fresh new corners, I wasn't in any hurry to change things.

It was only Chase's persistence which kept him from being just another of a long line of guys I'd have sex with once and subsequently crumple and toss their telephone numbers away. That wasn't going to happen to Chase. **He pursued me in a way I had never been pursued; my ego and I were no match for his irrepressible force.** It was also the early years of the AIDS epidemic and there was a lot of coupling going on. During that first week together he'd occupy my every waking minute. It was a perfect storm of timing for us. That evening at Sutter's Mill was the first time I'd purposely gotten all dolled up in my business drag to go out to a business bar. That evening Chase was celebrating his final day of work at an old job and it would be a week before he'd start his new one. He had time on his hands, as did I being in a similar circumstance. I had already left the company (long story about a short employment) that moved me to San Francisco and having just started a job search, I easily put the search on a short hold as we spent the week together. It was a week devoted completely to each other. We covered San Francisco and its surrounds in "The Beemer" as he liked to call it. He showed me his city and I showed him mine. We'd drive through The Castro with the sunroof open and Patsy Cline singing at full volume. As we crossed the Golden Gate and coursed our serpentine way around the Marin Headlands high above the Pacific Ocean. The honeymoon was on.

By the end of that first week, when we decided he should move in with me, it was a purely perfunctory decision as he really already had. When we went to his apartment to pick up his things, his "things" turned out to be a few pots and pans and whatever clothing and toiletries he'd not already brought over. That was it. When I registered my surprise at his few possessions, he said that he'd had some bad investments and had sold most of his things off to cover his losses. I accepted the reasoning, convenient enough for me as I had plenty of everything. Still in the back of my mind I thought, "Not even a mattress?" There was mystery surrounding this young man which I think served to make him even more attractive. To enhance the air of mystery, "Chase," I learned during that first week was in actuality, Christopher Michael Leon. "Christopher? Why Chase then," I asked. He replied, "My father always told me, 'Chase is to Christopher as Bill is to William.'" OK. **I came to learn (a little too late) that there were three distinct personalities attached to those three different names:**

Chase was the social guy. Chase always had a little too much to drink when we'd go out. With a swizzle stick stuck behind his ear, Chase could get a little bawdy, tell silly jokes (he had dozens of them,) and criticize the bad hair, bad bodies, bad clothes, bad grammar and bad manners of the less fortunate. Chase was the life of the party. And to some…just a little obnoxious.

Christopher was the business guy. I rarely saw Christopher and was grateful for that. Christopher could be hard and ruthless, especially in his negotiating skills. Christopher, upon entering a meeting, would place on the conference table a contract he'd been sent on which he'd emblazoned the words "HA! HA!" across the top for the person seated across from him (who sent the contract) to easily read and be intimidated. Christopher was direct and unvarnished. But still somehow, polished. He was all business and never lost an argument. Christopher occasionally slipped into our relationship (primarily during disagreements.) When he did show up I did my best to give him wide berth.

Mike was the nephew and cousin. I only heard the name "Mike" when his drop-dead gorgeous younger model-to-be cousin Jack would come to town from San Raphael, where the family lived. And with the exception of an occasional reference to one parent or the other's advice or life instruction, he would never ever talk about them. It was clear they were a subject totally off limits. Mike was where all the mystery lived.

The funny thing was, none of these three was the guy I had met and with whom I spent that first wonderfully happy week. That guy was the sweet, silly, happy-go-lucky young boy who was gracious, passionate, caring, funny, fun in bed and from all indications a total romantic who was head over heels in love with me. The one who had nicknamed me, "Little Treasure." That's right, Little Treasure. And I started calling him, "Chaser." So, inadvertently, to further complicate things, I added yet another name to the list. **Chaser was the guy I asked to move in with me. Unbeknownst to me at the time, the others, whom I'd yet to meet, came along with him.**

1983

Chase & Randy & San Francisco

BY THE TIME RANDY was ready to make his move west, Chase had already entered the picture. "Ya know, I really did like living alone," he said over the phone as we discussed the situation, "seriously, I don't mind at all. Will you help me look for a place?" So Randy came to the city and stayed with us in the Pacific Heights apartment until he found a suitable apartment of his own. And a job.

Randy and Chase, right off the bat were not the best of friends. They weren't enemies or anything close, just not friends. There was a rivalry for sure and an obvious overlap. Each had to share me with the other. They were always kind of wary of each other and how each affected the other's relationship with me. Not long after his arrival, after having found a good job, Randy met and fell in love with the younger, sexy and adorably incompetent Warren. Together they found a place in "The Planets" above The Castro. Neither Chase nor Randy were particularly sad to say goodbye to each other, but I was sad to see Randy head off to his new life. It had all happened so fast.

Having also fallen a bit in lust with the younger, very sexy and adorable Warren, I had come down with a rather nasty case of boyfriend envy; in truth, I was more attracted to Warren than to Chase. Warren was so damn boyishly cute and so damn sexy — my favorite combination. We had the wrong boyfriends! Warren was so *not* what Randy was usually attracted to. No, the happy go lucky Warren was much more my type. The analytical businessman Chase, now there was a boyfriend for Randy. In retrospect, though I hadn't thought of it at the time, I suppose we had found each other's perfect lover. And perhaps we'd found a little of each other in our new choices. That actually makes sense of it all. **This was also the first time for either of us to have a lover and a best friend; a whole new landscape to navigate.** Randy was busy with his new love, his new home, his new work and his new life and the same was true for me. We'd meet occasionally for dinner or brunch and speak on the phone several times a week staying in constant touch as always. We now, however, had our own individual pursuits and several San Francisco hills separating us.

1974...

BeachSex

MY FIRST NUDE BEACH experience was at Black's Beach near San Diego on my trip westward in the '70s with my wonky Steve McQueen. The beach lay at the end of a long circuitous walk and oftentimes precipitous climb straight down a steep mountainside cliff. Though sometimes dangerous, it was nevertheless a spectacular hike winding its way through scruffy coastal vegetation and stands of Cala lilies and fields of California poppies. As I made the downhill journey, it was in breathless anticipation hoping to find, at last, the beach I'd conjured up in my teenage dreams fueled by the nudist magazines I'd purchased as a young boy. I wasn't disappointed. There was sun, sand, and naked people as far as I could see.

Now about twenty-three, I felt instantly at home having visited this sunny place over and over, in my adolescent jerk-off fantasies. I'd finally made it. And…they were playing volleyball. There was always a volleyball game somewhere in the pages of those prized magazines and now, having so often fantasized myself in such a place, here I was, finally surrounded by naked people, and some of them actually playing volleyball. Let me tell you, there's a lot of bouncing going on in one of those games.

As we walked further along the beach the naked people became naked boys. Only boys. We had made our way to the nude gay beach. While I had certainly fantasized about such a place and had even written a few stories (for my own naive sexual gratification) my young self hadn't realized that such a place might actually exist. Scores of naked males dotted the sand, fully exposed to the sun, many with their legs spread wide for any appreciative passer-by like myself. Behind the beach were winding paths through scruffy vegetation being traversed by naked boys and men, their penises both hard and flaccid bouncing in front of them. There were dunes with little windswept hollowed out pockets where other naked men had set up camp, some sunning themselves and others laying there stroking themselves and waiting for a visitor or two or three. There were naked boys all over the place, walking, standing, posing, masturbating with and for each other, having sex and all of it right out in the open, observed only by the sun above. And, of course, me. **It was the dream-come-true, heaven-on-earth, gay-boy's-paradise that had obsessed my childhood imagination.** A great outdoors place full of naked and gay boys. And naked and gay me. I had finally made it.

There would be many other nude beaches and beach-like experiences after Black's Beach. Near Indianapolis were the quarries, big man-made holes in the earth filled with water. They had previously had been solid stone, quarried and carried away as Indiana Limestone, a precious material used for monuments and buildings in cities everywhere. Certain areas around the rim of these quarries were designated gay areas where all the above-mentioned activities occurred. With the quarries' proximity to Indiana University there were lots of horny college boys sunning their naked selves and I in my mid-twenties was ready, willing and waiting. During my Indy summers, I would visit the quarries quite frequently.

In Chicago, as I've already mentioned, there were the Belmont Rocks, an out of the way area near Lincoln Park right along Lake Michigan where gay boys would lie out and even have sex in the sun on the stone ledges stepping down to the water.

By the time I made it to San Francisco, in my early thirties, I had a fully developed sixth sense for sniffing out gay cruising areas and especially gay nude beaches. I am proud to say I discovered all of my favorite beaches in the area all on my own. My favorite such beach in San Francisco proper was Land's End. It was at the foot of Geary Street quite literally at the land's end. It took a bit of circuitous hiking down winding paths through all sorts of lush, fragrant vegetation — the fennel and eucalyptus almost overwhelming. You had to find a little opening in a fence, and once through it, follow the path further down the hill. When you reached a sign that shouted its upper-case warning, "CAUTION! CLIFF AND SURF AREA EXTREMELY DANGEROUS" and then in a quieter, more confidential, lower-case cautionary, "People have been swept from the rocks and drowned" you knew you were close. I always loved that sign imagining that, San Francisco being what it was in those days, a poet must have been drawn to the city but ended up, due to lack of finances, a sign painter who had applied his poetic sensitivity to a sign that, in the hands of a less artistic soul, would have simply commanded, parent-to-child, "STAY OFF THE ROCKS." **It was the "…swept from the rocks…" part that got me, in its almost romantic, whispered, lower-case**

warning. Down below, past the aforementioned dangerous rocks was a lovely little cove populated by gay boys all boldly naked and having a wonderful time together — see Black's Beach…above.

Once while I was enjoying the sun and fun there I saw, making his way down the path from above, a young naked boy. He was someone of indeterminable background, the type of person you see and wonder what in the world different ethnicities came together to create such a stunning exotic creature. **Adding to the vision of this naked boy descending with a dancer's grace onto the beach was the armful of Cala lilies he carried.** Now most Californians know that the flowers which grow wild along the cliffs and pathways along the shoreline are protected, not to be pulled up or cut down. It didn't bother me that the boy had transgressed this rule because the presentation he created coming down that pathway was so sublime I could never have found fault with it. There was another gentleman present however who was not so forgiving. He marched right up to boy and, arms flailing, began to admonish him about picking wild flowers. I watched the gentle boy's sweet face fall as he absorbed the loud, unnecessarily harsh, full-throated criticism. The boy was brought to tears and left standing there as the gentleman, his work complete, marched himself back to his beach spot. The boy stood in place for a moment, surely shaken by the assault, with the contraband lilies still in his arms. What to do with them now? I watched as he gracefully walked toward the water. He stopped about twenty or so feet from the water's edge and lay the Cala lilies on the sand. He then walked out to the water's edge and knelt down. I watched in curiosity as the naked boy (on his hands and knees…a lovely sight) methodically began to dig a small trench from the water's edge to where he had left the lilies. At the end of the trench he began digging a hole, deeper than the trench. Once the hole was deep enough, he one by one, placed each long curving Cala Lily stem into the hole, perfectly arranging them. As I watched the waves come in and rush up the trench to his flower arrangement, I realized the boy had dug a 'vase' for the flowers and a trench to systematically water them with each wave from the ocean. He stood up, admired his work, saw that his clever irrigation system was working and moved away from his Cala creation as gracefully as he had done everything else. I felt as though he'd given us a thoughtful gift and perhaps an apology, for his flower infraction.

Fog is always an issue in the San Francisco area so if Land's End was fogged-in, I'd head up to Baker's Beach, also a nude beach, but being a little more open and public, not quite as frisky as Land's End. If Baker's Beach was fogged-in, then I'd try Marshall's Beach just a little to the north of that, and a bit friskier than Baker's. Both Baker's Beach and Marshall's Beach had gorgeous views of the Golden Gate Bridge and a discernible gay presence. **If all of those beaches were fogged-in, it was time to head over the Golden Gate Bridge to the Marin Headlands.** I'd happily drive the winding one way coastal road way up above the Golden Gate with it's spectacular views of the dramatic, jagged coastline around every bend. Looping down and around the headlands, sometimes inland and then back out along the ocean, I would find Black Sand Beach. It was a long gorgeous and true to its name, black sand beach and at the southern end was the gay area which was always a fun destination especially beyond the rocks. Further up the coast was Muir Beach. It was a lovely, what I would call, "granola beach" as it had a naturist sort of population. Not much sex or exhibitionism there but a gorgeous beach and a perfect little unexpected authentic English Pub called The Pelican Inn for a bite at the end of a long beach day. You could order Shepherd's Pie and believe you were in The Cotswolds rather than Marin County. Still farther up the coast, just south of Stinson Beach was another favorite called (and I loved this) Michael's Beach. I sniffed that one out as there were unexplained parked cars along the Shoreline Highway. It lay well below road level and required a steep climb down the precipitous rocky cliffs. It was always worth the effort. A protected cove, Michael's Beach was definitely a beach for exhibitionists who were all over it. Showing off and getting off.

If all else failed and everything was fogged-in there was one last possibility. I found this place quite by accident on a particularly foggy day when there was sun to be found nowhere. I had continued driving north, past Stinson Beach just enjoying the drive having given up hope of finding any other beaches when the road had taken a turn inland. Just as I was contemplating turning around, I came to a spot with another group of unexplained parked cars. While well inland with no possibility of a beach, still, curious about the cars, I pulled in and parked. As I had done many times before in such situations, I waited to see if anyone else arrived and eventually someone did. It was a man who exited his car, crossed the highway and disappeared into the vegetation carrying a beach bag and a folding beach chair. Though there was still no sunshine, this was enough for me. I followed, finding the path the man must have taken. It took me through an open field of wildflowers and eventually to a split rail fence with a locked gate. I hopped it and followed the path into a cool forest. Only a few minutes into the forest I arrived at a clearing. To my surprise I found, surrounded by tall evergreens, a lake sparkling in the sunshine. Yes, sunshine. Around the rim of the lake were all sorts of naked men laying out in the sun. Yes, the sun. Though it was still a foggy day, there was, as if by magic, a clearing in the fog right above the lake with the sun shining through it. Floating in the middle of the sparkling lake was a big log and on it, or at least trying to stay on it, were two lithe, wet and glistening naked boys rapidly rolling the log with their feet, in a desperate attempt to stay vertical. **I had found a quiet tucked-away oasis of gay boys laying around sunning themselves naked with a sexy naked show going on in the middle of the lake.** Some were playing with themselves and some were having sex and all were enjoying the quiet, remote, peaceful environment with the occasional splashing sound of one or the other boy slipping off the log and hitting the water. I went back many times to that gorgeous sunny lake. I learned in time it had a Native American name (that I no longer remember) which meant "Lake Hole In The Sky." Apparently no matter how foggy the day, there was always a reliable patch of blue, a magical "hole in the sky" right above it.

1984

The Walking Wounded

I MOVED TO San Francisco at what was perhaps the worst moment in gay history to do so. I found a city already changed from the happy, electric, sexually free gay mecca I had known as a vacationing visitor throughout the seventies. **It was rapidly becoming a place trying its best to put on a brave face, desperate to retain its old sparkle while preparing to die.** The seams were showing and a rabid relentless monster was pushing its way through them, determined to destroy all those in its path, turning a playful, sexy city of joy into a cheerless, frightened city of suffering. And death. We were all just waiting to die as we watched our friends perish one by one. The City had been for so many years, home to a growing gay generation of hope and possibility and then, almost overnight, it became a broken-hearted hospital ward to a shrinking gay generation of fear and despair. It was the mid-eighties and the AIDS epidemic was growing exponentially. **There was a war being waged against gay men and we were losing it; proof in the**

walking wounded who were already everywhere. The Castro, perhaps the gayest neighborhood in the world and formerly a place with an around-the-clock party atmosphere of youthful sexual abandon, was suddenly studded with young old men. They were walking with canes, these formerly vital athletic gay boys were walking with canes. And barely so, oftentimes leaning against a friend — there was always a friend — as they painstakingly made their slow and halting way up the Castro hill towards Market Street, ghoulish ghostly reminders to all the other not-yet-stricken others, of their own inevitable futures. It was all so at odds with the sounds of Donna Summer or Gloria Gaynor happily spilling out of the open doors of one of the many bars just as they always had. How could they continue to sing on like that? As if they're was nothing happening? Didn't they know? "I Will Survive?" Seriously? Have you looked around?

Passing one of the new invalids valiantly trying to maintain the normalcy of his life amidst all of the horror of that horrible disease, you'd briefly glance into the recesses of his hollow eyes and wonder if you knew him. You'd try to recognize him in his frail altered-by-the-disease state. Not recognizing him, you'd feel sorrow and empathy but at the same time, a welcome sense of relief would wash over you realizing, if he wasn't familiar to you, then, in all probability, you hadn't had sex with him. And he hadn't infected you. Along with that sigh of relief, immediately came the inherent guilt attached to such a selfish thought.

Being gay in those early days of AIDS meant becoming a master of compartmentalization. You had to be aware and vigilant of the horrible specter of the disease and help your comrades wage the war against it, but you couldn't let the war rule your life. You had to continue, to 'soldier-on' as it were, ignoring as best you could, the storm gathering all around you.

You still had to pay your rent so you went to work and tried to do your best. But you'd sit in your office staring at the wall wondering if the nausea you were experiencing was just some bad tuna at lunch or was it a new malevolent opportunistic germ determined to end your life the way it had for that big beefy bearish guy who lived in the apartment right down the hall; or the sweet-faced young waiter down on Union Street who used to deliver your Saturday morning breakfast with a flirtatious wink and a sexy smile; or the tow-head blond in the building just down the hill who would sun himself naked on his roof and (you were quite certain) get hard just for your right-handed gratification. He was gone too, along with all the formerly healthy, happy, sexy, short, tall, fat, thin, hunky, ordinary and extraordinary others who were quietly disappearing all around you. You'd compartmentalize the thought, try not to think about the dead and dying or this new queasiness in your core and you'd go back to work.

You still went out to the bars and tried to pretend it was pre-summer of '81. This wasn't easy when all around you were faces showing the ravages of an illness nobody really understood. You would look at one of these familiar, formerly virile young boys, suddenly old, all skin and bones and swallowed up by his used-to-be-tight-fitting-muscle-t-shirt and jeans. You'd feel an overwhelming sense of sadness at this tragic transformation, knowing this would probably be the last time you saw him. At this, you'd contemplate your own potential future and pending mortality. Deciding you'd probably be next, you'd look away, compartmentalize the thought, override it with a "What the fuck," shrug of your shoulders and order another round of drinks.

You still did drugs and still shook your ass until way past dawn. But…you'd wonder if the sudden ache in your foot was just too much dancing or your new Adidas sneaks. Or, perhaps, it was some sort of treacherous opportunistic infection that caused a numbing peripheral neuropathy; like Jerry's, or Jeff's, or Jason's, and a harbinger of your own personal horror ahead. You'd compartmentalize that unsettling, inconvenient thought as well, and head off to the after party.

And you still had sex — thoroughly modified sex if you were smart. And strong. And when you were having this new modified 'safe-sex,' experienced as you were, you always knew the moment when he really wanted it. If he was the verbal type he'd be begging for it. You were always certain, once you'd worked him into a heavy-breathing, lustful frenzy of desire and need, when he was ready for you to fill that need. Your need to fill him was just as strong and you were just as ready. You'd used your mouth and tongue and fingers to get him open, wet, wanting and hungry for it. The pulsing head of your penis was right there, pushing into him, a needy knob teasing his needy hole. It was finally "the" exact moment to slip it in and take take him to total ecstasy…and yourself along for the ride. It was at that exact, fever-pitched moment, you'd have to stop. "Where's the condom?" If you happened to find where it had slipped between the sheets while you'd been rolling around, or had given up altogether and located another one, you'd desperately and against all odds, try to keep the momentum of the moment up. And his legs. And your erection. You'd try to keep that up too. Even if you were semi-successful at this, you'd still have to tear the condom package open (with your teeth probably though you'd even been warned against that.) Then, you had to unroll that ugly, rubbery, kinda smelly piece of murky-translucent latex onto your proudly pretty, happily exposed semi-erect penis, making it look like a bank robber in the movies with a stocking over his face, smashing down all his handsome features.

Worst of all, amidst all this condom-mania you'd try like hell to not think of the reason why you were doing it. You'd try not to think of terminal illness. You'd try not to think of your suffering friends dying from that illness. You'd try not to think of friends already dead from it. **Your only defense in that moment then, was putting it all out of your mind and pretending the disease didn't exist. Warning! Danger Ahead!**

Forget about AIDS and you forget about safe sex. You'd dial back your brain, if you could, at the absolutely wrong moment to do so. With your brain taking a back seat to your mindless needy dick and perhaps aided by weed, poppers, or some other altering substance, reasoning was out the window and along with it the specter of AIDS. **You were ready to take a chance, spin the cylinder in a game of sexual Russian Roulette and pull the trigger, banking against the odds, that you were not about to perform a lethal act on yourself or someone else.** At that moment, somehow, the risk seemed worth it. At that particular moment, to recapture the ecstasy you'd enjoyed, without fear, for decades, you would take the chance. You'd compartmentalize all that negative thought, forget about that awful condom you couldn't find anyway and the disease it represented. You'd take another hit of poppers and in the resultant rush, your mind would wipe itself clear of thought or reason and you'd just stick it in. As you always had. Without a thought or care, to satisfy your lust (and connect to a simpler, sexier time) you'd shove yourself deep inside, skin to skin, and pleasure-ride your way to heaven. In a moment of unbridled ecstasy you'd enjoyed without worry time and again, buried deep inside his hungry squeezing pleasure-giving hole, without any more thought, having a hunger of your own, you'd give that final thrust and release yourself into him, as you had done so often before, filling him with that precious milky-white, life-giving part of yourself that now just might be lethal. **The regret and worry would come later.**

All that compartmentalizing led to a lot of denial and pretending, not only with yourself but with your friends. Pretending, when your friend showed you a recently sighted dark spot on his leg you said, "It's just a bruise," though you'd seen that kind of 'bruise' before. Pretending another friend's soaked bed sheets were the result of a nightmare, or a recent "hot humid night," you'd deny the truth about the sheets and the reality of San Francisco nights. When you heard your friend's coughing spell and he asked if there was a cold "going around," you lied a little white lie and said, "Yeah. Everybody's had it." You found yourself pretending, with your friend at his first hospitalization, that everything was going to be alright; it wasn't going to be alright and you knew it. But still you pretended. And lied. **And when he got sick, really sick, you helped him and supported him and continued to lie to him and yourself, again with those ridiculous words that no one has ever really believed, "Everything's gonna be alright," and knowing it wouldn't, you would stay with him and love him and support him and care for him. And continue to lie to him.** Then, once home, you'd scan the bathroom mirror looking for your own first 'bruise.' And, finding one, you'd lie to yourself.

1985

Time To Move On

SO, the San Francisco I'd arrived in was a substantially changed place from the one I thought I was moving to. It was no longer the mythical Emerald City destination my inner-Dorothy had yearned for. **The party was over.** Nothing was carefree anymore. It was no wonder that when a relationship appeared, I grabbed it. It was "safer," a word on everyone's mind. While we were committed to focusing our sexual desires on one another, Chase and I were realistic enough to know we couldn't be exclusive, so, like many, we made a sort of monogamy pact. We could fool around with other guys but only 'safely.' Mutual jack-off. That sort of thing. With the challenges I'd faced staying hard in a condom, I'd already moved in that direction anyway. We would then save unsafe penetrative sex for each other only. Keeping us healthy. Assuming of course we could trust each other to be safe and assuming neither of us had already been infected as there was no HIV test yet. The other benefit of a relationship was, if god forbid, one of us did get sick, we'd have the other to take care of us. **Self-preservation was moving up the list of reasons to not be single.**

Chaser and I were good for each other in many ways. We were sexually compatible. He had the creamiest, smoothest, whitest, most translucent skin I had ever seen on a man. I loved just looking at him. And touching him. And those green eyes. Both of us tidy and neat, cohabited quite well together. We liked the same movies. We loved to dine in and loved to dine out. We loved to entertain. Brunch became our specialty. We traversed every square mile of the entire Bay Area together. We'd hop in the Beemer for road trips up and down the coast. I loved the beach but had always considered it a solitary pursuit. He was way too pale for the beach. Perfect. He was also good for my ego. I'd never had a boy so into me. Walking down Castro Street together, his hand in my back pocket, a small wet spot would develop in the hardened bulge in his jeans. Every time. You can't fake that. I was impressed…and flattered. We became a couple and for a while we rarely let the outside world in. And that was good as, when we did, things would begin to unravel.

I couldn't help but notice that in social situations, my adorably sweet Chaser wasn't as adorable. Or sweet. There was an edge that hadn't been apparent during all the time we spent just the two of us. Socially, Chaser would morph into someone I didn't quite recognize. He'd become caustic and judgmental. While he was funny and could get lots of laughs, his humor was chronically based in observations on the personal appearance and demeanor of others, something I suppose we all do from time to time but it seemed to dominate his social conversations. I didn't admire it. And, add just a little alcohol and it'd become worse. Much worse.

I didn't enjoy this guy, who I determined to be "Chase" nearly as much as "Chaser." It became apparent that "Chaser" was reserved only for me and no one else would ever meet him. Sad, really as he was best of the bunch. But no match for the dominant Chase.

San Francisco turned out for me to be a stepping stone. The company that moved me there changed hands (yes again) and I was left jobless. Well, in truth they'd offered me a position back in Columbus, Ohio where the home office was located but after having reluctantly left my beloved Chicago for San Francisco, I was certainly not going to move to Columbus. I wasn't crazy about the new job I eventually found down in Hayward California so when a job offer with a move to Boston came along, I decided to look into it. Chase had grown up in the Bay Area and was ready to live someplace else and had recently taken a vacation to Cape Cod and Boston. He had loved it. It was also one of the cities I'd targeted as a child. So a mere two years into my San Francisco stay, I interviewed for the job at The Talbots, got it and Chase and I made plans to move to Boston.

This time, Randy, comfortably settled into his new life with Warren, would not follow. We stayed committed to keeping in touch and we knew we would. We'd just be talking over a longer distance — rather than a few hills and the breadth of a small city, there'd be an entire country between us. This would be my first move to a new city without the prospect of Randy's following at some point. It wasn't an easy choice to make but we had our own lives now and mine seemed to be taking me away from my best friend. This saddened me no end and almost kept me in San Francisco, a city that hadn't quite worked out as I'd hoped, but the excitement of a new job and a new city, with a new partner — a new life really — balanced things out and drew me East.

BOSTON

We

were

inmates

of a virtual

death row,

each silently

awaiting

his

certain

execution.

1985...

Cedar Lane Way

SINCE BOSTON had been on my wish list of cities (New York, Chicago, San Francisco and Boston) I'd targeted as a boy, it seemed this was then, the right opportunity to try it out, especially since AIDS had rubbed the luster off my shining city by the bay. I moved to Boston on my own at first. Chase remained in the west until I could get us settled in the east. **My home environment has always been important to me and finding apartments is another area where things just seem to work out for me.** The charming little carriage house in Louisville; in Indy, the Art Deco Admiral; The sumptuous 2000 Building in Chicago, and the sprawling Pacific Heights apartment in San Francisco all just sort of presented themselves. With each move and each new city, the pieces would fall into place and I'd find myself in the perfect living situation. The universe was always accommodating and kind. Until Boston. Boston would prove to be a bit more challenging. For the first month of the move there, The Talbots had placed me in a corporate apartment in the Back Bay which was really lovely but I had my eyes on Beacon Hill. Not understanding the rather unique way things work in Boston I rather naively walked around that historic neighborhood looking for "For Rent" signs. There were none. I soon learned that unlike San Francisco where you'd just find a for rent sign on an interesting building in an interesting neighborhood, go in, have a look and rent it on the spot. In Boston, things were different. There were realtors and their agents to be dealt with, appointments to be made, applications to be filled out and approved, and of course, fees to be paid. This was an entirely new landscape but I had to remind myself that things do generally work out for me.

I can no longer say how or where but at some point I met a couple, Ed and Bruce who lived in a gorgeous — absolutely to die for — garden apartment on a tiny little Beacon Hill street named Cedar Lane Way. Not a street actually, but a "lane way" a term I'd never even heard before. I coveted the apartment and Cedar Lane Way, the most charming little street I'd ever seen. Ed's being in real estate explained to me why theirs must have been about the best apartment in all of Beacon Hill. I now knew what I wanted.

Ed happened to know of a tiny townhouse becoming available just down the street from their place. Having seen Cedar Lane Way and imagining life on it, I was in. The charming little house, on that charming little street, though a real "fixer-upper," was also a real find. Ed thought since he knew the owner, he could slip me right in to see it before it became available on the general market. The owner, Hardy was an old retired doctor. He was an eccentric — Beacon Hill is full of them — and lived next door to the tiny house. Hardy's much larger brick house which faced Mt. Vernon Street was actually attached to the little brick house on Cedar Lane Way by an added-on, greatly in need of painting, clapboard connector building. Ed got me in. I fell in love with the little house. It was a charmer and apparently so was I as Hardy seemed to fall in love with me. We hit it off. The little house had essentially one room per floor, each with a fireplace. There was a tight winding staircase and rather than a traditional handrail, it had a heavy nautical rope held onto the curving wood paneled wall by brass nautical fittings. It even had its own gas street lamp right outside the front door. I was in love. The fixer-upper part didn't bother me much as I had never shied away from this kind of challenge. I remained a firm believer in "potential." Ed negotiated a below-market rent because of the condition of the place and perhaps because Hardy had taken such a shine to me. **I signed on the spot and tried to ignore an indefinable, somewhat acrid fragrance my sensitive nose had picked up.** I wasn't overly concerned, certain that once I gave the place a good cleaning the 'fragrance' would disappear. I left out that small detail when I enthusiastically called Chase to let him know our good fortune and our new address.

With Chase and our stuff still out on the west coast, I bought a mattress and had it delivered to 30 Cedar Lane Way. Having easily cleared the most difficult hurdle of moving to a new city, I happily moved myself and my clothes into the charming little townhouse. Not everyone was happy with the ease with which I had accomplished this task. A long time Beacon Hill resident and Boston Blue Blood Brahmin real estate "honcho" (a word he wouldn't use) was furious that an "outsider" (a word he would use) had slipped into that hallowed neighborhood and scooped up such a prime property. "Outsider," I would find, was a word a lot of Bostonians felt comfortable using when referring to anyone not born in the city. Or in this case not born in the neighborhood. This was one of the many things I was to learn about Boston and its Bostonians, especially ones of the Beacon Hill Variety. The honcho pitched a fit and let Ed and me know in no uncertain terms that the lease "would not stand." He went directly to Hardy whom he was certain had been coerced into renting to me against his will. Hardy, bless him, took up for "the Professor" (the nickname he'd given me, I don't know why) and the lease remained intact. And just like that I was a Beacon Hill resident.

I threw myself into the place cleaning and repairing anything I could before Chase made his way east. Once he had, he wasn't quite as enamored with the charming little townhouse as I was. I saw potential. Chase saw work. While he loved Beacon Hill and Cedar Lane Way and even the little house, in theory, he wasn't ready for the fixing and cleaning involved. "My mother told me that if I was successful, I wouldn't have to do stuff like this," he'd say while steel-wooling the filthy metal trim on the kitchen counter. "Well, I guess you're just not that successful yet," I'd reply, "keep scrubbing!"

There was also that smell. While I'd tried my best to clean it away or even ignore it, it wouldn't let me. It was much too insistent. Chase (whose nose was even more sensitive than mine) had picked up on it right away. With a face registering something somewhere between concern and disgust, barely over the threshold, he said, "Do you smell something?" before even putting his bags down. I had to admit I did. And it seemed to be growing, assaulting both our noses. It wasn't so much a smell really as it was a feeling — a kind of stinging sensation that took up residence in your nose. It was acrid and ammonia-like and after burrowing it's way in, stayed there and made your eyes water. It seemed mostly to emanate from the bathroom which was in that shabby in-need-of-paint connector building that attached our little house on Cedar Lane Way to Hardy's big house on Mt. Vernon Street. Our bathroom was right above Hardy's floor below. Clearly the smell was coming from Hardy's house and that floor below ours.

I'd met Hardy's dog, a big enthusiastic Doberman named Lotah, Tah for short. "That's the thing about dogs, Professor," Hardy would tell me, "they need one syllable names. A simple name for a simple animal." Tah would gallop up and down Cedar Lane Way happily peeing on everything, including at least one understandably disgruntled neighbor. As she would be trying to enjoy her morning coffee and the *New York Times* at a table in her partially sub-grade kitchen with its grade level open window, a strong urine stream would come shooting in, drenching her and her newspaper. More than once. We, the residents of Cedar Lane Way, were indeed aware of Tah who spent a lot of time outdoors, but none of us knew about the cats, indoors. Lots and lots of cats. As it turned out not all of them still alive. The ones who were among the living apparently were allowed free reign over Hardy's place. Apparently without benefit of litter boxes. I believe the cats' primary residence was the floor below our bathroom in the little connector building. Separate from Hardy' residence it was convenient enough for Hardy and the cats, but a disaster for us. **The stench would travel from that** lower floor like some sort of evil specter, up into our bathroom and into our little townhouse permeating every molecule it crossed. You could almost see it. The second you entered the house it was there to greet you and immediately establish itself in your nostrils; like Hardy's cats had peed directly in your face.

It became clear the cats weren't going anywhere and neither was the stench. Chase, on the other hand was out. This was particularly difficult for me as I had put so much time and effort into the place. Hell, it wasn't 'particularly difficult,' it was a horror show! I loved that little house and I loved Cedar Lane Way. And Beacon Hill. Worse yet, Hardy had taken me aside early on and with "Professor, I'll sell you that little house one of these days and I won't charge you the crazy prices they're gettin' for things around here," he'd burnished onto my brain the dream of being a Beacon Hill land owner. And at the right price. That dream was falling victim to a bunch of damned cats. Beacon Hill had found a way to squeeze "the outsiders," out. The cats had won. I was devastated, forgetting for a moment that things usually just seem to work out for me.

Unbeknownst to us, Ed our realtor friend had a plan. He'd felt bad about the situation he'd (unwittingly) put us in and had devised a way out. He and his partner Bruce had decided they wanted to stop renting and buy a home in Boston's up and coming, increasingly gay South End. They'd found one they loved and were ready to move. That meant they would be vacating their gorgeous garden apartment just down Cedar Lane Way; the one that I had already decided must have been the best apartment in all of Beacon Hill. We'd visited Ed and Bruce several times and were both in love with the place. We jumped at the chance. It was easy getting out of the lease as the old Brahmin real estate "honcho" was there to snatch up the property. Let him deal with the cats. Hardy was disappointed in "the Professor." Having not taken a similar shine to Chase though, (nor Chase to him,) he seemed to adapt quickly. Ed and Bruce relocated to the South End and we moved from number 30 to number 24 just up and across Cedar Lane Way.

24 Cedar Lane Way was all about discovery. From Charles Street, the main street of Beacon Hill, just a half block up the hill on Mt. Vernon Street you'd turn left and discover Cedar Lane Way a street so narrow you could stand at its center and nearly touch the brick on either side of this shady quiet "lane way." **Tiny townhouses and gas lamps charmingly lined one side and on the other, garden gates set into high brick walls with trees and greenery spilling out over the tops.** Opening the large wood gate at number 24 you'd discover an ivy-walled "hidden garden" bursting with flowers. The two-level space, divided by a stone step and path, set on a diagonal wrapped around a dark brown painted clapboard building with a pair of ceiling to floor Palladian windows. An ancient wisteria, seemingly unsupported, stood over five stories high at the far end of the garden, centered between two windows of the red brick residence and provided a canopy over the entire width of the garden. Up about four steps, also on a diagonal, and through the door you'd discover the original kitchen of the house which was now a wood beam ceilinged great room serving as kitchen, living room and dining room. Under your feet you would discover the original 150 year old wide plank, worn-smooth, richly honey-colored pine floors. There was a large brick fireplace equipped with all the original built-in, still-intact colonial era copper kettles and iron doors. You'd walk through a brick archway to the rear of the apartment where the guest room, bathrooms and laundry room were. You'd then discover a curved bluestone stairway taking you below through an arched painted brick tunnel to discover the original cellar that was now the master bedroom complete with stone walls, wood-beamed ceiling and windows looking up and out into the garden. **Discovering 24 Cedar Lane Way was discovering a piece of heaven right in Beacon Hill. Heaven was home.**

1985...

Bi-Coastal Friendship

RANDY AND I stayed in touch in those days before cellphones, texting and email, by running up our long distance phone bills. I visited when I could. Occasionally work took me back out there as well. We remained each others' confidants and best friends. It's funny that no matter how he had matured nor how self-reliant he'd become, Randy still seemed to come to me for guidance and I guess, perspective. In some ways I think I may have been his other mother. He would talk to his mother in Louisville perhaps even more than with me. I'm sure his mom was just as used to hearing "Michael says…" as much as I was used to hearing "Mom says…" We would talk endlessly about our individual lives and the challenges we faced with our work, and especially our partners. We of course always shared our mutual appreciation of the absurdities in our respective lives and the world at large. Though we were both solidly pursuing our new lives with our new significant others, I think perhaps we each, without actually saying so, had one foot out the door, knowing we had each other if things went too far awry. We'd commiserate a lot and laugh endlessly, sharing all the mutual silliness we found in our new relationships. "He did it again," was an opening I'd become accustomed to, ("he" being Warren,) "last night when I opened the dishwasher, there they were, the knives, sharp end up again. That is grounds for divorce, right?" he'd ask as we'd share a laugh. Or he'd lament the dichotomy of Warren's blue collar attributes (something Randy had always found attractive in his men) with his own white collar needs, "You know, you really want them to have a little dirt under their fingernails but still know what fork to use at dinner." **Sharing laughs as we always had, was critically important at a time we'd also share our individual fears for an uncertain future where friends and acquaintances were continuing to get sick and were dying all around us.**

1986

Crane's Beach

THAT FIRST LONG NEW ENGLAND WINTER finally melted into spring and then, at last, summer. **Summer and New England are a perfect marriage.** The coast with its jagged cliffs and cloudless skies, sandy beaches and sweeping dunes, seagulls and sailboats, lobsters and lighthouses, grand houses with wide wraparound porches and tiny grey shingled cottages with crisp white shutters, pink roses and multi-colored hydrangeas and flowers, flowers, flowers everywhere, is, to my mind, the absolute quintessence of summer. **No place I've ever seen wears the season better.**

Crane's Beach, just north of Boston is one of the most expansive of New England's beaches and a personal favorite. It is near Beverly, Massachusetts and was part of the old Crane (plumbing) Estate which included a huge Baronial mansion on a hill that is now used for events. It is a seemingly endless white sand beach that, if you walked far enough (about forty minutes) became a gay nude beach (you knew that was coming) and well worth the effort. To me at least. My friends might have had a differing opinion. As we'd trudge along, to their complaints, I would remind them that if they ever put an ad in a personals column, it would surely include, "long walks along a beach" among their likes. This was always met with eye-rolls and groans as we'd press on, reminding me exactly why I preferred the beach as a solitary pursuit.

Leaving the crowds behind, on that long beach walk, you'd discover a pristine white sand beach devoid, for quite some time, of people. After a while, where the empty beach began to be dotted by a naked male here and there, you knew you were at the start of the gay beach. The more populated nude area lay just ahead. The sandy stretch would become studded (sorry) with more and more naked and gay boys. You could spread your things out there or take up residence behind the beach in its gorgeous windswept dunes. There you could be among all the requisite naked men with all the requisite naked activities. It was a sexy Sahara Desert with horny naked boys crisscrossing the sandy hills and valleys ever in the pursuit of sunny beach sex. Around every dune, or at every turn or dip in the terrain there were opportunities for sandy sex out in the open, under the blazing sun, with a stranger or four, right in Beverly, Mass adjacent. Or at that point was it Ipswich? I was never sure. **There were also small pine oases where, out of the sun, you could cool yourself and at the same time heat things up with someone else who'd come to the sheltering shade with the same two purposes. You'd happily do with each other as you wished while standing on a cool pine needle carpet, watched only by an occasional deer sharing the peaceful surroundings.** Crane's Beach, being all sun, sand and sex and as far away as one could get from the judgemental eyes of those easily offended or not so inclined, was one of those heaven-on-earth spots. For me and those like myself, who loved sex and beaches in equal measure, it was a perfect place.

Except, that is, in greenhead season. At the height of the beach season, mid-July to mid-August, the hungriest flies on planet earth, green eyed little monsters descend by the millions upon Crane's Beach, relentlessly determined to devour everything in sight. Everything with blood that is. They are voracious, mean-spirited little creatures, showing up in biblical numbers and intent on destroying your day at the beach. And your skin. No matter how beautiful the weather or how fun the sex, being eaten alive by these nasty hungry flying beasts was simply not worth it. So, when approaching the parking lot if I saw a sign reading "Greenhead Season — No Refunds" I would simply turn the car around and drive away, disappointed and horny. You'd only ignore that sign once. I suppose I could relate to those angry hungry little fuckers. If I had a lifespan of only a few weeks I'd be irritated too, and I'm pretty sure I'd hungrily devour everything in sight.

If you did disappointingly drive away from Crane's Beach because of the greenheads or if you were at the end of a perfect beach day, you could cap it off with a visit to the apple farm nearby. Headed home post-beach you'd pass an old weathered barn set way back off the road. It was rustic and crusty, perfectly bleached-out to a silver-gray, and all that a New England barn should be. Surrounding the barn was an apple farm with row after perfect row of identical looking apple trees growing in every direction and abundant with their red ripe fruit ready for picking. You had to stop for any one or more of a number of fresh apple products: apple tea, apple jams and jellies, apple cider and most famous, the apple donuts. Sugary, absolutely delicious, fresh-from-the-oven apple donuts smelling of ginger and cinnamon, warm and soft in your hand. You couldn't pass them up.

1986

Beach Bash

WHILE I LOVED Crane's Beach and all my nude beaches in California where I could be in my naked and gay glory, surrounded by like-minded souls, not all my nude beach experiences were good ones. Shortly after moving to Boston, while at a party I heard a conversation about a nude beach in South Boston. Not only was it a nude beach but there was apparently a wall separating the beach by gender. A designated all male nude beach? I'd never heard of such a thing and though it was the depths of winter, I was already there. With my love of nude beaches and love of naked men, though knowing nothing of South Boston, I knew, first chance I got, I'd try it out. So, one early summer day I rode my bike to "Southie" for the first time, located the beach, and found the "Men's Bathhouse." In the bathhouse as I was undressing the only other person I saw was a priest also undressing. Practically the moment he was out of his Roman collar and black pants the bald pink and portly naked cleric was hard and surreptitiously wagging it at me. I wasn't interested but the event did set a certain tone for the afternoon.

I headed out to the beach and as promised it was full of naked men. Only men. There was a long wall down the left side of the beach with presumably, women on the other side. I located a spot and spread my beach towel out and lay down. Lying on my stomach I could see naked men everywhere legs spread wide. There were some men surreptitiously playing with their hard and semi hard penises. It was all oddly covert though and something about it just didn't feel right. There was no casual open sexuality like I was used to in the relaxed nude beaches in California. Instead what was going on in this place felt inauthentic and dishonest. I began to feel increasingly uncomfortable and out of place and considered leaving as there was nothing sexy or fun about this new-to-me naked place. **I couldn't escape the feeling I didn't belong.**

Before I could gather my things, I heard in the distance someone yelling. I looked up, as did everyone, to see a red-faced, thoroughly sunburned whiter-than-white stocky young man, naked of course, yelling at the top of his lungs. Everything seemed to stop and sharpen and all focus (including my own) shifted to him. He was quite a distance away and pointing. "Faggot," he was screaming. "There's a faggot in here!" still screaming, "We got a fucking queer!" **Oh good god he was pointing at me!** I was now the focus as all eyes shifted my way. Again as loudly as he could, "There's a faggot in here, we got ourselves a fuckin' faggot!" With that he stopped pointing and started running. Toward me! Not knowing what to do, I got up just in time to feel a fist connect with my face. He was beating me in the face, fist after fist, right there in the middle of the beach filled with naked men watching — only watching. **No one, including the previously weenie-wagging priest, came to my aid or even seemed to acknowledge that anything out of the ordinary was happening.** The basher was still screaming at me as I fell back to the ground, naked of course, with blood spurting from my now broken nose. I was confused and disoriented. As he continued to hurl homophobic expletives at me, I didn't know what to do but lay there bleeding into the sand. As he turned and made his triumphant march away, I began to pull myself together to the sound of his continued obscenities being hurled indiscriminately to anyone who'd listen, the focus having been shifted back to him, away from me. Without one man acknowledging my beaten bloody presence, I began to gather my things. I got my naked and gay ass out off the beach and out of that hostile place as quickly as I could with the sound of his continued screaming fading behind me. Rushing through the bathhouse, blood pouring out of me, I hurriedly put on my shorts and sneakers, grabbed some toilet paper, stuck it in my still bleeding nose and rushed out to my bicycle.

Still shaken, I rode away as quickly as I could from South Boston, a neighborhood that, I found out later, is legendary for its bigotry and homophobia. I never knew what gave me away. I was simply lying there minding my own naked business — I thought. Perhaps I was just a new face (an "outsider") so suspicious eyes were already on me. Perhaps I was watching too intently all the covert sexual activity I saw around me, trying to figure out the place. I never knew, but something made it apparent that I was a gay interloper who had invaded the sanctity of their determinedly non-gay environment, upsetting its balance and in so doing, threatening to expose the existence of its potentially pernicious, homo-erotic underbelly. As such, I "didn't belong" there and had to be dealt with. Truly, I didn't belong there and I never went back to that beach or to South Boston. Ever.

1986

Boston On The Downside

WHILE CHASE AND I found heaven behind our garden gate, the other side would present some challenges beyond that one horrific South Boston experience. My job turned out to be a horror show. The CEO of The Talbots and the sole reason for my move (hoping for another Phil Kelly/ Marshall Field's sort of relationship) resigned the day I started. The very day! Had I lived then as I do now, assessing signs from the universe — I mean really, he resigned the day I started — with Chase still in San Francisco, I'd have turned and run. I didn't though. **I pressed on, even with Charlotte the boss-from-hell.** It was quite clear she did not like me and I did not like her right back. I was surely her employee-from-hell. My first review was something out of Mary Tyler Moore's first episode. "I've noticed," Charlotte stated resolutely glancing up over the top of her reading glasses, "you avoid confrontation." With my typical sense of pride in a job well done I replied, "Well, thanks, you know, I try…" Abruptly cutting me off mid-sentence and not allowing me to complete a thought that was clearly anathema to her, she fired back, "That was NOT a compliment!" Charlotte and I were clearly on different pages.

On one of my first weekends in Boston I did a little sightseeing with a helpful coworker. He took me across the Charles River to Charlestown to see the Bunker Hill Monument. I had chosen it because of what I perceived to be a similarity to Coit Tower in San Francisco. I was feeling a bit homesick for that other city by that other bay, on that other coast. It was a mistake. From Coit Tower in San Francisco you see a bright glistening pastel landscape rolling over hill after sun drenched hill. It's a sparkling white Mediterranean fantasy dotted in every season with greenery and flowers. From the Bunker Hill Monument all I could see was a flat, endless pile of bricks. Or at least that's how it looked to me. On that cold sunless January day, there were no leaves, nothing green in fact. All I saw was concrete gray or brick brown. I was instantly depressed at the thought of having left an evergreen city that gets even more lush and colorful in the winter, for this bleak colorless place. **As I was leaving the monument, a "trolley" of sorts — more of a bus actually, dressed up to look like a trolly — in sharp contrast to the beloved (and real) San Francisco cable cars — added to**

my transplanted state of depression. The night we went to a concert at Symphony Hall, having been to the Opera House and Davies Hall in San Francisco, I happily anticipated an evening of glitter and glamour. I was sadly disappointed. Never had I seen such a lackluster, colorless, under-accessorized bunch in my life; overcoats, boiled wool jackets from The Talbots and sensible shoes. No sparkle. Not a jewel to be seen.

Owning a car in Boston and especially Beacon Hill was no less horrifying. Not only is driving in Boston a blood sport but, at the time, BMW meant "Break My Window." I had had the "Beemer" delivered from San Francisco directly to my job in Hingham and took it to the nearby BMW dealership to be fitted with an alarm system — unnecessary in San Francisco. The close of business for the dealership that day, saw me driving off in my newly security-equipped BMW. Their first order of business the next morning, saw me driving it back in with a broken window, destroyed dashboard, and missing Bose sound system. **My BMW was broken into on its first night in Boston.** Parking on the hill was just as hideous. I who was accustomed to having a garage space right under my San Francisco apartment building (automatic garage door opener and all,) would circle Beacon Hill, after a long day of work, for as much as an hour, looking for a space. My BMW which was sparkling new in San Francisco, in Boston was unrecognizably old and covered in salt and dirt, snow and ice. I'd often walk right past it. The car was continually vandalized and when some lovely person named Vito decided to engrave his name across the hood in 18" high letters, it became clear to me that the car had to go. I needed it however for the long reverse commute to Hingham for my horror show of a job that also had to go. Things were deteriorating fast.

Worst of all, Chaser seemed to have stayed in San Francisco and sent the other personalities to Boston. The sweet charming boy I'd met and fallen for made only rare appearances. Chase and Christopher had pretty much taken over. We became very social in Boston and made a lot of friends. Chase had always been outgoing, even gregarious, and he hit his stride in Boston. The social environment there seemed to nurture a combination of Chase (the social guy) and Christopher (the business guy.) Those two personalities seemed to morph into a single sometimes funny, sometimes biting, upwardly-mobile, 'Chase-topher' (oh my god another one) perfectly suited to his new job and this new social landscape that seemed to be mostly about social standing and social climbing. Problem was, I had to live with this new guy who barely resembled the one I'd met out west. **He'd become exceedingly judgmental, of nearly everyone and especially of me; he was as upwardly mobile as I was not.** A basic incompatibility grew between the two of us. I think the difference was so obvious to others that quite frequently friends would take me aside and ask why we were together. If was difficult expressing back then, when I was so close to the situation, about my having fallen for someone who now didn't seem to exist. Sex dried up and that was as much my doing as his. I still hadn't developed the ability to sustain sexual interest over any length of time. In anyone. Chase's change of personality had sped up the process of my disinterest.

The greatest of all the challenges was AIDS, which, as it happened, we weren't able to leave behind in San Francisco. Friends were dying. In Louisville. In Chicago. In San Francisco. In Boston. Everywhere. No one knew who 'had it" or who would be next. As I watched these men meet their premature demise, certain I'd be next, somewhere from the dust collected in the darker corners of my mind would come the dark thought, "Why would I be spared when the others weren't? I'm not special. Why would I be passed over?" My not being special meant my days were surely numbered. Then, witnessing the most glorious generation this earth has possibly ever known (not an overstatement, I assure you) dying by the hundreds, then thousands and hundred thousands, as I'd continue to be spared, ever the man of extremes, I'd re-think things. "It's only the special ones that are being taken away." This line of reasoning actually made more sense to me. The supremely talented. The incredibly accomplished. The most beautiful. The superlative. They were the ones being picked off one by one. I was none of those things. I was the middle of the pack — in my own estimation, "just a garden-variety-gay." It made sense then, that my lack of being special would actually be my salvation. **Ironically the quality I thought would doom me, perhaps, would save me. I constantly vacillated between these two opposing thoughts.**

Hope, a former constant in my life was vanishing along with my friends. As they were taken away one by one, the childlike optimism that had been my signature had begun to evaporate. I might be next or I might be saved, but "for what?" This new negative hopelessness would creep in and dominate my every thought and act. **My old "things just seem to work out for me" mantra had taken a backseat to despair; my optimism along with my heart had been amputated like a diseased, worthless limb.**

So what to do? I began thinking short term rather than planning for a future I might no longer have. My whole existence, which had pretty much died along with my friends and the lifestyle we lived and loved, came into question. Things had taken turns I'd never have expected or imagined and I was at the depths of depression. A "what's the use" frame of mind developed, swung into high gear and took over. **I was in a state of mourning not only for lost friends but for the lost life I'd thought I was going to have and would now be denied.** My formerly happy social life of friends, parties, and sexual abandon where things generally went my way, had evaporated. Everything was wrong. No longer able to imagine a future, I lost my imagination. Along with it went my sense of optimism. Though 'hate' is a word I have since banished from my vocabulary, at the time I 'hated' Boston. I 'hated' The Talbots. I 'hated, Charlotte. I 'hated' winter. I 'hated' Chase." I 'hated' my life and life itself. Everything was indeed, wrong. There was no way out. Maybe this time, for the first time, things were not going to work out for me.

1986

Who's Next?

VIRUSES don't come more insidious than HIV. Horror fiction could not have devised a more evil disease. It is a virus that attacks the immune system, the same system that is actually meant to protect us from disease. I repeat: A disease that attacks the system of defense we have for disease. There is obviously no defense from such a thing. After the immune system had been attacked and sufficiently suppressed, left defenseless, you would fall victim to any number of "opportunistic infections." Opportunistic indeed. What a horribly descriptive word. You were, being left with no immune protection, simply laid exposed to whatever malady managed to come along and seize the opportunity to take advantage of your immune deficiency. No matter what is was, it would kill you. You wouldn't actually die of HIV or even AIDS itself. **But you would die.**

Death by opportunistic infection gave parents of many gay boys a smokescreen to shield their sons' sexual identities. And actual cause of death. Their obituaries would routinely state the cause of death as "cancer" or "pneumonia." Not AIDS. Not "The Gay Plague." Other craftier parents wouldn't state their sons' cause of death at all but would include in the obituary, "In lieu of flowers, please make a donation to the American

Cancer Society" or "The Leukemia Foundation" to throw people off the scent, suggesting their pride and joy had died from some other "acceptable" disease.

With other gay boys dying all around us, we — Randy, Chase, and myself — lived the way most gay boys did: in absolute uncertainty. We were all in peril. It was just a matter of time. **We were inmates of a virtual death row, silently awaiting our certain execution.** At first there was no HIV test. No one knew "who had it." You never knew when your health would suddenly take a turn and your days would be numbered. There were no drug cocktails or any medical procedures to save you from the certain death sentence of an AIDS diagnosis. Even when an HIV test had been developed you were just as likely to decide not to have one. With no viable treatment, what was the use of knowing? Friends and acquaintances were being diagnosed and were dying everywhere now. Our first friend to fall, oddly enough, was Randy's and my first mutual friend, handsome Ron Bianchi, in Louisville; the man who was the reason we'd known each other at all was the earliest casualty from our immediate circle. This big, handsome, accomplished, smart, popular, seemingly invincible man was cut down in his prime. Ron's passing was a foreshadowing of things certain to come. If it could happen to him, well, surely we were all toast. Who's next?

1986

Say It Isn't So

IKNOW exactly where I was when Randy called with the bad, and I suppose inevitable news. I was in my bedroom and picked up the phone where it was ringing on the nightstand by Chase's side of the bed. It was Randy which was nothing unusual as we'd talk in those days quite frequently. But it was mid-day when the rates were higher. That was unusual. I was looking out into our garden when Randy, clearly upset on the other end of that 3,000 mile line separating us gave me the horrible news. "Say it isn't so, please say it isn't so!" was my silent thought as he began telling me that he hadn't been feeling well and had gone to the doctor. He had pneumonia. "Say it isn't so." A diagnosis of Pneumocystis was sure to follow. "Say it isn't so." Pneumocystis and Kaposi Sarcoma were the two primary killer opportunistic infections associated with the AIDS virus, guaranteeing a diagnosis of full-blown AIDS. "Say it isn't so." He was hospitalized. He was scared. **Just like that my best friend was dying. "Say it isn't so!"**

I remember repeating that silent bargain with the universe. "Please, say it isn't so!" I don't remember the time of year of that horrible life-changing phone call. It's odd that I can't remember the season as I can so clearly recall standing there looking out into the sanctuary of our walled-in Beacon Hill garden. It's confusing. Was the garden green? Full of flowers? Were there the bright leaves of fall on the ground? I just don't remember. **I might have been looking out at the flowers and greenery of a quintessential summer's day but, with the harsh news of Randy's diagnosis, all I can clearly remember is the the cold feeling of death you associate with the harshest, bleakest winter.** Was there snow? I don't know. It didn't matter. What mattered was my best friend, the funny, silly, devoted, loyal still-young man I'd shared so much of my happy life with was 3,000 miles away in a hospital room...dying.

Please, please say it isn't so!

1986

Why Bother?

B
Y THIS TIME and especially with Randy's news, I had developed what I realize now was a "why bother" attitude. Up until this point, I would have considered myself an upwardly mobile achiever but a shift had taken place. Convinced of my own impending mortality, though only in my mid-thirties, I started making decisions from a new and different perspective. I was preparing to die. **With everyone dying around me and my best friend at death's door, I was just standing in line knowing my number would be called; just not knowing when. So, why bother?**

Why bother (even when an HIV test had finally been developed) to take it if there was no treatment? I didn't get tested.

Why bother beating my head against a corporate wall at a job I didn't like (and if I'm honest, wasn't doing a very good job at) if I'm as good as dead? I toyed with the idea of quitting.

Why bother with a huge monthly payment on a BMW I'd bought for a life I was now to be denied? I made plans to get rid of the BMW.

Why bother making new friends if they're just going to die and cause me even more grief? I stopped going out.

Why bother keeping my remaining friends close, if that closeness, upon my death is going to cause them pain and grief at my loss? I started distancing myself from all those close to me thinking that if I pulled away from them while still alive, after my death, not having me around wouldn't be difficult. With my new absence, I was curbing their grief.

Why bother going to the gym and looking good? I got lazy. I over-ate. I gained weight. Fat was the only defense against AIDS. Or so it seemed. HIV wasting was a reality. Nobody with AIDS ever died overweight. I reasoned: Staying fat = Staying alive.

Why bother looking sexy if sex can kill you? I no longer cared about my appearance. That was the surest way to insure a sexless life. I stopped a going out and I stopped looking for sex and I stopped having sex.

Why bother living at all if living meant being sex-less?

Why bother with anything that might increase the enjoyment of a life if that life was about to come to an abrupt premature end? Wouldn't it be easier to leave a life that was devoid of friends and fun? And sex. A life that was dull and uneventful would be a life to which it would be easier to say "goodbye." With nothing to look forward to, perhaps not having a future wouldn't be so bad.

Why bother?

1986

Hope In The Name Of Irene

IN THE MIDST of all the challenges presented by AIDS and Boston, my best work friend, Sharon came into my office at The Talbots gushing about a psychic she had seen. While Sharon highly recommended this lady, I at the time had no belief structure whatsoever in such things. As a survivor of Catholicism, I was still at a point where I equated spirituality with religion and I wanted nothing to do with either. Sharon who was my true confidant at work pressed on in her insistence I see the lady. Her name was Irene. I became a little more interested when Sharon produced a newspaper article saying that the police used the woman for missing person cases. That seemed to add a touch of credibility. And there was something else. The psychic lady lived in Plymouth, Massachusetts. That, I decided was a pretty cool place for a psychic to live. With the rock and all. **So, along with two of my female co-workers, and a healthy dose of skepticism, I booked an evening appointment with Irene, the psychic in Plymouth.** We were required to give her our full names in advance of our visit and that was all. I worked late that evening so when I arrived at the psychic's home, one co-worker had already seen her and the second was downstairs getting her reading. Clearly unhappy with her reading the first co-worker greeted me with a disgruntled "I coulda used the money to buy a new blouse." She rolled her eyes and said that the lady had told her nothing she didn't already know. My already low expectations were now lowered.

Shortly thereafter, Peggy, the second co-worker ascended from the lower level of the house followed by a tiny kewpie doll of a lady in a yellow flowered "duster" and equally yellow curly hair. She said her goodbyes to my c-workers and shifted her glance to me. Her eyes widened as she looked at me. She focused her eyes right on nine and with outstretched arms breathlessly exclaimed, "Michael, my Michael!" Taking my surprised hands in hers she said, "I'm Irene and I've been waiting all day for you Michael." She led me downstairs, sat the two of us down across from each other and instructed me to use a house-provided pad and pen to take notes. With her eyes fixed on mine she said "Now Michael, as you know when the appointment was made I asked for your full name. I do that so that I may meditate on your name the afternoon of your appointment. When I do this I get images and then I interpret those images. Now Michael, oh Michael," she said breathlessly still looking me straight in the eyes, "the images I received for you were, well, astonishing. I can't wait to share them."

The first image was that of a racehorse crossing a finish line first. I found that interesting since I grew up in Louisville, home of The Kentucky Derby. She told me the horse had a big blue ribbon, first place, another positive sign. She went on with a laundry list of nothing but positive images she'd received. **She told me the most wonderful things that were absolutely contrary to my current existence and state of mind. When I asked if it was a good idea to go out on my own and would I be successful she answered, "Yes. When you find your true calling, you will be successful beyond your widest imagining."** Her message of hope and optimism flew in the face of all I was currently experiencing and I really didn't know what to do with the information except write it down, store it away in my "For what it's worth" file, and close the drawer.

Irene's information, positive that it was, would have fallen on totally deaf ears had it not been for what happened next. At the end of her unbelievably bright accounting of my future, she asked if I wished to ask her about anyone else in my life. Predictably enough I gave Irene my mother's name. She clutched her heart dramatically and bent over as though in pain as she proceeded to describe my mother in every accurate detail, "Your mother has been burdened all her life with so much pain, sickness and suffering," Irene said still clutching her chest as if feeling my mother's pain. As she looked directly into my eyes she continued, "Her pain, so much of her pain and illness is self-inflicted. Your mother loves so truly and deeply and worries so much about all those she loves so intently that it's killing her." **Watching this little smiling yellow haired lady suddenly in pain, I was amazed at the way she'd managed to seem to know my mother.** I remained skeptical though as I decided she'd simply described the stereotypical Italian mother (though my mother was actually German and she should know that.) Still, she had totally nailed it.

Irene hadn't reeled me in however until I gave her my father's name. Hearing it, she immediately leaned back in her chair, arms flung to her basement ceiling and eyes widened. She seemed to grow and expand right in front of me and in a look of absolute astonishment and straight into my eyes she hooked me with the words, **"How has your mother managed to keep up with that man for all these years?"** Now I was the astonished one. In all my years living with and knowing my parents, I had never thought of nor had I ever heard anyone else characterize my parents' relationship so accurately. My mother was the tortoise to my father's hare. Dad was a whirling dervish of New York energy to my mom's sedentary Kentucky gal. The extrovert and the introvert. It was as if, at the mere mention of my mother's name, Irene had gotten to feel her and know her so well that when I gave her my father's name, instantly seeing who he was and the obvious contrast, she'd put it all in context of my mother. Talk about nailing it.

She'd reeled me in. If this tiny little psychic lady could so clearly see the reality of my parents, the two people who'd given me the world, then perhaps she could also see the reality of me, and my future. Could all the brilliant but unbelievably positive things she'd seen for me actually be believable? Perhaps. **A new glimmer of hope for the future crept in but was completely at odds with my current state of being and mind.** I had trouble wrapping my head around it all. I'd come to a level of acceptance of my current dismal situation which quite frankly if I were going to die soon, a fact of which I was quite certain, then so be it. I'd become comfortable with the thought. It might take a while for me to reconcile all of these suddenly new hopeful but conflicting concepts. The one thing Irene never mentioned and I was careful to not ask about was death. Or Randy. Or Chase. Curiously, the things most on my mind, oddly enough, I never mentioned. Just in case this little Irene really could foresee the future, there were some things I did not want to know.

On the long drive home that night from Plymouth to Boston, among all the uncertainties I knew one thing that was certain. I knew changes must be made. Still determined that death was imminent but also equipped with this new promise given me by a little kewpie doll psychic lady in Plymouth Massachusetts, unhappy in my relationship, unhappy with my work, and unhappy with my chosen city, at a time when I had been ready to close the book of my life, a long repressed survival instinct kicked in. I saw a glimmer of hope.

Irene had also told me that I possessed a "Silver Aura," her first she said and, "the highest attainable." I desperately wanted to believe it and all the other wonderful things Irene had told me. **I decided on that drive home, rather than close the book of my life, I would instead, at 35 years old, begin a new chapter.** While it may be my final chapter, I determined as I entered Beacon Hill and miraculously found a parking space, I, along with my "silver aura," though I didn't know exactly how, were going to make it a good one.

1986 – 1989

Going Out With A Bang

I QUIT MY JOB. The Talbots finally had a new president who was chopping heads and mine I was certain, especially with my boss's lack of love for me, was next. So I just went in one day and resigned. I felt instantly better. As I would leave Beacon Hill on my way to that dreaded job in Hingham, every morning I would wistfully observe, with more than a little envy, people with their coffee and scones at the outdoor cafes on Charles Street. **I wanted so much to be a "coffee and scone" person. That was my new goal: just a life that would afford me that one simple luxury. I didn't think to ask for more.** Chase wasn't happy with this decision and did not understand my giving up "a good job." He would also not have understood the "coffee and scone" argument either so I didn't even bring it up. I didn't know where the money would come from but somehow things had always worked out for me and with my renewed optimism I decided this would be one of those times. Also, encouraged by Irene to go out on my own, it just felt right. I quickly started a one man store design business and just as quickly, picked up two clients. I got rid of the BMW. What had been in San Francisco a dream, in Boston was a nightmare. A vandalized always needing a parking space burden of a nightmare. Apart from the seasonal ease with which it could get me to Crane's Beach, I never missed it. During the many months of malaise and depression, certain of my upcoming demise, I had gained a lot of sexless weight. I was unhappy and my physical state was a manifestation of that unhappiness. Or was it the other way around? It didn't matter. What did matter, was that my post-Irene thoughts were turning things around. My habits began to change. I began riding my bike. A lot. I started going to the gym. A lot. I discovered aerobics. I changed my diet. Within five months I had dropped forty lumpy pounds of fat and gained a lot of trim smooth hard muscle. My love handles were gone and my abs were back. And so was sex. But not with Chase.

New body or not, Chase wasn't much enamored with this new Michael. I had always suspected that the Pacific Heights address, the BMW, the high-paying job and the Brooks Brothers' suits were what he'd really fallen for. Taking all those upwardly mobile trappings away, there wasn't much about me he really seemed to like. I was changing. I was suddenly embracing the time I now had on my hands and the things that time afforded me. **I was learning the art of just "being" rather than doing.** This also didn't sit well with Chase, still the driven sort. "I never see you Do-ing anything," he angrily shouted at me during one of our many arguments. He really didn't comprehend or embrace the new me at all. I was learning introspection and for the first time ever started to learn who I really was. I happened to like the new me as much as Chase clearly did not. **He judged me harshly for all of these changes. It was clear to me that just as my edges were softening, Chase's were hardening.** I realized I was now living with Christopher, the sharp edged disapproving business guy who never lost an argument. I had so expertly avoided him prior to this period of time but there was no escaping him now. Chaser was long gone and Chase only showed up in bars or at parties. At home it was Christopher and Christopher was having none of this new Michael. We grew further apart. Sex between us remained nonexistent. I thought my new and improved body might have generated a spark but it didn't and that was probably just as well. I was feeling really good about my physical self again and learning a lot about the spiritual me as well. Chase showed little interest in either. I happily shifted focus to all the others who were interested. The new me was getting a lot of attention and along with it my ego, which I'd folded up and put away in mothballs, was out of storage and being given fresh life. I was going out a lot and being appreciated again. My old favorite pastime became my new favorite pastime — I was having sex again. A lot of sex. And, my other old favorite pastime was also back. I was dancing again. A lot.

1988

Party On

TIME PASSED and as a 36-year-old gay boy who hadn't died yet, self-employed with more time on my hands, I continued to shift gears. Ever the man of extremes, my "Why bother?" had morphed into a polar-opposite "Let's party!" Was it possible I just might live? And if I were going to live, I decided I'd live a life worth living. **If I wasn't going to die alongside my friends then I'd live my life for them.** Given a gift denied to so many, I'd better be grateful for it and use it to live my life for me as well. I was ready to party again.

There were AIDS fundraisers to attend; party after party to raise money to care for the victims and the research of that dreaded disease. My new store design business was doing well and providing me with enough money and more time to get involved in this worthy and all-consuming cause. There was also something about going out dancing during such a dark time that would lift me out of the depths of all the dying and allow me, all of us, to forget for awhile the pain and suffering going on around us. The Circuit (or at least as much of it as I could afford) had always been where I'd had the best time; where I'd found my family and where I'd found my self. It was also, eventually, as I became more and more aware of my spirituality, where I'd find my soul. I, along with my new body and developing soul, were ready to take each party that came my way with a new-found, party-til-you-drop attitude. I was having fun again. And growing.

Worst case, I figured, I could just party my way to the grave while I partied my ass off. Literally. I went out more and more whether the parties were fundraisers or not. If I were going to die anyway, why not have fun doing it? That meant drugs. Party drugs. Any minute now the doctors might be pushing prescription drugs on me, so why not do some fun ones while I'm healthy? Why not? There were Black Parties and White Parties and every color of the rainbow parties to attend in New York, Miami, Atlanta, San Francisco and Palm Springs. They were every color of the rainbow pills to take as well. And they worked. **I embraced The Circuit and The Circuit embraced me right back and in so doing reinstalled in me a reason to live and the hope that I just might.**

The sex I was having was not the sex I had so thoroughly enjoyed, pre-AIDS. It was the new "safe sex," not nearly as much fun but it was definitely better than the nothing I'd been having for the past two years or so. I adjusted and jumped right into this new "look but don't touch" world of gay sex. Ugly stinking condoms were not an option for me, neither was sex without them. But there were lots of things I could do beyond fucking. And a lot of it was a lot of fun. I just had to give up the one sex act I loved the most.

There were safe sex parties and safe sex venues and I attended as many as possible. Life seemed to be split right down the middle between the sadness of loss, both real and potential and the exhilaration of drugs and parties. I, like so many others, teetered on the line between these two facets of the AIDS era. **One night you'd be dancing til dawn with abandon, in denial. The next day you'd be consoling a dying friend at his hospital bedside or grieving at a memorial service for the loss of a dead one. All the while feeling sheepish and a little guilty, wondering if it was totally inappropriate to be cruising the orderlies or other grievers.** You'd spend the week with hospitalized dying friends and the next on vacation sunning and dancing with the living in Key West, or P-Town or Fire Island. It was a way of coping I suppose. The vacations and parties, already fabulous were made more fabulous by the drugs and the bonding of like-minded individuals with similar experiences, hopes and fears; our gay wagons circled against a formidable foe. I regretted not one moment of those party days — the dancing and the drugs — and began to grow personally and spiritually in ways I hadn't anticipated. Without my asking, the universe with its wonders, would reveal itself to me, up on a box or a stage, right above the dance floor.

1988

Sure Of Each Other

COINCIDING with my newfound sense of hope and positivity, the ever-accommodating universe that was opening itself and showering me with gifts had another one waiting. While I had remained close to my family in Louisville in some ways, they really weren't a part of my day to day existence. Since my coming out back in 1969 and my parents' subsequent desire to sort of pretend my homosexuality away, they knew little of my life and I think they preferred it that way. They just weren't equipped to deal with their gay son's gayness. I found I really missed having a family. Or at least a family with whom I could be myself and share the actual uncensored details of my life. But for one family member, my authentic self may have never been spoken of. Or to.

On one of my visits to Louisville I offered to take my niece Michelle back to school in Cincinnati. It was only an hour and a half drive but during that short time, two souls found each other and bonded permanently. Of course we were uncle and niece and I'd loved her since I first held her in my arms on her baptism day in 1969, but we'd never had the time to get to know each other as adults (she had recently turned 19.) We found we were kindred spirits and even with the 18 years of life experience between us, were in similar circumstances, each needing a family member who we could talk to. That's all. Just someone in our family with whom we could honestly share our real selves and not fear any sort of rejection or loss of love. On that drive we became that for each other creating our everlasting familial bond built on unconditional love. Like Pooh and Piglet, we could be "Sure of You."

Michelle, at 19, was at that time in life when we, shedding the influence of our parents, begin to realize just who we are, apart from them. As it was with me when I came out (the year she was born), she was determined to spread her wings and discover just who she was. I understood her. I understood the challenges she faced that made her want to get as far from Louisville as she could and find a place where she would find herself. I supported that search. The understanding and support bonded us as did the fact that we each, at last, had a family member with whom we could be completely honest. **We loved each other not in spite of who we are but because of who we are.**

Michelle chased down every one of her demons, all the while coming to me for guidance and support. I warily watched and supported my charge as she quit school (I had), went off to follow The Grateful Dead (I hadn't done that) and necessarily changed her name to Starr, relieving herself from the baggage attached to her given name. She also had to deal with parents, much as it had been for me when I came out, who wondered who this new person was and how to deal with her. I absolutely adored this new person who was very different from me and at the same time, so similar.

Starr was just as supportive of me as I was of her. I could tell her anything without her being shocked or judgmental. **It was a time of stormy seas of change and upheaval for both of us and we rode wave after wave together.** During our many long-distance conversations — she moved to San Francisco (as had I) and then Hawaii — as we'd exchange thoughts and philosophies, she would convince me to write, assuring me that others would want to hear what I had to say. Her words would be the ones that would stick in my head and cause me to begin one day to write.

1988

Cyclorama

I'VE ALWAYS had an affinity for circles. They are after all, the perfect geometric shape. No angles. No corners, just a curving line meeting itself. No beginning, no end. Infinite. Geometry was the only facet of mathematics that interested me. I suppose it was my visual sense. I could "see" geometry. The rest of it was just...numbers.

I also since childhood have had an affection for the suffix, -rama. As a Cub Scout I would attend an annual event called Scout-O-Rama. That suffix denoted to me not only a whole world of boys but also a whole world of anything. For a time, I would attach the suffix to everything I could. Dinner was "Food-O-Rama." A day in the park was "Fun-O-Rama." Biking with my friends was "Bike-O-Rama." Somewhere along the same timeline Cinerama came along. Cinerama was a big bold way of showing movies that wrapped nearly around you for an in-the-picture experience. I loved the experience and of course I loved the name.

I believe it was in the 4th grade that our teacher gave the art class assignment to create a piece of abstract art. With my love of circles I decided that the circle would be my motif. I found something round and drawing around it I filled the sheet of manila drawing paper with dozens and dozens of circles in every color in the Crayola box. It was really quite pretty and I was quite proud of the outcome.

I first named my abstract art piece "Circle-O-Rama" after "Scout-O-Rama" but decided it was too cumbersome. Next was "Circlerama" after "Cinerama" but that didn't look right either. I finally settled on "Cyclorama" and proudly turned it in to Sr. Mary Demetria who hailed it as a masterpiece. This was in sharp contrast with another piece of artwork and another not so generous nun just two years before. I had been vindicated and was praised for my grasp of abstract art. The success of "Cyclorama" stayed with me forever. As did the artwork which I am pretty sure I have packed away in some cardboard box somewhere.

So it was with great interest that I saw an advertisement for a dance party that was being held in a Boston space known as The Cyclorama. The name of course caught my eye immediately. I asked around and learned that The Cyclorama was a big round building housing a big round event space. It had been built in the late 1800s to house large painted dioramas about the Civil War that would wrap around you — an early Cinerama if you will. The dioramas were long gone but the big circular party space remained. I excitedly imagined a perfect circle housing a perfect party that shared its name with my long ago art project. Parties in the big round Cyclorama were wonderful. The space was huge but, with no corners, somehow, intimate, wrapping itself like embracing arms around the partiers. It was a big hug of a party space with a large domed ceiling too. High ceilings have always been my preference for parties.

Boston was a city of cliques — closed circles in the habit of excluding others. People seemed to group together by type and stayed in their circles. Others unwelcome. There seemed to be an odd suspicion of one group for another. It was strange really and created voids between communities. You could draw lines between the neighborhoods: the Brahmin Beacon Hill, the Yuppie Back Bay, the Italian North End, the Irish South Boston not to be confused with the Gay South End.

Sadly the gay community followed suit with lots of cliques. While I didn't like the idea of these exclusive circles of friends, I was fortunate (I suppose) to find myself in one. We were a really great group of gay boys. All handsome, all fit, all upwardly mobile and fun. I suppose, though I don't like admitting it, we were a clique. We had great fun together planning weekends on the Cape, weeks in Provincetown, camping weekends, parties and spontaneous gatherings and game nights at each others' homes. When we went out to clubs and parties it was probably clear we were a group — a clique — and I am sad to say, it was equally clear where the boundaries around us lay. **While it was nice to be on the inside rather than the out, I was never quite comfortable with it.**

At the end of an AIDS fundraiser at The Cyclorama, as the party was clearly coming to an end, the DJ played "United We Stand" by Brotherhood Of Man. It had been years since I'd heard the song that had ended so many a night in my first little gay bar in Lexington, KY. So here it was again that song of camaraderie and mutual support used so many years later to end a gay fundraiser. I was of course dancing with our group and instinctively we all pulled together in a tight circle, arms around each others' waists or shoulders and danced, heads together, slowly to the song. It felt familiar and good connecting to the past like that, arms around each other showing love and support just like the old days. Well almost. It occurred to me that unlike the old days when we'd be ending the night in long inclusive anyone-can-join-in lines, at the end of that Cyclorama party, my friends and I were in a tight little exclusive circle. It seemed so out of step with the song and with the event itself — raising money for the care of our foundering and fallen friends. I happened to look over my shoulder and saw a sweet face looking at us in what I had determined to be either longing to be part of a group or sadness at not. **Whatever it was that I saw on his face, drove home just how at odds our tight little circle was with that song of unity.** I took my arm away from whichever friend was to my left and smiling, I motioned to that sweet face to join us. He seemed surprised but did and our circle was a little wider. I looked to my right and finding another face, pulled my arm away again. I motioned him to join us and the circle increased. My friends took note of this and began doing the same. Our United We Stand circle grew wider, and wider and wider with each new member welcomed in to it. It expanded into the remaining dancing crowd as it continued to grow larger and larger.

I have since imagined the cinematic quality of this entire scenario as seen from above. An overhead shot shows a large circular room packed with dancers. Suddenly a small circle near the center of the floor appears. As the music continues, the circle begins to grow. Outside the ever-increasing circle, the floor is densely packed with dancers who, one by one, get gobbled-up by the circle as it continues to grow and fill the circular room creating one big all-inclusive circle.

1988

Who Does She Think She Is?

SINCE THE FIRST TIME I got up on a box to dance I have been hooked. On a dance floor you only dance with the person with whom you went out there or with the few people immediately surrounding you. But up on a box or a stage, with clear visibility over the entire party, everyone is available to you. You see things from up there and connect eye to eye, you especially feel things. Those who respond create an energy exchange that feeds me and can keep me going all night. Dancing up high, making eye contact and exchanging energy with other dancers has become something of a drug to me. There is nowhere else I have ever experienced it. **Connected that way to so many people at the same time, it is as if the entire party is moving through me — a kind of conduit of party energy — pulling that energy from the partiers and sending it right back, sharing it and magnifying it.** And in so doing, powering me all night.

There is magic that happens up there that's difficult to express in words but I can give one instance that made me an absolute believer. I was on stage at Metro (or Citi or Avalon — it changed incarnations and I can never remember which was when.) It was a Sunday night. Gay night. As the music hit a peak, my arms, always in the air, stopped, angled away, up and out in opposite directions, fingers pointed. At that instant two laser beams from way off hit the tips of my fingers. In that huge space those lasers had somehow found my tiny fingertips, extending the line of my pointed finger to eternity. Or perhaps it was the other way around. Whatever the case, it looked for that moment as if those lasers were coming out of the ends of my fingertips. I was mesmerized! What were the chances? The lighting guy could not have known my finger tips were going to stop there. Even if he did, no matter how good he was, he could not have engineered that. And I certainly didn't know the lasers would be there. It was to me, one of those miraculous moments divinely provided to reassure me of something at work greater than the music, the lasers, the lighting guy or me.

While I'd been up on boxes a few times in my early Chicago days my actual dancing up on boxes and stages got its start on the dance floor at Metro (or Citi or Avalon.) It was a big Boston dance club at which I rarely missed a Sunday night. During one of my first visits, I was dancing out in the middle of the floor and just in front of a box with a couple of boys dancing on it. I had my back to the box and, arms in the air, I was really going to town on some favorite song when I felt hands from behind me reach under my armpits and lift me up, backwards, onto the box. Suddenly I was dancing up there too. I turned to see who had done this and there was no one there. I was alone on the box. There was no indication as to who might have been the person or persons who helped me up there. Slightly confused, I turned back around and scanned the packed dance floor that lay below me. I continued dancing as a new world opened up to me. I could see from that slightly elevated position that suddenly the party was mine. I was able to connect with everyone below, everyone at least who was looking up at me. From that vantage point I could dance with a whole room full of people. I don't know who it was who lifted me up or why, but in that moment, my party life changed forever.

Life is energy and from that special moment on, addicted to the energy I'd spend most of my party time up high, feeding on it. Where there were no boxes or stages, I'd improvise. At the Boatslip in P-Town there was only a ring around the sunken dance floor, just a step or two higher. I'd spend the entire T-dance there, dancing along that edge. I was an early pioneer of "arms in the air" dancing and danced more with my arms and hands than with my legs and feet given I'd typically be up on a small box. Dancing on four square feet, down below ya gotta keep it small. But above the waist I was all movement. A Boston friend once named me **"The Human Metronome"** because of my arm movement and my ability to keep time with the music. I also realized early on that shirtless I look better with my arms up. We all do. Another Boston friend named Gordon, used to call me **"The Waring Blender."** I'd be out on the floor revving it way up, arms in the air, and he'd lean over to one of our other friends, nod to me and say, "Oh look, he's just turned it up to 'Frappe!'"

Those late eighties Boston years were the darkest of the AIDS days and dancing provided real relief from the constant struggle against that disease. It was a time of despair which can wreak havoc on one spiritually. Dancing on a box or a stage (or even the ring around a dance floor) repaired that damage for me and recharged my spiritual batteries like nothing else. **The dance club was my church and a box or stage, my altar.** That is where I found the strength to go on. And on and on and on.

There is another element to that spiritual energy exchange. For all the years since I started losing friends to that dreaded disease, before going out I have a little conversation with my departed party buddies. "Hey guys, lets go dancing," I always say, "Come with me. Let's party." They show up every time. I feel them there, around me and in me. **Filled with their energy, when I get up on stage and pull the energy from the dance floor, I am introducing them, my boys from the past to my boys in the present, connecting us all and creating an everlasting spiritual bond.** I do not take this lightly and am humbled by the power I feel. I dance with the strength of thousands.

I doubt there are many who have considered how much courage it takes to get up on a box and dance up high in front of hundreds of oftentimes judgmental homosexuals. Yes, we can be. There's always a moment of hesitation before I get up there but I don't let it stop me. The rewards are always greater than any fear I might have of exposing my less than perfect physical self in a province usually populated by so much physical perfection.

I do understand and have from the start, that while I love being up there, not everyone loves my being up there. I can feel their energy as well. It must seem to some, and understandably so, that I have an unquenchable need for attention. A friend once referred to me as an "attention whore" and to some I guess I am. If the casual observer doesn't know anything about me or hasn't experienced that special energy exchange, then I suppose I am just some guy who likes to get up on boxes and make a spectacle of himself in an unending need for attention. Those who think this way are not the ones who send me that great positive energy. It is quite the contrary. Surrounded by so much positive energy, I can usually feel the negative energy pockets. That kind of "attitude" especially in the time of AIDS always seemed so counterproductive.

At a time when we should have been supporting each other, instead there were those who just seemed to want to criticize and stand in judgement. I have come to think of these people as the "Who does she think she is?" boys. I see them, arms crossed over their chests and with looks that seem to range from disapproval to disdain. I can almost hear them saying, to themselves and each other, "Who does she think she is?" While I don't know these people, and they certainly don't know me, they still, somehow, seem to have an amazingly strong opinion of me.

One Boston evening, I accompanied my friend Phil into Mike's Video in the South End. Working there was one of my favorite people (and fuck buddies,) an adorable, sweet, sexy, always happy ginger boy named Michael. He helped us in his usual cheerful manner but working alongside him was one of the "Who does she think she is?" boys. I recognized him immediately. I had never met the boy but, out dancing, I had felt his stares and negative energy. And I could feel them in Mike's Video. I did my best to ignore the energetic slings and arrows being hurled my way but even though my sweet sexy Michael was working that night, I couldn't get out of that store fast enough. As we departed Mike's Video, I said to Phil, "That boy behind the counter hates me." Phil gave me a "seriously?" look and responded, "That is so like you, Michael. You think that boy has such a strong opinion of you when in truth he's probably never even noticed you. You know, not everyone has an opinion of you. You are not the center of the universe." Wow. Where did that come from? I thought it over and wondered if perhaps I was being too self-centered and making too much of this negative energy thing. Still, I couldn't escape my certainty that the boy was indeed feeling something for me and it sure wasn't love. The negative energy was there. I could feel it. And see it in his eyes. Later that evening at the rear of the Eagle Bar, also in Boston's South End, Phil left to go to the bar upfront for another drink. He returned after awhile, drink in hand with an odd look on his face. "Michael, I am so sorry for what I said earlier." I wasn't sure to what he was referring but quick to accept any sort of apology I thanked him. He continued, "I just ran into your red-headed friend...from the video store. He said that as soon as we left the store, the guy working next to him pointed to you and said, 'I hate that guy!'" Phil went on, "Michael said he said to him, 'Wait, that's one of my favorite people. Why would you say that? How do you know him?' And the guy said back to Michael, 'I don't know him. I just hate him!'"

The "Who does she think she is?" people will come and go and think what they will think. I really can't be too concerned. Happily there are others who think better things. I was recently searching for the Key West paper airplanes, I think, and came across a Christmas card circa 1989(ish) tidied away in a file full of memories. It was from two Boston party friends, Steven and Philip. They were a sweet, sexy, muscle couple who had sort of adopted me on the party circuit. I held them in very high esteem and, if I'm being honest, was always just a little surprised they'd even noticed me, much less taken me under their wings the way they had.

I opened the card to find, penned in Steven's hand, the loveliest message. I'd forgotten about the card and Steven's surprising words. Re-reading them so many years later, they still surprise me and remind me why I still do what I do. They also remind me that there was a time when I did care about the judgement of others. **It was the Stevens and Philips in my life, investing their energy in me, who helped me over that hurdle of self-doubt.** Steven's beautiful words of encouragement would suggest he and Philip had a pretty good idea of who I was, and what I was doing up there—at the time, better even than I. These many years later, with a greater understanding of who I am, I try my best to live up to the kind words in that touching message written on a Christmas card so long ago…

Dear Michael,

To that unyielding spirit that
you always seem to possess, a toast!
At any function in which you are
in attendance, may your personna
always provide a focus reminding others what joy
can be found in living each moment to the fullest.

May this holiday renew that spirit so that your
light will continue to shine brightly into the
new year and be a beacon for every man as we
approach the 21st century.

With all our love,
Steven/
Philip

1988 - 1990

The Truth About Gold Dust

GOLD DUST is hard to hold onto. **Impossible, in fact. That's the first truth about gold dust.** All too quickly it slips through your fingers. Try as you might to keep it from doing so...there it goes. You can try to hold on to whatever you can, as you see it sparkling away over your fingertips, but won't succeed. It's already off to hoard itself away as a memory like all the other gold dust. **That's the second truth about gold dust: memory is the one place where gold dust does remain — for a while.** You can visit it there, trying to polish up the old sparkle but as it begins to lose its luster you realize it's gone. **That gold dust often isn't recognized or appreciated in the present is the third and probably the most frustrating of its truths.** Immersed in gold dust it's hard to see until it begins to slip away. The second it does is the second you recognize it for the precious ephemeral commodity it is. But it's too late. It's already gone. Acceptance of these three truths is made easier knowing there is more gold dust ahead if you remember to look for it. Or better yet, allow it to find you. And when it presents itself, try to recognize it if you can, embrace it while you can, and always be grateful for it. But, when it's time...let it go. Letting go is one of life's hardest lessons but it comes with a blessing: **Letting go of gold dust is the surest way to get more. And that's the final truth about gold dust.**

Key West, having been pure gold dust, followed these golden truths. Times changed and so did that gold-dusted little island. With each visit I became more aware of the magic that had surrounded me because I could see it slipping away. Change is inevitable and changes were everywhere. The bridges of the overseas highway were widened and the airlines increased their flights making it much easier to get to Key West. Upstate, Ft. Lauderdale, being fed-up with the 300,000 or so spring breakers who would descend annually like a swarm of locusts wreaking havoc on their beaches and town, drove them away by upping the drinking age to 21, enforcing laws and limiting parties. Many of those college kids of course found their way to the most permissive little island in Florida, overrunning it. **I cannot fully express the anguish of strolling along quiet Fleming Street on a peacefully perfect Key West afternoon (as I had care-freely done so many times in years past) and having a beer bottle, thrown from a passing convertible over-filled with drunk college boys, whiz past my head and crash on the wall next to me, as I heard the word "faggot" shouted along with the sound of drunken laughter growing distant as the car sped away.** I also shed a tear when one of my favorite restaurants, formerly run by a sadly deceased gracious gay Jamaican gentleman, located in a spectacular Victorian mansion set way back from Duval and Caroline Streets on a tastefully landscaped corner filled with palm trees and twinkle lights, replete with peaked gables and a big wraparound porch where, while dining on something superb, I first heard the deep resonant sound of Morganna King wafting out to us from inside...had become a Hooters. A Hooters. In Key West. My Key West. Then came the cruise ships and the subsequent t-shirt shops and on and on. Ya gotta let go.

I can imagine that "the Conchs" as the Key West locals are called, found themselves in a similar predicament back in the early '70s as they saw their sleepy peaceful little island suddenly become overrun with homosexuals. Gay guest houses, restaurants, shops, sex venues, etc, certainly changed the landscape of their quiet sanctuary. It couldn't have been easy adjusting to their new reality. Property values soared along with the cost of living and surely many got priced-off their precious piece of paradise. Things change. The sparkle fades. **You have to let go.**

Along with the other disastrous changes of the '80s came AIDS. It was a confluence of events, a perfect tropical storm determined to blow away whatever gold dust still remained. Gay Key West was being decimated. AIDS was changing the playful sexy landscape of gay life forever and along with it, playful sexy gay Key West. An island dedicated to the type of sexual abandon that passed the illness on, was an island that would be vastly affected. The walking wounded were everywhere. It was 1988 (or '89 or '90) I can't really say as those years of uncertainty, suffering, and death run together in my memory. The sickening reality of that horrible uppercase acronym was inescapable. Boys who were dying understandably wanted to live out their final years, months, or days in the magical place they loved best. Perhaps some even thought Key West with all its gold-dusted magic might just sprinkle some of it on them, providing some life prolonging remedy or perhaps even a mystical cure. I'd have believed it. **Whatever the case, with the sick and all the other walking wounded — the exhausted caregivers and the survivors warily awaiting their own eventual fate — it was clear Key West was no longer an island of abandon. There were serious matters to contend with — primarily survival. Rather than a place to play, it became, for far too many, a place to die. An island of death. The thing about death though... wherever you find it, you will also find angels. In the wake of all the dying, Key West was becoming an island of angels.**

1989

The Messenger

I CONTINUED to vacation in Key West during those years because, though ravaged by the changes and that horrible disease, it still managed to retain for me, some of its old gold-dusted magic. As I learned to shift my focus from the physical to the spiritual — letting go of complaints, grief and whatever other negatives I'd been holding onto — the spiritual air began to open up, making me aware of the angels around me. Of course they'd be gathering post-mortem in Key West, the magical place that had supplied so many earthly joys before they'd made their premature departures. Others were arriving pre-mortem, ready to transition and earn their wings in their happiest of places. I would walk the streets, as always, cruising the boys, certain of the angel presence around me. I'd dance the night away surrounded by my recently departed friends. When I had sex, of course they'd be there too. I would see them in the faces of the new arrivals, especially the first-timers as I'd helpfully and happily tell them where to go and what to do. It was a challenge upon meeting a Key West newbie to *not* talk about how great the place *had been*. Tempted to relate tales of the good old days, I'd keep my mouth shut on the subject and allow them to enjoy the island without benefit of my own personal pre-AIDS perspective. **There was, after all, still magic to be had on that little gold-dusted island of angels if you were open to it; and to them.**

On one of my stays at the Oasis, having returned from dinner with friends, I was out by the pool alone (but for the angels) enjoying the quiet night and the ever present warm embracing breeze. The nearly full moon and the gently swaying palm trees were reflected in the pool's sparkling surface. Nowhere have I found quiet time as perfect as what I experienced sitting by that pool when all the others were all out dining or dancing or doing god knows what. **The pool, usually the social center and heart of the house, during a certain window of time every night, became a place to be blissfully alone.** There was always some light non-intrusive samba sort of music perfectly in tune with the environment, playing lightly in the background along with the rustle of palm fronds over head. Everything took on a soft surreal glow, cast from the tiny purple neon "Oasis" sign nestled into the greenery over by the hot tub. I would simply "be" there in the absolute serenity of the place. Open to anything.

Lost in my own personal reverie that particular night, I heard faint voices in the distance, growing closer, piercing the peace. **I was about to be no longer alone in my alone place.** Two thirty-something boys walked up to the pool's edge and gazed at the same reflection I had been enjoying. Seeing their faces reflected back I said "Hello." I was a surprise to them. They introduced themselves as Stephen and Bruce, "Best friends from Canada." As they took the lounger next to mine, they explained that they'd just arrived that evening and had run right out to dinner. "We decided on Key West at the last minute so we could only get the Oasis for a few days and then we're going to a place called The Brass Key," said Stephen who seemed to be the designated spokesperson and then he added, "we had to take what we could get." It was typical for a guesthouse, when they couldn't accommodate an entire desired stay, to call around to other guesthouses for reservations in as many places as was necessary. So their stay would be split between two guesthouses. Having planned most of my Key West vacations months in advance, I applauded their spontaneity. Having lived in Chicago and now Boston, I completely understood any last minute decision to vacate equally frigid Canada. After a delightful getting to know you chat in which I shared all my what's new around the island information, they politely excused themselves. "We're exhausted," exclaimed Stephen in a way that made me know it was true. As I watched them walk away, I couldn't have explained why, but I felt an instant connection, a true kinship with these two exhausted Canadian souls.

The next morning Stephen and Bruce joined me at the pool where we spent the day together. **They confided in me that when they'd gotten back to their room after our meeting the night before, they were astonished by how much I reminded them of a friend of theirs.** "What's really interesting though," said Stephen, "you don't really look like him or sound like him..." Bruce chimed in, "You're not as tall and have darker hair, yet somehow, you're just like him." After a brief pause, "We can't figure it out," they said in unison, Bruce shaking his head and Stephen with a shrug.

We spent our time together at the Oasis, bonded like old friends in, on and by the pool. Of course. They needed to rest, relax and unwind. Three of my island specialties. We got along fine. We had conversations about everything by that pool sometimes sharing the most intimate thoughts — things you'd typically share with only your besties. I would say something about something and they would once again be amazed at the similarities they saw between myself and their friend. They would repeatedly comment about it, sometimes saying in unison, "Just like him."

Stephen was yin to my yang, he being a more pragmatic sort and I, more spiritual. Once as I was sitting at the edge of the pool, my feet dangling in the water, Stephen, on his float, asked somewhat sarcastically, "So, does your crystal heal you?" He had spotted, the crystal I wore on a chain around my neck. **It was the late eighties and the New Age thing was at its peak. Shirley MacLaine was out on a limb and crystals were everywhere, according to *Time Magazine*.** Stephen enjoyed teasing me about my being too "new age-y woo woo" to use his words. "More spiritual" is how I might have described myself. In response to his slightly dismissive question about my crystal's healing capabilities, I gave him an equally dismissive answer. "Well, you see Stephen, I don't know about the power of a rock to heal but I am learning a lot about energy. I have been blessed with something, some special energy-something that I'm certain is a gift from the universe. It has kept me safe and healthy all my life, protecting me against all odds. I like to think I can wear this crystal and charge it up with whatever it is that keeps me safe and healthy and then, give it — energized — to someone less blessed, and maybe that energy-gift-from-the-universe, shared, just might do for that person what it's done for me and maybe...perhaps...even heal that person." And, after a slight pause, I added, "Makes perfect sense to me." Stephen's eyes narrowed with his usual skepticism. He was momentarily silent and, after sharing a glance with Bruce who was seated beside me, he paddled away, shaking his head and saying, "Just like him."

Stephen and Bruce's days were up at the Oasis and they moved to The Brass Key a few blocks away. We visited back and forth spending time at each others' pools.

On their last day they shopped and explored Key West while I, as usual, spent the time floating on the Oasis pool, a little high and mostly naked. In my favorite place, doing my favorite thing, feeling sexy and spiritual, the universe was, as was typical, opening itself, graciously sharing its infinite wisdom. I always trusted the truths I would receive in this manner and would adopt them as part of my own personal truth. Without question. **They were, in fact, answers before I'd even thought up the questions.** The information would typically be about harmony, balance and serenity, lovely things like that. But on that glorious Key West afternoon, in all my suntanned serenity and sexy contentment my thoughts turned to death. Death. "No, not death." Not now. Puleeeze not at the Oasis; especially not while floating on a pool. The whole point of Key West to escape the misery of death and dying back in cold gray Boston. To find it waiting for me at the Oasis, my favorite Key West playground was unacceptable. I fought the thought at the same time it was becoming more insistent. Death! Why now? Was I about to die? Why, while blissfully floating on a pool in Key West, of all places, would my thoughts suddenly turn to death? The more I tried to push the thought out, the more determined it was to push its way in. And ruin my afternoon. **On this otherwise perfect day, I was now consumed with the subject I had come to Key West to forget. Death.** The thought became one of those ear worms that, after digging its way in, replays itself over and over and over again. But now, instead of "My Sharona," or "1-8-0-0 Cars For Kids," it was "Death," dominating my brain, and wearing down my resistance. With no other choice, I gave myself over to it. At that moment the spiritual floodgates opened! What I had perceived as thoughts became rapid-fire shouts of information about death. "Death is nothing." Nothing? "Nothing!" And again, "Death is NOTHING!" And then, "It doesn't exist. It is not a thing. It doesn't happen. It is, in fact, a non-happening. Death isn't anything." Since I had long before learned to recognize as truth, these "answers before I had the questions," I shifted gears to process and store the information. Floating on the pool, and no longer resisting, I became a spiritual sponge soaking it all up. I started thinking differently about death. I realized that the great shared universal fear of what happens when it's all over, is, in actuality, nothing. Nothing. And therefore nothing to be afraid of. I lay there instantly comforted as the shouting began again more insistent than before and as crystal clear as the Key West sky above me. This time in a full-throated shout, "DO NOT BE AFRAID OF DEATH. DEATH DOESN'T HAPPEN. THERE IS NOTHING TO FEAR WHEN IT'S OVER…THERE IS NO OVER!"

"There is no over?" As I lay there still making my way around the pool, pressed into my float by the weight of this new information, at the same time lifted to an ethereal lightness that is hard to describe. It was like floating except I was already floating. On air perhaps instead of water. That's what it felt like living with this new universal truth. With all the death around me, I'd spent so much time thinking about death, wondering and worrying about it, fearing it and mostly trying to ignore it. Suddenly with this one unexpected spiritual transmission, I was faced with it and at the same time was being released from the fear of it. "There is no over," I repeated to myself and the next thought arrived as loud and insistent as the others, **"Tell Stephen!"** Stephen?

Stephen and Bruce had promised to stop by the Oasis with their luggage, before their departure from Key West. We'd visit awhile and then call the taxi when it was airport time. I was out by the pool, when they arrived. Together poolside, they shared the events of their last day along with their purchases and discoveries. Later, with the taxi waiting outside the Oasis, I walked them out. As the luggage was being loaded into the pink taxi's trunk, I knew I had to tell Stephen about my recent brush with death. I didn't know why and I didn't know how I'd even broach the subject but I knew in no uncertain terms, I had to tell my new friend who seemed more like an old friend what I'd learned just that afternoon. At the last minute I pulled him aside and looked directly into his eyes. "Steve I have to tell you something" I said in all seriousness. "OK," he replied somewhat warily to the gravity in my voice. I continued, "Steve…it's about death." At the word "death" I saw apprehension in his eyes. Then fear. As I tried to remember word for word what I'd been told I began to unload. "Death doesn't exist. It doesn't hurt. It isn't scary. It's nothing to be afraid of. It's nothing. There's not even a blip and we move on. Death is nothing Stephen so there is nothing to fear. Don't be afraid of nothing!" Hmmmm that last part didn't sound quite right. He was clearly agitated by all of this and I was clearly not getting through to him. I continued undaunted and more strident in my delivery. I was on a mission and focused directly on his eyes not allowing him to look away and nearly shouted, "DO NOT BE AFRAID OF DEATH, STEPHEN. DEATH DOESN'T HAPPEN." I was practically preaching now, "THERE IS NOTHING TO FEAR WHEN IT'S OVER, THERE IS NO OVER!" And one more time, "DON'T BE

AFRAID OF DEATH, STEPHEN, ITS NOTHING!" He was taken aback. Clearly he did not know how to respond to this barefoot person in his little speedo using his parting words on a Key West sidewalk, to tell him about death, of all things. He pondered all of this for a second and, as a car approached, he said a bit dismissively, "Well, I guess I could jump in front of that car right now and test your theory..." He trailed off not finishing the thought as his eyes darted back and forth from me to the disappearing auto and back to me.

At that moment I suddenly knew what should have been apparent to me all along. Did Stephen tell me or was it another message? I can't say for certain. Whatever the case, it was all suddenly clear. The friend — Stephen and Bruce's friend — the friend who I was "just like," even though I wasn't, the friend who I sounded like but didn't, the friend who's words I seemed to speak, the friend whose image I evoked over and over again, the friend we'd spoken of so frequently, was dead. Of course. Why hadn't I figured that out? He had died of AIDS...of course. Stephen and Bruce had taken care of him to his death...of course. After their friend's passing, broken with grief and exhaustion, Stephen and Bruce had to get away...of course. They made their last minute plans for Key West...of course. At the Oasis. Of course. And when they arrived, who was waiting out by the pool for them...? Their friend. Of course. Sort of. They had found, out by the pool that first night, their deceased friend. Looking like him though I didn't. Sounding like him though I didn't. Reminding them of him over and over again. We bonded like old friends which in a way we were. I became their friend. Or had he become me?

Whatever the case, the next realization came through as loud and clear as all the rest: the friend had had a plan. He needed to deliver on a promise and I was the right person at the right place at the right time. In appreciation for the love and care given him, the grateful friend, while still alive, knowing of Stephen's crippling fear of death had made a promise. As a thank you for caring for him and staying with him and loving him to the end, he'd promised to find a way to let Stephen know what death was like. This was something he could do for his friend Stephen after Stephen had done so much for him. He had a feeling dying wouldn't be so bad and when he found out for sure, he would deliver the good news to Stephen. Somehow. He would find a way.

And so he had. The friend had delivered on his promise making me his earthly voice. He'd found me at the Oasis in my spiritually open state-of-being, just waiting for his friends and slipped right in, creating an earthly version of himself, someone with whom Stephen could be totally at ease. Later when he'd gotten me alone, he'd take advantage of my floating on my pool openness, and shout the information at me in a way I could not possibly ignore. Once successful at that, he made certain I'd understand that the information was for Stephen. I had no choice but to deliver that information and make good on the friend's promise.

An angel messenger had used me, a mortal messenger as a spiritual conduit to deliver a vital piece of information from beyond, making good on a promise he'd made when still alive. I was the lucky person chosen to deliver a divine "Thank You" to a dear friend and hopefully assuage his fears (and mine in the process) forever.

1989

Ghost Writer

I MET JOEY at the gym, my third favorite place to meet boys after the beach and dance floor — not coincidentally all places of partial undress with the possibility of sex. From the start, he was as attracted to me as much as I to him. Nice. Also rare. We met in the sauna and consummated our relationship on the spot right there in the dry heat of that small, dimly-lit, cedar-lined room. He was quick to tell me how he had a thing for "thick-hipped men." He saw my least favorite physical characteristic as a plus. He had me.

Joey was Italian, younger and a little shorter than I with the kind of soft curly unkempt hair that somehow always fell perfectly over his forehead. He had a smooth, rounded, tanned, well muscled body. **He was made for sex; some people just are.** I was quite certain, I'd seen him in a Caravaggio painting with his darkly lashed amber eyes, richly blushed cheeks, dimpled chin and (my favorite) his impossibly full rosy lips, so full in fact, his lower lip actually had lip-cleavage. Joey once pointed out that his level of horniness could be accurately gauged by simply looking at his upper lip. There was a contrasting white line that would appear, separating the rosy-pink of his lip from the lighter tan of his facial skin tone. The brighter and more distinct that reliable thin white line, the hornier he was. That upper lip became the barometer of our sexual activity.

No longer at a nine to five job I had plenty of time on my hands and, starting with our sauna sex-meet, I spent a lot of it at Joey's house. It was a big old two story home, somewhere out beyond the South End, filled with antiques, dogs and people. In sharp contrast to the quiet increasingly tomblike atmosphere on Cedar Lane Way, Joey's home was filled with life. There was an ever changing cast of characters who came and went, seemingly at will. Did they all have keys or were the doors never locked? The enormous kitchen was the gathering place, a kind of wacky way station for any friend or friend of friend or just anyone who needed or wanted a place to hang out and be a part of Joey's off-kilter family. We'd hear them coming and going, smoking and toking, cooking and chatting as we'd be kissing and fucking right above them.

Joey was just what I needed — a ready, willing, self-described sex addict. "I'm addicted to sex and happy about it so we can work on anything but that," he had once gleefully warned a therapist on his first visit. We'd smoke some weed and make love for hours in his French antique bed, intertwined in each other. The afternoon sunlight would filter through the sheer curtains creating a soft chiaroscuro effect on the firm Caravaggio curves of Joey's smooth naked body and firing the crystal chandelier over our heads, casting tiny sparkling rainbows all around the room. At the foot of the bed, on the oriental carpeted floor of that elegant room, unpredictably, was a blow up kids' swimming pool, its shiny-bright primary colors at odds with the otherwise hushed cream and rose-gold tones of the room. Just as unpredictably, it was filled with a litter of newborn whimpering puppies. Post-sex, Joey would slip off the bed, still naked, scoop up a couple of puppies and curl up with them on the velvety wool of the carpet, their equally velvet pudgy little bodies slipping up and over his satin skin as he'd roll around with them, another, albeit larger, puppy. Watching over the edge of the French cane footboard I'd feast my eyes on all I saw, falling in love and lust for this unpredictable human being with the prettiest, smoothest, roundest, whitest, hungriest, most responsive and delectable bubble-butt I had ever enjoyed.

In that bed, during and post-sex, I learned so much about that boy. He'd been abused; psychologically, physically, emotionally, and sexually. I imagined him as a child, how sweet and pretty he must have been and because of those two qualities, in equal parts, how vulnerable he'd been to his abusers. **How they'd so thoroughly convinced this little angel that he was anything less.** The damage they'd inflicted went deep and was apparent in behaviors he seemed unable to control. Sex being one. Alcohol another. Weed and prescription medications as well. Though I didn't have the words to describe it then, Joey was bi-polar. When his highs kicked in, you knew it. That's when the sex was its manic best. It was also when he'd become reckless. Dangerous. On a dark narrow road to Cape Cod, the manic Joey's eyes would go wild. He'd press the accelerator to the floor of his Mercedes roadster til the speedometer could no longer register the miles per hour, terrifying me and making me wonder why I would risk myself this way. Then, of course, I'd remember the sex. And the tenderness. And the sex. Occasionally, during especially wild sex, I would see the manic Joey become the depressed Joey. In an instant, without warning, he'd shift from insatiable and eager to depressed and disinterested. We'd stop mid-fuck as he'd curl into a fetal position, a wounded puppy just needing to be held. **I was mad about both the boys.**

Once while we were curled up together post-sex, Joey hesitantly asked, "Can you do me a favor?" Knowing how much I'd enjoyed any favor I had ever granted him in that bed, I responded, "Yes. Of course. What can...?" Before I could complete my thought he was off the bed with, "Wait here." My eyes followed his naked body across the room intently watching his every move. I could not take my eyes off that boy. The sexy perfection of his form and movement never failed to mesmerize me. Squeezing my once-again-hardening penis, my eyes devoured as they always would, every curvy inch of him, appreciating along with his boyish beauty, his sturdy sexiness. Standing at an antique desk in the golden horizontal evening glow pouring through the large bay window, Joey was in silhouette, outlined by a warm shimmering golden line of light trimming the curve of his back, his rounded ass, muscular legs, his full pecs, perky nipples and equally perky penis. **I watched as this haloed being pulled from a heavy wooden drawer, a stack of letters tied with a thin satin rose colored ribbon.** Joey returned to bed, snuggled in next to me, and pulled at the satin bow. He opened one of the envelopes and held its contents out to me. I could read a combination of urgency, longing and need, in those big amber-eyes as he pleaded, "Read this to me."

I took the hand written letter from him, unfolded it and began to read aloud. "My dear sweet Joey,..." It became clear to me that this was a letter written to Joey by his deceased lover. I had known that his adored (also thick-hipped) lover had died of AIDS. It was a wound still fresh and Joey was in some ways lost without him. As he listened intently to the words lovingly written to him, I hadn't grasped why I was reading those very personal words out loud until it dawned on me that Joey couldn't read them himself. Joey was illiterate. His lover, an English teacher, had written and left behind at his passing, a stack of letters professing his love for a boy who, tragically, could not read them. This seemed to me to be, especially for an English teacher who'd clearly understand these things, the ultimate act of irony. Or perhaps Joey had hidden his reading disability from his lover. I didn't know, but from that day on, I became the from-beyond voice of Joey's deceased love. **We'd lie in bed together, Joey snuggled up to me and work our way through page after page as I poured someone else's heart out to him.** The letters were beautifully and lovingly written but were so personal, so incredibly intimate that at times I felt like an intruder. They had shared not only what appeared to be, in those letters at least, a fairy tale romance but also the very bed in which we now lay pressed together. It should have been he, not me, pressed up against that beautiful naked boy, expressing those words of love. His words of love. Glancing up now and then, I could see both the love and loss on Joey's face as he'd intently listen and I would feel just a little jealous or perhaps envious of the ghost who'd written them. I wasn't entirely sure in our subsequent sex whether it was me or the deceased lover Joey was giving himself to. **For certain, Joey and I were never alone in that room. There were three of us there; always. And of course, all those puppies.**

Joey was somewhat impatiently I think, waiting to join his ex and would do so in only a few short years when AIDS came to claim him. He would depart this world leaving his love letters behind along with the dog-and-friend-filled house where he'd created a life with a man of words who, just as impatiently I imagine, awaited him.

1989

A Change Is Coming

MY RELATIONSHIP with Joey made it quite clear that another change was way overdue in my life. I couldn't go on lying to Chase about my daily whereabouts and activities. Nobody can spend that much time at the gym. I had to come clean so one evening I just simply laid out the facts as I saw them. We weren't in love with each other, perhaps never had been. We had evolved into significantly different persons from the ones who had initially met that night some five years before at Sutter's Mill in San Francisco. And on top of everything else, I had met someone else with whom I was having a torrid sexual relationship. I didn't think it would amount to "anything long term" but sill there was someone else. It was time we move on. I had had my eye on an up and coming area of Miami called South Beach and thought I'd like to investigate living there and perhaps even opening a shop. I had a great idea for a store and thought it was the ideal time to put it in motion and South Beach the ideal location, location, location. **My head, full of thoughts of palm trees, beaches and sunny coastal retail had already moved on from Boston. And Chase.** It wouldn't be immediate, but without question, I was moving on.

Chase was not happy with this new development and I think the worst part was that he hadn't gotten there first. He'd have so wanted to be the one to break up with me; I imagine he'd been toying with the idea. Chase was most furious that I had had a conversation about it with our friend Jon before I'd spoken with him. Jon was a friend to both of us but was definitely Chase's best friend. In seeking his advice and trying to provide Chase with a friendly cushion of support I had unwittingly taken away his ability to say that it had been his idea. He was not happy with me now on so many levels. Living together without an exit strategy was difficult, to say the least. I moved to the upstairs bedroom and we began carving out our new lives both together and apart.

Not more than two weeks after "the talk," while in the throes of figuring out how to proceed with my life, Chase came home from work early having gone to the doctor. He hadn't been feeling well. He'd had a persistent shortness of breath and something "yeast-y" in his throat. **Tests were done and it turned out Chase was HIV positive. April 3rd, 1989 brought a diagnosis of pneumocystis and full blown AIDS.** My grandfather had died years before on April 3rd and the same day a year later a tornado had ripped through our Louisville neighborhood destroying a good portion of the entire city. "Did anything good ever happen on April 3rd?" I wondered.

We were both filled with a mixed bag of emotions: surprise, anxiety, bewilderment, guilt, sadness and mostly, fear. I wondered what part I had played in this. I hadn't been tested yet. Had I given it to him? Had he given it to me? I sat outside the room where Chase was getting his bronchoscopy and tried to forget the cough I'd had for the last three weeks. I tried to ignore the small dark spot that had appeared on my right bicep over a week ago and wouldn't seem to go away. It could be just a bruise. Or not. If only I could remember hitting my arm there. And the cough could just be a touch of bronchitis. Or not.

By this time Randy had been sick for a while out in San Francisco. We'd all lived with the cloud of AIDS gathering over our heads for the better part of a decade, one that I had wished away from its beginning. **We hoped for the day when the sky would clear; instead, the rain came.** Chase was hospitalized. We learned an entirely new vocabulary. Aerosol Pentamidine and Bactrim became everyday words. So would the words "double blind study." Horrible sounding words like: Kaposi's Sarcoma, Candidiasis, Toxoplasmosis, Coccidioidomycosis, Cytomegalovirus, Wasting, Lumbar Puncture, and so many others previously unknown to us, became critically important.

We got Chase through that first hospitalization and back home as the entire universe shifted beneath us.

1989

Surviving Chase
(Part 1)

TIMING, throughout my life has been critically important and never more so than at this point in time. Having spent the better part of a year contemplating such a step, I had finally broken up with Chase and not a moment too soon. Had we been together when he was diagnosed, I'm certain I'd have felt trapped. Without a choice, I'd have felt obligated to stay on and take care of him. I'm sure I'd have resented him for it. Since we had already made our split by the time he had gotten sick however, it was my choice to stay. An easy decision really. I couldn't have left him to fight this battle alone. I had seen too many of our friends go through it without the support of families and it was their significant others and best friends who got them through it. Chase needed someone to rely on and there was no question I was that person. He had no family to speak of and what little he did was on the west coast. My focus shifted from my future plans to Chase's survival. I promised him that I would stay for as long as it took for the death sentence that was an AIDS diagnosis to play itself out. I didn't use those words but that was the reality of the situation. Everyone diagnosed with AIDS died. That was the reality for all the others and now it was Chase's reality. Our reality. **I swore to Chase absolutely and unequivocally that he would not die alone. I would be there.**

Timing was also critical in that by the time Chase became ill, my business had pretty much dried up. Store design is totally dependent on retail expansion and post stock market crash of October 1987 and the subsequent disastrous Christmas that followed, all retail expansion stopped. I had gone into that Christmas with two or three really great clients and I came out of it with none. At 36 and without clients I had time on my hands and the ability to lavish it on Chase and his care. It was easy at first as there was a period, perhaps laced with denial, where he became a new person. He'd left his job with a sizable and hard fought for severance package. This was, as it turned out, one of the final sightings of the tough, supreme negotiator Christopher. Chase seemed healthy and was happier than I'd seen him in years. Odd how a death sentence (laced with a little denial) can do that for you. He seemed to be embracing his new found time the way I had in my own faux death sentence. The Christopher personality took a backseat to Chase and there were even glimmers of sweet Chaser here and there. **I found myself oddly attracted to this new person who showed a newfound joy of living and a carefree quality I had never observed in him before.**

We began to live together in harmony similar to our first days together in San Francisco and began to enjoy a non-romantic, non-sexual relationship that was not unlike the "platonic lover" situation I had shared with Randy years before. We found a kind of domestic balance with each other, doing a lot of things together and a lot of things on our own. We started seeing other people and eventually even felt comfortable bringing them home. I would get small jobs now and then that would bring in money and he had his severance and benefits. He also took advantage of his newfound time to travel. He loved getting away and I loved having the alone time. I was able to occasionally travel back and forth to San Francisco to help Randy with his AIDS related challenges.

1990

Good Work On Good Work

MY EXPERIENCE at Marshall Field's left a void later in my professional life that I tried over and over to fill. Having enjoyed such a close mentor/mentee relationship with the President and CEO, Phil Kelly, I sought time and again to replicate it. Sadly I was completely unsuccessful at this — it's a gold dust thing. Out on my own again, I was meeting with relative success at this in Boston and had a few recurring clients. While things were looking up, I still needed more work.

More work (or at least the potential for it) came with a phone call from a store design firm in Texas. They were getting ready to pitch a potential client and had been given my name as a possible designer to lead the project. They were making a trip to New York to interview potential designers. Would I meet them there? Assuming the project to be a department store, since department store design was my area of expertise, and, since the interview was in New York, I also assumed the store to be there. A department store in New York? I was in. I spread my entire portfolio out for them, most of which was Marshall Field's work and told them about those halcyon days and my relationship to Phil Kelly; how I had helped him "dust-off" the formerly dowdy Marshall Field's giving it a fresh bold look. They seemed interested in me and my work and though they were looking at "several store designers," I left New York feeling optimistic about my chances.

Back in Boston, a phone call the next day confirmed I'd been chosen for the project. I was delighted of course, but I was in no way prepared for what came next. The project they were getting ready to pitch, with me now as lead designer, was the total renovation of the Garfinckel's flagship store in Washington DC.

Though not New York, I was nonetheless thrilled. Just like in Chicago, I would be working on another old, venerable, grande dame department store. And then the news got even better. Miraculously better. It seemed the new President of Garfinckels was…wait for it…George P. Kelly, also known as Phil! When they called me into the interview they had no idea I had had any connection to Phil, but apparently when I began to show them all the Marshall Field's work and talked about my relationship with Mr. Kelly, it was a done deal. In the bag. They realized that, though unwittingly, they had brought in the exact designer that could help them get the job. And it had. **I was beside myself knowing that once again, I would be working alongside my mentor from those fabulous Chicago days and working on one of the oldest and greatest names in retail.** Somehow things just seem to work out for me.

I made my first trip with the design firm executives to DC to meet with Mr. Kelly. I think he was nearly as thrilled to see me as I was to see him. It would be just like the old days. Mr. Kelly had a great belief in my abilities. He once told me that I was one of the few people he knew "to have real talent." I say this not to brag but to illustrate the level of confidence this accomplished man was able to instill in me. He always gave me free reign with design and I always "exceeded" his "high expectations." Again, his words. And again there were his kind words keeping me under Marshall Field's protective umbrella until my business was up and running.

As we toured the flagship together he described his vision for the store. It was a vision we shared and I could visualize it immediately. I knew I'd be able to give him exactly the store he wanted. More than what he wanted actually. I think he knew it too. So here we were in Washington now doing the same thing we'd done in Chicago years before. Another field trip was planned, for New York this time. I met Phil in New York along with executives from both Garfinckel's and the design firm and together we limousine-d our way around New York City. **It was just like the old "walk with me" days at Marshall Field's looking at stores, picking each other's brain and getting ideas for the renovation.** We were back in business. Gold dust!

The Garfinckel's flagship was a jewel. It was designed by the same firm responsible for Lord and Taylor, Bloomingdales and best of all, Saks, the one actually *on* Fifth Avenue in New York. It opened in 1929 just two blocks from The White House and was on the National Register of Historic Places. **Though possessing the rather dowdy look of an old dowager sorely in need of some love, she was still a grand dame with great bones; I couldn't wait to get my hands on her.** I knew Phil wanted to do at Garfinckel's what he'd done so successfully at Marshall Field's recreating its image as a forward thinking fashion and trend-setting store. As we were touring the store Mr. Kelly asked me what I thought of it. I told him just what I wrote above, adding that it was a jewel that I couldn't wait to get my hands on it. And then I added, "You know, Phil, this is my favorite kind of work. Rather than starting from scratch and designing from the ground up, I prefer to work on something well-established with good bones, honoring the original design, doing my good work on the good work that came before me." I heard myself say those words, "Good work on good work," and the words stuck in my head. Since I had just stared my own business, I had been looking for a slogan, some sort of identification beyond my name and there it was, "Good Work On Good Work." My new business slogan went directly on to my cards, stationery and envelopes and in time became a slogan for living — a way of life. **There is always good work that has come before us and we all have the ability of add our good work to the good work of others; every day in every way making the world a better place.** And in turn there will be others to come after us to add their good work to ours.

I returned to Boston with architectural plans of the Garfinckel's flagship and full of ideas. I was in retail heaven again working for Phil Kelly and redesigning this grand dame of a store. Just a few weeks into the job I got the telephone call. I never understood exactly what happened but because of problems with "mergers and acquisitions" Garfinckel's suddenly declared bankruptcy and closed its doors. We'd barely gotten started and my dream project with my old mentor was over. It was all too familiar. Occasionally things don't work out for me.

1990

La Te Da

THE RELAXED ATMOSPHERE of Key West did not promote punctuality. The saying goes, "The only thing in Key West you have to be on time for is the sunset." The sun, which set spectacularly every night off Mallory Dock (never waiting for the latecomer) put on a show you didn't want to miss. Along with the show itself was a nightly festival to celebrate this every twenty four hour occurrence. With street performers, vendors, artisans and hoards of visitors (most of them gay and in the mood for a party) it was an event you didn't want to miss even, with the laxness of the environment, if you arrived too late and missed the sun actually setting. Jugglers, acrobats, performers of every stripe; The Parrot Guy and The Cookie Lady showed up nightly without fail to ply their trade, entertain or sell their goods. There was even one sweet smiling, handsome and oh so hunky, kilted bagpipe player — you waited and hoped for an accommodating gust of wind. Never before or since have I ever much cared for the sound of bagpipes but that boy...whew... he was music to my eyes.

The only other event for which punctuality was important to me was the Tea Dance every Sunday evening at La Terrazza de Marti, adorably shortened to La Te Da. It was simply the best tea dance ever. Or at least, my favorite — a gorgeous weekly event of which I would not want to miss a minute. **I would in fact, plan my Key West stay for a week plus two weekends and tack on an extra Monday just so I could do two tea dances at La Te Da in one wonderful vacation.** I was not alone in my love of this Sunday afternoon standard. It was so popular in fact that during the hour or so preceding its start, there'd be no water pressure anywhere in Key West as every gay boy on the island was showering at the same time. The city water service at the time, with its underachieving feed all the way from the mainland was no match for the demand. Water would just drool out of the shower and over your head in your futile attempt to wash the day's suntan products, sand, lube or whatever bodily fluids you'd produced or collected. No one was going to miss La Te Da and everyone was going to be pretty.

And why not? La Te Da was a pretty event. Magical even. La Terraza de Marti was a traditional Key West guest house which wrapped its white clapboard self around a lushly landscaped pool with up-lit palm trees and loads of flowering tropical vegetation spilling out everywhere. The lighting was a flattering, cosmetic pink, giving the entire place a romantic tropical La Vie En Rose quality. At the end of the pool was a small dance floor and wrapping itself around the rear of it were multi-level stepped-back white railed decks making it a sort of dance amphitheater. If you happened to be up on one of those decks you could look down on the whole splendid event — the happy dancing, the sparkling pool, the tropical flowers and plants, all of it washed in that lovely pink light. From that higher vantage point you'd also be treated to the Key West sun fabulously setting (that's the only way it knew how) at the other side of the small super-flat island. If you were on the dance floor and glanced up, your eyes would be happily filled with the sight of those same decks lined with boys, cocktails in hand. **Sporting their recently acquired, glow-in-the-sunset tans contrasted with every shade of white and pastel imaginable, they were all gloriously illuminated to a rich golden hue by the graciously dependable fireball descending in the west.**

It was no wonder I was full of impatience as I waited in our room at the Oasis for my friend Jay to get ready. He seemed to lack any degree of urgency (or pick up on mine) as he glacially pulled himself together for his first La Te Da tea dance. Clearly my description of La Te Da and the wonders waiting there had not impressed him enough to mirror my need to get there early. The all important life lesson that time and circumstance work in our favor not against it, at this point in my life, was still years away. I would come to learn that whatever time I happen to arrive, at a party for instance, is exactly the time I am supposed to arrive. It's a lesson that had I learned earlier would have saved me from a lot of angst; like the angst I was experiencing at that particular moment. So there I was fully dressed in my favorite trim white cotton shorts, tight white t-shirt, and blue and burgundy grosgrain belt. I had my favorite sun bleached baby blue bandana tightly rolled and tied at my neck and I was ready to go, tapping my fingers and tapping my feet. Occasionally going out by the pool and coming back, and going back out again, I waited for my dear friend to pull himself together, as slowly as humanly possible, for his first Key West tea dance. Jay clearly did not realize the enormity of the event that lay ahead.

We had arrived on Friday evening and had spent Saturday and Sunday in the absolutely essential task of acquiring our tans just for this event. One that was now upon us and we were going to be suitably suntanned but terribly late. Getting there on the early side I would always have a little time to check out each level and enjoy the view from up high before heading down to the dance floor. Once on the dance floor I'd rarely leave. I had never been late before and at this point I knew the place would be packed and the party in full swing. We were already missing precious party moments. I tried to stay on the positive side, imagining us making a fashionably late entrance right onto the dance floor of a full blown party. That'd be fun too, I tried to convince myself.

I really needed that particular party on that particular night. We were well into the AIDS crises by then and friends were sick and dying all around us. The horror show played on. Randy had been sick for more than a year and Chase had been diagnosed as well. It was a difficult time to say the least and I optimistically extricated myself from it to take some time away to get lost in what had always been the restorative magic that was Key West. I had been focused for months on the moment I would enter La Te Da as I had done so many times before. As I not so patiently waited back out by the pool, my only thought was, "I have to get to that party!" I was a man dying of thirst in the desert with the watering hole in sight but just out of reach. I had to get to it.

Jay finally made his coiffed and crisply linen-ed appearance and we were off. It was a bit of a hike from the Oasis to La Te Da which was pretty much on the other side of the island. It was a walk I usually relished, starting out early and taking at a snail's pace because of all the window shopping and all the cruising along the way. But there were no boys to cruise on Duvall Street; they were all at tea dance. It seemed to take forever to get there but we finally made it. We had heard the party from blocks away. High energy dance music was inviting us in and a crowded dance floor full of boys awaited us.

We finally arrived and we made our way through the thicket of boys to the dance floor. I was shocked to find the dance floor, which should have been packed, wasn't. There was no one on it. Not a soul. The party should have been in full swing by then but there wasn't a party at all. And not for a lack of partiers. The place was packed. The perimeter of the empty dance floor was filled with boys as were the decks above and, as usual, the upper-deck partiers were spectacularly illuminated by that glorious sunset lighting. At least we hadn't missed that. I looked up at the beautifully illuminated faces but saw none of the usual joy. The boys lined the terraces as always but they exhibited none of the joy that La Te Da was famous for. The liveliest place on the island had no life; the most joyful place, joyless. **"So this is it." I silently said to myself, "This is what it's come to. The joy is gone."** This was our new world. Our new reality. AIDS, as it took away our friends had also taken the joy. Those of us who hadn't yet been removed had become the living dead; weary of the caregiving and certain we'd be next. Most of us were convinced, with the dead and dying all around us, that our day of reckoning was right around the corner. Any trip to Key West could be your final one. Any tea dance, your last. **Whenever I heard Donna Summer's "Last Dance" I could think of little else; any dance could be your last.** It had already been that way for so many. We were going through the motions of what we used to do, trying to convince ourselves and others, that we hadn't given up long ago. **Even if our own lives were not immediately threatened, we were still collateral damage, witnessing all the death and dying while valiantly caring for our loved ones.**

I was saddened beyond words and disappointed. And angry. I hated what AIDS had done to my friends and me and our entire lifestyle. To La Te Da. Now it seemed, it had even taken that away. As I stood there looking at that empty dance floor, filled for the moment with an all-consuming anger and hatred for this new reality, I knew I had to do something. Scream? Cry? Leave in a huff? "This above all to thine own self be true." I heard the voice of Polonius giving his son, perhaps the most important words ever spoken. That single sentence had become over the years my own personal mantra serving me well in times of trouble, doubt, fear, anger and hate. It always brings me back. **The truth is, I am none of those things. The truth is, above all, I am a person defined not by what I hate but by what I love.** And what I love is to dance! As much as I love sex — if you've gotten this far you know I do — if I am at a party where there's both sex and dancing, you'll find me on stage, front and center, dancing. I am a dancer. Above all else. Have been since the first time I jumped up on a box and had a dollar bill stuffed into my speedo. I still have it. The dollar. Not the speedo. When the music is good it is my true nature to dance. I don't mind doing it alone; I have on many occasions on many boxes and stages. Dancing is where, above all, I get my energy and how I share it.

"To thine own self be true." I heard the words as a command — a call to arms. With all the courage I could muster, I headed out to the dance floor to dance. By myself. To be true to myself. In the process, I'd be making something of a spectacle of myself but I didn't care. Someone had to do something about the sorry state of this affair. I could do it. I knew I could change the energy; be the plug into the universal energy source. The energy was there — it always is — I just had to tap into it and share it. This was La Te Da — there had to be a party and I had to dance. Pure and simple.

With my signature arms in the air dancing, pure joy in my heart and a smile on my face, I began to dance, making direct eye contact with one boy I'd singled out at the edge of the dance floor. Focused on him, I danced, arms in the air until I got him to return my smile and then quite unexpectedly his arms went into the air as he mimicked me. We were dancing — he on the sidelines and I out on the floor. I did the same with another face I spotted on one of the terraces. He responded in kind, smiling and dancing, arms in the air. I did it with another and another. Some reluctant, or embarrassed and some enthusiastic. Upstairs, downstairs, the boys began responding one by one. A smile here. Arms in the air, there. The energy picked up. These boys all wanted to dance; they just needed some encouragement, though none would venture out, reluctant perhaps to get too involved with the crazy guy alone on the dance floor. Whatever the case, they all stayed put, arms in the air and dancing in place. This continued until I pretty much had the entire place dancing with me. Smiles were everywhere and the place was suddenly filled with the electric energy it had lacked only moments before. I spotted a foursome of enthusiastic lesbians who had moved to a corner of the dance floor in what I interpreted as a desire to join me. With a big smile, I nodded an invitation to them and in seconds they were out on the floor dancing. That's all it took. The place had been heated up, the ice broken and within minutes the dance floor was packed and pumped. It was a party. Just like the old days. Everything was alive as I danced my way from the center of the dance floor to the edge of the pool where I installed myself between two chrome railings — the ones that come up out of the water to get you out of the deep end. From there I had a better scope of the entire party as I continued to dance with everyone including all the levels above where boys were also dancing. **Now this was LaTeDa!**

I spotted, on the other side of the now crazily energized dance floor the face of an angel. It was staring directly at me. A quick glance over my shoulder (to see who he was actually looking at) reminded me there was nothing behind me but pool. He was looking at me, this perfect incarnation of the tow head Florida blond. With his corn silk hair thick and loose, surfer style, and nearly shoulder length, he reminding me of my beloved boyhood angels in our family bible. **This sun-tanned Florida angel's face glowed with the kind of beauty I've always held in absolute reverence.** His finely articulated features, perfect aquiline nose, full pink lips and a long lean body which exposed more of itself to me as he got nearer, were cutting a path right to me. Right to me! The blond-lashed eyes of this heavenly creature, which I could now make out as a pale morning sky blue, were fixed on mine. We were locked in a gaze I could not have pulled away from if I had wanted. As the dancing crowd parted for the Surfer Angel (the way crowds have a tendency to part for such beauty) I could see he was shirtless and barefooted, tan and lean and trim. His long baggy white linen pants, rolled up and showing off a pair of tanned, perfectly turned calves, seemed held up on his narrow hips by some invisible force. He was bronzed trim smooth muscularity. Of course. Angels always are. My eyes followed the sensual curve of his smooth oblique muscles down his narrow bronzed torso past a sharp tan line and over the subsequent stretch of pure white incandescent skin untouched by the sun, to the beginnings of a glowing golden pubic patch peeking over those impossibly low riding pants. **He and his personal presentation were so close to my own personal specifications, I could have designed him myself; indeed, I had been, I suppose, most of my life.** Those determined young eyes were still fixed on me and moving in a direct line to me. I could not widen my eyes enough to take in the fullness of the boy's approaching beauty as I committed every detail to memory. He finally made his sweet smiling way across the dance floor and right up to me. Eye to eye. Nose to nose. Lips to lips...almost. Kissing range. I could feel his breath. I could feel his heat. I could almost feel his heartbeat. I could feel his hands lightly touch my chest. I could feel their warmth. I could feel a push. A firm unexpected push...away. Was it the sound of angel laughter I heard over the music in the split second before I went head first right into the deep end of the pool at La Terraza De Marti? **That sexy little fucker pushed me into the pool!**

Freeze frame...

Being the classic chubby little boy, I had a childhood fear of being pushed by some athletically inclined boy-bully into the deep end of a pool. It was a fear that kept me away from summer camps or any activities where boys would gather near pools or other bodies of water. I was certain, should that happen that I would make a pool fool of myself, splashing and carrying on in front of all the other laughing taunting boys. Now here I was being pushed into the deep end of a pool, forced to face that childhood fear in front of the largest audience I'd ever managed to assemble for myself.

To say I was surprised would be a great understatement. Shocked is more like it. It was all so surreal and seemed to play out in slow motion. I remember hitting the water's surface and going under. Much to my surprise, I didn't panic. My feet found the bottom and I pushed off and quickly made my way up to the surface. By that time, Jay, who I hadn't seen since we first arrived, had made his way to the pool's edge. He was there for the save. I came up right where I'd gone in at the chrome railings. I grabbed the railings, used the steps and Jay's outstretched hand to extricate my soaked self from the pool. I looked up expecting to find, I suppose, people laughing at me, a party full of bullies pointing at dripping wet, embarrassed me. **Instead I saw the stunned faces of an entire party stopped in its tracks.** No one was dancing. The music had continued but the party was frozen in time. With the energy of the party suddenly stolen, everyone was still, standing in place, their expectant faces looking directly at me. I was once again tempted to look over my shoulder. The next move it seemed was up to me. "This above all to thine own self be true." Looking around and buoyed by the goodwill I felt, true to myself and without another thought, I gave the biggest smile of my life, stripped off my soaking white t-shirt, swung it above helicopter style letting it fly into the crowd as both my arms went up and I went back to dancing. Arms went up everywhere and La Te Da went wild. **It was once again a party.**

It was a tradition (or perhaps it became one that day, I'm not sure) that someone would end up in the pool at every La Te Da Tea Dance. I never saw the angel boy again.

1989

Coast To Coast...Ups & Downs...Hopes & Fears

COMFORTABLY SELF-EMPLOYED in Boston, and somewhat in command of my own time, with Chase still in his "HIV Honeymoon period," I was able to fly out to San Francisco with some frequency. Randy's partner Warren, while lots of fun and pretty to look at — really pretty and really sexy and really immature — could barely take care of himself. He was in no way able to carry the responsibility of a sick and dying lover. We got Randy through that first crisis and got him back to the apartment he shared with Warren. What we all came to learn about this insufferable disease was that dramatic changes were the norm. If the word "norm" can be used at all. Boys almost overnight became old men. Deterioration would come on so fast that death would seem to be imminent one day, and then suddenly, a full recovery would happen just as fast, giving hope. False hope, as the process would simply reverse itself. Over and over. **A weird combination of hope and despair guided our days.** You just never knew when any sudden plunge would be the last. Whether going up or going down the suffering was constant. The fear. The treatments. The trials. The procedures. The hospitalizations. The never ending medical horror show that was AIDS. When Randy was sick it was frightening and challenging, but when he had recovered it was just like the old days of laughing at the absurdities of life. We now had so many new absurdities concurrent with this awful illness and laughed our way through those too. And cried. Always together. During one of my visits, he introduced me to his new favorite TV personality, a likable woman named Oprah Winfrey. We'd watch her daily talk show together, enthralled, oftentimes high, just the way we had with Julia Child and Tammy Faye Bakker in the carefree Chicago days. We'd talk back to the screen with our own take on what was being discussed. Like straight guys watching a football game, we were armchair coaches of a different stripe. If we were apart we'd watch her show individually and then by phone, we'd share our thoughts and perspectives, both silly and serious.

After a while it became pretty clear that Randy's days were numbered at the same time Chase's challenges were mounting. It was attacking on every front. I'd be needed in Boston as much as I was in San Francisco. Knowing Warren couldn't provide the level of care he'd need, Randy made the gut-wrenching decision to go back to Louisville to die. It was a choice many young gay men had to make in those days and not an easy one for Randy. While he had a wonderfully supportive family on whom he knew he could depend (a rarity for gay boys, especially in the days of AIDS) this meant leaving Warren, his work (by then he had established his own accounting business,) his friends, and life in San Francisco. For all practical purposes, he'd be abandoning hope. It also meant leaving the healthcare support of San Francisco, a city along with New York, with the greatest number of AIDS cases. He had the best doctors and the best care. Most everywhere else, AIDS patients were treated as pariahs. Louisville, while pretty advanced medically speaking, would not be so advanced socially. He would not get the tolerant treatment he was used to getting from San Francisco's medical community. This was a decision and commitment we both met with a great deal of trepidation. Chase was stable as I made plans to go out west to help my friend with this new and frightening transition. Was this the beginning of the end?

1989

Going Home To Die

WITH CHASE STABLE and actually flourishing, I could fly out to San Francisco without worry, to help Randy close out his life there. I believe the ever-incapable Warren, left to his own devices, would have probably become homeless. Randy and I shopped for a smaller apartment which Warren would be able to afford on his own. Randy had been the primary breadwinner in their family. We arranged the lease for the new place in Warren's name so all he had to do was sign it. Randy paid the deposit, security and first month's rent. We then arranged the moving company and Randy paid for the move. Warren owned only his clothes and a few personal items, so, Randy left all his belongings behind for Warren's use with the exception of his grand piano (which was shipped to Randy's parents in Louisville) and some clothing and a few precious personal items. We moved all the rest along with Warren into his new Randy-furnished and Michael-decorated, apartment as we prepared to leave San Francisco forever. Randy was able to leave San Francisco knowing that he had done whatever he could to ensure Warren was taken care of. All of this was accomplished as Randy was clearly weakening. It was time to go home to die.

Don't be a gay man dying of AIDS and his gay friend boarding a plane in the late 1980s and expect to be treated as anything close to a human being. Most people in those days knew only enough about AIDS to be terrified of it. Most were not only scared of the disease but often contemptuous of those suffering with it. There was so much misinformation being tossed around to a generally uncaring and often hostile public that few outside those immediately affected actually knew how the virus was transmitted. No one wanted to know. Few seemed even to care as long as it was affecting someone else. "Killing all the right people" as an episode of TV's *Designing Women* had referred to it. Randy and I sat waiting for the plane, to Chicago actually, as there were no direct flights to Louisville. It was in the eyes of all the other passengers and personnel where I could see the fear was registered, or was it horror, or judgement or even hatred? It was clear Randy was sick. He sat there in the boarding area hunched over and skeletal swallowed up by his lumpy sweater. He was only 34 but seemed to be a frail old man. He wasn't old, he was sick. It was easy to read these people's minds. This was, after all, San Francisco, ground zero in the ever escalating AIDS crises. No one thought Randy had lung cancer or leukemia or some other "acceptable" disease. Did I misread what I determined to be hostile looks of disgust and judgement? You cannot get inside someone else's head but it was pretty clear these people did not want us on their flight.

Things got even worse once we boarded. Because Randy was so slow moving, we waited until the end to board (a tactical error I suppose.) First it was the icy looks from the flight attendants as I helped him onto the plane. Then as we moved down the aisle all apprehensive eyes were on us. They were not friendly eyes. These would not be friendly skies. As we made our way haltingly down the narrow aisle, I could read the "not here, not next to me" or the "please pass by" or "keep going" thoughts behind those eyes. The man in the aisle seat quickly got out of our way as I helped Randy into his window seat and I settled into my middle one. The man disappeared. I didn't know if he was was going to return (he didn't) but I quickly grabbed the barf bag from his seat pocket and added it to mine and Randy's. You can't be too prepared.

1989

In Flight

LADIES AND GENTLEMEN, "The pilot has turned on the 'Fasten Your Seatbelts' sign indicating our initial approach into the Chicago area..." The voice on the crackling PA jarred me awake and for a moment, I struggled to remember my whereabouts. The roar of the aircraft and the withering sight of my friend seated to my left snapped me back to reality.

Randy was sitting in the window seat, curled in on himself, his now rapidly balding head resting against the vibrating fuselage wall. I watched him intently as he sat there hunched over, swallowed up by his big over-sized beige cardigan. Eyes half-lidded. Staring blankly. Not asleep. Not awake, just something in between. I had seen him in that same state in that same baggy, ratty, threadbare sweater everyday for I don't know how long. **Studying the sloping curve of his formerly broad shoulders I got the image of one of those weak wire shirt hangers, how they bend down and in, under-qualified when over-burdened by the weight of a heavy winter overcoat.** Randy was like that now, his under-qualified body weak and over-burdened by the overcoat of existence itself. Or what was left of his existence, if you could even call it that. And by that sweater. That old nappy sweater that so perfectly matched his somber mood these days. Like the sweater, he was looking old. Very old. He knew it. He had said so just days before. As we were standing at the bathroom mirror brushing our teeth in an activity we'd performed together innumerable times, Randy said, "I look old." I remained silent as I brushed away. Glancing over to me he continued, "I look old. Don't I look old?" I tried to ignore the insistence of his question and continued brushing. He pressed on, "Don't you think I look old?" He poked my arm demanding an answer. "No," I lied, "You look thin. Too thin. You're not eating enough." He rolled his eyes at that one. He'd heard this from me too many times and had tired of it long before. "You barely touched your breakfast this morning." More eye rolling. "And," I hesitated with this one but proceeded anyway, unable to control myself, "you're still smoking." He'd heard this before too and I could see in the mirror, his lips mimicking my last words. I gave him my typical side-eye but I understood. In truth he'd never been much of an eater but smoking, well that was a different matter. **Smoking was the only activity that Randy actually enjoyed anymore and he was not about to give it up.** One of the advantages of having AIDS I suppose, was that other life threatening illnesses were no longer so threatening. He laughed at cancer and sneered down emphysema. Who was I to take the joy of smoking away from him? But there I was admonishing him and trying my best, I suppose, to have some sort of impact on his deteriorating state of health and on his... "Ladies and gentlemen, as we make our final approach..."

Another PA announcement brought me back to the present and as they finished preparing the cabin for landing, I leaned over Randy's hunched body and tried to catch a glimpse of Chicago from the air. I wondered if he even realized we were above the city we'd lived in and loved so much. **Did he even care that the rapidly approaching grid with its assemblage of buildings was the place that had shaped so much of our lives?** It made me think about the years we'd spent dreaming of some day living in that city which seemed, at the time, so out of reach and after we'd made it, all the wonderful carefree days and nights we shared there. The fabulous parties we'd planned together and given; the stacks of thank you notes received. The nights of cruising and partying. The boys we'd brought home and gone home with. The friends we made. The friends we had sex with. The friends we lost. It made me wonder where and when had Randy actually acquired this hideous acquired immune disease. Had it been as early as Chicago? Was it one of those nights we'd both gone out looking for a human connection? Looking for love, or sex or both. In our horny pursuit, had one of us actually brought back a disease instead? A disease no one even knew existed at the time. A malicious disease that could and would kill. Had there been another decision we could have made that would have changed the course of these events? Who knew? Was it one of those cold Chicago nights when we might just as well have decided to stay at home, turn on the TV, get high together and let Tammy Faye Bakker with her running mascara "save our souls" and in so doing, Randy's life? Who knew? **I guess you really never know when a seemingly insignificant decision will end up being a life saving one or life taking one...** "Ladies and Gentlemen, we will be on the ground shortly."

Once again a PA announcement brought me back. And back to Chicago. Momentarily. It felt strange that Chicago, "our Chicago" was now just a place to change planes; especially on a trip home to die. We deplaned and went through the whole horrible, demeaning experience of boarding again, this time for the flight to Louisville — a smaller plane and smaller minds.

Randy's condition continued to deteriorate and he was eventually hospitalized in Louisville close to death with pneumonia. It was Pneumocystis of course and only a matter of time now. I would sit for days and nights with Randy in the hospital, at his bedside wondering how long until the end, how many more days, hours or minutes. I looked at my friend so gaunt, so drawn and gray, in so much agony and gasping for breath and I wondered if it was apparent to the dying person that he was actually dying. If so, was it also apparent exactly when he would die or was it a mystery on his side as well? **I looked into Randy's eyes for a clue that my friend might hold some sort of wisdom about his future to which I was not privy.** He was looking back at me. Tears were welling up in his cloudy terrified blue eyes, the only place where life still showed itself. As a single tear overflowed his left eye and made its way down his misery-worn face, I reached out and wiped it away. Looking down at my dampened finger and seeing a recently acquired paper cut that lay just beneath the tear, I became instantly frightened. Of a tear. My friend's tear. With all the warnings about bodily fluids, I suddenly wondered if HIV could be transmitted through a tear. **I was just as suddenly horrified and ashamed of myself at the thought — the traitorous thought that my best friend's tear could possibly kill me. I briefly hated myself for even thinking it and still, I surreptitiously and guiltily wiped the tear from my finger as quickly as possible and felt smaller for the act.**

1989

The Trouble With Warren

RANDY'S WONDERFUL FAMILY was there in support, all of us waiting together at the hospital for the inevitable. Or what we thought to be inevitable. As it had happened before, this time against all odds, Randy pulled through. He not only pulled through but, after a series of ups and downs, and various courses of treatment, he began to flourish. Was it the new meds, new treatments, the support of a kind and loving family? A miracle? Was the horror show over? Should we actually be hopeful? Would gay boys, Randy included, stop dying now? We didn't know. What we did know was that he was actually doing better and getting healthier and feeling stronger than he had in a long while. I returned to Boston and Chase who was beginning his own downhill trajectory.

As Randy's health continued to improve in Louisville, out in San Francisco, Warren's health started to fail and of course it was AIDS. Randy was feeling so robust by this time that he decided to go back out to San Francisco and look after Warren who as it has already been established had trouble taking care of himself even in the best of circumstances. **Randy flew out and moved in with all his old belongings and Warren.** He was back home again in San Francisco, taking care of sick Warren in the apartment he'd rented for him. No one had imagined such a scenario back when Randy, facing imminent death, had left San Francisco forever to die. They were back together again, Warren, Randy and all of Randy's stuff, in the apartment we'd set Warren up in not so long before.

Randy's health stayed stable while Warren deteriorated with the usual ups and downs of any AIDS patient. He was not the fighter that Randy was. His course with the disease would be shorter. Warren's health began to deteriorate rapidly and he was hospitalized. Randy practically lived at the hospital watching the robust young man he'd loved, deteriorating now before him. Having been near death not too long before, Randy never imagined Warren going first. The irony of the situation was not lost on him.

Throughout their earlier years together, whenever questioned about his family, Warren would respond that they were no longer a part of his life. Period. Pressing on, Randy had managed to eventually get out of him that they were "Bible-thumping Christians" who lived "somewhere in Southern California." He had no relationship with them anymore. Period. No more questions. No more answers. When Warren was hospitalized at one point, death seemed to be imminent. His hospital records were consulted and information regarding his next of kin was somehow in there. Warren's "Bible-thumping Christian" parents were informed by the hospital that the son they didn't even know was gay, was in a San Francisco hospital, dying of AIDS. **I'd like to be able to write about a good, caring, loving, empathetic Christian family who arrived in support of their gay son but that was hardly the case.**

Though I was in Boston taking care of Chase at the time, Randy and I were in daily touch, sometimes hourly. He called and told me how Warren's mother and sister had appeared out of nowhere, stormed the hospital and, of course not wanting to know anything of Warren's homosexuality or of Randy's existence, tried to shut him out. While Randy had no legal rights to Warren's hospital bedside, it was San Francisco and the hospital staff already knew Randy and allowed him in whenever the mother and sister were not there. So the "family" was not entirely successful in keeping Randy away from Warren. At home it was a different situation. The mother and sister moved into the apartment with Randy for a few uncomfortable nights, taking over the bedroom and sanitizing everything in sight. Randy described to me how he'd found his prized sterling silver flatware soaking in Clorox and ruined. The next time he called, it was with the worst news. In Randy's absence they'd changed the locks. One night exhausted after a long day at the hospital, Randy returned to find he'd been locked out. The apartment which Randy had rented for Warren but paid for himself; the apartment for which Randy was currently paying the rent; the same apartment that was filled with Randy's belongings, even his clothes (and now, with Warren's mother and sister;) suddenly, due to the act of these "Christians," was locked; with Randy on the outside. When he'd set up the lease, Randy had done so in only Warren's name. He was on the street with absolutely no proof that anything on the other side of that locked door was his. **Randy was suddenly, unbelievably, without a moment's notice, at the hands of these supposed Christians, shut-out and homeless in San Francisco with nothing but the clothes he'd put on that morning.**

He made some phone calls and a female friend took Randy in. He continued to visit Warren every day coordinating with the nurses to learn when the "family" wasn't there. As I've mentioned before, you never knew if an AIDS patient was in his final moments or if he'd suddenly rebound and be discharged. Warren didn't rebound one evening. His mother (not Randy) was notified of her son's death. Randy had, that same evening, left a seemingly stable Warren not knowing they'd already spent their final hours together.

Warren's family moved quickly. They emptied the apartment, collected Warren's body from the hospital, presumably packed it up with all of Randy's belongings and disappeared into the night, returning to "somewhere in Southern California." Randy never had the chance to say "Goodbye." Randy's home was gone. His belongings were gone. His clothes were gone. His lover was gone. He was left with nothing. **Still terminally ill himself, Randy was homeless with only the clothes on his back, a dead and vanished lover, and AIDS. A small band of anonymous, marauding "Christians" had stripped him of what little he'd had left to hold on to.**

I think of Randy and the tragedy of this moment whenever I have problems or I'm listening to someone else recount theirs. I think of how cruel the world can be, especially to those with kind hearts. I think of the strength, the determination, the fortitude my kind-hearted friend exhibited in getting himself through this. I am still awed by my best friend William Randal ("though everybody calls me Randy") Riede.

I also think of those "Christians," the villains of this story. I try not to obsess on them and on what they did to my best friend. I have long ago set aside thoughts of revenge, preferring to believe with all my heart in karma. I do empathize with these people who didn't even know their son was gay, only to suddenly find out he was dying of the dreaded "gay plague." How that horrifying information fit nowhere into the format of their "Christian" existence. I do my best (with varying results) to empathize with them, try to hold them in my heart, and forgive them.

1989

Do Something Normal

ONCE AGAIN, 3000 miles separated me from my friend in distress. He felt hopeless and I felt helpless. It had all happened so fast; there was nothing I could do for him. No way I could help. Randy continued staying with his female friend. I can only remember her last name now, the rest of her information is in the address book I retired because of all the dead friends in it. A book of the dead. It was better to simply start a new one as I just couldn't bear to cross one more name out.

Weeks into his new living arrangement, one evening on the phone, believe it or not Randy and I were actually laughing. It was of course all about the absurdity of his situation. "You know this is going to make for great storytelling someday," one of us said to the other. It was big-drama and would be a great story to tell. Someday. If either of us survived. If we did manage to survive we'd have done so laughing our way through it. That's for sure. It was the only way. For us. When you've been slammed down to rock bottom, a good sense of humor is probably the best device to pull yourself back up. Or to be helped up. **Randy had died so many times in his head, in both our heads, that nothing was too serious anymore.** As I'd be wringing my hands in distress about his trials and tribulations on the other end of the line my friend with AIDS would respond with, "Hey, I've got my health," his voice dripping with irony. We'd break up.

During one of our calls Randy was asking for advice about his situation. What did I think? With Warren gone should he go back to Louisville? Should he stay in San Francisco? Should he start up his business again? Should he look for an apartment or a roommate? He had always been a planner and it seemed, since he was healthier these days, that perhaps, he just might have a future to plan for after all. A total fresh start. What had been a distant hope was suddenly possible. Or at least possibly possible.

With so many questions about his existence, I suggested that this might be a good time to take a backseat and allow the universe to take the lead. At the word "universe," I knew my pragmatic friend's eyes were rolling on the other end of the line. My turn toward the spiritual, developed during all those years of loss wasn't always in line with Randy's more practical view of existence. Things really did have a way of working out for me and I was learning to perhaps attribute those "things" to some higher power with a broader view than my own. I had also learned that I couldn't control everything and perhaps even better, I shouldn't try. **Randy wasn't always ready to embrace my new found philosophies and was skeptical of what he saw as a convenient repackaging of my old "things just seem to work out for me" philosophy.** In retrospect I imagine he was also none too eager to turn himself over to a universe that time and again had proved itself to be pretty damned hostile. I couldn't blame him really.

In an effort to bring him back from his questionable future, I tried to get him into the more certain present, asking him, "What day is this?" "The date?" he answered, pausing for a deep cigarette smoke exhale, "I dunno I've lost track." "Not date, day, what day of the week?" Thinking this over for a moment he said "Sunday." Having spent many a Sunday with Randy and Warren, I knew the answer to my next question but asked it anyway, "And what do you usually do an a Sunday afternoon?" "You know the answer to that as well as I do," was his quick response, "The Beer Bust at The Eagle." **I suggested that perhaps doing something absolutely normal in this extremely abnormal situation might be just the thing to center him a bit.** "Do something normal. Be true to yourself. Go to The Eagle. Have some fun. You deserve a beer bust," and then I added, "you need some normal right now." There was a long pause on the other end of the phone as his thoughts burned along with his cigarette. "I could use a little normalcy," he thought aloud. "Actually I could also use a beer!" Another pause and with another smoky exhale, "I don't have any clothes." He was right about that. The Eagle, a leather and Levi's sort of place had a strict dress code. Randy's and Warren's boots, jackets, harnesses — all things suitable to the Eagle scene were long gone with Warren's Christian family. We'd already had our share of laughs about this of course. "Who do you think's gonna wear the chaps?" I asked to Randy's snickers. "Ohmygod," Randy replied, "They'll be fighting over them but his Sherman tank of a mom'll win of course. Oh my god I just saw them in our harnesses! Saggy tits and all. Hanging over..." We both cracked up (and got a little nauseous.) "If they had any idea where those boots have been and all the things you've done in them..." Holding our sides, "...and on them!" he added, "...ohmygod...they'd burn them immediately." "Or hold an exorcism!" I added as we both rolled on the floor, laughing. "Yeah just a little 'nomine patris et filii et spiritus sancti...' and they could keep everything without compromising their good Christian integrity. Bless their hearts!" More laughing. "You know they found the porn!" A brief pause as we each pondered church ladies poring over all the hard core action. We cracked up. "Whaddaya suppose they did with it?" And in reply, "You know there's gotta be at least one closeted Christian homo brother or cousin who squirreled it away when no one was looking." More gasping for breath until we both quieted down. Ya had to be there.

"You know what?" Randy said at last with another long drag on his cigarette, "I'm gonna go to The Eagle and I'm gonna go in my white shirt, blue jeans and Weejuns," describing his signature look. "I have always wanted to do that but never had the nerve," exhaling, "...and Warren would never have allowed it anyway." "Well," I responded, "no worries there." It was true. Warren, long gone to somewhere in Southern California along with Randy's furniture, dishes and leather chaps, couldn't protest.

1989

Miracles Happen

A T THE LOW POINT of his life, Randy went that Sunday afternoon to the Beer Bust at The Eagle, an indoor/outdoor bar. He wore his white button down shirt, jeans and penny loafers and against all odds, they allowed his entry. Perhaps they'd softened their rules for those who it was clear "had it." Or perhaps it was a simple little miracle in preparation for another bigger miracle.

Whatever the case, against all odds, sometime during the evening, across The Eagle's crowded walled-in outdoor patio, my friend spotted the unlikeliest of things: someone else in a white button down shirt, jeans and penny loafers, staring right back. What were the chances? **His name was Art and he was a smiling, salt and peppered older "daddy-type," ex-priest, tailor-made-just-for-Randy, HIV-positive miracle.** And just when Randy needed one the most. The universe had suddenly turned benevolent. After all that had been thrown his way, it seemed Randy had received an apology. Or perhaps it was a reward for having gotten through it all.

Whatever the case, Randy went home with Art that night and never left. It was love at first sight. For both of them. Art was a wonderful man who adored Randy and was devoted to his care. I visited their apartment in the Castro and spent some wonderful times with them. My visits became less frequent as it became clear that Chase's needs back in Boston were ever growing at a time when Art had happily taken over the care of my dear friend. I no longer had to worry about Randy's existence. He was right where he was supposed to be, in good, kind and loving hands. He and Art were happy together. They shared a wonderful life right until the end.

1990

In My Undies At The Copa

THE COPA was the mid-to-late-80s, next generation Key West dance club after The Monster died. While it lacked the tropical indoor-outdoor quality of my much loved Monster, it was spacious and rowdy and always had great music. And with The Monster's sad demise, it was the only place to dance the night away in Key West. A converted theater, it had a lighted marquee over the sidewalk and a little ticket booth out front just like the small town movie theaters of old. Selling tickets in the little booth was a big (why are they always so big?) and slightly intimidating drag queen. **She might have been sweet but I'd fallen victim to so many drag queens that I had become more than a little suspect of the lot of them.** I do not know why but I was the guy that big scary drag queens loved to pull out of the audience and abuse during their shows. They were always fierce creatures, considerably bigger with their high heels and higher hair than my modest 5 feet 9 inches. The bigger they were, the scarier they were and I was more than a little terrified of them. There was also something about them that took me back to the big scary nuns of 1950s Catholic elementary school. Fierce and sometimes brutal, they — the nuns and the drag queens — seemed to revel in both characteristics foisting their brutality on the unsuspecting of us. I was no longer unsuspecting.

One particular evening as I stepped up to The Copa's ticket booth, Big Scary Drag Queen seemed especially friendly. While I had purchased tickets from her on many occasions, there was no reason for her to remember me but still she seemed especially warm that night and, though still on my guard, I felt especially welcome. But no less frightened. I handed over my entrance fee and her big scary drag queen hand pushed my ticket to me through the little opening in the glass separating us. I moved on with no further thoughts of big scary drag queen encounters. As I handed my ticket over to the sexy boy at the front door, he immediately asked me if I'd like to be in the wet underwear contest. Laughter was my only response as I waited for my hand stamp. He held the stamp over my hand but wouldn't stamp me. "Don't laugh," said Sexy Door Guy somewhat indignantly, "seriously, we want you in our underwear contest." "Seriously, no," I responded, wondering who "we" was. Still he wouldn't stamp me. "You should be in the contest man, c'mon!" He was almost pleading. "No, thank you. I am not going to be in your underwear contest tonight or ever!" I was more emphatic this time. **I had seen enough of those contests to know to stay away from them.** In every such contest up there on stage in the parade of beauties would always be one contestant who was older and decidedly less hunky than the rest. He was the one that everybody would look up at, point to and say, "What's he doing up there?" Or even worse, "What's she doing up there?" **At about thirty-five years old and a decade older than the average contestant, I wasn't going to be either of them and told Sexy Door Guy as much.** He remained unconvinced and I remained unstamped. I shook my hand at him as the stamp still hovered there. "C'mon," he continued his plea, "Be a sport. We need hot guys and you're adorable!" Oh god, flattery. It was so hard for me to stay strong in the face of "hot" and "adorable." Flattery which goes directly to my needy ego has always been my downfall. His also having that rangy lean torn-jeans-sleeveless-open-torso-revealing-plaid-shirt-country-cowboy-sexy thing going on didn't help in my resolve to stay out of that contest. Sexy Door Guy saw me waver and went for the kill. "Great! So you'll do it," he said with a sexy grin and a sparkle in his determined equally sexy eyes. "No" I once again protested though more weakly this time. Other people arrived behind me and he stamped them in and still I hadn't received mine. "You know you want to. It's a lot of fun. Really." He was selling hard now, "You'll really enjoy yourself. It's fun!" He was repeating himself. "Look, all that happens is you go on stage, stand in a kids' swimming pool, she pours a little water on your underwear, then she gives you a little pat and off you go." "SHE?" I blurted out. As I pointed my thumb over my shoulder toward the ticket booth, I think she was looking at me, "That big scary drag queen?!" "She's not that big," he quickly replied. "Nope, not doing it." I responded, "No way. Won't do it. Never. Ever." Now I was repeating myself. "And besides, you can't be in an underwear contest without underwear," I said with a shrug as I pulled the waistband of my shorts away, happily giving Sexy Door Guy a clear view inside my shorts and evidence of my free-balling claim. While I wasn't interested in his contest, I was interested in him. With a look of what I hoped was interest he said "No worries." He took the invitation to reach right in and give me a feel down there. Then, his eyes focused on mine and with a squeezing fist full of me he said, "We've got a bushel basket of underwear behind the stage, big boy," and with a good squeeze, "you can borrow a pair. Take your pick." More squeezing. "Keep 'em actually. As a thank you. A little parting gift…from me." One more nice firm squeeze. He knew the power of sexual persuasion and knew he could use it on me. "Please…do it…for me… we need you." Eyes…seducing. Lips…pouting. "Need." "Big Boy." The squeezing. Damn, he'd gotten to me. I was in and he could tell. "Great!" he said as he stamped my hand. "Now, later on around 1am we'll make an announcement. When you hear it just come to the back of the stage. We'll take care of everything." **I do not remember ever actually saying "yes."**

Backstage was more fun than I had imagined. There was a line-up of cute boys removing their clothing. Some, like me, had worn no underwear so they had to help themselves, as did I, to the bushel basket. While checking each other out, we made our choices. I chose a nice pair of euro-cut tightie-whities and along with my other naked contestants to be, tried them on. Nice snug fit and plenty of room in the pouch. I was thankful I'd worn my favorite chrome cock-ring (yes, I have a favorite cock-ring) as I could fluff myself right before going on stage and it'd hold the extra girth. You can never be too prepared. We all stood lined up managing our bulges just so and as I scanned my fellow contestants I couldn't escape the feeling that I was way out of my league. I was gonna be the "what's she doing up there" guy. These boys were really hot, especially one dark haired blue eyed smooth luminous young beauty I had my eyes on.

Sexy Door Guy, the one who had talked me into this was now Sexy Backstage Guy. He was giving instructions regarding onstage deportment. "Stand nice and tall, shoulders back, chests out. Engage. And remember, we're prettier when we smile," he said flashing his own sparkling pearly whites. During all this backstage preparation Big Scary Drag Queen to choruses of laughter had been on stage, entertaining. As she came to the close of her rather lengthy monologue it was suddenly showtime.

The first contestant was being summoned to the stage. I needn't have worried about fluffing myself, Sexy Backstage Guy was ready for the challenge. He enthusiastically reached into the first contestant's briefs, gave him a few jerks, fluffed him with one hand and with the other, deftly shoved him up the steps and out to the stage. Clearly he'd done this before. I watched from the wings. There were questions. He hadn't said anything about questions. We have to talk? To HER? **Conversations with big scary drag queens never went well.** Once again I could foresee myself being terrorized by yet another of these giant malevolent beings in front of god knows how many people. Why oh why had I agreed to this torture? A simple glance over at Sexy Backstage Guy reminded me why. Big Scary Drag Queen asked the first contestant as he stood there nearly-naked in front of all those people. "Where are you from? How long are you staying in Key West? How big's your dick? Have you been here before? Are you a top or a bottom? Which guesthouse are you staying at?" Stuff like that. She artfully managed to pull some sort of sexual innuendo from even the most innocent of answers. I was in trouble and I knew it. After the interrogation, things went pretty much as Sexy Backstage Guy (back when he was still Sexy Door Guy) had explained: fluffing, water pouring, more fluffing. After making several dick references about size and girth, Big Scary Drag Queen took the boy by the shoulders and began to... OH...MY...GOD...NO!

I watched in horror as she turned the boy around, butt to the audience and forced him to bend over. All the way over and touch his toes, feet spread wide showing off his underwear-clad ass. In the glare of the impossibly bright spotlights. She then poured water over it and pulled his underwear up the crack and proceeded to play with his butt cheeks. A sight that would be (had I been in the audience) a total turn-on only struck fear in my heart. No one had said anything about ass display. Or ass play. Since childhood I've had what I considered to be an enormous ass. My gluteus was maximus and I had never liked it. My thin hipped older brother used to tease me about my butt incessantly. It was way too big and way too round, and way too high and way too wide. **My big fat ass was my least favorite physical attribute and I had spent a lifetime trying to camouflage it. Now here I was waiting in line to get up on a stage and have a big scary drag queen bend me over and display it for all the world to see!** Or at least all the world that was at The Copa that night. No. No. This could not happen. I backed away in horror. Sexy Backstage Guy saw this and blocked my exit. "Cold feet?" He said. "No...BIG ASS!" I responded. He was puzzled. Since I was looking out to the stage he seemed to think I was referring to the boy up there. "No! MY ASS!" I blurted out much too loudly while pointing to my own butt and then leaning in to his ear in a quieter more conspiratorial but no less determined tone, "My ass is huge and I'm not getting up there and bending over for the whole world to see it! Nope! Not gonna happen. And besides you never mentioned turning around and showing off my ass." "Your ass is fine and yes I did," he snapped back, "I said she'd give it a little pat and send you off." I heard a slapping sound coming from the stage. "See, just like that and its all over." And with a firm shove, "Now...back in line!" My inner parochial school child forced me do as I was told. **I nervously awaited my**

fate, heart beating wildly, devising a possible last minute escape route, as one by one, the other contestants were led to the slaughter. The young boy I'd had my eye on was being interviewed. What do you know, he was from Louisville, KY. My hometown. Big Scary Drag Queen made a reference to K-Y Lube and horse sized cocks and I knew I was toast. She finished with Louisville Boy, annihilated one more victim and suddenly it was my turn. That enormous wigged creature was welcoming the next contestant to the stage. Me. Sexy Backstage Guy reached into my briefs and gave me a few friendly tugs and a couple of really nice warm squeezes. I had to admit the squeezes felt really good and they worked. They both fluffed me up and took my mind off what was about to happen to me. AND THEN IT HAPPENED TO ME.

I felt his other hand on my back and as with those who went before, a firm push sent me up the steps and right out onto the stage with the Big Scary Drag Queen. She was big and in the unforgiving glare of those lights, she was spectacularly scary — an enormous threatening tower of made-up malevolence, sequins and wig. I had to stop looking at her and cast my gaze to the audience. I was grateful that the blindingly bright lights made it impossible to make out individual faces. I was instructed to stand in the little swimming pool and self-consciously stepped into it. I was asked the requisite questions including my hometown. She'd taken note of the Louisville connection with "Well, whattaya know, two southern girls both from Derby City right here gracing our stage tonight at The Copa. What are the chances?" And then with a direct eye-line to my bulging crotch, "Are you hung like a Thoroughbred too, honey?" Why did she suddenly have a southern accent? With magnolia blossoms dripping off her vocal chords, she got off on a rather lengthy tangent about big horses with little jockeys with big dicks, horny stable boys and every other horse related cliche she could turn to her subversive advantage. **I stood silently through it all, exposed and embarrassed, on stage, in the bright lights, in someone else's underwear, in a kids' swimming pool, in front of all those people, silently cursing Sexy Door Guy.** As she went back to the business of speculating about my size, in her newly acquired southern accent she said, "Well let mama have a look for herself." She pulled out the waistband of my borrowed underwear and took a peek. She dramatically let it snap back, looked up and screamed, arm outstretched, grasping for support as she feigned lightheadedness. Then overstating the situation with a fanning motion first at herself and then at my crotch, "He's from horse country all right!" This to the hooting, applauding audience and my total embarrassment. She then reached right in, squeezed my dick, stroked it and fluffed my balls and entire package just as I'd seen her do with the other guys. Having it all arranged just so, she then poured water (warm thankfully) over my now bulging package. I looked down and could see how in the glare of those bright lights my penis, shining chrome cock-ring and all, had become visible as my thin white borrowed undies went from translucent to transparent. I have to admit, the exhibitionist in me took over and my attitude shifted from scared to excited. Quite excited. Big Scary Drag Queen took note and of course called attention to my cock-ringed, growing bulge. The crowd went wild again. My needy ego was being stroked and I was actually starting to enjoy myself. All the approval was really quite gratifying. I was suddenly having fun. Only briefly (pun, intended) though, as the moment of dread arrived. While in my fit of ego showing off my long suit, I had for just a moment forgotten about the part where I'd have to turn around and show off my other side: the body part of which I was not so proud. The fun was over. There was no getting out of it. Oh the degradation. I did as I was told, turned around and with her hand pushing my shoulders down, I slowly and ever so reluctantly bent over. All the way over, assuming the position, feet wide apart as instructed, wide-ass spread to the world. I felt warm water washing over my underwear and then a big drag queen hand smoothing the wet fabric down and patting my wet cotton-clad cheeks. To my dismay, I then felt my underwear being pulled up the crack of my ass exposing my big bare butt cheeks. She squealed with delight. I didn't recall her doing this with the others. She proceeded to go to town on my big spread ass. She caressed my cheeks. She jiggled my cheeks. She spread my cheeks. She bent down and kissed my cheeks! Well, one of them at least. Mortified I listened upside down as she kept me bent over like that forever — much longer, I was certain, than the others. What was she doing up there? I couldn't tell from my upside down vantage point but with all the hooting and hollering and cheering, my mind went to the worst. I imagined her making wide apart hand gestures and shocked and appalled faces about how horrible and huge my giant butt was and the unbelievability of its vastness. **She was up there making fun of me and my big fat ass. I was sure of it. I was mortified. I was worried. I was upside down.** She kept me bent over that way for what seemed an absolute eternity. The finale — and it didn't come a moment too soon — was a stinging, reddening ass-slap (not a little pat as described) to the hoots of the crowd. After that I was allowed to right myself and turn around red faced and a little dizzy. She asked for a big round of applause, kissed me on the cheek (my face this time, leaving a lipstick print there to match the one on my butt cheek) and off I went, lightheadedly de-wedgie-ing my underwear. There was another guy behind me and the parade of underwear contestants was over. We were brought back out on stage and judged by the applause we received. Predictably, luminous young Mr. Louisville won. Surprisingly, embarrassed old Mr. Louisville came in a respectable first runner-up. Second place. It was finally over.

The next evening as I approached The Copa, Big Scary Drag Queen was at her usual post in the little ticket window. As I pushed my money through the small arched opening in the glass separating us, she gently placed her Big Scary Drag Queen hand on mine, patted it a little and pushed it, with the money, back to me. "Darling," she said, "you have the most beautiful ass I have ever had the pleasure of having on my stage. You never again dear, ever have to pay at The Copa. Thanks for being such a good sport and sharing your pretty ass. You are a Doll!"

Thanks indeed. She called my ass beautiful! My big fat ass, beautiful! Pretty! She'd also said, "Pretty!" I was suddenly glowing. For the first time in my life I felt just a little more kindly toward my big fat butt. "Mount Everest Hiney Bucket" as my older brother with his athletically slim hips used to call it, had found an admirer in a big and as it turned out not so scary, maybe even benevolent drag queen. Ticket in hand, as I approached Sexy Door Guy I was feeling just a little better about myself, about drag queens and for the first time ever, about my big fat ass.

I kept the underwear.

1990

Funny The Things You Remember & The Things You Don't

THE END. Here's the thing. The end is fuzzy. **I can't actually remember my final conversation with Randy. That's difficult for me to admit.** I should have cherished every last word from my very best friend but I just can't seem to reassemble the words we exchanged that January evening, he in San Francisco and I in Boston.

It's funny, I can pull up the tiniest details of so many of our talks and adventures throughout all those years. The fun times. But a lot of the details of the painful times seem to have faded from memory. I suppose it has something to do with rote learning. As a parochial schooled child I was often taught by rote. Repetition. Drilling. The nuns were fond of drilling and it always worked on me. I can still recite much of what I learned that way. It stays with you. It occurs to me that repetition is perhaps responsible for the things I remember and the things I don't. Over the years, I've told the fun stories so often and I've replayed them over and over in my head, preserving for all time all the glistening details. Through repetition. Repeating with glee, those lovely stories, replaying them for my own enjoyment and others' amusement, has I think, burnished the details onto my brain right along with all the stuff the nuns managed to cram in there. On the other hand, memories that were too painful to re-live or too sad to re-tell have faded away, I think, simply because there was no repetition. I haven't replayed them in my head nor have I shared those stories often enough to have saved the details. They're either gone or buried so deep they're unwilling to surface.

Such is the case with my memory gap regarding that last phone call. The day before, January 19th, was special — Randy's 35th birthday — so I remember that conversation. "And you swore you wouldn't make it to 35!" "Did you get my card?" "Did you have a cake?" "How are you feeling?" "How's your mom?" She was visiting from Louisville. "How is Art?" Pretty standard stuff. Randy was so sick by then that I had a feeling he was going to die on his birthday. But he hadn't. So the next day, January 20th, was a day like any other. Just one more day that Randy hadn't died. Of course we knew any day could be his last, but it had been that way for months so our conversations rarely had any sense of finality to them. Nothing terminal. Given we spoke every day there wasn't much news to share. It was business as usual with the specter of death hovering; you just never knew how far away. What did I say to him in the final conversation? I wish I could remember our final words but they're either gone or possibly tucked away so deep I can no longer reach them. It's troubling. What do you say to a dying friend when you have no clue as to when he will die? What did I say? Did I have any words of reassurance for him? Anything to say to ease his fears? Any wise words to help him on his way to the next life? I just don't know. Of course, when you're having a final conversation you don't know it's *the* final conversation. Only later does that unfortunate fact become apparent. **The importance of the last phone call only reveals itself when it's too late to appreciate that it, indeed had been the last call.**

1990

Last Call

HOW MANY TIMES had Randy and I heard the words, "Last Call" blasted out at us and fallen victim to the subsequent flashing of lights forcing us from whichever (now suddenly and garishly illuminated) gay bar we'd happened to find ourselves? Time to go? Already? Last call always came as a surprise. It'd sneak up on you. Blissfully unaware of the time, you'd be doing god knows what with god knows whom — dancing, drinking, talking, kissing, fucking — and with little warning they'd fully amp the lights. Nothing could empty a gay bar faster than harsh, daytime-bright, unflattering fluorescents. **Fully illuminated, gay bars are not pretty and at 3 am neither were we.**

From Louisville's Badlands we'd head out for a short car trip around the corner for a 4 am stop at the White Castle. Early morning fine dining among the other somewhat suspect denizens of the night. Or we'd be off to the nearby "bookstores" which were actually peepshows (of which Louisville had several) still looking for a sexual encounter or two in a dimly lit, concrete floored, pine scented, sloppily painted plywood cubicle.

Or, from Chicago's Bistro, once again around the corner and across from the Gold Coast, this time on foot to The Machine Shop. "Le Shoppe Méchanique" as Randy had dubbed it, in an effort to upgrade the crowded, dimly-lit, plywood-cubicled after hours labyrinth-for-sex where you'd likely see graffiti on the wall that read "Blow Jobs 50¢, with Lipstick 75¢." Hey, a girl's gotta pay for her cosmetics.

We might also head way uptown (by bus this time) to 'The Tubs,' Man's Country gay bath house. There we'd spend the remainder of the early morning hours in and out of skimpy ever-dampening white towels, combing the hallways, disco, saunas, orgy rooms, steam rooms and showers in the relentless and hopeful pursuit of sex and who knows, maybe love, even if it was only for the night.

And failing any of those options, there was always the last resort, "The Second Story Emporium," another plywood cubicle-ed, glory-holed sex spot. This one was right in our neighborhood and was way too convenient. We frequented it regularly enough to have a nickname for it: "The 2SE."

No matter how, we'd always find a way to extend our night out, even if it just meant going home, smoking a joint together, laughing and talking, or simply sharing the silence in our gorgeous living room at either end of the sofa, toe to toe under a handmade-by-my-sister afghan, while watching that inevitable sunrise over our sparkling Lake Michigan. Last call wasn't about to end our night and we'd stubbornly see many a sunrise before we'd let go of it.

If those "Last Calls" had a way of slipping up on us, we certainly never anticipated the advent of a Final Last Call. Though here it was upon us. Really? Already? The lights had been turned up. Once again, too soon, and this time…forever. Our long night out together, the one that had started seventeen years before in Louisville to the sound of Diana Ross singing about love and loss, was about to come to an end. There'd be no more trips around the corner or way uptown. No more greasy burgers or wet towels. No more tricks and no more treats. There'd be no way to extend this night. The laughs were over. There would be no more joints to share and no more sunrises to watch.

1990

This Just In...

A MEMORY. A glimmer of a memory has seeped up from wherever it was hiding. It's about that last phone call. Writing can do that — resurrect a detail that can trigger an entire memory. I'm remembering…a fundraiser.

Though Randy had made it to his 35th birthday he wasn't cheered by that fact and I was in no mood to cheer him up. He, my best friend, was dying. Chase was sick and also probably dying. Most of my friends (our friends) were sick and probably dying. Many had died. They were Randy's friends as well. It was the worst of times. Neither of us was in the mood to share our current travails trying to put some sort of silly spin on it, as we'd always done. I had become really adept at pulling him from his moods but this time both our moods were black. There were 3,000 miles between us. Randy was dying. I knew that and there was nothing I could do about it. He knew it too. I remember...

"What day is it?" Randy asked out of the blue after one of those long pauses when there's nothing to say. I thought for a second wondering if he wanted a day or a date. "It's the day after your birthday," I answered, "the 20th." "I know that," he impatiently replied, "what day is it?" He stressed the word "day." "Saturday," I answered. There was another pause on his end, this one I recognized as a deep draw on a cigarette. I jumped in, "Are you..." Knowing I was about to chide him about his smoking, with a major exhale he cut me off with, "It's Saturday *night* then," acknowledging the time difference between us he continued, "what would you usually do on a Saturday night?" I knew he knew the answer to his question but I answered him anyway, "I go out dancing." "Go out dancing," he immediately responded and added, "Do something normal. Be true to yourself. You deserve it." He understood what I was going through, the level of loss. He knew surviving wasn't easy. We'd talked about it a lot. He was my friend. He knew me. **And even with one foot in the grave, there he was, my best friend, trying to pull me out of my own darkening mood when it should have been the other way around.** "Didn't you tell me the other day about a party this weekend?" Yes, I had told him about a dance party that night in fact. An AIDS fundraiser. But I was not planning to attend. I wasn't in the mood for a party. "Go," he said, "Go to your party. Go dancing. You need some normal right now." Those were his words to me. Now I remember. I also remember the warm glow when I realized they were my words. The words I'd used to get him to The Eagle that fateful San Francisco night. The night he met Art. He'd remembered them. Even memorized them. And gave them right back to me.

I have been so focused on what I said to Randy, trying to remember what pearl of wisdom I had imparted to my dying friend, I hadn't given much thought to what he might have said to me. Randy had become a man of fewer words by then, but there he was using a few more of them to make me feel better, reminding me in my own words to do something normal. I promised to go dancing and I promised to call him the next day and tell him all about my night out.

That brought another memory back. A more tuned-in-than-I friend had played for me (just that day) a Kate Bush song called "This Woman's Work." Knowing how audibly disinclined I was (I'd never even heard of Kate Bush) Glenn knew I would not likely discover her on my own. It was a song about the life we have in us and strength to go on. I think it was actually about giving birth but it was precisely what I needed to hear on that particular day. I immediately memorized one stanza and it became my mantra. Having not heard the words in decades, I can still bring them up verbatim. "I know you've got a little life in you yet, I know you've got a lot of strength left." I guess it's that rote thing again. Repetition. I repeated that mantra over and over that day and night and thought of Randy's deteriorating condition out on the west coast. With each recitation I tried my best to send the information and the strength and the life to my friend 3,000 miles away. It was all I could do.

I did go out dancing that evening, just as Randy had suggested and took those words with me. I said the words over and over to myself in the hopes of sending some sort of spiritual message across the miles, using that direct connection we had always shared. Dancing with my hands in the air and chanting my new chant,

I would send him a message of hope, strength and endurance given me by a singer I'd just heard for the first time. I would try to pass it on. I'd hoped he'd be hearing the words from me, feeling them somehow through that same energetic connection. That he would be saying them to himself along with me. And believing them. Believing he had a little life in him yet. Believing he had a lot of strength left. Over and over those same words. **We would connect spiritually across all those miles and together, do what we could to extend his time here on earth. Together, our unit of two souls, the way we'd done so much else would perhaps add another day.** There wasn't much else I could give my friend from so far away. I remember feeling him and our special connection. "I know you have a little life in you yet. I know you have a lot of strength left." We'd say those words over and over again, saying them...together, hearing them...together, believing them...together, staying alive...together, dancing...together, as we had for so many years...together, taking the two of us...together, into the dawn of a new day.

January 21, 1990

We Don't Have Tomorrow, But We Have Yesterday

THAT DAWN CAME for only one of us and with bitter news. It was early Sunday morning January 21, 1990. The party was over and I'd just gotten home. I was standing by the upstairs phone when it rang. I stared at it allowing it to insistently ring on, knowing it would be Art. Knowing the news he had to share. **When I finally picked up the receiver, just two words, "He's gone," confirmed what I already knew.** With his mother and Art by his side, Randy had just succumbed to that horrible upper case acronym, AIDS. The relentless disease that might have taken my best friend any number of times before, decided this would be the time. It was just two days after his 35th birthday. The party was over. "He's gone."

I was numb. My dear friend was gone. My confidant. My partner in crime. My roommate. My life partner. My student. My teacher. My dizzy, smart, athletic, talented, beautiful, laughing, smiling, sexy, silly, perpetually horny, endlessly capable, supremely focused, wonderfully loving, valiant, blue-eyed "platonic lover" had been taken away, severing a bond I thought, hoped, would last forever. "He's gone."

It suddenly all seemed unreal as if the whole illness thing had a been a terrible dream — a horrible AIDS-related nightmare. How could I accept the passing of this vital human being, this absolute piece of me with a phone call? Though I didn't understand it, I was moving rapidly into the first stage of grief — denial. He's gone? It couldn't be true. How could Randy have passed without my having been there to hold his hand? Without hearing his last breath? Without seeing the life leave my dear friend's body? Without witnessing this life-ending event, this new reality seemed much more an unreality. He's not gone. I hadn't been there to cry at his bedside so I wouldn't cry. Couldn't cry.

Days later in Louisville where our story began, as I walked up to a coffin in a funeral home and stared down at the silent suited-up remains of my sleeping friend, my thoughts were not about a horrible new reality but rather of his perfect nose. I focused on the nose job that I tried and failed to talk him out of in Chicago. Oh, I forgot about that story. Ask me some day. I'll tell you all about it. Anyway, there it was, the perfect nose he had wanted so badly and had gotten so few years from. That new nose should have lasted a lifetime. I guess, in a way, it had. A foreshortened lifetime. Now it served as a red herring — something else to focus on — to help me deny this tragic new reality and deny my tears.

A day later, at a Catholic funeral service that Randy would have hated, his being referred to as "your unworthy servant William" by his namesake uncle priest, added to the unreality. Surely the person in that closed coffin, to whom this priest (who Randy loathed) referred, was someone else. "Unworthy servant, William" indeed. **Randy never used his first name William and he most certainly was no servant, worthy or unworthy, to a god in which he did not believe.** The Randy I knew wouldn't willingly be in this church and couldn't be eulogized in such a manner. This all fed my willingness to deny this new hateful reality. That same January day, Louisville's Calvary Cemetery was too cold for a graveside service and the ground too frozen for burial. Somehow that too fed my denial, allowing me to dismiss the finality of it all. My tears would have to wait.

Back in Boston I wake to a new day. I open my eyes and stretch, fluff my pillow as usual and turn in the other direction hopeful perhaps of a little more sleep. The sun's already up so that's probably not going to happen. I glance at the cold light beaming in from my barren winter garden and begin to welcome the new day when suddenly the cold new reality of that new day hits. He's gone. Randy is gone. My sweet silly best friend with his perfect nose is gone. It's in the unforgiving light of those morning moments that I am faced with the glaring truth and forced to work my way through my denial and on to the sadness and anger and depression and then finally the grief, and acceptance. It's in that acceptance that my dear friend Randy dies again, every morning, morning after morning, severing our bond over and over again. I pull the covers up, shut my eyes and try to go back to those precious moments before I'm forced to face this awful reality but it doesn't work. It's like that every morning. I wake to a day just like any other has ever been and for a short while everything is as it has always been. **Those few precious blissful moments before I remember. And when I do, Randy dies again. Every goddamn morning. And that's when I cry.**

Once they finally came, the tears wouldn't stop. Processing my grief over Randy's loss added to the cumulative losses previous and to come. Art died within a year and I would cry for him. Within three years Chase would be gone and more tears would come. There'd be countless others in between. The collective grief and the constant crying, became too much. My tears dried up as I numbingly accepted death after death. They were all gone. And so were my emotions. I stopped feeling. I shut down. It was my only defense. What else do you do when your broken heart has been amputated?

There was an added sadness as well, the lonely feeling of having been left behind. They were all gone — my party boys — somewhere. While the party was over here on earth, I knew there was another one somewhere. I could guarantee it. A party to which I had cordially not been invited. Most of my favorite people were there. I was not.

1990

After Randy

WHILE OUR EARTHLY BOND may have been severed, there was, and still remains, another bond that connects me to Randy. While he lives on in my memories, certainly, there's something more. Even after thirty years. Or perhaps especially after thirty years. Though I can't see him or touch him, I know he's there. Around me and in me right inside my soul, I suppose where he always was. That is after all, the nature of soul mates. Our friends used to say we were "attached at the hip." I suppose "attached at the soul" would have been more apt. Certainly is now. As I sat writing all about Randy & me, I have felt him with me, guiding me through these memories, filling in details long ago forgotten or set aside, or buried. **I even had the thought that at some point, I was only taking dictation; that it was actually Randy writing our story.** His story. Might be. It'd be just like him. He always wanted to write and he and his red pen were merciless editing any of my own attempts at it.

I've become accustomed to that sort of help from beyond. I have learned so much about spirituality and how to use it. You can't lose that many people and not. It occurs to me now that perhaps many of my "aha moments," spiritual epiphanies I experience from time to time are actually Randy (or another lost friend) whispering in my ear, sharing with me some piece of universal truth to which he, well ensconced on the other side, is now privy.

Music connects us too. Randy wasn't the disco-bunny I was but he did have a favorite dance song: "When Will I See You Again" by The Three Degrees. There wasn't much that could move Randy from cruising to dancing (he was self-consciously uncomfortable with the latter) but this song could do it. The poignancy of the lyrics, "When will I see you again, when will our hearts beat together?" had escaped me until just recently when the song popped up somewhere. As I listened to those lyrics, it was as if I were hearing it for the first time. The title says it all. Was he singing to me? Or I to him? Whatever the case, it's Randy's song and he is with me whenever I hear it and I do wonder when will our hearts beat together again. I also feel his spiritual embrace whenever I hear "Whiter Shade of Pale," "Clair de Lune," "Laura" and especially "Touch Me In The Morning."

There are other things that connect us:

The mere mention of a **bachelor party** makes me laugh.

Abortion clinics which elicit smiles from no one, will get one from me.

Whenever I see someone knitting, I'm taken back to a gentler time in a tasteful gray living room well above the roar of lions, Lake Michigan and a glittering city. And I regret just a little my not having requested "the sweater" **Randy's first knitted creation**, when Art asked me which of my deceased friend's belongings I'd like to keep. Why hadn't I remembered the sweater?

When I cook he is right there over my shoulder helping me "clean as I go" and reminding me of all we learned together cooking, **baking and getting baked ourselves**, and laughing our way through all our triumphs and failures in our Chicago kitchen.

On the rare occasion I get high these days, we're back watching TV together, laughing til our sides split at **faith healers and chefs and quirky British sitcoms.**

When I use the word **"incongruous"** I smile a little and feel my heart warmed a lot.

When I'm faced with a challenge I imagine how Randy would have met it for, with his strength and courage, **he taught me so much in that arena.**

When I observe some small, silly oddity that I know he'd have also enjoyed, I want to share it with him immediately. **There's always a brief second, before reality hits, when I think I can.** I can see in my mind's eye, so clearly, the mischievous sparkle in those bright blue eyes and his wicked smile and hear him laughing, giggling along with me at our shared lunacy.

Whenever I see **little blue-haired old ladies** I'm reminded of those days we'd imagine ourselves as old friends sharing a bus ride on our way into town and I shed a little tear at the realization that only one of us was given the privilege of having gray hair.

When I make some new discovery, the type of thing I'd have shared with him, I can still see the appreciative boyish wonderment in his clear-eyed face. And when I'm imparting, to someone else now, some sort of something I know (or think I know) **I can still hear him say in astonishment, "How do you know these things?"**

And my heart, though broken, still bursts with happiness.

1990...

A Hidden Garden

I SPENT a great deal of my newfound time mourning my losses and recharging my batteries while tending our lovely little walled-in garden in Beacon Hill. It was the perfect place to grieve. And grow. **Shortly after moving to Cedar Lane Way, I learned that our garden had been for many years on the "Hidden Gardens of Beacon Hill" tour.** It was considered to be one of the prize gardens being home to "Miss Emerson's Wisteria" a six story apparently free-standing wisteria planted some 150 years before (so I was told) by a female relative of Ralph Waldo Emerson. Such provenance is highly revered in Boston and especially on Beacon Hill. The word provenance itself is highly revered.

Having grown up with flowers, and a mother who was an authority on roses, I was delighted when asked to be a part of the tour as a "Ribbon Garden," one that tour-takers can only stand at the gate and peek into. Knowing nothing of me — an "outsider" and a "transient" (meaning renter) — the ladies of the garden club were more than a little skeptical when they showed up to "Measure the garden gate for a ribbon." Measure for a ribbon? I had to laugh. Do they dole it out by the inch? I did pass their inspection and within a few years had been upgraded to full garden (non-ribbon) status. Over the ensuing years my garden became not only a staple of the tour but quite possibly its centerpiece. I was not a member of the property owning all female garden club, so on garden day with nothing better to do, while all the other garden member/owners were selling tickets, guiding tours, and tending to the porta-potties (that particular lady referred to, with a blue-blood snicker as "The Queen of The Latrines,") I would station myself at my garden gate and talk to all the (mostly) ladies taking the tour. I'd answer question about plants, flowers, gardening techniques, etc. Being in the antique business, my garden was furnished and decorated with perfectly weathered antique garden furniture and pretty much treated, with oil paintings and mirrors nestled into the ivy covered walls, as a well accessorized outdoor room. And then there was that wisteria which reliably hit its peak every third Thursday in May, tour day. Thank you Miss Emerson. I would stand at that gate speaking with all the touring visitors gaining a following of lovely ladies who would, year after year, queue all the way down Cedar Lane Way to Mount Vernon and then sometimes onto Charles Street to speak with "The lovely gentleman" and visit his garden.

In the spring of 1992 the wisteria was having its most abundant bloom ever. My neighbor who had lived in her Beacon Hill home next door for over thirty years confirmed this. While it did usually hit its peak, somewhat miraculously, right on Garden Tour Day, that year I could tell (though it's bloom had been more spectacular than ever for the tour) there was still more to come. It had never been this loaded with its pendulous lavender clusters. I had planned to spend the weekend after the garden tour in Provincetown with a group of friends. I loved those weekends and really looked forward to them but I really didn't want to leave town and miss the big bloom. I knew that once the wisteria would hit its peak, the next day a large percentage of its blossoms would drop right off. I didn't want to return from a weekend away and see most of the big bloom on the ground. I called my friend Phil who had organized the weekend to tell him I wasn't going and gave the reason why. "Michael, that is ludicrous!" was his immediate response. "You're going to miss a weekend in Provincetown to watch a plant bloom?" Clearly he didn't get it but there was no moving me. I was not going to miss my wisteria's greatest bloom ever. I was rewarded for that decision by a spectacular six story fountain of lavender flowers the like I had never before seen; or ever would again. I spent the entire weekend under it, a cascading waterfall of pendulous color more spectacular than it had ever been. I wouldn't have missed it for the world let alone a weekend in Provincetown.

A few days after the big bloom a friend named George came over to visit and we spent some time in the garden talking. Sitting under the still laden wisteria we were surrounded by a fluffy carpet of the lavender blossoms totally covering the ground. The effect was absolutely ethereal. It had been a particularly trying time with Chase who was being difficult and oftentimes just plain mean to me and I was pouring my heart out to my friend. "Why don't you just leave?" he asked, "What about the South Beach idea? Maybe it's time to resurrect that." He insisted, "If Chase is going to treat you this badly, he doesn't deserve you. Maybe it's time to just move on." I thought about it for awhile and toyed with the possibility of escaping. **Then, glancing up at the spectacular fountain of lavender blossoms overhead, I gestured to it and the soft carpet of lavender snow beneath us and said, "Well, even if I could leave Chase, how could I possibly ever leave this?"** And then with a look of resignation, I added, "I just might be stuck in Boston with this wisteria forever."

About a week or so later I was riding my bicycle on one of those perfectly clear blue sky days when all of a sudden I could see a wall of black clouds quickly moving in. There was a storm approaching and I raced home with barely enough time to beat it. As I came into the garden I saw the neighbors' cat Tigger who loved hanging out in our garden. I was rushing now as the skies had darkened to almost night and the storm was clearly bearing down on us. The wind and rain had already started. I took my bicycle into the house and ran back out to scoop Tigger up into my arms. Prone to talking to him, I hollered over the storm, "This is a big one Tigger, let's get in the house quick!" And with a nod to my favorite movie, added, "Auntie Em! Auntie Em!" as the screen door slammed behind us. I dropped Tigger to the floor and as I reached for the doorknob to close the inside door, it was sucked from my hand and the door slammed itself shut. I immediately looked out the small window by the door and into the sudden near-nighttime darkness to see the thick corkscrew shape of the wisteria trunk incredulously seem to grow. It stretched up, growing Jack In The Beanstalk style, and with one loud whoosh and a louder crack, it moved away. In a second, the entire wisteria along with the tree that had supported it for 150 years, came crashing down, taking out the garden wall and falling over the next three or four gardens. **Within a moment and right before my eyes, Miss Emerson's 150 year old wisteria, my wisteria, the centerpiece of The Hidden Gardens of Beacon Hill was gone.**

Minutes later the storm had moved on and the sky was clear again. That quick freak storm which had done no other damage in the entire city had taken out my glorious wisteria. I couldn't overlook the fact that just days before I had pointed to that gorgeous plant as my only reason for never leaving Boston. **The universe had spoken, "So there!"** I didn't know whether to feel personally persecuted or graciously grateful. In either case, I could not ignore the message.

During all the challenging days that followed, I would still be able to retreat into that wonderful garden sanctuary. With the wisteria gone, the garden wall repaired and a new tree planted, it still managed to maintain its magic. I'd lovingly garden my way through an afternoon, plucking spent blossoms, transplanting something, watering and feeding and caring for all the living flourishing life outside and at the same time, caring for a dying one inside. And in the stillness of that special sanctuary, with that special purpose, much as it had when I'd float on a pool in Key West, a very generous universe would open itself giving me answers before I'd ever thought up the questions. I'd reenergize my spiritual batteries in my hidden garden for whatever new challenge presenting itself.

1964

Miss Garrison & God's Work

I WAS NOT ALWAYS a fan of gardening. As a youngster, the word "gardening" meant one thing. Weeding. My mother had lovely roses by the hundreds growing in row after row of beds in our backyard, all of them requiring weeding. A lot of weeding. Constant weeding. The grass in the backyard of my not-so-old Kentucky home was primarily Bermuda grass and planted by the original owner for its fast growth, not its beauty. **If Kentucky Blue Grass was part of god's original plan, Bermuda grass, coming somewhat later, was most assuredly an add-on from satan himself.** Rather than growing vertically like regular grass, Bermuda grass grows horizontally, close to the ground, in all directions deep-rooting itself every inch or so, ensuring its absolute resistance to pulling of any kind. It is a thoroughly invasive nightmare species hell bent on breaking the back and spirit of any teenage boy given the task of its removal.

The wet, dirty, sweaty, job of ridding the rose beds of the Bermuda grass, and several other determined weeds, was one that typically fell on my shoulders. I suppose as kids we all had our jobs. My sister's I think were more indoor/household related — dusting and the like, and mine — the more boy-appropriate, outdoor yard work. Though I'm not absolutely certain, I can't quite remember my older brother doing either — a fringe-benefit no doubt, of his being the first-born-generally-away-at-school-seminarian-priest-in-training. Yard work was hard work. There was no arguing that. It was filthy work and not my favorite way to spend a summer day when I might otherwise be getting up to who knows what other more enjoyable activities.

It was with some skepticism then, as I listened to my mother tell me of a dubious job opportunity to earn some extra money. There was a woman — an unmarried neighbor lady of The Amshoffs, church friends of my parents — who was looking for help with some yard work. "She's a non-Catholic but still a good Christian woman," I believe was how Miss Garrison was described first to my mother and then to me, "and she needs help." I could always use extra spending money but there it was, that simple two word euphemism for hard labor, "yard work." Yard work could encompass anything, but all of it, surely, two things: dirty and back breaking. **Still, seduced by the almighty dollar and Miss Garrison's posh Audubon Park address, I said "Yes."**

As I bicycled my way around to the front of Miss Garrison's home on a shady slightly elevated corner lot, all I saw were trees, clusters of bushes, shrubs and high grass...and weeds, all screaming for attention. Somewhere in the middle of it all was a stone house only partially visible from the street. Quickly assessing the amount of work the place needed, I wanted to turn and hastily bike my lazy-ass away from all of it, but I forced myself instead up the curved stone walkway, deposited my bike on the front porch and rang the bell. An ancient old (probably my age now as I write this) woman in a flowered dress, her gray hair pinned up in a Gibson-style bun and, wiping her hands on a dish towel, opened the screen door, introduced herself and asked me in. As I took in the rather heavy Victorian living room, I was immediately reminded of a similar room in an old Shirley Temple movie and a wisecracking, big city gal's pronouncement, "I wouldn't like it if I was a moth." I had to suppress a giggle but, as I settled in a bit and answered Miss Garrison's many questions, I started to become quite comfortable in that grandmotherly room of this grandchild-less old woman. We got on just fine. I don't remember the details of our negotiations but we must have come to some agreement because I promised to show up the next day for work.

Arriving the next morning at Miss Garrison's I was feeling a bit overwhelmed by the task ahead. We started in the front yard surveying the property working our way around the side. It was autumn and she put me right to work raking leaves. She was trimming some lower hanging branches and I'd rake them up along with everything else. Raking my way along the side yard I suddenly let out a yelp! Having instantly dropped the rake, I was clutching my hand with an enormous painful splinter (from that ancient old rake) buried in it. Miss Garrison, quick to respond, was there in a flash examining my hand and said, "I can take care of that," and as she turned away, "I'll get the sandpaper!" With that she was off leaving me in terror. "That old lady thinks she's gonna sandpaper this splinter outta my hand," I thought out loud in horror as I tried as hard as I could to get the splinter out before she could get back with her abrasive sure-to-be-painful remedy. I couldn't get it out. It was buried way too deep. I watched in fear as the determined Miss Garrison came at me with a big piece of sandpaper and...The sandpaper it seemed was for the rough spot on the rake, not for my hand. She had also brought a needle, some tweezers, disinfectant and a band-aid.

When we broke for lunch, I followed her into the house through the front room and into her kitchen. She had prepared a lunch in advance and as we ate our tuna on toast and apple salad along with freshly made lemonade, we talked. Miss Garrison was kind. That much was clear straightaway. And, once we were past the splinter event, not scary at all, unlike most old people. My great-grandfather and both my grandmothers, German and Italian, for instance, were terrifying to me. Miss Garrison was not. She seemed genuinely interested in me and asked so many questions that I'm sure my little emerging ego was fed in a way it hadn't been before. Her questions weren't of the "Where are you going" or "what are you doing" variety I was used to from my parents or schoolteachers. Hers were more personal. She would ask what I thought about things, what I loved, what made me happy. What I would do when I got older. I'm sure I overshared but I'm just as certain she enjoyed it because she said so time and again. **"Oh Michael, I could listen to you all day," she'd say by way of encouragement as I'd happily prattle on with story after story of my not very eventful thirteen year old lifetime, "you are such a fine storyteller. When you describe something, I see it, plain as day"**

After lunch on that first day, we went back outside but this time through her back door just off the kitchen. It was then I first saw her backyard which at a glance was a big weedy mess. My instant fear of being cruelly overworked however gave way pretty quickly to other observations and their subsequent thoughts. As I followed Miss Garrison around her backyard, while she pointed out this flower and that, it became clear that this wasn't a backyard at all but a garden. A real garden if ever there was one. Though having gone to seed and thoroughly overgrown with weeds, it held the latent beauty of a formerly well-planned, well-tended, and thoroughly loved garden until the gardener had grown old and could no longer kneel or stoop or bend over or do so many of the things such a place requires on a day-to-day, year-round basis. I could see, though it had fallen on hard times, Miss Garrison's garden had been developed over years and decades of dedication to creating beauty, pure and simple. Trailing Miss Garrison through her garden and listening to her explain its former glory, I began to feel the magic there. I could hear that neglected place quietly crying out to me. Miss Garrison's magic garden wanted me. Needed me. As it revealed its need to me, my young inner-landscaper saw the potential and knew why I was there. That needy, untended space drew me in and begged my participation. **It was as if the milkweed vines that had overtaken just about everything else had taken the opportunity to wrap themselves around me as well, determined to pull me in and keep me there.** I'd be Miss Garrison's new back and knees. That is when a job turned into a mission — a destiny.

We'd spend hours together on a regular basis, Miss Garrison and I, growing our garden right along with our blossoming intergenerational friendship. She was winter and I was spring as we'd work season to season, side by side, raking autumn leaves, winterizing along with the first frost, planting bulbs for spring and in the summer, tending and transplanting — "There. It'll never know it's been moved," she'd whisper to me with a conspiratorial wink, as we'd lovingly relocate a flourishing flower to its new home. Through Miss Garrison I began to think of plants and flowers as sentient beings able to respond to us and our love for them. I liked that. We'd work together discussing not only plant life but life, not only love of flowers but love. How each reflected the other. Some of it I got and some of it would wait years or decades for the seeds my gardening friend had planted to take hold, grow and blossom, as my own spiritual development and awareness caught up. It was Miss Garrison who first sowed in me the seed of an idea that there is divinity in all things. Where there is life, there is beauty and where there is beauty there is god. "Just look around you," she'd say by way of explanation, taking in the beauty and life surrounding us as she'd prove her point with four words and a sweep of her hand. **Gardening became something much more meaningful with Miss Garrison; more than just pulling weeds and getting dirty, gardening became god's work.**

One Christmas Miss Garrison had a "special" gift for me. As I tore into the carefully wrapped package, as with any thirteen year old, my mercenary side took over. She did, after all, have a houseful of antiques. I could only imagine what treasure lay in that suspiciously lightweight box as I excitedly unwrapped it. Well, I have to say I was more than a little disappointed when all I saw as I lifted the lid of that box were a few pages that had been torn from a magazine. There wasn't even a magazine, just a few ragged-edged pages. Though thirteen year old boys aren't particularly adept at masking disappointment, I hope I managed some semblance of excitement for this gift which seemed to be so important to my dear old friend. Miss Garrison explained that it was an article she'd torn from a magazine years before and had saved it. "Michael, I really never knew exactly why I'd saved it. And then you came along," she said wanting me, I suppose, to be as excited as she was, "and then I realized, I saved it for you." I didn't really understand how you could save something for someone before you'd even met. Then I read the story. It was called, *A Christmas Memory* and had been written by Truman Capote, a name that meant nothing to me at the time. It was the story of an unlikely intergenerational friendship between an old lady and a young boy called Buddy. I could see right away that I was Miss Garrison's Buddy, though at the time I didn't fully appreciate the layers and textures and poignancy of this touching story and how it related to the two of us. That would take some time but I came to cherish those torn-from-a-magazine pages. Not long after, *A Christmas Memory,* was published in book form, and produced for TV. It is to this day my favorite hour of TV ever, partially because I consider it a visual work of art with Geraldine Page giving one of the greatest female performances I've ever seen, but also because every time I watch it (or read the book) Miss Garrison is alive again. There I am working right by her side learning life lessons and helping her do god's work, tending to life and creating beauty in her magic garden.

I am sorry to say that after coming out, going away to college and getting involved in so many activities: school, work, sex, as her garden returned to wild, my visits to the aging Chalia Garrison became less frequent and eventually stopped. I wasn't particularly good at keeping in touch and I can't remember the last time I saw her. I wish I could. She stays with me though, in my memory and in my heart. I remember so much of the beauty of her spirit. Her kindness, her friendship, her love and the wonderful things she taught me. Miss Garrison is with me whenever I'm in a garden doing "god's work." Whenever I carefully transplant a flower, sure of her presence watching just over my shoulder, I whisper a conspiratorial, "There. It'll never know it's been moved."

Surviving Chase
(Part 2)

MORE HORRORS would eventually present themselves. Chase's initial post-diagnosis golden period, laced with denial, ended with his next hospitalization, again for pneumocystis. Once again we got him through it but he was definitely compromised this time in a way he hadn't been before. There was no denying the same downward trajectory we'd witnessed with our other friends. Cancer. Cytomegalovirus. Yeast infections. Weight loss. Hair loss. Wasting. Lethargy. Mood swings. Along with all this came, predictably I guess, all the stages of grief one by one and at times in unison. There was anger, lots of it and generally directed at me if for no other reason than I was the only one around. Chase had started a sort of self-imposed seclusion and saw fewer and fewer people as he got sicker and sicker. All at once he was losing his hair and his looks, his patience, and his ability to cope with the outside world. Along with all of it came the resentment he felt for me as he knew that someday he'd be reliant on me. He had been a person self-reliant from an early age. I think sometimes he hated me for that even as I was dedicating myself to his care. I understood but that didn't make it any easier to deal with. He'd lash out at me and be contrite later on. He'd be surly and unhappy and downright mean and then the telephone would ring and an entirely different upbeat person would answer it carrying on a jovial laugh filled conversation. "Who are you?" I'd think. The phone would get hung up and there was the angry despondent victim again. By way of apology he'd explain that he was able to rally for a few minutes on the phone but he hadn't the energy to carry it off for long. With me he could be sad, depressed, and most of all angry. He seemed to be testing me. I think there was a part of him that never believed I would actually stay and I think at times he was determined to drive me away and prove himself correct. **While I had made an unwavering commitment that I would be with him to the end and that he would not die alone, I could have done a better job of convincing him that I didn't always have one foot on the way out.** I wasn't so sure, myself. I used his doubt to my advantage during those times when he was being particularly difficult. So I know I had a hand in feeding his basic insecurity. I was committed to staying but I always fell short of convincing him. Perhaps I wasn't convinced myself.

Those were horrifyingly difficult days. The hospitalizations, the chemo, the cancer on his leg that wouldn't heal. I would un-bandage his leg and together we'd look at this hideous looking sore right out of a horror film and say, "Well, it looks a little better here around the edges," trying to find even the tiniest improvement in that awful gaping sore that would not go away. Anything for a little optimism. I'd accompany Chase to all his doctor visits and I would sleep on a cot in the room during his hospitalizations. We'd grill the doctors for any new information they might have and demand to know about any new medications and treatments. And trials. And studies. Ever the corporate animal Chase managed his illness like a business, following up in writing with all his doctors in duplicate and triplicate. He'd arrange meetings, pulling them together and strategizing with them about his care and treatment. Every option was investigated and every trial explored. I stood in awe of his ability to do all of this in the face of pain, deteriorating health and the attendant despair it all brought. And the health insurance paperwork!

While Chase had brought his business skills to his care, I brought to it some of the more new age philosophies I was coming to embrace. As I was caring for that horrible leg wound, I would press the gauze against it and consciously force love and light into it. I'd visualize it getting better and even healing. When I did the laundry as I was folding his t-shirts, with my hands I would purposefully press love and healing energy into each of them hoping that when he wore them, some of that energy would provide a healing embrace. Perhaps it helped. It certainly couldn't hurt.

"OK, now close your eyes" I'd say to Chase as I eyed the tubes carrying the dreaded chemotherapy medication into his arm. "They've spent so much time telling us about all the negative side effects, they never mention the good that it can do. Forget about the side-effects and focus on the good stuff." All we'd heard about from Chase's legion of doctors was hair loss, lethargy and the most dreaded for Chase, nausea. He hated the thought of living with nausea and I'm certain he would rather have died. "Let go of the negative and focus on the good," I coached him. "Visualize a life saving liquid entering your bloodstream. Don't be afraid of it. Welcome it for the good it can do. Give it permission to help not harm. Empower it. Let it work its magic with no side effects." I can't say with certainty that it worked, but he never had any of the nausea expected with the therapy. Mostly after a chemo session he just wanted to sleep.

That's how we got through the chemotherapy sessions and everything else. Together. With hope. As Chase would sit with his eyes closed and visualizing with me, I'd take note of the changes in his appearance. The thinning hair. The facial wasting which made his already prominent cheekbones and jawline even more so.

Just as Randy had, he was rapidly aging right before my eyes. A whole generation of vital, beautiful individuals, at the end, looked frighteningly alike. This particular young man, my Chaser, who was seven years younger than I, seemed much older, slumped over and burdened by his remaining life. The eyes were the same. Though closed at the moment, I knew when opened they would still flash with the same mischievous green sparkle. But for how long? When would the sparkle fade and the light go out?

Throughout all of this we were a team. He became more and more dependent on me and I became more and more devoted to his care. I rarely left his side. As he weakened and dementia began to seep in, I took on an ever greater decision making role with his doctors. He was too proud to walk with a cane or a walker, so I became his support. As we'd walk down Charles Street together, he would be partially to the side and just slightly behind me with his hand on my shoulder. That's how we got places. While he could still walk that is. Then I would carry him. How many times had I carried him through our garden and out to a waiting taxi and at the hospital? I had hernia surgery which failed due to the fact I'd had to take Chase to the hospital that same night, lifting him into the taxi and out, onto a wheelchair, and off, onto a toilet, and off.

As more and more of my time was devoted to Chase's care, it was clear I needed an outlet. And some sort of income since store design jobs had dried up. I also needed to get away from Cedar Lane Way and Chase now and then but nothing had presented itself. Even if some sort of offer did come my way there was the problem of my inability to commit to anything long term because I never knew when Chase's condition would take a dramatic turn and all of a sudden I'd be needed full-time. I did get out socially now and then but anytime I was away from home it was with what I called "The Pot on the Stove Syndrome." **Chase was my pot on the stove and I never knew when he was going to boil over in my absence.** My mind was never far from Cedar Lane Way whenever I was anywhere else. Once while cooking dinner, I ran out for some ingredient or other and returning realized I hadn't brought my keys. Our garden gate locked automatically and I was on the outside of it with my literal and figurative pots on the stove. I was a madman as I finally found a locksmith to help me. Apart from a slightly scorched dinner, all was fine. Sleeping Chase was never the wiser, but it was a wake up call to be more careful and pay closer attention, always.

We did have friends who offered to give me a break and stay with Chase but he wasn't much interested. I don't know for certain if it was vanity (he knew he was not looking so great anymore) or his need to rally and put on a good face for others and just wasn't up to it anymore. Whatever the case, I was the only person he felt comfortable having about. Still, I needed an occasional break from what our friend Jon called "Michael's laser beam focus." I needed something I could do or a place that I could go to just get away. It had to be close by and hopefully I could have some sort of income from it. I didn't know what it would be but I firmly believed it was out there. After all, these things just seem to work out for me.

1991

Little Shop Of Treasures

HAD I TRIED, I couldn't have escaped the gravitational pull of the little Beacon Hill shop right around the corner.

On one of his better days, Chase and I were at a dinner party at the home of a neighbor who told me she had heard of a woman with a small antique shop right in Beacon Hill. The neighbor knew I was looking for work and this woman was looking for someone to shop sit a few days. I didn't pay too much attention as having been a resident of Beacon Hill for several years and with my involvement with the garden club ladies, I quickly assessed the type of woman who most probably owned the shop and the type of shop it most probably would be. I imagined a rich bored Beacon Hill empty nest housewife with nothing to do beyond her Junior League responsibilities. I also imagined a husband who happily set "the little lady" up with a little shop selling precious little items to other little ladies who were just like her. Beacon Hill was chock full of these women and I already knew too many of them who, for the most part didn't seem to want to know me. I certainly wouldn't want to work for one. Having pigeonholed the situation, I took the business card with the woman's name on it but gave it little thought.

It was only a day or two later when our good friend Amy dropped by to see Chase and happened to mention that she'd been to a dinner party where she met a young woman with a furniture refinishing business right in Beacon Hill. Amy told us the refinisher happened to mention that the woman who had a small antique shop upstairs from the refinishing shop was looking for someone to shop sit a few days for her. Hmmmm... could it be the same person? Amy remembered the name of the shop owner was Madeleine. I found the business card and there was the name, Madeleine Gens. Hmmmm...again... two disparate people having no knowledge of each other within a day or two telling me about the same woman needing help in her shop. And one of them Amy. Amy had started out a friend and coworker of Chase and had become during the challenging days with Chase, one of my closest confidantes. We would spend Tuesday mornings together just talking and sorting things out, each thinking the other was helping more. **Well, I had learned enough about the workings of the universe and its signage principles for guidance to know not to ignore a signpost like this one.** Especially one that Amy was holding up for me. Despite any earlier misgivings I checked out Charles River Street Antiques the next day.

The shop turned out to be a quick zig-zag from our apartment; just three half-blocks away. It was a charming little storefront on a quiet side street and so packed with merchandise it spilled out the door and onto the sidewalk. As I stepped into the shop expecting to see a prim Boston lady, I was met instead with the dazzling smile of a handsome, dark haired, blue eyed, muscle boy in a string tank top. Well, things were looking up at Charles River Street Antiques. So, *not* what I was expecting, he was a charming sweet sexy gay boy — did I mention the muscles? — who apologized for Madeleine's absence and told me she was out buying and would be in the shop the next day. As it turned out, the muscle boy's upcoming departure was the reason for Madeleine's need of a new shop sitter. As I looked around the small, rather dark, stuffed with merchandise shop, its haphazard hoarder-like merchandise presentation (if you could all it that) was an assault to my organized store design and Virgo sensibilities. It did strike me that it was the kind of place where, if you dug around enough, you might just turn up a treasure or two. I left the shop feeling that despite the disorganization it wouldn't be an altogether bad place to spend time. It had an interesting energy that I couldn't quite put my finger on — coulda been the muscles — too bad he was leaving. I left with the feeling that I already somehow knew the place, a feeling of familiarity that gave me an instant sense of comfort despite the mess. **I'd come to understand that I had been a missing piece in the magical puzzle that was Charles River Street Antiques. And it had been my missing piece.** But I'm getting ahead of myself.

The next day I returned to River Street and met Kurt who had merchandise in the shop. He was a blond haired gay angel of a man who was shop sitting in Madeleine's absence. Was she ever there? Madeleine arrived momentarily with her newborn baby on her back. She was a crystal clear blue eyed force of nature exuding energy, all of it positive. I had never before seen such good, sparkling, unfocused energy democratically beaming in every direction, from one human being. I just stood there taking in this whirling spirit that seemed to energetically rearrange every molecule around her — including a few of my own. "Hurricane Madeleine," as I later nicknamed her, was nothing like the bored Beacon Hill housewife I'd imagined. **From that first moment on, I was a willing captive to this lovely, kind, blue eyed force of nature with a baby on her back.**

I have always thought that we have such power over tiny impressionable minds and because of this, when I see a baby or small child I always like to get right in its little wide-eyed face and tell it how good it is. I'm pretty certain we can impress words on these impressionable little minds that they will come to identify with, once they learn the meaning of those words. I think babies see god in our faces and they believe whatever it is we have to tell them. Because god (as far as they can tell) told them that's what they are, that's what they are. Good or bad. The programming sticks. Tell a baby it's good and it'll believe it and behave accordingly.

I sadly report that most every parent who hears me tell the child how good it is, counters with, "Good? Are you kidding? He's a little devil!" Or, "Oh, you don't know. She's a horror show!" Right in front of the child. Over the years this had become my litmus test for parents and there have been few passing grades. Until I met Madeleine. She swept in, newborn on her back and while giving her attention to innumerable other things, took little Dylan and placed him in a carrier on the sidewalk in front of the shop. Seeing that happy wide-eyed innocence looking up at me, I got right down in his face and said, "Oh what a good boy you are." Among all the other things receiving her attention, Madeleine, without missing a beat said, "Yes he is, so good! He is the best little boy!" And then directly to little Dylan, "Aren't you a good boy!" **Yup, this Madeleine was special.**

We got along famously from the get go and it was decided I'd start shop sitting on September 5, 1991–the day after my 40th birthday, though she wasn't aware of that. I now had a job giving me a break from the sickness on Cedar Lane Way and I could make a little money as well. It was right around the corner, quite literally, from where I lived. Madeleine understood about Chase and his needs and my need to be there for him. I could sit in the shop, close it at a moment's notice and run around the corner to take care of any Chase related need and run back. I could close for lunch, run home, make lunch, eat with Chase and return. If he was well enough he always had a place nearby to visit. Best of all, if need be, my schedule could accommodate any doctor visits or hospitalizations. And when the time came and Chase required around the clock attention, I could simply step away. It was the perfect opportunity. To what extent I had no idea.

I did not show up for work the morning of September 5th but made a phone call to Madeline instead. Upon hearing me on the other end of the phone telling her I would be late for my first day of work she must have thought she had made a big mistake. "Oh no, I hadn't expected this one to be a flake," she thought, as I began to make my excuses for not starting as planned. When I told her I had just spent the night in the emergency room at Mass General Hospital having been hit by a car, she amended her thinking.

For my 40th birthday, my friend Jay had thrown a surprise party the night before. To this day I have no memory of that event or of what followed. Surprise! I guess, after enjoying my lovely surprise party — I've seen photos so I do know it was lovely — I must have decided to top the occasion off with a late night bicycle ride along The Esplanade. And some outdoor midnight sex. Sounds like me. The Esplanade was a nearby park along the Charles River and a popular gay cruising ground. Especially on hot humid nights when like-minded boys would have nighttime Boston to themselves. Feeling festive and ever-horny I must've changed into shorts and a tank top and set out on my bicycle to "celebrate the humidity," as a Chicago friend who knew me too well, would, with a chuckle, refer to it. On what must have been my return from what I hope was a successful visit to the Esplanade, an eyewitness saw me on my bicycle, on Mt. Vernon Street, coming through the intersection at Charles Street headed toward Cedar Lane Way. I was less than a block from home. His account said that he was in his car waiting on Mt. Vernon for me to clear the intersection so that he could turn onto Charles Street. As I came into the intersection, a speeding car on Charles Street ran the red light and hit me broadside throwing me along with my bicycle into the air. I landed on the hood of the car and as the driver sped up, onto his windshield, flew up into the air again and came down on a parked car. The hit-and-run took only seconds. The eyewitness later told me how scared he was as he had never seen a dead body and was certain I had to be dead. He pulled his car over and ran to my aid. A worker had come out of a manhole and rushed into a nearby 7/11 and phoned the police. I was clearly out of it and was trying, with not even a half block to go, to get home. They sat me down on a curb forcing me to wait for the EMS truck as I protested, blood gushing from my head, that I was fine. I of course was not fine.

My first memory, since sometime before the party, is that of seeing my silver hoop earring on my little finger. I remember staring at it and wondering what my earring was doing there, totally unaware of my surroundings. As I looked beyond my fingertip, I started to realize I was in a hospital bed with doctors and nurses rushing around me. I was confused. "Was I mugged?" I asked a passing nurse. "No sweetie. We've told you before, you were in an accident and you're at Mass General Emergency Room." With that a doctor came up and said, "That was a pretty nasty cut on your forehead." "Oh, no," I replied, "Am I going to have to have stitches?" "Oh you've had your stitches already. Eighteen of them. And an MRI." The MRI was the reason my earring had been removed to my little finger for safekeeping.

As excuses for not showing up to work go, it was a pretty good one. What a way to turn 40 and start a new job. A few days after the big accident, I began shop sitting and found the work a little less than stimulating. Being on a quiet side street there wasn't the foot traffic of busy Charles Street. Hours could go by with no one coming in. This gave me time to become acclimated to the space and all the stuff in it. As I looked around, I began to notice that the space was actually filled with hand-picked treasures. You couldn't tell at first because it was all so haphazardly displayed. The more I searched the shop the more treasures I'd find. I felt like I'd discovered Tut's Tomb. Madeleine as it turned out really knew her stuff. **This was not a store full of junk at all, but a hand-picked, carefully curated shop. It just didn't look like one.**

I was inspired and knew what I had to do. Somebody had to make all those items look like the treasures they were. My store design, merchandising background made me just the boy for the job. My time could be used to far greater advantage in merchandising rather than just sitting there. With Madeleine away for a few days of buying I threw myself into it, merchandising while shop sitting. I employed every tool I had in my store designer's arsenal. I knew all the tricks of merchandise presentation and applied them liberally all around Charles River Street Antiques. I shopped the store identifying categories of merchandise and making collections within those categories. I translated them all into individual stories to tell around the shop. The merchandise responded to the love. Every single piece began to sing and became the treasure it actually was, surrounded and supported by other familial treasures. By the time Madeleine returned, the shop had been transformed. Stepping through the door, Madeleine stopped dead in her tracks. I could tell she was shocked and speechless. As she made her wordless way around she would stop, right where I planned, her eyes surveying each merchandise story and every item in that story. I watched as her eye followed from item to item just as I'd intended. She moved on to the next story and did the same. Moving through the entire store this way, she stopped at each predesignated spot until she circled back to the front. She was flabbergasted. I think (or at the very least, hoped) she was seeing her merchandise with fresh eyes and understanding what a fine job she'd done in selecting it all. Still somewhat speechless all she managed to say was that the shop looked "beautiful." Years later, Madeleine confessed to me that when she first walked in she had felt a little violated that I had taken such liberty with her shop. She quickly realized however, that lacking the ability and patience for merchandise presentation, she could now focus on buying. That was the part she liked best. **We were a match made in heaven. I could do what I loved and Madeleine what she loved.**

Chase's illness progressed and just as planned, I was able to manage the shop and him without slighting either. All the time the little shop on River Street gained in popularity as people from all over the world found us. There was magic in that shop and people were drawn to it. Some were customers and some just needed a place to go. Mass General Hospital was close by and we were amazed at how many people, taking a break from their caregiving, out for a meal, or a stroll, found their way to us. They needed a place to get away and just as it had for me, the universe provided it. They would leave our shop recharged. An astrologer once told Madeleine that she did not open the shop to make money but rather to provide a place where people could find her. And they did. There were the lonely hearts, the scared, the ones with no one to talk to, oftentimes full of pain and sadness. It was a safe place which welcomed them with open arms and open heart — just like Madeleine herself. We had one sweet trans person who would visit frequently. She would stay sometimes for hours talking about antiques and anything else. **After her departure, Madeleine would say, "You know, she just needs someplace where she can be a woman."** Madeleine's open-hearted non-judgmental attitude provided her that. They all came to us, sharing their stories both funny and tragic and in so doing added to the magical energy of that little shop on River Street creating a family of friends, neighbors and customers.

As one of those in need, I had no idea when I took that shop sitting job just how great that need would be and how much, in the face of Chase's deteriorating condition, I would rely on Madeleine and her shop to get me through it. I don't exaggerate when I say, **"Madeleine Gens and Charles River Street Antiques saved my life." I had been looking for a place to just get away for a bit. I didn't think to ask for more.** It was a place of much much more, right around the corner where I could go every day to get away from the suffering and illness. I could be challenged creatively, make a contribution, be surrounded by beautiful things and supportive people, learn about antiques and even make a little money. I was also able to lock the door and run home to Chase at a moment's notice. And when the time came, as Madeleine promised, I could simply walk away in order to take care of Chase full time until the end. The strength I got from the little shop of treasures was vast, real and immeasurable and helped prepare me for the inevitable.

I made a discovery in Madeleine's shop that would serve me personally and professionally the rest of my life. I noticed there'd be an item that for whatever reason wouldn't sell. It'd sit there day after day, week after week, months even with no one paying it any attention. Then, someone would come in and fall in love with it. A vase for instance. They'd pick it up and hold it to the light and say things like, "This is the loveliest vase I've ever seen. I love it. Look at how it captures the light. Look at the cut, the clarity. What a jewel." And then for whatever reason — "I don't have my checkbook," "I really need to think about it," "I want to bring my husband in to see it" — they would walk out the door leaving it behind. The next person to walk in the shop would buy it! After it's having sat around for perhaps months with no one interested in it suddenly one person loved it and left it and the next bought it. It happened over and over. **I couldn't ignore this and came to understand that simply by loving something we energize it.** It is a loving energy another person will feel and respond to. Anything loved is more beautiful. It's that way with people too I suppose. You are never more attractive than you are when you're on the arm of someone who loves you.

Armed with this universal information, I began to actively employ it in my merchandising. I would press love into every single thing I touched and viewed and "love each piece into its proper place," hoping to use this technique for increased sales. I did the same in clients' homes, rearranging and loving all the furniture and possessions they'd fallen out of love with and at the same time reenergizing everything. Not only would my amazed clients return to a home reimagined using sound principles of design and space, but also to a home of previously unloved things that were now resonating with a glowing loving energy. Their home would spiritually wrap its arms around them for the first time and welcome them in, just as Madeleine's shop had after I'd merchandised it. I don't know if any were fully aware of this but I certainly was when I'd receive the loveliest thank you notes along with their payments.

Madeleine and I would do several antique shows each year, most of them in New York City. These were grueling weekends that saw us packing up what amounted to an entire household of furniture and furnishings, carefully loading it all into a huge trailer truck, driving it down from Boston to Manhattan (with Madeleine doing the driving,) unloading the truck into the exhibition space, unpacking everything, setting up, merchandising and decorating the booth, selling all day Saturday and Sunday, striking the booth at the close of the show, re-packing all the merchandise that didn't sell and loading all of it out of the exhibition space and back into the truck and then driving directly back to Boston. It was exhausting. One of the more challenging aspects of those weekends was, in the face of such exhaustion, getting ourselves back to Boston safely. It was a long nighttime drive with Madeleine at the wheel and I in the passenger seat. We had to keep talking because any lapse in conversation could lead to quiet and quiet could lead to nodding off and nodding off could lead to imminent death. **So in an effort to keep things lively, I would regale Madeleine with my sex stories.** I had lots of them and she ate them up. Madeleine is, as am I, an appreciator of all things pretty so I would describe in consummate visual detail each beautiful sexy moment embellishing these colorful stories with every pretty detail I could remember. She would say, somewhat breathlessly, "Michael, you should write gay porn for straight women!" I'd laugh. The kicker was, once back in Boston, Madeleine would be so "revved-up" by my stories when she'd finally crawl into bed with her husband Tim, even exhausted as she had been... well...let's just say...Tim always appreciated Madeleine's return from those shows. He thought it had something to do with her driving a truck.

And then there was Kathleen. Kathleen was Madeleine's five year old angel of a daughter. She was a young girl with an old soul. She had bonded with Chase in a way few people had. He adored her and though he allowed few visitors he would always see Kathleen. He in fact wasn't all that fond of children, generally speaking, but Kathleen was different. He loved her visits. She was able to see past the illness which of course she couldn't understand yet somehow did. Her visits brightened Chase's days. When Chase was near the end, he asked if he could see Kathleen one more time. He had deteriorated to such an extent by then as to be almost unrecognizable. We were concerned that she would not handle it well. "Kathleen, would you like to go see Chase and say goodbye to him?" Madeleine asked little Kathleen, and preparing her for his emaciated condition added "God is getting ready to call Chase home so he might not look like Chase anymore." As I tentatively opened the door for the two of them, Kathleen without hesitation, rushed right past me and into Chase's outstretched arms. She couldn't have known the power of that moment or it's significance but Madeleine and I did. I leaned over to Madeleine and said, "I always knew she was an angel."

1990

A Vision In White Linen

MY MOST VIVID MEMORY of Jay, oddly enough, isn't my own. Ever-visual Madeleine, appreciator of all things aesthetically pleasing, described him thusly, "I was in the shop down on my knees fussing over something in the showcase and through its glass I saw a pair of tan legs walk in and stop. I scanned up to see a tall, dark and handsome, absolute vision in crisp white linen." To this day, that is my favorite way to remember Jay — a handsome vision in white linen, a fabric that always seemed to have been invented just for him. Cashmere as well, now that I think about it. In a city famous for its rather dowdy personal presentation, Jay was always a standout. He'd shop the sales racks at Neiman Marcus and buy all their most fabulous pieces at a fraction of their original cost, the rest of Boston having passed them over as "too fashionable." As if there were such a thing. Tall trim and fit, he always looked smashing in everything.

Introducing himself, upon our first meeting, as having just relocated from Canada, my initial thought was, "Boston doesn't have enough boring bankers, we now have to import them from Canada?" He turned out to be barely a banker and never boring. That initial meeting happened auspiciously at the beach — my favorite place to make new friends. And we became friends. Fast friends. For life friends. It was a time when I needed as many outlets as I could find, to get away from the cares and sorrows of Cedar Lane Way. Jay and I could hang out together at his Back Bay apartment only blocks away, listen to some great jazz — he knew all about jazz while I did not — share a joint, Chinese food, Häagen-Dazs ice cream and our personal philosophies of life. And we could make each other laugh. We got each other, much in the way that Randy and I had. It was great being able to share our quirky mutual sense of humor. And all that laughter.

I'd be making a sandwich for Jay, asking the same litany of preferences that I would ask Chase, "What kind of bread would you like? Toasted or plain? How many slices of turkey? Ham? Do you want mayo or mustard or both? Lettuce? Tomato? Sliced thin? What kind of cheese? How many slices?" I could see his growing impatience about something and by the time I got to, "How do you want it sliced, vertically or on a diagonal? he'd scream, "HOW DO YOU LIVE LIKE THIS?" We'd both break up with laughter knowing the special challenges I had in the care and feeding of my own AIDS victim, Chase. His validation of my current state of affairs was invaluable during those challenging days, making it possible to get through so much of what I was going through. **He was a loving lifeboat in my swirling sea of cock-eyed caregiving for an often unappreciative and not very patient, patient.** Though a full decade my junior, somehow, Jay seemed to me, senior. He was like a protective older brother — someone whose opinion I could solicit and follow.

1992

The Birds & The Bees & The Boys

THE VICTORY GARDENS in Boston is a patchwork garden community made up of several hundred small plots, each fenced-in and tended by various gardeners. Some are vegetable gardens. Some are floral gardens. Some are both. Every little patch of green has its own personality. Many are lavishly laid out and romantically furnished for their intrinsic beauty, while others are simply working gardens meant only for production and harvesting. And most, I presume, for the inherent joy they provide the gardener. The individual gardens, each reflecting the personality of its gardener, when viewed together create a charming crazy quilt of flowers and vegetables, patterns and colors. The Victory Gardens conveniently located on the way from our apartment to the hospital, became a refuge during that challenging time. **I found myself on my bike stopping there going to or from the hospital or headed there whenever I could, to get away, clear my head and recharge my batteries.**

The gardens, established during World War II when similar gardens were created all over the country, are located in an area of Boston called The Fenway. The Fenway is one of the jewels in Frederick Law Olmsted's "Emerald Necklace" a system of treelined parkways and parks that runs throughout Boston much as it does in my hometown of Louisville, another Olmsted "Emerald Necklace" city. I had a great fondness for The Fenway and spent a lot of time biking in and around it much as I had done in Louisville's Cherokee Park where I had my first sexual encounter.

The Fenway was also a great place for sex. Rather than the forested hills of Louisville's Cherokee Park or Chicago's Lincoln Park (or any of the other urban park pre-internet,) The Fenway's distinction was its tall rustling reeds rather than trees. There were paths carved out by gay men tramping their way deep into the reeds which were right along the edge of The Victory Gardens. Day and night it was a popular destination for anonymous recreational sex. Just a bit of outdoor-boy-fun. There were risks involved. You would hear the occasional story of a knifing or a police raid, bicycles being stolen, tires slashed and, worst of all, bands of roving homophobic teenage boys. While such stories heightened your sense of awareness, and kept you on guard, they rarely kept you away as the lure and excitement of anonymous outdoor sex, day or night, was stronger than the potential threat. The adjacency of The Victory Gardens to the reeds created a particularly combustible sexual environment as so many gay boys, like myself, are attracted to gardens and so many of the gardeners themselves happened to be gay. One could cruise the narrow paths through the tall reeds meeting up with another cruiser in a reed-enclosed out-of-the-way cul-de-sac for a quickie, while some other paired-off or group activity would be happening just around the bend at another dead end spot. One could also cruise the labyrinthian paths around the individual gardens and if lucky be invited in, privacy kindly provided by fences overgrown with vines and tall stands of dahlias, hollyhocks, delphiniums, foxglove and the like. **The Fenway was tailor made for a gay man in love with beauty, the outdoors, and sex in equal parts. Seriously, I love a man who makes things grow.**

I was fortunate to have a friend with a particularly lovely Victory Gardens plot. It was a larger than average parcel surrounded by a tall fence overgrown with honeysuckle. There was an old weathered garden gate set into the honeysuckle fence and despite what a big old tarnished brass padlock hanging on it might suggest, the gate was never locked. I doubt there was a key. Inside the garden was an equally weathered wood arbor with a built-in bench below and a canopy of pink roses wrapping it. The bench's lift-up seat kept hidden the trowels, clippers, gloves and other tools of gardening along with the poppers, lube, condoms and other tools of sex. What a good friend my gardening friend was. He also had a 9–5 job which left his garden unattended most weekdays. Knowing my home situation, he generously allowed me access to his garden whenever I wished. It was the perfect place to get away from the sickness of Cedar Lane Way and I would spend many an afternoon clipping, pruning, deadheading, and toking up. I'd soak up the sun and appreciate the beauty of my borrowed surroundings, baked while baking my tan-lines. Always horny and hopeful.

There was a small grassy clearing just big enough to stretch out in; and, just big enough to accommodate one other, if one other happened to wander by. I'd lie there in my smallest of speedos surrounded on three sides by walls of natural flowering vegetation. The 'fourth wall' was an opening which provided a view toward the gate. And if you were on the outside of the gate, a view of me. From my vantage point, I could keep track of anyone who might be passing by and if anyone of particular interest happened to pass and perhaps linger for a prolonged look, I could invite him in. It was "pretty sex," my favorite kind, in that little outdoor clearing, naked together, surrounded by glorious nature in full bloom. **Having sex in that gorgeous garden was not unlike being in a sexy naked and gay version of an animated Disney cartoon.** There were birds happily chirping and singing and bees buzzing around us doing their daily work. There were flowers everywhere, swaying in the breeze and anointing the air with a fragrance that would blend with that of freshly-cut grass and freshly-had sex. All of nature it seemed, conspired in support of this summertime, somewhat subversive but lovely, sexy, semi-private, socially-forbidden, outdoor activity.

One hot still summer afternoon as I lay there soaking up the sun in my favorite spot I heard something off in the distance. The sound, though indefinable, was at odds with the quiet serenity of the day and made me sit up and take notice. My defenses were engaged even though I could not make out exactly what I was hearing. As the sound approached I could hear it was voices, several voices. Male voices. Young male voices that I instantly recognized as a group of teenage boys. **There are few things more terrifying to a gay man than roving gangs of teenage boys; they are capable of the worst combination of homophobia, peer pressure, mob behavior and violence.** There was no real reason for their presence in the Victory Gardens but malevolence. It is a time-worn story. The Victory Garden is a "fag" hangout and no doubt they were looking for "fags" to beat up. I may have already picked up the word in fact as their single voice got closer and more threatening. I jumped to my feet instantly aware of my own vulnerability. There wasn't time to escape or even time to locate and put on my clothes. They were steps away. There was no way out and no place to hide. I was nearly-naked, alone in a small secluded space with only one means of egress soon to be blocked by a rapidly approaching malevolent male mob. I was trapped and I was about to be gay-bashed. In Boston. Again.

Gay Boy's Life

Along with the voices came the birds. There were birds suddenly flocking in from all directions and fluttering around me. Now I'm gonna be attacked by birds? Trapped like Tippi Hedren in the attic? Before I could make any sense of this and even more threatening, the bees came. Bees, out of nowhere, swarmed around me. What was happening? A sudden triple-threat. Bashers and birds and bees...oh my! (I can make jokes now but this was all truly frightening!) If I'd had no time to exit before, it would be impossible now through that swarm of angry bees. The gang of boys was suddenly at the gate; I saw three or four hostile faces sneering at my nearly-naked gayness and more heads visible over the honeysuckle fence. More than a gay bashing, there was about to be a gay massacre.

We stood there, eye to eye, homo to homophobe. Staring. Just staring. **That's when I realized the swarming wall of bees that was keeping me in was keeping them out.** One boy put his hand on the gate to open it but was swarmed by the bees. He backed off, swatting at them and looking for another way in. His friends behind still staring at me, began swatting them as well. The buzzing wall between us would let nothing pass. I was being protected. The gang stood there dodging and swatting, and then, apparently deciding a good old fashioned gay-bashing wasn't worth tangling with a swarm of aggressive bees, one by one the boys moved on, heads down still swatting away the bees. As they made their departure the voices returned. I could hear an occasional "faggot," "queer," and "homo" being spat back at me as they and their voices trailed off into the distance.

I sat back down emotionally drained, appreciating the buzzing swirling life around me. What had just happened? Had all those creatures come to protect me? It certainly seemed so. At first. As I thought this through it became clear that more probably they had come to me for protection. They are small creatures of instinct, in the habit of using those instincts for survival. In the quiet balance of that garden space, hearing those voices they must have sensed a threat. Seeking out the most benign presence in the area, they came to me, I think possibly, for protection; and in so doing, actually provided protection. They may have saved my life.

I sat back down appreciating more than ever a beautifully balanced universe that uses its own to take care of its own. This was one of many life events which made me increasingly comfortable with the thought that no matter what challenges and even danger may lay ahead, in harmony with the universe, I would be taken care of. I began to understand and appreciate a little more about how and why things just seem to work out for me.

1993

A Letter From Mikey

Feb 23, 1993

Dear Mom & Dad —

A letter from Mikey; this is probably causing terror in your hearts right now. RELAX! I'M FINE! I am, however, moving toward a time in my life when I'll be needing your love and support more than I ever have.

There is so much about me and my life that I have not shared with you because, like you, I don't like making people feel uncomfortable — especially those I love. But in doing so, I've separated you from so much of my life and that hasn't been fair to either of us. To spare your feelings I haven't offered a great deal of information about me; and to spare mine, you haven't asked questions.

I want you to know that there is nothing about me that I wish to keep a secret. There is nothing about me for which I am ashamed. I am proud to say that you both raised a good son who tries his best to simply do good things that are true to his own nature. You have allowed me to be who I am — and I love you so much for that.

It's been 24 years since we have actually discussed my homosexuality. I guess I've been waiting for you to bring it up to let me know that is was OK to discuss it — I more than anything did not want to force my sexuality upon you. During that same 24 years (we don't move too fast, do we?) you've probably been waiting for me to bring it up. So we've been waiting for each other — living our lives in tandem but not sharing everything.

At last, last summer, the silence was

broken. You broke it Mom when you brought up the subject of Louisville's Gay Rights Ordinance. I love you so much for that. It was an act that nudged open a door for me. At the same time Dad, you did the same in warning me about possible gay-bashing in Louisville. I love you for that too. I'm using these two acts as indications from you that the time is long overdue to open wide the doors to my life and allow myself to be simply, who I am with both of you. Correct me if I'm wrong here, but I think you'd like to know more about me and my life.

Since there is nothing in my life for which I am ashamed, there is nothing that I would wish to keep from you. I promise you honest answers. Please feel free to ask any questions.

There are a few unasked questions that I would like to answer right now because it is very important that you know these things.

The first, and it's good news: I am HIV neg. This means that I am not infected with the virus that causes aids. I've wanted you to know this for quite some time and it's been very selfish of me to not share this information. I'm sure you've been worried. These tests are not 100% conclusive, it's pretty likely I have not been infected. Having practiced safe sex before most people even knew the rules existed.

Chase however has not been so fortunate. He was diagnosed with full-blown Aids nearly four years ago — April 3rd (what is it about that date?) He has done quite well throughout the past four years, but he seems surely on a decline over the past several months. As I watch his health deteriorate I realize that I will need all the strength I can get — strength derived from the support of loved ones. I am page 3

fortunate to have many loved ones who are with me in this — I would love to know I can count you among them — that is the main reason. Please don't worry, this information with you until now. I knew this was a situation that would take years to play itself out. And I didn't want you worrying for years. I just don't want you to worry now. I just won't you to know.

My first priority for quite some time has been Chase and his health. I made this commitment four years ago — as he has so few people in his life on whom he can depend. I'll be with him to the end. This hasn't been easy and it's likely to become far more difficult in the future. He could still live to his 80's for years, or the disease could be gone next week — let's that kind of disease.

So I am here caring and supporting for myself. I am asking for your care and support for that. I know I can depend on it and for that I am eternally thankful.

Funny, I'm suddenly feeling so grown up. ☺ I guess it's about time — I am over 41 years old — but even at 41 I have always felt like the baby of the family — and I guess I'll always be that — but at some point I guess all baby boys become men. I hope you are as proud as I am of the man your baby has become.

Thanks,

I love you,

Mikey

My parents called as soon as they received the letter and were their usual loving selves.

1993

Desert Rain Of Gifts

FROM BEGINNING TO END, 1993 was a roller coaster ride of ups and downs. When I would mention (read: complain about) this, my ever-wise friend Shani would be quick to point out, "People pay a lot of money and stand in long lines to ride roller coasters so enjoy it." There were times when I could enjoy the ride but more frequent than not the ride was at best, challenging. Just as with Randy, there were times when I was certain Chase was in his final days and then suddenly he'd rebound. And seem to be healthy again. There was no rhythm to this. No reason. And no knowing when, after having successfully built him up, the next collapse would come. Never knowing if perhaps it'd be the final one. Spring was on its way (for someone who grew up in the south, Boston springs arrive notoriously late) and things seemed to be going pretty well with Chase. We had gotten through the long, challenging winter and with his heath steadily improving right along with the change of the season, we were guardedly optimistic.

My Boston friends Jay and Phil were going to Palm Springs for the big White Party held annually on Easter weekend. They had a reservation in a gay guesthouse and had space for one more. Would I like to join them? White Party Weekend, a series of parties actually with the huge White Party as its centerpiece, was legendary. I had never been but had always wanted to go. I hadn't visited Palm Springs since the mid-70s. I had loved it then and was pretty sure I'd love it even more now, especially on White Party weekend. The offer was too good to refuse. Chase was stable and I was exhausted. **It was the perfect opportunity to get away and I grabbed it.**

Most cities are vertical places. The Palm Springs of my memory was a horizontal one. Layers stacked, one on the other, creating an expansive, uniquely horizontal desert-city-scape. Set into a horizontal line of mostly desert sand and colorful tiles was the horizontal blue of sparkling pools. Just above that glistening blue line was another glistening line, this one oiled bronze and made up of naked or nearly-naked suntanning boys. This horizontal line of gay horizontal bodies was set against a predominantly green and multi-colored band of tropical and desert vegetation. Above that soft floral band, another one, hard and pastel, stucco and steel, sleek and rectilinear, made up of one and two story buildings, all low and wide and horizontal. These mid-century modernities, street after street of them, sat end-to-end spreading their way over the desert sand. Above their flat roofs, still another horizontal line made up of row after row of palm trees gently swaying to whatever breezes the mountains allow in. Most dramatic of all, the wherever-you-look horizontal line of those majestic mountains providing an all embracing 360 degree hard-to-believe-it's-real Hollywood-backdrop. Topping the mountains and in sharp contrast to their craggy gray darkness, if you happened to catch the season right, was one more horizontal line, this one white, made up of the pure untouched snow capping them. Above the heat of the desert; snow. Finally, overhead, extending endlessly beyond the jagged line of those snow caps, the reliably clear sky lighting everything below it to perfection. Dependent on the time of day, that infinite sky changes from turquoise to gold to yellow to crystal clear blue to orange to pink to red to purple with every variation and combination. And of course, above it all, creating all of this is the ever-present ever-generous Palm Springs sun whose light gets caught within the circle of mountains and bounces back and forth and back again. There is nothing like the continually changing light of Palm Springs that washes everything in its magic. That is how I remembered Palm Springs and I couldn't wait to see it again.

The Palm Springs of my memory was also a sexy place. A young man's playground, an oasis overrun with horny young gay baby boomer boys like myself. The extreme heat, dry as it was, caused a sort of sleepy sexuality. Languid and lazy and hot. Always hot. A laissez-faire kind of hot. Too hot in fact to concern oneself with social conventions like…clothing or privacy. **There was a naked-permissive, over-heated desert-sexuality that not only allowed but encouraged any flame that might ignite, to flare up, right there, fanned by the surroundings, and explode until it burned itself out.** Within the privacy of the gay guesthouse walls, sex was 'public' and ubiquitous. I couldn't wait to experience it again.

As we drove in from Los Angeles for White Party Weekend there was much that was new to me. We passed a sandy sea of spinning wind turbines, all moving and gleaming in kind. They created a luminous outdoor gallery of kinetic sculptures spilling their way down the sandy brush of the desert hills. I was dazzled and energized. Sadly gone were the "date shacks," tiny roadside clapboard cottages tucked into thickets of palm trees where you could pull over and enjoy a date shake freshly made from dates harvested right there, probably that morning. Sitting at a sun-bleached and sun-heated picnic table sipping your cold treat you'd take in the sweeping majesty of the endless desert around you happy to be alive…and there. While the shacks and shakes were gone, the mountains remained; just as tall and majestic and ubiquitous as I'd remembered. That was good news. Severe and jagged, they still encircled the city creating a magically lighted dramatic desert bowl that you can drive right into. I'd forgotten just how impossibly high and formidable they are, dwarfing all else including the mid-century masterpieces that I was happy to see still lined the streets. There seemed to be more of these Palm Springs gems, in fact, and all fixed up too.

The Palm Springs we drove into on White Party Weekend, some seventeen or so years since my first visit, had grown older. It was still a boys' playground, just…older boys. We were no longer 20 but pushing our 40s. The new Palm Springs was also still plenty hot but not quite as sleepy. It had grown bigger and, especially being White Party weekend, busier. Would it still be as sexy?

As we pulled into the parking area of our suitably mid-century guesthouse, it was my fervent hope that I would find on the other side of the wall that separated it from the outside world, a place as fun and frisky as the guest houses from my Palm Springs and Key West past. I needn't have worried. Post-check-in, we passed the pool area chock-full of sexy, naked and nearly-naked boys. Boys swimming, floating, lying in the sun, reading, drinking, and socializing. I could see within the desert tropical landscaping, pathways that undoubtedly led to all sorts of playgrounds within this playground within a playground where I was certain to be getting up to all sorts of frisky business. **This was most assuredly a place to be my naked and gay self; my favorite version of me.** I realized I was home and breathed a sigh of relief. Palm Springs would be my desert Key West where, aligned with the universe, and in tune with all its energetic forces, it would once again, I hoped, open up to me. In Palm Springs rather than providing the spiritual information I'd become accustomed to, as it turned out, that ever generous universe seemed insistent on providing something else; sex.

Perhaps the decision to go to Palm Springs was so appropriate that the universe just simply said "yes" and "yes" and "yes" and "yes." It was a well-deserved respite away from all the caregiving attendant to the constant needs of an AIDS patient. It was the right thing at the right time, putting me in tandem with the universe and all its balance and harmony. Making no demands of this universe I was happy to let it take over and provide what it might while fulfilling its design for happiness. I hadn't asked for anything specific of that long weekend trip. I was just happy to be away from it all. I didn't think to ask for more. But I'd get more. Much more; rewarded I think, over and over, for all the constant caregiving, the constant emotional support, the constant medical championing for someone who could no longer fight his own battles...the constant. Period. Back in the cold of pre-spring Boston, taking care of a dying man, I was also a dying man (of sorts.) I was in the middle of a metaphorical desert, parched and weary, desperately thirsting for water. In need of an oasis. Palm Springs, in the middle of a real desert, became that made-for-me oasis. As the weekend progressed, the rewards tailored to my specific likes and loves presented themselves again and again. **With grateful outstretched arms, my parched self soaked up this desert rain of gifts, thanking the universe for every one of them.**

Making that initial post-check-in walk past the pool, I spotted among the tanned naked bodies surrounding it, my first gift. He was a stand-out. One of those golden boys for whom, it seems, the sun only shines. As if all the others fall somehow into the shadow. I feasted my eyes on his perfectly tanned perfectly proportioned body and got a really good look at his perfectly fluffed penis. I of course could not take my eyes away from my newly found golden boy. With a gentle tug on my tank top and, "This way darling," my friend Jay (who knows me all too well) put me back on track before I made an unintended splash right into the pool. Our room was big and spacious and thoroughly mid-century. There were two queen size beds and only three of us. The fourth person with whom I'd be sharing a bed was the "boyfriend of a friend of a friend." His name was Eric and like me, was a last-minute fill-in. He'd be arriving later.

Back at the guesthouse after dinner and dancing, in the still-warm Palm Springs night, I set out for the hot tub. Of course. In a setting like this one, it is the only sensible thing to do. As I approached, I could see from some distance a silhouetted figure alone there in the moonlight half submerged in the bubbling water. As I got closer, to my delight, I saw that it was the poolside golden boy I'd spotted post-check-in. Apparently the moon also shone only for him as he was actually glowing in its cool soft light. Fluffing first and then dropping my towel, I allowed myself a moment to just hang there, goods on display, before easing into the hot bubbling water. Our eyes met, our toes touched, we shared a smile and that's all it took. Right there, on my first night in Palm Springs, embraced by those gorgeous mountains, under a galaxy of stars and that same generous moon, all set like jewels into the deep-blue of a Maxfield Parrish sky, I enjoyed my first Palm Springs gift of many to come. And come. And come. It was the perfect start to the perfect weekend and would prove to be only the beginning.

Eventually extricating myself from the hot water and my hot friend, I made my relaxed way back to the room to find that Eric, the "boyfriend of a friend of a friend" had arrived during my absence and was already fast asleep in our bed. The covers only partially hid a spectacular body and the face of a sleeping muscular angel. I happily crawled right in. Lucky me, he was a cuddler. His cuddling along with the enervating effect of the hot tub and the post-sex afterglow made my first night's sleep in Palm Springs the best I'd had in recent memory. I met my bedmate the next morning and he was as stunning standing up as he had been lying down. Really nice too. He pretty much went his own way that weekend but was reliably in bed at some point each night for more cuddling. I couldn't and wouldn't have asked for more.

Out by the pool with Jay and Phil, on our first afternoon, I was floating, naked, when I spied four boys, all cute collegiate types, checking in. I floated my way to a see-and-be-seen position, making sure I was well-fluffed, awaiting their walk-by. Was it interest I saw on their faces? As I continued paddling my way around the pool I did so full of hope. Within minutes they were into their speedos and out by the pool. My kind of boys. Shortly thereafter they were out of their speedos and into the pool. Yes, definitely my kind of boys. **I've spent a good portion of my life (and I do mean it's been good) in the pursuit of the all grown-up adult versions of the boys I wanted but couldn't have when I was a boy myself.** These boys fit that blueprint perfectly. From that moment on, I had the constant companionship of four of the most adorable boys I could have wished for. Had I been so bold, that is, to wish for four adorable college boys. I'd wished only for a fun vacation. I didn't think to ask for more. We did everything together. Everything. One of the four, a smooth strawberry blond, blued eyed sexy charmer with freckles across his nose and shoulders became my instant favorite. We were inseparable. One evening as the two of us were waiting out by the pool for the others to join us before going off to a party, blond boy reached over and began feeling my recently groomed legs. "You shave your legs," he said, still stroking them, "I like how they feel." I was an early adapter of manscaping having already done it for a decade at this point. "No, actually I clip them." He looked over at me a bit puzzled, "with a barber's clippers. Works great and you don't get razor burn or stubble," I said. "I like how they look too; shows off your leg muscles," he said through a sexy smile running his fingers up my leg where he was getting the desired reaction between them. "Where else do you groom?" I heard as I felt the warmth of his breath in my ear and the grip of his fist on my crotch. "Do me." he said with a squeeze, "Groom me. I need it. Please? Now?"

I don't need to be asked twice. Rushing hand in hand to the room he shared with his three buddies, as we burst through the door my sexy young friend announced, "Guess who's getting groomed!" Turns out they all wanted it. Within minutes all four were naked on their hands and knees; four shining collegiate boy butts lined up for grateful groomer, me. Electric clippers humming, I went to work transfixed on those smooth white boy butts committing the image to memory. There might be videos somewhere.

That same night while at the party, we were either too early or it was one of those parties that takes a while to get going. Whatever the case, at a point when things were finally kicking in, my collegiate group appeared. "We're getting ready to leave. Wanna ride back to the guesthouse?" asked my favorite blond boy. "Gosh, I don't think so. The party's just getting started," I replied honestly, "I think I'll stay. I'm sure I can get back one way or another." **My blond boy did not seem pleased with that answer. "Let me re-phrase that," he continued, "we're going back to the guesthouse. If you come with us, you and I are going to have sex on one bed and they (gesturing to his smiling friends) are going to be on the other bed watching."** Back at the guesthouse that's pretty much exactly what happened. Oh the things I did to that boy right in front of his friends. It was mattress-slipping-off-the-frame sex, all to the enthusiastically vocal appreciative cheering section of three. There might be videos somewhere.

As the week progressed and these "adventures" continued to mount up, I of course would regale my friends Jay and Phil with the stories of whatever of my good fortunes (both on and off-campus) they hadn't witnessed themselves. Jay in particular would just look at me and shake his head in what (I wasn't quite sure) was either amazement or envy or disgust or perhaps just resignation to my behavior. Whatever the case, I was having the well-deserved time of my life.

The final party we attended, in Cathedral City, was one of those nights when I walked into the party and said to myself, "This is the night of nights!" I actually said those exact words out loud as we entered. I could feel the energy. It happens sometimes. I have often referred to big gay dance clubs as my church, well this night it seemed appropriately enough, I'd found, in Cathedral City, my cathedral. The energy all around was positively electric. It was clear this would be a night to remember. It didn't take long to find my way out to the middle of the crowded dance floor and I started dancing there alone losing myself in the energy and the music. After awhile a circle opened up around me creating a void between me and all the other dancers.

As a child who grew up on film musicals of the 30s and 40s, I had always loved when Fred and Ginger, or some other couple would start dancing and a circle would form around them by others who would pull away to admire the dancing duo. I often fantasized that once grown up, such a thing might happen to me. Once grown up such a thing did happen, quite frequently in fact. As I'd start dancing on a crowded dance floor, an open circle would form around me. Every time. Rather than finding delight in this as I had in my childhood fantasies, I would actually find it more than a little unnerving. I'd be embarrassed at the thought that perhaps the other dancers were repelled and wanted to get away from "the crazy guy out there dancing by himself." Over time though, I became less concerned about what they might be thinking and decided the space around me, emptying of any negative (perhaps judgmental) energy, was opening up to accommodate all my angel buddies from beyond; those I had danced with before they'd made their premature departure from this world. They would fill the void with their from-beyond positivity and dance with me once again, surrounding me and enjoying the supernatural night alongside their still mortal buddy. I was the one they'd left behind, but they were in the habit, of coming back, leaving for awhile their heavenly angel parties, encircling me and dancing the night away with me, right here on earth. To the casual eye it might look as if I am dancing alone but I am not. I am in fact surrounded. Chase, Randy, Warren, Art, Scott, the Jimmies and legions of others… they're all there, the ones I knew and the ones I didn't. **I came to think of that space around me as my "Angel Circle."** The circle fills itself in eventually by the living — anyone drawn to that kind of angel energy, but the void lasts long enough to remind me of my departed friends and assure me of their joyful unwavering presence around me.

So there I was, in Cathedral City, dancing in my angel circle when I noticed someone else dancing in it. There were two of us in that small clearing. This was new. My dance partner was a tall, muscular, long haired, nearly-naked Tarzan Boy. Tarzan, always well-muscled and also nearly-naked on TV, first in black and white and eventually in "living color," was a youthful fantasy of mine. Of many young gay boys, I'll warrant. In my fantasy we'd swing from tree to tree in our loin-clothed nearly-naked state playing our jungle Tarzan games and living together naked in our tree house undisturbed by the outside world. This Cathedral City Tarzan, muscled and magnificent, actually reminded me of one of my favorite Tarzans, Miles O'Keeffe, from the 1980s Bo Derek film version. Sometimes you can't quite get your eyes open wide enough to take in and record extraordinary beauty. This was one of those times.

I noted right off we were "twinning." My new Tarzan's "loincloth" was a tiny, skin tight, tropical print, square cut swim suit. Hanging from it's waistband was a white tank top no doubt removed upon entering the party and looped there for safe keeping. He was wearing white "Chuck's" — Converse high-top sneakers. My "loincloth" was my favorite 1950s Key West-purchased clingy boxer-style swimsuit. It was a tropical print virtually identical to the one sexily clinging to my new Tarzan. I also had a white tank top that I'd taken off when entering the party and had looped it through the waistband of my suit for safe keeping. And, I was wearing my favorite white high-top Chucks. But for the size and proportion differences (and a lot of muscle) we were the mirror image of each other. Dancing together in that circle our eyes fixed on each other's eyes, we moved toward one another. I couldn't tell whether he was minicking me or whether he danced just like me but whatever the case, our moves were identical as we closed the gap between us. Practically nose to nose, a breath's distance but never quite touching, as I moved in, he moved out. As he moved in, I moved out. We worked together like that in unison, like some sort of sexy binary organism, each anticipating and accommodating the other's movement. It was a perfectly choreographed, in-sync, sexy impromptu pas de deux. **I had never seen anyone who danced exactly like me, until I danced that night with a tall,**

spectacularly well–muscled, similarly and scantily clad Tarzan in an open circle filled with angels on an otherwise crowded dance floor in the middle of the desert in Cathedral City, California.

We eventually left the circle. As he took my hand and led me through the crowded dance floor, the dancers parted for this enormous God Of The Jungle. He led us to the bar where he ordered drinks and we got to know each other. His name was Miles. "Miles?" I said, "like Miles O'Keefe? The actor who played…" "Tarzan?" he said finishing the question and answering it at the same time. "I get that a lot. I'm not him. Or he's not me. Or whatever. I've never been Tarzan. Or played him." He pondered a moment and then added, "I kinda felt like Tarzan today, though. My buddy and I went up to Joshua tree…" I didn't have a clue what Joshua Tree was but played along imagining it anyhow. "We found this waterfall. Actually it was a series of waterfalls, one spilling into another and so forth. Down the mountain. Anyway, we took off our clothes, climbed up to the top and jumped down the first one into the water below. We did this with each one til we got to the bottom and climbed back up and did it all again." My already active imagination went into overdrive seeing these naked Tarzan twins jumping through waterfall after waterfall, splashing into each waiting natural pool, frolicking there together and perpetuating my naked Tarzan fantasy.

Through the haze of that happy naked daydream, a bit lost in it, I heard the words "My friends are scared of you." Snapped back from my fantasy, I was puzzled and he could tell. "Didn't you notice when you were out there dancing by yourself they all backed away?" "Yes," I responded with a nod and before I could add that this was not new to me, he continued, "Well, I was out there with all my friends and you joined us and started dancing by yourself." OK… "Well," he continued, "they took one look at you and said, 'Oh good god no, there's another Miles!'" At that moment I couldn't focus on anything but the flattery I felt hearing that anyone would think I was anything like this godlike man. He continued, "They were afraid of what was gonna happen when two of us got together so they told me they'd see me later. They couldn't get outta there fast enough. We scared them all away," he said with a big sparkling self satisfied grin. "Left just the two of us out there alone…together…dancing…" He made an explosion sound that he echoed with his widened eyes and bursting-open hands, "Better than sex!"

I was mesmerized by this sweet, gentle gorgeous hunk of Tarzan as we sat at that bar talking, kissing, groping and getting to know each other until it was time for him to go. He had driven up from San Diego with his friends. It was the end of the weekend and they were headed back that night. As we were kissing each other goodbye, I became aware of Jay and Phil standing there in their continued disbelief of what they were witnessing. It was time for us to go too. On the drive back, there were about a million questions about my Tarzan Boy and several comments (many of them snarky) about all my good sexual fortune that weekend. I'm sure they were happy for me, to an extent, but I also think they were secretly glad that the next day it would all be over.

We were leaving Palm Springs late in the afternoon giving me time to float on the pool, catching my last naked rays before heading back to the cold Boston Spring-that's-not-Spring. Once again I spotted, a pair this time, of boys checking in. I stretched out, hands clasped behind my head as they passed by. From behind my Ray Bans I caught a couple of glances that made me pretty sure they'd be back out shortly. Within minutes they were in their speedos and out by the pool. Minutes later they were out of their speedos and in the pool… with me. My new friends were standing in the pool on either side of my blue float, one gently playing with my balls and the other stroking my hard penis. I in turn had my hands under the water squeezing both theirs'.

At that moment, Jay came out of our room, took in the all too familiar situation, shook his head, rolled his eyes heavenward, turned and walked right back into the room.

1993

Roman Holiday

CHASE wanted to spend his final years traveling and being ever the businessman, had business cards printed that said "Christopher Leon — Traveler." The focus of his traveling became Italy and more specifically Florence. He'd fallen in love with Florence and would go there a couple of times each year. He'd fly to Milan, rest for one night and take the train to Florence the next day. His residence of choice in Florence was The Tornobuoni Beacci, a wonderful little pensione where they took especially good care of "Signore Leon."

As time and the disease progressed Chase's trips became more challenging and we decided that I would accompany him on what, though we didn't actually say the words, would be his final trip to his beloved Italy. We both knew it. Conversely it would be my first trip to Italy — actually my first trip to Europe. While I did have a passport, with my limited funds and affection for Key West, San Francisco, Palm Springs and New York, I never seemed to get out of the country. We planned the trip with a few nights in Milan, a week in Florence and then another week in Rome. Prior to this, Chase had avoided the larger cities because with his illness he could become easily overwhelmed. Given he'd have assistance, he felt more comfortable in exploring both Milan and Rome.

While I was thrilled by the entire plan, it was Rome that held the greatest excitement for me. It was after all the city of Audrey Hepburn and Gregory Peck and I was so looking forward to my own Roman holiday. While we knew of course where we'd be staying in Florence and our Milan accommodations were not critical to me, Rome was vitally important. **In addition to *Roman Holiday*, I'd seen many films set in Rome and I had a rather romantic view of the eternal city; I wanted to stay in a hotel and location that reflected that view.** I was quite definite about that. I researched travel magazines — there was no internet then — and had come across several small boutique hotels that fit the bill. I had over time whittled my list down to just one, a wonderful little place called the Hotel Teatro di Pompeo. It was all I had imagined a little out-of-the-way albergo in Rome to be. It was built over the ruins of the ancient Roman theater of the same name. The photos showed it to be part crusty ancient and part stylish contemporary, a combined Italian esthetic which I would come to love. It was small, chic, affordable and tucked away on a tiny piazza in the vicinity of the grander Piazza Navona and just around the corner from the famous Campo de' Fiori outdoor market. It was, in a word, perfect. For me at least.

There was just one problem. Our good friend Jon. Well, Jon wasn't the problem. The fact that he had recently been to Rome on business and had stayed at The Hotel Canada and recommended it, was the problem. The Hotel Canada was "conveniently located" in the vicinity of the train station and had all the creature comforts of any large business hotel. So for Chase and his increasing disability, it was, in a word, perfect.

Hotel Canada? Who goes to Rome and stays at the Hotel Canada? By the train station. I somehow allowed my displeasure about this unappetizing possibility to seep out. Actually I threw a bit of a fit. The thought of making my first visit to Rome, the Eternal City and staying at something called the Hotel Canada was horrifyingly unthinkable. **No one would ever expect to find Audrey and Gregory in a place like that.** Chase was quick to recognize the approaching storm and came up with a Solomon-like decision. He'd fax both hotels with a request for the nights required and see what rooms were available. We could then make our decision or perhaps it would be made for us depending on cost and availability. Well of course with the corporate efficiency expected of it, The Hotel Canada responded immediately with a lovely note saying that it would be the hotel's "delighted pleasure" to accommodate Mr. Leon and Mr. Anastasio for the nights required. And from The Hotel Teatro di Pompeo? Nothing. The fax machine sat silent. Chase, being well aware of my developing philosophies about the universe and its signs, seized this as an opportunity to point out that this was indeed confirmation that we should stay at The Hotel Canada. I was without argument but held out hope that we'd eventually hear from the good people at The Hotel Teatro di Pompeo. The fax machine however refused to cough up so much as a sentence on the subject. Much to my disappointment, the reservation was made at the Hotel Canada.

Now, to add insult to injury, well after our plans were set, Chase's friend Paul announced he'd be in Rome on business for a couple of days during our stay. You know how in relationships while some friends are shared by the couple, other friends belong to one or the other? Well Paul, never a favorite of mine, was definitely Chase's friend. So, for me, it wasn't particularly good news that we'd be spending part of our precious time in Rome with Paul. It got worse. To further aggravate the situation, Paul, aware of the great hotel debate, had faxed the Hotel Teatro di Pompeo for a reservation. He of course received quick confirmation for his two night stay. Paul then, would be staying at my Hotel Teatro di Pompeo and I would not. The top of my head almost blew off.

Our Italian adventure in Milan went well with the small exception of our being set upon on arrival by a band of aggressive gypsy children; shopkeepers all around coming to our aid. I thought Milan was magnificent with its Galleria and Duomo. Everything I saw was more beautiful including the subway cars and even the radiators in our hotel room. Why did this surprise me? I knew, in theory at least, about Italian design, I just hadn't experienced it first hand or been so immersed in it.

And then there was Florence which was beyond anything I could have imagined. The chill of the dark narrow passageways and the warmth of the sun washed open piazzas; the gently winding Arno River with all its bridges; the way, when you got away from it and looked back, the entire city seemed to be some sort of warm living being that had found a beautiful hushed river valley to curl up in for a prolonged peaceful slumber; the church bells that resounded in a sort of cushioned echo throughout that same valley; the Italian museums, the Italian art, the Italian shops, the Italian food, the Italians themselves; the way the chic and glamorous salesperson, when questioned about the super-small handbags in her shop, said in her gorgeous Italian accent, **"A lady's handbag need only be big large enough for lipstick and lire;"** the great big giant naked David (two of him actually — an outdoor copy and the indoor original, both with that perfect gleaming marble butt;) an underground gay dance club down a long dark passageway and steep steps, where I danced on stage to a disco "Carmina Burana;" and a chic and modern out-of-the-way gay bathhouse where I taught a very enthusiastic Italian boy the word, "Daddy." All of this totally exceeding my high expectations.

And then there was Rome. Rome, the eternal city. We were finally there. We checked in to the Hotel Canada and it was nice enough and exactly what you would expect a corporate hotel to be. It was pretty and comfortable but it certainly wasn't my idea of charming, quaint or any other of the adjectives I might have used to describe my idea of a perfect Roman hotel. After settling ourselves in, Chase called Paul who had arrived before us. Paul, gushing (to my slow burn) over the Hotel Teatro di Pompeo, insisted we come right over as he wanted to "show it off." He went on and on about the "charming little piazza" just outside his lovely windows. He also insisted we go out to dinner in his neighborhood as it was so "delightfully charming." Or some such words as that. (Grrrrrr, slow burn heating to near boiling as I thought about our neighborhood with the train station not far from our own lovely windows.)

The Hotel Canada's ever efficient front desk provided us with a map and bus directions that would get us in the vicinity of the Hotel Teatro di Pompeo. Off we went. The bus did deposit us somewhere near the hotel but we had a little trouble finding it…a lot of trouble finding it…actually we couldn't find it. The map seemed pretty clear and while I've always been a good map reader, I just couldn't see how to get there. It was a sweltering cloudless summer day, one that had us packing up in Florence, checking out of our pensione, getting to the train station, training down to Rome and checking in to our hotel. Chase, who was quickly wearing down and also having some pain with the peripheral neuropathy in his feet, was losing patience. He spotted a Tabacci (convenience store) and suggested that while he went to rest his feet and himself on a low wall in the shade, I should go to the Tabacci and ask for directions. I proceeded toward it rehearsing my Italian just as two white haired women were exiting the store. In my best and limited use of the language I asked "Dové Albergo Teatro di Pompeo?" They both simultaneously began to answer in rapid fire Italian complete with hand gestures and each with arms waving in opposing directions. I stood there totally confused as I heard a deep masculine voice speaking English in the most velvety Italian accent say, "May I help with directions in English?" Music to my American ears.

I could not immediately see the source of the voice as it came from the dark shadowy interior of the Tabacci in contrast to the blazing glare of the sun where I stood shielding my eyes. As the voice emerged from the darkness, the sunlight illuminated a handsome Italian face. Still shielding my eyes I looked him over and realized the face was not only handsome it was also, quite improbably, familiar. A familiar face? In Rome. A city I'd never been to. Couldn't be. Not only had I never been to Rome but I had not, knowingly at least, ever met anyone from Rome yet here was a familiar face. Who was this man? He looked at me somewhat quizzically and said, "Do I know you?" I was apparently familiar to him. And then, "Have we met?" I was about to answer in the negative as I studied his face and tried to connect the dots, if there were any. It suddenly hit me. Incredulously I said, "Yes! Yes we have, last year, a little antique shop on Beacon Hill, in Boston," I continued, "You purchased three Venetian paintings from me." He pondered this information for a moment and I saw the look of recognition cross his face. "Si, certo!"

Even for me and my "things usually work out for me" experiences, this was amazing. Mind-blowing! **There I was, in Rome, for the first time, on my first day in desperate need of help to find a hotel and the only Italian I'd ever met in my life was waiting there to direct me!** Let that sink in. And…add to that the timing. He had closed his shop right around the corner for only a moment — just long enough to make a quick run to the Tabacci to get some cigarettes and return immediately. I had shown up at that precise moment, during that short, almost infinitesimal window of time. A moment earlier or later and we'd have missed each other entirely. While I have become accustomed to pieces falling into place around me working things out in my favor in ways I could never dream, still, this was extraordinary! I was just looking for directions. I didn't think to ask for more.

I stood thankful to and in awe of a universe that would work this kind of magic in my favor, giving me, against all odds, exactly what I needed exactly when I needed it. This was further proof of my developing philosophy that the universe is designed this way — to accommodate us — to embrace our needs. **Though I call it "magic," and some say "coincidence," I was beginning to understand that it's actually, quite simply, the way the universe was designed, the way it works — if we allow it to.** Understanding this fact, getting out of the way and letting the universe do its job and then, when it has, recognizing it and being grateful is all it takes to be showered with unexpected gifts.

Our Roman friend insisted we come for a cold drink at what turned out to be one of the most unique and interesting antique shops I'd ever seen. We visited for awhile, seated near an enormous gurgling white marble fountain filled with lemons and artichokes as I pondered another antique shop back in Boston and its part in the magic of that afternoon. Refreshed now with our drinks finished and Chase's feet rested we were off to find the Hotel Teatro di Pompeo. Our antique dealer friend showed us the way. Well, no wonder I couldn't find the hotel. What appeared on the map as a street was actually a tunnel through a building. It had a gate closing it off making it seem to be the entry to the building or even a private residence, not the public corridor it was. Once we made it through the cool dark passageway, the hotel of my dreams was standing in front of us. I could not escape the thought that all of what had just transpired had to be a far greater positive sign from the universe than the small negative of an unanswered fax.

The Hotel Teatro di Pompeo was, though not in any way lavish, still all I'd dreamed it to be. Located on a classic little Roman piazza with a huge church dome hovering above, it seemed ancient and modern at the same time and once through the doors the same feeling persisted. A glass core gave it the quality of being indoors and outdoors. A handsome gentleman greeted us at the front desk and it was immediately clear to me that we were in the right Roman hotel and our luggage was in the wrong one. The gentleman graciously (of course) directed us to Paul's room. We ascended the stairs taking us outdoors and then back in and reached Paul's floor. He opened the door to our knock revealing a lovely room absolutely Franciscan in its simplicity. Stuccoed and stone walls, an enormous once-gilded antique chandelier hanging from a high inclined ceiling beamed in ancient wood, large windows overlooking that lovely piazza and perfectly Italian antique pieces all came together to fill me with one very nasty case of hotel envy. The Hotel Teatro di Pompeo was indeed all I had hoped it would be and there wasn't a train station or businessman in sight. I stood there listening to the soft muffled sound of church bells, suffering the double indignity of not staying there ourselves and being forced to listen to Paul rave on and on about all its virtues. "Wait'll you see the breakfast room," he gushed, "It's like an ancient catacomb!" Yeah, just wait. That was supposed to be my breakfast room. Once again, side-glancing Chase, I may have allowed my unhappiness at this unfortunate situation to leak out. Chase, looking appropriately sheepish, had become enamored with the Hotel Teatro di Pompeo himself. I experienced a modicum of remorse for making him feel doubly bad about it all, but not enough to actually improve my selfish behavior. I was unhappy with the entire Roman hotel situation. Period.

We returned to the lobby on our way out to dinner. As Paul turned in his key I was speaking to Chase, about what I don't recall, but what I do remember is at the end of whatever it was that I was saying, for some reason, probably because I was still somewhere between annoyed and angry, I chose to address Chase with a firm "Mr. Leon." Hearing this, the gracious gentleman behind the desk looked at us and said "Mr. Leon? Of

Boston?" We both looked at him somewhat quizzically. This guy knew Chase? Was this yet another Roman who'd somehow intersected our lives before? In unison we responded "Yes." To which he replied, "We have been waiting for you, Mr. Leon. Are you checking in? Your room is ready."

His room? Our room? What room? We have a room? At this hotel? It's ready? They're waiting for us? Chase and I looked at each other puzzled and quickly back to the gentleman for more information. He showed us a reservation in Mr. Leon's name for our entire stay in Rome. The hotel had apparently received the fax from Chase and the gentleman assured us that a confirmation had been faxed right back. Somewhere in the ether between Rome and Boston the fax had simply evaporated. Or…I really didn't want to go there but…had Chase maybe tossed it out? I tried not to think like that because we had a room at The Hotel Teatro di Pompeo! It was just sitting there all prepped and waiting for us. I glanced at Chase who was as amazed as I. Just one problem. The Hotel Canada. We discussed our situation with the gentleman who promptly made a phone call and spoke at some length in his gorgeous Italian. He hung up and informed us that The Hotel Canada was quite understanding of our situation and that we'd only have to spend one night there and then we could move over to the Teatro di Pompeo. We'd still have to pay to secure the room at The Teatro di Pompeo, meaning we'd have to double-pay for that first night. Fine. But then, a young English speaking couple with long hair and backpacks popped in and asked if there might be a room available for only one night. **Chase looked at me incredulous as I cast my eyes heavenward, did a little happy dance and once again thanked a universal design much greater than anything I could ever come up with.**

1993

Don't Ask Don't Tell

IN 1992 we elected a president who promised that one of the first things he would do as president would be to lift the armed services ban on homosexuals. I was in LA when Mr. Clinton won the election and there was literally dancing in the streets of West Hollywood. The new President had gotten a lot of gay votes because of his stance on gay issues — enough to help put him in the White House. Once in office Mr. Clinton learned the harsh reality that even for the Commander In Chief things don't go quite so easily. The opposition was far stronger than expected and sadly the battle was lost to small-mindedness, fear, bigotry and ignorance. Perhaps Mr. Clinton shouldn't have made campaign promises he couldn't keep.

Now I personally don't give a rats ass about joining the military. **I have always thought that along with not getting married and not having children, being exempt from the military was one of the best things about being gay.** But there are others who don't share that sentiment. They (many of whom are already in the military) should be allowed to serve. And have kids if they want, but that's another discussion.

The President, along with the joint chiefs of staff and congress, was responsible for creating a policy called "Don't Ask, Don't Tell" which, making things even worse than before, effectively required gay servicemen and women to lie about their sexuality. It was OK to be gay as long as you kept quiet about it. You will stay invisible.

The new policy effectively said, "You may exist, but shhhhhh... keep it to yourself. You may be within our ranks but we do not want to acknowledge your existence. Stay in your closet and we'll all just ignore the whole inconvenient thing. You will stay invisible.

That also meant that the military wanted to know nothing about the contribution that gay servicemen and women were making. It as much as said that you may contribute as gay people but we, the heterosexual majority will just pretend you're straight and conveniently tally up all your contributions in our column. Take credit for everything. No one will ever know the accomplishments of gay people. You will stay invisible.

Furthermore, in order to ensure your complete invisibility, we're not even going to ask if you're gay. We will pretend you aren't among us and won't even bother you by asking. If by any chance you are asked, you will deny your existence. You will stay invisible.

Infuriating! Imagine, being required by law to lie about who you are, to deny who you are. BY LAW! This was considered a step in the right direction? The philosophy extends well beyond the armed services and has for ages. Keeping gay people in the closet, has always been a convenient way for heterosexual society to not have to acknowledge our contribution to society. Since there is the presumption of heterosexuality unless otherwise notified, if we don't come out, all our accomplishments become a credit to the heterosexual majority. A society that doesn't see us teaching its children, healing its sick, building its bridges, running its corporations and especially in this instance, fighting its fucking wars and defending its people will never give us credit for any of it. Without our being out, the heterosexual majority can ignore all the many ways we make their lives better every day. And take all the credit. With Don't Ask Don't Tell, the government finally found a way to write this unkind, unsound philosophy into law. And keep us and our contribution invisible.

The christian wrong, **(I can never bring myself to call these people the "christian right" as their behavior would indicate the accuracy of neither word)** would have the world believe there is some sort of gay agenda. Well, if there is a gay agenda it can be summed up in a word: honesty. Our goal is to live life honestly being true to who we are in the open light of day not the darkness of a closed closet, the polar opposite of what Don't Ask Don't Tell required. We want and need visibility.

I expected some day there'd be a big old karmic kick in the butt delivered to the person most responsible for "Don't Ask Don't Tell." Bill Clinton who was voted into office as a (self-proclaimed) advocate for gay people, though I believe well-meaning, failed us miserably, and the "Don't Ask Don't Tell" buck stops with him. As President he was most responsible for creating a law requiring people to lie about their sexuality. **Proving the universe not only believes in karma but has a sense of irony as well, Mr. Clinton would eventually, under oath, very publicly lie about his sexuality.** He was impeached for it. What goes around does come around. The balance restored.

On a more positive note, most of Mr. Clinton's policies were good for the LGBTQ community. When the AIDS Quilt was shown on The Mall in Washington DC, President and Mrs. Clinton visited it. It was validation from a sitting president that up until that time, we hadn't enjoyed. Totally ignored by Mr. Reagan and dismissed by Mr. Bush, we'd finally been acknowledged in a decidedly public, important way. So thanks for that Mr. Clinton.

Gay Boy's Life

1993

On The Edge Of Despair

MADELEINE had kindly given me two tickets to Cirque de Soleil for my birthday. She knew I had always wanted to see it but hadn't had the opportunity to do so. The tickets were purchased way in advance and there was a specific time frame for their use. I had held on to them thinking always that a better time would present itself in the future. When the final date for their usage had arrived, Chase, who the second ticket was optimistically intended for, was in the hospital. To make matters worse, this was the hospitalization that occurred right after my failed hernia surgery. I spent the nights in the hospital in pain trying to get a little sleep on my cot in Chase's room while still monitoring his through the night care. When Cirque day arrived, after having spent a particularly sleepless night on that cot, I had a morning full of tending to Chase's needs and dealing with doctors and nurses. I left mid-afternoon to run home because prior to 'le Cirque' that night, there was a memorial service for a recently deceased friend, Preston. **This was gay life circa 1993: hospitals and memorial services. And circuses.**

As I arrived at Cedar Lane Way frazzled, worn out, in pain and late, our friend Jon who was patiently waiting for me, took one look and 'knew' I'd never be able to pull my weary, unwashed, unshaven, disheveled stinky self together in time for the memorial. I rushed past leaving him sitting out in the garden and flew into a whirling frenzy of self-restoration. In minutes, I appeared at the door showered, shaved, coiffed and in my Brooks Brothers best. I pulled my finest Holly Golightly on him, fastening an invisible earring to my right ear and saying, "How do I look?" He eyed me up and down and happily, right on cue, he was the perfect Paul Varjak with, "Very good. I must say I'm amazed.," or something close to that. "You were a darling to help. I could never have done it with out you," I replied, giving it my best Audrey Hepburn, reprising one of my favorite scenes from one of my favorite films, *Breakfast At Tiffanys*. And off we went, Audrey and George to honor our dearly departed friend, Press, at his memorial.

That's the way it was then. You just couldn't be serious all of the time. With all the suffering and hospitalizations, deaths and memorial services you had to hold on to what made you the person you were before all the horror began. You had to find humor in it. Gay humor. **A gay sense of 'camp,' that special sort of homosexual humor that danced on the edge of despair, had gotten gay generations of men through tough times before. As the epidemic grew, it became even more important serving as a glittering rainbow lifeline connecting us to each other and those who came before and those who would come after, helping us laugh through our tears, shining hope and light in the dark skies of AIDS.**

Sometimes you just had to laugh. And be gay. That is, after all, who we were. And who we would remain. If we lived through it all. It is our heritage and it is how we cope. And how I coped, with the hospitals, and the memorial services, and later that particular evening, with Cirque de Soleil, the pain in my groin and that empty seat beside me.

1993

A Comfy Chair

IT IS NOTABLE how disease can change a person's wants and needs. During his earlier days Chase might have coveted a gold watch from Tiffanys or a pinstripe three piece suit and tassel loafers at Brooks Brothers. As the disease progressed, as I had seen with Randy before him, Chase's needs leaned more toward survival and comfort. During his final months, Chase made a special request for a "comfy chair." He had become so thin, so skeletal that he could not find comfort anywhere in our home. A super comfortable chair seemed to be the answer and I passed this request on to Madeleine. It took no time for her to show up with an enormous antique hybrid between a wing chair and a club chair stripped down to its original muslin base. It was sturdy and wide-seated with a rounded back and when fitted with cushions (also provided by Madeleine) and wrapped and linen-tied (by me,) it was the perfect answer to Chase's needs. **More than a chair, it was a big, soft upholstered hug on four beautifully turned mahogany legs.** Chase's new comfy chair supported his frail aching body like nothing else had and became home to him for the remainder of his life.

One evening while watching the film *My Fair Lady* together, Chase in his comfy chair and I on the floor, with my head resting on his knee, Eliza Dolittle started to sing:

> "All I want is a room somewhere
> Far away from the cold night air
> With one enormous chair
> Oh wouldn't it be loverly?"

I thought of Chase in the warmth and comfort provided by his own enormous chair and decided Eliza was singing for him. And then:

> "Someone's head resting on my knee
> Warm and tender as he can be
> Who takes good care of me
> Oh wouldn't it be loverly?"

I felt the warmth of his hand press softly on the top of my head and the gentle pat of his fingers as it occurred to him just as it occurred to me that Eliza was now singing about us. There I was his caregiver with my head resting on his knee. The funny thing was, I'd heard that song innumerable times and that line never made sense to me. I couldn't visualize someone's head resting on someone else's knee. It didn't seem comfortable or likely. Lap, yes; knee, no. And yet there I was sitting on our bedroom floor with my head resting on his knee, warm and tender and taking good care of him. "How loverly." For many months after Chase's departure when I was missing him I would take my own hand and lay it gently on the top of my head as Chase had done with his and pat lightly. That gentle touch would bring him back for a moment or two.

1993

Surviving Chase
(Part 3)

AS IT HAD BEEN WITH RANDY, and all the others, there were no clues as to whether Chase was in his final hours or if he'd live on for weeks or even rally and get healthier for months. All I really knew for sure was that he was going to die. They all died. I would pour Chase a glass of milk and, looking at the expiration date, wonder whose date would come sooner. **Which would last longer, Chase or the milk?**

Over the progression of the illness I had seen significant changes in Chase's personality. Again. The sweet Chaser of days gone by seemed to return and slowly take over toward the end. Perhaps it was the onset of dementia or perhaps he was simply mellowing. Perhaps he was becoming more appreciative. I didn't know for sure but I found the closer to the end we got, the more and more I was feeling for this increasingly sweet suffering young man. Gone were the snide remarks and harsh judgements. He was kinder, gentler, more compassionate. He was grateful and gracious in a way I had never before witnessed him to be. I was drawing closer and closer to him at a time when I knew this would just make losing him harder. I could have lost the unpleasant Christopher of nearly five years before, barely batting an eye. Things had changed. It became clear that an unexpected downside of having cared for him for so long was that I now cared for him more than I had ever cared for him before. The loss would be enormous. I was finally finding him just as I was losing him. Had I spent so much time hating him would there be no time left for love?

During this time, I came to understand the kind of love a mother has for an infant child and how losing that child would be devastating. Chase became that infant absolutely dependent on me for absolutely everything. I washed and folded his laundry, dressed and undressed him. I would intently study the nurses aides at the hospital and learned how to change his bed linens with him in bed and hardly disturb him. I bathed him. I changed his IV drips. I gave him shots. I wiped his bottom and changed his diapers remembering the high esteem I had formerly held for those particular body parts as I was now dutifully cleaning them. I cooked for him and — his worst fear, I think — I fed him. He was always so worried about a time in his future when he might have to be fed "like a baby." I'd devised, because of that fear, a way to do so that didn't quite seem to be 'feeding.' I would sit in bed with my back against the wall (we didn't have a headboard) and have him lean back against me, both of us facing the same way. I'd then place the dining tray across his lap, place the fork in his hand, his hand in mine and together we would scoop up the food. Then stabilizing his shaking hand together we'd bring it to his mouth. He could not see me and he was mostly feeding himself.

That is how that final night found us as Chase polished off his breakfast. Breakfast always had to be his first meal no matter the time of day. Or night. He had slept all day so it was late night, just after "breakfast," when I heard Chase's whispered words and finally fell in love with him. After ten challenging years. It was the night I heard that simple sentence, "You're so comfortable. You're so comfortable I'd like to take you into the past with no judgement." He'd even repeated it. Was I over-interpreting his words as tears streamed down my face? I wasn't sure but I wrapped my arms around his bony skeletal frame as the baggage from the past simply melted away. He had released me, with that one lovely sentence, or so I had determined, from the burden of all the judgment he had held over me through the years we'd spent together. **"No judgement." I had never imagined those words from him but with them I felt he'd accepted me, finally, for who I was. I fell in love right then and there pulling him even closer as I shed tears both happy and sad onto the back of his neck.** It had all come so late. And just in the nick of time.

We stayed that way for a while and I eventually got up, rolled him on his side and cleared the tray of food away. I turned off the lights and crawled into bed behind him both of us laying on our sides with me spooning him. I, while the smaller of the two of us, had always been the "big spoon." I kissed him and, knowing I had been given a bottle of morphine to administer for pain, asked him if he had any. "No pain," he said. I held him tight and said, "I love you." "I love you," he said right back. He drifted off to sleep. I couldn't sleep but continued to hold him hearing guttural sounds coming from somewhere deep within him, sounds I had not heard before. I remembered having heard the term 'death rattle' and I recognized it instantly. After hours of this frightening rattle, thinking that each labored breath might be his last, his breathing became easier, softer and more normal. He was quietly sleeping. It was early morning, still dark outside, as I slipped out of bed, lay his long body pillow up against him in my place and went upstairs to take the food tray to the kitchen and turn off all the lights. I lay down on the foot of the upstairs bed, feet still on the floor, to close my eyes for just a minute. I was exhausted having not slept for several nights. Thinking each moment might be Chase's last, I had spent every minute with him. Monitoring his every breath. I had promised him I would be there at the end and be there I would. I fell soundly asleep with my feel still on the floor. I have no idea how long I had been asleep, but, when I woke with a start, it was light outside.

In a panic I ran downstairs to check on Chase. He was gone. Dead. I had let him die alone. The greatest unwavering promise I had ever made to Chase and myself, the one unbreakable vow that I would not let him die alone had been broken. **I had let Chase die alone. It was that simple. I had failed him.** Instead of being there, lovingly holding him, caressing his body and encouraging his soul to depart it, gently letting go of him and reassuring him all would be right and good as he transitioned to the other side, rather than all of that, I was upstairs. Asleep.

How could I? I had let him down and momentarily hated myself for it. A cry came from deep within me, deeper than anything I'd ever expressed in my life. It was a painful wail of loss and sorrow, disappointment in myself but mostly an apology to Chase for leaving him to die alone. I hadn't been there for him and I screamed out a deep guttural apology to him. "I'm sorry Chaser! I am so sorry!" I apologized out loud, uncontrollably crying it out from somewhere deep inside me to his lifeless body and the lifeless room and the lifeless air around us. Dropping to my knees I rested my head on his body and took his cool lifeless hand in mine and cried into it. "I'm sorry, Chaser. I am so so sorry!"

October 23, 1993

It's All Over

ONCE I HAD COLLECTED MYSELF, I stood over Chase' lifeless corpse and asked, "Is it over?" And then, "It is. It's all over." All the suffering, all the care-giving, all of it was suddenly over. I couldn't quite wrap my head around that. I heard the words in my head and even said them out loud but couldn't entirely grasp their meaning. While I might have told myself prior to Chase's passing that I was prepared for this moment, clearly I was not. I stood in awe of the finality — at least on this, the mortal side — of death. There may be "no over" on the other side but it was "over" over here. Now what? I called my friend Shani who had been standing ready to put things in motion regarding the disposition of Chase's remains. I slowly stripped and lovingly washed Chase's body for the last time and dressed him in his favorite double breasted pinstripe Brooks Brothers suit, high polished cap-toe shoes (I had seen to that much earlier) and because I was not able to completely close his eyes, his favorite pair of Ray Ban Wayfarers. **He looked so peaceful and so smart lying there dressed to the nines, the sunglasses giving him an almost movie star coolness as though he were on his way to a premiere rather than the crematorium.** I called Madeleine who came right over to pay her last respects. After her departure, with Shani waiting upstairs, as I waited for the funeral people to pick up Chase's body, I put on Linda Ronstadt's *What's New*, the romantic album that, in my San Francisco living room the night we met, had played us into our relationship. I cried sitting on the bed next to him as I listened to Chase's favorite track, 'Someone To Watch Over Me.' I listened to the lyrics I had heard so many times before with a fresh perspective. I suddenly realized the significance Chase had held in them. Perhaps I was hearing them now with new ears. Chase's ears. I suddenly understood his connection with that song. Perhaps he always knew he would need someone to watch over him. I became that someone. And now it was his turn. He would now be the someone to watch over me.

My favorite track was next. As Linda sang "What'll I do when you are far away and I am blue what'll I do… What'll I do with just a photograph to tell my troubles to…when I'm alone with only dreams of you that won't come true what'll I do?" I appreciated the new poignancy of those words as I heard a commotion upstairs and realized they'd come to collect Chase. I wasn't ready. But the song was over. Everything was over. All of it — the laughs, the tears, the joy, the sorrow, the anger, the frustration, mostly the pain and suffering. Over.

Hearing voices overhead, I lifted the arm off the record appreciating the symmetry of Linda's singing us into and then, exactly ten years later, to the day, heartbreakingly out of our relationship. **I wordlessly said my final goodbyes to the man I thought I loved and didn't love and then finally loved with a greater love than I had ever expected.** I held his hand, kissed it, laid it back down on his other hand and said, "I don't like boat whistles," referring to a line from one of our favorite films, *An Affair To Remember*. Just before I headed up the stairs I turned, and, in resignation to his long battle with that horrible disease I whispered, "It's over Chaser, it's all over."

I waited upstairs with my friend Shani as they rolled a big black body bag through the kitchen past us. I had asked that they not use a body bag. I suppose there are regulations that require them to do this but it just seemed to me to be a giant garbage bag and I hated the image of Chase's being garbage hauled out to the curb. In the movies people were always taken out on a stretcher with a white sheet over them, shoes showing.

Much more civilized, elegant and sensitive to those of us left behind. More like our loved ones are asleep. Not dead. Not garbage. Not ready for the incinerator. I briefly considered Hindu widows and how they were known to throw themselves on their husbands' burning funeral pyres. I understood them and their grief for the first time. I wasn't suicidal but still, I understood. **Eyes on the black bag I once again broke down as I watched Chase and Randy and all the others, along with an entire lifestyle and most everything I loved about being gay, bagged-up and carried out through my living room and garden; gone forever.**

1993

What'll I Do?

IT'S A NEW DAY. I open my eyes and stretch, fluff my pillow as usual and turn in the other direction hopeful of perhaps falling back asleep. The sun's already up so that's probably not going to happen. I glance at the cold light coming in from my barren winter garden and suddenly the new reality hits. Chase is gone. It's like that every morning. I wake to a day just like any other and for a short while everything is as it always has been. Just as it was with Randy. Those few precious blissful moments before I remember. And when reality sets in, my partner of ten years, Chase dies all over again...every goddamn morning. And I get up and start my day. What'll I do?

In life there are always questions. Basic existential questions like: "What should I be doing with my life?" "Where should I go?" "Where do I belong?" "What should I do?" "What is right for me?" "Who is right for me?" During the years of taking care of Chase I was never bothered by any of those questions about my existence. **I knew, simply knew, without a doubt, that in the entire universe I was exactly where I was supposed to be and doing exactly what I was supposed to be doing.** That kind of knowledge gives you great balance. And strength. And power. To go through life with absolutely no question about your existence is a gift really, a gift given me by the commitment I had made to Chase. I was able to accomplish whatever I had because all doubt about my being had been removed. For a time at least. Until Chase died.

At the moment he was gone it was suddenly all questions. I had given myself completely to a purpose and in a heartbeat that purpose was gone. Over. Finished. Funny thing was, during all the time taking care of Chase I never projected forward to the end. I had never given any sort of consideration to the moment when he would no longer be around. I suppose it has to do with denial. Somewhere inside I had to know he was going to die. Of course I knew. We both knew. He was certainly going to die but somehow, I just never gave a thought to that reality and what it might bring. Would bring. Suddenly it was all about "Where should I go? What should I do?" Now where do I go? What do I do? I had put myself on hold for years devoting my life to the care of another and suddenly that other was gone and now it was time to move on. But where? I had had a purpose and now the purpose was over. I was the glue that held Chase together but now without him what was I? What'll I do?

1993

Postmortem Man Of Mystery

CHASE rarely spoke of his family and his accounting of childhood experiences — tony north shore of Chicago upbringing and New England prep school education — were detail free and inconsistent. I never pressed for information because this was clearly a part of his life with which he was visibly uncomfortable. Upon his death I was required by law to contact his next of kin. I telephoned his California cousin Jack who was the only family member I had met. Jack informed me, much to my surprise, that he was not actually related to Chase (who he referred to as Mike.) This was news to me! He told me the story. It seems Mike was an orphan who had been passed around from foster home to foster home until he had landed in the home of Jack's aunt and uncle. It apparently wasn't a happy home and when they found out the never-adopted Mike was gay, at 16 years old, they threw him out. Jack's mother who was the foster mother's sister took Mike in.

The story Chase had told me about his early days in Lake Forest, Illinois and his school days at Exeter were a total fabrication, a smokescreen to cover the real story. It broke my heart to think that he felt he had to cover up the story of an orphan who had been pretty much self-sufficient from the age of sixteen and had put himself through high school and college. **His real life story was much more impressive than the made up one.** The foster home part of his story explained so much about Chase's abandonment issues and why he never really felt I would be there for him until the end.

I was told another curious story by Chase's friend Kathy in Sacramento. I had met Kathy several times and she was his closest girlfriend. He considered her and her twin sister to be family. Kathy told me how Chase had called her one day and said he was moving in with someone he'd just met (me) and if she rented a van and got herself to San Francisco pronto, she could have all "this old stuff." Everything. She did. That explained the empty apartment when we moved Chase's few remaining things in with me. I can only guess that his "old stuff" didn't match the person he had created so he just got rid of everything before I had a chance to see it.

Christopher Michael (aka Chase) Leon had been a man of mystery in life and took many of his secrets to the grave.

1993

Memento

A WEEK OR TWO after Chase's death I was cleaning the apartment. On my hands and knees while washing the bathroom floor, my sponge picked up a fingernail clipping. This had happened countless times before and would usually fill me with anything from annoyance, to disgust, to rage depending on how I happened to be feeling about Chase at the time. Fastidious about most other things, somehow he didn't give a thought to his nail clippings which would end up everywhere in the bathroom except in the garbage can. His eyesight wasn't so great so perhaps he couldn't see the clippings. Whatever the case, they were always there, in the sink, on the vanity top, on the floor. Tiny little ubiquitous slivers of crescent moon-shaped annoyance. I would even convince myself at times that he would leave them there on purpose, just to annoy me. And they did, annoy the hell out of me. "This is disgusting. Can't he clean up after himself? Do I have to do everything around here?" **Chase's errant nail clippings never brought out the best in me.**

It was not until Chase was gone that I realized that I had nothing of him. No piece of him at all. I hadn't thought about this when he was still alive. He was gone entirely. I had come to understand why people save locks of hair of their departed loved ones. I could have cut a lock from what little hair he had left but it just never occurred to me to do so. It wasn't until he was gone that I realized he was completely gone without any physical trace of his having been here. There could have been some piece of him, some piece of physical evidence that he had once inhabited this planet and my life that I could have saved and cherished but I hadn't. Once they'd taken him away it was too late. There were his ashes, when I would eventually get around to collecting them, but they weren't the kind of physical memento I was feeling a need for. I had so desperately wanted a piece of him. Something that proved his existence here on earth, with me. And now here it was, sticking to a wet bathroom sponge — a nail clipping.

Funny how things change. Here was a piece, albeit a tiny one but still a piece…of Chase. The only actual physical piece of him. The memento that I had longed for and had given up hope of ever having, I was now picking out of a dirty sponge and cradling in my palm. Cherishing it. **The tiny little crescent shaped sliver that used to drive me up the wall, annoying the hell out of me, was now a tiny little treasure.** What was once a throwaway annoyance, now resides in its own little brown velvet ring box like the tiny treasure it is. Suppose there's a lesson in there?

1993

Don't They Know?

W HEN I WOULD VENTURE OUT in public those first few weeks after Chase's passing, I would be surprised that life was going on just as it had before. Didn't they know? Weren't they aware of what had happened? Life had stopped yet those around me were going on as if nothing had happened. **How could everyone and everything keep going when my entire world had been turned upside down?** I know its a self-centered way of thinking but that is exactly how I felt. Life goes on and that is a fact. Everything continues. The world moves on and I needed to as well. I was not the only person to lose another and I would have to face each morning and the subsequent realization that Chase was gone and my life had changed.

By the time Chase had died I'd lost so many friends along with the lifestyle they represented. It was all too much to bear. I was full of grief and at times full of guilt for not feeling grief, relieved that it was all over. There were even glimmers of joy as I anticipated my new life but the subsequent guilt attached to those feelings would overwhelm them and the grief would take over. I found myself pretending for the benefit of others that I was doing better than I was. I really didn't know where to put all my conflicted emotions. So I just shut them down. I tucked them all away somewhere within myself as I holed up in my Beacon Hill apartment. I withdrew surrounded by all my ghosts but at the same time, intent on ignoring them. **Chase had been the last straw on — a haystack of dead friends — the one that broke my camel's back.** I knew I had to find a way to go on but I just couldn't throw myself back out there where life was continuing, just like normal, for everyone else. Life was anything but normal now and I wasn't ready to jump back in. It was easier to recede and so I did. A New England winter was on its way; a perfect time to hibernate with my sadness. Bury my grief.

1993

Four Boxes

CHASE DIED on October 23, 1993, ten years — to the day — of our first meeting. The warm glow of autumn was quickly replaced by the gray brutality of winter. Or did it just seem particularly brutal that year? I'm not quite certain. Withdrawing, physically and emotionally exhausted, I settled into a general malaise, sheltered from the cold and most of life outside the walls of our Beacon Hill apartment. **I'd cried all my tears. The cumulative loss of Chase along with Randy and so many other close friends and party friends, all of them bright and promising and cut down in their prime, had left me with a sort of paralyzing numbness.** I was living something of a half-existence no longer feeling much of anything. Feeling had become too painful. As the cold got colder and the snow started to pile up, I withdrew further into the protective sanctity of our Cedar Lane Way home.

I'd had Chase's body cremated. While I had been contacted several times and asked to "Please collect Mr. Leon's ashes," I couldn't quite bring myself to make the trip to the crematorium to do so. Perhaps it was the cold. Or the snow? Perhaps it was my not wanting to leave the solitude and protection of my inner sanctum. More likely, it was the finality of it all that kept me from picking up the cremains of my deceased partner. For months "Mr. Leon's ashes" had sat in four boxes on a shelf somewhere in South Boston (where I hadn't been since my beach bashing) waiting for my reluctant self to collect them.

Mr. Leon's wishes regarding the disposition of his ashes:

1. To be spread in the Pacific Ocean off the Marin Headlands near San Francisco...
2. To be spread at Crane's Beach north of Boston...
3. To be spread into the Arno River off the Ponte St. Trinita in Florence, Italy...
4. To be saved and combined with my own ashes someday.

With the above post-mortem wish list, I had foreseen a time when I'd be required to divide Chase's ashes into four packages. Not wanting any part of such an activity, I had asked the professionals to do the dividing. Hence the four boxes. **So Chase's ashes remained in those four boxes in the hands of those used to dealing with such things and I who was not, did my best to ignore the whole ash situation.** Until I was emotionally ready to deal with them, South Boston could keep those four boxes of Mr. Leon's remains.

Christmas that year was a challenging one. In the wake of Chase's demise my usually shining holiday had lost its luster. I was typically a Christmas maniac of the "If It Doesn't Move, Decorate It School of Christmas Decorating," but that particular season found me less than enthusiastic about my favorite holiday. I baked no Christmas cookies, bought few presents and decorated nothing. As the holiday grew nearer, I realized that I'd never had a Christmas without a Christmas tree — a realization that saddened me even more. **Thinking that a tree might be just the thing to get me out of my funk and into the Christmas spirit, I went out, bought one and started the process of putting it up and decorating it.** This was an activity that usually gave me great joy. I'd have carols on the stereo, spiced mulled wine on the stove, Chase by my side and a child's enthusiasm for all things Christmas. Typically Chase, not being the decorator I was, would contentedly sit on the sofa, hot mulled wine in hand getting a little toasted by both the wine and the fire in our fireplace. He'd patiently listen to the story of each ornament old and new (I'd been collecting them since childhood) as I'd hang it on the tree and create before his eyes, to use his words, "My Little Treasure's Real Christmas Splendor." This year however, his "Little Treasure" just wasn't in the real Christmas splendor spirit. My usual enthusiasm was nowhere to be found. My heart was not in it. Had I planned ahead on having a tree, perhaps I'd have invited some friends over and wouldn't have found myself decorating this one alone, wallowing in self pity. But there I was, doing just that. Alone. Wallowing. Numb. As numb as I can ever remember being. As I somnambulistically strung the lights and hung the ornaments it was clear that even with the Christmas music playing in the background, a log on the fire and the aroma of hot mulled cider wafting through the air, the mere act of decorating a Christmas tree was not going to lift me out of my sad state. With a what's-the-use sigh, I sat down, ornaments in hand amidst the mess of boxes, tissue paper, unused strands of non-working lights, and other detritus of the tree-decorating process. Slumping in the chair I scanned it all and stared blankly at my half finished creation and all that Christmas crap around me. I don't know how long I'd been that way when the doorbell rang.

I got up, went out the door of our apartment, and made my shivering way through our walled-in garden. I opened the big heavy wooden gate I'd been hiding behind for months. It revealed a tall, thin, positively Dickensian looking man. He had a high forehead, higher cheekbones, sunken eyes, and was (a prerequisite for the job?) dressed all in black. **I eyed, in his outstretched arms, four boxes. Chase's ashes. I recognized them immediately.** He explained that he had had some errands to run in the area and thought he'd take the chance I might be home, saving me a trip to Southie (and I expect more to the point, finally getting rid of those four boxes.) I thanked him and apologized for causing him to make a personal delivery. He was quite gracious about it.

Well, if I was looking for something to cheer me up, this certainly wasn't it.

Here they were, Christopher Leon's ashes tidied away in four small identical cream colored cardboard cubes each about the size of the tissue box in our bathroom. Four boxes of proof of my partner's exit from the planet and out of my life forever now cradled in my arms just the way I'd cradled Chase himself two months before as he drifted off to a sleep from which he'd never awaken. The finality I'd been avoiding, now, suddenly delivered to my doorstep at a moment when I was already as sad as I could ever recall.

Burdened with this unexpected and unwanted delivery, I walked back into the apartment and sat down right where I'd been surrounded by all the Christmas crap, before the unanticipated doorbell. With the four boxes of ashes weighing heavily in my lap, I eyed the half finished tree. It was all suddenly more than I could bear. The tree. The mess. The four boxes. Their untimely arrival. The loss. It all came in on me at once. Chase dead.

Randy dead. So many others dead. An entire lifestyle dead. The countless memorials, the exhausting care-giving, the endless tests and procedures and hospitalizations. The wounds that wouldn't heal. The trials and procedures that didn't help. The hopes given and dashed. The unspeakable agony of that unspeakably horrible disease, AIDS. The indelible memory of the soulless skeletal remains of the man I loved, lying in our bed one horrible morning, awaiting removal. **The image, burnished onto my brain, of a big black body bag being wheeled through the same room where I now sat with a half decorated tree.** If I'd thought I'd cried all my tears I was wrong. In the midst of stacks of open boxes of ornaments, Christmas decorations and that damned tree, as some unending unwanted Christmas Carol played on in the background, I broke down into wails of sadness. Loud uncontrollable convulsive sobs of grief poured out of me. As tears streamed down my face, my entire body seemed to be shaking with the sadness and grief I'd held in until this awful inevitable endless moment of release. I wept not only for the loss of my lover's life, my best friend's life and the lives of so many other friends close and not, but also for the loss of an entire lifestyle. **All I loved and all I'd cherished about being a gay male had been stripped away, incinerated and tidily boxed up just like those damned ashes in those damned four boxes on my lap.** I couldn't stop. I sat there crying, wailing actually, and shaking uncontrollably as I stared down at those four damned boxes, containing what was left of the man I had finally loved, cared for and nurtured to his untimely demise — four boxes — final and unavoidable proof of his inevitable end and the end of an entire way of life resting now in my lap as I wept over them.

As I sat there still convulsing and bleary eyed, through my tears I noticed a square piece of yellow paper affixed to the top of one of the boxes. Wiping my eyes, I studied the post-it note which was clearly meant to have been removed before the boxes were handed over to me. It read:

"Four Boxes of Leon"…"Four Boxes of Leon?" I let out a sur-prised chuckle and immediately suppressed it. I didn't mean for it to happen, it just slipped out. **Right in the middle of my grief, feeling suddenly inappropriate, I quickly looked around for who's disapproval I don't know.** And I contin-ued snickering. Four boxes of Leon? Now I was really tickled. Four boxes of Leon? Oh my god! Hilarious! Chase, all four box-es of him, would have agreed. Remembering my joke-telling Chase's often silly sense of humor I could see his reaction to that post-it note. I was suddenly howling.

As uncontrollable as the crying had been only moments before, now, much to my embarrassed amazement, the laughter was just as out of control. Still wiping away the tears from my earlier collapse, I looked down at those "Four Boxes of Leon" and howled knowing how much Chase adored a good punchline. Oh my god he'd have loved this! All Four Boxes of Him! More howling! I thought of all of Chase's awful jokes and how, after hearing them I-don't-know-how-many-times, I refused to laugh at them. I was laughing now. With him — finally sharing the punchline and a greatly needed laugh. It had been way too long in coming.

There were tears again but these new tears came from an entirely different place. And, in this case, brought on by a little yellow post-it note penned by a well-meaning office worker of few words, working in sync with a beneficent universe whose altruistic gifts I was beginning to understand and appreciate. That life-saving

Deliver
Four Boxes of Leon
to Michael Anastasio
24 Cedar Lane Way

post-it note somehow brought back to life my departed lover and me along with him. It resurrected in an instant, life-of-the-party Chase's wicked sense of humor. I hadn't always found it so funny but now I was in hysterics. I could hear his laugh again. It filled me. It filled the room which suddenly was alive with him. He was there with me, laughing and sharing the silliness. Chills ran through my entire body as I felt his presence in me and around me. Everything came alive. I was suddenly aware of all the beauty and life surrounding me and by Chase's eternal sparkling presence in every single molecule. By his eternal life. By his eternal love. By his eternal assurance. By him. He was everywhere. How had I missed this before? How had I not seen him? Had I overlooked him or had he just arrived? With the ashes? Or with that Post-it note. Or the laughter. That was it. The laughter. It was back and we were connected once again. A connection that, as it turns out, was unwavering. I hadn't seen it. Or felt it. Or realized it. It was there though, not only unbroken by death but actually, I now realize, strengthened and enhanced by it and made more beautiful. And real. It was all so clear. There was no more stuff in the way.

Embracing those four boxes, I finally began to compose myself. I looked back at that half decorated tree and was suddenly surprisingly enthusiastic in my resolve to once again create Christmas in my home, our home, the home Chase and I had made and shared together. I could smell the rich aroma of the mulled cider. I was aware now of the carols sweetly playing on in the background and the crackle of and warmth from the log in the fireplace. The lights and ornaments suddenly had a sparkle I couldn't see before. That cold, dead empty living room overburdened with so much pain and suffering and heartache and a half decorated tree was suddenly warm and full of sparkle and life. I got up and began working on the tree again, this time with a renewed vigor. There we were, the two of us in our living room, just like always: me decorating the tree and Chase as always, sitting patiently on the sofa where I'd just deposited him.

All four boxes of him.

1993

Four Boxes Post Script

I FINISHED DECORATING the tree and it was indeed a sparkling "Real Christmas Splendor!" I then found the prettiest Christmas wrapping paper I owned, carefully wrapped the four boxes of my dearly departed, tied him up with the finest ribbon I could find, fashioned from that same ribbon, four of the most festive bows I'd ever created, tied the bows to the boxes and put him under the tree.

All four boxes of him.

Before I departed for Christmas in Louisville with my family, standing at the door of our apartment, luggage in hand, I took one last look at the "real Christmas splendor" in all its glistening glory. As I reached for the light switch to turn off the lights on the tree, I eyed the four lovingly wrapped boxes nestled under its lower branches, ready to say good bye to them. I was suddenly reminded of a story I'd seen on our local nightly news about some Grinch-style Christmas thieves who were breaking into homes and stealing presents from under Christmas trees. I knew those carefully wrapped, expensive looking packages weren't expensive presents but any potential Christmas thief wouldn't. I panicked! Dropping my bags I ran over to the tree and hurriedly scooped up my four little treasures. With the Boston Coach driver waiting outside our garden gate, I frantically searched for a hiding place — some place a thief wouldn't think to look. But where? Under a bed? No, first place he'd look. In a closet? Nope, second place he'd look. In the kitchen cabinets? No space. In the oven? Ew...ashes...No! Why hadn't I thought of this before now? **This hypothetical anti-Christmas thief had to be outsmarted.** As I darted around the apartment like a man possessed, a thought came to me. I ran to the wooden accordion style door that hid the laundry area and quickly pushed it aside. Opening the door of the clothes dryer I carefully placed the four boxes into it. I tossed in a couple of waiting-to-be-laundered bath towels, fussed them around a bit so they'd totally obscure the boxes and slammed the dryer door shut. Happy with my chosen hiding place, and breathing a sigh of relief, I closed the accordion door, marched out to my bags and with a final glance at the tree, switched off its lights. Heading out the door, my parting hope was that if a thief did break in during my absence, he wouldn't be doing any laundry.

1974

Surviving

ON APRIL 3, 1974, about nine months after Randy and I met and just before we moved in together, there was a tornado. Actually there were many tornadoes throughout the midwest that day but this one in particular devastated a huge portion of our hometown of Louisville, Kentucky. Entire neighborhoods were wiped out. Walking through the demolition zones and looking at the newspaper photos of the unbelievable devastation, there would be, in an otherwise flattened neighborhood, a lone house, standing amidst the rubble, untouched by the storm. All by itself; one house that for whatever reason, had been spared. I remember thinking "Why? Why would one house be spared when all the others were destroyed?" Without an adequate answer to that question, the next thought was, "How lucky! How lucky to be spared when all the others were taken." Lucky...yes...I suppose. I'm sure the owners of these spared homes did feel lucky. At first. But later when a new reality began to set in, perhaps not so much. Sure they survived but then...look around. Take in the situation from their new point of view. **Yes, they'd been spared, but were left to stand alone in a devastated landscape.** The neighborhood they'd built and tended so carefully, was gone.

About a decade later, as the tornado of AIDS swept through our gay neighborhoods, those of us who were spared were similarly grateful, of course. We were allowed the continued gift of life when most were not. But all around us was devastation. The landscape of friendship and family had changed. Vanished. We'd lost, it seemed, nearly everyone. We'd stand there, grateful to have been passed over; then we'd look around and all that could be seen in every direction was devastation and in the middle of this devastation you stand alone. And begin to feel less fortunate. Where we formerly had carefully tended neighborhoods of friendship — families we'd created and nurtured, there was now nothing but loss. Most everyone...gone. The families we so carefully built, the friends we simply expected to grow old with had left. The neighborhoods we'd tended, in a whoosh, were gone. Left behind to clean up after the storm, alone, we'd begin to feel not quite so fortunate.

You have to suffer not only the loss but also the grief without your support system — a system taken away just when you needed it the most. **AIDS decimated the immune system, the very system in place to take care of us and defend us from such diseases. Similarly, AIDS decimated our support system, the very system there to take care of us in our hour of grief.** AIDS took away the ones who should have been there to take care of us, those who survived, in this time of grieving for their loss. You've got to start over and rebuild your ravaged neighborhood but you have to do it now without the help and support of those you held dearest — your support system. It is they who you mourn and they who are no longer there to help you through the ordeal of losing them. It's a metaphor that turns in on itself again and again. You were there for each one nurturing him, one by one, to his peaceful transition to the next world. **You were there for them with your love and support but now that you are in need, like the neighbors in those tornado-torn neighborhoods, they have all moved on.**

With time, you also move on. You rebuild. You have to. I did. We all did. We learned to live with the loss and the grief. I did that too. Randy was gone. Chase was gone. Scores of other good friends — gone. It wasn't just the lovers and close friends but also the legions of party friends — boys whose names I never knew but whose faces I would always see and spirits I would always feel as we'd party together through the years. And have sex together. One by one they'd vanish and I'd wonder where they'd gone but in my heart I knew. They were lost forever and missed nearly as much as those I held close.

Other people step in. I learned to rely on these others and along with them, I began to build a new family, and neighborhood. I was afraid at first, afraid to re-create something that could so easily be taken away, just like before. I had to get over that and start anew. I would never forget the old family — the old neighborhood, but I would come to embrace the new one and cherish it, perhaps even more, appreciating now post-tornado, it's potentially ephemeral nature. There could be more tornadoes out there.

Also with time, I began to realize that there are support systems and, there are support systems. I started noticing the magic that surrounds me everywhere, everyday. **I would see the individual signatures of my seemingly lost souls in these reassuring little bits of divine intervention.** They're still here. They never left. They show themselves over and over. They are the ever-optimistic voices inside my head. I am not alone. As it turns out, I never was. I am reminded constantly of their ever-presence. Their spiritual fingerprints are everywhere. They have become part of that all encompassing all embracing universe I've come to understand and appreciate — a universe I may have formerly called "God" that is ever-protecting. I was there for them in their hour of need and now these friends are here for me, in all my hours of need; sharing, guiding, watching, advising and especially protecting. Quid Pro Quo.

Turns out I am actually the fortunate victim of the tornado that was AIDS. Fortunate not only to have survived but also for all the lessons learned. It gave me an understanding and acceptance of loss and change that most people don't develop until their golden years. It made me mature and kept me young. It caused me to look at an age spot on my hand and not regret getting older but instead think of all my friends denied the gift of growing old and the gift of age spots and I'd kiss mine and be thankful for it. It gave me challenges I couldn't have imagined and it made me grow. It swept me out of an existence I didn't appreciate or try to understand and dropped me right into a new world where, with a little help from my friends, I'd find a yellow brick road to awareness and appreciation of the miraculous universe that surrounds me, embraces me, protects me and has, throughout my life, ensured that things would just simply work out for me.

1940 – 1970

The Code

PRE-STONEWALL there weren't many venues for gay men to meet other men certain also to be gay. There were a few bars, where you could meet and drink and dance and be arrested. There were parks where you could meet and have sex and be bashed and be arrested. Or public bathrooms where you could also meet and have sex and be bashed and be arrested. **Your options were few, sometimes smelly (I was never a fan of bathroom sex) and quite frequently dangerous.**

Identifying each other away from these venues was particularly challenging but enterprising gays have always found ways to find each other well in advance of the Internet and Grindr. One of the most sure-fire methods was to ask, "Are you a friend of Dorothy?" It was a kind of verbal secret handshake and of course, a nod to Dorothy in *The Wizard Of Oz*. Judy Garland who played tornado-victim Dorothy was, in those days, the perennial gay favorite. Some might say, obsession. A tuned-in gay would get the reference immediately and answer, "Yes." And off he'd go with his new friend to do god knows what, secure in the knowledge that this mutual friend of Dorothy was not likely straight, a basher, or a police officer. An astute gay male, even if he was unaware of the code, might still pick up on it's Judy Garland reference and answer "Dorothy? Doro...oh... yeah...of course, Dorothy...yes, yes I am." Once again, off they'd go. The answer, "Dorothy who?" would get a, "Sorry, I thought you were someone else," and the questioner would move on, leaving the unsuspecting straight guy to go on his unmolested Dorothy-friendless way. **Pretty clever, these friends of Dorothy.** It worked *almost* every time.

When I was living in Boston during the late 80s and self-employed, under the recommendation of a friend named John, I was hired by a store design firm in Cincinnati. On my first day of work, I found myself in an elevator with the President of the company. He introduced himself and when I did the same, he answered with, "Are you a friend of Dorothy?" I was taken aback and really didn't know exactly how to answer him. I mean, there it was, the gay (if by then slightly outdated but hey it's Cincinnati) code. It seemed unlikely though that the president of the firm would open with that. Still... as I stood there hesitant (and response-less) there was a pregnant pause between us which he then, to my relief, filled with, "Oh wait, you're John's friend, not Dorothy's" and continued, "from Boston." Seems another employee whose name was Dorothy had a friend who'd started that same day. The code wasn't fool-proof.

1994

A Friend Of Dorothy's Guide To The Wizard Of Oz

"It's always best to start at the beginning..."

LONG BEFORE DISCOVERING THE CODE, I was already a friend of Dorothy. From my first viewing of *The Wizard of Oz*, Dorothy Gale of Kansas captured my young heart and spoke to me (through Judy's sweetness and vulnerability) in a way few movie characters have. Living her black and white farm existence, this gullible, pigtailed, always-in-the-way kindred spirit is certain of a technicolor world out there beyond the black and white limits of her sepia-toned Kansas sky. She knows there's a place, somewhere, where she will fit in. She is also, I think, pretty certain it'd be a lot more fun than Kansas.

"Somewhere over the rainbow..."

When Dorothy in her cute little gingham dress sings so sweetly and with such yearning about a place where "Dreams that you dare to dream really do come true," I could tell she believed in such a place and she made me believe it too. She can make me believe just about anything, this girl who, in her black and white world, believes in the colorful magic of rainbows. The purity of her voice and the sincerity of her longing touched me somewhere deep within my being. Dorothy was singing for both of us. I didn't fit in either. Long before I learned about sexuality, I knew I was different. As I began to understand more about myself and my same-sex attraction, I dreamt of a place where I'd find others like me. A place where my dreams really would come true. A place where I wouldn't be so alone. I'd look around my Louisville existence, as Dorothy had on that Kansas farm, and there was nothing that told me I belonged. Nothing in my family (no matter how much they loved me), nothing in my neighborhood, nothing on TV or in any advertising — nothing anywhere to indicate I wasn't alone in my same-sex interests. Or in my love of Judy Garland or even my love of blue and white gingham, for that matter. **I was a technicolored boy living in a sepia-toned world.** A gullible little alien presence; I might just as well have been in pigtails and gingham myself. So of course, like my friend Dorothy, I dreamt of somewhere else — anywhere else — where I could find others like me and no longer alone, I too would fit in. I was pretty certain it'd be a lot more fun than Kentucky.

"...to the Young in Heart..."

It would be decades after my first childhood TV viewing of (a black and white from start to finish) *The Wizard of Oz*, that I, in my Boston bedroom, while mourning my losses and feeling sorry for myself, would turn once again to my old friend Dorothy. Trying to find some constancy in a world that would take Chase's young life along with the lives of my best friend Randy and so many other wonderful young friends, I would, as I have innumerable times, pop into the VCR my favorite classic film. This time, watching it with a fresh set of eyes and seeing the parallels between my friend Dorothy's story and my own, I would finally get it and promise myself to someday write about it.

"Well, bust my buttons! That's a horse of a different color!"

Suddenly understanding the film version of *The Wizard of Oz* in a new way, I began to wonder if it has ever revealed itself to anyone else, the way it did to me that afternoon. Has anyone else

ever taken note of the very simple all-important message — two of them actually, that I saw in it that day? Its timeless "kindly philosophy" that had escaped me before had been there all along. This time, sharing my friend Dorothy's journey, rather than simply watching, I'd enjoy a brand new experience with my favorite old film. Alone in my Chase-less bedroom, surrounded by my ghosts and licking my wounds certain I'd be the last to go (having seen all the others go before me) I was trying to understand, as I did most days, a god that would allow such suffering and death among the "Young at Heart." Applying my own experiences to Dorothy's, I'd find we had a lot more in common than just our yearnings and problems and a love of gingham. **Our parallel journeys, rather like a set of concentric rainbows, would reveal much more than either of us had been searching for, pulling back the curtain on the two greatest truths of existence.** I don't know if Dorothy got it but I sure did. I couldn't miss it. Somewhere over my rainbow, I found there really is no place like home.

"Do you suppose there is such a place, Toto?"

It may have been tough growing up a sweet young girl on a 1930s Kansas farm where you're not appreciated; but try growing up a little gay boy in a 1950s Louisville where you don't even exist. And when you begin to figure out that you do exist, everything and everyone is intent on telling you you're bad, pitting you against yourself. **They actually warned me about people like me!** The mean-spirited Almira Gulches of the world or even a well-meaning Aunt Em can do a real number on a kid, convincing you of your inner "badness," while never acknowledging your inherent goodness. Religion was most thorough at trying to pound that "badness" out of you all the while much more thoroughly (and ironically) pounding it into you. In an effort to save my soul, they were actually burying it, making my own search for me even more challenging. Where I should have been taught to find the goodness within, I was only taught there was evil. They may have called me a "Child of God," but they spent a lot more time treating me like the spawn of Satan. I was a little sinner, pure and simple. **It's no wonder then that, little devout Catholic I, upon discovering my true homosexual self, couldn't figure out where I fit into all of this — somewhere between "angel" and "abomination."** I was forever looking to a god who would approve of me because theirs clearly didn't.

"I've a feeling we're not in Kansas anymore."

When Dorothy gets her wish and a tornado sweeps her up and deposits her with a little "Oh!" (presumably somewhere over the rainbow) she finds herself in the strange land of Oz, a technicolor place as full of magic and wonder as she is full of questions. And a healthy modicum of fear. Right away, Dorothy meets Glinda The Good Witch of the North (in, by the way, one of the great movie entrances of all time.) After sorting out the good witch/bad witch thing — "Only bad witches are ugly" — our puzzled Dorothy finds she's dropped her house on The Wicked Witch of the East, killing her and forever freeing the Munchkins from her evil tyranny. **Having just arrived in town and being told she's a killer, and at the same time being hailed a hero, Dorothy is understandably conflicted. And confused.** The Munchkins (who it has to be said can put on one damned impressive celebration at a moments notice) hail Dorothy as their savior. At this point she's feeling pretty special and everything's going really well until...

"What a smell of sulphur."

The Wicked Witch of The West arrives, full of fire and brimstone. She is pure evil and scares our Dorothy (and any kid watching the movie) half to death. This sweet little girl in pigtails is up against someone who, we later find out, has an air force of flying monkeys. This green-skinned horror-show of malevolence is after one thing: Dorothy's ruby slippers. Ruby slippers? With everything else going on, Dorothy is surprised to find she has ruby slippers but "there they are and there they'll stay." Somehow, gazing down at her glittery new shoes she becomes suspiciously adept at modeling them. I always thought if she'd known about the ruby slippers in advance, she probably wouldn't have worn those unfortunate anklets. But then again, she is from Kansas. Anyway, Glinda assures Dorothy her ruby slippers (though kinda stolen from a dead lady) are everlasting and all powerful and if she keeps them on, (simple enough, really) they will protect her from The Wicked Witch. She believes it. **You don't argue with someone who just arrived in a big pink bubble.**

"I'll get you my pretty..."

I could relate to this wicked witch thing. I had the constant fire and brimstone threat of "Satan" in my young life. Though there were no pyrotechnics and I never actually saw this alleged horned resident of the evil underworld, nevertheless, the priests and nuns assured me of the hellacious threat from this pointy-tailed, cloven-hooved adversary. I was just a little kid. I'd seen the pictures. Mission accomplished: I was scared to death! **They loved using the devil to scare us little 1950s baby boomer kids and did so with great regularity.** I was told in no uncertain terms, that Satan was after one thing: my eternal soul. Soul? After all the "badness" programming I was surprised to find I had one. Yes, they assured me, I did still have a soul and though unfortunately "tainted by sin," it remained everlasting and all powerful. And "Satan" was after my soul just as sure as the Witch was after Dorothy's ruby slippers. As long as I kept my imperfect little soul intact, and free from mortal sin, it would keep me safe from "Satan." Though my initial reaction to all of this was laced with a healthy dose of kid skepticism, you don't argue with a scowling veiled tower of black and white 16th century garb with a giant rosary hanging from her waist.

"My! People come and go so quickly here!"

With the Wicked Witch gone, it becomes clear that Munchkinland (which looks a lot like Bloomingdales in the 1970s) is not Dorothy's final destination. Glinda, who despite her goodness doesn't have all the answers, tells Dorothy, reverentially to the bowed heads of the Munchkins (along with some intentionally impressive background music,) about the "Great and Wonderful Wizard of Oz." He lives in the Emerald City, and is "Very good but very mysterious" (an implied threat?) The Wizard, Glinda assures her, does have all the answers, is all powerful and grants all wishes. Dorothy believes it. Once again, who's gonna question someone who answers to "Glinda The Good," has the devotion of legions of lovable little people, waves a magic wand, and wears a big pink lucite crown and more pink tulle than anyone has ever seen in one place.

So...if she wants to find the Wizard, Dorothy will have to continue her journey; to wit, Glinda instructs her to "Follow the yellow brick road" that will lead her to the Wizard. Apparently there's no other way. "All you do is follow the yellow brick road..." Glinda once again assures her as she makes her pink bubble exit, taking no more questions. All the little Munchkins agree — in song, as they are wont to do — that this is indeed the way, the only way as they sing the phrase over and over and over and over...

"Follow the yellow brick road."

My naive and gullible self was similarly deposited in the strange land of Catholicism, a place also as full of magic and wonder as I was full of questions. And a healthy modicum of fear. We were told by priests and nuns reverentially to our little bowed heads (along with intentionally impressive church music) about god, resident of heaven who, though good, is also full of mystery (a definite threat.) God, like the Wizard, is all powerful, has all the answers and grants all wishes. It was pretty clear to me that neither church nor religion class was my final destination. Like Dorothy, if I was gonna find god, I'd have to take my religion on the road. **If I was good and followed the yellow brick road of Catholicism (and the Catechism) I was told I would get to Heaven and there I'd find god, with all the answers.** Apparently there was no other way. I believed it. Who was I to question someone, ordained by god, who changes bread and wine into the body and blood of Jesus Christ right in front of your eyes every Sunday morning.

"We're off to see the Wizard..."

As we set off on our similar paths, both surviving tornadoes by the way, my friendship and identification with Dorothy would deepen right along with my gingham envy. The search was on. We were off to see The Wizard, or in my case god, each on a journey with the constant threat of evil around every corner but armed with the assurance we'd be protected against that evil. We'd have to stick to the program and the yellow brick road, and grovel a bit but hey, protection doesn't come cheap; ya gotta do whatcha gotta do. And after we did what we had to do, Dorothy could enter The Emerald City and find her Wizard while I could enter The Kingdom of Heaven where I would find god.

"It's a man!"

Together on our quest, Dorothy and I would make friends along the way, some helpful and some as lost as we. Dorothy's new friends (one I'm pretty sure was gay and the other two questionable though none of them ever mentioned the anklets) seem as thoroughly programmed against themselves as we; self-esteem issues abound. They, like we, were convinced by their own Almira Gulches or Aunt Ems, of their imperfections: brainless scarecrow, heartless tin man, cowardly lion, bothersome farm girl, godless homosexual. **We'd been ill-defined by those who had had control over us; someone else's definition of who we were not.** Even though our day to day existence proved over and over the inaccuracy of those mis-definitions, we'd all been too thoroughly programmed to see the actual truth of our inherent perfection. They hadn't told us about that. Rather, they'd most effectively left their own dirty fingerprints all over our previously perfect clear pink bubbles — the ones we came into this world with — so much so we couldn't see our true selves through their residue. I thankfully did possess a tiny little whisper of a reassuring inside-voice with a different message, telling me I was a good boy. I suppose we all do. They are sadly no match for the full throated shout of the insistent outside-voices determined to overwhelm that little voice of truth in an effort to prove it wrong. **Mine would remain hushed but it would remain.** For me, religion was the loudest and most insistent of those outside voices.

"Lions and tigers and bears, oh my!"

There'd be bumps on that winding yellow brick road for Dorothy and her new friends; for me too. There'd be plenty of scary stuff along the way. For Dorothy: lions and tigers and bears. For me: Christians and preachers and nuns. Oh my. There were also temptations. Apples were forbidden fruit (first and most famously offered to Adam and Eve by that snake, satan) and Dorothy finds (just like Adam and Eve who suddenly had to put on clothes) when snatched, there's instant, ferocious retribution. Gay sex was my forbidden fruit and though I didn't have anything as dramatic as angry trees throwing apples at me, I did have hateful "Christians" angrily waving their placards, shouting obscenities and throwing their bible full of a judgmental god my way. "Hate the sin not the sinner," they say. Yeah...right. The hate for the "sinner" is all too obvious.

"Unusual weather we're havin' ain't it?"

A field filled with poppies could have delayed Dorothy's journey, perhaps sidetracking her forever. Instead, Glinda appears, makes it snow and before you know it, ("Curses! Curses! Somebody always helps that girl!") Dorothy wakes from her poppy-induced slumber. Refreshed, she is on her way again, mostly unaware of the help she's received from beyond. The nap, rather than derailing her, actually seems to have done her some good, preparing her for what lay ahead.

Parties filled with poppers and drugs could have thrown me off my path, perhaps sidetracking me forever. Instead, just like Dorothy, there was always some unseen protective force ("Things just seem to work out for me") pulling me back from any drug-induced unconsciousness. Energized, I'd be on my way again, mostly unaware of the help I'd received from beyond. The parties and drugs, rather than derailing me, actually seem to have done me a lot of good, opening me up and preparing me for what lay ahead.

"You're out of the woods you're out of the dark you're out of the night..."

To the accompaniment of a chorus of optimistic voices, excitedly arriving at The Emerald City, Dorothy and her friends are greeted by the city's Doorman. After a bit of a trip-up with a doorbell which clearly works, though a sign he hurriedly hangs out says otherwise, (what's that about?), The Doorman (aka Gatekeeper) after Dorothy's compliant knock, opens the gates to The Emerald City to her. Once inside with her friends, there's a jovial Cabby who drives them around and eventually takes them all to The Wizard's residence where Dorothy pleads for entry to the Guard who will, after some initial misgivings, give her access to the Wizard's residence. **Dorothy doesn't seem to notice a striking familiarity that all these guys share. Though just a kid, I spotted it instantly.**

"Nobody's ever seen the Great Oz!"
"Well then — how do you know there is one?"

Inside the Wizard's residence, Dorothy and her friends proceed down a long hallway that will ultimately lead them to The Wizard. It's deco-gothic style, though beautiful, seems designed to be intimidating. A lot like church. The terrifying voice of The Great and Powerful Oz is beckoning Dorothy in along with her companions. She has finally made it and is about to see The Wizard. Nobody has ever seen the Wizard of Oz. "Not nobody — not nohow." And yet they all seem to believe in him. A lot like god. The Wizard as it turns out, is all shouting and booming, complete with pyrotechnics and a disembodied head floating over an altar, right where the suffering crucified Christ was in our church. The entire spectacle seems intent on scaring Dorothy "The small and meek" and her friends; and frighteningly familiar to easily intimidated little Catholic me.

"You should be ashamed..."

When The Wizard succeeds in scaring the most vulnerable of her friends, Wizard or no Wizard, Dorothy angrily strikes back. **"You should be ashamed of yourself! Frightening him like that when he came to you for help!" And there it is. If there has ever been a more concise condemnation of organized religion, I haven't heard it.** Dorothy nailed it. Frightening instead of helping. Ashamed indeed! My brave friend Dorothy with those few well-chosen words, reveals The Wizard to be exactly what he is: a bully intent on scaring those who come to him for help. And in so doing, she exposes religion for exactly what it is: an institution intended to scare those who come to it for help.

Oh, if only Dorothy had been around for my 1950s Catholic education to defend me from those who'd used their religion to terrify me. I went to church and school a vulnerable, devout little

boy looking for help, needing to find a kind and loving god and all the nuns and priests could do was scare me with their disapproving vengeful one. They seduced me with pomp and pageantry, organ music, and pretty statues and when under their influence, they told me of my inherent badness and of a vengeful god needing to be worshipped and feared. Who was I to question them? I did once, and was branded a heretic. At seven. These people were intent on making me a good "god-fearing" Catholic and they almost succeeded. They preached of a god ready to punish me for all my young sins. How many could I have had? They sent me to confession. They tried to convince me that I was pretty much rotten to the core and that my only salvation was in groveling before this judgmental vindictive presence; just like The Wizard. I came to them for help and all they could do was frighten me. They, right along with the Wizard, should have been ashamed of themselves. Thank god (literally) for that tiny but insistent inside voice that knew better.

"I can't wait forever to get those shoes!"

Even after all of this, the Wizard gives Dorothy and her friends a test to prove their worthiness. Girl, I've been there too. The Catholic Church was great at throwing big challenges at little kids. Martyrdom was held in high esteem and I imagined myself more than once, in defense of their ridiculous religion, riddled with arrows or worse. Dorothy's challenge is simple. Basically, kill the Wicked Witch, the same woman who's intent on killing Dorothy and taking her shoes. After she's dead, then take her broomstick back to the Wizard as commanded. Is that all? **This little girl in anklets, dispatched to vanquish the evil force of darkness was pretty much me as a "Soldier of Christ" in a parochial school uniform sent to stamp out satan and all his evil.** Fortunate for our Dorothy, the witch's threat of evil is so thin it is vanquished by a mere bucket of water. Who knew it could be so easy?

"Oh rubbish! You have no power here. Be gone..."

Similarly, satan, that ever-present malignant "force of evil," drilled into me from original sin on, turned out to be just as thin and just as easily dispatched. **Once I came to realize that the devil (and the threat of evil "he" represented) simply does not exist, the "force of evil" was just as easily vanquished by a divine bucket of truth.** Once the force of darkness was dispelled, so was the possibility that it could have ever lived in me. Who knew it could be so easy?

"Pay no attention to that man behind the curtain."

Somehow, liquidating the Wicked Witch as commanded, isn't enough to appease this unappeasable deity. This too is familiar ground. Religion taught me I could never be enough. God could not be satisfied. Somehow, no matter how I might try to prove myself worthy, I would always be a "sinner" and despite the many trips I'd make to the confessional, I would remain ultimately unworthy. Similarly unworthy, Dorothy and her friends are put off once again by the Wizard who tells them to return another day. Dorothy, who's understandably had enough at this point, is in no mood. The Wizard pulls out all the scary stops, every frightening, threatening device in his wizardry arsenal to scare Dorothy and friends one more time just as her little dog Toto runs off and literally pulls back the curtain. Whaddaya know...turns out a mere mortal (perhaps well-meaning, perhaps not) is running this scary scam. It's all pomp and theatrics. **Somewhere along my own yellow brick road, the truth was revealed to me as well: religion and in my case, Catholicism turned out to be a scary scam.** It's all pomp and theatrics, run by mere mortals (perhaps well-meaning, perhaps not.)

"Times being what they were, I accepted the job..."

Curtain pulled back, when the "Wizard" is finally revealed, there it is again. The same face. It's the same guy! OK. As a boy this small detail bothered me, as it would any little gay Virgo. Why, I wondered, would they use the same actor to play five roles? And to my personal dissatisfaction, an actor I was not particularly fond of: Frank Morgan, who played Professor Marvel, The Gatekeeper, The Cabby, The Guard and the Wizard himself. I didn't get it. This was a big budget film. It's not like they couldn't afford to cast individual actors for each role. Why would they use Frank Morgan in so many roles? More than a little annoyed, I once asked my mom about it and her response was something like, "Well, I don't know. Maybe Frank Morgan was down on his luck and needed the work." Plausible enough though I wouldn't have hired him. True it wasn't long after the Great Depression — but still, the question remained...**why?**

"No, I'm afraid it's true. There's no other Wizard except me."

While watching "The Wizard of Oz" in my Boston bedroom that day, I suddenly had an answer. An epiphany if you will. It all became crystal clear. Why hadn't I seen it before? They had cast those roles in that fashion so that I, some seventy-plus years later, could use their casting choice and a timeless film that practically everybody has seen or will see, to illustrate an all important truth. It's all so simple. As all important truths are. It's the simple truth about the existence of God.

And there's good old Frank Morgan to help me illustrate this simple truth. Every character Frank Morgan played was there for Dorothy at an important transition for her, helping her along the way. Professor Marvel dealt with her kindly and sent her back home to the safety of Aunt Em, away from the approaching tornado. The Gatekeeper opened the doors of Emerald City to her granting her the protection from the world outside. The Cabby happily drove her around seeing that all her needs were met before taking her to her destination — the Wizard. The Guard granted her entrance to the Wizard's residence, which apparently he'd never done for anyone else. Dorothy accepted the help provided by each of these individuals without (apparently) giving any of them much thought. Then, having reached her destination, she finally meets The Wizard and whattaya know — there it is again — that same face!

The presence that our Dorothy had so desperately been seeking on her long journey, had shown itself to her time and again. She simply hadn't noticed. So fixated on a godly presence in some high-exalted place, she'd missed that same presence in those she'd met and been helped by along the way. So blinded by the search for something greater she'd missed that greatness right in front of her eyes. She simply hadn't seen it. **In the those she'd met along the way to find the Wizard, that is where The Wizard was.**

Similarly, I'd been told about a god in heaven. If I were a good boy, someday I'd get there and that's where I'd find him. Yet everywhere along my own path to find God, there were those who'd been there to help and guide and protect me. God had already been revealed, present in every person I'd met on my own journey. Just like Dorothy, I hadn't noticed. I hadn't been taught to find God's ever-presence in everyday people. Rather, I'd been taught to look to Heaven. **A religious red herring.** Had I not been handed the primitive, almost infantile concept of some bearded father figure who lives in the clouds, loves to be worshipped, grants wishes, judges us and who I would someday find in Heaven, I might have been able to see the true divinity that lies in others and find it all around me. And in me. So programmed to find god in heaven, it's no wonder I missed God in my Mom or Dad or Frank or Carmen or Randy or Dawn or Steve or Chase or Shani or Shelton or my employers or my teachers or in that guy I had sex with last night...or in you. That is where to find God.

No one ever taught me that one important truth. But Frank Morgan and his five roles simply and elegantly illustrate that critically important truth better than any religious training ever has.

"There's no place like home."

There is one more critically important lesson waiting for us in that wonderful film, this time from Glinda The Good. At the end of the film when Glinda tells Dorothy to click her heels three times and repeat "There's no place like home, there's no place like home," what is she telling Dorothy? Don't travel? Don't grow up? Don't ever leave home? I don't think so. "There's no place like home. There's no place like home." With that one phrase, repeated over and over burnishing it onto our communal psyche, Glinda was giving Dorothy (and me and all of us) a profound truth; the most important truth there is. I don't know if Dorothy picked up on it — I certainly hadn't for decades of watching *The Wizard of Oz* — but I suddenly got it — right between the eyes! **"There's no place like home." If you go looking for God, rather than in a church, or in Heaven, look in your own backyard; find God in you.** If we don't find God there first we won't find God anywhere. "There's no place like home."

Dorothy said it, "If I ever go looking for my heart's desire again, I won't look any farther than my own backyard." My own backyard. Searching for my own heart's desire — God — I need only look inward. Not in Heaven but in my own backyard. In me. It's that simple. Click. Click. Click. "There's no place like home." Click. Click. Click. Home.

"The horse of a different color you've heard tell about."

Like Dorothy, I had to find this most important truth for myself, this lesson of my own divinity. No religion. No dogma. No priest. No nun. No bible. No catechism. No self-help book. **Nothing in my religious education could have taught me this important undeniable fact about myself.** I suppose it's that way for all of us. We each must look within to find God for ourselves. In ourselves. Once I began to understand that God isn't some judgmental vindictive paternal presence in some lofty place somewhere, but instead a force that resides in me, my little inside voice grew and shouted what it knew all along, the infallible validating news, "God is in here," and with it all those outside voices determined to keep that good news from me, were silenced. God resides in me. I would never be alone again. How nice to have a great classic film and Glinda in all that glitter and tulle to validate it with a wave of her magic wand.

"Oh dear — that's too wonderful to be true!"

And if God is in me then God is you. Also simple. Everything after that falls right into place. God is in everyone. That's what makes it easy to accept Frank Morgan's five character lesson. To find God in ourselves is to find God in everyone.

"And you — and you — and you — and you were there."

It's all there in my favorite classic three strip technicolor film masterpiece, *The Wizard of Oz*, with its timeless, eternally true, critically important and incredibly simple message to us all. I sat down that day in Boston to watch my favorite film, be entertained by all my old friends in Kansas and Oz and didn't think to ask for more. **What I got was so much more: all the theology this friend of Dorothy will ever need.**

Glinda summed it up best...

"That's all it is!"

1981

Saved

WHY DO YOU THINK you were saved? It's a question I'm asked a lot. Why indeed. I've given a lot of thought to this over the years, have some ideas about it but in the end, I always answer the question with the same question, **"Who knows?"**

The most practical answer to the question is that I have always been a "top." Sexually, especially when it comes to anal sex, I was and remain an unwavering top. During my early days of being out I gave bottoming a shot but didn't like it. Given I was living in a world of bottoms, I didn't have to. Although I was mistaken quite frequently for a bottom — I think it was my small stature and my big butt — I was a total disappointment in that department. It isn't as though you can't contract HIV as the top, it's just less likely you will. It was the "bottoms" or the "versatile" guys, recipients in anal sex who were more at risk. Since most of my friendships started with sex, it follows that most of my friends were bottoms. Or at least versatile. So while most of my friends were contracting HIV, I didn't. Perhaps, being an unrelenting top saved me. **Who knows?**

A more metaphysical answer might have to do with aging. I remember sitting around with some Chicago friends in a conversation about growing old. Of that particular group I was the only one who was looking forward to becoming an older gay man. To a one each of my friends expounded on how he didn't want to become "some tragic old queen" (their words not mine) "predatory" still "trolling the bars" and "trying ridiculously to be young" (again, their words.) It might have been Randy who said, "First time you see me in a caftan, shoot me!" I was shocked at how my friends seemed to take such a negative view of growing old as a gay fait accompli. I was also amazed that so many of my friends had bought into the myth of "the lonely old homosexual," a myth by the way, perpetuated and hard-sold to gays by the straight world. During my formative early-out years, I was fortunate to have had older gay men (I have mentioned them before) who I sincerely wanted to be like when I got to be their age. They were smart, tasteful, accomplished, youthful but not ridiculous, sexual but not predatory, and they were most certainly not lonely. **Their houses were full of gay boys coming and going and I could see myself, someday, just like them.** Even before that, when as a young boy I saw the film *Operation Petticoat*. I wanted to be Cary Grant and have Tony Curtis, spending the better part of the eighth grade in fact, trying to develop a cleft chin. I was always the older man. Even then. There was a part of me that believed I'd be better old than I had been young. That part of me was looking forward to getting older. I seemed to be alone in this and, of that Chicago group, I was the lone survivor. Perhaps the simple desire to grow old allowed me to grow old. **Who knows?**

The third answer is also a metaphysical one. I was fortunate to never feel guilt with sex. Not even when I was a little Catholic boy and the largely hostile world around me seemed so convinced that I should feel guilty, I didn't. Religion tried really hard to make me hate myself but they couldn't do it. They tried to convince me that I had "impure" thoughts but I was happy with those thoughts and encouraged every one of them. They taught me about "the sin of self-abuse" but I didn't see the "sin" or feel "abused." Just excited and happy. And good. How could it be bad? As I got older the rhetoric got stepped-up: sick, depraved, pervert, aberration, and that all-time favorite: abomination; all in an effort to make me hate myself. They didn't get away with it. They tried so hard to convince me of the evil within me but when I got around to looking inside, I only found

Gay Boy's Life

good. **And when I did finally have sex with a man, it was as if I had located the missing piece that completed the puzzle of happines that is me.** At long last I was whole and no one could convince me this was bad. Sex had to be a gift from God; how could it be bad? Along with that realization would be a total lack of guilt. Could that have saved me? **Who knows?**

Now a word from "Michael's Legal Department" as my friend Shelton used to call it whenever I'd explain or amend something I've said:

I can't know why my friends were taken. I can try to understand why I was not. I have written the above in an effort to illuminate my own experience of surviving. I do not in any way blame any one of my friends for his illness. I won't speculate why they are no longer among us. I only speculate what, against all apparent odds, saved me.

1994

Shadow Chase

CHRISTMAS HAD PASSED. It was a new year and I was feeling a need to get back to life. I redecorated the room where Chase had died. I had to. It had been our room, then his room, then his room to die in. It now had to be my room to live in. And heal in. I had become increasingly aware of my ability as a designer (with a spiritual edge) to employ certain devices during my work to sort of 'spiritually heal' my clients' spaces and in so doing help spiritually heal them. **As I'd rearrange their things, I'd "love each item into its proper place," re-energizing each piece, which would re-energize their entire spaces and as it followed, their spaces would energize them.** I don't expect they were fully aware of this but I certainly became aware. Employing these same devices for my own need, I re-created a bedroom fresh and new, getting rid of all that spoke to the anger and pain, suffering and dying that had gone before and replaced it all with positive loving energy. I not only made the space much prettier and more suited to me, but I also energetically refurbished it, loving every precious thing in it and about it and giving it the power to re-energize me. And heal me.

One day while sitting with my feet up on my desk happily enjoying my newly refurbished room, I found myself awash in a sudden wave of grief. These bouts of sadness and the subsequent tears would occur without warning. I'd be going about my daily business as usual and...suddenly an overwhelming sense of loss would consume me; a sudden loneliness for Chaser. Some sweet memory would flash through my brain and trigger it. You spend a lot of time post-mortem remembering the good times, burnishing them onto the brain. It helps you forget or at least diminish the bad times. The effect is that you end up canonizing your departed loved one. **So there I was, sitting and remembering Saint Chase and longing to see him again.** I found myself, as I had become accustomed, speaking to him out loud. Unaware at the time of the irony, I called out into the empty redecorated room from which I had removed all evidence of him, "Chaser, I want to see you. Show me that you're here. I need to see you," cried out the ever-visual me, "...just one more time. Even if its only for a second, I just want to see you again. Let me know you're here."

Since the loss of so many beloved friends I'd become accustomed to their from-the-other-side brand of magic so, with my request in, I fully expected to see him. Somehow. I don't know what I was expecting — a vision perhaps — a kind of floating hologram? We were both *Star Trek: The Next Generation* fans so why not? Perhaps he'd get beamed-in. Anyway, at the same second I finished verbalizing my need, outside, a cloud must have moved away from the sun because a beam of light suddenly came through the bedroom window, shining into the room and illuminating the wall just to the left of the bed. And I saw Chase. Right there. Created by that beam of light.

I had given Chase as a stocking stuffer one Christmas, a peg strip to hang clothes on. At each of the three pegs was a cute wood pastel animal cutout. It was actually made for a child's room but I quite frequently liked to bring out the little boy in Chase. He was there, that little Christopher, buried deep within and Christmas was the perfect time to draw him out. In the room redo, I had hung the peg strip next to the bed and hanging on it was a favorite t-shirt and pair of orange boxer shorts — my morning at-home wear.

The ray of light suddenly beaming through the window had illuminated the t-shirt and shorts creating a shadow on the wall just to their left. **It was Chase's shadow. His profile. I recognized it immediately.** I had gotten my wish. Instantly. "Asked and answered," as he'd have said. So clear and sharp I couldn't have missed it. Chase was in our bedroom again, visibly as asked, right by the bed. Our bed, his bed, my bed. On demand. I sat there in awe, staring at this instant answer to my request, committing it to memory, afraid that at any second it would go as quickly as it had arrived. With my eyes never leaving the shadow I reached for the phone with the thought that someone else had to see it. To validate it.

"Madeleine, get over here now!" I said to the dead air at the other end of the phone line, then, in a tone a little less demanding, "Sorry. What are you doing? Can you come over here? Now? Immediately? Please?" I added, "Nothing's wrong. Just come. You have to see something." I didn't know how long this beam of light might last and with the movement of the sun and clouds if it went away would it ever reappear. Ever dependable Madeleine was over in a flash. I answered the door telling her nothing as she followed me downstairs. The shadow had remained unchanged by cloud or sun. I pointed in the general direction of the bed and said, "Do you see anything over there?" At a glance, without missing a beat she said, "Oh my god it's Chase!" **Madeleine, who always saw the magic, saw him too.**

I stopped wearing my favorite t-shirt and orange boxers for quite awhile after that not wanting to disrupt the shadow that would reliably appear at that same time every sunny day. I'd go downstairs, coffee mug in hand and wait for it. I'd have little chats with it now and then. Or just be with it. With him. He was always there, Shadow Chase, defined by the light, resurrected in a way, in that redecorated room right along with the new decor. The shadow gave me the warmest feeling assuring me of his constant presence. I was in no hurry to wear that t-shirt and boxers again and had no idea how or when I'd let go of Shadow Chase. He came and went for months with the t-shirt and boxers remaining there undisturbed, illuminated by the ever-dependable sun. I found other shorts and shirts to slip my just awakened nakedness into each morning.

One night as I finished packing for a greatly-needed Key West respite from the cold and grief, I scanned the room for any forgotten thing. I eyed the t-shirt and boxers I'd been careful not to touch or disturb in any way. It was nighttime so of course there was no shadow. In an instant I decided it was time. "Chaser, lets go to Key West," I said as I snatched the t-shirt and boxers from their pegs, folded them and put them in my bag.

Peaches & The Perfect Suit

O N EACH VISIT to Key West I would find the perfect swimsuit. While most of my friends would shop for their swimwear before their vacation, I'd wait as I knew that Peaches would have just what I wanted. Peaches, a charming little one-of-a-kind shop never failed to produce the perfect suit. It was located on Duval Street along with the restaurants, clubs and all the other one-of-a-kind stores. Peaches sold only swimwear and only their own private label. No Jantzen. No Speedo. No any other brand that could be found anywhere else. They had the best fabrics and always the perfect fit — for me at least as I didn't have a speedo-body; you know, the mesomorphic, wide-shouldered, narrow-waisted and narrower-hipped, classic athletic swimmer's build I loved and coveted in equal parts. To my eternal annoyance, I was a bit more "generously" proportioned from the waist down so the right cut on a swimsuit was critically important to me and my thunder-thighs. You had to feel sexy in a swimsuit and every Peaches suit, with its unique cut, clingy-without-an-inner-liner-probably-too-revealing fabric, and perfect stretchiness made me feel very sexy. Consistency was also key as there were tan lines to be considered. I liked my tan lines masking tape sharp and sticking with the same Peaches cut, I could be assured of tan line sharpness with day to day and season to season conformity. This was vitally important.

Key West was a place of ritual behavior and Peaches was for me, an important part of that ritual. From the airport I'd take a pink taxi (the taxis in Key West were my favorite color) to whichever guesthouse I'd decided to try that year. Having arrived, I'd pass a pool area checking out the sun bathing beauties checking out the new arrival — me. I'd waste no time checking in and getting out to the sun. In my carry-on would be a swimsuit (no doubt last year's Peaches purchase,) a tube of Bain de Soleil Gelee, a baseball cap and sunglasses. When traveling to Key West you couldn't depend on your checked luggage getting there with you. In fact, quite to the contrary, you could typically depend on its not getting there with you. Many of the Miami to Key West flights used small planes with the attendant weight allowances. Filling the plane with passengers was the first priority. Luggage was last. Bags left in Miami were flown out on later flights, ones presumably with few or perhaps no passengers. Once your bag did finally arrive on the island, it'd be whisked off to your guesthouse, also in a pink taxi. Grateful for what I considered to be a complimentary Key West luggage delivery service, I always happily packed accordingly.

I couldn't strip my cold weather gear off fast enough, excommunicating those layers of nasty dark woolen fabrics to rear of the closet to be forgotten for the next ten days. I'd quickly slip into my old Peaches suit, take a toke or two of weed, grab my baseball cap and toss the Bain de Soleil, room key and sunglasses into it. I'd snatch up a pool towel and within seconds would be stretching my winter-white body out on a sun lounger, poolside, with all the bronzing boys. I would spend the next few hours stretched out in the sun, sometimes socializing and sometimes not; sometimes on a lounge chair flipping over at intervals and sometimes floating on an aquamarine pool float. **Pool floats in Key West were as reliably aquamarine as the taxis were pink.** Floating on a pool at a gay guesthouse in Key West, as far as I could be from the eyes of the straight world, baked by the sun and the weed, wearing my baseball cap and sunglasses, in and out of my little wet clingy Peaches swimsuit, surrounded by naked and nearly-naked sexy gay boys was, not surprisingly, my all-time favorite activity. **It is where I would achieve my own perfect balance; I'd be doing it right this**

minute if I could. I would float there feeling sun warmed and sexy lusting for the other tanned exposed boys surrounding me. Some of their eyes might be lusting for me as well. Excited by the thought, I'd breezily paddle my contented way around the pool, soaking up the sun and admiration in equal parts while my own eyes would be devouring them.

At one with this tailor-made-for-me environment, with my brain dialed back by the weed and connected to the universe that had provided it all, I'd grow spiritually while the bulge in my Peaches suit would also grow. Tuned in and turned on; enlightened and sexual. Two supposedly opposing forces working in concert with each other. God and Sex. Yin and Yang. I'd float on those pools in Key West, horny just being there, soaking up the sun and all that the universe had to offer along with the sexy smiles and glances of the other sun baked boys. I'd be centered: horny and spiritual, finding pure magic for my body and my soul. **I'd learn the secrets of the universe growing spiritually, all the while getting the perfect tan and hopefully preparing for my next sexual encounter or whatever challenges, good or bad the universe had in store.**

After enjoying an hour or two of this magical activity I'd force myself to move on. Overdo your exposure to the South Florida sun on your first day and you risk ruining your entire vacation. A rookie error. So after nearly not enough time, continuing my first day ritual, I'd head for the outdoor shower which, no matter the guesthouse, was always strategically placed with exhibitionists and voyeurs in mind. I'd thoroughly enjoy my shower, hoping others would too and head back to my room. There I'd put on my favorite 1950s rayon trunks (purchased years earlier in Key West,) and perhaps a tank top. Shirts were optional and, especially in Key West, I so loved being "one item of clothing away from naked." I'd slip into my flip flops and off I'd go with my destination being Duvall Street and more specifically, Peaches. Year after year, it'd be there, waiting for my return. On one particular vacation as I strolled up Duvall Street checking out the shop windows (and boys) my eyes searched ahead for Peaches. It wasn't there. My heart nearly stopped. OK, that's an exaggeration but it's safe to say I was taken aback and not happy. I was sure of the spot. No Peaches. I went into the the new shop-that-wasn't-Peaches and spoke with the person behind the counter who politely told me Peaches had moved up the street and on the opposite side. Disaster averted. What would I have done? Where else would I have found my perfect suit? Peaches, grown larger in its new and expanded corner location (formerly a gas station I think) was better than ever and I of course found my perfect suit.

On one of my latter Key West visits, staying at the Oasis, I went through my whole routine. As I strolled up Duvall Street in Peaches pursuit, once again checking out the shop windows and the shirtless boys, I passed the old Peaches location giving it a nostalgic glance. I continued up the street to the new location and looking ahead I saw Peaches wasn't there. Not again? The person behind the counter of this new-shop-that-wasn't-Peaches politely gave me the bad news. Peaches had gone out of business. No!

Over the previous few years there had been subtle and not so subtle changes occurring all over Key West and here was another one. A Key West institution and purveyor of every swimsuit I'd purchased for the past I don't know how many years was gone. I exited dejected and unhappy. Now, I know, in the grand scheme of things, a swimsuit is not of much importance, but for me, seeing so much of my beloved Key West slipping away, it seemed monumental. In a time when AIDS had already taken so much from the gay community and from Key West itself, this was about more than a swimsuit. It was about the continued diminishing of the soul of the place I loved the most.

I left the shop-that-wasn't-Peaches on a mission, determined to find the perfect swimsuit. I scoured Duvall Street, walking in one shop and out the other, empty handed. Up and down Duvall Street there was nothing that appealed to me. Wrong fabric. Wrong cut. Wrong size. Wrong elastic at the leg openings. Wrong everything. My last resort was Fast Buck Freddie's. Being more of a department store, I thought it less likely to have what I wanted but I strode in anyway, still a man on a mission. As I approached the swimwear department, I saw a wall of hundreds — perhaps thousands — of swimsuits. My fingers quickly flipped through all the suits in my size, medium. After a protracted search, they stopped at a little yellow and white striped number that was a lot like the suits I'd get at Peaches. I became hopeful. Nice fabric. Nice cut. I looked at the tag. Small. Damn. I lost hope. I looked for and located a salesperson who could not find the suit in any other size. I decided to try the small which didn't really seem too too small but it's kind of difficult to make a rear assessment on yourself. Especially my rear. Anyone knows that the wrong elastic can create love handles where love handles don't exist. And you can't depend on the honesty of a salesperson working on commission. I got dressed and disappointedly returned the suit to the wall. **As I exited Fast Buck Freddie's swimming suit-less, I wondered, along with all the other changes, "Was Key West's magic slipping away with its soul?"**

The next day as I was doing my Oasis pool thing, as would so frequently happen, fresh arrivals showed up. I really hit it off with one of them. He was a retailer and owned a clothing store in LA. Since I was a retail store designer; both of us being retail junkies on holiday had a lot to talk about. We loved the same stores and it was fun sharing similar feelings about so much in the retail world. After talking shop around the pool for the better part of the day, my new friend suggested we smoke a joint and shop Duvall Street together, high. Excellent idea! I loved shopping in Key West, high. I loved doing anything in Key West, high.

As we giddily moved from store to store, we were appropriately appalled by what we thought they were doing badly and we mutually applauded what they were doing well. As we entered Fast Buck Freddie's I spotted the swimwear wall and remembered the yellow and white suit I'd seen the day before. I'd already related the Peaches story so I asked him, if the suit was still there, would he give me an honest opinion? He agreed. As I fingered my way through the suits I located the yellow and white one and pulled it out for him to see. As I held it up, I didn't know how to read what I perceived to be a look of disapproval. How stoned was I? We'd agreed on most everything. Did he think it was wrong for me? Pushing the waistband down with his index finger to reveal the inside label, he said, "That's mine." I didn't understand. His? He wants it? Seeing that I was puzzled, he continued, "That's my suit. I own the company that made it."

And I was afraid the Key West Magic had slipped away. **I stood there astonished. After all my angst about Peaches closing, the hours spent in the quest for the perfect swimsuit, after finding one, on the entire island, just one (in the wrong size,) I managed to meet, the very next day, and take into the store, the owner of the company that made it!**

I tried "his suit" on and he agreed that I should have a medium. He assured me he could call LA and have a medium sent out next day air. He did just that and while he was at it, had them send a few other styles he thought I might like. The yellow and white striped suit in medium was a perfect fit. So were the others. I had an array of new swimsuits, gifted by the manufacturer himself. I couldn't have asked for a tidier solution to my Peaches problem. Apparently the Key West magic was still intact.

1994

Lying Flying Lesbian

IN THE HEAT AND HUMIDITY of a Key West afternoon I am standing in line behind an enormous lesbian waiting to check in for our Miami bound flight. Staring at a wall of suffocating plaid flannel in front of me, as I pull from my shoulder bag my boarding card, dampened by my still wet swimsuit, I inch my way toward the little makeshift looking counter for PBA Airlines which runs tiny planes from Miami to Key West and back.

The PBA gate agent asks the enormous lesbian: "What's your weight?"
The enormous lesbian answers the PBA gate agent: "160 pounds."
I stand there in total shock while the PBA employee's face registers nothing as he checks her in, scribbling something down without even a glance at her.
I approach the little makeshift looking desk and hand over my boarding pass.
The PBA gate agent, as he looks at my boarding pass asks: "What's your weight?"
I answer the PBA gate agent: "310 pounds."
Now he looks up, eyeing me suspiciously: "You're not 310 pounds."
I answer the PBA gate agent: "No I'm not but (discreetly signaling with my thumb toward the mountain of plaid that had just moved away) she's not 160. If she's gonna lie her weight down and I'm getting on that tiny little airplane with her, I'm lying mine up!"
Chuckling, smiling and shaking his head, the PBA gate agent scribbles something on his log and returns my boarding pass to me.

1994

Take The Roses

THE FIRST SUNDAY in June was a special day in Boston. Or in 1986 it became a special day with the first AIDS Walk. The yearly fundraiser 'From All Walks of Life' was held that year and every year thereafter. It was a 10K walk that raised money for the local AIDS Action Committee. **Always an emotional event, it became more and more so with each passing year and each passing friend as the already long list of names lost to the hideous disease grew longer.** We walked not only to raise money but also to remember and honor those we'd loved and lost and those who had walked before but were no longer physically able or no longer alive.

The Walk was also the unofficial start of summer. The morning of The Walk, Chase and I would host an annual brunch since our home in Beacon Hill was close to the walk's start (and end) on the nearby Esplanade. We'd have twenty or so friends in for quiche, mini-muffins, yogurt, fruit salad, mimosas, bloody marys and friendship. Post brunch it'd be off to the walk which started at the Esplanade's Hatch Shell. It was a sometimes sad but mostly joyful event of bright colors and balloons as we'd wind our way along the Charles River out to Brookline, returning through Cambridge and back to The Hatch Shell. Being Boston at its best, historic and mostly along the sparkling Charles River with its graceful bridges, it was also a favorite bicycle route of mine. I was only too thrilled to walk it with thousands of others in awareness-raising and remembrance.

I loved everything about the walk. I loved the friendship. I loved raising money for a good cause. I loved that it was spring and the near-endless New England winter had finally passed. I loved that it ushered in summer. I loved, in the wake of lost friends to be surrounded by fellow survivors; surviving for now at least as we never knew who among us wouldn't be around for next year's walk. I loved the celebration of these friendships. I loved the bonding. I loved being gay. I even loved how it brought back memories of the springtime loveliness of the May Processions of my Catholic youth. I especially loved one particular feature. At the end of the walk waiting at the far end of the final pedestrian bridge leading to the Hatch Shell, were people handing out roses. Those who completed the walk were presented, in a simple gracious act of thanks, a long stemmed rose by a smiling volunteer, arms laden with and surrounded by buckets of roses. Everybody got one. **The tradition of being thanked with a rose, a symbol of beauty and life, always struck me as so sweet, so special and so intrinsically…gay.** No sticker slapped on your t-shirt. Just a single full of life rose from one hand to another in appreciation for a walk well walked. I imagined it was a gay man who thought of handing out roses as a reward and I looked forward to receiving mine every year. Having been raised by a mother who grew roses and was an authority on them made me a rose lover all my life and this particular reward all the more special. Coming at the end of what was always an emotional walk, that rose, representing to me, life and beauty and so much of what I held precious in the world, had become over the years increasingly precious.

After the roses, back at the Hatch Shell there was a festival with informational booths, sales booths and of course food booths. There would also be musical entertainment and speeches both political and emotional. And balloons — rainbows of balloons. Toward the end of the event, when the walkers in the Hatch Shell area, arms wrapped around one another sang "That's What Friends Are For," there was hardly a dry eye. That song had become an anthem of the AIDS movement, honoring the way in which people, primarily gay people had come together to take care of their own in a world that at the time was at best dismissive of those suffering with the disease and at worst openly hostile. The communal singing of "That's What Friends Are For" created year after year an emotional, bonding moment. Tears were shed in sadness for friends lost and in joy remembering their lives. The pain and the suffering of the AIDS era — still going strong — were real and horrifying but on that one afternoon every year we all stood together and celebrated life. **For one afternoon you overlooked the possibility that this could be your last AIDS walk.** Year after year as the names added up, the impact of that song grew and took on greater and greater significance. As did, for me, the roses.

The AIDS Walk in 1994 was the first held after Chase's death. Gone for only eight months this would be the first 'first Sunday in June' that he would not be with me to host our annual brunch or walk the walk. I carried on without him, aware with each step, of his absence. It was a day to celebrate life and I was determined to do just that. It was also a day of remembrance and there'd be no question that I would indeed remember. It was one of those days when every minute held a different emotion. Walking surrounded by friends there were moments of profound sadness while other moments brought extreme joy. When at last, surrounded by the living, arms wrapped around each other and singing 'That's What Friends Are For,' the dead were there too. I was saddened to tears by the loss and grief I still felt while also relieved and grateful that the suffering (at least Chase's) was over. By the time they played that song, I couldn't distinguish between the sadness and the joy. I just stood there crying and singing surrounded by the living, grieving for the dead, shedding tears of happiness and grief, while clutching my long stemmed roses. **Yes roses...plural.**

At the end of what, though I didn't know it at the time, would be my final Boston AIDS Walk, as I crossed the last bridge before the Hatch Shell, I peered around the walkers trying to see if there were roses. Sometimes, especially I suppose in times of loss when so much is taken away, you worry that even something as seemingly insignificant as a rose at the end of a walk, will be taken away. No rose could be the last straw that would break my camel's back. As I searched up ahead I was relieved to see, as always, the volunteers, arms full of roses, happily handing out their long stemmed beauties. As I got closer, I saw that my rose-bearer was a boy, not just beautiful but almost supernaturally so. I studied his face the way I have always studied such faces trying to figure out what exactly makes them so beautiful. We all have two eyes, a nose and a mouth. How can there be that much difference? There is, and I continued to study the extraordinary difference of this twenty-something boy. He was dressed, just like me, all in white. White was an AIDS walk tradition of mine. His too maybe. **I locked eyes on him — of course — and approached reverentially as I always do when presented with such beauty whether it be a man, a woman, a piece of architecture, a sunset, a flower, or...a boy.** Not being able to avoid my penetrating gaze, he fixed his gaze right back on mine. We stayed that way locked on each other as I slowly among my friends and other walkers, made my way to him. Not taking his crystal-clear blue heavily lashed eyes from mine, he extended his hand with a rose. Not removing my eyes from his, I took it. We stayed that way his hand wrapped around the rose stem and mine around his, sharing it for a moment. I sadly, with the crush of walkers behind me, had to pull my hand and the rose away. As I made my way past him, our eyes were still locked on each other as our heads rotated in unison, looking back over our shoulders maintaining our gaze. As I got farther from him and almost out of sight all of a sudden those electric eyes flashed and he bolted toward me. As he reached me, that impossibly gorgeous face leaned in and planted a kiss squarely on my lips. With his lips pressed against mine, he pressed into my hands all the remaining roses he held in his. **Shocked by this unexpected act and still locked on those eyes, I stood freshly kissed and holding all those roses, frozen, in awe of this impetuous blue-eyed angel in white.** Our locked gaze was finally broken as he turned and dutifully rushed back to his station to continue handing out his roses. I was breathless as I ran to catch up with my friends.

I kept an eye on that boy during the festival, looking back toward the bridge to make certain he was still handing out his roses. There were walkers trailing in most of the afternoon keeping him at his post. After the emotional singing of "That's What Friends Are For" the trickle of walkers had pretty much dried up so I went back to the boy before he could get away. He was standing there arms still laden with roses waiting for a few stragglers. The eyes flashed again as they saw me approach. I immediately committed to memory the image of that angel in white with those eyes and that smile, and all those roses. We talked. Happily he was as charming and delightful as he was beautiful. I told him I lived on Beacon Hill just over the Fiedler Bridge and asked if he'd like to come see my place. **The agreeable angel said yes.**

On the other side of the Fiedler Bridge in my ivy-walled hidden garden in Beacon Hill surrounded by trees and flowers under a brilliant blue sky, my agreeable angel and I sat on a weathered antique English garden bench kissing and touching. There were stacks of roses scattered to either side of us — with so many leftovers what were we to do but take them with us? After removing his shirt I realized we'd gone as far as we could in that outdoor space which was only semi-private. While in the nighttime, under the cloak of darkness, I could pretty much do anything out there — and did — I didn't want to shock my Beacon Hill neighbors who in

Gay Boy's Life

the light of day, might have been peering out of a high window or two. I suggested we go inside. We stood and as I took the boy by his hand and began to step away, I had a thought. **I turned and whispered, "Take the roses."** He turned back to the bench and scooped them up. As he turned back toward me I studied that half naked angel of a boy surrounded by my carefully tended garden, his arms again laden with roses. I once again committed to memory, every perfect detail of him and of that precious moment.

I led my angel boy back to the rear bedroom, a summery sun-bleached, white-washed wood-paneled room with a white painted floor and pale blue ceiling. I flipped the switch that turned on the strands of twinkle lights that lined the walls and washed the room with warm sparkling light, and quite honestly had been installed there in hopeful anticipation of just this kind of moment. I took the roses from the angel, dropped them at the foot end of the bed and moved him around the side of it kissing him all the way. We stood there devouring each other and removing our clothing. When he was completely naked, I stepped back to appreciate the new view. He was all tan, smooth, trim naked perfection. His sharp speedo tan lines (just how I like them) framed the purest white skin clearly never touched by the sun. As I stood and appreciated the dazzling sight of a naked angel in my bedroom, he sat down on the edge of the bed never taking those sparkling baby-blues away from my own hungry appreciative eyes. He lay all the way down on the bed stretching out his tan body in sharp contrast to the crisp white linen sheets. His head was at the foot end of the bed and those impossibly blue eyes were looking up at me. Taking in the sight of this naked boy lying upside down on my bed and all those roses at his head, I asked "Have you ever been kissed upside-down?" He looked at me quizzically as I moved to the end of the bed and knelt down among all those roses. I leaned down and pressing my lips to his, we began to kiss. Passionately. Just like that. Upside down to each other. As we kissed, and our tongues explored each other's mouths I reached down and with each hand found a rose. I squeezed the rose heads tearing them away from the stems. Still kissing him I began sprinkling the rose petals all over and around his lithe body. I did this again and again while we kissed dropping more and more rose petals. I glanced up to see the pastel petals fluttering in the air and coming to rest on his smooth translucent skin and the crisp white sheets on which he lay. I was mesmerized by the sight of his perfect erect penis standing proudly from his wispy pubic patch and all those rose petals. **The smooth skin of the dick shaft was as pale as the lightest of the the blush colored petals and the swelling emerging head revealed itself to be a deeper rosier pink that matched the darker ones.** Leaning in closer and taking in a sweet spicy fragrance I couldn't quite tell was the boy or the rose petals or likely a combination of both, I immediately took that sturdy, rock hard piece of pink flesh into my mouth, devouring it before eventually devouring every one of his other rosy pink parts.

Lying there on my back, spent, with the boy's head on my chest, my arm cradling him and my fingers stroking his lower back, while removing an occasional crushed rose petal or two, I wondered if this angel hadn't somehow been sent to me by Chase. It was all too perfect: the extraordinary beauty of the boy in white, his having been tailor made to my own precise preferences including those dazzling blue eyes and speedo tan lines, his immediate response to me, the roses and especially the timing — on a day celebrating life and remembering loved ones, and in particular one special loved one, my recently departed Chase. Knowing about my since-childhood obsession with angels had he sent this one? It was all too perfect to have been a natural occurrence. Surely there was some supernatural force involved here and I half expected the boy to vanish at any second. **"It is good to have friends in high places," I thought with a satisfied smile as I sent a silent note of gratitude heavenward.**

The angel sighed a contented sigh and snuggled in a bit closer. Feeling his warm breath on my neck, I surveyed the smooth landscape of his naked body pressed against mine as my fingers found their way farther down his back and began to revisit a furrowed moist sweet spot I'd enjoyed only moments before. He groaned a little, pushed back against my finger, wriggling a bit to let it in and, nuzzling my neck, said in a sexy pleasured whisper that came from way down deep, "Yes, please," and then, "This is so wonderful. No, better than wonderful, this is…just…perfect." I kissed the top of his head, moved my lips to his ear and whispered, **"This is what happens when angels have sex."** In response he let out a contented purr accepted more of my finger and nuzzled his face in closer. "You know," I said to him in a whisper, "You have the most beautiful eyes I have ever seen." "No, you do," was his immediate response as his breathing deepened. "Mine? Mine are brown," I responded a little too quickly in a self-deprecating tone referencing my life-long dissatisfaction at not having blue eyes, "plain…old…brown." "You're kidding, right?" He said and then, in all earnestness, without even looking at them, "Your eyes aren't brown at all. Your eyes have deep green rings around the outside that change to gold with tiny flecks of green and brown and then they change again at the center to a kind of golden hazel. They are not "plain old brown" at all, and they are beautiful." He made me believe it.

The boy *was* an angel.

1958

Second Grade Saint

MICHAEL ANASTASIO, "you are a heretic!" That was the ancient old Sister Maria Thomas with one short sentence condemning me to burn in the eternal fires of hell for all eternity. Of course from a second grader's frame of reference, the "ancient" frowning face glaring its judgement over me may have been anywhere from 30 to death. I don't know. **What I do know is that I, only a second grader, had been deemed a heretic.** Quite a burden to try to place upon the dutiful shoulders of a well meaning gullible little boy of seven; all for the simple offense of questioning the concept of Original Sin.

For those who don't know about Original Sin, it's the sin with which we as good Catholic children were born. Apparently we came into this world not in a perfect state of grace but with a black stain on our white milk bottle souls. That's how our souls were illustrated to us back then. Three milk bottles drawn on a parochial school blackboard. One bottle was pure white — the perfect soul untouched by sin. Apparently the Blessed Virgin Mary was the only one to ever have one of these. How she got it I still do not know. The second bottle had the black stain of not-so-bad venial sin in the milk. Or was it on the bottle? **I was never quite sure.** The fact that it was white chalk on a black board made the whole enterprise backwards creating even more confusion. Anyway, it was just a single blotch. The rest of the milk was nice and white. The third bottle was entirely black with mortal sin. Black milk. Bad. Straight to Hell kinda bad.

So Original Sin had us entering the world with a black stain on (or in) our little white souls. That's why they came up with baptism. In order to cleanse our souls of this terrible stain and have any hope of entering the kingdom of Heaven, you had to be hauled into church in an over-sized, over-starched, embroidered white gown that somebody before you probably wore. **I'd always been secretly happy to know I had once**

been to church in a pretty white dress. Once there, they'd pour holy water over your little forehead and, with a couple of prayers, as if by magic, poof, you are now a child of god. Baptized, with a new set of potentially gift-giving "godparents." And what about the unlucky little children who happened to die before they got to partake in this wet, mystical event? Limbo. That was the best those poor little unbaptized unfortunates could hope for. Limbo was a nebulous place that, in my child's mind, was full of chubby, colorless, naked dead babies winglessly floating around in some murky, grey on grey, purposeless eternity.

I took issue with this. I hadn't done anything to earn a black blotch on my soul. I hadn't sinned. Someone else apparently had. Yet I got stuck with it. Their "original" sin. When pressing Sister Maria Thomas further for specific information regarding this "sin" (and our unfortunate inheritance of it,) she gave the class a colorful but dubious answer about the Garden of Eden…Adam and Eve…an apple…and a snake. Apparently "God" had expelled Adam and Eve from a garden for eating an apple and we ended up with their sin — The Original Sin. Seriously? All this over a snake? And an apple? God could really hold a grudge. It just didn't make sense. I could tell there was some critically important information being left out. **I had the feeling it probably had more to do with the fact that Adam and Eve were both naked. Yep. Naked.** I'd seen them that way in our big family bible and their nakedness interested me greatly. Well, Adam's did; Eve just looked lumpy. Naked Adam was shiny and muscle-y, and looking at him with his goods on display, gave me a very special feeling, but even at seven, I was wise enough not to bring any of this up in class. But when I did press further for more of an explanation as to why I, a little boy of seven, was being held accountable for some far-fetched, something a man a woman and a snake had done with an apple a long long time ago, naked, in a garden far far away (with the subtext that I thought this was exceedingly unfair and couldn't be correct,) I was summarily dismissed a heretic. At seven. I also knew better then, to even mention how I thought Adam and Eve could have saved us a lot of trouble if they'd just eaten the snake instead of the apple. First, god wouldn't have missed the snake. Second, there probably wouldn't be any snakes in the world today. Third and most important, we'd all still be naked in the Garden of Eden, and I wouldn't have to sit through this stupid class. And of course, there'd be no Satan. And no hell. I didn't bring this up either. **I just knew Sister Maria Thomas wouldn't be interested in any discussion of a world without hell.**

Heretic that I was, apparently headed in the opposite direction, I guess I could kiss goodbye to my eventual ascension into heaven. During the less interesting parts of the Mass, I'd quite frequently visualize this miraculous and (up until this heretic thing) inevitable event. I'd imagine the ceiling of our church opening to accept my glorious saintly departure from this mortal world. The architecture of our modern (some-day-it'll-be-a-gym) church worried me a bit as I couldn't quite figure out where the flat, beamed ceiling would open. There was no seam down the middle where it could elegantly separate, so the best I could figure was its awkwardly opening up on one side. Details like this always drove my little gay-Virgo-in-training crazy. I secretly wished we lived in a more Gothic parish with a church of a more inspiring style of architecture that would lend it's rib and groined-self better to my heavenly departure. However it would occur, after my saintly separation from the mortal bounds of this earthly existence, would come my inevitable canonization. Saint Mikey! So Sister Maria Thomas, standing in judgement over me, seemed intent on crushing my second grade sainthood plans. **The woman was incredibly accomplished at crushing things, especially little souls.**

Earlier that school year Sr. Maria Thomas had similarly trounced on my hopes of becoming an angel. When in class one day she asked "What do you want to be when you grow up?" I enthusiastically responded, "I want to be an angel!" I was immediately told, in no uncertain terms, that one could not *grow up* to become an angel. "Angel? You will never be an angel, Mr. Anastasio. One can not *become* an angel. Angels just are!" **This was not good news.** I was absolutely obsessed with angels and certain (up until I was presented with this new, dubious and unfortunate information) that I would someday become one. I was firmly convinced of the presence of legions of guardian angels that went everywhere with me protecting my every move and had been just as convinced that someday I too would become an angel and protect other little boys like myself. "What you can become if you live a very good life, Mr. Anastasio," pausing for stoic reverential emphasis, "is a saint." Nuns were quite fond of addressing seven year old boys as "Mr."

My lifelong obsession with angels had started with that previously mentioned family bible, a large, leather bound, gilded edition with full-color illustrations of Matthew, Mark, Luke, and John, the four evangelists, right on its front cover. Pretty magnanimous of the publishers to put the four authors on the cover (in gilded frames no less,) rather than on a flyleaf in the back of the book where most authors get stuck. Matthew, Mark, and Luke were old grey bearded guys but the younger John, my personal favorite with his long wavy hair, deep blue eyes and full pouty lips was really cute. I'd later, happily find out he was Jesus's favorite too. Anyway, our top of the line bible had, scattered throughout its pages, lustrous classical paintings reproduced in full glossy color. My favorites were the ones illustrating angels. Male Angels, typically depicted as haloed, extraordinarily beautiful young men with flowing golden blond hair, crystal-clear eyes, chiseled facial features, naked (or nearly-naked) ripped muscular gleaming bodies, perfect supernaturally glowing skin and always a set of ethereal white feathered (at times even gilded) wings attached to their impossibly muscular glistening backs.

Who wouldn't want to be an angel?

This was Catholic porn to the eager young eyes of a little gay boy in search of his identity. Given the endless hours I spent with our family bible, my parents must surely have been convinced they had on their hands the most religious, reverent little kid ever and (every Catholic parent's dream) a certain candidate for the priesthood. Little did they know my interest in that humongous book began and ended with its pictures of these heavenly, naked or nearly-naked male creatures. All I knew was that those pictures made me feel really really good and I couldn't stay away from them. **My favorite angel was my namesake, Michael, the finest example of these gorgeous role models.** He was an Archangel in fact — there were only three of them — and I was quite certain he was my own personal guardian angel. Michael was always depicted using his muscular sinewy legs to stomp on Satan — the treasonous newly demoted fourth archangel — driving him and all evil out of heaven forever. Saint Michael did this wielding a glorious silver sword while attired in the sheerest second skin of armor accentuating his squared-off pecs, protruding nipples, ripped abs and obliques with the merest suggestion of a short cute little gilded skirt barely obscuring his genitalia and emphasizing those spectacular thighs. **I was happy my name was Michael.**

So when Sister Maria Thomas announced one day that she would be having a class on angels, I was right-at-the-ready with my freshly sharpened yellow #2 Ticonderoga pencil (and two spares) firmly and eagerly grasped in my anxious little fist, feverishly awaiting any information she could give me on these ethereal winged beings. Finally a class I was interested in. **I was not much of a student and found a slight resentment in the concept of my needing to be taught things.** But here was a class I could really sink my teeth into. I was ready as a brand new kitchen sponge to soak up any information coming to me. There were things I wanted to know. Crucially important things. Were angels naked (or nearly-naked) all the time? Did they like being naked (or nearly-naked) all the time? Did god like them to be naked (or nearly-naked) all the time? Did they just fly around and sit around heaven naked (or nearly-naked) all day? Did they get to do other things naked (or nearly-naked?) Did they get to have naked (or nearly-naked) angel parties in heaven? If so, did the saints get to go too? If I become a saint do you think I can go? If so, is there any chance the saints get to be naked (or nearly-naked) at the angel parties? How did they get their naked (or nearly-naked) angel bodies so muscle-y? And shiny? And finally, who got to design and make their skimpy little angel outfits? Like I said, all the important stuff.

The class ended up being a little dryer than that. Devoid of any information regarding angel parties or angel nudity, it was mostly about angel hierarchy. **Catholics (especially nuns) it seems, are very big on hierarchy and nudity, not so much.** According to Sister Maria Thomas there are three spheres of angels encircling God with the first containing the Seraphim, Cherubim and Some-other-im that I could never remember. That was the ring closest to God. There were two more rings. The second I also don't remember much about but the third ring contained the Archangels and your garden variety messenger angels. This is where my greatest interest lay as Saint Michael was an Archangel and all my other favorites in paintings were frequently delivering news. This was the ring, it seemed to me, where all the beautiful boy angels probably hung out — naked (or nearly-naked.) And where I wanted to end up — (naked or nearly-naked) with them. It was also the likeliest ring to have all the best angel parties. Seemed logical.

While all of my unasked questions went unanswered, at least the description of the circular angel motif had given me a glimpse as to how their angel parties might be set up. So...even with this lack of all the important angel intelligence that I had hoped for, I was still spurred on to do some "extra-credit" work at home after dinner that night. I had rarely (if ever) been so motivated but this was, after all, about angels. Armed with all my second grader art supplies I went to work recreating in full-crayola splendor, what Sister Maria Thomas had tried to illustrate on her black chalkboard with one single piece of underachieving white chalk. Row after colorful row of angels were being sumptuously illustrated in a fashion unmatched even by my cherished family bible. I used every item in my second grader's artistic arsenal to create the finest example of angel art a seven year old had ever imagined. Surely the same supernatural power that influenced those great classical artists' creations in our bible was at work here. **The saints and angels themselves were guiding my chubby little boy fingers flying over the manila drawing paper as my masterpiece took shape.** Just before bedtime, my creation was complete and with great pride I studied the outcome. Row after lavishly illustrated row of heavenly haloed and winged beings encircled God in the glorious heaven of a seven-year-old's mind. Rays of golden light emanated from the center, clouds of white and pink and blue along with dozens of gold lick-and-stick stars encircled the entire angel extravaganza. I was astonished that I could have created anything of such beauty and grandeur. This was certainly a great artistic achievement worthy of the pages of our family bible.

I went to bed that night as I always had, firmly convinced of the legions of angels surrounding and protecting me. I could barely get to sleep consumed by a combination of pride in my great artistic accomplishment and my unbridled enthusiastic anticipation for the moment tomorrow morning when I would proudly place my extraordinary masterpiece into Sr. Maria Thomas's outstretched, grateful hands!

Sometimes actual events don't quite match up to our level of expectation.

So excited was I to hand in my extra credit project that I didn't even remove my coat and hat before marching right up to Sister Maria Thomas's enormous wooden desk and proudly presenting her with my drawing. Never had I so boldly approached that dark brown massive, frightening piece of authoritarian furniture with its starched, ever-disapproving black and white presence seated behind it, but I was on a mission. She snatched it from me without, as far as I could see, even a glance at it and promptly told me to take off my coat and sit down. The day played out as pretty much every second grade day had ever played out. Classes, recess, classes, classes, lunch, classes, classes, and more classes. While I had had fantasies of my masterpiece being enthusiastically shared with the rest of the class, it just stayed on that desk getting buried under layer after layer of the detritus of a teacher's day. I eventually lost track of it while I remained ever hopeful that at some point it would be pulled out from wherever it had gone, and would be presented and appreciated for the great work it was. **As the day waned so did my enthusiasm for Sister Maria Thomas's appreciation for and sharing of my great artistic effort.** Maybe tomorrow. That's it! Of course. She hadn't actually even seen it yet. When she gets back to the convent tonight and has a chance to really study my extraordinary masterpiece in all its glory and splendor she'll certainly share it with the class tomorrow. In fact, it'll probably already be displayed on the bulletin board when we arrive tomorrow morning. Of course. That's it. I could see it there already. I'd just have to be patient, wait and go about my business.

My business. **Nuns were famous in those days for their use of child slave labor.** We kids were enlisted for all sorts of menial chores and mine, quite frequently, was to take the garbage outside at the end of the day and empty it into the Dempster Dumpster. I do not know why, but the nuns, to a one, always referred to it as the "Dempster Dumpster" as if the big green waste receptacle that took up a significant piece of real estate at the rear of our school had a first and last name. I wasn't the perfect candidate for this task. Being quite small for my age, I had always experienced some difficulty in getting the garbage from the can to the dumpster's square opening which was well above my head. The nuns never seemed to take into account such physical limitations when assigning tasks. I was much better suited to things like, say, clapping erasers, putting chalk back into the boxes and into the storage cabinet or straightening the rows of desks — tasks a little closer to the ground.

That particular afternoon was especially cold and blustery and I was coatless and shivering. As I reached the dumpster, I did a little sign of the cross and gave it my best thrust trying to propel the garbage out of the can aiming it right at the opening. At that moment a big gust of wind came up and I stood there being showered with all the garbage that didn't make it to the opening, which is to say, all of the garbage. I threw down the can and immediately scurried all over the asphalt trying to retrieve as many pieces of airborne paper as I could, knowing the punishment I would surely receive for littering the playground. The wrath of the nuns for such simple infractions was legendary in the days of baby-boom parochial school education. We were all victims at one point or another. The larger crumpled pieces of paper were easier to chase down, grab and place back into the can but the smaller tiny torn shreds of paper swirling in the air around me were almost impossible to catch or gather. Having eventually settled to the ground, the papers were everywhere, requiring me to get down and crawl around picking up each tiny piece individually. On the cold grey asphalt of the St. Stephen Martyr Grade School playground/parking lot, on my hands and knees, pinching the small shreds of paper now stuck to the ground, the colorful mosaic of garbage under me began to look familiar. **The tiny shreds of crayoned artwork covering the pavement revealed an angel wing here, a halo there, a piece of a ray of light, a gold star, a haloed head, pink and blue cloud parts, Angel parts and more gold stars.** I realized with a jolt, tears welling in my eyes, that the garbage surrounding me, the small bits of colorful paper I was retrieving were actually, unbelievably, the tiny shredded scattered pieces of what had once, just that morning in fact, been my great artistic masterpiece. My glorious creation had in a simple ruthless act been ripped to shreds and turned into mere litter by an insensitive teacher's hand.

I knelt there surrounded by an angel-littered landscape. Tears streaming down my seven year old face and staring at the shredded bits of my great artistic achievement, I had no choice but to treat my cherished angels, now in pieces, as just so much garbage littering the ground. I had to suffer the indignity of pinching each little piece of what was left of my masterpiece off the ground and toss it into the can. My angel art was now garbage and had to be dealt with as such.

Sr. Maria Thomas had torn my precious work to shreds, summarily tossing it into the garbage and with it, a portion of my childhood exuberance and naiveté. I understand now that along with my masterpiece she had also tossed into that garbage can her own credibility. As Catholic children we were taught that in the spiritual hierarchy of the church, nuns and priests were somewhere between us and God, giving them a kind of near-infallibility and granting them exceptional power to influence our impressionable questioning young minds. When they spoke to us they spoke with the voice of God, or so we were told. With her one callous act she had begun to relinquish her power over me (and that of so many who came after her) for I think I understood, even at such a young age, that this could not have been the hand of God at work. God wouldn't tear a second grader's artwork to shreds. No that was not God's work but instead the work of a flawed and fallible human being.

So later in the year, during a discussion of original sin, when Sister Maria Thomas branded me a heretic, her remark fell hollow on my young but wizened ears.

1994

John Hancock Lights

WHENEVER I would spend Gay Pride in New York City, I loved The Empire State Building's changing it's crown lights to lavender washing the top dozen or so floors and needle in that signature gay color for the entire weekend. It was such a positive, affirming and validating gesture by those in charge. Unlike today, it wasn't easy back then to change such lights. It was a big deal. I mean really, if The Empire State Building would go through all the trouble to change it's lights for us then we must really be making headway in the culture of acceptance. In New York City at any rate.

After New York Gay Pride 1993, as I was making my way through Boston's Public Garden, I glanced up at The John Hancock Tower. Not the newer sixty story I. M. Pai minimalist skyscraper, but the older 26 story Art Deco treasure just next door. It's a building I had always loved — both it and its reflection in the newer, angled, glass monolith next to it. In the hypodermic-looking needle topping that lovely building — what I always referred to as "The Top of the Cock" — are glass panels, lit from within, that tell by the change in color, the weather for all of Boston, or at least all those in Back Bay, who could see it. There was a poem about it:

> Steady blue, fair skies for you,
> Flashing blue, a change is due,
> Steady red, rain ahead,
> Flashing red, snow instead.

And if the lights were flashing red during the summer that meant, in true Boston form, that the Red Sox game had been cancelled.

Looking at that illuminated needle, and having recently seen the Empire State Building lavender-lit, it occurred to me that both colors necessary for lavender were there. The red and blue lights, if turned on together, were both pale enough to make lavender. Wouldn't it be great if the John Hancock followed The Empire State Building's lead and lit itself up lavender to commemorate Gay Pride? And it'd be so easy.

I became obsessed with the idea but did nothing about it allowing my typical can't-do attitude to mix with another voice of negativity reminding me that this was not New York but Boston. And conservative John Hancock. There'd be no convincing those starched Boston businessmen to use their landmark building in commemoration of pride in anything but insurance. And the weather. And the Red Sox.

Still, I remained obsessed. Every day as I would walk through The Public Garden or through the streets of the Back Bay and look up at that needle I would imagine it lavender. It became a thing. **Each time the John Hancock Tower caught my eye, I would visualize its needle, lavender.** My mind would change the colors. Steady blue — lavender. Flashing blue — lavender. Steady red — lavender. Flashing red — lavender. No matter the day, the month, the season, the weather, or the state of the Red Sox, I would visualize lavender. This went on for an entire year. Everybody needs a hobby.

When Gay Pride weekend finally arrived in Boston, that Friday as I was walking once again through The Public Garden on my way to the gym, I glanced up as usual to The John Hancock needle ready to visualize it lavender. I didn't have to. It was lavender! I had to take a really good look to make absolutely certain that I was seeing what I was seeing. I thought for a moment that perhaps I had visualized it that way so often that my eyes were playing tricks on me. They weren't. **The needle lights were lavender.**

Oh my god I thought, someone else had the idea and had done something about it. Whoever it was had gotten through to the John Hancock hierarchy and they had obliged. Or perhaps they'd come up with the idea on their own. How wonderful. I wondered who it was and spent the entire weekend pointing the lights out to friends and acquaintances asking if they had any idea who was responsible. I wanted to thank whomever it was for so graciously granting my unexpressed wish. No one knew. The lights remained lavender for the entire Gay Pride weekend and my questions as to the who and the how of it went unanswered. No one seemed to know anything about those lavender lights.

Weeks went by without answers and I had pretty much let go of the whole thing. One day on my way to the gym I swung past my friend Jay's apartment to pick up his out of town friend who wanted to work out. We headed off to the gym together and while walking through Back Bay I pointed out the needle on The John Hancock Tower and told him about the lavender lights. "Do you think it was your visualization that did it?" he asked in all seriousness, "you might have manifested it." I made a mental note of the word "manifested" as I answered, "Well, the thought had crossed my mind. I do believe in visualization so I guess I'd have to accept the possibility," I replied, "though I'm putting my money on an enterprising gay custodian who got his way." "Even so," he continued, "you could be responsible for triggering him to do it."

Later at the gym while working out, I spotted a copy of Bay Windows, the local gay rag that someone had left on the floor next to the machine we were using. Sitting there in between sets, I glanced down, ready to be annoyed by the inconsiderate person who'd left it there. The headline, **"John Hancock Lavender Lights**

Still a Mystery" practically shouted at me. The gist of the article was about how no one at John Hancock was responsible for changing the lights to lavender that Gay Pride weekend. No one had taken responsibility and no one knew how it had happened. Whether it was a fluke, some sort of malfunction, or an overzealous gay person with access (my imagined custodian?) the gay pride lavender lights remained a mystery. **A mystery to everyone, that is, except perhaps, to me.**

1994

A Hidden Garden Opens Up

THERE WAS ONE FINAL GARDEN TOUR after Chase passed away. Even without the wisteria the garden had never looked better. The new tree had taken hold and was a beauty. I had planted a new wisteria and a white clematis where the old wisteria had been. They had taken hold and were growing well and blooming together. The white azalea was in full bloom lighting the center of the garden. I had the table set for tea and had made a ridiculously large abundant flower arrangement for the center of it. **At the last minute I made a little tribute to Chase.** Using a black and white smiling photograph of him, I affixed a tiny red AIDS ribbon to it and put it on a small gold easel. I placed the easel on the little triangular porch with a miniature flower arrangement I'd made, and next to it a small lighted votive candle. Just to the right of the easel I attached a note that said, "In Dedication to My Partner Chase Who for Ten Years Shared My Life, My Love, and My Garden."

24 Cedar Lane Way was more popular than ever that last year of the tour. As people (mostly women) left the garden, having seen my little tribute, they hugged and kissed me. Some pressed hurriedly written notes of condolence into my hands. Many had visited my garden before, and this time they learned more about me than about my flowers. They were moved. And so was *The New York Times*. The paper had come that year to do an article on The Hidden Gardens of Beacon Hill. Part of the article, which appeared in the next Sunday's edition across the banner on the back page of the front section above the Bloomingdales ad, was about my garden. They made special mention of the dedication to Chase. **We made *The New York Times*!**

In addition to its being a once a year showplace, that peaceful hidden garden became my refuge and my strength. It was in that garden that, for the first time in fact, I became still. In that stillness, now dedicated to a life of service and surrounded by all the blossoming life I'd nurtured around me, the universe began to open up to me much as it had while floating on a pool in Key West. **Turns out contrary to what the nuns of my youth were famous for saying, an idle mind is *not* the devil's workshop, but rather God's playground.** While not being a questioning person, in the nurturing balance of that garden, much the same as the nurturing balance of a Key West pool, sometimes a little high, with my brain dialed back by the weed and my observational skills enhanced, I would receive answers before I'd even thought up the questions. Seeds planted long before by my gardening friend Miss Garrison, also took hold. I embraced all this information as fact as it came, I was certain, from a voice inside me, not a process of my mind but of the spirit, connecting me to overall undeniable truths that lay deep within me (as they do within us all) connecting me with the universe itself and all its universal truths. I didn't think to ask for more.

Some of the truths I learned in my garden:

Racism and Intolerance:
I noticed that in the middle of a bed of pink impatiens, a single little lavender petunia had somehow managed to spring up. The majority impatiens did not squeeze out that brave little minority petunia. The impatiens didn't seem at all threatened by the existence among them of a volunteer flower that was different but instead seemed happy to allow that little petunia to grow and flourish. **The impatiens seemed content simply providing a background for that one single petunia who was different to stand out.** Weeds on the other hand, when allowed to grow, once a majority and by virtue of their preeminence, will overtake a single flower, strangling it and pressing it into nonexistence.

Parenting and Acceptance:
I would buy what I thought to be a full flat of not yet blooming begonias. Once planted and blossoming, a plant would turn out to be something else — surprise — not a begonia at all but let's say, a zinnia. **Just because it turned out to be different from what I'd expected it to be I didn't love it any less.** I had to accept that it could not change nor could I change it. There was no way that little zinnia was ever going to be a begonia. I didn't turn my back on it or pull out that determined blossoming little individual. Even though it didn't turn out as expected, I gave it all the love and care I'd have given it otherwise and all the love and care I gave the others.

Aggression and Peaceful Coexistence:
Working in the garden going about my business of deadheading or weeding or feeding or watering, I would do so with bees flying here and there all around me. We, the bees and I would work side by side, each aware of the power we had to inflict pain and suffering and even death on the other. We never exercised that power. We didn't need to. There was no aggression from either side as we went about the same task of tending our garden. And there was no fear. The bees could have swarmed and attacked me but didn't knowing instinctively I am at one with their world. I could have swatted them away or sprayed them with some chemical but chose not to as I know just as instinctively that they are not threatened by my presence among them. **We would go about our business happily devoted to the same task peacefully coexisting with each other.** At harmony sharing the same universe.

Free Will and Acceptance Of A Greater Power:
A flower doesn't know its place in the garden. It doesn't have the perspective of the gardener to understand its participation in the overall design of the garden. It's point of view is limited to its immediate surroundings. **A flower must be content in knowing there is an overall plan and accept its place in that plan.** That individual flower's job is to grow and blossom to the best of its ability wherever the gardener has placed it. That is all that is required of it. If each flower in a garden decided it wanted to be somewhere else and relocated itself accordingly, the gardener's design would be lost.

Patience:
Don't rush things. **A flower will bloom when a flower will bloom.**

1994

Angels & Aircraft Carriers

IT WAS THE LAST WEEKEND IN JUNE 1994, just eight months after Chase's passing. It was also the Twenty-fifth Anniversary of The Stonewall Rebellion and Gay Pride Weekend in New York. Add to that the Gay Games which were also in town and New York City was GAY. Or for that one weekend, it certainly seemed so. Clued-in straight New Yorkers had fled the city — it was their only defense — and gay people overran it. I had travelled to New York with a group of friends from Boston and, as we made our way to the big White Party on the top deck of *The Intrepid*, an aircraft carrier moored on the Hudson River at 46th Street, we were all dressed in our requisite white, or more precisely undressed in our requisite white. It was still the age of the short short so making our way past London Terrace, to a one, we wore tiny white shorts (well, in truth there was one tutu; thank you, Jay.) As we were coursing through the streets of Manhattan en-masse in this nearly-naked state, everywhere I looked I could see similarly undressed boys in their abbreviated white shorts, little more than underwear really, all making their white sneakered and black booted way through the sultry New York night. **As we got closer to *The Intrepid* there were more and more boys filtering in from all the side streets, gay fireflies studding the night and lighting the darkness of the Westside Highway with their party whites.** The sight of all this, believe it or not, snapped me back to my Louisville childhood.

Having a father who was a native New Yorker, my family and I, during my youth, were occasional visitors to the city. I had a deep fascination with all things New York and considered myself to be a displaced New Yorker, my Kentucky existence merely a holding pattern until I could eventually land where I knew I belonged. Horny kid that I was with a particularly vivid imagination, New York worked its way into many of my little boy fantasies about the things that might go on in that big sexy city and how I might happily participate in them. The walk to *The Intrepid* that night brought back one of my favorite little boy fantasies that I'd put to paper about one hot summer weekend in a New York populated only by boys in their underpants. **An already well-established fan of outdoor near-nudity, my most vivid fantasies took place in the heat and humidity of summer where people often ran around in as little as they could get away with.** And people wonder about my love of heat and humidity. Anyway, this particularly naive, juvenile fantasy had boys (myself included) running all over the streets and neighborhoods of New York nearly-naked in our little tighty-whities doing all sorts of things that at the time I could only imagine. On that walk to *The Intrepid*, warmed by the memory of my heated summer fantasy, I looked around and marveled at the accuracy of my current circumstance compared to what I had conjured up and written about so many years before. Boys, everywhere, boys in their underwear overrunning the streets of New York. I was living my little boy dream. Perhaps, I wondered, could I have actually manifested the entire thing? Was it a child's wish so heady and pure it couldn't help but be fulfilled by an accommodating universe? A universe that is, with its own sense of timing as it only took thirty or so years of my patiently waiting for it to work its wondrous ways. Whatever the case I could consider that particular fantasy — fulfilled, along with yet another universal lesson in patience.

Fantasy fulfillment aside, white parties were always my favorite of the big gay circuit events for another very real reason. I love dancing amidst thousands of boys clad only in their skimpy white. As an early fan of black light (since my 1960s high school dance decorating days,) I love how it takes white and gives it a glowing luminescence. Being surrounded in the dark by nearly-naked dancing boys awash in the day-glow light, their glistening sweat adding to their ethereal sheen is nothing short of pure magic. Glowing-white and dancing the night away was so positive, so uplifting and so much at odds with the dark days of AIDS. It was an era of pain. Suffering and death were everywhere. The white parties would wash you in that ethereal light, driving the darkness somewhere out beyond the perimeter of the parties. For those few hours of escape and complete abandon, it was as if none of the horrors of that dreaded disease existed. With so much death around, it was great just to be alive. And dance. We could put on something white, get a little high and for a night step out of the real and terrifying world of AIDS. **We'd joyfully dance the night away with friends and pretend that we'd all be alive for the next white party.** All the circuit parties (most of them ironically fund raisers against the disease) were escapist like that but the white parties especially had the ability to lift me up and take me away completely from the AIDS horror show. I could focus, for a short time at least, on joy rather than sorrow. Light rather than darkness. Life rather than death.

And then there are the angels. With my childhood angel obsession instigated by our family bible and it's gorgeous illustrations, white parties are the closest I have ever been to my naive youthful fantasies about angels and their heavenly parties. It is no secret that the gay community is populated with some of the most gloriously beautiful boys on the planet. Well-groomed and well-gym-ed, they bear a striking resemblance to my beloved bible angels. **Dress these gorgeous boys in white-practically-nothing and surround me with them on a dance floor and I am right in the middle of the angel parties my actively gay young mind conjured up and tried to illustrate so many years before in the quiet privacy of my upstairs bedroom.** As I survey the glowing dancing boyscape surrounding me, I can almost see the shining halos appearing above the heads of these incandescent golden boys and the wings sprouting from their broad muscular backs. They are the near-naked angels of my heavenly childhood desire dancing at the near-naked angel parties I'd so hoped to attend.

Suffice it to say then, I love a good white party and the party on the top deck of *The Intrepid* that very special June night was no exception. It was in fact the Nth degree of white parties. Had I thought to make a list of favorite things as a youngster, boys in their underpants, sleek jet airplanes and New York City would have been right at the top. Dancing among jet aircraft then, perched around the perimeter of the top deck of an actual aircraft carrier with a thousand (more or less) nearly-naked boys in their tiny whites, all of it wrapped in the glittering embrace of New York City, was a night tailor made to my own rather precise, youthful specifications. Add to that some of my newer favorite things; high-energy music, ultra-violet light and laser beams shooting off into the dark blue eternity of a New York City night sky and there I was at my perfect party.

It was a supernatural night of pure New York City magic with the Angels out in abundance. The music was high energy and so were the boys. It all played out against the sparkling New York City midtown skyline dominated by The Empire State Building bathed in lavender by its crown lights once again kindly color-adjusted just for Gay Pride weekend. The stars above us, the city to the east, the Hudson River to the west, the airplanes and the boys — angels all, whether mortal or immortal — made it a night to go down in party history and one that would etch itself permanently in my memory. It was a warm summer night of airplane wings and angel wings and it could have happened only in New York.

Sadly, parties can't go on forever — well, at least, not the earthly ones. So as this particular one drew to a much-too-early-end and the last dance was over, the partiers, myself included, reluctantly started to move toward the exits. I was not ready to let that special evening go but the party was over. Or so I thought. Unexpectedly (and happily) the music started again. **A solo clarinet slid into a series of notes piercing the nighttime sky over the top deck of** *The Intrepid*. I recognized the notes immediately, as the bar of music that opens George Gershwin's "Rhapsody In Blue" or as I called it when I was a little boy, "New York Music."

I don't know why but that particular semi-classical piece was New York City to my young ears. It embodied all I imagined about that big bold mythical city and it was my favorite piece of music in our family library of record albums. I'd play it incessantly on our big wooden console stereo while laying on our living room floor wrapped in the lavish orchestrations and piano virtuosity of Mr. Gershwin's classical/jazz masterpiece. Eyes closed, I'd dream of New York City and the magic it would someday hold for me.

So there I was on the top deck of *The Intrepid* Aircraft Carrier at the end of the most fabulous party ever, with a sparkling CinemaScope New York City skyline as a back drop. **Still surrounded by legions of boys no longer moving to the exits, and with my favorite piece of music ever, my New York music, playing, I had no choice; I had to dance.** Lost in my own little world with that gorgeous New York night and that fabulous piece of music I'd grown up with and cherished, I began to move. Having listened to "Rhapsody In Blue" god knows how many times, I knew it by heart in its sixteen minute thirty–one second entirety. I don't know that I'd ever imagined choreography for the piece but I certainly knew it well enough to attach my own right then and there and so I did. Buoyed by the supernatural evening and the energy surrounding it, I flew into what can only be described as a performance! Well, some might have described it as making a spectacle of myself but I didn't care. **I was on the top deck of a fucking aircraft carrier in New York City Harbor at the end of the most fabulous party I'd ever attended, surrounded by angels, dancing to my all-time favorite piece of music — "Rhapsody In Blue" — my New York Music!** The most vivid of my childhood fantasies could not have matched this night or this moment as I danced, arms flung to the heavens and fingers flying across the keyboard of some unseen air–piano. The boys not proceeding to the exits pulled away and formed that inevitable angel circle around me. Some were, I suspect, simply staring, at what, they weren't quite sure, but others were cheering me on, engaged as was I in the energy, the music, the spectacular setting and the magic of the night.

Among the cheering circle I noticed one boy so focused on me that even in my almost trancelike state, I could not have possibly overlooked him. Or his angelic beauty. Yes, another one! He with his dazzling smile and bright sparkling eyes, was focused on my every move. His energy, which he generously lavished upon me, perfectly matched my own. It's not often enough that I capture the gaze of such a boy so when I do, I am not about to lose it. Every time I turned his way, our eyes would meet and I'd stayed locked on him. We were one. He'd flash that smile, beam his energy at me and cheer me on. Connected, I'd simply absorb him and his glowing energy and send it right back. **We remained energetically connected that way throughout the entirety of "Rhapsody In Blue."** Fed by his energy and the cheering others, as the music swelled into the lushly romantic main theme (my favorite part), I turned my focus specifically toward him, continuing to send his generous spirit right back, as we energized each other and shared the final moments of that heavenly music and that heavenly night.

As the music moved through its final crescendo, and came to an end, so did my dancing. The circle burst into applause and suddenly, back down to earth, I became more self-aware and a little embarrassed. The applause ended and as the rest of the group began to move away, the smiling boy left his friends and moved toward me. He came right up to me and leaned in. Close. We were eye to eye. I thought I was about to be kissed… but his mouth went instead to my ear. **Slowly and deliberately, his warm breath caressing my ear, in** a hushed whisper meant only for me, he said, "I saw your wings." I pulled away just far enough to look him in the eyes, wondering if I'd heard what I'd heard. He smiled and once again, leaned into my ear and this time he spoke even slower and more deliberately. **"While you were dancing... I... could... see... your... wings."** He pulled away, looked me right in my surely astonished eyes, gave an affirming nod and once again flashed that dazzling smile. He then turned, joined his waiting friends and disappeared into the New York night.

NEW YORK

I'm

just

throwing myself

into

the universe

and

I

expect

to be

embraced!

1951 & 1961

Aunt Jean At Idlewild

MY CHILDHOOD FASCINATION with airplanes has never died. More than a fascination, actually it is an ongoing love affair. I was an early flier, my first flight at three months old, being well before my ability to remember. That flight was on a Constellation, for my money, easily the most romantic of all airliners. The Constellation was used in countless films of the 1950s sitting majestically on the tarmac with its swooping dolphin-like fuselage and elegant triple fin tail, waiting to be boarded by some glamorous movie star or, in flight — soaring above equally glamorous New York City, or Paris, or Rome. **It was pure romance at 30,000 feet.** Having no memory of that first flight, I cherish the airline ticket that my mother so graciously saved for me. It was more of a book, really, with a gorgeous drawing of the Constellation on its cover and inside, its pages were all handwritten. Eastern Airlines. Dec 25. Child's Fare. Forty five dollars.

I have often wondered if, on that first flight, I might have been the screaming baby that everyone dreads. It's an image that flies in the face of the romantic notion I have of my mom, dad, brother and sister all dressed to the nines and me wrapped in blankets and nestled asleep in my mother's arms blissfully unaware we were making our way in that great airliner to that great city, winging our way over it just like in the movies I would love in years to come. New York City was the destination that Christmas 1951, and more specifically, Columbus Ave at 68th Street. That was where my father had grown up and where my Positano-born grandmother still lived in a walk up railroad flat.

My childhood fascination with New York City also has never died. More than a fascination actually, it too is an ongoing love affair. **Seeing New York in all those glamorous movies and having a father who grew up there, I was ever that displaced New Yorker just waiting until that great city called me home.** Like Dorothy from Kansas, I had my own childhood Emerald City — New York, and I couldn't wait to get there. It was a dream place that appealed to my young gay boy sensibilities. It was big and sophisticated and glamorous. And sexy. People dressed up there and did interesting things. I knew that. Once again, I'd seen the movies. Thankfully we made many subsequent trips to New York, ones that I would actually remember. Every few years in fact, we would fly there to sightsee and visit my Italian grandmother, aunts, uncles and cousins. And every few years there was a new type of airliner to get us there. Airplanes and New York went hand in hand. For my youthful purposes you couldn't have one without the other.

On those trips to New York we would always change planes in Washington, DC as there were no direct flights to New York from Louisville. That was fine by me as it meant more opportunities for more planes. One year while waiting in the Washington airport in the middle of the night for our flight to NYC — it was always the middle of the night as night flights were more affordable for families — my older brother Frank took me to the window and pointed to the plane we were going to be boarding. "Look," he said excitedly, "that's our plane. It has jet engines!" I could hardly believe my ears or contain my excitement. Jet engines! Down the side of the plane was written, "Eastern Airlines Prop-Jet Electra." Prop-Jet! Electra! All of it written in gold lettering trimmed out in red. And it was a "Golden Falcon!" It said that too. **Golden Falcon and Prop-Jet Electra instantly became my new favorite words. With its gold and red propellers and a red-trimmed stylized Golden Falcon logo on the tail, it became my new object of desire. I was in**

love at first flight. It was quite possibly the most exquisite thing my young eyes had ever seen. And it was ours. For the next couple of hours at least. I didn't know that an airplane could have both propellers and jet engines but this glamorous airliner did. I couldn't take my eyes off it and I was so glad I didn't because as I stood there, nose pressed up against the glass with my hands shielding out any offending light, I saw the door of that gorgeous aircraft suddenly slide up under its metal skin and disappear completely; like the futuristic spaceship in *The Day The Earth Stood Still* — a favorite film that just happened to come out the same month and year as my birth — September, 1951 — also the year of my first flight. Once the door was out of sight, just as suddenly, a set of steps magically unfolded out and down to the tarmac revealing not alien robot Gort, but a stylish stewardess framed by the doorway. I stood there mesmerized by the sight, as the sound of my name being called brought me back to earth. It was my mom. This incredible flying machine was now ready to board and we were the lucky individuals who got to board it. My heart was beating wildly as we stepped out onto the tarmac and approached that heavenly airliner just sitting there ready to gobble us up and take us to Idlewild Airport in New York, the city of my dreams.

Upon boarding we were given an area in the front of the plane where the seats faced each other. Was there no end to the surprises this aircraft held? I eagerly surveyed the cabin, wide-eyed and captivated by the sleek ultra modern interior with gold trim everywhere. Every feature of this luxurious airliner sparked my little gay boy sensibilities. I was a sucker for pretty details and this plane was full of them. There were even gold brocade curtains at the windows. The inflight food and drinks were served on real china and glasses with the same Golden Falcon logo as on the tail of the plane. **I forced myself to stay awake for the entire flight as it was clear this would be the most glamorous experience of my short life and I was not about to miss one gorgeous minute of it.** After landing at Idlewild, the smiling immaculately turned out stewardess in her smart little stewardess pumps, with her smart little stewardess hat perched over her French twist stewardess hairdo, let me push the button that would make the sliding door and stairs do their magical thing. Me! I got to open the door! I was so excited I'm sure I almost passed out.

We walked down the magic steps out onto the tarmac and into the terminal where my Aunt Jean and her boyfriend were waiting to collect us. I was surprised to see my Aunt Jean was wearing a black sequined cocktail dress and her boyfriend was in a tuxedo. I was dazzled but confused. Aunt Jean, an executive secretary in a cosmetics firm, was easily the best dressed, most sophisticated and worldly of all my New York relatives but this was way beyond anything I had expected even of her. When I had the opportunity, I pulled my mother aside and asked why Aunt Jean and her friend had gotten so dressed up to pick us up at the airport. "Oh, Mikey," my mom said with a chuckle, "they didn't dress like that to pick us up. They went out last night all dressed up. They must have stayed out all night and just came straight to the airport."

A moment passed as I processed this information. Stayed out all night! Dressed like that! Came to the airport! WHAM! My ten year old mind was blown! **That precise moment was the Big Bang of my young life; my concept of the world changed with that one sentence from my mother.** Oh my god, there are people, real people, who get all dressed up and stay out all night long and then go off to the airport in the morning to pick people up! Still up from the night before! Still in sequins and black tie! And a place where this is possible. New York! My world had stopped for a moment and then expanded exponentially as I pondered my mother's wonderful words. I and my little world would never be the same. I mean, I had seen movies where people would go out in New York all dressed up and names like "Tropicana," "Latin Quarter," and "Copacabana" would flash by. But they were movie people and I never imagined them staying out all-night-long. Was there no end to the glamour of New York City? **This was indeed crucially important new information and I knew at that moment, someday, I would get all dressed up and stay out all night long, dining or dancing or doing whatever it was that kept my aunt and her boyfriend up all night; things that at the time I could only imagine.** Someday, most assuredly, I would leave my little Louisville existence and do all these things. In New York City. My New York City. I could see it so clearly I wouldn't have doubted it for a moment. And I'd no longer need a plane to get there because "there" is where I would live.

1994

Moving On

I LEARNED SOMETHING about making blanket statements. Don't. **A blanket statement is a challenge to the universe — a universe that typically has other ideas.** It was time to move on from Boston and when asked where I was headed my only response was, "I don't know where I'm going but I know one thing is for certain, it'll have palm trees." After enduring ten New England winters, I was over cold weather and was tropically certain of my next warm weather home. Don't ever be so sure.

I planned a huge yard sale — a "House and Garden Sale" is how I advertised it. I overheard a boy at my gym say to his friend, upon seeing one of my meticulously crafted posters (complete with copies of 18th century engravings) on the bulletin board, "**Oh look, Martha Stewart's having a yard sale.**" It was actually very Martha. I had used every tool in my merchandising handbook to turn the entire apartment into a kind of department store... or as I referred to it, an "Apartment Store." The living room was a gift shop/world bazaar. The upstairs bedroom was a men's sportswear department. The downstairs bedroom a men's haberdashery complete with a shoe department and outerwear. The kitchen, obviously enough, was a kitchenware/dining department. The office was office equipment, bags, luggage and all sorts of collected odds and ends. The garden was a garden center with implements, furnishings, planters and plants. **I beamed with pride as I overheard one shopper say to her friend, "This isn't a yard sale, it's an affordable Bergdorf Goodman."** It was a huge "held-over-for-a-second-day" success.

Post-sale, I packed up the leftovers, put it all in storage and, untethered, excitedly began traveling to any place I thought I might potentially call home. Los Angeles was first. I visited my friend Jay who had moved there earlier but the City of Angels just didn't spread its wings for me. San Francisco was next. Nope. I had apparently not left my heart there. I did, however, leave a quarter of Chase's ashes in the Pacific Ocean. My beloved Key West was next but the magic was no longer there. Of the warm weather cities, I had saved Miami's super-gay South Beach for last because I really thought it the most likely. While five years before I had been gung-ho about it, it was no longer so super or gay and just didn't vibe for me anymore. Having exhausted the palm treed options, I tried Chicago where I had at one time been deliriously happy. It was no longer my kind of town. I even tried Louisville. Nope, not home anymore. **I had expected to just show up to one of these cities and have its arms reach out and embrace me, all the pieces falling neatly into place, letting me know I had found home.** It didn't happen. None of these cities opened its arms to me. Concerned friends would ask me over and over where I was going to end up. My only answer was that I didn't know but I was certain I would eventually find out. And then I would add with a shrug my usual, "These things just seem to work out for me." And I would see in my own mind's eye, Randy rolling both of his.

My lifelong love of New York would make it the obvious choice. However, I had said for decades, on the possibility of living there, "I don't want New York to ever be a place where I do my laundry." I couldn't quite imagine glamorous New York as everyday. It was a fun and sexy city always on holiday — a fantasy place — an Emerald City dream destination for my inner-Dorothy. And there were certain practicalities to be considered. New York has always been an expensive place to live. Who doesn't know that? It also has a well-earned reputation for being exceedingly hard to establish yourself in business. Still, its glamorous gravitational pull was strong and its "If you can make it there..." challenge, enticing. **Could I actually be, after all the years of waiting, a "New Yorker?"**

With my long-time friend Sidney from the Indianapolis days now living in New York, I decided this would be the perfect opportunity to say "yes" to her invitation to visit her in her Upper West Side, corner of Central Park West and 75th Street apartment. She invited me to stay as long as I'd like. People have a tendency to do that and I did just that. Once there, the pieces began to fall into place and New York gave me a welcoming hug. It seemed New York, even with its lack of palm trees (well, there was one indoor clump in the Winter Garden near World Trade) just might be the place. There was work to consider and given all the antique shows I had done in New York with Madeleine, I had something of a presence already established there. Should I perhaps try my hand at having my own antique business?

I had been at Sidney's nearing a year when I met a boy named Shelton. We became instant boyfriend/fuck buddies. **Ready to move on from Sidney's apartment, I began looking, along with Shelton, for a new living situation we could share. If we could find a place large enough to live and work in, all the better.** Shelton found an ad in The Village Voice for a "live/work" loft in West Chelsea. The location was a little dodgy — way west on 29th St between 10th and 11th Ave, adjacent to an old abandoned, derelict looking elevated freight railroad track. Affixed to it and spanning 29th Street was a huge lighted billboard introducing a brand new TV personality named "Judge Judy."

It was a desolate warehouse district south of Hell's Kitchen bereft of charm or anything pretty, with lots of gas stations, taxi repair stands, auto and tire repair facilities, truck rental outlets and parking lots. **"Hell's Carport" as I liked to call it.** It was a no man's land (save for some incomparably big chested, likely trans, nighttime prostitutes) but the price was right. The space was huge, totally raw but the sketchy looking kind of tweaky prospective landlord promised to build it out for us. Or at least divide the space into three live/work lofts of which we had the first choice. Against my strong misgivings about the sketchy location, and the even sketchier landlord, we took it. If I'd only thought to ask him if he actually owned the building. I was new to all things New York — what did I know?

1979...1995

Fifth Avenue Sidney

WITH SIDNEY'S STELLAR SUCCESSES behind the cosmetics counter, both in West Lafayette and Indianapolis, her years of teaching and her Masters in Education, the company execs were quick to offer her a position in their education department. She would be teaching the salespeople who worked, as had she, behind the counters. Her combined teaching and selling experience made her the perfect fit for the job. She took it and of course, as with everything else, excelled.

She was eventually promoted to a regional position, still in the education department but now over the people who teach the people behind the counters. They moved her to Chicago. By this time I had moved to San Francisco. Of course Sidney was just as successful there and was eventually made Director of Education for all of Canada. She moved to Toronto around the time I moved to Boston. **She was eventually offered the job heading their International Education Department, a move that landed her in New York City. She was by now a high powered cosmetics executive.** The president of her company came to her one day and said they were starting a new cosmetics line and they wanted Sidney as the Director of Education for the new line. She took the job.

When Sidney invited me to visit her, I jumped at the chance. It was great being together again talking and and laughing about our days in Indianapolis along with Steve and all the adventures we'd shared. With all her upward mobility, she was still the naive midwestern girl I'd known back then. And she still had that laugh. The timing turned out to be perfect for both of us. Sidney had met a man who lived on the other side of Central Park and was spending more and more time with him on the Upper East Side and less and less time with her two cats on the Upper West. It didn't take long for Sidney to realize that she had a built-in cat sitter and she could move in with Bill on Fifth Avenue without making the commitment of bringing the cats and all her belongings. With all my belongings in storage and no fixed address, I was essentially homeless and could easily move into her place and take care of her cats while she moved across the park. **She'd be able to test the waters of living with Bill on Fifth Ave and with a park between us, I'd be testing my own waters in New York.**

I was now living rent-free in an apartment at 75th and CPW. With maid service. With Sidney's boyfriend in no hurry to seal the deal, I had an open invitation to stay on. Thank you Sidney. It was a win-win for all. Cats included. Around the same time on a mid-afternoon cruise through Central Park, I met Shelton. We had sex right there in The Ramble, a famous gay cruise ground, and began seeing each other. A place to live and a boyfriend. Done. The New York pieces were clearly falling into place. It had all worked out so easily. Was all this New York's way of wrapping its expensive arms around me?

Eventually Shelton and I found the loft and Sidney moved the cats and the rest of her things in with Bill, a divorced father of two, who had both moved away. He lived alone in his Upper East Side Fifth Avenue duplex which was both fabulous and sad. It was a family residence where clearly all the family members but one had moved on. One and a smelly, incontinent, at death's door cat. The place needed work; a lot of work. Sidney hired me to help her fix up "The hell-hole on Fifth Ave" as she called it. Together we made it more than livable and Indy Sidney was quickly becoming Fifth Avenue Sidney.

An avowed feminist raised by an avowed feminist way ahead of her time, Sidney insisted on paying her own way during her entire courtship with Bill and continued to do so well into their marriage. With therapy she was eventually able to let go and have him take the greater financial role. He was from a fabulously wealthy New York family. I remember having conversations with her about quitting her job, which was keeping her from being able to fully enjoy their life together. "You know," she'd tell me, "I am beating my head against the corporate wall working for a really good six-figure salary, which took me years to get to and is just a rounding error for this man." **Sidney did quit her job and eventually became the Fifth Avenue Grande Dame she is today.**

For a few years we would see each other for an occasional lunch — always at some fabulous New York City venue (that I couldn't afford) for which she would always graciously insist on paying — but as time went on, it was clear we'd come to live in completely different worlds. The last time we had lunch together there were a few rather worrisome Republican rumblings. Also knowing that I like photography, she showed off a couple of "recently acquired" rare antique photographs. She and Bill love photography and even have their own dark room. She once mentioned their touring Europe "with the Hasselblads" and I thought she was referring to another couple. They're cameras. Anyway, proudly pointing out their new photographic acquisitions Sidney announced, "It's nearly impossible to find anything under six figures anymore." **Clearly we had become denizens of separate worlds; the only overlap being the memory of our former friendship.** Over time the lunches ended. We became Christmas card friends and eventually even the Christmas cards dried up.

I ran into Fifth Avenue Sidney quite some time ago — two years? five perhaps? — at the green market in Union Square. In a city New York's size, these chance meetings are anything but chance. She opened with, "I think I owe you an email." Which she did. I can't remember much of anything else we talked about. I was too busy eyeing her gorgeous trench coat, which was lined (if my usually dependable-in-these-things eye was correct) in sable, turned out tastefully and modestly around the edges. As I mentally tallied up the total cost of my former first grade school teacher friend's personal presentation: hair, makeup, manicure, earrings (Tiffany & Co?), sunglasses (Prada?), loafers (Tods?), handbag (Hermès?), that coat; all I could think of was the enormous chasm that had grown between us. With me in my hoodie, jeans, sneakers and gym bag, it must have been even more obvious to her. There was a lot more than a park separating us now. **I said something funny…I don't remember what…and suddenly out of nowhere there it was — that loud, enormous, spontaneous laugh, unbridled and unexpected, bursting from within — and just like that, to my delight, my cherished midwestern school teacher friend from our Indianapolis Admiral days magically reappeared for a happy few seconds before her Fifth Avenue composure took over and reigned her back in.** Sidney had learned how to suppress the un-suppressible.

She still owes me that email.

1995

Loft Life

SHELTON AND I HAD MOVED whatever possessions we had in New York into that big raw loft space and together we headed off to New England in an enormous rented truck. We scoured Maine for antiques and, using a large chunk of the money I'd inherited from Chase, we filled most of the truck with treasures to be marked up and sold in New York. We then swung by Boston where we filled up the remainder with all my worldly belongings left behind when I'd set off to travel the country. We returned to New York with a very full truck packed with my old and new life.

Added to all the booty brought back from New England were the treasures I'd pick up in New York on weekends at the various flea markets on or near 6th Ave and 26th St. I'd get up before dawn (or in some cases still be up from the night before — Limelight was only a few blocks away) and get to the flea markets as the vendors were setting up. That's when you were sure to find the best treasures. Sometimes you could buy right off the trucks as they were unloading. I had my favorite merchants with all the best stuff. One in particular, who dealt only in paintings, was the seller to most dependably have something I'd love. He'd always hold paintings he thought I'd like as he knew my eye and that I'd be coming through early.

The loft was full. And huge: big enough to live in, work in, play in and settle in for the long run. But the task ahead was daunting. **As I looked around at a huge completely raw space filled with a sea of furniture, clothing, personal belongings and a shitload of merchandise, I thought "What have I done?"** Shelton and I would smoke some weed and run around the place naked in our crazy, unfinished, full of potential and antiques playground. Usually high, sitting in two big weathered English antique garden chairs, with our feet propped up at the windows overlooking the wildflower and weed-covered abandoned railway curving right around us, we would take in our portion of a glittering city. We'd ponder our existence and the existence of the entire universe, all the while trying to ignore the chaos behind us. There were floors and walls to paint, lighting and shelving to install, boxes and boxes and more boxes to unpack with their contents to organize. How would I ever manage to sort this place out?

Once while unpacking a box, Shelton pulled out *A Catholic Baby's Record*, my "Baby Book" in which my mother, in lovely parochial school cursive penmanship, meticulously documented my every baby milestone. Falling from the slim, slightly tattered, pastel-colored volume was a card with my birth hospital's instructions for the new mother and the care of me, her newborn infant. Perusing it, Shelton said, "Well this explains a lot!" I was all ears. He continued, "It says here, under 'Special Instructions' that there's a tub of white Vaseline to rub daily on the circumcision." We looked up at each other and shared a silent pause before he laughed out, "Your mom was giving you little finger jobs practically from birth!" Now we were both laughing. Rolling on the floor laughing, "Oh my god," I cried out, "it does explain so much!" And from Shelton, "Probably everything!" More laughter. What Shelton was specifically referring to was my near-legendary Vaseline dependency. Pretty much as long as I can remember, I have had an almost-addiction to Vaseline. I never masturbated without it and couldn't understand anyone who could. Or at least use some oil-based lubricant. During sex, this dependency was a constant annoyance to Shelton because, in the days of safe sex, a petroleum-based product like Vaseline could not be used with a condom, so, once I pulled out the Vaseline and greased myself up — to help keep myself up — certain other penetrative acts were off the table. My annoying Vaseline dependency had now been explained to Shelton's satisfaction. At least that much was clear. The mind reels at any other things those "little finger jobs" could possibly explain.

Before we could begin to do anything about the loft we had to prepare for our first antique show. It was the outdoor Mulford Farms Show in East Hampton. We were sharing a tent with Madeleine who'd be coming down from Boston. We got all the merchandise ready, packed up what amounted to an entire houseful of furniture and decorative items and drove it all to East Hampton. We set up our side of the tent the night before the show. It was a richly romantic mix with a lot of gold and cream and rose colors. Proudly surveying our work, I christened it our "Gilded Blonde Collection." We were back in the morning to help Madeleine set up. There'd been a nasty overnight storm — wouldn't you know? — which sadly damaged some of our merchandise. Not a great start.

As the gates opened, we were ready to sell. I watched the crowd pour through the gates and disperse in every direction. Making a bee-line to our tent was a woman I'd had many dealings with while helping Madeleine during her shows in The Hamptons. She was not my favorite person. In fact she was our least favorite customer. Something about her was terribly grating. She'd try to get you down to bottom dollar (usually by demeaning the item she had interest in — a technique that never worked with me), and then once there she'd try harder to go even lower and then she'd refuse to pay tax. She was focused on our tent and I thought, "Oh, good god no. Not her. No, she can't be my first customer!" **I really didn't want my first sale of my new business to be to my least favorite customer.** She gave her usual dismissive hello as she came into the tent and began poking and prodding her way around, lifting an item here, fingering it awhile and depositing it there. I saw her eyeing a small painting — one of my favorite items in the entire collection. "Oh no," I thought, "not that!" It was purchased from my favorite vendor on 26th St for no more than fifty or sixty dollars. I did not want it to go to her. She picked it up and continued to inspect every piece of merchandise in our tent, never putting the painting down. I tried to remember what price I had put on it but couldn't. I loved that little painting — a turn of the century French-looking beach scene with ladies in long flowing white dresses with blue satin sashes (really) and men in top hats. I really didn't want her to have it. In fact my need for her *not* to buy it grew with each passing second. I'm not proud of any of this but I just didn't want that lady to be my first sale and especially not with that particular painting. She finally made her way over to me with the painting. With her typical snarky attitude and her eyes still darting around the booth and not at me, she asked, "Whattaya want for this?" She waved "this" at me not even honoring it with the word "painting." This wasn't going to go well. "Let me see," I said as I got it away from her, checking for a price tag, hoping I'd marked the price high enough. No price tag. Miracle of miracles I hadn't priced it! "Six hundred and fifty dollars!" I blurted out without even thinking. **She was shocked. I have to say so was I.** Where had that come from? "What in the world makes this tiny little painting worth six hundred and fifty dollars?" she asked in disbelief as she snatched it back from me. "Because," I responded, "I love that 'tiny little painting' so much," now with my hand on it trying to get it back, "that $650 is the least I could get for it and be happy to see it go." She looked unhappily at the little painting and with a full-on tug-of-war between us, knowing what was coming next, I cut her off with a firm, "Final price! Plus tax!" There was a long pause before she looked back up to me and said, "I'll take it." So she was going to be my first sale after all but at least I'd be getting ten times my investment. She handed me the painting and went back to shopping. She found several items more and my first sale was a big one. **The funny thing is she actually turned out to be a nice person, one**

of my best customers. She'd follow up purchases with thank you notes and sometimes with her own little drawings. You never know.

With Mulford Farms a success, we returned to the city and I threw myself into making the loft not only a nice place to live but a great place to shop. I systematically worked my way from the windows back and created an absolute Martha Stewart dream of a place. I divided the loft into Living Room, Garden Room, Dining Room, Kitchen, Bedroom, Showroom, Interior Design Office, Bathroom and Laundry Room. I even had a gift wrapping area — a personal dream.

Our wall of windows faced north with an unimpeded view across the depressed railroad tracks leading into Penn Station, now built over and called "The Hudson Yards." We could see the Queen Mary and all the ships sailing up and down the River. With the abandoned elevated railroad, now revitalized and called "The Highline," curving right around our loft on the same level, just outside our windows were wildflowers, trees and fields of Queen Anne's lace. In midtown Manhattan. During the winter, with an entire wall of glass, we'd find ourselves in a super-sized snow globe and in the spring there were all those wildflowers popping back up along with the grass and weeds on the old rusty railroad tracks. **During the summer we'd go to bed to the sound of crickets and have our morning coffee in the garden corner with wild pheasants strutting right outside the window.**

Shopping the flea markets at dawn or dancing the night away at Limelight on 6th Ave, I'd make my way back to the loft via the 28th Street flower district just as they'd be preparing for business. **Still a little high from the night before, I was Eliza Doolittle in the opening scenes of *My Fair Lady* with the abundant flowers of Covent Garden all around me being uncovered and set out for sale.** It was a "loverly" floral fantasyland. One such morning, having gone instead to the flea market, I bought a couple of paintings from my favorite vendor. While concluding the sale I noticed a small painting of a male ballet dancer. It was one of those ethereal works that instantly touched my soul. The fact that it was a romantic rear-view and showed the dancer's round muscular butt covered by the sheerest of flesh-colored tights didn't hurt either. The painting was damaged. It had a small L-shaped tear in it. That is why it was off to the side and why my vendor buddy hadn't shown it to me. I asked how much he wanted for the painting. I'm sure he could see how much I loved it and he could have asked almost any amount. Instead he told me it was mine. Free of charge. He said in its condition he couldn't sell it — I disagreed — and he wanted me to have it since I clearly loved it so much. On that we could agree.

Later that day, still out and about with my purchases, I stopped by the Walter Kerr Theater where Shelton was handing out headsets for the hearing impaired at one of his "rent jobs." Rent jobs were how Broadway hopefuls (which Shelton was) would sustain themselves in an expensive city while they trained and rehearsed and auditioned. This particular rent job allowed him access to the theater on a nightly basis, something that was important to any Broadway hopeful. The show that day was *Love! Valor! Compassion!* a play about a group of gay friends in the time of AIDS. You could get cheap balcony seats at about twenty dollars. I had seen it many times and would visit with Shelton at his console before the show and at intermission. One of my favorite performers in the show was an actor named John Glover who, in an extraordinary performance, two of them actually, played identical twins with dissimilar personalities. When Shelton exited the theater and joined me on the sidewalk. I pulled the painting of the ballet dancer out and began telling the story of how I'd come by it. Mr. Glover came out the stage door and saw me showing off the painting and came right over. He clearly loved the painting and I could see in his eyes that he had connected to it the way I had. He said he thought it was lovely and that I should be pleased to own such a beautiful work. As I thought about it that evening I decided to gift wrap it and leave it for him at the stage door at the next performance. **I enclosed a note which said, "Dear Mr. Glover, I think you saw in this painting exactly what I saw in it this morning at the flea market. In appreciation for your work in this show and your inspirational performance, I hope you'll accept it as a gift."** I included my name and telephone number on the card. When I answered the phone the next day it was to Mr. Glover's voice. "Hello Michael, this is John Glover. I wanted to thank you for the unexpected gift," and to my delight he added, "I thought perhaps you'd like to come see the show again as my guest. There will be a ticket at the box in your name for whichever performance you'd like. Then, after the show, you could visit backstage to see the painting in its new home." At the next evening's performance, certain he knew exactly where I was seated, I was sure he'd directed one of his monologues right to me. Backstage after the play, I was taken to Mr Glover's dressing room. He was so gracious, and an absolute gentleman as he showed off the painting in its new surroundings. Upon seeing it again, if I'm being perfectly honest, I had a tiny twinge of regret still feeling about the painting the way I had at first sight. That painting of a dancer was perfect hanging on a wall in such a theatrical setting so I knew it was where it ought to be. **Mr. Glover took me out onstage, a first for me. We sat down and talked, mostly about AIDS, being gay, and the theater, just the two of us and the ghost lamp behind us in the quiet of the otherwise empty Martin Beck Theater.**

Loft life as it turned out was fun. It was a big lively place filled with antiques, friends and love where everybody seemed to want to hang out. We had Thanksgivings and Christmases. Pre-White Party parties. Pre-Black Party parties. Sex parties. There was an ever-changing array of out of town houseguests. We were rarely alone. Customers also showed up and the loft was the perfect selling tool for my interior design business. A woman from *House Beautiful* magazine showed up and took a bunch of polaroids anticipating a possible article on the loft and me. Life was good and things were going really, really well when, quite unexpectedly, a determined little dog showed up.

1996

Puppy Love

I T WAS A DARK AND STORMY NIGHT. No, really. It was. Having visited Shelton many times at his work handing out headsets at Broadway shows, I had sort of fallen into the job as well. **I was working headsets for the final evening performance of *A Delicate Balance*.** It had received rave reviews and I had asked to be assigned there before it closed. The Broadway Flea Market, an outdoor fundraising event for Broadway Cares/Equity Fights AIDS was being held that day so I was in the theater district early to shop it before heading off to the Plymouth Theatre. Shelton and I had recently (and mostly amicably) broken up. I was looking for something as a housewarming gift for his new place. I knew he'd spent the better part of the day, in my absence, getting the last of his things out of the loft and I thought it'd be a nice gesture to take him a gift in exchange for his loft keys. I purchased an autographed glossy b&w photo of Bernadette Peters that I knew he'd love, just in time as it had started to rain and the venders were quickly packing up. By the time I made it to the theater the skies were opening up for what turned out to be a super-windy, lightning-studded gully-washer of a storm.

Opening and closing nights on Broadway are always special and so it was with *A Delicate Balance* that night. By the time I left the theater the rain had pretty much subsided but still I was glad that Bernadette was in a plastic protective sleeve as I made my way to Shelton's new place. He loved his gift and I got my keys back. **He excitedly told me that there was a surprise waiting for me in the loft. A puppy of indeterminate breed and gender had, in my absence, apparently made its way into my home.** I had a friend named Jerry — another antique dealer — visiting from Paris and somehow he had come into possession of a little dog. I had thought many times about getting a dog, especially now that I'd be living alone. Both the companionship and security a dog would provide appealed to me. And I love dogs. I just wasn't sure I was ready to care for one. Nevertheless, with Shelton's departure, a dog had gone to the top of my wish list. Given the dog arrived the exact day of Shelton's final departure, I felt a message had been delivered from the universe telling me that yes, the time had come, I was ready once again for the responsibility of caring for another being. Things really do seem to work out for me.

I headed home excited with nothing but puppy thoughts in my head. I couldn't wait to see this furry little four-legged creature that had somehow, in my absence, installed itself into my loft and life. It was after midnight when I returned to a dark loft. Jerry was sound asleep in my bed and I quietly went around the loft looking for the little fella. I softly called out, "Here puppy puppy, here puppy puppy." Nothing. I checked every nook and cranny, mostly on my hands and knees, searching around all the furniture and other merchandise. Nowhere other than in my bed was there evidence of another living creature. There was a bowl of water and another with some uneaten food but no sign of a puppy who might be interested in either. My excitement waned as I gave up my search, feeling pretty sure that an owner must have presented him or herself and the dog was already gone. I went to bed disappointed. Well actually, I went to sofa disappointed. **After my fruitless puppy search I curled up sad and puppy-less on the living room sofa for "just a minute," and fell asleep.**

I awakened to a brightly morning-lit loft. As I wiped my eyes and blearily surveyed the landscape around me, over in the far corner of the garden room in its deepest darkest corner under a piece of furniture I saw something move. My first thought was "rat," but then I remembered the potential puppy. I put on my glasses to see two eyes warily looking back at me. On closer inspection they were two terrified eyes staring at me and belonging to something very black and very dirty and cautiously inching its way out from its protective cover. I slipped carefully as I could off the sofa and onto the floor and, with hand outstretched and another, "Here puppy puppy. Here puppy puppy," started to make my way over toward the tiny creature on the other side of the loft. In the sweetest kindest least intimidating voice I could manage I tried to coax it toward me but it quickly returned to its place of safety where it stood trembling. "It's OK, it's OK," I kept repeating as I tried to convince the little critter it was safe. It moved toward me just a bit but as soon as I did the same, it receded again. This dance went on for awhile. I don't know what word or gesture from me did it but the little skin and bones creature finally emerged and made its halting way over to me. It was filthy, all covered in dirt and grimy black oil. In sharp contrast with its tiny emaciated frame, were the biggest ears dripping with long oily spikes of hair nearly touching the floor. Continuing with the "It's OK, it's OK's" I pulled its frightened shivering little body to me and held it close to my chest. **I could feel the fear in its trembling body and, as I continued to hold it, caress it and talk to it, I could feel the fear melting away.**

It was love at first sight. For both of us. I looked down at two of the most enormous brown eyes bulging from that filthy skeletal frame. Those eyes, previously full of fear were now full of…what…soul? They seemed wise, somehow, and looked right through me. As that little body melted into mine, I realized without question, that I had found a soul mate. Or, a soul mate had found me. I didn't know that a non-human soulmate was possible but in that moment I did and after, I never doubted for a second. We were simply connected and that was that. This wasn't our first time together. I knew it. I could feel it. She relaxed into my arms (it was at this time I could tell "it" was a "she,") and we continued to forge our everlasting bond. **She was mine and I was hers.**

When Jerry awoke he filled me in on the particulars of this little girl's journey into my home and heart. Though I didn't know it, I actually had neighbors (in addition to Judge Judy) in that desolate warehouse area, one in fact also named Michael. He had been walking up 10th Avenue near 26th St and had seen a little animal dart out into the heavy uptown traffic. Though it was storming and he was in a hurry to get home, he rushed out into the traffic risking life and limb and scooped the little critter up from the crush of vehicles and certain death. He was then faced with the question of what to do with this tiny, drenched, dirty, nearly dead dog. He couldn't take it home as he owned a big Akita that didn't like other dogs. He remembered a doggie day care center on 29th St (in my building) and headed there. They refused the dog on health issues. By law they could not take in strays. So Michael was stuck with a dog he couldn't take home. As he was exiting the building, my Parisian friend Jerry was entering. Michael told Jerry how he'd come by it and why he couldn't keep it. "Well, I don't actually live here," said Jerry, "but I'm pretty sure my friend Michael who does, wouldn't mind my taking it in." With that Jerry took the dog off Michael's hands. "I'll put some flyers around the area to see if we can locate the owner," said Michael as Jerry wrote down my phone number for him.

That first Sunday morning together was a total bonding experience. Jerry had gone off on his day leaving me with my new filthy little friend. She would not leave my side. I got her to drink and eat. Bath time was next. I washed her thoroughly three or four times before the water in the tub ran clear and she was finally free from all that dirt and oil. Where had she been to get that seriously filthy? I put her on my lap and gave her a thorough grooming and a proper haircut. After blowing her dry — she was already learning the travails of being a gay man's dog — I could see she was not only a full bred Yorkshire Terrier but a real beauty. She was skin and bones but what great bones. You could see them all. **When I put her back down on the floor, after having spent her first grimy night in the darkest dustiest corner of the loft, now clean and fluffed, she ran right out to the living room and jumped up on the white sofa.** "Cool dog," I said to myself as I watched her do a couple of circles on it before sitting down and contentedly looking up at me. From that moment on she always knew just what to do to fit in and never upset the delicate balance of my home and my life. It was now her home and her life too and she'd be part of that balance. She had worked so hard to get to me and she was clearly determined to stay.

Sitting down next to her and stroking her soft fur, she quickly hopped into my lap and curled up there. I sat pondering her arrival and the Broadway show I'd seen the night before, a play about a woman with a perfectly well-ordered household upset by the appearance of friends frightened and scared out of their own home and determined to live with her forever. There I sat with, on my lap, this tiny creature who'd shown up on that same night, frightened and determined to live with me. That play had prepared me for her. And just in the nick of time, at its final evening performance. **I needed no other evidence that we were simply made for each other.** As I thought about that play, I became amazed by the confluence of events: her having shown up the day that Shelton moved out and the split second timing of Jerry and Michael's meeting. I also realized that it was Sept 29th, the feast of St. Michael the Archangel, my namesake. Michael One (as I call him.) Your saint name day is a big deal in the Italian culture. Not only had she shown up on St. Michael's day, she was found by a Michael and ended up with a Michael. It was all written in the stars.

The honeymoon was on. Taking my new little nameless girl for a walk at the end of an improvised rope leash, I spotted one of Michael's notices taped to a street lamp. Not a praying person I nevertheless made a silent wish that no one would answer it as I was already so in love I couldn't imagine giving her up. I was encouraged that all the little tear-off phone number strips were still intact. The call came a day or so later. It was Michael. He introduced himself and said, "I heard from the little dog's owner" he continued, "apparently his sister was institutionalized and he 'got stuck' (that sounded like a quote to me) with her dog. He was keeping the dog in a warehouse on W 26th St where she had two puppies. One (or both, he wasn't sure of that) had escaped. You've got one of the escapee puppies." He gave me the man's phone number with a warning, "There's something off there. I got a bad feeling about this guy and don't think he really gives a shit about the dogs. If you contact him, be careful," and then he added, "I asked and he said they haven't had any shots and have never been to a vet." I pondered the possibility there was another neglected puppy and mother in a warehouse somewhere on 26th St that might need rescuing but with Michael's warning and thoughts of possibly losing my new little treasure, I tore up the telephone number and tossed it.

I would walk my little girl late at night just before bedtime and, this being New York and a desolate warehouse district, there were several prostitutes who worked the block. **There was an especially big-chested pair, always together, who were quite friendly and seemed to work as a sort of hooker tag team.** After it had been established without question that I was not their customer they had shifted their interest to my little dog. "Oh my god she is precious. What is her name?" They spoke in unison. They really were a pair. "I just got her. She doesn't have a name yet," was my inadequate answer. They crouched down — my god I'd never seen such huge boobs — and one of them took my little girl's face into her enormous hands. **"Well, there is only one name for this beautiful little girl,"** and then looking up at me, **"you should call her Princess."** Her friend agreed. "Princess, that's her name." I wasn't convinced. "I am a gay man who has suddenly found himself with a little foofy dog," I told them in no uncertain terms, "I won't be naming her Princess!" They were clearly unhappy with this, "Well, all I know is that little dog is a princess," and once again, in unison, "You should call her Princess." I'd see them on my nightly walks and it was always the same, "Have you named that little dog yet?" I'd shake my head and she'd say "Princess, she's a princess if ever there was one." Her friend would always agree.

The truth was, I had tried several names and my determined little pooch wouldn't respond to any of them. In fact it was as if she was determined to *not* respond to any of them. She had proven herself to be a smart little critter, potty training herself and sitting up and begging without ever being shown how. Once, early on, when I was ignoring her she barked at me. In a stern voice she hadn't heard from me before, I said, "You have to understand that there's no place in my life for a dog who barks for attention." She never did it again. She could always tell strangers outside the door from the actual neighbors. She was smart and for whatever reason, she wouldn't allow herself to be named. As a fan of *A Streetcar Named Desire*, my first choice was Stella. I could see myself Stanley Kowalski style in a sweaty t-shirt yelling, "Stella!" She was clearly not into it. As a big Audrey Hepburn fan I, one by one, gave her a series of Audrey-related names: Audrey, Eliza, Holly, Regina, Joanna, Jo, and Ann. Whenever she was away from me, I'd call, "Here, Audrey," or any other of the list of names I liked. **She wasn't having it and would actively ignore me.** It was the strangest thing. Every name I tried fell on those big, deaf and disinterested ears. Then one day we were playing together and she got up on her hind legs to dance — another thing she'd taught herself. When I saw this I said, "Oh boy let's boogie!" With that she went crazy, running around and jumping, happier than I'd ever seen her. What did I say? Boogie? I thought to myself, "Is that your name, Boogie?" It wouldn't have been my first choice but I thought, especially with my love of dancing that it was kind of cute. She certainly loved it. The next time she was away from me in the loft, I called out, "Here, Boogie!" She came instantly, running to me so excited to hear her name. **Boogie had named herself.** The next time I took her walking my prostitute pair were at their post. Before they could ask, I said, "She has a name. Her name is Boogie." "Boogie?" they spat out in unison, disgust and disbelief showing through the layers of make-up on their appalled faces, "that's no name for a Princess!" "Well, don't blame me, she named herself," and I added, "but she will always be Princess Boogie to you." They were only partially satisfied.

Boogie and I were inseparable. I would look at that little life in my arms and think of all that she had gone through to get to me. I realized that as long as she needed to be taken care of, I'd be taken care of. **At a time in my life when everything was up in the air, her confidence grounded me and made me feel safe.** And loved. We went everywhere together. She'd travel by plane and train and automobile. She became the toast of Barney's uptown and was loved by shopkeepers in Chelsea, Soho and elsewhere throughout the city. Once while meeting with prospective interior design clients, I sat across from them in my living room with Boogie on my lap. As I looked into the large Venetian mirror hanging above the sofa on which they were seated, I saw reflected in it a gay New York interior designer, surrounded by antiques, talking to his clients while stroking his foofy little dog. I was a social stereotype. How had this happened to me? I hadn't set out to be either an interior designer or to be a little foofy dog owner yet here I was both.

Not long ago I was going through some old photos and came across one of my childhood dog Huggie and me. Huggie was named before we got him and though we didn't much like the name, he seemed pretty attached to it. Despite our best efforts he would not be renamed so he remained Huggie. Huggie, a feisty little terrier, became mostly my dog. My older brother and sister were off living their lives while I was at home and spent more time playing with him, so we bonded. I adored that lovable little dog who died when I was away at college. I sadly never got to say goodbye. The photo that I came across was of 15 year old me lying on the floor on my stomach, watching TV the way I always would. Burrowed in between my legs was Huggie with his head resting on my butt the way he always would. That is how we watched TV together. It reminded me of another photo taken more recently. In that photo, taken during a Christmas visit to Louisville, I am lying on my stomach on my parents' living room floor and Boogie is burrowed in between my legs with her head resting on my butt. I placed the photos next to each other. Both dogs, terriers about the same size, in the same pose (on my butt) and both photos taken at my parents' house. **The photos and the dogs in them were practically identical. Why hadn't I seen it before? Huggie. Boogie. Even their names were alike. Could Huggie who I loved so much and had never said goodbye to, actually be Boogie? Had he made his way back to me? As a she? Born in a warehouse, escaping, being on the mean streets of Hell's Carport for days and then against all odds somehow finding her way into my apartment when I wasn't even there, had come home. That horny little Huggie who'd escape our Louisville home as often as he could for some sort of neighborhood mischief would always return to me. Had he returned once again? As Boogie? Why hadn't I seen it before? It certainly confirmed my early feelings of our having been together before and of my having found a soul mate. That little dog so determined to keep his name was once again just as determined to do so. Exhausted af-**

ter all the girly names I'd thrown at my reincarnated puppy, when I finally said, "Boogie," worn down, she must've thought, "Close enough." And Huggie became Boogie.

1992 – 1997

Self-Healing Homo

IT WAS SPRING OF 1997 and I had a loft-full of friends in for the annual Black Party — The Rites Of Spring as it was called. I was suffering with my hernia, by this point, a nearly five year chronic condition that had been particularly problematic for weeks. It was more tender than ever and was not responding to my visualization therapy. What was I going to do? I did not want to miss that party. It was time for a showdown: Black Party vs Hernia. Which would win? I lay there thinking back to the unfortunate day I'd inherited this annoying condition and how I'd tried to get rid of it.

I should have listened to my mother. Good lord, how many of my stories could start with that sentence? Anyway, I really should have listened. "Slow down!" "Make two trips!" "Don't rush!" "You're gonna get hurt!" Any one of those oft-shouted instructions might have helped as I impatiently closed the shop on River Street in Beacon Hill that night back in 1992. I was running late for something and in my haste I had forgotten to put away a small concrete urn planted and overflowing with ivy and annuals. I had already set the alarm as I angrily spied it sitting there on the brick sidewalk, mocking me. I considered leaving it there. But I imagined some miscreant stealing it or worse, using it for some sort of vandalism. I knew it had to be put away. This meant waiting the minute or so for the alarm to set, then reopening the shop, disarming the alarm and hauling the planter in, then resetting the alarm and re-locking the door. I was doubly unhappy because of my rather contentious relationship with the alarm. I was also in a hurry. I waited for the beep that would tell me the alarm was finally set and then unlocked the door. With the door reopened and alarm off, as I went to pick up the urn I did so way too quickly and, without thinking, jerked the heavy concrete annoyance up off the ground. It was heavy. Very heavy. I heard something rip. Or pop. Or tear. Or, I don't really know how to describe it. It was part sound and part feeling. And it was in my groin. And it hurt. Oh no. What had I done?

What I had done was give myself a hernia. One quick stupid move and I instantly had a chronic medical condition. My father had had hernias and though I never really understood what they were (I remembered having heard the unglamorous word "truss" several times) I knew they weren't pleasant. I learned from my friend Shani who was in medical sales, that a hernia is a piece of intestine pushing through a weak spot in the muscle of the abdominal wall. I know, gross. Even grosser was the possibility a hernia could be strangulated (lovely word) and cause great harm or death...also from Shani. The only treatment for a hernia, I was told, was surgery. Oh no.

I now had to be careful with everything I lifted. I had to be extra cautious at the gym where I was used to lifting heavy weights. No more. I imagined my newly acquired and cherished muscles deflating, my body deteriorating and my sex life right along with it. How would I have sex now without the right bulges in the right places and with an unsightly wrong bulge in exactly the wrong place? The groin. Not the groin. This was a disaster. And that bulge. That ugly bulge was a constant annoyance. It'd push out and I'd push it back in.

It'd stay in for a short while, long enough to give me hope, and then suddenly there it was again with a mind of its own, pushing right back out, a determined and unsightly alien taken up residence in my body. Once again I'd press it back in. It might stay put for a moment giving more false hope but then it would pop right back out in an unending back and forth. **It became habitual with a frequency somewhere between pastime and hobby.** Along with it came discomfort — constant, and pain — intermittent. Sitting, standing, walking, running, lifting, lying, I was ever-aware of its presence by an ever-insistent throbbing in my groin. And that bulge. I couldn't ignore it and it would not go away. The hernia had become a chronic condition taking on a personality of its own. We began to live together in a state of detente. I came to think of it as an uninvited and insistent houseguest. A guest that no matter what I did or said to it or how uncomfortable I made it, absolutely refused to leave.

I considered naming it.

Being in the antique business, a living that requires heavy lifting didn't help things. I had to be extra careful with every piece of furniture I'd lift and carry. The condition persisted with no relief as the word "strangulation" hovered somewhere in the back of my brain. I considered surgery to get rid of it but I just didn't want to go the medical route.

Irene, the Plymouth psychic had told me among many other things that I was a "self-healer." The term "self-healer," though tidied away in the back of my mind, had firmly established itself there. I liked the idea. As a son whose mother had a near obsession with doctors, their treatments and their drugs, I had gone the other extreme, entirely eschewing the medical world as much as was possible. The self-healing philosophy appealed to the part of me that wanted nothing to do with medicine. The hernia gave me the perfect opportunity to test Irene's self-healer theory. Could I heal myself? Irene had said so and she had been correct on so many things, in fact just about everything she'd told me had proven to be true. But this was a big one. Self-healer. It was after all, a New Age. I began to visualize. While lying on my back, I'd press the bulge in flat, send healing energy to that spot and visualize it staying that way — flat. I'd do the same as I was walking around town. Hand in my pocket I would press and hold, making myself aware of it, sending energy to it and visualizing. Always visualizing. With each piece of furniture I'd move, with every step I'd take, I'd visualize it away. This went on for months. Healing energy. Flat. Healing energy. Visualize. Flat. Sometimes the bulge would disappear and I'd think I'd been successful but it would eventually come back. It would vanish entirely for perhaps hours and I'd be filled with hope and a self-healing job well done and then each time, to my disappointment, that damned ugly bulge would return. Over time I became less certain of my self-healing ability to visualize it away. That didn't keep me from trying, however increasingly futile the attempt seemed to be. I was walking the razor's edge of certainty in my ability, working in concert with an all-powerful universe, to be able to heal myself, and the alternate certainty that I couldn't. I was sure the universe was doing its part but not so sure of my own contribution.

I was a self-healing failure.

Nothing changed. I continued to resist naming the damned thing since I feared naming something gives it power. The visualizing continued. The bulge continued. The pain continued. And the malevolent voice inside my head that kept repeating "strangulated hernia" continued in a chorus of other disappointed voices that assured me I'd never heal myself. I gave up and made a doctor's appointment. Along with that came the surgeon's appointment. And the subsequent surgery. I had held onto my self-healing hope up until the moment I went under anesthesia. Do you know that before having anesthesia you have to meet with the anesthesiologist who will say, "Now, you understand there is no guarantee you will survive the anesthesia experience. Please sign here." What?!

Happily I survived the anesthesia experience. Having finally peed after being catheterized, an excruciatingly painful experience and no small feat, I was sent home, hernia repaired, with the instructions to lie flat the rest of the day and the next day. No lifting. No physical exertion of any kind. The timing could not have been worse as Chase's condition that evening took a nasty turn. I found myself carrying him out to and putting him in a taxi, hauling him out of the taxi and into a wheelchair, then spending hours in the emergency room waiting for his admission and an empty bed, all the while hauling him in and out of the wheelchair and on and off the toilet. **Unhappily the hernia repair failed.**

The lump was back and more insistent than ever. I couldn't believe I had gone through the entire surgical process and was right back where I had started. Bummer. After getting over the anger and despair of this new unfortunate fact of my life I became philosophical about it. I had once been convinced of my self-healing ability but had given up on that conviction. This was, I decided, the universe's way of giving me a second chance to prove that together, we could get the job done and repair that damned bulge. The visualizing continued. Day and night. Everywhere I went, vertical or horizontal, I resurrected my old pastime, over and over again pushing the bulge flat. I visualized beams of healing light and energy permeating the damaged tissue and knitting it together. I pressed on it and visualized the fissure healing, mending itself. And through it all, that damned lump, my ever more annoying uninvited houseguest, persisted.

I was encouraged to make an appointment with another surgeon. Mine went out on maternity leave — perhaps, I thought, a sign. I did see another surgeon but never scheduled the surgery, remaining firmly convinced that I would, when the planets aligned or some other piece of timing that I could neither predict nor understand, with the help of the universe, heal myself. These things after all did have a habit of working out for me. Within a month Chase died and I was in neither a head space nor spiritual space to deal with self-healing or anything else that required a positive attitude. I became hopelessly mired in grief and self-pity and a new feeling of being adrift in the world. The lump in my groin, the only thing at that time of which I could feel absolutely certain, was now a chronic, annoying and painful condition that simply amplified my current state of negativity. Healing took a back seat as a towering snit of self-pity took over and drove me and my unsightly chronic condition inward to endure a long bleak New England winter, alone. Well, except for lumpy companion.

Ten months later when I relocated to New York City, I did so with my chronic condition but without health insurance. This would be the acid test of my self-healing abilities. I had made the decision to not have surgery while still under a Boston area group policy that I would lose as soon as I left the city. Foolhardy? **Perhaps, but I was ever more determined to heal myself.**

I lived with my chronic condition and continued to press it in only to have it pop right back out. Every time. As before, I would visualize it flat, focus healing light and energy on it, in it and around it, and with fierce determination visualize the light-filled tissue coming together, knitting itself and healing. Like before, the lump would go away for perhaps an hour, or two, or maybe more. But it would always return. The pain was intermittent and the discomfort constant. The threat of "strangulation" was ever on my mind. This went on for two and one half more health insurance-free years. Though I had learned how to obscure it best I could during sex, the whole hernia thing had gotten really old.

So back to spring of 1997 and my loft full of friends in for the annual Black Party. I'd been attending "The Daddy of All Circuit Parties" for years and wouldn't think of missing it but the hernia had been particularly problematic for weeks. It was more tender than ever and was not responding to my visualization therapy. The pain was worse than it had been in a long time. I was becoming worried and increasingly depressed. And I had a loft full of friends. I couldn't spend the entire weekend in bed but I did spend the better part of Saturday, the day of the party, horizontal, in bed pressing the bulge and doing all my visualizations and hoping against hope that I'd be able to make it go away at least long enough to allow me to attend part of the event. I did not want to miss that party. **It was time for a showdown: The Black Party vs The Hernia.** By the time we were ready to leave for the party, my groin had sort of flattened a bit. The tenderness and discomfort were still there but at least I wasn't bulging too much. I figured I'd be good for awhile, so I slipped into my black latex jeans, harness and boots and off I went to The Black Party, hopeful I'd be able to dance with my friends for at least a few hours. As we taxied up a dark 10th Avenue with only green lights as far as the eye could see, I began to think less about my annoying lump and more about energy — the energy I experience dancing onstage and connecting with the party. There is, without a doubt, something mystical to it. **Could it also be miraculous?**

As I entered Roseland Ballroom and was hit with the familiar wall of hot, humid, male sexuality, I did so with a purpose. In that moment I committed myself to using that sublime party energy to my own advantage. What if, rather than taking the energy in and simply returning it as was my wont, I channeled it first, through me, with the express purpose of healing? Myself. I had experienced that mystical energy so many times, knowing it, without question, to be real; why wouldn't I be able to use it? **I would visualize the energy as pure healing light flowing through me.** I would send it to my groin as miraculous strands of light knitting up the internal tissue, creating an illuminated mesh of healing energy to repair it and heal it...forever. I could see it.

As I made my way to the edge of the stage and carefully lifted myself up on it, I did so with a purposeful sense of self-healing optimism tempered by a history of self-healing failure. Feeling the usual tugging in my groin I cautiously began to dance. And dance. And dance. The energy was there as always and I put it to good use. I connected with the crowd and took the energy in but this time, rather than just throwing it back, I concentrated it and focused it on the sensitive area of my groin with one purpose: to heal that bulge forever. All night long, for hours I took the energy and visualized it as a healing sparkling light, creating a mesh of golden threads weaving their way over that insistent painful bulge, pressing it down and flattening it, knitting it up with light. I visualized the energy healing me before flinging it back to the dancing crowd. I visualized myself healed and imagined there might be someone else out there that needed healing and might just come along with me.

By the time I left the party, a five-year, annoying, painful, chronic condition, in a ten-hour (or so) night of dancing was gone. Vanished. Permanently. The bulge was gone. The pain was gone. The discomfort was gone. My uninvited guest, the lump, was gone. At The Black Party of 1997 I became a firm believer in our ability to heal ourselves, and more specifically in my ability to heal myself. With a little help from Irene and the universe and all that extraordinary energy so lavished upon me.

Post-Black Party I developed some other sure-fire techniques for self-healing. Feel free to call me "crazy," but I'm convinced they help me stay healthy today and everyday. Here are a few.

Scrubbing Bubbles:

TV commercials have been very helpful in giving me the visuals to use in my own self-healing visualizations. There are TV commercials with drawings of veins and arteries and what they look like with plaque building up narrowing them and threatening to clog them. There are also commercials that show scrubbing bubbles that clean your kitchen sink. I put the two together and visualize tiny microscopic bubbles with even tinier ultra-fine brushes covering their entire bubble surface and sticking out as the bubble spins. I then visualize the bubbles coursing their rapid-fire way throughout my entire circulatory system one after the other, spinning and scrubbing and removing all the nasty plaque that might be building up along the inside walls of my veins and arteries as shown in the commercials. The first round of scrubbing bubbles have tougher bristles to get at the hard stuff, the next round, slightly softer to continue the removal process and the final round super-soft brushes to polish the walls, making them less likely to hold onto any future plaque. I do this daily. It's especially effective on those nights when I'm having trouble getting to sleep. Somehow the visual of those scrubbing bubbles spinning and working their cleaning way, one after the other, is better than counting sheep and all the while I'm nodding off, I'm also cleaning my circulatory system. Call me crazy, but my cholesterol is great and I'll just bet I never have to have stents.

Toilet Training:

OK this one might be a little gross but we're all grown-ups here. Before the iPhone, I'd be sitting on the toilet with nothing to do but be. Well, there are the skin mags in the wall-mounted rack, but I've seen those guys a million times by now. So, deciding that I could use the time to better effect, I began, while seated there, to visualize all negativity, all germs and disease, any elements of darkness associated with illness or pain, etc, sucked (from wherever they were holed-up) and replaced with healing light. All that negative whatever would be washed through my system and right out of me into the toilet with all the other waste being eliminating. Then, I concentrate on specific parts of my body, the ones that happen to be a challenge at the moment, and I visualize anything that might be detrimental to them, dislodging itself and being replaced with the same healing light. Then I see it forcing its way down and out, eliminating with it any polyps or other bad stuff it might encounter on the way and flushing it all out right along with the all the poop. Given, like most people, I'm a dump-a-day guy, (too much information?) this is a great way to take otherwise down-time and put it to the good use of self-healing. Call me crazy, but it seems to work for me. I just have to leave the iPhone out of the bathroom or all bets are off. The same goes for urinating. I do that several times a day. Why not visualize germs and anything that might be detrimental to my health flushing away in my urine stream? Also works for farts and even sneezes. No bodily function goes to waste. Hey, it can't hurt.

Little Fat-Pricks:

I have had a weight issue since birth. Thanks Mom. My weight, I was told, doubled before I'd even left the hospital. It's been a constant struggle since. This is especially difficult for a gay man who loves sex and partying. One technique for controlling my weight is to visualize my fat cells being attacked by tiny microscopic needles that prick the cells all over their fat little selves so that the fat can ooze its nasty way out and be flushed away (see above.) If you can believe the internet, once you develop a fat cell, it's there for life. They won't be gotten rid of. Your only hope is to drain the fat out of them. Call me crazy, but that's what I see these "Little Fat-Pricks" doing. Sometimes they seem to work. Though they're probably not as effective as liposuction, they're certainly cheaper.

Pain Management:

All of a sudden I'll have a pain. "Oh good god, what fresh hell is this," will be my first thought. Then I remember what I've learned. When there's a sudden pain, let's say in my knee as I'm walking along somewhere, it is actually a reminder of how much I use that knee, depend on it and take it for granted. The pain then, is just my knee saying, "Hey! I'm down here! I'd like a little attention! Maybe some gratitude, some validation or even a thank you for a job well done!" I thank it immediately and continue walking. I'll even say aloud, though under my breath so others don't think me absolutely crazy, "Thank you knee. Thanks for going and going and going and never letting me down. I really appreciate all your hard work." I then consciously send loving healing energy to it as I continue to walk. Before you know it, the pain is gone. It pretty much works for any pain anywhere, not just knees. Call me crazy, but it sure seems to work for me and it's a lot easier and cheaper than knee replacement surgery or any other horrors the medical community is ready to foist upon us.

1998

Brenda, Don Juan, Mr Boss & Me

HANDING OUT HEADSETS for the hearing impaired at Broadway shows was just about the best gig you could get in the theater district. It was an easy job, just taking driver's licenses in exchange for headsets. Best of all, it allowed me to see just about any Broadway show I wanted, as many times as I wanted. If I like a show or a movie, etc, I've always been of the "until I have it memorized I haven't seen it enough" school, but high Broadway ticket prices don't allow you to see shows multiple times. So this gig was a great way to do just that and be paid for it. And, if there happened to be an empty seat — usually an orchestra one worth in excess of $100 — I could take it. I could watch most any of my favorite shows as many times as I'd like.

One of those favorites was *Smokey Joe's Cafe*. It was a "jukebox" musical, which are typically not my favorites. But... what *Smokey Joe's Cafe* had that made it a favorite, was Brenda Braxton. I had first seen Brenda Braxton at the *Annual Easter Bonnet Competition*, a fundraiser for Broadway Cares Equity Fights AIDS. Shelton and I managed to score two last-minute tickets to the event. **We were in the last row of the rear balcony — nosebleed territory — of the Palace Theater but when Brenda Braxton came onstage, even from way back in those cheapest of the cheap seats, she knocked my socks off.** I had never been so dazzled in a Broadway theater. Ever. She had a million dollar megawatt smile that read all the way to the rear of the top balcony — not an easy feat. I christened her the most beautiful woman I'd ever seen on a Broadway stage. She was a mesmerizing Broadway Goddess.

The first time I worked headsets at *Smokey Joe's Cafe* I could hardly contain my excitement at finally seeing Ms. Braxton in an actual Broadway show. I wasn't disappointed. In addition to all the numbers in which she was wonderful, she had one big show-stopping solo. Dragging a chair behind her, Ms. Braxton strode out onto a black stage, a black woman in a shorter-than-short black dress and higher-than-high black heels. **She was all lipstick, legs, confidence and attitude.** And that same megawatt smile. Over her shoulder matching her crimson lips was an equally crimson feather boa trailing her for, I don't know, about a mile.

She deposited the chair center stage, sat down on it and began to sing a song called "Don Juan" about an ex-boyfriend and how now that his money's gone, she's gone. It was a performance that was smoldering sex one minute and high comedy the next. **That long red boa became another performer in her extraordinarily capable hands. It took on a life of its own as she cuddled it and flung it and wrapped it and waved it and whipped it. She caressed it and somehow made it caress her. In a sexy pas de deux between performer and prop, she seasoned and peppered every line of the song and milked it for every drop of sex and humor it contained.** Mounting and dismounting the chair she had so unceremoniously dragged out there, this extraordinary performer who was to me the absolute quintessence of Broadway musical theater would always bring the house down with her sexy comic "Don Juan." Stop the show. I worked *Smokey Joe's Cafe* so often that after awhile I might not watch the entire show, but I was always in the house for Brenda and Don Juan.

With a few exceptions, at most theaters when you worked headsets you had to use the stage door and then find your way to the house (the actual theater), which is where the headset console was typically located. Since most people who use the stage door are either actors, musicians, stagehands or any other of a number of behind the scenes workers, there's really no reason to have a direct route from stage door to house. Almost no one besides, say, the headset guy needs one. That meant in most theaters it was a winding, circuitous path you had to follow, back of the house, to get to the front of the house. The upside of this was that while making your way upstairs and downstairs and this way and that, you passed through virtually every component of backstage Broadway, something that I, a real "Broadwayphile," found endlessly interesting and entertaining. I'd see the wardrobe women pressing clothes and feel the steam as I passed by their racks and racks of costumes. I'd pass by row after row of wigs on wig stands and people fussing over them. There were chorus girls and chorus boys headed to and from their dressing rooms, set pieces here and there and backdrops overhead. I'd pass by all sorts of indefinable sound equipment and electronic gadgets and the people working them. **It was a back-of-the-house dream journey past every realm of Broadway theater that only a fortunate few ever got to experience.** When I was lucky, there'd even be an occasional Broadway star. I loved it. The part I didn't love as much, was getting lost. Sometimes the path was marked with yellow arrows or the like and other times there was nothing other than the complicated directions given by the guy, probably called "Pops" at the stage door.

The Virginia Theater where *Smokey Joe's Cafe* was playing had a particularly circuitous route from stage door to house. Oftentimes I'd get turned around and end up in some sort of dead end. One day I arrived for my headset job wearing a brand new suit — it's first wearing. I'd gotten it at a Hugo Boss sample sale. It was a Baldessarini — their top of the line label — which I had purchased for next to nothing. It was a perfect fit and I felt pretty damned good about myself in my new should-have-been-a-thousand-dollar-suit as I greeted "Pops" and made my way to the back of the house. As had happened before, I took a wrong turn and found myself in a break room. **I scanned the dimly-lighted space for a way out and saw some tables and chairs, a kitchen counter, a coffee maker, a microwave, a refrigerator and Brenda Braxton. Brenda Braxton!** I stood there star-struck and frozen as I beheld my Broadway Goddess face to face. There she was in all her goddess glory, standing before me, illuminated from within as only gods and goddesses are. She was wearing a short bathrobe, mules and full make-up. I was a deer in the headlights, unable to do anything but stare. After an eternity, I managed to squeak out that I was looking for the house and made some sort of shaky apology about "barging in" on her like that. There was a long pause as those huge eyes slowly and dramatically scanned me up and down and up again as I stood frozen in her presence. **Then, flashing that**

megawatt smile she said, "Honey, looking like you do, you can barge in here anytime!" I truly did not know what to say to that and stood there processing it all, still frozen in place, open-mouthed and gawking. She mercifully broke the silence with another smile and then "The house? I think if you go right through there, honey…" She pointed the way to a door that led me, heart beating wildly, to a hallway that took me right out to my console.

1996 – 1997

Loft Lost

IT FELT VERY "NEW YORK" living in a loft in such a desolate area of the city. It was also a little intimidating but apart from my own imaginings I don't think I was ever in actual danger. There was just the potential of it given the remoteness of the address and the vulnerability of being alone on the street. Especially at night. There were a lot of trucks but little foot traffic save the prostitutes on my block. On the long walk from the 7th Ave subway, once past 10th Ave, almost home, I would cross under the threatening darkness of the derelict abandoned elevated railroad. **There was not another human in sight but for the giant Judge Judy, arms crossed, gavel in hand, smiling down from the billboard above.** I would quickly enter my building, just as derelict and abandoned looking as the elevated railroad and the entire neighborhood. A quick trip up the stairs and on the other side of my police-locked door, I breathed a sigh of relief. Every time.

As I'd sit in my garden room enjoying my unique view, I'd appreciate the fields of Queen Anne's lace, the unexpected pheasants, the chirping crickets, the generous space and the cheap rent. The desolation and threat of danger all seemed worth it. One night as I was pondering the desolation and the abandoned railroad, a thought occurred to me. Perhaps the word "epiphany" might be more accurate because as I sat there pondering my cheap third floor rent and thought about how many other un-leasable third floors were adjacent to the twenty or so blocks of that old elevated railroad, my active design imagination took over. I could see the old railroad transformed and with it, the entire neighborhood. **I imagined the entire length of the old railroad turned into a pedestrian walkway with gorgeous landscaping, paving, lighting, fountains, and sculpture gardens, all of it with glass elevator and stair access from the cross streets below. The retail designer in me saw in all those nearly worthless third floor spaces, the potential for high-end retail.** Just fill in the few feet between the railroad edge and my loft and the outside wall of my loft could be a storefront for Saks Fifth Avenue or Tiffany's or some other high-end retailer. It would be a twenty-block upscale outdoor mall. Property values would skyrocket and the entire neighborhood would be revitalized. I imagined the railroad line as an eastern border and anything west of it (then dirty and dingy) painted white. The new thriving area would become known as Manhattan's West Coast or "WECO." I even dusted off the plans from my Boston days for a store I wanted to open back then in Miami's South Beach. The store's name "Coast" would fit perfectly with the West Coast identity so of course this new neighborhood would be the perfect location for my flagship. As I sat down and drew conceptual plans and sketches I wondered how one would go

Gay Boy's Life

about making something like this happen. The thought overwhelmed me at the same time I was about to be overwhelmed by something else.

Long story short: my sketchy tweaky landlord went to jail and I had to move. At a time when everything was new and hopeful it all came to an abrupt end. After living in the loft a short time it became apparent that the landlord did not own the building. Back when we first looked at the space, he had gotten the keys to the floor of the building, presented himself as the owner, showed it to prospective renters, wrote leases and rented the spaces to us. It was only then that he had actually rented the floor from the real owner of the building. At this point with other buildings and other tenants he'd usually disappear with the money (first month, last month, security) without renting the space. He had done just that many times before. For whatever reason, our lofts were the only ones he had ever actually followed through on. That was his down-fall. He would collect the rent every month. In cash. In person. That's when the police nabbed him. First of the month. He had taken so many people for so much money it was easy to put him away. So one day after having lived in the loft a couple of years and unaware of any of this, I came home to an eviction notice posted on my door. The other two lofts had the same. The actual owner of the building was throwing us out. While we had been paying rent to our landlord, our "landlord" wasn't paying his. The owner of the building was not only throwing us out but was also suing for back rent. Two years worth! And the others who took our "landlord" to court were suing us for the rent we owed him. It was a nightmare. On the advice of my lawyer, I invited the building owner over to meet in person to see what I had created from that raw warehouse space. He saw what I was losing and though he had no choice in evicting me (it was a commercial building and I was there illegally) he dropped his lawsuit for back rent. We were both victims. The same held true for all the other lawsuits. I managed to talk my way out of them. All were eventually dropped. My lawyer jokingly said her firm wanted to make me a job offer.

My hand-wringing friends who were in love with the loft as a fun hangout were concerned for my future. I was after all losing my home and my workplace all at once. They were less accepting of my fate than I. I held my usual view of things generally working out for me. **When asked where I was going to go and what was I going to do, my response was always the same. "I don't know," I'd say in all earnestness, "I'm just throwing myself into the universe and I expect to be embraced!"**

Enter Robyn. Robyn was my first client in New York. She had met Madeleine at an antique show in The Hamptons and Madeleine had recommended me to her. We hit it off instantly. I redid her apartment and from that moment on, I was in business. Robyn was not only extraordinarily well connected but also a firm believer in my abilities and a great networker; I never had to look for a client in New York. Ever. To this day. I could make a genealogical chart over the past nearly 25 years of my New York clients and most of them could be connected back to Robyn. So in the middle of all my troubles, Robyn called one day. She hadn't heard from me in awhile and was wondering what was up. I told her, "Don't ask. You don't want to know." She responded, "Of course I want to know. What's going on?" **When I told her what was happening, without missing a beat, she responded, "Move in with me."** I told her I was pretty desperate and she should be careful. She repeated, "Move in with me. I'm serious. I know what living with you would be like." And then once again, "Move in with me. And your little dog too."

I rapidly sold off as much merchandise as I could and then, along with Shelton, packed up and moved two truckloads of what remained to a storage space way up in Hudson, New York where I once again stored my life away. With the loft emptied and the storage space packed full, back from Hudson sometime after 1am, I dropped Shelton off, returned the truck, and along with my little dog Boogie, exhausted, without a clue as to what my next step would be, spent my first night in Robyn's apartment. She was in The Hamptons. It was August 31, 1997. The next morning I walked Boogie to a little bodega down the street to get a coffee and glanced at The New York Times headline. **Princess Diana was dead.**

1999

Robyn's Nest

WHEN I MOVED IN WITH ROBYN at one of the lowest points in my life, it was with the intention of staying perhaps a couple of months; just long enough to get my bearings after the traumatic loss of my loft. Losing both my home and workspace, practically overnight, put me right back where I'd started in New York. Worse actually; having invested all my funds into my now deceased business, my bank account had died as well. No money. No prospects. A packed tight storage space with rent due monthly. Once again I had no idea what I was going to do with my life.

I continued with my mantra, "I'm throwing myself into the universe and I expect to be embraced," and in so doing would continue to remind myself of the philosophy I've developed over a lifetime of things going horribly wrong and yet to my amazement, working themselves out. Often miraculously so. **I once again did my best to just get out of the way, be grateful for my current state, aligning myself with the universe and allowing it to do its job; the way it was designed.** I knew that accepting my current circumstance, no matter how at odds it was with what I'd wish, would put me in synch with the universe that gave me this challenge. Aligned with it then, rather than fighting it, we could work together in harmony and get through this, as we had before. Many times before.

My acceptance of the tragic loss of my home and business and my willingness to go along with the universe (though it certainly didn't seem to have my best interests at heart) redirected my thinking. I began to look at the loss as a sort of correction. I decided that, with the loft and the antique business, I perhaps had gone off in an inappropriate direction and the universe was simply redirecting me. I had to admit that selling antiques was a back-breaking business that wasn't producing nearly the income I'd hoped for. This was just the way things had to be to put me on the right path. And save my back. That level of acceptance had brought me Robyn. Her offer to live with her became the initial embrace I had hoped for and expected. I had a place where I could stay in New York, be safe and gather myself for whatever was next. Once under her roof, during the first week, Robyn said I could stay with her the rest of my life if I wanted to. While I did not doubt her sincerity — that's just who she is, I knew I couldn't stay forever. **I had to get a life again and move on from the comfort, contentment, fun times and instant family I'd found with her.**

My father died in the spring of 1999. I went back to Louisville to be with him and my family prior to his passing and stayed with my mom for about six weeks after his death. The loss of her ever-adoring husband was of course devastating to her. I was "Little Mike," there to keep her company and help her over the inevitable hurdle of loneliness she experienced at the loss of her "Big Mike." After a sickness of less than two months, the constant companionship of a 54 year marriage was gone. During my stay, in addition to keeping my mom company, I also helped her in any way I could, including getting her rose garden in shape for the summer. This was work she and my father had done together for decades and now she was left to do it on her own. A love of flowers, roses in particular, along with our shared hatred of Bermuda grass, was one of the many bonds I shared with my mom. By the time I headed back to New York, her rose garden looked spectacular and she was adjusting to her new life alone. My sister and brother were the local constants, always in her life and available at a moment's notice, while I was the long-distance son who came and went as regularly as I could.

By the time I returned from spring in Louisville it was summer in New York. My cohabitation with Robyn was going on two years — rather than the two months I had originally anticipated. Boogie and I had so settled in to life on King Street that Robyn's home really did feel like our own. Robyn was out to work typically by 7am each weekday and not home until around 11pm as she would go out to dinner and drinks with clients or friends. She was such a *Sex in The City* girl. During the summer, on the weekends, it wasn't unusual for her to head off on a Friday morning and then after work head straight to her share in The Hamptons, stay through Monday morning and go to work from there. I wouldn't see her from Friday morning at 7am until Monday night at 11pm. We'd then have Tuesday, Wednesday, and Thursday evenings to catch up with each other and *Frasier* and *The Guiding Light*. Then, she was back out to The Hamptons. And that was summer. **It was really as if Boogie and I lived on King Street and Robyn was visiting us.** I was comfortable. Being comfortable, for me, can be a blessing and a curse in equal parts.

Even though I felt at home and comfortable (there it is again) at Robyn's, I knew I couldn't sleep on her sofa forever. **So I bought a futon.** But even off-sofa, I couldn't get rid of that nagging voice telling me I needed to move on. I knew myself all too well. If I'm comfortable and safe, I'm settling in. I was in very real danger of staying forever. Two months had turned into two years. In the blink of an eye, those two years could become a decade. She might just be stuck with me forever. I'd have to force myself from this safe and happy Robyn's nest and get a life.

I just couldn't quite figure out what that life would look like. And where would it be? New York was out of the question. Way too expensive. My investment in a lost business and a lost life had left me with nothing. My fledgling interior design business was not yet nearly enough to support me. In New York that is. But that's where the clients were. I could no longer afford my favorite city. I also could not envision leaving it. So after my return from Louisville, I decided to have a heart-to-heart with myself — a real "Come To Jesus Moment" — one that would force me to come to terms with my current state in life and make a plan for my future. This was not something I did with any regularity or comfort. The AIDS era had taught me to live in the present. Not believing I had a future, I had become unaccustomed to planning for one.

My inner Scarlett O'Hara who had happily embraced the "Tomorrow is another day" philosophy of procrastination, had put off thinking about tomorrow for far too long. I had to think about it now. And make a plan. Did I want to see the year 2000 and a new millennium in while sleeping on a futon on the floor of someone else's home? No matter how comfortable that home might be? **I had to strip down to my naked and gay self, take a hard look in the mirror and plan for a New Millenium.** I did just that. Literally naked. Staring into the mirror I became distracted. "Not bad," I thought, turning this way and that,. "At least I haven't let my body go." On the contrary. That was something positive to focus on. It was true. I'd had a lot of time for the gym and all those hours left me looking pretty good. Damned good actually. Thoughts about my current situation faded as I surveyed the firm, trim, smooth muscular curves of my naked, freshly tanned-from-Louisville-yard-work, summer-ready body. Of course I got horny, grabbed my hardening penis and jacked off.

Normally that would have been the end of it but my tried and true method of problem avoidance hadn't worked this time. After a quick windexing, I went right back to the question at hand, so to speak. This was one time I wouldn't let myself off by getting off. Rather than taking my usual post-ejaculation nap, I began instead to ask the really hard questions. What had brought me to this sorry state? Had I chronically masturbated myself into this situation? How did I end up with an empty bank account and no future? How did I end up sleeping on a friend's floor? What did I have to show for my life? How had I managed to get to nearly fifty years old and skip right over what should have been my most productive years? Those were the same years when "most people" have their greatest financial success, the years I "should have" had my greatest financial success. How had I managed to squander all of those years? **Had the relentless pursuit of sex and fun been so all-consuming that I had allowed everything else to take a backseat?** What had I done wrong? Everything of course.

I beat myself up for all the "wrong" choices I'd made. All the times I turned left when I "should have" turned right. The decisions I made to slow down when I "should have" sped up. To drop out when I "should have" stayed in. All the time spent "being" rather than "doing." Chase's frustrated words, "I never see you DO-ing anything," echoed in my brain. I even blamed myself for the things that had been out of my control. How had I allowed it all? I thought of all the time I spent chasing boys instead of a career; all the time "wasted" on sex rather than work and money; all the hours spent jerking off, putting off my life, waiting to die rather than actually living and making a living. All the orgasms instead of income. The hours at the gym. The nights partying. I blamed myself for it all, angry, and worse, disappointed with what I saw in the mirror. "How, Michael, did you do this?" I could never get those years back. I had nothing to show for them. I questioned every decision and action that had brought me to this moment. "How did you miss your 'best' years?" I asked over and over, "The years, nearly two decades of them, when you should have been at your most productive? What have you got to show for it? Michael, what have you done?" **Not much.**

There weren't any easy answers. I stood there momentarily ashamed of my reflected image and the near-half of my life gone in the blink of an eye. I had "squandered" too many of those years, somehow allowing them to slip right through my fingers and had nothing to show for them. **I had met the promise of the "underachiever" status assigned early-on to grade-schooler Mikey. Standing naked in the unforgiving light of self-examination, I looked into the mirror and saw a failure.**

1999

Things Just Seem To Work Out For Me

I N THE MIDST of all the negativity, something began to happen. After all the self-examination, self-shaming and self-judgement, still standing there naked and staring at myself in that unforgiving mirror, a higher power kicked in. I continued to think of those same years, the past fifteen or so that I had "lost" and "wasted," the same years I'd dropped out to die but instead had lived to take care of my dying partner and friends. **I began to see those years differently.** The years I'd spent loving those same friends over to the other side and mourning the losses. Years hardly lost. I thought about all the time spent learning how to deal with the loss and recover from the heartbreak. The wounds that had healed and the scars that remained. The years during which I had learned to "be" rather than do. The spiritual growth I'd enjoyed from just "being." And how that growth had helped me to deal and cope with the heartbreak and loss. The things I'd learned that I couldn't have possibly learned under some corporate umbrella. All the years I hadn't spent at a desk in some mind-numbing job navigating company politics but had instead enjoyed being in command of my own time. All that I'd learned while gardening in Beacon Hill or floating on a pool in Key West. All the life lessons. All the great sex. All the new friends. All the clients whose stores and homes and lives I'd made better. I began to appreciate the many ways in which I had grown.

Light started to seep in and illuminate the shadowy corners of my negativity, my doubt and self-hating. My perspective began to shift. I started thinking a bit more kindly about those years and, in turn, about the naked "failure" I saw in the mirror. Perhaps a bank balance wasn't that important compared to my newly acquired spiritual wealth. Perhaps the years hadn't been wasted after all. Perhaps I'd just taken another path. I had survived hadn't I? That was something. Especially when so many hadn't. When had I ever been just like everybody else anyway? My negative thoughts began to dissolve one by one as positive ones took over. I began to instinctively employ all the devices I'd learned over the years about acceptance. Perhaps my wrong turns had been right ones. **It's possible.** The "bad" choices good ones. **Also possible.** Perhaps every little thing that had led me to this moment had been right and appropriate, and that the road I had travelled was exactly the one I should have been on all along. **Possible.** Perhaps I was exactly where I was supposed to be at that particular moment in time. **That too was possible. Perhaps after my house had been torn down by a tornado, I had managed to construct a new foundation, this time on solid ground.** Perhaps it was time to begin building on that foundation and go about the business of living again. Preparing to die, I had put my life on hold, but, having not died, I needed to once again think of the future. These were much happier thoughts. I accepted them all and began to see the choices that brought me to that point as right and appropriate. "Perhaps" grew into certainty and the possibilities became actualities as I accepted that I was right where I belonged and became grateful for the journey that had brought me there.

I think of my old friend Dorothy who, at her big moment, as instructed, had taken the yellow brick road. **I had often wondered, given there was also a red brick road right alongside the yellow one, what if she'd chosen it instead?** The one that hadn't been recommended. The one "less travelled." Would the red brick road have been easier? Harder? Who would she have met along the way? Would she have regretted not taking the yellow brick road, as she'd been told, and beaten herself up for her red brick journey? How far off course would she have strayed, if at all? What other things would she have learned, or not? Most important of all, where would the red brick road have taken her? I suppose she'd still have ended up right where she belonged.

If the journey leads to self-realization, there are no wrong choices or wrong roads, for the destination is always the same.

Accepting my own journey and, in so doing, realigning myself with the universe that had given it, my inner-Scarlett was back to join my inner-Dorothy. No longer the procrastinating Scarlett but the planner, I heard her ask, "Where shall I go? What shall I do?" Hmmmmm. "I don't need to go anywhere. I am right where I belong." OK, first question answered. My eyes focused on the eyes in the mirror and I asked the second question, "What shall I do?" Oh geez. "Do." That word. Be-ing is easy. Do-ing is hard. It came to me. "Find a way to stay in New York." Easily said. Not easily done. What would it take to stay in New York? Manhattan preferably. What would it take? Oh lord. I thought about it. What would it take? I thought some more. I almost had it but it slipped away. What would it take? A job? Unlikely. Where would I find one that would pay enough to keep me in New York? And by this time, nearly 50 and self-employed for 15 years, had I become one of the "hardcore unemployable?" A boyfriend? Even less likely. **Sofa-sleeper that I was, body or no body, I wasn't much of a catch at this point and couldn't quite imagine anyone wanting to commit to the current me.** And in my state of flux, I clearly wasn't ready for the commitment. I thought some more. Still nothing. It occurred to me that even though I wanted to stay in the city, perhaps I wasn't supposed to stay. What I wanted, I had learned over the years, is irrelevant. What I need is what I'd get. I knew I could trust the universe to give me that at the very least. What did I need? **Perhaps a sign.**

A sign. "Yes!" What I needed was a sign. That was it. Something to tell me that yes, in fact, I was supposed to continue my life in New York City. Or not. I tried to keep an open mind but I really didn't focus much on the "or not." **The years had taught me to be aware of signs — especially the positive ones — and I had become a firm believer in them.** They are always there and I had become accustomed to all the signposts large and small, guiding the way. I could depend on them. I'd learned that much. I need only to pay attention and be grateful. They will always be there. And waiting for a sign allowed old procrastinator Scarlett to put it all off to "another day."

What kind of sign? Should I look for something specific to tell me I should stay? If so then what would it be? Yes, I decided, something specific. Something I'd recognize instantly. Something that most certainly would keep me in New York. But what? I thought it over some more and then it came to me. **A rent-controlled apartment in Greenwich Village. The New York City Holy Grail. It was all I could afford and the only way I could afford to stay in New York.** I decided on the spot, if a rent-controlled apartment in Greenwich Village presented itself, that would be my sign.

Greenwich Village, The West Village in particular, is my favorite neighborhood in all New York. I'd gotten glimpses of it in movies as a small boy and had fallen in love with its quirkiness and sense of mystery. There were things going on in that "interesting" place and I could see my grown-up self living there and exploring them all. I fantasized about it regularly. Since Greenwich Village was one of the gay capitals in the 70s and 80s, I visited often during those decades. It was all that I'd hoped for and more. I had sex with a lot of boys in that neighborhood and got to know it. Sort of. It's a crazy quilt of streets, at odds with the New York grid; Waverly Place actually crosses itself at Waverly Place, so you can get a bit turned around. I would walk its quiet tree-lined streets visualizing myself actually living some day in that quirky, charming, sexy playground, reinforcing my childhood dream. Buttressing it. By the time I'd finally made it to New York, the neighborhood had become too expensive, well beyond my reach. But for the possibility of finding a rent-controlled apartment, I could no longer even fantasize myself there. Now, any New Yorker will tell you that a rent-controlled apartment in Greenwich Village is a fantasy, on the rarity scale right up with the Gutenberg Bible and the Hope Diamond. There are urban legends built around these apartments. **They're the unicorns of the real estate world.** I wasn't even certain they still existed, having never met anyone who actually lived in one. Two of the friends on the TV show *Friends* lived in one but apart from them (and they were fictional), I had never met anyone who even knew anyone who actually lived in one. I was god knows how many degrees of separation from any prospect of a sign.

Nevertheless, I decided on the spot, still looking into that mirror of truth, that my sign would be a rent-controlled apartment in Greenwich Village. If a rent-controlled apartment in The West Village should fall in my lap, then I would know with absolute certainty that I was meant to stay in New York. This would be a challenge and I tossed it right off to the universe, the same universe that had embraced me so many times before. The universe that gave me Robyn would give me this if this was the right thing for me. I knew I could depend on that universe. It would come through. I mean, things, after all, do usually work out for me. **This was a big request and I couldn't ask for more. Still standing there naked, I got excited by the possibilities and I gave myself one more good wank.**

Days later, I was walking on shady tree-lined Grove Street, as I had so often, given it's my favorite street in the Village. **Just at its intersection with Bleecker Street, I saw a handsome, somewhat older and quite dapper-looking man.** Now handsome, older and dapper wouldn't typically catch my eye. My usual "type" would be better described as cute, younger and sexy, but there was something special that did catch my eye about this well-dressed man. And then he smiled. That handsome face with its sparkling baby blue eyes lit up with a dazzling smile and it was directed right at me. Returning his smile with mine, I walked up to him. We began to talk. He introduced himself as "Eric." Within the first minute or two, among many other things, he told me he lived "right down the street," (pointing down Grove Street) and added with what seemed to be great pride, "I've been in the same apartment for twenty-five years." **"Twenty-five years,"** I repeated. **"Wow! That's a long time."** As I digested this information he handed me his business card and said he had "to go to work." I thanked him and we parted ways. Twenty-five years.

Any New Yorker will tell you that saying you've lived in the same apartment for twenty-five years is tantamount to saying you live in a rent-controlled apartment. A rent-controlled apartment! This man had just told me in New York City shorthand, that he was living in a rent-controlled apartment. **Not only that, his rent-controlled apartment was on my favorite street. The same street, by the way, where the TV *Friends* lived in theirs.** What were the chances? My mind reeled. Make no mistake, when I put my request in to the universe for a sign, had I thought to be more specific, I'd have asked for a rent-controlled apartment on Grove Street. I hadn't wanted to be pushy. But there it was, right there on Grove Street, the answer to my universal request, my sign, only a few days after I'd made it. Asked and answered.

It seemed I'd found the apartment, but there was someone in it. It was surely rent-controlled, but also occupied. What was I to do with this information? Later as I placed Eric's business card by the phone in Robyn's kitchen (this was still a time when a phone was on a wall, not in a pocket) I wondered, "Is this truly the sign I'd asked for?" How could it not be? How else was a rent-controlled apartment going to present itself? And the timing. And Grove Street. *Friends!* This had to be my sign. But I'd asked for an apartment, not a relationship. This was obviously a stable kind of guy. Very stable. Too stable. Twenty-five years at the same address kind of stable. As I stood there running my finger over Eric's engraved name on his card, I started counting on my other hand my own corresponding twenty-five years and the seventeen addresses I'd had in seven cities. I was not so stable and demurred at the thought of interjecting my mutability into this man's stability. I did not want to get into a relationship for the housing it would provide. Even though I was pretty desperate and this housing was rent-controlled. Even though it happened to be on my favorite street in my favorite neighborhood. Even though it seemed to be the immediate answer to my "sign" request. I couldn't ignore the timing. I'd asked and within days I had been given an answer. Sort of. I wasn't sure.

I needed another sign, a follow-up sign, to validate the first one. That was it. Something, anything, to tell me to make a phone call and pursue this. Weeks went by. Nothing. Every day I would look at that business card next to Robyn's yellow wall-mounted trimline phone, listen to my gut and ponder the name printed on it and ponder my next move. My gut told me nothing. I kept my eyes and ears open but nothing told me to pick up that receiver and call. I'd stare at that business card (he was also called Richard, which brought back thoughts of Chase and his many names) wondering what I should do.

About six or so weeks after that initial meeting, on a hot and humid mid-July evening, I was feeling horny and frisky. It's always the heat and humidity that get me. I smoked some weed, put on a pair of shorts and my sexiest tank top and, after Boogie's walk, I kissed her goodbye and headed my horniness out into the summer night, a little high and looking for trouble. I walked up 7th Avenue and turned left onto Bleecker Street headed toward 8th Avenue, one of my usual routes to gay Chelsea. As I approached Bleecker's intersection with Grove Street, there he was again. The handsome Eric with the sparkling eyes was standing on the street corner where we'd met the first time. The same street corner. **In a city of so many people, and so many corners, there he was, the same man on the same corner; this was my sign.** I needed no other confirmation. He hadn't yet seen me so I walked right up to him and said, "Eric." He focused those baby blues on me for a second or two before an unhappy look of recognition crossed his face. The blue sparklers cooled and narrowed. He was quick to admonish me in a deeper-than-it-had-been-before voice, "Oh...you're the guy who never called me. I was sure I was going to hear from you that night." I guess I couldn't blame him for his lack of enthusiasm. I responded with, "No I didn't. But...your card's right by the phone. I look at it everyday." He wasn't convinced and responded, "Oh sure it is..." I cut him off, "It is! Right by the phone." We chatted a little. He explained that his real name is Richard but he used that name primarily for business. So he was Richard to some, Eric to others and Richard Eric to still others. "Oh good lord," I thought, flashing back to Chase and his multiple personalities, "not another one." Happily, though answering to several names, Eric thankfully turned out to have one all-purpose personality. He asked me what I was up to. I told him I had no plans. He asked me back to his place.

I woke up the next morning in New York City's Greenwich Village, on Grove Street in Eric's arms in his rent-controlled triplex. Yes, triplex. That's three floors. From the film *Notting Hill*, as if reading my mind he quoted Hugh Grant, "You can stay forever." "Hmm, stay forever," I thought as I remembered Robyn's same words. With my designer's eye making its way around the top floor of that split-level apartment, I thought, "I could do something with this space." Was I home? It had all been so quick and so specific, it had to be home. I would just have to relax into this and know that it was right. Or perhaps I should look for a sign. Yes, another sign. That was it! One more little nod from the universe that this was indeed the right direction. Something quick so I wouldn't waste the time and emotions of this lovely Eric lying next to me. **If I were going to upend this man's life, I was going to need one more sign before I did it.** Like the others, I was certain I'd know it when I'd see it.

I awakened that morning, as I do every morning, with two things: morning wood and a need for coffee. We happily took care of the first and when I mentioned the latter, to my surprise, though a coffee drinker, Eric didn't have a coffee maker. What adult human being doesn't have a way to make coffee? He shrugged it off with, "I just go around the corner to the deli." I was instantly charmed and amused by his quintessential New Yorker response.

I told him about Boogie who I'd left alone. She'd desperately be needing a walk. I had to get back to Robyn's. He suggested that I go to Robyn's, collect Boogie and walk her back. We could have brunch at an outdoor cafe that allows dogs. Walking Boogie along Grove Street that gorgeous Sunday morning, as I glanced ahead there he was, big handsome smiling Eric waiting for us on the stoop of his building. As we approached I saw, waiting next to him on the steps, a large coffee, a bowl of water and some carefully placed doggie biscuits. **My sign. Apartment or no apartment, he had me at the doggie biscuits.**

I took Eric up on his Hugh Grant offer, bought a coffee maker and settled in to stay forever. With the Millennium approaching I was safe and secure in our rent-controlled triplex apartment, on my favorite street, in my favorite neighborhood, in my favorite city, with a man to love and to love me. And my little dog too.

Things just seem to work out for me.

2001

One More Year

ALL I'VE EVER WANTED is to be one year older. It's been that way all my life. Just one more year. As a child, when asked about my age, I would answer, "On my next birthday I'll be __ years old," always going to the next year. I suppose it's typical of children to wish to be older but for me it was a mission. **Just one more year.**

In grammar school I looked up to the eighth graders. Ever-immature for my age, I couldn't wait to be like them. Eighth graders were grown up. Mature. Until I got to be one. Somehow when I arrived at the lofty age of twelve — the oldest kids in school — I wasn't grown up like all the other eighth graders before me had been. I was still a kid. What happened? They grew up. Why hadn't I? I had fallen victim to what I would later name, "The Eighth Grader Syndrome." For whatever reason, those who preceded me had managed to mature into eighth graders, but I hadn't. I would tell myself, "Just one more year. In one more year I'll feel grown up...at last."

Moving on to high school, The Eighth Grader Syndrome followed me. Different school. Same story. During my underclassmen years, I looked up to the upperclassmen and couldn't wait to become a senior and be mature, just like them. Grown up at last. Didn't happen. Somehow what had worked for them hadn't worked for me. Finally a senior but not very senior. **Why had the maturing process been designed for everyone but me?**

Perhaps it had something to do with birth order. As the youngest in our family I saw myself as such and within that familial context, resisted the growing up process at every turn. I was immature. I'd been told this on every occasion by everyone around me. My teachers, my brother and sister and even my parents had pronounced me immature over and over again. Immaturity became part of my self-identity. I was after all "the baby" of the family and referred to as such constantly by my mother. "And this is our baby," she would say, adding the diminutive "Mikey" as she introduced me to someone or anyone. Baby. Mikey. Baby Mikey. It made me feel loved, cuddled...babied. Being the baby is what made me special in our family and

I guess I wasn't about to let go of that identity. **My need to hold onto my babyhood was at odds with my desire to shed it.**

Being gay has played a part as well in my inability to grow up. Like most gay boys, I was denied a gay childhood. I wasn't encouraged to be the gay boy I was. I wasn't even *allowed* to be the gay boy I was. I couldn't play dress-ups with my sister, have dolls, draw ladies' clothes or arrange flowers the way I had wanted. I was discouraged away from much of what I found "pretty" and was encouraged to be a "regular boy" with regular boy pursuits. And have a regular boy's childhood. **Someone else's childhood. I was given *Boys' Life* magazine, which proclaimed on its cover, "For All Boys," but I found little of *my* boy's life in its pages.** They gave me baseball bats and gloves. Footballs and helmets. Guns and little green army men. Trucks. They discouraged me away from designing evening gowns and my ladies' fall collections and encouraged me toward the more manly-appropriate architecture. A large part of my gay manhood, then, has been about pursuing the gay childhood I was denied. **A precious part of me remains a little gay boy who dresses up now and then — whether black leather or a pink tutu — and parties with all the other little gay boys who also never quite grew up.** Together with them — doctors, lawyers, designers and pilots, I am the little gay boy I was meant (but never allowed) to be. As an adult, no matter how deferred, I am finally living my own Gay Boy's Life.

And still, there remains an undeniable need to grow up. Like all the other kids. Become an eighth grader. Become a high school senior. Become an adult. Give me one more year and I'll finally shed my babyhood. Just one more year and I might finally be and see myself as the adult I'm supposed to be. That the world expects me to be. Just one more year and perhaps I will shed my inner Peter Pan and might even start to think of myself as an actual grown-up rather than a grown-up baby. Just one more year.

Just one more year took on an entirely new meaning during the AIDS era. Suddenly it wasn't about getting older, it was about staying alive. Just one more year. Give me just one more year to live. That's all. For a while, maturing was no longer the focus. Simple existence was. Year after year, against all odds, I'd be blessed with one more year and another and another even as I watched my younger friends grow old and die. But in the face of it all, I kept getting my wish for more of those years, as horrible as they were. I suppose there is a certain sense of optimism in wanting one more year. In one more year, things will be better. In one more year, problems will be solved. **In one more year, perhaps it'll all be over and my friends will stop dying.** It's a hopeful sense of optimism that served me well those dark years of sickness, death and loss. Just one more year.

You'd think the challenges presented by those hellish years might have given me the maturity I'd sought but even after all the loss and all the horrors, somehow I still wasn't as grown up as my peers. That same old feeling of immaturity persisted as I happily approached my gay "daddy" years. Unhappily the Eighth Grader Syndrome persisted. It was pointed out to me by several younger daddy-oriented boys that I just wasn't daddy enough. **I saw myself in the daddy role long before I grew into it.** While I had the years, I didn't have the maturity to pull it off. Not daddy enough? "Ya gotta behave like a daddy to be a daddy." I'd heard time and again. Just like in grade school, everyone managed to grow up but me. I'd been a daddy-in-training most of my life; would I ever achieve true daddy-dom like all the other daddies? I stayed optimistic though and still firmly believed that given one more year I would finally grow up and find my inner daddy. Go from Gay Power to Gray Power. Just one more year.

There is an upside to immaturity. It seems, somewhere along the way — I think it was during my forties or perhaps fifties — though still technically immature, I had become "youthful." **It seems if you hang onto immaturity long enough, you become suddenly youthful.** Who knew? That big negative cloud of immaturity that hung over me and identified me, sometime during mid-life, lifted. I am now youthful. I can live with that. And one more year.

So, I arrived at the dawn of a new century and a new Millennium, nearing my own mid-century point, youthful. The greatly anticipated year 2000 arrived without so much as a ripple. Y2K never happened and the new century seemed pretty much the same as the previous century. I still hadn't grown up, but I was "youthful" now, so I no longer cared.

At the end of the first year of the new Millennium, I found myself at New Year's Eve 2000. Fifty years since the New Year's Eve I was conceived. Thirty-one years since my first New Year's Eve gay kiss and twenty years since the New Year's Eve when I sat at a friend's party sharing with Randy my dread of the decade ahead. 2001 (of *A Space Odyssey* fame) was just about here and I was looking forward to whatever changes that fabled year might bring. I'd be turning fifty the coming September. AARP, which began its mailings at the first of the year, would decide that on September 4, 2001, I'd reach maturity. According to them I'd be a senior citizen. **I knew better.** I was still nowhere near as senior as all the other seniors and nearly seniors I saw around me. Deciding that maturity is grossly overrated, I would happily and youthfully accept and embrace, at long last, The Second Grader Syndrome. And one more year. I wouldn't think to ask for more. In September I would turn fifty youthful years old, officially taking me into my senior years still lacking the maturity of my peers. So what? Who cares?

What could September 2001 in New York City ever bring that could possibly change that?

BONUS CHAPTER

From My Next Book With the Working Title...

I DIDN'T THINK
TO ASK
FOR MORE

I

remain

constantly amazed

by

an accommodating

universe

that works

in

such wonderful,

magical,

and sometimes

miraculous ways

and

I

am eternally grateful.

1998

The Man With The Ball

PROMISE ME SOMETHING! The bearded angel flashing his beatific smile intermittently illuminated by multi-colored pulsing lights was beaming goodness up at me. I didn't know who he was or what the promise might be, but kneeling now at the edge of the stage at the 2015 Rapido Amsterdam Pride Party I could not have denied such a face any request. I leaned in a little closer and trying to make myself heard over the loud techno music, I responded, "Sure. Anything. What is it?" With his sparkling eyes fixed on mine he continued, **"Promise me you will never stop doing that!"**

"That" started some eighteen years before. Walking up Varick Street in New York City and glancing into a shop window, an unusual looking sphere caught my eye. It was on a coffee table in a printing shop, the type of place where you have stationery or business cards, things like that, custom-made. I watched as a young man picked up the sphere and it instantly expanded from perhaps ten inches in diameter to nearly three feet. Just like that. This intrigued me as he played with the sphere, making it expand and contract. I went in to investigate further. The young man had moved on, so I picked up the dark blue plastic ball and began to play with it, increasing and decreasing its size. It handled so easily. Taking it over to the sales counter I asked a young woman what it was. She said a coworker had found it in a shop in the West Village. As she went off to procure the name of the shop, I continued to play with the expanding sphere.

Later I sought out the shop, Tah-Poozie, on Greenwich Ave and the owner, a lovely man named Sam introduced me to The Hoberman Sphere. It was a toy designed by an engineer who lived right in Greenwich Village and specialized in expandable structures for use in places like outer space or under the ocean. Sam carried an inventory of spheres in varying colors. One was a bright neon green. "It glows in the dark," I thought, "perfect." **I bought my first Hoberman Sphere on the spot.**

If you've made it this far in "Gay Boy's Life" you know that by this time, I had spent decades dancing on boxes and stages. Along with me there'd be other guys, some dancing with big fabric flags — oftentimes glow-in-the-dark. I had never been a "flagger" but I saw in the sphere its potential as a dance apparatus similar to the flags. Especially since it also glowed in the dark. Having spent an entire gay lifetime dancing with my arms overhead it seemed I had spent the better part of my dancing years preparing for this. The sphere had been the missing component. **My entire dancing style had been designed just for the Hoberman Sphere.** I was complete. Well, almost. One day while strolling along Canal Street, I stopped in a plastics store and bought several dozen diamond shaped mirrors, took them home and glued them onto all the pivot points inside and out. If I ever got up the nerve to take this thing on stage with me, I'd be a great big human disco ball. Now I was complete!

I decided to premiere my sphere at The Black Party 1998 in NYC, the granddaddy of the gay circuit. Held annually in Roseland Ballroom on the Saturday night closest to the Vernal Equinox, it drew a large, 5,000+ crowd of black leather barely-clad gay men. It was a drug-fueled, nearly-naked sexy event that I had been attending for years. It would be the perfect venue for the ball. Its green neon glow would surely be a standout against all that black, and the mirrors reflecting the lasers…well, I could see it.

As I went through security at Roseland, the ball caused quite a commotion with the security staff. They allowed me in and after penetrating the dense heated wall of masculinity that greets you (and the always lengthy coat check) I made my way to the stage via the back stairs. I danced in the shadows at the rear waiting until it felt right to approach the front. After dancing awhile hidden behind other partiers, the music shifted just as a path opened to the front edge of the stage. I took this as an invitation and moved forward. I danced front and center, as is typical for me, hovering above the dense sea of men, but this time with my new neon ball. I kept my new toy compressed waiting for the best moment to show it off. I danced this way for quite awhile with the small glowing ball between my hands waiting for my moment. Even though compressed I could see it catch the ultra violet light and an occasional partier taking note of the glow. I kept the sphere small and then, all of a sudden, the music suddenly exploded and so did my Hoberman Sphere! Almost involuntarily, I expanded it right along with the music, to its full spinning circumference. The lighting guy cooperated with an ultraviolet spot that set the sphere on fire! As I danced, I opened it. I closed it. I spun it. All in time to each beat of the music. **It became a blazing ball of light in my hands — more than I'd anticipated.** Faces in the crowd were wide-eyed and open-mouthed. Arms went in the air and fingers pointed. An actual wave of upturned faces and outstretched pointing arms coursed it way across the crowded dance floor. The arms then began to open and close with each expansion and contraction of the ball — waves of motion mimicking my movements. I could see the word, "WOW" mouthed over and over again throughout the crowd as friends jostled friends alerting them to my spinning ball of light. Many moved in for a closer look and those in front tried to reach up and touch it. The dancers to either side on the stage applauded and cheered, trying to get a better look.

My first outing with the ball had been a huge success. I had handled it as if I had been doing so all my life. This was indeed my missing piece. I could have danced all night and practically did. I was hooked. I was accustomed to the enormous energy exchange I'd feel while dancing on stage at these parties but the energy the crowd fed me that night was beyond any I had experienced before. **That ball was an energy collector!** I connected with the party in an amped-up way greater than I'd ever experienced before. I had arrived onstage at about 3am and danced I am quite certain to at least 3pm the following afternoon — 12+ hours of non-stop dancing, spinning my big glowing expanding sphere, drawing energy from the crowd and sending it right back. My new ball was my new drug and I became an addict. I couldn't wait for the next fix. I brought the ball out at Gay Pride, did the entire length of the parade with it and the response was spectacular.

Over the years I've developed a following, an expanding sphere (if you will) of people who crowd the dance floor in front of the stage, dancing with their arms up going in and out following my moves and my expanding sphere. **People would come up to me at parties and tell me that they'd hoped I would be there and thank me.** And then there were the gifts. Guys would come up to me with neon bracelets and necklaces and rings and all sorts of glowing, flashing and blinking accessories to wear. Once, two boys danced up to me with pineapples on their heads and placed the two pineapples at my feet. Pineapples! I remember looking at the boy dancing next to me with a queried look on my face as if to say, "What the...?" His response as he shrugged and leaned into my ear was, "Offerings." The most memorable 'offering' came at one of the Black Parties when I could see way off at the far left edge of the dance floor two guys dancing with something on their heads. Was it the pineapple guys again? I couldn't tell what the items were — they were not pineapples — but the dancing figures kept getting closer and closer bouncing their way through the almost impenetrable black clad crowd. As they got closer I saw they were two glowing jugs, one green and the other orange. The boys danced their way to the edge of the stage. placed the glowing jugs at my feet, pointed to them and mouthed the words, "For you." They were two big jugs of frozen Gatorade in two flavors, enough to keep me cool and hydrated all night. In the frenzy of the moment, I thanked them as they moved on before I could ask, "Who are you?" "Why do you have frozen Gatorade at The Black Party?" "How did you get Frozen Gatorade into The Black Party?" "Why me?" "Are you the pineapple guys from before?"

Not everyone is so enamored with me and my ball. The flaggers as they are called didn't know what to do with me. There are so many of them and only one of me so they unwittingly became a background to me and my ball. I guess I didn't have to take center stage but it just seemed to be a better arrangement symmetrically speaking, one ball in the center surrounded by all those whirling flags. Really a thing of beauty. They didn't quite see it that way and would occasionally try to flag me right off the stage. It worked. I would retreat to far stage left or right. Sometimes this wasn't enough as they just seemed to want me gone. I stood my ground and over the years we seem to have come to a place of mutual respect. Being (as I have been called) "relentlessly friendly' I have even made friends with several flaggers. There have been others not so in love with me and my ball — guys who just don't understand what I'm up to up there. One good friend good-naturedly calls me the "attention whore" and I guess to some, I am. There's one European party promoter in particular who comes to mind... I'm getting ahead of myself. More on that story later.

Once at a White Party in New York I was dancing on a platform when I felt a tug at my pant leg. I looked down the see a young man signaling that he wanted to tell me something. I squatted down and he said he had a message from the lighting man up in the booth. It was either Guy Smith or Steve Revlon — both are listed on the poster. He wanted me to be aware of the spinning, circular images being projected on the ceiling, and that he had turned off the spinning circle over my head because, he said, I was that spinning circle down on the floor. A tribute from the lighting guy. That was a first. Later at that same party after hours of constant dancing, music and lights, all of a sudden the music stopped and the room went dark. **This is a rare occurrence and when it happens you know something special is on its way.** I stood there on my platform in the dark silence, my ball and me, waiting anxiously just like the rest of the room. What's it gonna be? All of a sudden an ultra-violet spot pierced the darkness and blinded me. Oh good lord, in that darkened room the spotlight was on me! I froze. At the same time, the DJ, Warren Gluck, started playing "Someday I'll Fly Away" by Nicole Kidman. It is a richly orchestrated piece of music and my favorite song from the film *Moulin Rouge*. With its quiet, softly romantic passages it suddenly swells into great big emotional bursts and is perfectly suited to the high drama I can capture with that ball. I knew it by heart. It was time for a performance and I went to town. **All that could be seen in that darkened room in the narrow glow of a single ultra-violet spot, was a glowing sphere being spun in time, to that beautifully romantic song.** All eyes were on that ball of light reducing with every quiet part and expanding with every swell of that gorgeous piece of music until together we hit its final crescendo! The crowd went wild as we finished, Mr. Gluck, Mr. Smith (or Revlon,) Ms. Kidman and I, and the party went on.

Shortly after my husband Eric and I first met in 1999, he took me to Paris for my birthday. It was Fashion Week and the City of Lights was pure magic for new lovers. We went out to a disco on the Champ Elysees and of course I took my ball. Yes, I took it to Paris; I rarely went anywhere without it. The club was packed but kind of dead when we arrived. Eventually I got up on stage and did my thing. The response was great and the energy of the club shifted. It was suddenly a party. We danced for hours with all our new Parisian party friends and as we departed, we took a significant part of the party with us. **At 3am, through the dark quiet streets of Paris, there was a little impromptu parade of gay boys dancing down the Rue de**

Something or Other, behind a man with a big sphere still glowing from the light and energy it had picked up earlier. It must have been quite a sight for any early-morning Parisian passerby.

I had been a party boy for most of my gay life. Nearing 50 when I met Eric, I decided it was probably a good time to put away my party boots. Ya gotta grow up eventually, right? It was so nice just snuggling in with my new love rather than heading out each weekend to party my ass off. Creature of habit that I am, I became more and more comfortable with being a homebody. It was a nice habit and I happily settled right in with Eric and Boogie. Rather than vacationing in Key West (it had changed so much anyway) and spending my money doing the gay circuit, we'd spend our summers in Positano, where my Italian grandparents were from and where I still have a lot of fabulous family. **It wasn't gay, but "summering" for anywhere from four to ten weeks, in one of the most beautiful places in the world and an international jet-set resort, well, no eyes would weep for me.** Still, over the years, I came to recognize what an essential piece of me the party life and especially the dancing and the gay camaraderie and energy had been and just how much I missed it. My party life had become limited to The Black and The White Parties in New York and then after the White Party died, it was only the Black. It wasn't enough. I wanted to be gay again (for more than one night per year.) I wanted to dust off my party boots, go out and be surrounded by gay boys and gay energy on gay vacations. At the same time I didn't want to seem whiny and unappreciative, ungrateful for our yearly trips to the always fabulous Amalfi Coast. How could I complain?

I had a dream and a plan: to go on a gay cruise. I thought a gay cruise might be a sort of combination package of a Key West guest house and a circuit party. I imagined my three S's of a perfect vacation all on one boat. And maybe some naked sunning and floating, too? Perhaps some European nude beaches on excursions? And dancing! I thought back to the White Party on The Intrepid and imagined partying on the top deck of a cruise ship to be similar to that flawless New York night: music, nearly-naked boys dancing all around us and laser beams shooting off into the eternity of a night sky. Only on a cruise, we'd me moving through the Mediterranean or some other body of water. And, I'd have my ball. I hoped I could perhaps get Eric interested, stressing the camaraderie, ports, fine dining and the less intense party scene I imagined there to be onboard. On a cruise, it seemed, a party wouldn't be the full-on commitment it is in the city. If you weren't into it, you could just go back downstairs to your cabin or anywhere else on the ship. Later, after a late-night meal, or a drag show or a movie, or even a nap, you could try the party again. No commitment. I was sold and presented the option to Eric but he wasn't so sure. This was clearly my dream, not his. I didn't give up however, and over the next couple of years as I continued to work on him, I held out hope for a change. Then something amazing happened. We learned, that "our" apartment in Positano would no longer be available. What seemed like sad news actually gave me hope. Things had become so easy with Positano, after eight straight (pun intended) years, it seemed perhaps we'd never move on from our familial paradise. Now, this would give us good reason to start looking elsewhere for our summer vacation.

I continued to check the gay cruise sites to see what was new and would pass along the information to Eric in a sort of soft-sell way. I eventually came across an Atlantis Gay Cruise with a South American itinerary. Well-travelled Eric had not been to South America and I knew he wanted to go. This cruise which started in Buenos Aries and ended in Rio de Janeiro was perfect. It was smaller and more upscale than the typical party boats. It was also a February cruise (summer down there) and wouldn't disrupt our summer vacation once we got around to planning it. He gave it some thought and acquiesced. We had a fabulous time and met some great guys. Of course I took my ball.

Our first gay cruise was such a success, and with our mindset shifted from Positano, within seven months we were on another cruise, this time in the Mediterranean. The first stop, in Mykonos as it happened, was on my birthday. We also, conveniently, had several friends who all just happened to also be in Mykonos that night. We set up a big birthday dinner. Funny thing is, my birthday is almost always on Labor Day weekend. Just try to get a group together in New York then. But in Mykonos… Eric and I were a bit early for our table so we went into an art gallery across from the restaurant where we spotted two guys who looked familiar. They approached us with their arms in the air moving their hands in and out — the international sign for the man with the ball. They recognized us from the South American cruise, remembering the ball. Henk and Dick from Amsterdam became fast friends on that cruise. As luck would have it, our vacation that year ended with a week in Amsterdam, so we made plans to meet up there. Henk and Dick showed us around their beautiful city, introduced us to some friends and thus began our love affair with Amsterdam and its people. We now have more Dutch friends than American ones and our circle has grown to include friends from all over Europe. **The ball had been the catalyst for this new chapter in our lives.**

Now, the real kicker to that story is that when we got off the plane in Buenos Aries for the first cruise, and were standing in a long line at Passport control, I realized with a jolt that I had left my ball on the plane! I panicked and told Eric to go on through and I'd meet him on the other side. I bolted back through that long serpentine line and found my way the best I could remember, back through the labyrinth of corridors that had led us from the plane. Miraculously I found the right jetway and even more miraculously (this would have never happened in the USA) I got back on the plane and found my ball right where I'd left it under the seat. I snatched it and ran back to Passport Control breathless with my ball tucked under my arm. I wonder what our lives would be like right now if I hadn't been able to retrieve the ball that made our Amsterdam friends recognize us in Mykonos. **I remain constantly amazed by an accommodating universe that works in such wonderful, magical and sometimes miraculous ways and am eternally grateful.** With a little help, things just seem to work out for me.

The Hoberman Sphere has brought so many wonderful people into our lives. Eric frequently says, "Between my mouth and Michael's ball, we meet everyone." He's right. Super-friendly Eric will go up to anyone and introduce himself. I on the other hand, tend to let people come to me. The ball is a sure draw. One year at the Rapido Party two adorable speedo-clad boys came up to me with, "You are the best entertainment at this party!" My heart did flip-flops as this was a party with some pretty fine shiny muscular nearly-naked entertainment. The two spent the remainder of the evening flanking me as we danced the night away. As I was leaving the party with Eric and some friends, the boys, Christiaan and Ernesto came up to me and asked where I was going. I told them home. "Oh no you aren't," they said as they whisked me off to the bus for the after party. They are now, years later, like sons too us. **But for that glowing piece of expandable plastic, we might never have met these boys and our lives would be less full.**

Once when I was on a box at a party in San Francisco I felt a tug on my jeans. I looked down to see one of the most gloriously beautiful faces that to this day I have ever seen. He asked if it would be OK if his friend joined me on the box. Of course I said, "Yes," and since it was a small box, I pulled his (also gorgeous) friend up and hopped off. The gloriously beautiful boy thanked me and introduced his also gorgeous and sexy boyfriend. He said pointing to his friend now up on the box, "He has been wanting to get up on that box all night but I said to him, 'There's no way you're going to ask that man with the ball to get down. He's too fabulous!'" Me? Too fabulous? From the likes of this glorious creature? Days later on on our drive down the coast of California, we needed information regarding gay accommodations so I pulled out the International Spartacus Gay Guide for help. What do ya know…right there on the cover were the two beautiful boys at the San Francisco party. Spartacus cover boys! Gay Royalty!

I have enjoyed over the years the lower-case sort of celebrity status that the ball has afforded me. Performing with it all over the country and the world, it has become my signature. Strangers come up on the street and ask if I am the man with the ball. People say some of the nicest things as well and compliment me, my energy and my handling of that big ball. **"You are the heartbeat of the party," I have been told more than once.** After a party in Amsterdam I received the loveliest message asking me if I understood the effect I have on people; if I understood what I was doing energetically. I wrote back that it was definitely a spiritual experience on my end but wasn't sure if others felt it. He assured me that others did and that quite frequently it was the talk of the party. After a Black Party in New York one year a friend once said, "Michael, there were two Black Parties this year…before Michael and after Michael!" I am both proud and humbled.

My current favorite of all parties is the Rapido Party in Amsterdam. Rapido (I even love the name) is held in an old gothic church — not a fan of organized religion, I can't think of a better use for one — that reminds me of another favorite of mine, the now defunct Limelight in NYC, also a converted church. Dancing front and center stage at a Rapido party, high, surrounded by Eric and all our Dutch (and other European) friends, dancing to great music and washed in UV lighting is, well, appropriate to the location, it is my church and my pulpit. **There aren't many places I would rather be, or where I feel more alive, more complete or more at home and filled with that special universal energy than at Rapido.**

The organizer and promoter of the Rapido parties is a man named Edgar Bonte, and while I'd never met him, I stood in gratitude to him for making my favorite party possible. Now, our good friend Dick *did* know Edgar and from time to time had passed along, a few comments he'd heard Edgar make over the years about me and my ball — things like, "Is he still doing that?" Emphasis on the word *still* and "He hit me at a party with that thing years ago." Ouch! Not the most complimentary of remarks. Preferring to focus on the positive, I tried to forget the words as I would party on but they did lodge themselves somewhere in the back of my mind.

Fast-forward to Amsterdam Pride 2014. As we were just settling into our B&B, I received a message from Will, an Amsterdam friend whose husband Erik (also our friend) was DJ-ing that night at party called "Funhouse." He wanted me to come. We had just come off a week-long LaDemence Cruise which is seven days of non-stop parties and the next night we'd be going to the Rapido Party. I needed a night off. I also did not have a ticket. Though Will thought there'd be some available at the door, I wasn't convinced. Will would not take "no" for an answer…oh why do I have such trouble saying "no" to cute boys? I said, "OK, I'll go," and added, "should I take my ball?" "Of course," he responded without hesitation, "it's your signature!"

So, with my ball in its bag, off I went on foot, to a party that, as it turned out, was not in walking distance. **Arriving long last at the venue, I saw a line quite literally a mile long; I imagined waiting in it for hours only to reach the front and be told there were no tickets available.** I walked past the line, and walked, and walked and walked until I made my way to the front of it. I needed only to ask a simple question about ticket availability (then I could go home) but the guys at the front of the line were way too busy to deal with me. There was a VIP line as well but the man attending it was also swamped. The only other person I saw who might help was sitting a way off on the other side of the ropes at an elevated desk. He was thoroughly involved, never looking up from his computer screen, so he was a no-go as well. I stood there perplexed contemplating my next move when I glanced to my right to see our friend Dick. Right next to me.

Where had he come from? I hadn't seen him approach yet there he was like some genie from a bottle. **This was typical Dick — always the right person at the right moment with the right information.** I told him about my ticket predicament. He said, "Stay here," and with that, he stepped over the rope and walked up to the man at the computer. They began to chat. Something about their conversation made me uneasy but I continued to watch, hoping for a way into that party or, better yet, a good reason to drag my tired ass back to the B&B to bed. I watched as Dick put his hands in the air going in and out making the sign for 'The man with the ball.' They were laughing and having a great time when Dick turned and signaled for me to step over the rope and join him. The man at the computer had returned to his work when Dick, smiling broadly said, "Come with me," and together we bypassed even the VIP line and went directly into the party. Without even buying a ticket! Thank you Dick. And thank you man at the computer.

I was feeling pretty good about myself since apparently the ball had been my ticket in. I couldn't contain myself, and, as we waited in line for our locker keys, I had to ask, "Dick, did that man at the computer let me into the party because of my ball?" Dick chuckled a little and said, "Well, I wasn't going to say anything but since you asked, 'that man at the computer' is Edgar Bonte, the party promoter and he said to me, 'Do you think if I let him in he'd promise NOT to use that ball?'" I was crushed. And insulted — by the man responsible for the party itself. He had kindly let me bypass the lines, giving me access to the party for free. **The latent price however, had been a baseball bat to the knees of my self-esteem.** And my ball, which I stored away in the locker along with my excess clothing and my newly bruised ego. As I entered the party it was with a reminder that not all are so enamored with me or my ball.

Post-party I sent Edgar a message thanking him for allowing me into the party and I noted his not being a big fan. He wrote back thanking me for my participation, and added that even though he indeed was not a big fan, he recognized that others were and it wasn't his place to interfere with their fun. He also graciously offered his help any time in the future. A year later in 2015, after the Rapido Pride Party, I sent Edgar another thank you note. His kind response ended with, **"Amsterdam is in love with you."**

One of the most frequently asked questions is, "Have you had the same ball over all the years?" The answer is "No." The balls wear out and they can break easily in the hands of others. For awhile when it was time to replace a worn out sphere, I'd just go to Tah-Poozie where I'd bought the first one. Sam always knew when I'd been out dancing as his Hoberman Sphere sales would spike. I would always carry his business cards with me giving them to those who asked where to purchase one. After several years though, Tah-Poozie closed its doors and I had to turn to the internet for help. There were Hoberman Spheres galore but no "Glow Spheres" the one that glows in the dark. I searched in vain as I kept repairing my last ball with parts salvaged from older ones. Things were looking bad as we were preparing for our summer 2015 vacation which would be full of parties. The old one was just not going to make it. As a last ditch effort I sent off an email to the Hoberman corporation asking for help. The next day I was surprised to receive an email response from Carolyn Hoberman, the wife of the sphere's inventor with the news they had sold the toy division to another company which decided that the Glow Sphere was too costly to manufacture. They had stopped making it. This was not good news. The potential good news however was that while she was currently traveling she would be back in New York in a few days. She said she'd be happy to check her archive and if she had more than one Glow Sphere, she'd sell me one. I anxiously awaited word from her. She called several days later but the news wasn't good. There was only one Glow Sphere in the archive. It was from the original run and she just couldn't give it up. I understood. In the same email I told her a little about myself and what I, over the years, had done with the sphere — the dancing, the parties, etc. We emailed quite a lot back and forth and then all of a sudden in another email she said that I had inspired her to place a minimum order of 700 Glow Spheres so that I might have one. I was flabbergasted by her generous act and promised I'd help her sell them when I'd go out dancing. I waited patiently to hear news of the shipment. Nothing. It was just a week before we were ready to leave for vacation and still no word. I dashed off an email. When Carolyn wrote back, it was with bad news. The spheres were "literally on a slow boat from China" and would not make it in time. There was however good news. She would give me the sphere from her archives and replace it with one from the new shipment. **That meant not only would I have a new ball to take to Europe for the summer of 2015 but it would be one of the first ones ever manufactured — for all practical purposes, the original Hoberman Sphere!** I only needed a new sphere; I didn't think to ask for more. Things just seem to work out for me.

It was at the 2015 Rapido Pride Edition Party in 2015 then, with my brand new original sphere that the beatific face smiled up at me and asked for his favor: to "Never stop doing that." That beautiful man named Gerrald had no idea of the gift he had just given me. Having done this "ball thing" for over twenty years now I often wonder when enough is enough. I have thoughts that even the "fans" must be tired of the ball by now. Tired of the same old show. Tired of me. I imagine them looking up, rolling their eyes and saying, "Is she still doing that?" Emphasis on the word "still," or "Oh my god, get her down from there!" **Whenever I go out I look for some indication that my act is past it's sell-by date, that I've gone stale and it is indeed time to leave the ball at home. Gerrald gave me permission, no, he actually made me promise I wouldn't stop and I can't go back on my word.** There was no greater validation than that smiling face at Rapido. He rushed off to get his husband telling him, "I did it! I talked to the man with the ball!" As if that were something special. He brought his sexy husband Peter back to meet me. I called Eric over to meet them and Eric in turn introduced them to our "family" who inevitably fill the angel circle around us. Gerrald and Peter have become two of our closest friends. I hope that someday I might just be able to give Gerrald a gift as precious as the one he gave me.

Rapido two years later (Sept 4, 2017 — my birthday, to be precise) found me in my same spot on that same stage doing, of course, the same thing surrounded both on the floor and up on stage by our family of friends. There was a spectacularly beautiful young boy dancing next to me. He was the kind of boy, so in keeping with what I consider to be perfect male beauty, that I could have designed him myself — long, lean upper-body, low-waisted, tan, boyish, slightly exotic and nearly-naked. **His tiny tiny tiny speedo clung straight across his impossibly narrow hips, so low it defied gravity.** He was the kind of boy that at a glance I will reliably hear myself say, "Oh…just one hour…that's all I'd need…give me just one hour with him…" I wouldn't think to ask for more. As he danced next to me, I was consummately aware of his presence there and he seemed somewhat focused on me as well. Studying me actually. I was flattered and a bit giddy as we shared glances and smiles all the while I'm twirling my big day-glowing ball. I was dazzled by this magnificent creature and his apparent interest in me. During a particularly extended glance he leaned over to me and asked, "Could I play with it?" **The ball. Of course. He was interested in my ball. Not me.** This happens a lot.

I am usually reluctant to turn the ball over as it is fragile and, if handled improperly will easily break. Try as I might to give some quick instructions on its usage, once in the hands of the novice (usually high) it is instantly mishandled and returned with at least two or three fractured parts along with the complaints, "It's too heavy" or "That's hard."

At a party on a LaDemence cruise, a boy snatched the ball from my hands and started playing with it way too roughly. Not wanting to be a buzz-kill, I just stood back and let it happen. As I watched and worried, (that ball had to get me through a lot more parties that summer) out of nowhere our friend Eduardo appeared, went right up to the boy and declared, "That ball is very fragile and you have to give it back this minute!" With that, he snatched the ball away and returned it to me as our friend Christiaan rushed up with a horrified look on his face and announced, "The room was in a panic!" But the ball was unharmed. SuperEduardo (as I christened him) to the rescue.

I had a good feeling about the dazzling boy at Rapido asking to play with my ball and handed it over without hesitation or, as I recall, any instruction. I couldn't have said no to him no matter. He was a natural. He twirled and spun it like a pro so handily and elegantly that I could not take my eyes away. **He and my ball together were a thing of beauty. I was mesmerized.** As I delightedly watched him, another less delightful thought, prompted no doubt by my easily-threatened ego, crept into my head. "Wait. He's too beautiful. He looks too good. He'll ruin my brand! If I don't get that ball back, no one will ever want to see me with it again!" I was suddenly a selfish, "It's my ball, give it back," six year old. I'm not proud of this reaction but there it was. I think he must have sensed a change in my mood because he brought his glorious performance to an end, and with a quiet thank you, he handed the ball back to me. I felt a bit smaller as I returned to dancing with my ball, but not before he extended his hand and introduced himself with, **"I'm Randy." Randy. Of course it would be Randy.**

Rapido the next year found me in the same spot on the same stage and dancing right next to me once again was beautiful Randy. We shared a glance and I immediately offered him the ball. I watched again in awe as he so gracefully moved the ball about giving it his own special spin. Pun intended. He put on such a beautiful show I didn't think to snatch it back as I had done the year before. I was in love and in lust as I watched, mesmerized by the sheer beauty of it all, the sexy elegance of his long, lean, golden, nearly-naked body topped by that magnificent glowing ball. Over the years, I had been likened with my big expansive ball, to the Emmy Award statuette — a gorgeous long lean golden angel supporting, high above her, a big gleaming sphere. I'd always meet this comment with a slightly self-deprecating smile and "Thanks." Now, all long and lean and golden and gleaming I saw that statue in Randy. **I could almost see his wings.** As it had been with me, the ball seemed to be an extension of him. Not an accessory. When he finished his performance, he returned the ball. **As he placed it in my hands he leaned in to my ear and said, "I hope you live forever, but when you do decide to depart this world, I would be honored if you'd leave your ball to me and I promise to use it until it's time for me to pass it on to some other young boy and together we will carry on your legacy forever."** Wings indeed. Of course I enthusiastically said, "Yes," to which he replied with his hand extended, "Then we have a gentlemen's agreement?" To which I, as I took his hand in mine to shake it, replied, "Yes we do." And that was that. The torch, or in this case, the ball, has been passed. Or it will be…eventually, as my dancing days are surely numbered. I will, someday, decide it's time to end my commitment to Gerrald and honor my commitment to Randy and I will, at long last, stop "Doing that."

I

even

had

the thought

that

at some point,

I

was

only taking dictation;

that

it was

actually

Randy

writing our story.

His story.

Might be.

It'd be just like him.

ACKNOWLEDGMENTS

I**T IS SAID** that writing is a lonely profession. For me at least, it's true that I require a quiet place where I can write alone, undisturbed, in order to do my best work. Having said that, I have found that no book is completed alone. Without those who have supported and encouraged me to write and then enthusiastically read what I have written and given their invaluable feedback, this would not be the book you have just read. **I gratefully stand with all those who have inspired and helped me in this effort.**

To Randy Riede, my Best Friend, whose life was so interwoven with mine that I couldn't write your story without it turning into a memoir all about me. Surprise. **Thank you for being the divine spark that ignited *Gay Boy's Life*.** I wish you were alive to read it but somehow I think you may have written it; or at least, great big chunks of it. Since your departure, I have felt your presence but never more than when I would sit down to write. Thank you for the gift of your undying (sorry) love and for any heavenly help you may have provided from beyond.

To Starr Anastasio, my loving niece-who-is-more-of-a-daughter, who, for decades, asked me to write my stories, thank you. Your everlasting belief that I have something worthwhile to say that others would want to (and "should") hear, gave me the confidence I needed to actually write. **Your loving, gentle, (sometimes unrelenting) words of encouragement were ever in my head.** The journals you gave me are filled with notes that went word-for-word into *Gay Boy's Life*.

To Richard Eric Weigle, my loving husband, who gave me that first iPad, the invaluable tool which made it possible to, at long last, gather my thoughts in an organized manner and write, no matter where I was or what I might be doing. Thanks to you, much of *Gay Boy's Life* was born at the gym, on subways, airplanes or wherever a thought happened to cross my mind. **Thank you Eric for the safe haven of your constant love, your steadfast support, your continued generosity and your boundless positive energy.** I am especially grateful for your years of patience while exiled to our upstairs bedroom as I quietly wrote below.

To Warner Thijssen, Michelle Watt, Frank Naumann and Warren Smith, it was with each of you right inside my head, that I wrote chapter after chapter. **Typing out each sentence, I could see you reading along and hear you laughing with me at the funny moments and, at the sad, shedding your tears with mine. You are my audience. My Four Muses.** The fact that some of you have read *Gay Boy's Life* multiple times already, amazes me. Thank you for your inexhaustible need for more, unwavering loyalty and your ever-enthusiastic feedback. You inspire me and helped me find my voice.

To Frank Naumann, Warner Thijssen, Terry Greenberg, Gerrald Suurd, Peter Snellenburg, Eduardo Valencia, Warren Smith, Karen Merson, Ariane Qureshi, Blair Fell, George DeMarco, Jonathan Pepoon, Greg Amend, Paul Poux, David Gerard, Christiaan Elings and Ernesto Medina Alcaraz, who patiently listened as I read aloud chapter after chapter. Over the years, in addition to listening, each of you has continued to show interest throughout this entire process (which must have seemed at times, endless.) It did to me. **You have continually checked on my progress, given me invaluable feedback and cheered me on.** Thank you for your thoughtful words, your patience and your kind encouragement.

To Adam Waring, Robyn Borok, George Lucien, Jay Waterham, Max Klaus Quoß, Warner Thijssen, Michelle Watt, Sander Maas, Jay Katz, Carolyn Livingston, Karen Merson, Margaret Healy, Jack Hines, Jim Pierce,

Karen Snow, Brooke Schooley, Alice Kim, David Cynn, Anthony Lacey, Cathryn Lewin, Suzanne Guglielmi, Len Kraig, Carolyn Shain, Maureen Walker, Dean Egan, Vicki V. P. Guffey, Juan Carlos Gutierrez, Frank Russo, Richard Eric Weigle and MJ Miarecki, who all took the time to read *Gay Boy's Life* in any one of its many developmental incarnations. Thank you so much for the gift of your time and for your all-important feedback. I took every comment, both praise and criticism to heart. **Your thoughtful responses helped me write a better book than it would have been otherwise.** If you're reading this, it must mean that, having already read it, you still decided to buy *Gay Boy's Life* and read it once again. I thank you for that as well.

To Robyn Borok, Richard Eric Weigle, Jay Katz, Starr Anastasio, Kim Thorstenson, Malcolm Woodworth, Margaret Healy, Madeleine Gens, Shelton Dominici, Gerrald Suurd, Peter Snellenburg, Eduardo Valencia, Christiaan Elings, Ernesto Medina Alcaras, Michael Rohr, Frank Anastasio, Carmen Carter, Amy Yentsch, Jim Trowell, Edgar Bonte, Randy Grofstein, Brenda Braxton and Steve Wilcox, each mentioned within these pages, I thank you. Each of you has made a special contribution to my story — our story. **Over the years, you have all enriched my gay boy's life by your love and friendship.** I am so grateful that you have remained in my life through all these years and even decades and your presence within the pages of *Gay Boy's Life* brings me great joy.

To those no longer a part of my life, I thank you as well. **I have chosen to include you because you were an essential part of my story.** Our story. I've changed your names and some details to protect your privacy. If you happen upon *Gay Boy's Life*, and read it, I'd be delighted to hear from you. Further, if you would like me to use your actual name, I'd be happy to do that for later editions. If you don't wish to be included in the book, I'll consider editing you out at your request; reluctantly, as the stories are really good.

To Michelle Watt, thank you for all your thorough proofreading. Your laser-like ability to hone in on each word and punctuation mark, catching mistake after mistake has kept me from eternal embarrassment and shame. How could I have missed so many? As a devoted wife and mother of three young children, how you have managed to devote so much of your interest and time to me, and to *Gay Boy's Life* quite frankly, astonishes me! **The fact that you even found me from way on the other side of the planet, still amazes and delights me.** You are a friend for life and more—I'm pretty confident this is not our first time around.

To Bert Green, thank you for your patience, your expertise, your eye, your consummate attention to detail and the grace you've shown in dealing with each amendment, change, addition, etc. **I could not have navigated the waters of self-publishing without you — period.** But for your expert help, *Gay Boy's Life* would still be locked inside my iPad or in the cloud or wherever it is these things get holed-up.

To my Cover Boys, Warren, Daniel, Christiaan and Thor, I thank you for your permission to use the photos I took of you in Gran Canaria. **Thanks to you boys, I have the happy, colorful sexy cover I wanted for *Gay Boy's Life*.** I'd sure buy a book with all of you on the cover.

To Patrick Phillips, thank you for graciously giving me permission to use your beautiful poem. **I have never read a lovelier, more hopeful description of "HEAVEN."** With each reading, it still touches me deeply and continues to fill my broken heart with joy.

To Vincent Ford, thank you for the use of your very funny "Gay In The Womb" act-opening joke. **It is not only spot-on accurate but has allowed me to open *Gay Boy's Life* with a laugh.** That's a good way to start anything.

To Victor Mignatti, thank you for appearing at exactly the right moment, with exactly the right information and producing exactly the right person — Bert Green. **You made all the difference in the world, moving me from editing to publishing.**

To Damien Mittlefehldt and Nathan Manske, thank you for making it possible for me to tell my stories on video, helping in their written development. Thank you also for creating *I'm From Driftwood* and being interested in what older LGBTQ people had to say. **You are doing the good work of helping current and future generations be more comfortable with and accepting of themselves.**

To The Dominican Nuns at St. Stephen's elementary school, thank you for so thoroughly teaching me how to write. **You've taken a lot of beatings in *Gay Boy's Life*, at your own hands as it turns out, since without your excellent teaching skills, this book may have never been written.** Apologies for the abundant alliteration and abject adjective avalanche within these pages and especially the run-on sentences throughout from cover to cover but I still really like them not to mention I could still diagram the hell out of them and it is after all *my* book.

To The Older Gay Men in my young gay life, who, when I was newly-out and impressionable, became my sexy surrogate single parents. I thank you. **By your example, without even realizing, you gave me a blueprint for my future.** Just living your lives as graciously as you did, balancing sex, love, friendship, guidance, taste and so much more, you made me want to become you. I could see myself being gay and growing old. Without that effortless influence, perhaps I wouldn't have so easily seen my future as an older gay man and just perhaps, would never have become one. Who knows?

To The Caregivers, especially the dying who took care of the dying. Thank you. In a world that was largely indifferent and even worse — contemptuous, you compassionately cared for your own when few others would. **You nurtured them through all the pain and suffering while bravely watching your own certain future playing out in front of you.** As you selflessly loved each soul over to the other side, you knew, if you weren't next, your time was surely coming and still you soldiered on. That was valor of the highest order.

And finally...

To My Fallen Comrades, My Gay Angels, you'd have changed the world had you been allowed to stay in it longer. You were the best of us. **Those left behind, the rest of us, carried on in a world diminished by your departure.** You left us in numbers that, all these decades later, seem too great to be believed, even for those of us who were there. We who were there and who witnessed your valiant response to the pain, suffering and inevitability of your death, carry the responsibility of telling your stories. With the many years (and now decades) distancing us from the horrible nightmare that was AIDS, it becomes increasingly important for the world to understand the horror of that time and to learn from it. To learn from you. **It is important to me that the world understands the enormous loss it suffered as you left us, taking with you your collective promise and possibility.** *Gay Boy's Life* **was written to keep your individual flames alive not only as a reminder of what might have been, but also to remind others that, until you were so brutally removed from us, for one glorious, all-too-brief moment in time, you did dance upon this earth, lighting the way for the rest of us.**

Thank you.

This book is for you.

Printed in Great Britain
by Amazon